D1871850

THE

USEFUL PLANTS OF INDIA

THE

USEFUL PLANTS OF INDIA

WITH NOTICES OF

THEIR CHIEF VALUE IN COMMERCE

MEDICINE AND THE ARTS

COLONEL HEBER DRURY

GYAN

Published by

Gyan Publishing House
5, Ansari Road
Daryaganj, New Delhi-110002
Phone: 011-47034999, 9811692060
E-mail: books@gyanbooks.com

Distribution Network
gyanbooks.com
India, USA, Canada, UK, Australia, France

© Publisher
All rights reserved. No part of this work may be reproduced, stored, adapted, or transmitted in any form or by any means, electronic, mechanical, photocopying, micro-filming, recording or otherwise, or translated in any language, without the prior written permission of the copyright owner and the publisher.

ISBN : 978-81-212-9150-7 (PB)
First Published, 1873

2nd Impression 2023

Printed at: Gyan Press, Delhi.

The book is sold subject to the condition that it shall not, by way of trade or otherwise, be lent, resold, hired out, or otherwise circulated without the prior publisher's written consent.

THE USEFUL PLANTS OF INDIA
Author: COLONEL HEBER DRURY

THE

USEFUL PLANTS OF INDIA

THE

USEFUL PLANTS OF INDIA;

WITH NOTICES OF

THEIR CHIEF VALUE IN COMMERCE, MEDICINE, AND THE ARTS.

BY

COLONEL HEBER DRURY,

AUTHOR OF THE 'HANDBOOK OF THE INDIAN FLORA.'

" *Simul et jucunda et* IDONEA *dicere vitæ.*"
—HOR.

SECOND EDITION.

WITH ADDITIONS AND CORRECTIONS.

LONDON:
WILLIAM H. ALLEN & CO.
13 WATERLOO PLACE, S.W.
1873.

CONTENTS.

PREFACE TO THE FIRST EDITION.

An increasing demand for everything relating to the vegetable productions of India has of late years been the means of eliciting from various quarters much useful information, tending to a more extensive acquaintance with, as well as improvement of, the natural resources of the country. The idea that a collection of ascertained facts regarding the uses of Indian plants is still a desideratum, led to the compilation of the following pages. A vast quantity of miscellaneous matter is scattered throughout the pages of Rheede, Ainslie, Roxburgh, Wallich, Wight, Royle, and others who have written on the subject of Indian botany; and it frequently occurred to me, that were an attempt made to collect in a single volume the various notices on the chief uses of plants as recorded in their works, it would form a somewhat useful and desirable handbook to a knowledge of our botanical resources. Undoubtedly, many of the so-called uses of Indian plants are now either entirely obsolete, or, owing to the advancement of science and more extended investigations in the departments of medical and economical botany, have been tested and corrected by recent observers; while numerous doubts and errors have been either cleared up or exploded.

The reports of the juries on the timber, vegetable oils, drugs, &c., submitted to the Madras Exhibition in 1855, are so many evidences of the richness and variety in these important sections of the natural products of the Indian Peninsula; and further show how well that exhibition was calculated for the attainment of the best results, the development to a great degree of resources hitherto so little known.

With a view to render more familiar the knowledge of subjects so replete with interest and utility, I undertook the present compilation. I have not aimed at the production of a scientific work, for which I do not consider myself qualified; but have merely endeavoured to offer a guide to the amateur, especially to those sojourners and residents in India whose leisure hours may induce them to follow a pursuit than which few are more attractive or delightful.

The short descriptions, which it is hoped are sufficient to identify the plants enumerated, are taken from the best authorities; and in this, as in every other instance, I have acknowledged the sources from whence I have drawn my varied information. At the same time, it will be found that some new facts have been adduced, drawn from personal observation or inquiry, especially regarding plants growing in Travancore. Furthermore, whenever practicable, I have been particular in making references to the works of Indian botanists; and in regard to the plants of this Presidency, no one could desire more sure or safe companions than Drs Roxburgh and Wight.

It required both patience and consideration to arrange much contradictory and useless matter, without hastily rejecting anything that might be of importance; while I laboured under great disadvantage, from the want of access to any public library or collection of botanical works and treatises — for numerous isolated notices on botanical subjects are scattered in various periodicals, which would not only have assisted me with increased information, but have enabled me to remedy the many omissions and defects which, I fear, will be detected in these pages. When I first commenced the undertaking, I was little aware of the obstacles I had to encounter, and soon had reason to see how extremely difficult it was to render a book of the kind so complete as the title would lead one to expect. Feeling the impossibility of gathering the facts requisite for the purpose, I had the alternative of relinquishing my labours at the commencement, or of collecting such information as I was able from the scanty materials at my disposal.

To determine those limits which should constitute the *ne plus ultra* of Indian plants was not the least difficult portion of my labours. I could not in a small volume embrace the varied flora of the Himalaya; yet there are some plants growing in those regions, the uses of which are so important in a commercial point of view in this country, that I could hardly omit them,—viz., the Aconites, the Berberries, and others. I resolved, therefore, to make my plan so far arbitrary as to include those plants of the Himalaya, Silhet, Assam, and other countries bordering on India, which have special and acknowledged uses, and whose importance and commercial value are recognised in Hindostan and the Lower Provinces. Again, with respect to naturalised plants, if I determined to mention only those which were in point of fact indigenous to India, I must have omitted many which have in course of time become naturalised, and cannot with propriety be separated from the Indian flora. Of these I may mention *Linum usitatissimum*, *Cæsalpinia coriaria*, *Panicum*, *Italicum*, *Ipomæa batatas*, and others which have been introduced, though perhaps from remote times, but, independently of position, soil, and culture, have so adapted themselves to the climate as to have become as it were Indian plants. Not so *Theobroma cacao*, *Caryophyllus aromaticus*, and others, which only thrive under certain conditions of soil and climate, and therefore cannot strictly be included in a work professing to deal almost exclusively with the flora of India.

Those who have never considered the subject are little aware how much the appearance and habit of a plant become altered by the influence of its position. It requires much observation to speak authoritatively on the distinction in point of stature between many trees and shrubs. Shrubs in the low country, small and stunted in growth, become handsome and goodly trees on higher lands, and to an inexperienced eye they appear to be different plants. The *Jatropha curcas* grows to a tree some 15 or 20 feet on the Neilgherries, while the *Datura alba* is three or four times the size on the hills that it is on the plains. It is therefore with much diffidence that I have occasionally presumed to insert the height of a tree or shrub. The same remark may be applied to flowers and the flowering seasons, especially the latter. I have seen the *Lagerstrœmia Reginæ*, whose proper time of flowering is March and April, previous to the commencement of the rains, in blossom more or less all the year in gardens in Travancore. I have endeavoured to give the real or natural flowering seasons, in contradistinction to the chance ones, but, I am afraid, with little success; and it should be recollected that to aim at precision in such a part of the description of plants is almost hopeless, without that prolonged study of their local habits for which a lifetime would scarcely suffice.

I gladly take this opportunity of recording my grateful sense of the assistance I received from General Cullen, British Resident in Travancore and Cochin, who, with his usual liberality, permitted me free access to the valuable botanical works in his library,—an advantage, the importance of which was invaluable, and which I might in vain have sought elsewhere in any private collection in this country. My best acknowledgments are due to the Honourable Walter Elliot and Dr Hugh Cleghorn, who kindly undertook the labour of revising the work during its progress through the press, my distance from the Presidency not admitting of personal superintendence. I am also indebted to Surgeon Edward Balfour, of the Madras Army, who kindly placed at my disposal a list drawn up by him of the commercial products of the Presidency, with reference to their exports and imports, to which I have made frequent reference in the following pages.

H. D.

TREVANDRUM, *September* 1858.

PREFACE TO THE SECOND EDITION.

TWELVE years have elapsed since this work was first published, and during that time many important advances have been made in the knowledge of the vegetable treasures of our Indian possessions. Among the principal causes which have tended to develop an inquiry in the resources of the Forests of India have been the several local Exhibitions, which have probably done more than anything else to foster and maintain an interest in the acquisition of all information bearing on the uses of plants available for domestic or commercial purposes. At the same time, the attention of the local governments was called to the neglected state of the forests, and under the able superintendence of Dr Hugh Cleghorn of the Madras Medical Department, the Forest Department sprang into existence, and rapidly became one of the most usefully organised institutions of the State. The preservation of the valuable timber-trees, hitherto so recklessly neglected and destroyed, became at once an object of paramount importance, and especially since the adoption of the railway system into the country, which necessitated the constant and unvarying supply of timber. Side by side with this determination to preserve our valuable resources of timber and fuel, Government resolved to stimulate and encourage the introduction of such products of foreign growth as appeared most capable of being turned to good account in a social and economic point of view. Chief among these was the Cinchona experiment, which has been so successfully carried out under the original designs and guidance of Mr Clements Markham, and which now promises the happiest results in producing and manufacturing, in a country where it is so much needed, an abundant supply of excellent quinine at a very reasonable cost.

To the above important measures—Forest Conservancy and the introduction of the Cinchona plant—may be added the encouragement given by Government to the extension and opening of new tea-plantations, especially in the North-Western Provinces and the Assam territories. European capital is now being largely employed in reclaiming vast tracts of waste forest-land, and, at the present rate of progress, it would be difficult to estimate the commercial advantages which must accrue some years hence from the continued application of labour, energy, and wealth by the British capitalist to these plantations.

The Author trusts that this volume may show to some extent what are the chief resources of India in the above respect, and how they may be made available with the best effect; and, furthermore, what advantage has hitherto been taken of them. A work like the present, to be of any value, must keep pace with the discoveries of the day; and however imperfect and meagre in detail some of the articles unavoidably are, yet the Author has spared no pains to render the information on each subject as full and complete as the materials at his disposal admitted of.

In the present edition a wider range has been given to plants of foreign origin introduced and now largely cultivated in the country, the omission of which, inasmuch as they yearly become of more commercial importance, would have been inexcusable. Among these may be mentioned Cinchona, Tea, Cacao, Tobacco, the Australian Eucalyptus, and others which may reasonably be admitted, as they are now so extensively cultivated in the country.

It would have given the Author more satisfaction if he could have given a more uniform nomenclature of the native names of the plants described, but the subject is one of difficulty; and as complete uniformity is not—at present, at least—attainable, it has been considered best to defer so desirable an end until some future time, when perhaps a better result may be secured.

It only remains for the Author to record his thanks to those who have assisted him in the collection of materials made use of. Among those he would particularly mention Dr Hugh Cleghorn, so happily designated the 'Father of Forest Conservancy in India,' and Dr E. J. Waring, the able editor of the 'Pharmacopœia of India,' a work replete with valuable information, which has frequently been laid under contribution in these pages.

MONMOUTH, *October* 1872.

PRINCIPAL ABBREVIATIONS

EMPLOYED IN THIS VOLUME.

Ainsl. ....Ainslie's Materia Indica. 2 vols.
Ait. ....Aiton's Hortus Kewensis.
And. Bot. Rep.....Andrew's Botanical Repository.
Aubl. ....Aublet, a French traveller and botanist.

Beauv. ....Beauvoir, Essai d'une nouvelle Agrostographie.
Beddome, ...Flora Sylvatica.
Beng. Disp. ......Bengal Dispensatory, by Dr W. O'Shaughnessy.
Benth. ....Bentham, Labiatarum genera et species—Schrophularineæ Indicæ.
Bl. ....Blume (C. L.), Flora Javanensis.
Bot. Mag. ....Curtis's Botanical Magazine.
Bot. Misc. ....Hooker's Botanical Miscellany.
Buch..................Dr Francis Hamilton, formerly Buchanan, whose 'Journey,' MSS., and Herbarium are well known among botanists.
Burm. Ind. ......Burmanni Flora Indica.
Burm. Zeyl. ......Burmanni Thesaurus Zeylanicus.

Cav. Ic. ....Cavanilles (A. J.), Icones et descriptiones plantarum, quæ aut sponte in Hispaniâ crescunt aut in hortis hospitantur. 6 vols. fol. 1791—1800.
Cav. Diss. ....Cavanilles's Monadelphiæ classis dissertationes decem.
Choisy, ...A Swiss botanist who elaborated several of the Natural Orders for De Candolle's Prodromus.
Cleghorn, ...Forests and Gardens of S. India.
Comm. Prod. ...Commercial Products of the Madras Presidency, as shown by its Exports and Imports.
Corr. ....Correa (F.) de Serra. A botanical writer.

Dec. ....De Candolle (A. P.), Prodromus Systematis Naturalis Regni Vegetabilis.
Deless. Icon. ......Delessert, Icones selectæ plantarum, quas in systemate naturali descripsit De Candolle.

Desrouss......................Desrousseaux. An eminent botanical writer in Lamarck's Encyclopédie.
Desv. ....Desvaux (N. A.) A French botanist, editor of the Journal Botanique.
Don (*D.*), ...Prodromus floræ Nepalensis.
Drury, ...Handbook of the Indian Flora. 3 vols.

Endl. ....Endlicher, Genera plantarum.

Forsk. ....Forskal (Peter). A famous Swedish naturalist; author of Flora Ægyptiaco-Arabica, and other works.

Gœrtn........................Gœrtner (J.), De fructibus et seminibus plantarum. 2 vols. 4to, 1788.
Grah. Cat. ....Graham's (J.) Catalogue of Bombay Plants.

Ham. ....Dr Francis Hamilton (formerly Buchanan). Author of a Journey to Mysore, and several papers in the transactions of the Linnæan Society.
Herb. Mad. ....Herbarium Maderaspatense formed by Drs Klein, Heyne, and Rottler.
H. B. Kth. ....Humboldt, Bonpland, and Kunth; authors of Nova genera, et species plantarum æquinoctialium orbis novi.
Hook. Bot. Misc. ....Hooker's Botanical Miscellany. Also his Journal of Botany.

Jacq. ....Jacquini icones plantarum rariorum. 3 vols. 1781.
Jury. Rep. Mad. Exh....Jury Reports of the Madras Exhibition, 1855.
Juss. ....Jussieu (Bernard de), Genera plantarum.
Juss. ....Jussieu (Adrien de). A celebrated botanist.

Kth. ....Kunth. An eminent Prussian botanist.
Koen. ....Koenig, a Danish botanist. Physician to the Tranquebar Mission in 1768.

Lam. ....Lamarck (J. B.) Editor to the botanical portion of the Encyclopédie Méthodique (*Enc. Meth.*) Paris, 1783.
Lesch. ....Leschenault de la Tour. A French botanist who travelled in the Moluccas, Java, and Sumatra. He was director of the Botanical Gardens at Pondicherry.

L'Herit. ....L'Heritier (C. L.) A French botanist, author of a work entitled Stirpes novæ aut minus cognitæ.

Lindl. ..,............Lindley (Dr J.) A celebrated English botanist, author of the Vegetable Kingdom, Flora Medica (*Flor. Med.*), and other works.

Linn. ....Linnæus. The founder of botanical science. His principal works are Species plantarum (*Linn. Sp.*), Mantissa plantarum (*Linn. Mant.*), Flora Zeylanica (*Fl. Zeyl.*) His son published a Supplementum plantarum.

Lour. ....Loureiro, Flora Cochinchinensis. 1 vol. 1790.

Pers. ....Persoon (C. H.), Synopsis plantarum.

Pers. Obs. ....Personal Observation and Inquiry.

Pharm. of Ind....Pharmacopœia of India. Edited by E. J. Waring, M.D.

Pluk. ....Plukenet (L.), an eminent botanical writer. His works are published in 4 vols. 4to, Lond. 1696-1705.

Poir. ....Poiret (J. L. M.) A writer in Lamarck's Encyclopédie.

Powell, ...Baden-Powell's Punjaub Products. 2 vols.

R. Br...............Robert Brown. The most famous of living English botanists.

Retz, ...Observationes botanicæ, 1774.

Rheede, ...Author of the Hortus Malabaricus, 12 vols. fol., 1686-1703.

Rich. ....Richard (L. C.), and his son, Achille Richard, two eminent French botanists.

Roem. et Schult...Roemer (J. J.) and Schultes (J. A.), authors of Linnæi systema vegetabilium.

Roth, ...(A. W.) Author of Novæ plantarum species præsertim Indiæ orientalis.

Rottl. ....Rottler (Dr). An Indian botanist, for a long time residing at Tranquebar.

Roxb. ....Roxburgh (Dr W.) One of the most indefatigable of Indian botanists. His principal works are Flora Indica (*Fl. Ind.*), 3 vols. An edition was published by Carey and N. Wallich at Serampore (*Ed. Car.*) Plants of the Coromandel Coast (*Cor.*) Hortus Benghalensis. He left behind him also drawings of plants in the East India Company's Museum (*E. I. C. Mus.*)

Royle Fib. Plants,.Royle on the Fibrous Plants of India. He also wrote on the cultivation of Cotton in India.

Rumph. ....Rumphii Herbarium Amboinense.

Ruiz e Pav...........Ruiz (H.) and Pavon (J.) Authors of Flora Peruviana et Chilensis.

Simmonds, ...Commercial Products of the Vegetable Kingdom.
Sim's Bot. Mag. ...Sim's Botanical Magazine.
Stewart, ...Plants of the Punjaub.
Swz. ....Swartz, Flora Indiæ occidentalis. 3 vols., 1797.

Thunb................Thunberg (C. P.), Flora Japonica.
Tourn. ....Tournefort, Institutiones rei herbariæ.

Vahl Symb...........Vahl (M.), Symbolæ botanicæ. Enumeratio plantarum.
Veg. Subst. ....Vegetable Substances. 3 vols. 12mo.
Vent...................Ventenat (S. P.) A famous French botanist.

Wall. ....Wallich (N.), Plantæ Asiaticæ rariores. Tentamen Floræ Nepalensis.
W. & A. ....Wight & Arnott's Prodromus Floræ Peninsulæ Indiæ orientalis.
Wight's Contrib. ..Wight's Contributions to Indian Botany.
Wight's Ill..........Wight's Illustrations of Indian Botany.
Wight's Icon. ......Wight's Icones plantarum Indiæ orientalis.
Willd. ....Willdenow (C. L.), Linnæi species plantarum.

THE

USEFUL PLANTS OF INDIA.

A Ram turâ-i

(1) **Abelmoschus esculentus** (*W. & A.*) N. O. MALVACEÆ.

Esculent Okro, ENG. Bhindi, Ramturi, HIND. Bhendi, DUK. Venday, TAM. Benda, TEL. Vendah, MAL. Dheuroos, BENG.

DESCRIPTION.—Biennial; stem herbaceous, hairy, without prickles; leaves on longish petioles, cordate, with 3-5 obtuse lobes, strongly toothed, scabrous on both sides, with short appressed rigid hairs; pedicels very short; involucel-leaves 10, deciduous; capsule pyramidal, furrowed, elongated, acuminated; petals pale yellow, dark crimson at the base. *Fl.* All the year.—*W. & A. Prod.* i. 53.—Hibiscus esculentus, *Linn.*—H. longifolius, *Roxb. Fl. Ind.* iii. 210.——Cultivated in gardens.

MEDICAL USES.—Valuable as an emollient and demulcent, also diuretic. Used in catarrh, dysuria, and other cases requiring demulcent remedies. A decoction of the fresh immature capsules is inhaled with good effect in hoarseness and other affections of the throat. The dried capsule may be used when the fresh ones are not procurable. The fresh capsules bruised, as well as the leaves, form good emollient poultices.—*Pharm. of India. Dr Gibson.*

ECONOMIC USES.—Though indigenous to the West Indies, this plant has long been naturalised in India. The capsule known familiarly as the Bendi-Kai is an excellent vegetable, and much esteemed for imparting a mucilaginous thickening to soups. The young pods are often gathered green, and pickled like capers. The stem yields a strong, silky, pliant fibre, well suited for the manufacture of ropes, string, gunny-bags, and paper. They are exported to a slight extent as hemp, to which they bear considerable resemblance. A bundle of them tested by Dr Roxburgh bore a weight of 79 lb. when dry, and 95 lb. when wet.—*Roxb. Royle. Jury Rep. Mad. Exhib.*

(2) **Abelmoschus moschatus** (*Moench*). Do.

Musk-mallow, Eng. Mushk-bhendi, Duk. Kasturi-Venday, Kathe-Kasturi, Tam. Kasturi-benda, Tel. Katta-Kasturi, Mal. Mushak-dana, Beng.

Description. — Stem herbaceous, hispid with spreading hairs, not prickly; leaves, and long petioles, hispid with rigid hairs, but otherwise glabrous, unequally and coarsely toothed, deeply 5-7 lobed; lobes all spreading, oblong or lanceolate; pedicels harshly pubescent, axillary, about as long as the petioles; involucel-leaves 6-10, linear, hairy; capsule oblong, acuminated, hairy; petals sulphur-coloured, dark crimson at the base. *Fl.* July—September.—*W. & A. Prod.* i. 53.—Hibiscus abelmoschus, *Linn.*—H. longifolius, *Willd.*—*Rheede Mal.* ii. *t.* 38.—*Wight Icon. t.* 399.——Bengal. Peninsula.

Medical Uses.—The highly-scented seeds are cordial and stomachic. When bruised, they have been given for the purpose of counteracting the effects of the bites of venomous reptiles, being applied both externally and internally. In the West Indies they are first reduced to powder, and then steeped in rum, and in this state are administered in snake-bites.

Economic Uses.—The plant abounds in mucilage, and is used in Upper India to clarify sugar. The seeds are used in Arabia for giving a perfume to coffee, and are also used in Europe as a substitute for animal musk in scenting powders and pomatums. The stem yields a strong fibre. Dr Roxburgh cut the stems while in flower, and immediately steeped them in water; these broke at an average weight of 107 lb., both when dry and wet. Among other fibre-yielding plants of this family may be mentioned the *A. ficulneus* (W. & A.), the bark of which contains a large proportion of very strong white fibre.—*Royle. Jury Rep. Mad. Exhib.*

(3) **Abroma augustum** (*Linn.*) N. O. Byttneriaceæ.

Oolut-kumbul, Beng.

Description. — Small tree, 10-12 feet; branches soft, velvety; adult leaves ovate-oblong, serrulate, under side tomentose, or scabrous with stellate pubescence; lower leaves roundish-cordate, 3-5 angled; calyx 5-partite; petals five, with dilated claws; flowers darkish purple, drooping; wings of the fruit truncated at the apex, with the exterior angle acute; peduncles terminal, leaf-opposed. *Fl.* Aug.—*W. & A. Prod.* i. 65.—*Roxb. Fl. Ind.* iii. 156.——Interior of the Peninsula.

Economic Uses.—This plant, known familiarly as the "Devil's Cotton," is a doubtful native of India, though the above locality is given on the authority of Roxburgh. The bark yields a tough fibrous tissue, from which cordage is manufactured, and is considered a good substitute for hemp. The tree succeeds well in most parts of the country, and grows quickly, yielding three or four crops annually fit for peeling. Dr Roxburgh called special attention to the plant, inasmuch as it was more easy of cultivation than Sunn (*Crotalaria juncea*), and the average produce almost three times greater. To prepare the fibres, the bark is steeped in water for about a week, beyond which they require no further cleaning; and in this state, without any subsequent preparation, they are one-tenth stronger than Sunn, and not liable to become weakened through exposure to wet. A cord made from these fibres bore a weight of 74 lb., that of Sunn only 68 lb.—*Roxb. Royle's Fib. Plants.*

(4) Abrus precatorius (*Linn.*) N. O. Leguminosæ.

Wild or country Liquorice, Eng. Ghungchi, Gunj, Hind. Gumchi, Duk. Gundu-mani, Kunri-mani, Tam. Guri-ginja, Guru-venda, Tel. Kunni-kuru, Mal. Kunch, Gunj, Beng.

Description.—Twining; young shoots with a few adpressed hairs at the apex; leaves alternate, abruptly pinnated; leaflets 8-20 pair, linear-oval, obtuse at both ends, glabrous or slightly hairy; calyx campanulate, obsoletely 4-lobed, upper lobe broadest; racemes axillary, peduncled, many-flowered; flowers pale purple or rose-coloured; legumes oblong, compressed, 4-6 seeded; seeds roundish, distinct. *Fl.* April—October.—*W. & A. Prod.* i. 236.—*Roxb. Flor. Ind.* iii. 258.—Glycine abrus, *Linn.*—*Rheede Mal.* viii. *t.* 39. ——Southern Peninsula. Mysore. Hindostan. Assam.

Medical Uses.—The root yields an extract similar in medicinal properties to Liquorice, though somewhat bitterish. The leaves yield even more than the root. The latter, mixed up with honey, are applied externally to swellings; and, pulverised and chewed with sugar, are given to mitigate coughs. Lunan states that in Jamaica they are used instead of tea. In Java the roots are considered demulcent, and the mucilage is there combined with some bitter. The seeds are occasionally employed externally in ophthalmia. The white seeds are considered to act as a poison, producing vomiting and convulsions, but not unusually fatal to man. The smallest fatal dose is one tolah. The expressed juice of the leaves is said to be useful in aphthæ.—*Ainslie. Powell's Punj. Prod.*

Economic Uses.—There are five varieties of this creeper, with scarlet, black, white, yellow, and blue seeds. The scarlet are most common. These, which have a jet-black spot at the top, are used by jewellers and druggists as weights, each weighing almost uniformly one grain. The goldsmiths reduce them to a fine powder, and in this state use them to increase adhesion in the more delicate parts of manufactured ornaments. They are also used for beads and rosaries, whence the specific name. The Hindoos prize them for necklaces and other ornaments. In Hindoostan they are known as the Retti weights.—*Lindley*. *Ainslie*.

(5) Abutilon Indicum (*G. Don*). N. O. Malvaceæ.

Country mallow, Eng. Kanghi, Hind. Kangoi, Duk. Tutti, Perun-tutti, Tam. Tuttura-benda, Nugu-benda, Tuttiri-chettu, Tel. Pettaka-putti, Tutta, Uram, Mal.

Description.—Shrub, 2-3 feet; leaves cordate, somewhat lobed, soft, shortly tomentose, unequally toothed; calyx 5-cleft, without an involucel; pedicels erect, axillary, longer than the petioles, jointed near the flowers; corolla spreading; capsules truncated; carpels 11-20, acute, not awned, hairy; flowers longish, orange-coloured. *Fl.* July.—*W. & A. Prod.* i. 56.—Sida Indica, *Linn.*—S. populifolia, *Lam.*—*Wight Icon. t.* 12. ——Bengal. Southern Provinces. Common in most parts of the country.

Medical Uses.—The leaves contain a great deal of mucilage, and are used in the same manner as the marsh-mallows in Europe. A decoction of them is used both by European and native practitioners as an emollient fomentation; and an infusion of the roots is given as a cooling drink in fevers.—*Ainslie*.

Economic Uses.—The stem yields a strongish fibre, fit for the manufacture of ropes. Wight remarks that there is no character of any importance to separate this species from *A. Asiaticum*. Another species, the *A. polyandrum* (W. & A.), found on the Neilgherries and about Nundidroog, yields a long silky fibre resembling hemp, also fit for making ropes; and samples of it were submitted to the Madras Exhibition.—*Roxb. Jury Rep. Mad. Exhib.*

(6) Acacia Arabica (*Willd.*) N. O. Leguminosæ.

Babool, Kikar, Hind. Kali-kikar, Duk. Kuru-veylam, Karu-vel, Tam. Nallatumma, Barburamu, Tummachettu, Tel. Karu-velakam, Mal. Babûl, Beng.

Description.—Tree, 30-40 feet, armed with stipulary thorns; leaves bipinnated; pinnæ about five pair; leaflets 15-20 pair, glabrous; peduncles aggregated, axillary or forming a raceme by the abortion of the leaves; heads of flowers globose; stamens distinct; legumes stalked, thickish, contracted on both sutures between the seeds; flowers small, bright yellow, fragrant. *Fl.* May—Oct.—*W. & A. Prod.* i. 277.—Mimosa Arabica, *Lam. Roxb. Fl. Ind.* ii. 557. *Cor.* ii. *t.* 149. ——Bengal. Coromandel. Deccan.

MEDICAL USES.—This tree, like others of the same genus, yields a transparent gum, which is used as a substitute for real gum-Arabic, which is the produce of *A. vera.* The gum is procured by making incisions in the bark, and the sap running out hardens in lumps of various sizes and figures. It exudes principally in March and April. The red kind is the most efficacious. It is used in coughs, rheumatism, and mucous discharges, and is also a useful food in diabetes. The bark is used as a tonic in infusion, and a strong decoction of it is employed as a wash for ulcers; and finely powdered and mixed with Gingely oil, is recommended as an external application to cancerous affections. It may be used as a substitute for oak-bark, and especially as a local astringent in special diseases. Poultices made of the bruised tender leaves are an excellent astringent and stimulant application to ulcers attended with sanious discharge. The leaves are also used in mucous discharges. The pods are used in coughs.—*Ainslie. Pharm. of India. Powell's Punj. Prod.*

ECONOMIC USES.—Mixed with the seeds of *Sesamum,* the gum is an article of food with the natives. The seeds and pods are of great value to the shepherd in the hot season, as food for his flocks when grass is scarce. A decoction of the bark makes a good substitute for soap, and is used to a great extent for tanning leather and dyeing various shades of brown; and, moreover, is employed in Mysore in the process of distilling arrack. The timber is useful for various purposes, such as wheels and tent-pegs, and in some districts is made into charcoal for gunpowder. The tree grows rapidly, and requires no water. There is a variety or distinct species in Candeish called *Ram-kanta,* and another in the Buglana districts which abounds more in gum than the common Babool, and differs from it in the form and colour of its legumes. Dr Balfour mentions in his 'Cyclopædia' the *A. cineraria,* the rind of whose fruit, known as Babbak or Neb-neb, is used as a substitute for the more expensive dye-stuffs, and for communicating shades of drab to cotton. It is a native of Senegal and the East Indies.—*Roxb. Gibson. Ainslie. Balfour's Cycl.*

In Sind, the Babool is the chief yielder of lac. The "Coccus Indica" attaches itself to the smaller and half-dried branches of the trees. The branches, when thoroughly punctured by the insect, lose all vitality, and are then cut off from the parent tree, and the lac gathered. Other trees, when suffering from drought, may yield it; but in Sind, as a rule, it is only gathered from the Babool. The product in its raw state realises about 10 to 12 rupees a maund. Fine Babool timber is annually sent from Sind to Bombay for the use of the gun-carriage manufactory.—(*Fenner's Report to Bomb. Govt.*, 1862.) The Babool has frequently been recommended as a good roadside tree. It is of quick growth, and would speedily form a shelter for travellers. The young trees would require but little care at first, and after a few years of pruning would often more than cover the cost of looking after them. After the cuttings begin to throw out young shoots, they should be carefully pruned, two or three of the strongest near the top being selected as leading shoots to form the future tree. They require water regularly in the hot and dry weather. To raise the trees from seed is a slower process, but is the best and most natural method. The trees are more regular in their growth, and last thrice as long as the cuttings. The Babool is a very hard wood. It is used extensively all over India, but more particularly in Bengal. The timber is only large enough for small purposes. In Sind it is found to be well fitted for railway-sleepers.—(*Cleghorn's Forests of India.*) It has been recommended to Government that more attention should be paid to the despised Babool. If suitable localities be enclosed, the growth of this tree is almost spontaneous, and most rapid; its timber is very useful for all ordinary purposes, and it makes excellent firewood.—(*Rev^t. Comm^r. Report to Bomb. Govt., Feb.* 1868.) With respect to firewood, several Australian Acacias have been thickly sown and planted in the neighbourhood of Ootacamund, where fresh supplies of fuel have become so great a desideratum. Among these are the *A. stricta* and *A. mollissima.* It is a curious fact that hares rarely touch the latter, whereas they destroy the *A. stricta* by hundreds. The reason is supposed to be that the one is more bitter than the other, the roots of the *A. mollissima* emitting a powerfully unpleasant odour. The bark of this latter is useful for tanning, and a tar has been obtained from the wood.—*Major Morgan's Report to Madras Govt.*, 1861.

(7) **Acacia Catechu** (*Willd.*) Do.

Khair-babûl, Khair, Kath-khair, Hind. Katthè-ki-Kikar, Duk. Vodalai, Vodalam, Tam. Podali-manu, Khadirama, Tel. Kadaram, Mal.

Description.—Tree, 30-40 feet; branches armed with stipulary thorns, occasionally unarmed; leaves bipinnated; pinnæ 10-30 pair; leaflets numerous; young shoots, petioles, and peduncles more or less pubescent; petioles sometimes armed below with a row of prickles; spikes axillary, 1-4 together, shorter than the leaves; corolla 5-cleft; petals united; stamens distinct; legumes thin, flat, glabrous, 4-8 seeded; flowers small, white, or pale yellow. *Fl.* June—Oct.—*W. & A. Prod.* i. 272.—A. Wallichiana, *Dec.*—Mimosa catechu, *Linn. Suppl. Roxb. Fl. Ind.* ii. 562. *Cor. t.* 175.——Malabar. Various parts of the Peninsula. Bengal. Delhi.

MEDICAL USES.—The substance formerly known as Terra Japonica is yielded by this tree. It is now better understood as one of the kinds of Catechu prepared in India—the word being derived from *cate*, a tree, and *chu*, juice. It is extracted from the unripe pods and old high-coloured wood, and the mode of preparation in some of the northern parts of India is minutely described by Dr Royle. The chips of the inner wood are put into an earthen pot over the fire; they are then boiled, and the clean liquor is strained off; when of sufficient consistence it is poured into clay moulds. This is usually of a pale-red colour, and in quadrangular pieces. Catechu has been successfully used in cases of intermittent fever in conjunction with infusion of Chiretta, in doses from ten to twelve grains. Dr A. Ross found it very useful in scurvy, both locally applied to the gums, as well as on the constitution. Finely-powdered Catechu has also been successfully used in ointments, mixed with other ingredients, in the treatment of obstinate ulcers and leprous affections.—*Ainslie. Pharm. of India.*

ECONOMIC USES.—Catechu is used in Berar in the process of dyeing chintz and other cloths. It is occasionally mixed with plaster to increase its adhesion, and is also, in conjunction with certain oils, applied to beams, to preserve them against the white ants. The most celebrated Catechu is that obtained from Pegu, and this brings £4 or £5 a-ton more than other astringent extracts. Catechu contains a greater proportion of tannin than other astringent substances, and it has been found that 1 lb. of this is equal to 7 or 8 lb. of oak-bark for tanning purposes. The manufactured article is brought down in considerable quantities from Berar and Nepaul, and thence to Calcutta, from whence it is exported to Europe. Other kinds of Catechu are prepared in India, the commonest of which is that from the nut of the Areca palm (*V. Areca Catechu*). As a timber, the wood of the tree is less hard and durable than that of other species of Acacia. It is of a red colour, heavy, close-grained, and brittle. It polishes well, and resists the attacks of white ants. It is used for agricultural purposes, sugar-mills, and pestles. — *Roxb. Powell's Punj. Prod.*

(8) **Acacia concinna** (*Dec.*) Do.

Siki, DUK. Shika, TAM. Shikaya, TEL. Chinik, MAL. Kochai, BENG.

DESCRIPTION.—Climbing; branches irregularly angled, tomentose, armed with numerous recurved prickles; leaves bipinnated; pinnæ 6-8 pair; leaflets numerous, linear, somewhat semi-hastate, mucronate; petioles with hooked prickles below; panicles terminal and axillary, with globular heads of flowers 3-5 together in the axils of a small bract or leaf, peduncled; stamens distinct; legumes large, succulent, contracted between the seeds; valves wrinkled on the surface when dry; flowers small, white. *Fl.* July—October.—*W. & A. Prod.* i. 277.—Mimosa concinna, *Willd.*——Bengal. Assam. Mysore.

Economic Uses.—A considerable trade is carried on in some parts of the country in the pods of this shrub, which resemble the soap-nut, and are used, like it, for washing the head. The Hindoos also use them for marking the forehead. The leaves are acid, and are used in cookery as a substitute for tamarinds.—*Roxb. Nimmo.*

(9) **Acacia Farnesiana** (*Willd.*) Do.

Guh-babool, Hind. and Beng. Gú-kikar, Duk. Piy-vélam, Tam. Piyi-tumma, Kampu-tumma, Naga-tumma, Tel. Pivelam, Mal.

Description.—Shrub or small tree, armed with stipulary thorns; calyx 5-toothed; corolla tubular; stamens distinct; leaves bipinnated; pinnæ 4-8 pair; leaflets linear, 10-20 pair, nearly glabrous; petioles and peduncles more or less pubescent; legumes cylindrical, fitted with pulp and two rows of seeds; flowers globular, 2-3 together, each on an axillary peduncle, small, yellow, fragrant. *Fl.* Dec.—Jan.—*W. & A. Prod.* i. 272 (under *Vachellia*).—Mimosa Farnesiana, *Linn.*—*Roxb. Fl. Ind.* ii. 557.——Bengal. Assam. Peninsula.

Economic Uses.—This small tree exudes a considerable quantity of useful gum. The wood is very hard and tough, and is much used for ship-knees, tent-pegs, and similar purposes. The flowers distilled yield a delicious perfume.—*W. & A. Roxb.*

(10) **Acacia ferruginea** (*Dec.*) Do.

Shimai-velvel, Tam. Vuní, Anasandra, Tel.

Description.—Tree, 20-25 feet, armed with conical stipulary thorns, occasionally unarmed; leaves bipinnated, glabrous; pinnæ 3-6 pair; leaflets 10-20 pair, oblong-linear; spikes of flowers axillary, usually in pairs, many-flowered; corolla 5-cleft; stamens slightly united at the base; legumes flat, lanceolate, rusty-coloured, 2-6 seeded; flowers small, pale yellow.—*Fl.* April—May.—*W. & A. Prod.* i. 273.—Mimosa ferruginea, *Roxb. Fl. Ind.* ii. 561.——Coromandel Coast. Courtallum. N. Circars.

Economic Uses.—The bark steeped in jaggery water is distilled as an intoxicating liquor. It is very astringent. A decoction of the same, in conjunction with ginger and other ingredients, is frequently employed as an astringent wash for the teeth. The wood is very hard and useful.—*Ainslie. Lindl.*

(11) **Acacia leucophlæa** (*Willd.*) Do.

Panicled Acacia, Eng. Sufed-kikar, Hind. Ujlee-kikar, Duk. Vel-vel, Vel-veylam, Tam. Tella-tumma, Tel. Vel-veylam, Mal. Suphaid-bábul, Beng.

Description.—Tree, armed with stipulary thorns; leaves bipinnated; pinnæ 7-12 pair; leaflets numerous, oblong-linear, slightly pubescent; panicles terminal or from the upper axils; branches and peduncles shortly tomentose; corolla 5-cleft; stamens distinct; legumes narrow, long, curved, shortly tomentose when young; heads of flowers globose; flowers small, pale yellow. *Fl.* June—Sept.—*W. & A. Prod.* i. 227.—Mimosa leucophlæa, *Roxb. Cor.* ii. 15. *Fl. Ind.* ii. 58.—A. alba, *Willd.*——Sholapore. Woods and hills on Coromandel coast.

Economic Uses.—The natives distil a kind of ardent spirit from the bark, mixed with palm-wine and sugar. A fibre is also prepared from the bark by maceration after four or five days' beating. It is used for large fishing-nets and coarse kinds of cordage, being tough and strong. The timber of the tree is hard and dark-coloured. —*Lindl. Rep. Mad. Exhib.*

(12) **Acacia sundra** (*Dec.*) Do.

Karungall, Tam. Sundra, Tel.

Description.—Tree, 20-30 feet; branches armed with recurved stipulary prickles, sometimes unarmed; leaves bipinnated; pinnæ 15-20 pair; leaflets numerous, small, linear; spikes 1-3 together, axillary, peduncled, shorter than the leaves, many-flowered; corolla 5-cleft; stamens distinct; flowers small, yellow; legumes thin, flat, lanceolate; seeds few. *Fl.* July—Aug.—*W. & A. Prod.* i. 273.—Mimosa sundra, *Roxb. Cor.* iii. *t.* 225.—*Bedd. Flor. Sylv. t.* 50.——Travancore. N. Circars. Bombay Presidency. Mysore.

Economic Uses.—A resin similar to that yielded by *A. Catechu* is procured from this tree. In fact, the two species are much alike. This one principally differs in being perfectly glabrous. The timber is close-grained, very hard and durable, very heavy, and of a dark-red colour. It is excellent for piles and sleepers; and the natives prefer it for posts in house-building, though, owing to the unyielding nature of the wood, it is apt to split when nails are driven into it. The tree is abundant, and grows to a fair size.—*Wight. Bedd. Flor. Sylv. Rep. Mad. Exhib.*

(13) **Acalypha fruticosa** (*Forsk.*) N. O. EUPHORBIACEÆ.

Birch-leaved Acalypha, ENG. Sinnie, TAM. Chinnie, DUK. Tsinnie, TEL.

DESCRIPTION.—Shrub, pubescent, with sessile, waxy, golden-yellowish glands; leaves rhomb-ovate, acute at both ends, serrated, beneath covered and shining with golden glands; spikes unisexual, very shortly peduncled, or androgynous and males; males commonly shorter than the leaves, erect, hoary; androgynous ones increased at the base by 1-4 female bracts; female spikes lax-flowered, 5-8 bracteate; female bracts 1-flowered, exceeding the capsule; male calyx externally pubescent; ovary densely hairy; capsules hoary tomentose; seeds smooth; flowers greenish.—*Forsk. Descr.* 161.—*Dec. Prod.* xv. *s.* 2, *p.* 822.—A. betulina, *Retz.*—A. amentacea, *Roxb. Fl. Ind.* iii. 676.——Peninsula. Mysore.

MEDICAL USES.—The leaves are prescribed by the native doctors as a stomachic in dyspeptic affections and cholera. They are also reckoned attenuant and alterative. The dose of the infusion is half a teacupful twice daily.—*Ainslie.*

(14) **Acalypha Indica** (*Linn.*) Do.

Indian Acalypha, ENG. Koopa-mani, MAL. Cupamani, TAM. Koopi, DUK. Mukto-juri, BENG.

DESCRIPTION.—Annual, 1-2 feet; leaves ovate-cordate, serrated, on long petioles; spikes axillary, as long as the leaves, male flowers uppermost, enclosed in a cup-shaped involucre opening on the inner side, striated, serrated; stamens 8-16; styles 3; capsules tricoccous, 3-celled, 1-seeded; flowers small, greenish. *Fl.* April—June.—*Roxb. Fl. Ind.* iii. 675.—*Wight Icon. t.* 877.—*Rheede,* x. *t.* 81-83.——Bengal. Peninsula.

MEDICAL USES.—The root, bruised and steeped in hot water, is used as a cathartic, and the leaves as a laxative, in decoction. Mixed with common salt, the latter are applied externally in scabies. A decoction of the whole plant mixed with oil is antarthritic; and mixed with chunam, forms a good external application in cutaneous diseases. A simple decoction of the leaves is given in ear-ache.—(*Roxb. Ainslie.*) The expressed juice of the leaves is a safe and certain emetic for children. It has also been usefully administered as an expectorant, and in bronchitis in children. A cataplasm of the leaves is applied as a local application to syphilitic ulcers, and as a means of relieving the pain attendant on the bites of venomous insects.—*Pharm. of India.*

(15) **Achyranthes aspera** (*Linn.*) N. O. AMARANTACEÆ.

Chirchirà, Chikrà, HIND. Agárá, DUK. Na-yuriol, TAM. Utta-rèni, Antisha, Apa-marganiu, Pratyak-pushpi, TEL. Katalâti, MAL. Opang, BENG.

DESCRIPTION.—Shrub about 6 feet; branches somewhat 4-sided; stem erect, pubescent; leaves on short petioles, obovate-rotund, abruptly attenuated at the base, pubescent; spikes virgate, acute, at first horizontal, afterwards reflexed; flowers purplish-green; bracts at first soft, soon becoming rigid and prickle-like; capsules 5-seeded, reddish. *Fl.* nearly all the year.—*Roxb. Fl. Ind.* i. 672.—*Wight Icon. t.* 1777.—*Rheede,* x. *t.* 78.—A. obtusifolia, *Lam.*——Bengal. Peninsula.

MEDICAL USES.—The seeds are given in hydrophobia, and in cases of snake-bites, as well as in ophthalmia and cutaneous diseases. The flowering-spikes rubbed with a little sugar are made into pills, and given internally to people bitten by mad dogs. The leaves taken fresh and rubbed to a pulp are considered a good remedy applied externally to the bites of scorpions. The ashes of the burnt plant mixed with conjee is a native remedy in dropsical cases. Astringent and diuretic properties are assigned to this plant, and Dr Cornish states having employed it largely in dropsy with favourable results. The whole plant, when incinerated, yields a considerable quantity of potash. These ashes, in conjunction with infusion of ginger, are likewise esteemed in dropsical affections. The flowering-spike has the repute in Oude and other parts of India of being a safeguard against scorpions, which it is believed to paralyse. It has also been used successfully as a local application in scorpion-stings and in snake-bites.—*Pharm. of India. Long in Journ. of Agri. Hort. Soc. of India,* 1858, x. 31. *Madras Quart. Journ. of Med. Sc.,* 1862, iv. 10.—*Wight. Ainslie. Hamilton.*

(16) **Aconitum ferox** (*Wall.*) N. O. RANUNCULACEÆ.

Bustnab-bish, Bish, BENG. Mahoor, HIND. Bachnag, DUK. Vasha-navi, TAM. Vasa-nabhi, Valsa-nabhi, TEL.

DESCRIPTION.—Stem erect, 2-3 feet, slightly downy above; tubers 2-3, blackish, white inside; branches villous; leaves roundish-cordate, deeply 5-parted; lobes pinnatifid, cuneate at the base, hairy on the brim beneath; racemes terminal, downy; flowers large, deep blue, hoary; helmet gibbous, semi-circular, slightly acuminated in front; cucullate petals slightly incurved.—*Dec. Prod.* i. 64.—*Lindl. Flor. Med.* 12. ——Himalaya. Kumaon.

MEDICAL USES.—This plant is found at high elevations in the Himalaya and Nepaul, sometimes at 10,000 feet above the sea. Dr Wight asserts that wherever within the tropics we meet herbaceous forms of Ranunculaceæ, we may feel assured of having attained an elevation sufficient to place us beyond the influence of jungle fever. The root of this species of Aconite is highly poisonous, equally fatal whether taken internally or applied to wounds. By Indian practitioners it is used in cases of chronic rheumatism. Dr Pereira found that a drop of the spirituous infusion applied to the tongue produced numbness, which lasted eighteen hours. Its action appears to be similar to that of *A. napellus*, which is found in mountainous parts of Europe.

"Although," says Dr Royle, "the acrid principle existing in most of the plants of the Ranunculaceous order is very volatile, yet the effects attendant on the roots of the *A. ferox* after it has been preserved for ten years was remarkable, as showing that it is more permanent than has been supposed." In the Taleef-shireef it is directed never to be given alone; but mixed with several other drugs, it is recommended in a variety of diseases, as cholera, intermittent fevers, toothache, snake-bites, and especially in rheumatism externally applied. The root is imported in considerable quantities into the plains, and sold at the rate of one rupee the seer.—*Wallich. Royle. Hamilton's Nepaul.*

Dr Fleming's experiments prove that the roots are more active immediately after the period of flowering than at any other time, and that the leaves lose their power when the seeds begin to form. The seeds themselves are comparatively weak (*Lindl. E. B.*) The terms Bish, Bikh, or Vish, merely mean poison. In Dr Playfair's translation of the Taleef-shireef the names *Sindia* and *Bechnak* are applied to poisonous medicines, undoubtedly the Aconite.

In Dr Pereira's experiments the effects were tried by introducing the extract into the jugular vein, by placing it in the cavity of the peritoneum, by applying it to the cellular tissue of the back, and by introducing it into the stomach. In all these cases, except the last, the effects were very similar—viz., difficulty of breathing, weakness and subsequent paralysis, which generally commenced in the posterior extremities, vertigo, convulsions, dilatation of the pupils, and death apparently from asphyxia.—*Wallich, Pl. As. Rar.*, i. 35.

(17) **Aconitum heterophyllum** (*Wall.*) Do.

Atis, HIND. **Atvika, Vajjê-turki**, DUK. **Ativadayam**, TAM. **Ativasa**, TEL.

DESCRIPTION.—Shrub; stem obscurely angled, smooth

below, pubescent above; tubers oblong-oval; fibres numerous, spreading; lower leaves long-petioled, round or sagittate-cordate, acuminated, 5-ribbed or more; helmet arched, slightly acuminate; wings equal to the helmet in size, obliquely triangular; lower sepals lanceolate, smooth; flowers blue.—*Royle Ill. t.* 13.——Himalaya.

MEDICAL USES.—The root of this species of Aconite, known by the name of Atees, has long been celebrated as a tonic and valuable febrifuge. It is generally sold in the bazaars as a fine white powder, but is somewhat expensive. There is a spurious substance called by the same name, which is only the root of the *Asparagus sarmentosus.* The true Atees is intensely bitter and slightly astringent, with abundant farina, which is free from any noxious qualities. It is probably not so injurious a poison as the *Bish*, as it is attacked by insects, while the other is not. There are two kinds, one black and one white, both bitter and astringent, pungent and heating, aiding digestion, useful as tonic medicines and aphrodisiac. The present species is found also on the Himalaya at elevations from 9000 to 10,000 feet.—*Royle. Annals of Med. Science,* 1856.

The roots are about an inch long, of an oblong-oval pointed form, light grey externally, white inside, and of a pure bitter taste.

Modern experience confirms the value of Atees as an antiperiodic. Dr Balfour was eminently successful in many cases of fever which came under his treatment with its employment. He, however, stated in his reports the necessity of selecting the best specimens, as much of inferior quality is sold in the bazaars. He advises that every root should be broken across, and all which are not pure white be discarded. The other species of Aconite found on the Himalaya, and yielding similar properties, are, *A. palmatum* (Don) and *A. luridum* (H. & T.)—*Pharm. of India. Indian Annals of Med. Science,* v. 548.

(18) **Acorus calamus** (*Linn.*) N. O. ORONTIACEÆ.

Sweet-flag, ENG. Bach, HIND. Vach, DUK. Vashambu, TAM. Vasa, Vadaja, TEL. Vashampa, MAL. Bach, Saphed-bach, BENG.

DESCRIPTION.—Perennial, semi-aquatic; rhizome thick, with long roots; leaves erect, 2-3 feet, sword-shaped; stalk leaf-like, but thicker below the spadix; spadix a foot above the root, spreading, 2-3 inches long, covered with a mass of numerous thick-set pale-green flowers, fragrant when bruised; petals six; capsules 3-celled. *Fl.* May—June.—*Roxb. Flor. Ind.* ii. 169.—A. odoratus, *Lam.*—*Rheede,* xi. *t.* 60.——Damp marshy places. Malabar.

MEDICAL USES.—An aromatic bitter principle exists in the rhizomes, for which reason they are regarded as useful additions to tonic and purgative medicines, being much given to children in cases of dyspepsia, especially when attended with looseness of bowels. Beneficially employed also in chronic catarrh and asthmatic complaints. Dr Pereira has remarked that the rhizomes might be substituted for more expensive spices or aromatics. The flavour is greatly improved by drying. In Constantinople they are made into a confection, which is considered a good stomachic, and is eaten freely during the prevalence of epidemic disease. They are supposed, moreover, to be an antidote for several poisons.—(*Pereira. Thomson. Ainslie.*) In low fevers they are considered an excellent stimulant diaphoretic, and also very serviceable in atonic and choleraic diarrhœa, and as a useful external application in chronic rheumatism, the powdered rhizome being rubbed up with Cashew spirit. Dr A. T. Thomson notices the root-stock favourably as an antiperiodic, and Dr Royle employed it successfully in intermittent fevers. It is also highly useful for destroying and keeping away insects.—*Pharm. of India.*

ECONOMIC USES.—The leaves contain an essential oil, to which they owe their fragrance, and which in England is used by the perfumers, mixed with the farina of the rhizomes, in the manufacture of hair-powders. They are also used for tanning leather and perfuming various substances.—*Ainslie.*

(19) **Acrocarpus fraxinifolius** (*Wight*). N. O. LEGUMINOSÆ.

Shingle-tree, Pink or Red Cedar, ENG. Mallay-Kone, TAM.

DESCRIPTION.—Large tree, deciduous, often having large buttresses, bark light grey, young parts golden pubescent; leaves glabrous, bipinnate; pinnæ 3 pairs with a terminal one; leaflets equally pinnate, 4-6, opposite pair ovate, acuminate; racemes many-flowered; flowers dull greenish-red; calyx and corolla minutely golden-pubescent outside.—*Wight Icon. t.* 254.—*Bedd. Flor. Syl. t.* 44.——Travancore Mountains and Western Ghauts. South Canara.

ECONOMIC USES.—A tree of rapid growth and worthy of cultivation. The timber is flesh-coloured and light. It is much used by the planters at Conoor and Wynaad for building purposes and furniture, and in Coorg is largely used for shingles. It is known by the Burghers on the Neilgherries as the Kilingi.—*Bedd.*

(20) **Adansonia digitata** (*Linn.*) N. O. BOMBACEÆ.

Baobab or monkey bread-tree, ENG. Gorak Amli, HIND. Hathi-Khatiyan, Bara-Khat-yan, DUK. Anai-puliyamaram, Papparap-puli, Puri-maram, TAM.

DESCRIPTION.—Tree of moderate height; trunk enormous,

30-40 feet in circumference; leaves digitate, quinate, glabrous, petioled; leaflets elliptical, slightly acuminated; petioles and peduncles pubescent; calyx 5-partite, pubescent, silky inside; petals 5, spreading, at length deflexed; flowers axillary, solitary on long pedicels; stamen tube adhering to the base of the petals; fruit a large oblong downy pericarp 8-10 celled, cells filled with farinaceous pulp; flowers large, white, with purplish anthers. *Fl.* July—*W. & A. Prod.* i. 60.——Naturalised in India. Negapatam. Madras.

Medical Uses.—The fruit is somewhat acid, but makes a cooling and refreshing drink in fevers. The acid farinaceous pulp surrounding the seeds is used in dysentery and diarrhœa; failing this, the rind of the fruit beaten into a paste and mixed with water may be substituted. Adanson found the fruit a great preservative against the epidemic fevers of the western coast of Africa, and especially beneficial in promoting perspiration, and attempering the heat of the blood. In Guadaloupe the planters use the bark and leaves as a febrifuge. Among other uses in Africa, the leaves are made into fomentations and poultices for rheumatic affections of the limbs and irritable inflammatory ulcers. Dr Hutchinson considers that the action of the pulp is not due to any astringent properties, but to its virtues as a refrigerant and diuretic. Duchassaing (*Pharm. Journ.*, 1845, p. 89) proposes the bark as a substitute for quinine in low intermittent fevers. He prescribed it in decoction, and found it effectual in cases where quinine had failed.—*Pharm. of India. Graham, Bomb. Flora. Adanson.*

Economic Uses.—This tree is a native of the western coast of Africa, about Senegal and Sierra Leone. It has, however, long been naturalised in India, and from its many uses is deserving of a place among the more useful plants of this country. The large fruit resembles a gourd, and contains many black seeds. In Senegal the negroes use the bark and leaves powdered as we do pepper and salt. The fruit supplies the natives of Africa with an excellent soap by boiling the ashes with rancid palm-oil. It is in the hollowed trunks of these trees that the negroes bury their dead; and it is a remarkable fact, that shut up in these, the bodies become perfectly dry, without the necessity of the process of embalmment. Humboldt, in his 'Aspects of Nature,' remarks that the Baobab or monkey bread-tree is the oldest organic monument of our planet. The earliest description of these trees is that of Aloysius Cadamosto, a Venetian, in 1454, who found one growing at the mouth of the Senegal river, whose trunk in circumference was 112 feet. Adanson himself saw them at 29 feet in diameter and 70 feet in height, and remarks that other travellers had found trunks of 32 feet diameter. As a timber-tree it is quite useless, the wood being soft and spongy. Dr Hooker says, "the tree is emollient and mucilaginous in all its parts." Along the sea-coast of Guzerat the fisherman use the large fruit as a float for their nets. The leaves are eaten with their food, and are considered cooling, and useful in restraining excessive perspiration. M. Mollien, in his Travels in Africa, states that to the negroes the Baobab is perhaps the most valuable of vegetables. Its leaves are used for leaven, its bark furnishes indestructible cordage, and a coarse thread used for cloth and ropes. Ropes made from the bark are said to be very strong, and there is in Bengal a saying, "As secure as an elephant bound with a Baobab rope."—*Hooker. Humboldt. Lindley.*

(21) **Adenanthera pavonina** (*Linn.*) N. O. LEGUMINOSÆ.

Anat-kundamunie, TAM. Bandi gooroovinza, TEL. Rukta-chundun, Ranguna, BENG. Munjatie, MAL. Kúchun-doona, HIND.

DESCRIPTION.—Large tree, unarmed; leaves bipinnated; pinnæ 4-6 pair; leaflets oval, obtuse, glabrous, 10-12 pair, on short petioles; calyx 5-toothed; petals 5; racemes terminal or from the upper axils, spike-like; legumes somewhat falcate, twisted, 10-12 seeded; flowers numerous, small, yellow and white mixed, fragrant. *Fl.* June—Aug.—*Roxb. Fl. Ind.* ii. 370.—*W. & A Prod.* i. 271.—*Rheede,* vi. *t.* 14.——Peninsula. Northern Circars. Travancore. Bengal.

ECONOMIC USES.—Although this tree is called *Rukta-chundun*, which means Red Sandal, yet the real red sàndal-wood is the produce of the *Pterocarpus Santalinus.* It is to be met with in most forests in India. The timber is valued for its solidity. The inner wood of the larger specimens is of a deep-red colour, very hard and durable. It yields a dye which the Brahmins use after bathing for marking their foreheads. They procure it by merely rubbing the wood on a wet stone. The seeds, which are of a shining scarlet colour with a circular streak in their centre, are used as weights by the jewellers, each of them weighing four grains. The natives in Travancore assert that they are poisonous if taken internally, especially when in a powdered state. A cement is made by beating them up with borax and water.—*Roxb. Ainslie.*

(22) **Adhatoda Tranquebariensis** (*Nees*). N. O. ACANTHACEÆ.

Tavashù-moorungie, Poonakoo-poondoo, TAM. Pindi-konda, TEL.

DESCRIPTION.—Fruticulose, hoary-pubescent; leaves small, roundish; bracts orbiculate, retuse, bracteoles equalling the calyx, linear; flowers axillary, solitary, ascending on a terminal spike, yellowish, purple-dotted. *Fl.* Feb.—March.—*Dec. Prod.* xi. 399.—Gendarussa Tranquebariensis, *Nees ap. Wall. Pl. As.*

Rar. iii. 105.—Justicia Tranquebariensis, *Linn.*—J. parvifolia, *Lam.*—*Wight Icon. t.* 462.——Eastern coasts of Peninsula.

Medical Uses.—The juice of the leaves is reckoned cooling and aperient, and is given to children in small-pox. The bruised leaves are applied to blows and other external injuries.—*Ainslie.*

(23) **Adhatoda Vasica** (*Nees*). Do.

Malabar nut, Eng. Adalsa, Arusa, Adarsa, Hind. and Duk. Adatodai, Tam. Adasaram, Tel. Atalotakam, Mal. Arusa, Beng.

Description.—Shrub, 8-10 feet; leaves opposite, lanceolate; corolla monopetalous, irregular; stem much branched; flowers on short spikes, terminal; flower whitish, spotted, sulphur-coloured at the throat, and at the limb with dark purple lines. *Fl.* Feb. —April.—Justicia Adhatoda, *Linn.*—*Roxb. Fl. Ind.* i. 126. ——Peninsula. Bengal. Nepaul.

Medical Uses.—The juice of the leaves is given in a dose of two drams with one dram of the juice of fresh ginger as an expectorant in coughs, asthma, and ague. They are bitterish and subaromatic, and are administered in infusion and electuary.—(*Journ. Agri. Hort. Soc. of India*, x. 28. *Ainslie*). The leaves, flowers, and root, especially the flowers, are considered antispasmodic, and are given in cases of asthma and intermittent fever. They have also been successfully employed in chronic bronchitis, and other pulmonary and catarrhal affections when not attended with fever.—(*Pharm. of India. Ind. Annals of Med. Science*, x. 156.) The leaves are given to cattle as medicine, and to man for rheumatism. The fresh flowers are bound over the eyes in cases of ophthalmia.—(*Stewart's Punj. Plants.*) The leaves are given in conjunction with other remedies by the native doctors internally in decoction, as anthelmintic.—*Ainslie. Roxb.*

(24) **Ægle marmelos** (*Corr.*) N. O. Aurantiaceæ.

Bael or Bel tree, Eng. Bel, Siri-phul, Hind. Vilva, Tam. Maredoo, Bilva-pandu, Tel. Kuvalam, Mal. Bel, Shri-phul, Beng.

Description.—Tree, middling size, armed with sharp spines; leaves pinnate; leaflets oblong or broad-lanceolate, crenulated, unequal, middle one petiolate, lateral ones almost sessile; petals 4-5, spreading; stamens distinct; style short, thick; flowers in panicles, axillary, on long pedicels, large, greenish white, fragrant; berry with a hard rind, smooth, many-celled, many-seeded; seeds covered with a transparent glutinous matter. *Fl.* May.—*W. & A. Prod.* i. 96.—*Roxb. Fl. Ind.* ii.

579. *Cor.* ii. 143.—Cratœva marmelos, *Linn.*—*Wight Icon. t.* 16.—*Rheede,* iii. *t.* 37.——Peninsula. Bengal.

Medical Uses.—The fruit of this tree is somewhat like an orange. The cells contain, besides the seeds, a large quantity of tenacious transparent gluten, which becomes hard on drying, but continues transparent. The fruit is nutritious, and occasionally employed as an alterative. It is very palatable; and its aperient qualities in the removal of habitual costiveness have been well ascertained. The root, bark, and leaves are reckoned refrigerant in Malabar. The bark of the root especially is given in compound decoctions in intermittent fevers, and the leaves made into poultices in ophthalmia. When dried before it is ripe the fruit is used in decoction in diarrhœa and dysentery; and when ripe and mixed with juice of tamarinds, forms an agreeable drink. A water distilled from the flowers is reputed to be alexipharmic. A decoction of the bark of the tree is given in palpitation of the heart, and of the leaves in asthma.—(*Roxb. Ainslie. Rheede.*) According to Dr Green, a sherbet of the ripe fruit taken every morning proves serviceable in moderate cases of dyspepsia. He further adds that the unripe fruit baked for six hours is a powerful astringent.—(*Ind. Ann. Med. Sc.*, ii. 224.) The fullest accounts of the properties and uses of the Bael are given in the papers by Grant and Cleghorn in 'Indian Annals of Med. Science,' ii. 222-234.

Economic Uses.—The mucus of the seeds is used as an excellent addition to mortar, especially in the construction of wells. A yellow dye is procured from the astringent rind of the fruit.—*Roxb.*

(25) **Æschynomene aspera** (*Linn.*) N. O. Leguminosæ.

Shola, Tola, Hind. Phool-sola, Beng. Attekudasa, Mal. Attoonette, Tam.

Description.—Perennial, floating, erect, sometimes branched; leaves unequally pinnated; leaflets numerous, linear, obtuse; racemes axillary, few-flowered; calyx 5-cleft, 2-lipped, bibracteolate; peduncles and pedicels rough with hairs; legumes 4-7 jointed, on long stalks, with prickly tubercles on the middle of each joint, margins striated, crenulated; flowers brownish orange. *Fl.* June—Aug.—*W. & A. Prod.* i. 219.—*Wight Icon. t.* 299.—Hedysarum lagenarium, *Roxb. Fl. Ind.* iii. 365.——Peninsula. Bengal. In tanks and lakes.

Economic Uses.—The pith is much used for the manufacture of hats, bottle-cases, and similar articles, it being a bad conductor of heat. It is cut from the thick stems and made up into artificial flowers, models of temples, and fishing-floats. The plants are gathered for this purpose in April and May, being abundant in the marshes in Bengal, and the borders of jheels and lakes between Calcutta and Hurdwar.—*Roxb.*

(26) **Agathotes chirayta** (*Don*). N. O. Gentianaceæ.

Chirayit Gentian, Eng. Shayraet, Tam. Chiraeta, Duk. and Hind. Sheelassettoo, Tel. Kiriyatha, Mal.

Description.—Annual, 3 feet; stems single, round, jointed; branches decussated, occasionally angular at the extremities; leaves opposite, amplexicaul, lanceolate, very acute, entire, 3-5 nerved; flowers numerous, stalked, the whole upper part of the plant forming an oblong decussated panicle; calyx 4-cleft; petals spreading, 4-parted, divisions equal to those of the calyx; capsules 1-celled, 2-valved, slightly opening at the apex; seeds numerous; flowers yellow.—*Roxb. Fl. Ind.* ii. 71. ——Nepaul. Kumaon. Northern India.

Medical Uses.—This is one of the most esteemed of Indian medicinal plants, being especially valuable as a tonic and febrifuge. The whole plant is pulled up at the time the flowers begin to decay, and is thus dried for use. Its febrifugal properties are in high estimation with European practitioners in India, who use it instead of Cinchona when the latter is not to be procured; and in most cases wherein Gentian is prescribed, this is recommended as a good substitute. The root is the bitterest part of the plant, and the bitter principle is easily imparted to water or alcohol. According to Battley's analysis of its chemical properties, "it contains a free acid, a bitter resinous extractive with much gum, and chlorates, with sulphates of potass and lime. No alkaloid has been detected in it; what is therefore sold as a sulphate of chiraytine is well known to be only the disulphate of quinia." It is best recommended in preparation as an infusion or watery extract, or a tincture, but not in decoction; even infusion made with warm water is denounced as producing violent headache. To form a cold infusion, a pint of water should not stand more than twenty minutes on half an ounce of the bruised plant. Chirayta possesses the general properties of bitter tonics, but has at the same time some peculiar to itself, which fit it well for certain forms and complications of disease. Unlike most other tonics, it does not constipate the bowels, but tends to produce a regular action of the alimentary canal, even in those subject to habitual constipation. During its use the bile becomes more abundant and healthy in character. The tendency to excess of acidity in the stomach, with disengagement of flatus, is much restrained by its use. These qualities fit it in a most peculiar degree for the kind of indigestion which occurs in gouty persons. It may, when necessary, be associated with alkaline preparations or with acids ; the latter are generally preferable. The same remark applies to its employment in the treatment of scrofula. As a remedy against the languor and debility which affect many persons in summer and autumn, nothing is equal to the cold infusion of this plant. It may be taken twice or even more frequently daily for a considerable time ; then discontinued, and afterwards resumed. Children take it more readily than most other bitters. It is found to be a very efficacious remedy in India against intermittents, particularly when associated with Guilandina, Bonduc, or Caranga nuts. The debility which is apt to end in dropsy is often speedily removed by infusion of Chirayta ; to which is added the tincture formed of it with orange-peel and cardamoms. Its efficacy in worm-cases has procured for it the name of worm-seed plant. The extract is given with great benefit in some forms of diarrhœa and dysentery, particularly if combined with Ipecacuan, the emetic tendency of which it very markedly controls. In Dr Fleming's Notes on 'Indian Medicinal Plants,' as quoted by Wallich, it is stated, "The dried herb is to be met with in every bazaar of Hindoostan, being a medicine in the highest repute with both the Hindu and European practitioners. It possesses all the stomachic, tonic, febrifuge, and antarthritic virtues which are ascribed to the Gentiana lutea, and in a greater degree than they are generally found in that root in the state in which it comes to us from Europe. It may therefore on every occasion be advantageously substituted for it. The efficacy of the Chirayta, when combined with the Caranga nut, in curing intermittents, has been already mentioned. For restoring the tone and activity of the moving fibre in general debility, and in that kind of cachexy which is liable to terminate in dropsy, the Chirayta will be found one of the most useful and effectual remedies which we can employ. The parts of the plant that are used in medicine are the dried stalks with pieces of root attached. A decoction of these, or, which is better, an infusion of them in hot water, is the form usually administered."—*Don in Lon. and Edin. Phil. Mag. Wallich, Plantæ As. Rarior.*

(27) **Agati grandiflora** (*Desv.*) N. O. LEGUMINOSÆ.

Agathee, TAM. Anisay, TEL. Agati. MAL. Buko, BENG.

DESCRIPTION.—Tree, 30-35 feet ; leaves abruptly pinnated, leaflets numerous ; calyx campanulate, slightly 2-lipped ; corolla papilionaceous, vexillum oval, oblong, keel large, falcate, with petals free at the base and apex ; racemes axillary, 2-4 flowered ; flowers large, scarlet or white ; legumes pendulous, very long, many-seeded, contracted between the seeds. *Fl.* March —April.—*W. & A. Prod.* i. 215.—Æschynomene coccinea, *Linn.*—Æ. grandiflora, *Roxb. Fl. Ind.* iii. 331. *Rheede*, i. *t.* 51. ——Travancore and elsewhere in the Peninsula in gardens.

Medical Uses.—The bark is very bitter, and is used as a tonic, and an infusion of the leaves is a useful cathartic. The natives put the juice of the leaves in the nostrils in bad fevers on the day of the paroxysm. The juice of the flowers is squeezed into the eyes for expelling dimness of vision.—*Lindley. Pharm. of India.*

(28) **Agave Americana** (*Linn.*) N. O. Amaryllidaceæ.

Bakas-pattah, Halhi-sengar, Barà-kanvar, Jungli-kanvar, Hind. Rakkas-pattah, Duk. Anaik-katrazhai, Tam. Rakashi-mattalu, Tel. Panam-katrazha, Mal. Jungli-ananash, Bilatipat, Beng.

Description.—Stem very thick, scaly at the bases of the leaves, very fibrous; scape erect, tapering, thick; scales alternate, sublanceolate, half stem-clasping, lower ones longer, approximated, upper ones more remote; radical leaves incumbent by turns, lanceolate, channelled, smooth, dentately spinous at the edge, glaucous, mucronate, stiff, 6 feet and more, juicy, outer ones reflexed, intermediate ones spreading, inner ones obvolute into a straight very acute cone; leaf-spines straight, chestnut, marginal ones incurved of the same colour; panicles very large, nodding, composite; peduncles recurved, bent inwards, decompound, many-flowered; flowers peduncled, greenish-yellow.—*Kunth Enum. pl.* v. 819.—*Linn. Spec.* 461. —*Andr. Repos. t.* 438.—*Wight Icon. t.* 2024.——Naturalised in India.

Medical Uses.—The roots are diuretic and anti-syphilitic, and are brought to Europe mixed with sarsaparilla (*Lindley*). Diuretic and alterative properties are assigned to the roots by the Mexicans. A thin slice of the large fleshy leaves makes a good poultice.—*Pharm. of India.*

Economic Uses.—The common American Aloe, although not indigenous, is now common in every part of India. It is a native of America within the tropics from the plains to elevations of 10,000 feet, and is now naturalised in the South of Europe. It is much valued as a hedge plant, but its chief importance arises from the excellent fibres which it yields. Not only are these procured from the leaves, but a ligneous fibre is contained in the root, familiarly known as the Pita thread. This is much used in the Madras Presidency. It is manufactured at a very slight expense, the mode of preparation being usually to cut the leaves and throw them into ponds for three or more days, when they are taken out, macerated and scraped with a bluntish instrument. It has been found that the leaf fibres are liable to rot owing to a milky viscid juice contained in them. This defect has, however, been considerably obviated by very hard crushing, or pressure between heavy cylinders, which, by getting rid of all the moisture, renders them more pliable for weaving and other purposes. In Calcutta, the fibres being submitted to experiments, were found equal to the best Russian hemp. They are much used for lashing bales of calico. As log-lines for ships they are found to be very durable, and far superior to ropes of hemp. In several experiments that have been made, especially by Drs Royle and Wight, Aloe-fibre rope has been found to be more powerful than either coir, country hemp, or jute. A bundle of the Agave fibre bore 270 lb., that of Russian hemp only 160 lb. Dr Wight found some cord of it bore 362 lb. In Tinnevelly it sells from 20 to 40 rupees the candy of 500 lb., and at Madras for 7 rupees a maund. There is no doubt that these Aloe fibres deserve more particular notice. They are admirably suited for cordage, mats, ropes, &c., and the tow might be advantageously used in the manufacture of paper. In Mexico they prepare a fermented liquor from the stem by incision, called Pulque, and from this they distil an ardent spirit. In that country, too, the dried flowering-stems are used as impenetrable thatch. An extract of the leaves is used to make a lather, like soap, and the leaves, split longitudinally, are employed to sharpen razors on, performing the duties of a strop owing to the particles of silica they contain.—(*Royle's Fibrous Plants. Jury Rep. Mad. Exhib. Lindley.*) An important discovery has recently been made, that plaster impregnated with the juice and pulp of the Aloe leaves will save walls from being attacked by white ants. The experiment was made in jails, and other buildings where white ants abounded, and those parts of the buildings where the Aloe juice was mixed with the plaster were free from the depredations of those destructive insects.—*Corresp. in Agri. Hort. Soc. Jour.*, June 1864.

(29) **Agave vivipara** (*Linn.*) Do.

Bastard Aloe, Eng. Kathalai, Tam. Peetha kalabantha, Tel.

Description.—Stemless; leaves ovate-oblong, acute, stiff, thick, recurved, spreading, pale green, hoary, prickly at the edges; prickles collected, very small, orange brown; scape branched, bulbiferous.—*Linn. Spec.* 461.—*Kunth Enum. pl.* v. 822.—*Ait. Kew*, i. 471.——North-West Provinces.

Economic Uses.—A good fibre, which is long in the staple, is procured from the leaves. The latter are allowed to rot in water for twenty days, and then beat on a plank, and again thoroughly washed. A strong and useful cordage is made from them, as well as mats and ropes. In South Arcot these fibres sell at 30 rupees the candy. Generally they find a ready sale in this country, and pay the expense of manufacture.—*Jury Rep. M. E.*

(30) **Ailanthus excelsa** (*Roxb.*) N. O. XANTHOXYLACEÆ.

Peroomarum, TAM. Perumarum, MAL. Peddamanoo, TEL.

DESCRIPTION.—Large tree; leaves abruptly pinnated, tomentose when young, afterwards glabrous; leaflets 10-14 pair, coarsely toothed at the base; petals 5, almost glabrous in the inside; filaments glabrous, shorter than the anthers; calyx 5-cleft; samaræ linear-oblong, 3-5, one-seeded; panicles terminal; flowers fascicled, green. *Fl.* Aug.—*W. & A. Prod.* i. 150. —*Roxb. Fl. Ind.* ii. 454. *Cor.* i. *t.* 23.——Northern Circars. Coimbatore.

MEDICAL USES.—The aromatic bark is used by the natives in dyspepsia. Dr Wight mentions that in the Circars the bark is regarded as a powerful febrifuge, and as a tonic in cases of debility.—*Ainslie. Wight Ill. I.*

ECONOMIC USES.—The wood is light and not durable, but is used for catamarans and made into sword-handles and sheaths for spears in Western India.—*Roxb.*

(31) **Ailanthus Malabarica** (*Dec.*) Do.

Peroomarum, MAL. Perumarum, TEL.

DESCRIPTION.—Tree, leaves abruptly pinnated; leaflets quite entire, ovate-lanceolate, unequal-sided, oblique at the base; panicles large, terminal; peduncles and calyx pubescent; petals glabrous, obovate, much longer than the calyx; samaræ oval, oblong, obtuse at both ends.—*Wight Icon. t.* 1604.—*W. & A. Prod.* i. 150.—*Rheede,* vi. *t.* 15.——Travancore. Malabar.

MEDICAL USES.—The bark has a pleasant and slightly bitter taste, and is given in cases of dyspepsia, and moreover considered a valuable tonic and febrifuge. It yields a fragrant resinous juice known as *Muttee-pal,* which was first noticed by Buchanan, who found the tree in the Annamullay forests. The resin reduced to powder mixed with milk and strained is given in small doses in dysentery, and also in bronchitis, and reputed to be an excellent remedy, owing chiefly to the balsamic properties of the resin. The fruit triturated with mango and mixed with rice is reckoned useful in cases of ophthalmia. Wight states that the bark is rough and very thick, studded with bright garnet-looking grains apparently of a resinous nature, which do not dissolve either in spirit or water. —(*Ainslie. Wight. Gibson.*) Mr Broughton, Quinologist to Government, reported upon the resin as follows: "This resin, as commonly met with, is dark brown or grey in colour, is plastic, opaque, and has an agreeable smell. It contains much impurity. The pure resin is very soft, having the consistence of thick treacle; and this is doubtless the reason why it is always mixed with fragments of wood and earth, which make it more easy to handle. The sample which I examined contained but 77 per cent of resin, the remainder being adulterations. Alcohol readily dissolves the resin, and on evaporation leaves it as a very viscous, transparent, light-brown, semi-liquid, which does not solidify by many days' exposure to a steam heat; when burnt it gives out a fragrance, and hence it is sometimes used for incense. Its perfume is, however, inferior to that produced by many other resins employed in the concoction of the incense employed in Christian and heathen worship. The peculiar consistency of the resin would enable it to substitute Venice turpentine for many purposes, though its price (6 rupees for 25 lb. in the crude state) forbids an extensive employment."

(32) **Alangium decapetalum** (*Lam.*) N. O. Alangiaceæ.

Sage-leaved Alangium, Eng. Alingie-marum, Tam. Angolam, Mal. Akola, Akarkanta, Hind. Bagh-ankra, Beng.

Description.—Tree, leaves alternate, narrow-oblong; petals 6-10; branches occasionally spinescent; stamens twice the number of the petals; filaments hairy at the base; flowers solitary or aggregate in the axils of the leaves, whitish yellow, fragrant; drupe tomentose, 1-seeded. *Fl.* April and May.—*W. & A. Prod.* i. 325.—*Rheede,* iv. *t.* 17.—*Wight Icon. t.* 194. —A. tomentosum, *Dec.*—A. hexapetalum, *Roxb.*——Rocky places in Malabar. Coromandel. Assam.

Medical Uses.—The juice of the root is reckoned anthelmintic and purgative. It is also employed in dropsical cases; and, pulverised, is a reputed antidote in snake-bites.—*Roxb.*

Economic Uses.—The timber is very beautiful and strong, according to Dr Wight sustaining a weight of 310 lb. The wood of the *A. hexapetalum* is also considered valuable. This latter is called *Kara-angolam* in Malayalum, and *Wooduga* in Telugu. It is a native of Bengal and Malabar.—*Wight.*

(33) **Albizzia amara** (*Willd.*) N. O. Leguminosæ.

Nalla-eenga, Nalla-eegoo, Narlinjie, Tel. Woonja, Tam.

Description.—Tree, unarmed; branches terete; young shoots, petioles, and peduncles, and under side of the leaflets clothed with yellowish tomentum; leaves bipinnate; pinnæ 8-10 pair, with a gland on the petiole and between the last pair; leaflets 20-30 pair; stipules lanceolate; peduncles solitary or aggregated, long and filiform in the axils of the upper leaves, and racemose from the abortion of the leaves; flowers small in globular heads; corolla 5-cleft; stamens long, numerous, monadelphous; legumes flat, thin, broadly linear, 3-6 seeded.—*Bedd. Flor. Sylv. t.* 61.—Acacia amara, *Willd.*—*W. & A. Prod.* i. 274.—Mimosa amara, *Roxb.*——Mysore. Bombay. Madras Presidency.

Economic Uses.—A tolerably large tree, with a maximum height of about 30 feet. The wood is dark brown, mottled, and very handsome, strong, fibrous, stiff, close-grained, hard, and durable, superior to Sal and Teak in transverse strength and cohesive power. It is much used by the natives for building purposes, and in the construction of carts, ploughs, and beams. It also makes excellent fuel, and for this purpose is extensively used for the railways in Southern India. The natives use the leaves for washing the hair.—*Beddome.*

(34) **Albizzia Lebbek** (*Benth.*) Do.

Sirissa tree, Eng. Siris, Hind. Kattuvagai, Tam. Dirisana, Tel. Velu-vâke, Mel. Siris-gachh, Beng.

Description.—Tree, 30-40 feet, unarmed; young branches flexuose; leaves bipinnated; pinnæ 1-4 pair; leaflets 4-9 pair, obtuse, oval, glabrous, unequal; peduncles axillary, each with a globular head of flowers on short pedicels, 1-4 together; calyx long, tubular; petals 5, united to beyond the calyx; stamens very long, monadelphous; legumes flat and thin, remotely 8-10 seeded; flowers small, white, fragrant. *Fl.* Aug.—Sept.—Acacia speciosa *Willd.*—*W. & A. Prod.* i. 275.—M. Sirissa, *Roxb. Fl. Ind.* ii. 554.——Travancore. Coromandel.

Medical Uses.—The seeds are used by the natives in the treatment of piles, and as an astringent in diarrhœa. The flowers are employed in the cure of boils, eruptions, and swellings, and act as antidotes to poisons. The leaves are useful in ophthalmia, and the powdered bark in ulcers, and especially in snake-wounds. The oil extracted from the seeds is given in cases of white leprosy.—*Powell's Punj. Prod.*

Economic Uses.—A considerable quantity of gum is yielded by this tree, valuable for many ordinary purposes. The timber is very durable, hard, and close-grained, and is employed for furniture. It is of a light colour, and is well adapted for picture-frames and similar work. In Northern India it is considered unlucky to employ the timber in house-building.—(*Roxb. Rep. Mad. Exhib.*) It is a frequent tree by roadsides, and has a large and umbrageous head. The tree is pollarded, and the cuttings used as firewood. It is now extensively planted on the Ganges Canal. It is of rapid growth, and flourishes in almost any soil. The leaves afford good fodder for cattle.—*Bomb. Govt. Rep.*, 1863.

(35) **Albizzia odoratissima** (*Willd.*) Do.

Karinthakara, MAL. Kurroo-vaga, TAM. Shinduga, TEL.

DESCRIPTION.—Tree, 30-40 feet, unarmed; leaves bipinnated; pinnæ 3-4 pair; leaflets 10-40 pair, narrow, oval, oblique, glabrous, pale on the under side; panicles terminal and axillary, the ultimate divisions cymose, or somewhat umbellate; heads of flowers small, globose; stamens monadelphous; legume flat, thin, thick-margined, about 10-seeded; flowers pale yellow, very fragrant. *Fl.* May—June.—Acacia odoratissima, *Willd.*—*W. & A. Prod.* i. 275.—A. lomatocarpa, *Dec.*—Mimosa odoratissima, *Roxb. Fl. Ind.* ii. 546. *Cor.* ii. *t.* 120.—*Rheede,* vi. *t.* 5.——Malabar and Coromandel. Common everywhere.

ECONOMIC USES.—The timber of this large and handsome tree is particularly hard and strong, and is well suited for naves and fellies of wheels. The tree is very abundant, and grows in almost any soil. It is one of the most valuable jungle timbers.—(*Roxb. Jury Rep. Mad. Exhib.*) It attains a large size at Vellore, Arcot, and in the Carnatic generally, and in the ghauts running towards Salem. The tree grows rapidly, and the wood is hard, heavy, and dark-coloured. It is excellent for all purposes requiring strength and durability, and should be planted where required to remain.—*Best's Rep. to Bomb. Govt.*, 1863.

(36) **Albizzia stipulata** (*Dec.*) Do.

Konda-chiragu, TEL. Amlooki, BENG.

DESCRIPTION.—Tree, 40-50 feet, unarmed; leaves bipinnated; young shoots irregularly angled; pinnæ 6-20 pair; petioles tomentose; leaflets numerous, semi-hastate, sides very unequal; peduncles aggregated; panicles terminal and in the upper axils; heads of flowers globose; corolla tubular, 5-cleft; stamens very long, monadelphous at the base; legumes thin, flat, glabrous; seeds 6-12; flowers white and rose-coloured. *Fl.* April—June.—Acacia stipulata, *Dec.*—*W. & A. Prod.* i. 274.—M. stipulacea, *Roxb. Fl. Ind.* ii. 549.——Travancore. Courtallum. Bengal.

Economic Uses.—This is one of the largest trees of the genus. The timber is close-grained and strong, rendering it valuable for furniture and other purposes. It is a native of the mountains north of Bengal, but it is to be met with in most parts of the Peninsula. —*Roxb.*

(37) **Aleurites triloba** (*Forst.*) N. O. Euphorbiaceæ.

Belgaum walnut, Eng. Jungli-akhrot, Duk. Nattu-akrotu, Tam. Natu-akrotu, Tel. Bangla-akrot, Beng.

Description.—Large tree; leaves petioled, very large, cordate, with entire or scalloped margins, 3-5 lobed; panicles terminal; flowers small, white; fruit roundish, somewhat compressed, pointed, very hard, 2-celled; cells 1-seeded. *Fl.* May.—*J. Grah. Roxb. Fl. Ind.* iii. 629.——Belgaum. Travancore. Mysore. Northern Circars. Bengal.

Medical Uses.—An oil is extracted from the kernel of the nut, which is employed medicinally as a sure and mild purgative, approximating nearer in its effects to castor-oil. It has neither taste nor smell, nor does it produce nausea, either administered pure or in emulsion. It has been pronounced superior to linseed-oil, especially for purposes connected with the arts. It is easily extracted, being separated from the kernel with less labour and simpler machinery than the oil from the Cocoa-nut, which requires great pressure.—*Pharm. of India. O'Rorke, Ann. Therap.*, 117.

Economic Uses.—This is a large tree, the newly-formed parts of which are covered with a farinaceous substance. The natives are fond of the nut, which is palatable, and something like our English Walnut. In the Sandwich Islands they are employed for candles. A number of them strung upon a stick will burn for hours, giving a clear and steady light. The tree grows most readily from seed, and might be extensively cultivated. The cake after expression of the oil is a good food for cattle, and useful as manure. According to Simmonds, "31½ gallons of the nut yield 10 gallons of oil, which bears a good price in the home market." About 10,000 gallons are yearly produced in the Sandwich Islands. In Ceylon it is manufactured, and there known as the "kekuna" oil. It is supposed to be a good substitute for rape-oil.—*Lindley. Simmonds. Comm. Prod. Jury Rep. M. E.*

(38) **Aloe vulgaris** (*Lam.*) N. O. Liliaceæ.

Barbadoes Aloe, Eng. Kattalay, Tam.

Description.—Stem short; leaves fleshy, stem-clasping, first spreading, then ascending, lanceolate, glaucous-green, flat, obovate, convex below, armed with distant reddish spines perpendicular to the margin; the parenchyma slightly coloured brown, and very distinct from the tough leathery cuticle; spike cylindrical-ovate; flowers at first erect, then spreading, afterwards pendulous, yellow, with the three inner segments at the apex somewhat orange, not longer than the stamens.—*Lam. Enc.* i. 86. *Rheede,* xi. *t.* 3.—A. Barbadensis, *Mill.* ——Common in the Peninsula.

Medical Uses.—The above species of Aloe, which is properly a native of Greece, or, as some say, of the Cape Colony, has long been naturalised in both Indies. It yields what is known as the Barbadoes Aloes. This substance is of a dark or reddish-brown colour, and has a most unpleasant odour. In quality it is far inferior to the real Socotrine Aloes (*A. Socotrina*). As a drug, Aloes is reckoned extremely valuable, and its medical properties are very numerous. Although aperient, yet, unlike other cathartics, the effect is not increased, if given in large doses, beyond a certain point. To persons predisposed to apoplexy it is more beneficial than most other purgatives. The compound decoction is a valuable emmenagogue, particularly when combined with preparations of iron. One of the best modes of covering the unpleasant taste of Aloes, when given liquid, is in the compound tincture of lavender. Aloes are produced by most of the varieties of these plants, but Dr O'Shaughnessy remarks that the quality of the product is apparently more dependent on soil, climate, and preparation, than on any specific difference in the plant itself. A great deal depends on the mode of preparation. The usual mode of extracting the substance is by making a transverse incision in the leaves, or cutting them off at the base, and scraping off the juice as it flows if done in the former way, and allowing it to run in a vessel placed for the purpose if in the latter. Pressure is made occasionally to assist the flow; but, as Dr O'Shaughnessy observes, "by this means large quantities of the mucilage are forced out and mix with the proper bitter juice, which is proportionately deteriorated;" for it must be recollected that the Aloe contains a great deal of mucilaginous matter, abundant towards the centre of the thick fleshy leaves. The Aloes after being received into a vessel are exposed to the sun or other heat, by which means they become inspissated. The greater portion of Aloes sent to England is from the Cape Colony. Of late years the importation of the true Socotrina Aloes has considerably decreased. What is now shipped to Europe is sent usually round by Bombay; but Simmonds says, "Socotrine Aloes, although long considered the best kind, is now below Barbadoes Aloes in commercial value." The several kinds of Aloes are the East Indian or Hepatic Aloes, so called from its liver colour, and said to be the produce of the *A. Arabica;* and the Horse-Aloes, which is only used in veterinary medicine. This latter product is said to be obtained by boiling the leaves that have been previously used for producing a finer sample. The greater part of Cape-Aloes is the produce of *A. Spicata*, which is of a yellowish colour, and has a heavy disagreeable odour. —(*Ainslie. Lindl. Bengal Disp. Comm. Prod. Mad.*) The other species yielding Aloes are the *A. Indica*, Royle (*A. perfoliata, Roxb.*), inhabiting dry sandy plains in the North-Western Provinces, and the *A. litoralis* (Koenig), found on the sea-coasts of the Peninsula. A good kind of Aloes is procurable from the latter. The natives attach much value to the juice of the leaves, which they apply externally in cases of ophthalmia, and especially in what are commonly termed country sore-eyes. The mode of administering it is to wash the pulp of the leaves in cold water and mix it up with a little burnt alum. In this state it is applied to the eyes, being previously wrapped in a piece of muslin cloth. An ink is prepared by the Mahometans from the juice of the pulp.—(*Ainslie.*) It appears certain that, with a little care, Aloes of good quality might be obtained from this source in considerable quantities, at a cost far less than that of the imported article. The freshly-expressed juice is in almost universal use as an external refrigerant application to all external or local inflammations.—*Pharm. of India.*

(39) **Alpinia galanga** (*Swz.*) N. O. ZINGIBERACEÆ.

Bara-Kulinjan, HIND. and DUK. Pera-rattai, TAM. Pedda-dumpa-rashtrakam, TEL. Pera-ratta, MAL.

DESCRIPTION.—Perennial; stem 6-7 feet when in flower, with leafless sheath up to the middle; leaves short-stalked, lanceolate, white, and somewhat callous on the margin, smooth; panicles terminal, spreading, dichotomous, each division with from 2 to 6 pale-greenish, fragrant flowers; calyx smooth, white, 1-toothed; exterior limb of corolla of 3 nearly equal recurved divisions; interior one unguiculate, oval, deeply 2-lobed, white with reddish specks; capsule size of a small cherry, obovate, smooth, deep orange-red, 3-celled; seed 1, much compressed, deep chestnut colour, a little wrinkled, arillate, except at the apex. *Fl.* April—May.—*Roxb. Fl. Ind.* i. 59.—Maranta galanga, *Linn.*——South Concan. Chittagong. Travancore.

MEDICAL USES.—The tubers, which are faintly aromatic, pungent, and somewhat bitter, are the larger galangal of the shops, and are used as a substitute for ginger. They are given in infusion in fevers, rheumatism, and catarrhal affections. The galangal root is much used in China, and is one of the articles of commerce, realising in London 12s. to 16s. per cwt. It has an aromatic pungent taste; the outside is of a reddish-brown; internally it is reddish-white.

An inferior sort of galangal is got from *A. Allughas* (Roscoe), the root of which is considerably aromatic. Of this latter species Rheede says, that the juice of the root is applied externally in gout, and is also used internally. The root itself macerated and mixed with wine is a good external application for pains in the limbs; and, pulverised, is administered in colic. It is the *Mala Inschikua* of Rheede.—(*Ainslie. Simmonds. Rheede.*) The *A. Khulinjan*, a variety of the *A. Chinensis*, is found growing in several gardens at Madras; and its rhizome, when dried, resembles that of the lesser galangal. It is supposed to be a distinct species by some, though closely approximating the *A. Calcarata*. It is stimulant, carminative, stomachic, and expectorant. It is useful in all diseases where ginger is used, and also in most nervous disorders. It has also proved useful in incontinence of urine.—*Suppl. to Pharm. of India.*

(40) **Alstonia scholaris** (*R. Br.*) N. O. Apocynaceæ.

Ezhilaip-palai, Tam. Edakulapala, Pala-garuda, Edakula-ariti, Edakula-ponna, Tel. Pala, Mukkan-pala, Mal. Chhatin, Beng.

Description.—Tree, 50 feet; leaves 5-7 in a whorl, obovate-oblong, obtuse, veins ribbed, approximating the margin; calyx 5-parted; corolla salver-shaped, with roundish segments; cymes on short peduncles; limb of corolla a little bearded; flowers greenish white, follicles very long, slender. *Fl.* Nov.—Dec.—*Rheede*, i. *t.* 45.—*Wight Icon. t.* 422.—Echites scholaris, *Linn.*——Travancore. Coromandel. Assam.

Medical Uses.—The wood is bitter to the taste, and the bark is a powerful tonic, much used by the natives in bowel complaints. It is astringent, anthelmintic, and anti-periodic. It has proved a valuable remedy in chronic diarrhœa and the advanced stages of dysentery, and also effectual in restoring the tone of the stomach after debilitating fevers.—*Pharm. of India. Gibson in Pharm. Journal*, xii. 422.

Economic Uses.—This tree has obtained the trivial name *Scholaris* from the fact of its planks being used as school-boards, on which children trace their letters, as in the Lancastrian system. The children assemble half-naked under the shade of the Cocoa palm, place themselves on rows on the ground, and trace out on the sand with the forefinger of the right hand the elements of their alphabet, and then smooth it with their left when they wish to trace out other characters. This method of teaching writing was introduced into India 200 B.C., according to Megasthenes, and still continues to be practised. The wood is white and close-grained. In Assam it is much prized for beams and light work, such as boxes, trunks, and scabbards. The whole tree abounds in milky juice.—*Nimmo. Roxb.*

(41) **Amarantus frumentaceus** (*Buch.*) N. O. AMARANTACEÆ.

Poong-kirai, TAM.

DESCRIPTION.—Stem herbaceous, erect; leaves long-petioled, broad-lanceolate, acute; panicles terminal, erect; sepals subulate, acute; stamens five; stigmas three; seed subcompressed, smooth; utricles wrinkled. *Dec. Prod.* xiii. s. 2, p. 265.—*Roxb. Flor. Ind.* iii. 699.—*Wight Icon. t.* 720.——Mysore. Coimbatore.

ECONOMIC USES.—This plant is extensively cultivated in the Coimbatore district, chiefly for the flour of its seeds, which is a great article of diet among the natives. Besides the above, there are several other species of Amaranths used as vegetables by the natives, such as the *A. polygonoides* (Roxb.), considered very wholesome, especially for convalescents; the *A. oleraceus* (Linn.), of which the several varieties are cultivated for diet, especially the *Var. giganteus*, which is about 4 to 8 feet high, and with a thick succulent stem, which is eaten as a substitute for asparagus.—*Roxb. Ainslie.*

(42) **Amarantus spinosus** (*Linn.*) Do.

Kanta-mat, DUK. Mulluk-kirai, TAM. Mundla-tota-kura, Nalla-doggali, TEL. Mullan-chira, MAL. Kanta-mari, BENG.

DESCRIPTION.—Erect, 1-3 feet, somewhat striated, glabrous, reddish; leaves long-petioled, rhomb-ovate, or lanceolate-oblong, with two spines in the axils; panicles sparingly branched; spikes erect, cylindric, acute, terminal ones long, stiffish, lateral ones middle-sized; flowers dense, green; utricles 2-3 cleft at the top, somewhat wrinkled; bracts unequal, bearded; seed lenticular, polished, black.—*Dec. Prod.* xiii. s. 2, p. 260.—*Roxb. Flor. Ind.* iii. 611.—*Wight Icon. t.* 513.—*Rumph. Amb.* v. *t.* 83, fig. 1.——Peninsula. Bengal. Malabar.

MEDICAL USES.—Emollient poultices are made of the bruised leaves. In the Mauritius a decoction of the leaves and root is administered internally as diuretic.—(*Bouton, Med. Pl. of the Mauritius.*) The *A. campestris* (Willd.) is considered demulcent, and is given in decoction in cases of strangury—(*Ainslie*). The *A. polygamus* (Linn.) is used in bilious disorders, and as an aperient.—*Long, Indig. Plants of Bengal.*

(43) **Ammannia vesicatoria** (*Roxb.*) N. O. LYTHRACEÆ.

Dàd-mári, HIND. Agin-búti, DUK. Kallurivi, Miumel-neruppa, TAM. Aqui-vender-paku, TEL. Kallar-vanchi, MAL.

DESCRIPTION.—Herbaceous, erect; stem much branched, 4-sided; leaves sessile, opposite, lanceolate, attenuated, smaller nearer the flowers; calyx 4-cleft to the middle, lobes acute, accessory teeth very small; flowers very minute, aggregated in the axils of the leaves, almost sessile; tube of the calyx at first narrow and tightened round the ovary, in fruit cup-shaped; petals wanting; capsule longer than the calyx, 1-celled; flowers red. *Fl.* Oct.—*W. & A. Prod.* i. 305. *Roxb. Flor. Ind.* i. 426.—*Dec. Prod.* iii. 78.——Peninsula. Bengal.

MEDICAL USES.—The whole plant has a strong muriatic, not disagreeable smell. Its leaves, being extremely acrid, are used by the natives in raising blisters in rheumatism. Bruised and applied to the affected parts, they perform their office most effectually in about half an hour—(*Ainslie*). The pounded leaves are applied to herpetic eruptions—(*Fleming*). It is said, from the great pain the leaves cause as blisters, they cannot be recommended.—*Pharm. of India.*

(44) **Amoora Rohituka** (*W. & A.*) N. O. MELIACEÆ.

Chemmarum, MAL. Hurin-hura, or Khana, HIND. Tikhta-raj, BENG.

DESCRIPTION.—Small tree; leaves unequally pinnated; leaflets 6 pair, opposite, obliquely-oblong, glabrous; young petioles slightly hairy on their lower part; male flowers in panicles shorter than the leaves, subsessile; calyx 3-leaved; female flowers numerous, sessile, solitary, erect on spikes, which are rather more than half the length of the leaves; petals three; capsule pale yellow, 3-celled, 3-valved; seeds solitary, enclosed in a fleshy scarlet aril; flowers small, white, or cream-coloured. *Fl.* July—Aug.—*W. & A. Prod.* i. 119.—Andersonia Rohituka, *Roxb. Fl. Ind.* ii. 213.——Travancore. Bengal.

ECONOMIC USES.—From the seeds, where the trees grow plentifully, the natives extract an oil which they use for many economical purposes.—*Roxb.*

(45) **Amorphophallus campanulatus** (*Blume*). N. O. ARACEÆ.

Telinga potato, ENG. Karuna, MAL. and TAM. Muncha Kunda, TEL. Ol, HIND.

DESCRIPTION.—Stemless; leaves decompound; flowers small, dark-coloured, sessile with respect to the surface of the ground, and appearing when the plant is destitute of leaves; spathe the length of the spadix, campanulate, margins curled; nectary none; club broad-ovate, lobate, anthers 2-celled. *Fl.* June.—*Wight Icon. t.* 782.—Arum campanulatum, *Roxb.*—*Rheede, Mal.* xi. *t.* 18, 19.——Bengal. Peninsula.

MEDICAL USES.—The acrid roots are used medicinally in boils and ophthalmia. They are very caustic and abound in starch, and are employed as external stimulants, and are also emmenagogue.—(*Lindley.*) The fresh roots act as an acrid stimulant and expectorant, and are used in acute rheumatism.—*Powell, Punj. Prod.*

ECONOMIC USES.—The roots are very nutritious, on which account they are much cultivated for the purpose of diet. They are planted in May, and will yield from 100 to 250 maunds per beegah, selling at the rate of a rupee a maund. The roots are also used for pickling. Wight says that "when in flower the fetor it exhales is most overpowering, and so perfectly resembles that of carrion as to induce flies to cover the club of the spadix with their eggs." A very rich soil, repeatedly ploughed, suits it best. The small tuberosities found in the large roots are employed for sets, and planted in the manner of potatoes. In twelve months they are reckoned fit to be taken up for use; the larger roots will then weigh from 4-8 or more pounds, and keep well if preserved dry. The natives employ them for food in the manner of the common yam. The plant is the *Chaneh* or *Mullum chaneh* of Rheede.—*Jury Rep. M. E. Roxb.*

(46) **Amphidonax karka** (*Lind.*) N. O. GRAMINACEÆ.

Naga Sara, Maitantos, TEL. Nar Nul, BENG.

DESCRIPTION.—Culms erect, 8-12 feet, round, smooth, covered with the sheaths of the leaves; leaves approximate, ensiform, smooth; mouths of the sheaths bearded; panicles erect, oblong, composed of many filiform, sub-verticelled ramifications, bowing to the wind; rachis of the branches angular and hispid; florets alternate; calyx 3-5 flowered; glumes unequal. *Fl.* Sept.—Feb.—*Roxb. Fl. Ind.* i. 347.—A. Roxburghii, *Kth.*—— Peninsula. Bengal.

ECONOMIC USES.—The common Durma mats at Calcutta are made of the stalks of this reed split open. Pipes are made of the culms, especially those used by people carrying about dancing-snakes. This grass is more luxuriant in Bengal than on the coast. In Scinde the culms are made into chairs, and the flower-stalks are beaten to form fibres which are there called Moonyah. These are used for string and ropes.—*Royle. Roxb.*

(47) **Anacardium occidentale** (*Linn.*) N. O. TEREBINTHACEÆ.

Cashew-nut, ENG. Kaju, HIND. and DUK. Mundiri-marum, TAM. Jidi-mamidi, Munta-mamidi, TEL. Paranki-mava, Kappa-mavakum, MAL. Hijli-badam, BENG.

DESCRIPTION.—Tree; leaves oval, alternate, with roundish or emarginate apex; calyx 5-cleft nearly to the base; petals

5, linear-lanceolate, pale yellow with pink stripes; stamens usually nine, with one longer than the others; style solitary; panicles terminal, with male and hermaphrodite flowers mixed together; flowers greenish red; fruit a kidney-shaped ash-brown nut, sessile on the apex of a yellow or crimson-coloured torus. *Fl.* Feb.—March.—*W. & A. Prod.* i. 168.—*Roxb. Fl. Ind.* ii. 312.—*Rheede,* iii. *t.* 54.——Coasts of the Peninsula. Chittagong. Trichinopoly.

MEDICAL USES.—The fruit is sub-acid and astringent. The pericarp of the nut contains a black acrid oil, known as Cardole, which is a powerfully vesicating agent. It requires, however, to be cautiously used. It is applied to warts, corns, and ulcers, but it is said that the vapour of the oil when roasting is apt to produce swelling and inflammation. Martius says, "The sympathetic effect of the nut borne about the person upon chronic inflammation of the eyes, especially when of a scrofulous nature, is remarkable." The astringency of the fruit-juice has been recommended as a good remedy in dropsical habits. The bark is given internally in infusion for syphilitic swellings of the joints.—*Lindley. Pereira.*

ECONOMIC USES.—The acrid oil stated above as Cardole is often applied to floors or wooden rafters of houses to prevent the attack of white ants, and most effectually keeps them away. A transparent gum is obtained from the trunk of the tree, useful as a good varnish, and making a fair substitute for gum-Arabic. It should be collected while the sap is rising. It is particularly useful when the depredations of insects require to be guarded against. For this purpose it is used in S. America by the bookbinders, who wash their books with a solution of it in order to keep away moths and ants. The kernels are edible and wholesome, abounding in sweet milky juice, and are used for imparting a flavour to Madeira wine. Ground up and mixed with cocoa they make a good chocolate. The juice of the fruit expressed and fermented yields a pleasant wine; and distilled, a spirit is drawn from it making good punch. A variety of the tree grows in Travancore, and probably elsewhere, the pericarp of whose nuts has no oil, but may be chewed raw with impunity. The tree flowers twice a-year. The juice which flows from an incision in the body of the tree will stain linen so that it cannot be washed out. An edible oil equal to olive or almond oil is procured from the nuts, but it is seldom prepared, the kernels being used as a table-fruit. The wood is of no value.—*Lindley. Pereira. Don.*

(48) **Anamirta cocculus** (*W. & A.*) N. O. MENISPERMACEÆ.

Pen-Kottai, Kaka-coollie, TAM. Kaki-chempoo, TEL. Kakmari, HIND. Polla or Kaandaka-conuveh, MAL.

DESCRIPTION.—Twining; bark deeply cracked; leaves alternate, slightly cordate, roundish, acute, whitish beneath, with 5 digitate ribs; calyx 6-sepalled; corolla none; racemes of female flowers, lateral, whitish green; drupes 2-3; seeds globose.—*W. & A. Prod.* i. 446.—Menispermum cocculus, *Linn.*—Cocculus suberosus, *W. & A. Prod.* i. 11.—*Rheede*, vii. *t.* 1, *and* xi. *t.* 62.——Malabar. Circar mountains. Concans.

Medical Uses.—The berries of this plant, which are very disagreeable to the taste, are known as the Cocculus Indicus seeds, and have been extensively used by brewers in the adulteration of malt liquors. In overdoses they are highly poisonous. An oil is produced from them used for poisoning fish and game. In a powdered state they are employed for destroying pediculi in the hair, and in ointment are reckoned of value in cutaneous diseases. The juice of the fresh fruit is applied externally to foul ulcers, and is esteemed a good remedy in scabies. Ainslie states that "the berry is employed by the Vytians as a useful external application in cases of inveterate itch and herpes; on which occasions it is beat into a fine powder and mixed with a little warm castor-oil." Marcet proved by experiments that it is also a poison for vegetable substances, a solution prepared with an extract made from the seeds having killed a bean plant in twenty-four hours. The poisonous properties reside in the seeds, which contain a large percentage of the virulent principle called Picrotoxine. And the pericarp yields another dangerous alkaloid called Menispermine. Its chief influence, as a poison, is upon the nervous system, and leaves scarcely any trace of its action upon the coats of the stomach. The ointment made from the powdered berries is very efficacious in allaying inflammation, but requires to be cautiously used.—*Ainslie. Pharm. of India.*

Economic Uses.—That the seeds are illegally employed in the adulteration of beer by the lower class of brewers in England is an undoubted fact, although the penalties imposed by the Legislature are very severe. It is said that 1 lb. of these berries is equal to a sack of malt in brewing, and it was even recommended, by a person who wrote on the 'Art of Brewing,' to add 3 lb. of seed to every ten quarters of malt. A considerable quantity of "Cocculus Indicus" is exported from Malabar and Travancore, and shipped for the London market, where the price varies from 18 to 24 shillings per cwt.—*Ainslie. Lindley.*

(49) **Ananas sativus** (*Schult.*) N. O. Bromeliaceæ.

Pine-apple, Eng. Anasa, Tam. Pooreethee, Mal.

Description.—Perennial, 2-3 feet; leaves ciliate with spinous points; calyx 3-parted; petals 3; spikes tufted; flowers small, bluish. *Fl.* April—May.—*Roxb. Fl. Ind.* ii. 116.—

Ananassa sativa, *Lindl.*—Bromelia ananas, *Linn.*——Naturalised in India.

Economic Uses.—The Pine-apple has long been domesticated in the East Indies, and is now found in an almost wild state in most parts of the Peninsula, Northern Provinces, and Ceylon. The Portuguese appear to have first introduced the seeds from the Moluccas. It is abundant in China and the Philippine Islands. The plant succeeds well in the open air as far north as 30°, while in the southern parts of the Peninsula it forms hedges, and will grow with little care and in almost any soil. The flavour of the fruit is greatly heightened by cultivation, being somewhat acrid in its wild state. The plants are remarkable for their power of existing in the air without contact with the earth; and in South America they may be seen in abundance, hanging up in the gardens and dwelling-houses, in which situations they will flower profusely, perfuming the air with their delicious fragrance. The most important use of the Pine-apple plant consists in the fine white fibres yielded by the leaves. These have been formed into the most delicate fabrics, as well as fishing-lines and ropes. Unlike other fibres, they are not injured by immersion in water—a property much increased by tanning, which process is constantly used by the natives. In Malacca and Singapore a trade is carried on with China in these fibres, which are there used in the manufacture of linen stuffs. As a substitute for flax they are perhaps the most valuable of Indian fibres. Dr Royle states "that a patent was taken out for the manufacture of thread from the pine-apple fibre, because, when bleached, it could be manufactured in the same way as flax. The process of bleaching by destroying the adhesion between the bundles of fibres renders it much finer, and hence enables it to be extended between the rolls in the process of spinning." Specimens of pine-apple fibre were sent to the Madras Exhibition from Travancore, South Arcot, and other parts of the country; upon which the Juries reported,—"The above samples are nearly white, very soft, silky and pliant, and the material seems to be a good substitute for flax, as it is known to be strong, durable, and susceptible of fine subdivision. It has also the advantage of being as long in the staple as flax, and it can be worked upon with the same machinery." According to experiments by Dr Royle, pine-apple fibre prepared at Madras bore 260 lb., and some from Singapore 350 lb. A rope of the same broke at 57 cwt. In other experiments a 12-thread rope of plaintain fibre broke at 864 lb., and a similar rope of pine-apple fibre at 924 lbs. —*Royle. Ainslie. Jury Rep. Mad. Exhib.*

(50) **Andromeda Leschenaultii** (*Dec.*) N. O. Ericaceæ.

Indian Wintergreen, Eng.

Description.—Shrub, glabrous, branches somewhat 3-cornered; leaves petioled, ovate or obovate, terminating in a gland, crenulate, punctuate beneath; racemes axillary or lateral, pubescent, shorter than the leaves, erect; bracts concave, acute, glabrous, one under the pedicel, two near the flower; flowers pure white; berries blue. *Fl.* All the year. —*Dec. Prod.* vii. 593.—A. Kotagherrensis, *Hook. Icon. t.* 246. —Leucothoe Kotagherrensis, *Dec. l. c. p.* 606.—Gaultheria Leschenaultii, *Dec. l. c. Drury, Handb. Ind. Flor.* ii. 116. *Wight Icon. t.* 119 5. *Spicil.* ii. *t.* 130.——Neilgherries.

Medical Uses.—The oil procured from this plant, which grows abundantly on the Neilgherries, is identical with the Canadian oil of wintergreen (*Gaultheria procumbens*). This latter oil is of some slight commercial value, and is used in medicine as an antispasmodic. Mr Broughton, the Government Quinologist, in a report to the Madras Government on the subject of this oil, says: The oil from this Indian source contains less of the peculiar hydrocarbon oil which forms a natural and considerable admixture with the Canadian oil, and therefore is somewhat superior in quality to the latter. The commercial demand for the oil is not, however, considerable enough to make its occurrence in India of much direct importance.

It occurred to me in 1869 that methyl-salicylic acid would, however, under suitable treatment, furnish carbolic acid according to a decomposition described by Gerhardt. After a few experiments I was successful in preparing considerable quantities of pure carbolic acid.

The method of manufacture is as follows:—

The oil is heated with a dilute solution of a caustic alkali, by which means it is saponified and dissolved, methylic alcohol of great purity being liberated. The solution of the oil is then decomposed by any mineral acid, when beautiful crystals of salicylic acid are formed. These are gathered, squeezed, and dried. They are then mixed with common quicklime or sand, and distilled in an iron retort; carbolic acid of great purity, and crystallising with the greatest readiness, passes into the receiver.

This acid is equal to the purest kind obtained from coal-tar, and employed in medicine. It, of course, possesses all the qualities which have rendered this substance almost indispensable in modern medical and surgical practice.

I had hoped, from the inexhaustible abundance with which the plant grows on the Neilgherries, that the carbolic acid from this source could be prepared at less cost than that imported. I have not yet had an opportunity of working on a large scale with an itinerant still, as would be necessary for its cheapest production; but from some calculations I have lately made, I am led to think it can scarcely be prepared for less than the price of that procured from coal-tar. The purest kinds from the latter source cost four shillings a-pound; I estimate the cost of that from this indigenous source at from rupees 2.8 to rupees 3.8 (five to seven shillings) per pound *in this country.*

The carbolic acid from the same source has certain advantages over the coal-tar acid, consequent on its extreme purity. It is less deliquescent, and cannot possibly be open to the suspicion of contamination with certain other products of coal-tar which possess injurious qualities.

In conclusion, I am led to the belief that it would not be advisable to prepare carbolic acid from this singular source, when the comparative cost shows that the gain must be very small or non-existent. But it appears to me well worthy of record, that should circumstances render the supply of the English product difficult or uncertain, as in the case of war, or the English price increase, a practically inexhaustible source exists in this country from which this indispensable substance, in its purest state, can be obtained at a slight enhancement of the present price.—*Broughton's Report to Mad. Govt.*, Jan. 1871.—*Pharm. Journ.*, Oct. 1871.

(51) **Andrographis paniculata** (*Wall.*) N. O. ACANTHACEÆ.

Shirat-Kuch-chi, Nela-vembu, TAM. Nella-vemoo, TEL. Nila-veppa, Kiriatha, MAL. Mahatita, Charayetah, Kiryat, HIND. Kalafnath, DUK. Cherota, Mahatita, BENG.

DESCRIPTION.—Annual, 1-2 feet; stem quadrangular, pointed, smooth; leaves opposite, on short petioles, lanceolate, entire; calyx deeply 5-cleft; corolla bilabiate, lips linear, reflected, upper one 3-toothed, lower one 2-toothed; flowers remote, alternate, on long petioles, downy, rose-coloured or white, streaked with purple; capsules erect, somewhat cylindrical; seeds 3-4 in each. *Fl.* Nov.—Feb.—*Lindl. Flor. Med.* 501.—Justicia paniculata, *Roxb. Fl. Ind.* i. 118.—*Rheede*, ix. *t.* 56.—*Wight Icon. t.* 518.——Bengal, in dry places under trees. Cultivated in Tinnevelly.

MEDICAL USES.—This plant is much valued for its stomachic and tonic properties, especially the root, which is one of the chief ingredients in the French mixture called Drogue amère. The whole of the plant is very bitter, and is occasionally used in cholera and dysentery. It is also said to be alexipharmic.—(*Ainsl. Lindl.*) It has been found serviceable in general debility, and in the advanced stages of dysentery. The expressed juice of the leaves is a common native domestic remedy in the bowel-complaints of children. The tincture of Kariyat is said to be tonic, stimulant, and gently aperient, and to prove valuable in several forms of dyspepsia. Roxburgh remarks that its Hindustani name, "Mahatita," signifies "King of

Bitters," and a very powerful and much-esteemed one it is.—*Roxb. Pharm. of India.*—*Fleming, As. Res.* xi.—*Waring, Indian Ann. of Med. Sci.* v. 618.

(52) **Andropogon citratum** (*Dec.*) N. O. Graminaceæ.

Lemon-grass, Eng. Akya-ghas, Hind. Hazar-masaleh, Duk. Vashanap-pullu, Karpura-pullu, Tam. Nimma-gaddi, Chippa-gaddi, Tel. Vasanap-pulla, Sambhara-pulla, Mal. Agya-ghans, Beng.

Description.—Root perennial; panicles somewhat secund; spikes conjugate, ovate-oblong; rachis pubescent; floscules sessile, awnless; culms 5-7 feet, erect, smooth; leaves many near the root, bifarious, soft, pale green, 3-4 feet long; spikelets in pairs, on a common pedicel furnished with a spathe; rachis articulated, hairy; flowers in pairs, one hermaphrodite and sessile, the other male and pedicelled.—*Rheede,* xii. *t.* 72. —A.schœnanthus, *Linn.*—*Roxb. Fl. Ind.* i. 274.—Cymbopogon schœnanthus, *Spreng.*——Travancore. Bengal. Cultivated in Coromandel.

Medical Uses.—An infusion of the fragrant leaves, which are bitter and aromatic, is given to children as an excellent stomachic. It is also diaphoretic. An essential oil is prepared from them, which is a most valuable remedy in rheumatism, applied externally. Mixed with butter-milk, the leaves are used in cases of ringworm. It is a remedy of considerable value in affections of the bowels. It allays and arrests vomiting in cholera, and aids the process of reaction. Externally applied, it forms a useful embrocation in chronic rheumatism, neuralgia, sprains, and similar painful affections.—(*Pharm. of India.*) The rhizomes and flowers have similar qualities.—(*Lindley.*) The essential oil, when first distilled, is of a high colour, owing to the quantity of resin in it. To remove this, as also to have the oil clear, it is saturated in charcoal grits that have been previously well washed and thoroughly dried. The grits saturated with the oil are thrown into the still with the required quantity of water, made slightly sharp to the taste and distilled. The oil thus obtained is not only clear, but in a great measure free from resin, and this passes in England as essence of Verbena or Citronelle. The oil of the first distilling, which is of a high colour, is known as the Lemon-grass oil. Mr C. Kohlhoff, for some time Conservator of Forests in Travancore, has used the double-distilled oil as an embrocation in cases of rheumatism, and found it a most efficacious remedy, and has also administered it in cases of cholera with great advantage. The dose is from 12 to 20 drops on a lump of sugar, repeated till the symptoms abate, at the same time applying it externally to the lips, back, and stomach, to prevent the cold and cramp so invariably accompanying that disorder. A decoction made from the fresh leaves is used by the natives to allay thirst in various disorders.—*Pers. Obs.*

Economic Uses.—When fresh and young, the leaves are used in many parts of the country as a substitute for tea, and the white centre of the succulent leaf-culms is used to impart a flavour to curries. In Bengal, large tracts of waste land are covered with this grass. The export of Lemon-grass oil from Ceylon amounts in value to nearly £7000 annually.—*Roxb. Simmonds.*

(53) **Andropogon Iwarancusa** (*Roxb.*) Do.

Iwaran-kussa, Beng.

Description.—Root perennial, fibrous; culms erect, 3-6 feet, smooth, filled with a light spongy substance; leaves near the root longer than the culm-points, margins hispid, otherwise smooth; panicles axillary and terminal, consisting of numerous fascicles of pedicelled, thin, 5-jointed spikes, with a spathe to each pair of spikes; flowers on the rachis in pairs, one awned, sessile, the other one awnless, male, and pedicelled; the terminal florets are three, one hermaphrodite, two male; glumes two, 1-flowered, with which the rachis and pedicels are woolly at the base.—*Roxb. Fl. Ind.* i. 275.—*Lindl. Flor. Med.* 611.——Skirts of the mountains of N. India. Hurdwar.

Medical Uses.—The roots of this fragrant grass are used by the natives in Northern India in intermittent fevers. In habit and taste it is similar to the *A. schœnanthus.* Dr Royle denies that it yields a grass oil.—*Pereira. Royle.*

(54) **Andropogon Martini** (*Roxb.*) Do.

Roussa-grass, Eng. Ganjni, Hind. and Duk. Kamakshipullu, mandap-pullu, Kasattam-pullu, Shunnarip-pullu, Tam. Kamakshi-Kasuvu, Kamanchi-gaddi, Tel. Kamaksha-pulla, Chora-pulla, Mal. Khama-kher, Beng.

Description.—Root long, fibrous; culm erect, branched, 5-6 feet, glabrous; leaves elongated, very delicate, soft, glabrous, acuminate; ligula membranaceous; panicles linear, subsecund; spikelets twin; rachis jointed, woolly; corolla of the hermaphrodite floret 1-valved, awned, male muticous.—*Roxb. Flor. Ind.* i. 277.—A. nardus, *Linn.*——Balaghaut highlands.

Medical Uses.—A fragrant oil is extracted from this species. It is of a pale straw colour, and is very aromatic. It is known as the grass-oil of Nemaur. It is valuable as a rubefacient, and is employed as a substitute for Cajeput oil, being frequently applied externally in rheumatic affections, also as a stimulant and diaphoretic. It has the power, in a remarkable degree, of preventing the hair of the head from falling off after acute diseases, such as fever, or after confinement or prolonged nursing. It even restores the hair; but it must be strong and pure, and not such as is usually sold by perfumers. It is obtained by distillation from the fresh plant. It closely assimilates in characters, properties, and uses, with the analogous product of *A. citratum.—Lindley. Pereira. Pharm. of India.*

Economic Uses. — This grass is a native of the highlands of Balaghaut, whence the seeds were brought by the late General Martin, and taken to Lucknow as well as to the botanic garden at Calcutta. He was induced to take particular notice of this long grass by observing how voraciously fond cattle were of it, notwithstanding its strong aromatic and pungent taste, insomuch that not only the flesh of the animals, but also the milk and butter, had a very strong scent of it. It is universally spread over the trap districts of the Deccan, though seldom found on the ordinary granite of those tracts. It is much used in perfumery—(*Royle*). A volatile oil, resembling in characters the two preceding oils, is the produce, it is believed, of the *A. pachnodes.—(Trin.)* It has obtained considerable repute as an external application in rheumatic, neuralgic, and other painful affections.—*Pharm. of India.*

A correspondent in the 'Bombay Gazette' writes as follows, while sending specimens of paper made from the Roussa-grass: "It may be had almost for the cutting throughout the Deccan. It costs about an anna a hundredweight, and twelve seers (= 24 pounds) has been found sufficient to make sixty quires of paper, equal in quality to that used by Soucars for writing their hoondies upon." Remarking upon the two specimens forwarded with the above, the editor observes that the material of which the best is formed might be converted, by proper processes and machinery, into as good paper as ever might be required for newspapers or book-work. It is after the oil has been extracted that the fibres are used for conversion into paper.

(55) **Andropogon muricatum** (*Retz*). Do.

Cuscus-grass, Eng. Balah, Hind. and Duk. Vetti-ver, Vizhal-ver, Ilamich-cham-ver, Viranam, Tam. Vatti-veru, Awuru-gaddiveru, Vidavali-veru, Ouru-veru, Tel. Vetti-ver, Ramach-cham-ver, Mal. Bala, Shandaler-jar, Beng.

Description.—Root perennial, fibrous; culms numerous, smooth, slightly compressed at the base, 4-6 feet; leaves bifarious near the base, narrow, erect; florets in pairs, awnless, male and hermaphrodite, the former pedicelled, latter sessile.

—*Roxb. Flor. Ind.* i. 265.—Anatherum muricatum, *Beauv.*—Phalaris Zizania, *Linn.*——Bengal. Peninsula.

Medical Uses.—An infusion of the root is used as a gentle stimulant, and makes a grateful drink in fevers. Reduced to powder, the roots are employed in bilious affections; and, mixed with milk, are used externally as cooling applications to skin irritations. Antispasmodic, diaphoretic, diuretic, and emmenagogue properties have been assigned to this grass, but it is not reckoned a valuable medicine.—*Ainslie. Pereira. Pharm. of India.*

Economic Uses.—The roots are made into fans, and being thinly worked into bamboo frames, are employed for the purpose of cooling the heated atmosphere in dwelling-houses during the hot winds. These are known as the Cuscus tatties. The grass is used for thatching bungalows and for covering palanquins.—*Roxb.*

(56) **Aneilema tuberosum** (*Ham.*) N. O. Commelynaceæ.

Description.—Root perennial, composed of several smooth elongated tubers; stem none, except the sheathing bases of the leaves which appear after the flowers; leaves ensiform, waved, acute, smooth; racemes radical, erect, smooth, straight; scape branched above, branches each with a sheathing bract, branchlets with several pedicelled blue flowers, rather large. *Ham. in Wall. Cat.* 5207.—*Dalz. Bomb. Flor.* 255.—Commelyna scapiflora, *Roxb.*—Murdania scapiflora, *Royle.*——Southern Concan.

Medical Uses.—The tubers are considered by the natives hot and dry. They are employed in headaches and giddiness, also in fevers, jaundice, and deafness. Also as an antidote to animal poisons and the bites of venomous serpents.—*Powell's Punj. Prod.*

(57) **Anethum Sowa** (*Roxb.*) N. O. Apiaceæ.

Dill or Bishop's weed, Eng. Suvà Soyah, Hind. Soyi, Duk. Satha-cooppa, Tam. Sompa, Tel. Shatha-koopa, Mal. Soolpha, Beng.

Description.—Annual, 2-4 feet, erect; glabrous; leaves decompound, alternate; leaflets filiform; petioles sheathing below; stem smooth, covered with whitish pubescence; petals roundish, entire; umbels terminal, without involucels; stamens about the length of the petals; fruit oblong, compressed, almost destitute of a membranaceous margin; seeds two; flowers yellow. *Fl.* Feb.—April.—*W. & A. Prod.* i. 372.—

Wight Icon. t. 572.—*Roxb. Flor. Ind.* ii. 96.—A. graveolens, *Wall.*——Bengal. Cultivated in the Peninsula.

Medical Uses.—The seeds are to be met with in every Indian bazaar. They form one of the chief ingredients in curry-powder. They yield a valuable oil, prepared by distillation, and used medicinally. Bruised and boiled in water and mixed with the roots, these seeds are applied externally in rheumatic and other swellings of the joints. The leaves, applied warm and moistened with a little oil, are said to hasten suppuration.—*Ainsl. Roxb.*

(58) **Anisochilus carnosum** (*Wall.*) N. O. Lamiaceæ.

Thick-leaved lavender, Eng. Panjiri, Hind. and Duk. Karpuravalli, Tam. Roga-chettu, Omamu, Tel. Chomara, Kattu-Kurrka, Patu-Kurrka, Mal.

Description.—Small plant; stem erect, tetragonal; leaves petiolate, ovate-roundish, crenated, cordate at the base, thick, fleshy, tomentosely villous on both surfaces; spikes on long peduncles; calyx with upper lip, with ciliated edges, lower lip truncate, quite entire; corolla bilabiate, upper lip bluntly 3-4 cleft, lower lip entire; flowers lilac. *Fl.* June—Sept.—*Rheede Mal.* x. *t.* 90.—Plectranthus strobiliferus, *Roxb. Flor. Ind.* iii. 23.——Clefts of rocks among mountains in N. Circars and Malabar. Mysore.

Medical Uses.—The fresh juice squeezed from the leaves of this plant, and mixed with sugar and gingely oil, is used as a cooling liniment for the head. The leaves and stems are given in infusion to children in coughs and colds. The plant also yields a volatile oil.—(*Ainsl. Rheede.*) A stimulant, diaphoretic and expectorant, is used in cynanche, and by the native doctors in Travancore in catarrhal affections. Dr Bidie states that as a mild stimulant expectorant it is particularly useful in coughs of children.—*Pharm. of India.*

(59) **Anisomeles Malabarica** (*R. Br.*) Do.

Malabar Cat-mint, Eng. Péyamératti, Tam. Moga-bira, Tel. Karintoomba, Mal.

Description.—Shrub, 2-5 feet; branches tomentose; leaves ovate-lanceolate, crenately serrated at the upper part, entire below; calyx 5-cleft, thickly covered with long, white, somewhat viscid pubescence; upper lip of corolla entire, white, under one 3-cleft, with the lateral divisions reflexed; anthers deep purple; whorls disposed in simple racemes. *Fl.* July

—Aug.—*Wight Icon. t.* 864.—Nepeta Malabarica, *Linn.*—Ajuga fruticosa, *Roxb. Fl. Ind.* iii. 1.—*Rheede,* x. *t.* 93.——Travancore. Peninsula.

MEDICAL USES.—The juice of the leaves in infusion is given to children in colic, indigestion, and fevers arising from teething, and is also employed in infusion in stomachic complaints, dysentery, and intermittent fevers. Patients suffering from ague are made to inhale the vapour arising from an infusion of this plant; copious perspiration ensues, which is kept up by drinking more of the infusion. The leaves, which are bitter and astringent, are taken to assist digestion, and to impart tone to the stomach. A clear reddish oil is distilled from the plant, of heavy odour, acrid and slightly bitter. A decoction of the whole plant is antarthritic, if the body be washed with it.—(*Wight. Ainslie. Lindley.*) An oil obtained by distillation from the leaves is likewise stated to prove an effectual external application in rheumatism. The *A. ovata* partakes of the physical characters of the preceding, and, according to Burman, a distilled oil prepared from it in Ceylon is useful in uterine affections.—*Pharm. of India.*

(60) **Anona squamosa** (*Linn.*) N. O. ANONACEÆ.

Custard-apple, ENG. Atta-marum, MAL. Seeta-phul, DUK. Ata, HIND. Loona, Meba, BENG. Sita-pullum, TAM.

DESCRIPTION.—Shrub or small tree, 15-20 feet; leaves oblong, or oblong-lanceolate, glabrous, pellucid-dotted; calyx 3-sepalled; petals 6 in a double row; exterior ones narrow-lanceolate, three-cornered near the apex; inner ones scarcely any; peduncles axillary; flowers whitish green. *Fl.* March—April.—*W. & A. Prod.* i. 7.—*Rheede,* iii. *t.* 29—*Roxb. Fl. Ind.* ii. 657.——Domesticated everywhere in India.

MEDICAL USES.—The leaves gently bruised and mixed with salt, and reduced to the form of a plaster, and in this state applied to malignant tumours, will act powerfully in ripening them. The seeds of the *A. reticulata* may be swallowed whole with impunity, though the kernels are highly poisonous. The bark is a powerful astringent, and as a tonic is much used in medicine by the Malays and Chinese. —*Long, Indig. Plants of Bengal. Rheede.*

ECONOMIC USES.—The Anonas are all South American plants. This species, as well as the *A. reticulata* (Sweet-sop or Bullock's-heart) and *A. muricata* (Sour-sop), has long been naturalised in the East. "The only place," says Royle, "where I have seen it *apparently* wild, was on the sides of the mountain on which the hill-fort of Adjeegurh in Bundelcund is built, and this it covers in company with the teak-tree, which only attains a dwarfish size. The fruit is delicious to the taste, and on occasions of famine has literally proved the staff of life to the natives. It is not generally known that the leaves of this plant have a heavy disagreeable odour, and the seeds contain a highly acrid principle fatal to insects, on which account the natives of India use them powdered and mixed with the flour of gram (*Cicer arietinum*) for washing the hair. When in fruit, the Custard-apple is easily distinguished from the Bullock's-heart. They are well known as *Seeta-phul* and *Ram-phul*. The Sour-sop or rough Anona is sparingly cultivated in Madras; the fruit is muricated with soft prickles.—*Royle. Gibson.*

(61) **Antiaris saccidora** (*Dalz.*) N. O. ARTOCARPACEÆ.

Nettavil-marum, TAM. Araya-angeli, MAL.

DESCRIPTION.—Large tree; leaves alternate, ovate-oblong, acuminate, entire, glabrous above, slightly villous beneath; capitule axillary, aggregated; drupe, shape and size of a small fig, covered with purple down. *Fl.* Oct.—*Wight Icon. t.* 1958. —Lepurandra saccidora, *Nimmo in Grah.'s Cat.*——Malabar. North Concan. Travancore.

ECONOMIC USES.—The natives strip the bark of this tree into large pieces, soak it in water, and beat it well, when it becomes white and furry. In this state the hill-people use it as clothing, and also make it into large bags by making a single perpendicular incision in the bark, and one above and below, and then sewing the sides together again. Paper is also made from the bark. It is a very large tree, 18 feet in circumference at the base. On wounding the fruit a milky viscid fluid exudes in large quantities, which shortly hardens, becoming of a black and shining colour, and of the consistency of bees'-wax. The inner bark is composed of very strong tenacious fibres, which seem excellently adapted for cordage and matting. The nuts are intensely bitter, and contain an azotised principle, which may prove an active medical agent. In the N. Concans, the natives call the tree Juzoogry and Kurwut. Sacks made from the bark are used by the villagers for carrying rice, and are sold for six annas each. The tree was first noticed by Dr Lush at Kandalla in 1837. The native name given in Graham's catalogue is Chandul, and there described as having dentate serrulate leaves.—*Dalzell in Hooker's Journ. of Bot.* iii. 232. *Nimmo. J. Grah. Cat.*

(62) **Antidesma bunias** (*Spreng.*) N. O. STILAGINACEÆ.

Nolai-tali, TAM. Nuli-tali, MAL.

DESCRIPTION.—Middle-sized tree; leaves alternate, entire, lanceolate-oblong; spikes axillary and terminal; male flowers triandrous, with an abortive column in the centre; flowers green; fruit red. *Roxb. Fl. Ind.* iii. 758.—*Wight Icon. t.* 819. —*Rheede,* iv. *t.* 56.—Stilago bunias, *Linn.*——Coromandel. Malabar. Nepaul.

MEDICAL USES.—The shining deep-red fruit is sub-acid, and esteemed for its cooling qualities. This is one of the numerous plants reckoned as a remedy against the bites of snakes. The leaves are acid and diaphoretic, and when young are boiled with pot-herbs, and employed by the natives in syphilitic affections.—*Lindley.*

ECONOMIC USES.—The bark is used for making ropes, especially in Travancore. In Assam the tree grows to a large size, the trunk being 12 or 14 inches in diameter. The timber is greatly affected by immersion in the water, becoming heavy and black as iron. Another species, the *A. diandrum,* found on the Circar mountains, yields a tolerable timber, useful for many purposes. Ropes are also made from the *A. pubescens,* a native of the Northern Circars, where it is called Pollarie. The succulent drupes are eatable.—*Roxb.*

(63) **Aponogeton monostachyon** (*Willd.*) N. O. JUNCAGINACEÆ.

Parua-kalanga, MAL. Ghechoo, HIND. Kotee-kalangoo, TAM. Nama, TEL.

DESCRIPTION.—Perennial, aquatic; roots tuberous; leaves radical, linear-oblong, cordate at the base, pointed, entire, 3-5 nerved; scapes slightly striated, as long as the leaves; spikes single, closely surrounded with flowers; capsules 3, smooth, 1-celled, 4-8-seeded; anthers blue.—*Roxb. Fl. Ind.* ii. 210.—*Rheede,* xi. *t.* 15.——Peninsula. Concans.

ECONOMIC USES.—This aquatic plant is found in shallow standing water and the beds of tanks, flowering during the rainy season. The natives relish the small tubers as an article of diet. They are said to be as good as potatoes, and esteemed a great delicacy.—*Roxb. Ainsl.*

(64) **Arachis hypogæa** (*Linn.*) N. O. LEGUMINOSÆ.

Earth-nut, Manilla-nut, ENG. Vayer or Nelay-cadalay, TAM. Nela Sanagalu, TEL. Velaiatee-moong, DUK. Moong-phullee, HIND.

DESCRIPTION.—Annual, diffuse; stem hairy; leaves abruptly pinnated; leaflets 2-pair; calyx tubular, long; corolla papilionaceous; stamens and petals inserted into the throat of the calyx; flowers above ground sterile, aggregate, axillary, yellow; legumes long-stalked, indehiscent, 1-celled, 2-3-seeded.

Fl. June.—*W. & A. Prod.* i. 280.—*Roxb. Fl. Ind.* iii. 280. ——Cultivated in the Peninsula.

Economic Uses.—Properly indigenous to South America, but extensively cultivated in the Peninsula for the sake of the oil yielded by the seeds. This plant obtained its specific name from the pods burying themselves in the earth, where they ripen their seeds. These latter are roasted in America, and are considered a good substitute for chocolate. The oil which is expressed from them is much used in China and India for lamps. The poorer classes eat the nuts. An experiment was made in France as to the relative consumption of the ground-nut oil and olive oil in a lamp having a wick of one-eighth of an inch in diameter, when it was found that an ounce of the ground-nut oil burned 9 hours and 25 minutes, while olive oil under similar circumstances burned only 8 hours. It has the additional advantage of giving no smoke. In Europe a bushel of ground-nuts produces one gallon of oil when expressed cold; if heat be applied a still greater quantity is procured, but of inferior quality. The nut, according to Dr Davy, abounds with starch as well as oil, and a large proportion of albuminous matter, and in no other instances had he found so large a proportion of starch mixed with oil. The leaf is something like that of clover, and affords excellent food for cattle, and the cakes after the expression of the oil form a good manure. Under favourable circumstances the nuts will produce half their weight of oil, and the quantity is much increased by heat and pressure. It is cultivated in the neighbourhood of Calcutta, the oil being used for pharmaceutical purposes, and especially for lamps and machinery. A great quantity of the oil is exported annually from the Madras territories. It does not seem to be consumed to any large extent in this country, although the nut itself is much eaten by the poorer classes. It is said to be used for adulterating gingely oil in North Arcot, where it costs Rs. 1-8 to 2-12 per maund. In the Nellore district the seeds are procured at Rs. 1-8 per maund, and in Tanjore about 200 acres are cultivated, producing annually 75 candies of oil, at Rs. 2-6 per maund. The seeds yield about 43 per cent of a clear straw-coloured edible oil, which is an excellent substitute for olive oil, and makes a good soap. Simmonds has remarked upon this useful product: "This oil is good for every purpose for which olive or almond oil is used. For domestic purposes it is esteemed, and it does not become rancid so quickly as other oils. Experiments have been made on its inflammable properties, and it is proved that the brilliancy of light was superior to that of olive oil, and its durability was likewise proved to be seven minutes per hour beyond the combustion of the best olive oil, with the additional advantage of scarcely any smoke." And further: "That the culture of the Arachis in warm climates, or even in a temperate one under favourable circumstances, should be encouraged, there can be but one opinion, especially when it is considered that its qualities are able to supersede that of the olive and the almond, which are but precarious in their crops. . . . I am informed by an American merchant that he cleared 12,000 dollars in one year on the single article of ground or pea nuts obtained from Africa. Strange as it may appear, nearly all these nuts are transhipped to France, where they command a ready sale; are there converted into oil; and then find their way over the world in the shape of olive oil, the skill of the French chemists enabling them to imitate the real Lucca and Florence oil, so as to deceive the nicest judges. Indeed, the oil from the pea-nuts possesses a sweetness and delicacy that cannot be surpassed." There are two varieties of this plant grown in Malacca; also in Java—one with white, the other with brown seeds. It is there known as the Katjang oil. So useful a plant should be more extensively cultivated in this country. It thrives well on a light sandy soil, and is very prolific. In some parts of America it yields from thirty to eighty bushels of nuts per acre. On the western coast of Africa it is planted to a great extent. —*Ed. Phil. Mag. Simmonds. Comm. Prod. Mad.*

(65) **Areca catechu** (*Linn.*) N. O. Palmaceæ.

Areca or Betel-nut Palm, Eng. Paak-marum or Camooghoo, Tam. Poka-chettu, Tel. Suparie, Duk. Adaka or Cavooghoo, Mal. Gooa, Beng.

Description.—Palm; spathe double; spadix much branched; male flowers numerous, above the female, sessile; calyx 1-lobed, 3-cornered, 3-partite; petals 3, oblong, smooth; stamens 2-partite, inserted round the base of the style; female flowers 1-3 at the base of each ramification, sessile; calyx 5-lobed, flowers small, white, fragrant. *Fl.* April—May.—*Roxb. Fl. Ind.* iii. 615.—*Cor.* i. *t.* 76.—*Rheede,* i. *t.* 5, 6, 7, 8. ——Cultivated.

Medical Uses.—The nut is used as a masticatory in conjunction with the leaf of Piper Betel and Chunam. It is considered to strengthen the gums, sweeten the breath, and improve the tone of the digestive organs. The seed, reduced to charcoal and powdered, forms an excellent dentifrice. Dr Shortt states that the powdered nut, in doses of ten or fifteen grains every three or four hours, is useful in checking diarrhœa arising from debility. The dry expanded petioles serve as excellent ready-made splints for fractures. —*Pharm. of India.*

Economic Uses.—In appearance the Areca Palm is perhaps the most graceful and elegant of Indian Palms. Its native place is unknown, but it is extensively distributed in India. It yields the betel-nut of commerce. A tree will produce annually, on an average, three hundred nuts. The catechu which they yield is of a very inferior quality. There are two preparations of it, which are respectively called by the Tamools, Cuttacamboo and Cashcuttie; in Teeloogoo, Kansee; and in Dukhanie, Bharab-cutta and Acha-cutta. The first (Cuttacamboo) is chewed with the betel-leaf. Like most of the Palm tribe, the trunk is much used for ordinary building purposes; and in Travancore is especially used for spear-handles, &c. The spathe which stretches over the blossoms, which is called Paak-muttay, is a fibrous substance, with which the Hindoos make vessels for holding arrack, water, &c.; also caps, dishes, and small umbrellas. It is so fine that it can be written on with ink. The Areca Palm is found chiefly in Malabar, Canara, North Bengal, the lower slopes of the mountains of Nepaul, and the south-west coast of Ceylon. It will produce fruit at five years, and continue to bear for twenty-five years. Unlike the Cocoa Palm, it will thrive at high regions, and at a distance from the sea. In the Eastern Islands the produce of the tree varies from two hundred to one thousand nuts annually. They form a considerable article of commerce with the Eastern Islands and China, and are also one of the staple products of Travancore. The nuts are gathered in July and August, though not fully ripe till October. In the latter country the nuts are variously prepared for use. "Those that are used by families of rank are collected while the fruit is tender; the husks or the outer pod is removed; the kernel, a round fleshy mass, is boiled in water: in the first boiling of the nut, when properly done, the water becomes red, thick, and starch-like, and this is afterwards evaporated into a substance like catechu. The boiled nuts being now removed, sliced, and dried, the catechu-like substance is rubbed to the same and dried again in the sun, when they become of a shining black, ready for use. Whole nuts, without being sliced, are also prepared in the same form for use amongst the higher classes; while ripe nuts, as well as young nuts in a raw state, are used by all classes of people generally; and ripe nuts preserved in water with the pod are also used." When exported to other districts, the nuts are sliced and coloured with red catechu, as also the nut while in the pod. The average amount of exports of the prepared nuts from Travancore is from 2000 to 3000 candies annually, exclusive of the nuts in their ordinary state, great quantities of which are shipped to Bombay and other ports. According to the last survey there were upwards of a million trees in Travancore. The following mode of extracting the catechu from the nuts in Mysore is taken from Heyne's 'Tracts on India:' "The nuts are taken as they come from the tree, and boiled for some hours in an iron vessel. They are then taken out, and the remaining water is inspissated by continual boiling. This process furnishes Kossa, or most astringent terra japonica, which is black, and mixed with paddy-husks and other impurities. After the nuts are dried they are put into a fresh quantity of water and boiled again; and this water being inspissated like the former, yields the best or dearest kind of catechu, called

Coony. It is yellowish brown, has an earthy fracture, and is free from the admixture of foreign bodies." The nuts are seldom imported into England. The catechu has of late years superseded madder in the calico-works of Europe for dyeing a golden coffee-brown, 1 lb. of this being equal to 6 lb. of madder. On the mountains of Travancore and Malabar, a wild species, the *A. Dicksonii*, is found in great abundance. Of this the poorer classes eat the nuts as a substitute for the common betel-nut, but no other part of the tree appears to be employed for any useful purpose.—*Ainslie. Lindley. Simmonds. Rep. on Products of Travancore.*

(66) **Argemone Mexicana** (*Linn.*) N. O. PAPAVERACEÆ.

Yellow thistle or Mexican poppy, ENG. Bramadandoo, TAM. Brahmadandi, TEL. Feringie-datura, or Peela, DUK. Buro-shialkanta, or Thialkanta, BENG. Bherband, HIND.

DESCRIPTION.—Annual, herbaceous; leaves alternate, sessile, repand-sinuate, sharply toothed; sepals 2-3; calyx prickly, glabrous; petals 4-6; stem bristly; flowers solitary on erect peduncles; capsules prickly; seeds roundish; flowers yellow. *Fl.* Oct.—Nov.—*W. & A. Prod.* i. 18.——Coromandel. Malabar in waste places.

MEDICAL USES.—This plant is a native of Mexico, but is now found abundantly in Asia and Africa over a very extended area. The stalks and leaves abound with a bitter yellow juice like Gamboge, which is used in chronic ophthalmia. The seeds are used in the West Indies as a substitute for Ipecacuanha. An oil is also expressed from them, which in South America is much used by painters, and for giving a shining appearance to wood. It has also been employed as a substitute for castor-oil, and is applied externally in headache by the native practitioners. The juice of the plant in infusion is diuretic, relieves strangury from blisters, and heals excoriations. The seeds are very narcotic, and said to be stronger than opium. Simmonds says, "The seeds possess an emetic quality. In stomach complaints the usual dose of the oil is thirty drops on a lump of sugar, and its effect is perfectly magical, relieving the pain instantaneously, throwing the patient into a profound refreshing sleep, and relieving the bowels." This valuable but neglected plant has been strongly recommended as an aperient, anodyne, and hypnotic, by Dr Hamilton and other experienced practitioners in the West Indies.—(*Vide* Pharml. Journal, iv., v., and xii.) Samples of the oil were produced at the Madras Exhibition. It is cheap, and procurable in the bazaars, being used chiefly for lamps.—(*Ainslie. Lindley. Simmonds.*) Age apparently affects its activity, the freshly-prepared oil proving more energetic and uniform in its operation than that which has been kept some time. It has a soothing influence on all herpetic eruptions; and as a local application to indolent ulcers the expressed juice is much esteemed by the natives. The native practice of applying the juice to the eye in ophthalmia is dangerous. The plant was introduced into India from Mexico some three centuries ago. It is covered with strong prickles, whence the Spaniards called it Figo del Inferno—the Fig of Hell. The fresh root, bruised and applied to the part stung by scorpions, is said to give relief.—*Pharm. of India. Agric. Journ. of India*, ix. 403.

(67) **Argyreia bracteata** (*Choisy*). N. O. CONVOLVULACEÆ.

DESCRIPTION.—Twining shrub, branched; leaves alternate, on long petioles, broadly cordate-ovate, dark shining green above, beneath hirsute and somewhat silky; calyx 5-cleft; sepals hairy; corolla campanulate, hairy externally, purplish white, with a deep purple eye; peduncles axillary, dividing at the extremity in two or three branches with a sessile ebracteated flower in the fork, each of the pedicelled flowers with three bracteas at the base of the calyx; berry 3-4 seeded, deep orange colour; seeds embedded in pulp.—*Dec. Prod.* ix. 328.—*Drury Hand. Ind. Flor.* ii. 296.——Madras. Coromandel.

MEDICAL USES.—This plant is filled with milky juice. Decoctions of the leaves are used by the natives as fomentations in cases of scrofulous enlargement of the joints, the boiled leaves being used as poultices at the same time.—*Wight.*

(68) **Argyreia Malabarica** (*Choisy*). Do.

Kattu Kalangu, MAL. Paymoostey, TAM.

DESCRIPTION.—Twining shrub; stem downy; leaves roundish-cordate, acute, furnished with a few scattered hairs on both surfaces, paler below; corolla campanulate; peduncles as long as the leaves, many-flowered at the apex; sepals 5; exterior ones clothed with hoary villi with revolute edges; petioles and peduncles villous; flowers small, cream-coloured, with deep purple eye. *Fl.* July—August.—*Dec. Prod.* ix. 331. Convolvulus Malabaricus, *Linn.*—*Rheede*, xi. *t.* 51.——Mysore. Malabar. Common on the ghauts.

MEDICAL USES.—The root is cathartic. This plant is considered by farriers a good horse-medicine. The leaves beaten up with the

Codi Avanacu (*Tragia chamælea*) and fresh butter promote the maturation of abscesses. The root is used externally in erysipelas. —*Ainslie. Rheede.*

(69) **Argyreia Speciosa** (*Sweet*). Do.

Elephant Creeper, Eng. Samundar, Hind. and Duk. Shamuddirap-pachchai, Kadal-palai, Tam. Samudra-pala, Chandra-poda, Kokkita, Pala-samudra, Tel. Samudra-yogam, Samudra-pala, Mal.

Description.—Twining, tomentose; leaves cordate, acute, glabrous above, thickly nerved beneath, and silky silvery; sepals 5; corolla campanulate; peduncles equal in length to the petioles, umbellately capitate; corolla nearly two inches long, deep rose-coloured, hairy in the plicæ outside. *Fl.* July —August.—*Dec. Prod.* ix. 328.—Convolvulus speciosus, *Linn.* —Lettsomia nervosa, *Roxb. Fl. Ind.* i. 488.—*Rheede,* xi. *t.* 61. —*Wight Icon. t.* 851, 1360.——Malabar forests. Hedges in the Peninsula.

Medical Uses.—The leaves are used by native practitioners in the preparation of emollient poultices, and also in cutaneous complaints, being applied externally to the parts affected. The upper side of the leaves is used by the natives to act as a discutient, the under or white side as a maturant.—(*Ainslie. Gibson.*) In a case which came under Dr Wight's observation they acted as a powerful vesicant.—*Wight, Ill.*, ii. 201.

(70) **Aristolochia bracteata** (*Retz*). N. O. Aristolochiaceæ.

Worm-killer, Eng. Addatinapalay, Tam. Gadida-guda-pa, Tel. Kera-mar, Hind. and Duk.

Description.—Trailing; roots perennial, fibrous; stems striated, waved; leaves alternate, petioled, kidney-shaped, curled at the margins, glaucous below; petioles channelled; flowers axillary, solitary, peduncled, drooping; calyx with the upper part of the tube and tongue erect; colour dark purple; covered on the inside with purple hairs; capsules ovate. *Fl.* Nearly all the year.—*Roxb. Fl. Ind.* iii. 490.——Coromandel in cultivated places. Travancore. Banks of the Jumna.

Medical Uses.—Every part of this plant is nauseously bitter. In cases of gripes, two of the fresh leaves are rubbed up with water and given once in twenty-four hours. An infusion of the dried leaves is given as an anthelmintic. Fresh bruised and mixed with castor-oil, they are considered a valuable remedy in obstinate cases of that kind of Psora called in Tamil *Carpang*. It is also said to be anti-periodic and emmenagogue. The fresh leaves applied to the navel of a child are said to have the effect of moving the bowels. The same, fried with castor-oil and made into a ball the size of an orange, relieves horses when suffering from gripes. The leaves beaten up with water are given internally in cases of snake-bites; also in infusion for boils and inflammatory attacks. The plant grows abundantly on dark red or black soil in the Deccan. The natives squeeze the juice into wounds to kill worms, hence its name "Keeramar."—(*Roxb. Ainslie. Gibson. Lindley.*) Dr Newton says that in Scinde the dried root, in doses of about a dram and a half, in the form of powder or in infusion, is administered to increase uterine contractions.—*Pharm. of India.*

(71) **Aristolochia Indica** (*Linn.*) Do.

Indian birthwort, Eng. Isharmul, Hind., Duk., and Beng. Ich-churamuli, Peru-marindu, Perum-Kizhangu, Tam. Ishvara-veru, Dula-govela, Govila, Tel. Karalekam, Karukap-pulla, Karalvekam, Ishvaramuri, Mal.

Description.—Perennial, twining; leaves stalked, wedge-shaped or obovate, 3-nerved, pointed, waved; calyx tubular, nearly globose at the base; racemes axillary, shorter than the leaves; flowers erect; corolla purplish; capsule roundish, hexagonal, 6-celled; seeds numerous. *Fl.* Sept.—Oct.—*Roxb. Fl. Ind.* iii. 489.—*Wight Icon. t.* 1858.—*Rheede*, viii. *t.* 25. ——Copses and jungles in Travancore. Coromandel. Bengal. Hills throughout the Concan.

Medical Uses.—The root is nauseously bitter, and is said to possess emmenagogue and antarthritic virtues, and to be a valuable antidote to snake-bites, being applied both externally and internally. For particulars regarding the alleged efficacy of this remedy, see Journal of the Agri. Hort. Soc. of India, v. 138 and 742. Mixed with honey, the root is given in white leprosy, and the leaves internally in fever.—*Ainslie. Lindl.*

(72) **Artemisia Indica** (*Willd.*) N. O. Compositæ.

Majtari, Mastaru, Hind. Machipattiri, Tam. Machipatri, Tel. Tiru-nitri-pachha, Mal. Mastam, Beng.

Description.—Suffruticose, erect; leaves white, tomentose below, pinnatifid, upper ones trifid, uppermost and branched ones undivided, and with the lobes oblong, obtuse, mucronate; capitules spicately panicled, oblong, panicle leafy and spreading, younger racemes nodding; outer scales of the younger pubescent involucre leafy, acute, of the inner ones scariose, obtuse; flowers small, greenish white. *Willd. Sp.* iii. 1846.—*Roxb.*

Flor. Ind. iii. 449.—*Rheede,* x. *t.* 45.—A. grata, *Dec.*——Common on high lands. Mysore.

Medical Uses.—The strong aromatic odour and bitter taste of this plant indicate tonic and stomachic properties. Dr Wight states that the leaves and tops are administered in nervous and spasmodic affections connected with debility, and also that an infusion of them is used as a fomentation in phagedenic ulceration. Dr L. Stewart describes an infusion of the tops and leaves as a mild stomachic tonic.—(*Pharm. of India.*) All the different species of Artemisia are aromatic bitter tonics, and most of them have anthelmintic properties. They contain an essential oil, a bitter principle called Absinthine, and a peculiar acrid. They are principally used in intermittent fevers and dyspepsia, also in epilepsy and chorea. The present species is used as an antispasmodic in hysteria. It might be used as a substitute for Cinchona, though inferior in intermittent fevers.—*Powell's Punj. Products.*

(73) **Artocarpus hirsutus** (*Lam.*) N. O. Artocarpaceæ.

Anjelee, Tam. Ayenee, Anajeli, Mal.

Description.—Tree; leaves elliptic, obtuse, or rounded at both ends, glabrous, hairy, especially on the nerves beneath; male catkin long, cylindrical, ascending, afterwards pendulous; females oval, size of a hen's egg; fruit globose, echinate. *Fl.* Feb.—March.—*Roxb. Flor. Ind.* iii. 521.—*Rheede,* iii. *t.* 32.—*Wight Icon. t.* 1957.——Forests of Malabar and Travancore.

Economic Uses.—This tree yields the Anjely wood so well known on the western coast for house-building, ships, frame-works, &c. The tree attains a large size in the forests on the western coast, where it abounds. The fruit is the size of a large orange, and abounds in a viscid juice, which freely flows from the rough rind if touched; this is manufactured into bird-lime. The pulpy substance which surrounds the seeds is much relished by the natives, being almost as good as the Jack-fruit. The bark is occasionally used in Canara for preparing a brown dye.—*Roxb. Wight.*

(74) **Artocarpus integrifolius** (*Linn.*) Do.

Indian Jack-tree, Eng. Pila, Tam. Panasa, Tel. Phunus, Duk. Pilavoo, Mal. Kantal, Beng.

Description.—Large tree; young branches hirsute; leaves alternate, petiolate, ovate-oblong, glabrous, pale below and hirsute with stiff hairs; flowers male and female on the same branch; peduncle pendulous, arising from the trunk or branches; amentum of male flowers cylindrical; calyx none; petals 2;

fruit ovate, muricated. *Fl.* Nov.—Dec.—*Roxb. Flor. Ind.* iii. 522.—*Cor.* iii. *t.* 250.—*Rheede,* iii. *t.* 26-28.—*Wight Icon. t.* 678.—A. heterophylla, *Lam.*——Malabar. Peninsula. Bengal.

Economic Uses.—The timber of this tree, so well known as the Jack-wood, is much esteemed for making furniture of all kinds, for which it is well adapted. At first it is somewhat pale, but afterwards assumes a darker tinge approaching to mahogany, and when polished becomes one of the best fancy woods for tables, chairs, and frames. The root of the older trees is dark-coloured, and admirably adapted for picture-frames and carving-work of all kinds. Like others of the same family, the tree abounds in viscid, milky juice. The fruit, which grows to an enormous size, and hangs by a peduncle springing from the trunk, is a favourite article of food among the natives. There are several varieties, but what is called the honey-jack is by far the sweetest and best. The seeds when roasted are also much prized as a diet among the poorer classes. The leaves are given to goats and other cattle, and are said to be very fattening. In Travancore the Jack-tree is a monopoly, and yields an annual tax to the Sircar. The wood yields an abundant yellow dye, the sawdust being generally boiled for this purpose. The kernels contain a quantity of oil. The tree, if planted in stony soil, grows short and thick; if in sandy ground, tall and spreading; and if the roots happen to come in contact with water, the tree will not bear fruit. Bird-lime is manufactured from the juice. The word Jack is a corruption from the Sanscrit word "Tchackka," which means the fruit of the tree. The situation of the fruit varies with the age of the tree, being first borne on the branches, then on the trunk, and in very old trees on the roots. In Travancore the mode of propagation is as follows: The natives put the whole fruit in the ground, and when the seeds germinate and grow up they tie the stems together with straw, and by degrees they form one stem, which will bear fruit in six or seven years.—(*Roxb.*) The other species worthy of mention are the *A. Chaplasha,* a native of Chittagong and the forests east of Bengal. It grows to be an immense tree, and canoes for river use are made from the trunk. The timber is also useful for other purposes, especially when required for anything under water. The *A. lakoocha* is a native of Bengal. The roots are used for dyeing yellow. The male spadix is acid and astringent, and is eaten by the natives in their curries.—(*Roxb. J. Grah.*) The *A. Echinata* is a large tree, growing on the Neilgherries, and yielding a good timber, but hitherto little known.

(75) **Arum montanum** (*Roxb.*) N. O. Araceæ.

Konda-rakis, Tel.

Description.—Stemless; root a cylindrical tuber; leaves

cordate, repand, polished; spadix nearly as long as the hooded coloured spathe; anthers many-celled. — *Roxb. Fl. Ind.* iii. 497.—*Wight Icon. t.* 796.——Northern Circars.

Economic Uses.—A native of the mountainous parts of the Northern Circars, where the root is employed to poison tigers. Among other useful plants of this genus may be mentioned the *A. lyratum* (*Roxb.*), also a native of the Circar mountains, the roots of which are eaten by the natives, and reckoned very nutritious. They require, however, to be carefully boiled several times, and dressed in a particular manner, in order to divest them of a somewhat disagreeable taste.—*Roxb.*

(76) **Asparagus racemosus** (*Willd.*) N. O. Liliaceæ.

Shakakul, Hind. and Duk. Tannir-muttan, Shadavari, Tam. Challa-gaddalu, Pillipichara, Pilli-tega, Satavari, Tel. Shatavali, Mal. Sat-muli, Beng.

Description.—A straggling climbing shrub; branches striated; leaves fascicled, linear, falcate; thorns solitary, reflexed; racemes many-flowered, axillary; flowers small, white. *Fl.* Nov.—Dec.—*Roxb. Fl. Ind.* ii. 151.—*Wight Icon. t.* 2056. ——Travancore. Deccan.

Medical Uses.—This plant, says Roxburgh, will perfume the air to a considerable distance, owing to the delightful fragrance of its flowers. The root boiled in milk is given in bilious affections. It is necessary to remove the bark previous to administering it, as it is considered poisonous. The leaves boiled and mixed with ghee are applied externally to promote suppuration in boils and tumours.—(*Roxb. Ainsl.*) It acts also as a diuretic, and is used in special diseases. It increases the appetite and removes pains in the bowels, and is also considered to prevent the confluence of small-pox.—(*Punj. Prod.*) The *A. sarmentosus* (Willd.), also a native of the Peninsula, has also medicinal qualities. It is known as the Sufed Mush; and on this Modeen Sheriff remarks (*Suppl. to Pharm. of India*, p. 59): "There are two kinds of Sufed Mush, one found in the bazaars of Southern India, and the other elsewhere. The former is the dried and split roots of *Asparagus sarmentosus*. Dried it is useless as a medicine, but when fresh it is nutrient and demulcent. The Sufed Mush of all other parts is the real drug to which the name is applicable, and is the root of *Asparagus ascendens*. It is a useful medicine, and is better than Salep, for which it is used as a substitute. It is known under the Dukhanee name of Shakakul-hindi. It grows in Rohilcund (*Pharm. of India, Suppl.*) The roots of the *A. sarmentosus* are often candied, in which state they are occasionally brought from China. They are also pickled in vinegar, and used as tonics, and also boiled in oil and applied in diseases of the skin."—*Ainslie. J. Graham.*

(77) **Asteracantha longifolia** (*Nees*). N. O. Acanthaceæ.

Neer-moollie, Tam. Neer-goobbie, Tel. Gokshura, Hind. Kanta-koolika, Beng. Wahel-schulli, Mal.

Description.—Annual; stem erect, bluntly quadrangular, hispid; leaves opposite, ensiform, very long; calyx 4-cleft; corolla funnel-shaped, 5-cleft, one division deeper than the rest; flowers in whorls, axillary, blue or bright violet; spines, three on each side of the stem, equal in length to the whorls. *Fl.* July—Dec.—*Wight Icon. t.* 449.—Barleria longifolia, *Linn.* —Ruellia longifolia, *Roxb. Fl. Ind.* iii. 50.—*Rheede,* ii. *t.* 45. ——Malabar. Bengal.

Medical Uses.—This plant may commonly be met with by the side of paddy-fields and other damp situations. The roots are considered tonic and diuretic, administered in decoction. They are also employed in dropsical affections and gravel. The leaves boiled in vinegar are reckoned diuretic.—*Ainsl. Pharm. of India.*

(78) **Atalantia monophylla** (*Dec.*) N. O. Aurantiaceæ.

Wild-lime, Eng. Cat-ilimicham, Tam. Malnaregam, Mal. Adivi-nimma, Tel.

Description.—Shrub, 8 feet; thorns small; leaves ovate or oblong, more or less emarginate at the apex; calyx 4-toothed; petals 4; racemes short, sessile; pedicels long, slender; berry globose, size of a lime, 3-4 seeded; flowers axillary and terminal, small, white. *Fl.* Oct.—Nov.—*W. & A. Prod.* i. 91.—Limonia monophylla, *Linn.*—*Roxb. Fl. Ind.* ii. 378.—*Cor.* i. *t.* 82.—*Rheede,* iv. *t.* 12.——Malabar. Coromandel.

Economic Uses.—The wood is hard, heavy, and close-grained; of a pale yellow colour, and very suitable for cabinet-work. In the forests of Coromandel it grows to be a small tree, flowering about the rainy season.—*Roxb.*

(79) **Averrhoa bilimbi** (*Linn.*) N. O. Oxalidaceæ.

Bilimbi-tree, Eng. Wilumpi, Mal. Bilimbi, Beng. Kamarunga, Hind.

Description.—Tree, 15-20 feet; leaves alternate, unequally pinnated; leaflets oblong, lanceolate, acuminated, entire; calyx 5-cleft, pubescent; petals 5; flowers reddish purple, in racemes from the trunk; fruit oblong, obtuse-angled; seeds without aril. *Fl.* May—June.—*W. & A. Prod.* i. 142.—*Roxb. Fl. Ind.* ii. 451.—*Rheede,* iii. *t.* 45, 46.——Goa. Travancore. Cultivated.

MEDICAL USES.—The juice of the fruit has a pleasant acid taste, from which a syrup is made, given as a cooling drink in fevers. The leaves are slightly sensitive to the touch. The tree is a native of the Moluccas. The fruits are pickled or preserved in sugar.

(80) **Averrhoa carambola** (*Linn.*) Do.

Carambola-tree, ENG. Tamara-tonga, or Kamaranga, MAL. Cumurunga, BENG. Meetha-kumarunga, DUK.

DESCRIPTION.—Tree, 15-20 feet; leaves alternate, unequally pinnated; leaflets ovate, acuminated, 2-5 pair on small petioles; calyx glabrous; stamens 5; flowers disposed in short racemes arising from smaller branches on the trunk; corolla 5-petalled, campanulate; petals yellowish purple; fruit acutely 5-angled, with a smooth yellowish rind; seeds with aril. *Fl.* April—June.—*W. & A. Prod.* i. 141.—*Rheede,* iii. *t.* 43, 44.—*Roxb. Fl. Ind.* ii. 450.——Travancore. Coromandel. Cultivated.

ECONOMIC USES.—This beautiful tree originally came from Ceylon and the Moluccas. It is now commonly to be met with in the Peninsula. The fruits, which contain an acid watery pulp, are good when candied or made into syrup. They also make good pickles, and the juice is very useful in removing iron-moulds from linen. The leaves are a good substitute for sorrel. The root, leaves, and fruit are medicinal, and the latter is used for dyeing and other purposes.—*Rheede. Don.*

(81) **Avicennia tomentosa** (*Linn.*) N. O. VERBENACEÆ.

White Mangrove, ENG. Oepata, MAL. Bina, BENG. Nalla-madu, TEL.

DESCRIPTION.—Small tree; leaves opposite, obovate or oval, slightly tomentose beneath; flowers terminal, small, dingy yellow. *Fl.* April—May.—*Roxb. Fl. Ind.* iii. 88.—*Rheede,* iv. *t.* 45.—*Wight Icon. t.* 1481.——Soonderbunds. Salt marshes in the tropics.

ECONOMIC USES.—A preparation is made from the ashes of the wood which natives use for washing and cleaning cotton cloths. Painters mix the same with their colours to make them adhere more firmly. The kernels are bitter but edible. In Rio Janeiro the bark is used for tanning.

(82) **Azadirachta Indica** (*Ad de Juss.*) N. O. MELIACEÆ.

Neem-tree, ENG. Aria-bepou, MAL. Vaypum, TAM. Vepa, TEL. Neem, BENG.

DESCRIPTION.—Tree, 20 feet; calyx 5-partite; petals 5; anthers ten on the throat of the stamen tube; leaves pinnated; leaflets ovate-lanceolate, unequal-sided, acuminated, serrated; panicles axillary; flowers small, white; fruit, when ripe, purple, size of a small olive, 1-celled, 1-seeded. *Fl.* April—July.—*W. & A. Prod.* i. 118.—*Roxb. Fl. Ind.* ii. 394.—*Rheede,* iv. *t.* 52.—*Wight Icon. t.* 17.—Melia azadirachta, *Linn.*——Malabar. Peninsula. Bengal.

MEDICAL USES.—The bark, which has a remarkably bitter taste, has been much employed of late years as a fair substitute for Cinchona. The natives consider it a most useful tonic in intermittent fevers and chronic rheumatism, administering it either in decoction or powder. The dried leaves, added to common poultices, act powerfully in preventing glandular tumours from coming to maturity. The same discutient effect is produced after the application of leeches, in all kinds of bruises and sprains, by a watery or vinous infusion of them, particularly when spirit of camphor is now and then sprinkled over the cloth, steeped in the infusion. The greatest benefit has been derived from the application in the worst cases of compound fracture. A *sacculus aromaticus* of these leaves, with a few grains of powdered camphor, seldom fails to afford relief in rheumatic affections of the ears, eyes, and teeth. Dr Wight says, "The leaves beaten into a pulp, and externally applied, act like a charm in removing the most intractable form of psora and other pustular eruptions." On the decline of the small-pox, it is almost invariably the custom of the natives to cover the body with the leaves of this tree. From the pericarp of the seed an acrid bitter oil is expressed, which is a useful remedy in leprosy, and is, moreover, anthelmintic and stimulant, being used externally in cases of bad ulcers, and as a liniment in headaches and rheumatic affections. It is obtained either by boiling or expression; is of a deep yellow colour. The seeds after being skinned are employed to kill insects, and the kernels powdered and mixed with water for washing the hair. A gum is also got from the bark, used medicinally as a stimulant. A kind of toddy called Vaypumkhulloo, is procured from the young trees, which is said to be a good stomachic.—(*Ainslie. Roxb. Wight.*) Of this tree there are two kinds; one of them, which has a black appearance, is called Karin-veppa; the other, with green prickly leaves, which have an exceeding bitter taste, is known under the name of Arya-Karin-veppa. The latter properly is that which produces the real Malabar China. The bark of this tree, however, is employed by the natives only in cases of necessity; for a decoction of the leaves, if the coarser parts which subside to the bottom of the vessel be used, produce as powerful an effect. The Brahmins are accustomed to prepare from the juice of these leaves what they call *Karil*—that is, a sauce which they eat with their rice. This medicine is of excellent service in tertian fevers, in cases of worms, and in all disorders arising from indigestion and weakness of the nerves and stomach. If the green leaves be bruised and applied to wounds and ulcers of long standing, they cleanse them, and prevent from spreading or becoming cancerous. In a word, they answer the same purpose as the China bark, and in a much shorter time, because more power is contained in the juice of the leaves than in the woody parts of the stem and the branches.—(*Bart., Voy. to E. Ind.*, 413.) Major Lowther, writing to the Agri. Hort. Society, says: "I noticed a curious fact connected with the flow of sap in the Neem-tree, presenting the animal phenomenon of discharging a copious fountain of juice into a sort of natural basin at the roots, accompanied by a curious pumping noise within the trunk. Such was the repute in which this natural medicine was held, that natives came in crowds and carried away the liquor in their vessels. In the epidemic cholera which ravaged the station of Berhampore more than twenty-five years ago, a strong decoction of the leaves was given with much success to European soldiers. In some parts of India the Neem will not grow on its own roots, but comes to great perfection when budded on its congener, the *Melia sempervirens*. The expressed oil is much used and sold in the bazaars as an application to the sores of camels and other animals. Probably a decoction of the boiled seeds will be found a good application to the roots of vegetation attacked by white ants."

Economic Uses.—The wood is very like mahogany, beautifully mottled, hard, and heavy. The old trees yield an excellent wood for furniture, and it is so bitter that no insects will attack it. It is also used for ship-building, carts, and other purposes. The oil extracted from the seeds is used for lamps, and also for imparting colours to cotton cloths.—(*Bedd. Flor. Sylv. t.* 13. *Rep. Mad. Exhib.*) It is not generally known that the timber is equally durable with Camphor-wood, and makes imperishable trunks and chests, the contents becoming in a short time insect-proof. A handful of dried Neem-leaves are useful in packing collections of seeds and in guarding dried plants. In the latter case they should be renewed frequently.—*Lowther in Punj. Agri. Hort. Soc. Proc.* 1857.

B

(83) Balanites Ægyptiaca (*Delile*), **var. Indica.** N. O. AMYRIDACEÆ.

Hingen, BENG. Garee, TEL. Nunjoonda, TAM.

DESCRIPTION.—Tree, 20 feet; leaves alternate, bifoliate; spines axillary; calyx 5-parted; sepals villous; petals 5, lanceolate; pedicels 1-flowered; flowers aggregate, small, green; drupe ovoid, acute, 1-celled, 1-seeded, with a woody 5-angled nut. *Fl.* April—May.—Ximenia Ægyptiaca, *Roxb. Fl. Ind.* ii. 253.—*Wight Icon.* 274.——Deccan. Goozerat.

ECONOMIC USES.—This is a variety of the Egyptian plant which is found in the plains of the Deccan. The flowers are very fragrant. In Egypt, the fruit, according to Delile, passes for chebulic myrobalans. The nut is covered with a soft pulpy substance like soap; bitter to the taste, and with an offensive, greasy smell. It is very hard, and used in fireworks. For this purpose a hole is drilled in it, the kernel extracted, and the shell filled with powder; when fired, it bursts with a loud report. In Africa, the wood, which is very hard and of a yellow colour, is used for making furniture. An oil is also extracted from the seeds. The unripe drupes are bitter and violently purgative, but are eaten when ripe without any unpleasant consequences. The ryots use the bark medicinally for their cattle. This is one of the few trees which flourish on black soil.—(*Roxb. Lindl. J. Grah.*) It is interesting, says Royle, to find this plant in the country about Delhi, and in the Dooab as far as Allahabad, especially on the banks of the Jumna, as it serves with other plants to show an analogy in the Flora of this part of India with that of Egypt, where also this plant is found, as well as in the interior and western parts of Africa. This was first discovered by Dr Roxburgh as belonging to the Indian Flora, when he suggested that it should be formed into a new genus rather than be referred to *Ximenia*, and described it as common on the driest and most barren parts of the Circars. It is found only in similar situations in the north of India, and is one of those plants which show the great uniformity of vegetation over a great extent of the plains of India.—*Royle, Himal. Bot.*

(84) Balliospermum montanum (*Muller*). N. O. EUPHORBIACEÆ.

DESCRIPTION.—Undershrub; upper leaves lanceolate, acute at the base, lower ones broader, ovate, and often cordate at the base, sinuately toothed or deeply 3-lobed, marked with long scattered hairs; inflorescence commonly bisexual, males more loose than the females, and longer peduncled, all shorter than the petioles; fruit-bearing pedicels deflexed; sterile bracteoles numerous; segments of the male calyx orbicular-ovate, of the female lanceolate; capsules sub-globose, tridymous, puberulous; seeds smooth, at length marbled. *Dec. Prod.* xv. s. 2, p. 1125.—Jatropha montana, *Willd.*—Croton polyandrum, *Roxb.*—B. polyandrum, *Wight Icon. t.* 1885.——Hills in Bengal. Northern parts of the Peninsula. Malabar.

MEDICAL USES.—The seeds are cathartic, and probably furnish the greater part of the Jumalgota of the drug-sellers. East of the Sutlej its leaves are in high repute for wounds, and its sap is believed to corrode iron.—*Stewart's Punj. Plants.*

(85) **Balsamodendron agallocha** (*W. & A.*) N. O. AMYRIDACEÆ.

Googul, BENG.

DESCRIPTION.—Tree; trunk crooked, and clothed with many drooping crooked branches down to the ground; branchlets often ending in thorny points; calyx 4-toothed; petals 4; leaves alternate, petioled, oval or elliptic, serrulate, smooth on both sides; at the base or apex of the petiole on each side is generally a small leaflet giving the appearance of a ternate leaf; flowers on short peduncles, axillary, small, red, aggregate on the buds by the former year's leaves: berry drupaceous, red, smooth, size of a currant; nut 2-celled, 1-seeded. *Fl.* Feb.—March.—*Wight Ill.* i. 185.—Amyris commiphora, *Roxb. Fl. Ind.* ii. 244.——Silhet. Assam.

ECONOMIC USES.—This tree is said to yield the Indian bdellium, a substance like myrrh. Dr Royle has remarked that all the species of this genus require to be carefully examined from good and authentic specimens, accompanied by their respective products, so much doubt still remains in the opinions of botanists regarding the tree producing this substance. From an interesting paper by Dr Stocks in Hooker's 'Journal of Botany' (vol. i. p. 257), it would appear that this plant is not identical with the *B. Mukul* which grows in Scinde, and which, from the similarity of the native name 'Googul,' has been mistaken for it. It is important to notice this fact, especially when so much doubt exists as to the true plant yielding Indian bdellium, though in all probability the exudation of both species is similar in its properties. Of the one under notice, Dr Roxburgh observes, that the whole plant while growing is very odoriferous, and if broken in any part diffuses around a grateful fragrance, like that of the finest myrrh, yet that the juice never congeals, but is carried off by evaporation, leaving little or nothing behind; and all that he could procure was a minute portion of gummy matter, which certainly resembles myrrh both in smell and appearance, but has no tendency to be even tenacious or elastic. The Googul is collected in the cold season by making incisions in the tree and letting the resin fall on the ground. This accounts for the dirty condition in which it is found in the shops. Bdellium is properly a gum-resin, of which there are several kinds. It occurs in brittle masses of different sizes and shapes, of a red, yellow, or brownish colour, sometimes transparent, with a bitterish balsamic taste like myrrh. It is soluble in potass, and contains resin, gum, bassorine, and a volatile oil. It is often used as a substitute for myrrh, to which it has some resemblance in its effect upon the human frame. The odour is more faint and more agreeable than myrrh, by which it may be distinguished. It will melt in the mouth, while myrrh, when chewed, adheres to the teeth and imparts a milky colour to the saliva.—*Roxb. Royle. Hooker's Jour.*

(86) **Bambusa arundinacea** (*Willd.*) N. O. Graminaceæ.

Bamboo, Eng. Veduru, Tel. Kull-moollah, Mal. Bhans, Duk. Mungil, Tam. Bansh, Beng.

Description.—Stems erect, bending at the summit, jointed, hollow between the joints; branches alternate; thorns two or three, alternate on the joints; when double, a branchlet occupies the centre; when triple, the largest is strong, sharp, and somewhat recurved, occasionally wanting; leaves sheathing, linear-lanceolate, upper sides and margins hispid, sheaths downy; when in flower, the tree is leafless and the extremities are covered with flowers like one large panicle composed of numerous verticillate spikes, each verticel composed of several oblong, jointed, sessile spikelets; calyx 2-6-flowered, 3-valved; flowers hermaphrodite and male; seeds size and appearance of oats; male flowers 1-3 above the hermaphrodite ones. *Fl.* March—May.—*Roxb. Fl. Ind.* ii. 191.—*Cor.* i. *t.* 79.—Arundo bambos, *Linn.*——Forests of the Peninsula.

Medical Uses.—The siliceous concretion known as *Tabasheer* (*Tavakshiri*, a Sanscrit term meaning cow's milk) is only procured from the female plant. It so far resembles silex as to form a kind of glass when fused with alkalies. It is also unaffected by fire and acids. It is employed medicinally in the cures of paralytic complaints and poisonings. Sir D. Brewster (*Phil. Trans.*, 1819. *Ed. Journ. of Sci.*, viii. 286) made some singular discoveries on the optical properties of this substance. It is called by the Hindoo physicians, he says, bamboo manna, milk, sugar, or camphor of bamboo, and appears to be a secretion from the joints of the reed in a state of disease, malformation, or fracture. The ordinary quantity produced by a disorganised joint or internode is four or five grains. It consists of silica, containing a minute quantity of lime and vegetable matter. Its physical properties are remarkable. Its refractive power is lower than that of any other body, when solid or fluid. With certain oils, which it imbibes, it becomes as transparent as glass. It absorbs water, and becomes as white and opaque as if it had been covered with white-lead. It is highly prized in native practice as a stimulant and aphrodisiac. Among other reputed medical properties of the bamboo, the root is said to be a diluent, the bark a specific in eruptions, and the leaves as anthelmintic and emmenagogue.—*Ainslie. Pharm. of India. Madras Journ. of Med. Sci.*, 1862, p. 245.

Economic Uses.—These gigantic arborescent grasses, which cover the sides and tops of the mountains throughout the continent of India, form one of the peculiar as well as most striking features of Oriental scenery. Few objects present a more attractive sight in the wild forests of this country than a clump of these beautiful plants, with their tall bending stems and delicate light-green foliage. With the exception of the cocoa, and some other palms perhaps, the bamboo is the most useful and economical of all the vegetable products of the East. In no other plant is strength and lightness combined to that degree which renders this so important an article in building houses, lifting weights, forming rafts, and a thousand other uses which might here be enumerated. It attains a considerable height —some 70-80 feet—and has been known to spring up thirty inches in six days. At the age of 15 years the bamboo is said to bear fruit—a whitish seed like rice—and then to die. These seeds are eaten by the poorer classes.

The purpose to which different species of bamboo are applied are so numerous that it would be difficult to point out an object, in which strength and elasticity are requisite, and for which lightness is no objection, to which the stems are not adapted in the countries where they grow. The young shoots of some species are cut when tender, and eaten like asparagus. The full-grown stems, while green, form elegant cases, exhaling a perpetual moisture, and capable of transporting fresh flowers for hundreds of miles. When ripe and hard they are converted into bows, arrows, and quivers, lance-shafts, the masts of vessels, bed-posts, walking-sticks, the poles of palanquins, to floors and supporters of rustic bridges, and a variety of similar purposes. In a growing state the spiny kinds are formed into stockades, which are impenetrable to any but regular infantry, aided by artillery. By notching their sides the Malays make wonderfully light scaling-ladders, which can be conveyed with facility where heavier machines could not be transported. Bruised and crushed in water, the leaves and stems form Chinese paper, the finer qualities of which are only improved by a mixture of raw cotton and by more careful pounding. The leaves of a small species are the material used by the Chinese for the lining of their tea-chests. Cut into lengths and the partitions knocked out, they form durable water-pipes, or, by a little contrivance, are made into excellent cases for holding rolls of papers. Slit into strips, they afford a most durable material for weaving into mats, baskets, window-blinds, and even the sails of boats. Finally, the larger and thicker truncheons are exquisitely carved by the Chinese into beautiful ornaments. No plant in Bengal is applied to such a variety of useful purposes as the bamboo. Of it are made implements for weaving, the posts and frames of the roofs of huts, scaffoldings for buildings, portable stages for native processions, raised floors for granaries, stakes for nets in rivers, rafts, masts, yards, oars, spars, and in boat-decks. It is used for building bridges across creeks, for fences, as a lever for raising water for irrigation, and as flag-poles. Several agricultural instruments are made of it, as are also hackeries or carts, doolies or litters, and biers, the shafts of javelins or spears, bows and arrows, clubs, and fishing-rods. A joint of bamboo serves as a holder for pens, small instruments, and tools. It is used as a case in which things of little bulk are sent to a distance. The eggs of silk-worms were brought in a bamboo-cane from China to Constantinople in the time of Justinian. A joint of bamboo answers the purpose of a bottle, and a section of it is a measure for solids and liquids in bazaars. A piece of it is used as a blow-pipe, and as a tube in a distilling apparatus. A small bit of it split at one end serves as tongs to take up burning charcoal, and a thin slip of it is sharp enough to be used as a knife in shelling betel-nuts, &c. Its surface is so hard that it answers the purpose of a whetstone, upon which the ryots sharpen their bill-hooks and sickles.—*Roxb. Lindley.*

When travelling in the Himalaya, Dr Hooker observed a manufactory for making paper out of the bamboo. Large water-tanks were constructed in the fields for the purpose of steeping the bamboo stems. They appeared to be steeped for a length of time in some solution of lime. They were then removed and beaten upon stones until they became quite soft, or till all the flinty matter which abounds in their stems was removed.—*Hooker, Him. Journ.*, 311.

A correspondent from Burmah furnishes the following very interesting account of the flowering of the bamboo, and of its uses: The flowering of the bamboo is considered to be a very rare occurrence. Once in eighteen, twenty, and even twenty-five years, does it flower, and still less seldom does it produce seed. We have shown the seed to Burmese of 75 and 80 years old, and they could not tell what it was. They had seen none before. Among the hill-people and the tribes who are buried away in the recesses of our forests, they have a very superstitious dread of this phenomenon. They mention that when the bamboo flowers, fevers and sickness will be prevalent. Their traditions have taught them so, and hence they always fear the appearance of this particular flower. Of course their apprehensions are based purely on superstition and ignorance. The flowering of the bamboo may be ascribed to natural causes.

It is one of the most valuable, as it is the most useful, kind of plants, adapted to supply the wants of mankind. It is employed in a great variety of ways—for houses, furniture, utensils, and for fuel. Colonel Nuthall, who spent many years on this coast, was of the deliberate opinion, from his great experience of the country, that no branch of industry would yield a capitalist more handsome profits than the growing of the large-size bamboo. All that is needed is to put the young shoots down, and they will run up rapidly of themselves without any care or attention to them whatever. They would proportionately fetch higher prices than the smaller kinds, for which there is a constant demand all over the country. The use of bamboo will never go out of fashion in Burmah, at least among the rural population. Often there is found a small whitish fungus growing on the sides of the bamboo, which is called by the people "*Wah moo*," which the late Dr Judson makes synonymous with "*Than moo.*" It is a mushroom growth, and when rasped or bruised down to a powder it is administered as a vermifuge by Burmese physicians. It is said to be a very effectual remedy in cases of worms, with which children are so liable to be troubled in infancy. We have no doubt that if this Burmese remedy was known in Europe, it would at once be introduced into the British pharmacopœia. It is a more manageable article than some of the substances now classified as vermifuge medicines.

Immense quantities of fine bamboos are floated down the various rivers of the western coast. They are usually 60 feet long, and 5 inches in diameter near the root. These are readily purchased, standing at 5 rupees, and small ones at 3½ rupees, per 1000. Millions are annually cut in the forests, and taken away by water in rafts, or by land in hackeries. From their buoyancy they are much used for floating heavier woods.—*Cleghorn's Forests of S. India.**

(87) **Barleria prionitis** (*Linn.*) N. O. Acanthaceæ.

Coletta-veetla, Mal. Shem-muli, Tam. Mullù-gounta, Tel. Kantha-jathi, Beng.

Description.—Shrub, 4 feet; stem herbaceous; leaves opposite, entire, lanceolate-ovate; between the branch and the leaf there is a spine with four sharp rays from the same centre;

* For further accounts of the bamboo, see Appendix A.

flowers sessile, axillary, orange-coloured. *Fl.* Nearly all the year.—*Roxb. Fl. Ind.* iii. 36.—*Wight Icon.* ii. 452.—*Rheede,* ix. *t.* 41.——Peninsula. Bengal.

MEDICAL USES.—The juice of the leaves, mixed with sugar and water, is given to children in fevers and catarrhal affections. The ashes of the burnt plant, mixed with water and rice conjee, are employed in cases of dropsy and anasarca; also in coughs.—*Ainslie.*

(88) **Barringtonia acutangula** (*Gærtn.*) N. O. MYRTACEÆ.

Karpà, TEL. Sjeria-samstravadi, MAL.

DESCRIPTION.—Tree; leaves crowded about the ends of the branches, cuneate-obovate, serrulated; racemes long, pendulous; pedicels very short; calyx 4-cleft; ovary 2-celled; fruit oblong, 4-sided, sharp-angled; flowers small, reddish white, with scarlet filaments. *Fl.* April—May.—*W. & A. Prod.* i. 333.—*Rheede,* iv. *t.* 7.—*Roxb. Fl. Ind.* ii. 635. Eugenia acutangula, *Linn. sp.*——Bengal. Peninsula. Travancore.

MEDICAL USES.—The root is bitter, and said to be similar to Cinchona, but also cooling and aperient. The seeds are very warm and dry, and are used as an aromatic in colic and parturition.—*Powell's Punj. Prod.*

ECONOMIC USES.—The wood is hard and of a fine grain, red, and equivalent to mahogany.—(*M'Clelland.*) It is suited for ordinary work.

(89) **Barringtonia racemosa** (*Roxb.*) Do.

Samutra-pullum, TAM. Samudra-poo or Sam-stravadi, MAL.

DESCRIPTION.—Tree; leaves alternate, short-petioled, cuneate-oblong, acuminated, serrulated, smooth on both sides; racemes terminal, or axillary from the large branches, pendulous; flowers on short pedicels, large, white with a tinge of rose; calyx 2-3 cleft; petals four; filaments longer than the petals; style long; fruit ovate, drupaceous, bluntly 4-angled, smooth, brownish red; endocarp scarcely separating from the epicarp; seed 1. *Fl.* May.—*W. & A. Prod.* i. 333.—*Wight Icon. t.* 152.—*Roxb. Fl. Ind.* ii. 634.—*Rheede,* iv. *t.* 6.—Eugenia racemosa, *Linn. sp.*——Malabar. Coromandel.

MEDICAL USES.—The medicinal properties are said to be similar to the preceding species. The roots are slightly bitter, but not unpleasant. They are considered by Hindoo doctors valuable on account of their aperient, deobstruent, and cooling properties. The fruit, powdered, is used to clean the nostrils in cold as a snuff, and is also applied externally, in combination with other remedies, in sore-throat and cutaneous eruption.—*Ainslie. Roxb. Lindley.*

(90) **Basella rubra** (*Linn.*) N. O. Basellaceæ.

Malabar nightshade, Eng. Rukhto-pooi, Beng. Alla-batsalla, Tel. Pol, Hind.

Description.—Stem scandent, 3-4 feet, angular, brownish purple; leaves ovate, acuminate, purplish; spikes nearly equalling the leaves, long-peduncled; flowers purple; outer divisions of the calyx oblong-elliptic; berries dark purple, obsoletely 4-lobed, greenish and purple at the apex before ripening; seeds pale brown. *Dec. Prod.* xiii. s. 2, p. 222.—*Wight Icon. t.* 896.——Bengal. Peninsula.

Medical Uses.—The juice of the leaves is prescribed by native practitioners in doses of a teaspoonful thrice a-day to children suffering from catarrh.—(*Faulkner.*) The *B. alba* is merely a variety.

Economic Uses.—This esculent herb is cultivated in almost every part of the country. The succulent leaves are dressed and eaten like spinach. An infusion of the leaves is used as tea. The *B. cordifolia* is also cultivated as a pot-herb. It yields a very rich purple dye, but is difficult to fix.—*Lindley. Roxb.*

(91) **Bassia butyracea** (*Roxb.*) N. O. Sapotaceæ.

Indian Butter-tree, Eng. Phulwara, Beng.

Description.—Tree, 30-40 feet; leaves obovate, tomentose beneath; corolla 8-cleft; stamens 30-40 on longish filaments; pedicels aggregate, and, as well as the calyx, woolly; drupes oval; flowers smallish, white. *Fl.* Jan.—Feb.—*D. Don. Fl. Nep.* p. 146.—*Roxb. Fl. Ind.* ii. 527.—— Almora Hills. Nepaul.

Medical Uses.—A pure vegetable butter called Choorie is produced by this tree; the mode of extraction Dr Roxburgh has fully described in the 8th vol. of the 'Asiatic Researches.' The kernels of the fruit are bruised into the consistence of cream, which is then put into a cloth bag with a moderate weight laid upon it, and left to stand till the oil or fat is expressed, which becomes immediately of the consistence of hog's lard, and is of a delicate white colour. Its uses in medicine are much esteemed in rheumatism and contractions of the limbs. It is also an excellent emollient for chapped hands.

It resembles piney tallow in its chemical properties, and is of a pale yellow colour.—*Pharm. of India. Roxb.*

Economic Uses.—The pulp of the fruit is eatable. The juice is extracted from the flowers and made into sugar by the natives. It is sold in the Calcutta bazaar, and has all the appearance of date-sugar, to which it is equal if not superior in quality. The butter which is obtained from the kernels of the fruit is reckoned a valuable preservative when applied to the hair, mixed with sweet-scented oil, and thus sold and exported. Being cheaper than ghee, it is used to adulterate that article. By experiments in England, a specimen was found to consist of solid oil, 34 of fluid oil, and 6 parts of vegetable impurities. The original specimen dissolved readily in warm alcohol, a property which may render it of great advantage in medicinal purposes. It makes excellent soap. When pure, it burns bright without smoke or smell, and might be advantageously employed in making candles.

It is a peculiar characteristic of the seeds of the Bassia trees that they contain at the same time saccharine matter, spirit, and oil, fit both for food and burning in lamps. The butter procured from this species of Bassia is not liable to become rancid, even if kept for some time. It is completely melted at a temperature of 120°.—*Roxb. Royle. Simmonds.*

(92) **Bassia latifolia** (*Roxb.*) Do.

Mahwah-tree, Eng. Poounum, Mal. Caat-elloopei, Tam. Ipie, Tel. Moola, Hind. Mahwah or Muhoon, Beng.

Description.—Tree, 40 feet; leaves alternate, oblong or elliptic, crowded about the extremities of the branches, smooth above, somewhat whitish below; stamens 20-30 within the gibbous tube of the corolla, on short filaments; corolla thick, fleshy, with a more than 8-lobed limb; lobes cordate; sepals 4; pedicels drooping, terminal; flowers white, with a tinge of green and cream colour, numerous, crowded from the extremities of the branchlets, peduncled, and bent with the mouth of the flowers directly to the ground; berry size of a small apple, 1-4 seeded. *Fl.* March—April.—*Roxb. Fl. Ind.* ii. 526. —*Cor.*, i. *t.* 19.——Circar mountains. Bengal. Concans.

Economic Uses.—The timber of this tree is hard and strong, and is in request for naves of wheels, carriages, and similar uses. An ardent spirit is distilled from the flowers by the hill tribes (where the tree is abundant), which makes a strong and intoxicating liquor. The flowers are sweet-tasted, and are eaten raw. Jackals are particularly fond of them. The seeds yield by expression a large quantity of concrete oil, which is used in lamps, to adulterate ghee, and for frying cakes. The kernels are easily extracted from the smooth chestnut-coloured pericarps, when they are bruised, rubbed, and subjected to a moderate pressure. The oil concretes immediately it is expressed, and retains its consistency at a temperature of 95°. The oil is, however, thick and coarse, and only used by the poorer classes.

The following account by Dr Gibson is given of this plant in Guzerat and Rajpootana, where it abounds: "This flower is collected in the hot season by Bheels and others from the forests, also from the planted trees, which are most abundant in the more open parts of Guzerat and Rajwarra. The ripe flower has a sickly sweet taste resembling manna. Being very deciduous, it is found in large quantities under the trees every morning during the season. A single tree will afford from 200 to 400 lb. of the flowers. The seeds afford a great quantity of concrete oil, used in the manufacture of soap. The forest or Bheel population also store great quantities of the dried flowers as a staple article of food; and hence, in expeditions undertaken for the punishment or subjection of those tribes when unruly, their Bassia trees are threatened to be cut down by the invading force, and the threat most commonly insures the submission of the tribes."

"In Guzerat and Rajpootana every village has its spirit-shop for the sale of the distilled liquor from the flowers. In the island of Caranja, opposite to Bombay, the Government duty on the spirits distilled (chiefly from this flower) amounts to at least £60,000 per annum; I rather think that £80,000 is most generally the sum. The Parsees are the great distillers and sellers of it in all the country between Surat and Bombay, and they usually push their distilleries and shops into the heart of the forest which lines the eastern border and hills of those countries. The spirit produced from the Bassia is, when carefully distilled, much like good Irish whisky, having a strong, smoky, and rather fetid flavour; this latter disappears with age. The fresh spirit is, owing to the quantity of aromatic or empyreumatic oil which it contains, very deleterious; and to the European troops stationed at Guzerat some thirty years ago, appeared to be quite as poisonous as the worst new rum of the West Indies has generally proved to our soldiers. It excited immediately gastric irritation, and on this supervened the malarious fever so common in those countries."—*Hook., Journ. of Bot.*, 1853, p. 90. *Roxb.*

In 1848 a quantity of Mahwah oil was forwarded to the Secretary of the E. I. and China Association, with the view of ascertaining its market value and applicability for the manufacture of candles and soap. The managing director of Price's Patent Candle Company stated in reply: "I beg to inform you that the 'Mowah' oil, of which you furnished us samples, is worth in this country, for the manufacture of candles, £8 per ton less than Petersburg tallow. We have tried a great many experiments upon it, and found it to be of the same value as cocoa-nut oil, as its being harder makes up for the colour being inferior. Large quantities could be used in this country at about £35 per ton. I send some candles and oil, but fear that the former will not remain in a solid state through the voyage to India. We have, however, processes secured to us by which we can make candles from Mowah oil sufficiently hard for the Indian market."

(93) **Bassia longifolia** (*Linn.*) Do.

Elloopie, MAL. Elloopa, TAM. Ippa, TEL. Mohe, HIND.

DESCRIPTION.—Tree, 40 feet; leaves ovate-lanceolate, entire, crowded about the ends of the branchlets, immediately above the peduncles; young shoots and petioles slightly villous; calyx of two opposite pairs of leaflets; corolla 8-cleft; filaments scarcely any; pedicels axillary, drooping, crowded, 1-flowered; stamens 16-20, within the gibbous tube of the corolla; flowers whitish; fruit olive-shaped, yellowish when ripe, 8-9 seeded; seeds solitary. *Fl.* May.—*Roxb. Fl. Ind.* ii. 523.——Coromandel. Malabar. Circars.

MEDICAL USES.—Like most Sapotads, this tree abounds in a gummy juice which exudes from the bark. It is employed by the Vytians in rheumatic affections. The bark itself is used in decoction as an astringent and emollient, and also as a remedy in the cure of itch.—*Ainslie.*

ECONOMIC USES.—The flowers are roasted and eaten, and are also bruised and boiled to a jelly, and made into small balls, which are exchanged by the natives for fish and rice. An oil is expressed from the ripe fruits which is used for lamps among the poorer classes, and is one of the principal ingredients in making country soap. It is to the common people a substitute for ghee and cocoa-nut oil in their cakes and curries. The cakes which are left after the oil is expressed are used for washing the head, and are carried as articles of trade to those countries where the tree does not grow. The oil is solid at a moderate temperature, but will not keep any length of time—not more than a fortnight or three weeks in the warm season; it then becomes rancid, emitting a disagreeable odour. If, however, it be well corked and secured from contact with the air, it will in cold weather keep for some months. In England it is used in the manufacture of candles. The price of this oil is about three rupees and a half a maund. The wood of this tree is hard, and nearly as durable as teak, but not so easily worked, nor is it procurable of such length for beams and planks. It thrives best on deep light soils.—*Roxb. Hunter on Veg. Oils of S. India.*

(94) **Batatas edulis** (*Choisy*). N. O. Convolvulaceæ.

Sweet or Spanish Potato, Eng. Kappa-kalenga, Mal. Shukar-kundoo-aloo, Beng. Chillagada, Grasugada, Tel.

Description.—Stem creeping, rarely twining; leaves variable, usually angular, also lobed, cordate; sepals 5; corolla campanulate; peduncles equal in length to the petioles, 3-4 flowered; flowers white outside, purple inside. *Fl.* Feb.—March.—*Rheede*, vii. *t.* 50.—Convolvulus batatas, *Linn.*—*Roxb. Fl. Ind.* i. 483.—Ipomæa batatas, *Lam.*——Cultivated.

Economic Uses.—This plant is said originally to have been found wild in the woods of the Malayan Archipelago, from whence it was introduced into this country. There are two varieties, one with red, the other with white tubers. The red variety is considered the best; both are very nutritious and palatable, though slightly laxative. This esculent root was brought to England from Spain and Portugal before the common potato became known. "The sweet potato," says Sir Joseph Banks, "was used in England as a delicacy long before the introduction of our potatoes. It was imported in considerable quantities from Spain and the Canaries, and was supposed to possess the power of restoring decayed vigour." In India they are cultivated by all classes. They require very little care; the ground being merely cleared of weeds, the plants will grow on any soil. In taste they are sweet and palatable, possessing a quantity of saccharine matter. The natives eat the tubers, leaves, and tender shoots. The former are considered as nourishing as the potato, and a lighter food. The tubers yield a large proportion of starch. They must be kept dry, or they decay soon. The herbage is employed for feeding cattle.—*Don. Simmonds.*

Batatas betacea, the *Beet-rooted sweet Potato*, figured in the Bot. Reg., t. 56 (1840), has been lately introduced. The following particulars are given in the Jury Reports, Mad. Exh. 1855:—

"Four small roots were sent from Australia by Mr Dowdeswell, and planted by Mr Rohde at Guntoor, whence it has been already largely distributed. It has been in daily use as a vegetable for the last six months, and is preferred to the common sweet potato, as being less sweet and more farinaceous."

The large turnip-shaped roots of the *B. paniculata* dried in the sun, reduced to powder, and then boiled with sugar and butter, are said to promote obesity. They are also cathartic, and as such are used by the natives. Cattle are very fond of them.—*Roxb.*

(95) **Bauhinia racemosa** (*Lam.*) N. O. Leguminosæ.

Bun-raj, Beng. Arree, Tel.

Description.—Small tree, unarmed, bushy; branchlets

drooping; leaves cordate at the base, upper side glabrous, under villous, or pubescent, or nearly glabrous; leaflets roundish or broadly ovate, united to about the middle, 3-nerved; racemes solitary, terminal or leaf-opposed, leafless, much longer than the leaves; flowers scattered, small, white; calyx spathaceous, at length reflexed, 5-toothed, pubescent; petals linear, lanceolate, slightly hairy outside; stamens all fertile, united at the base; filaments and anthers bearded; style none (!); stigma flat, sessile; legumes linear, straightish or curved, scarcely dehiscent, many-seeded. *Fl.* May—June.—*W. & A. Prod.* i. 295.—B. parviflora, *Vahl.*—*Roxb. Fl. Ind.* ii. 323.——Mysore. Concan mountains. Bengal.

Economic Uses.—This tree has a thick bark, of which matchlockmen make their matches. It burns long and slowly without any substance being mixed with it. To prepare the bark it is boiled, dried, and beaten. Strong ropes are made from the bark stripped from the green branches, used for cots, tying fences, and various other purposes. The fibre is not exported, and the price is very low. Among other Bauhinias which yield fibres may be mentioned the *B. diphylla*, which is common about Cuddapah and Guntoor, where it is known as the Authee nar, Yepy, and Apa.—*Roxb. Jury Rep. M. E.*

A fibre is also procured from the *B. scandens*, a large climber, growing in the Concans and Travancore. A line made from it was tested by Captain Thomson, who found that it sustained a weight of 168 lb. for the space of forty-five minutes, thereby equalling in strength the best Sunn hemp.—*Royle.*

(96) **Bauhinia tomentosa** (*Linn.*) Do.

Caat-attie, Triviat-putrum, Tam. Chanscheha, Mal.

Description.—Shrub, 6 to 12 feet; unarmed; leaves ovate or roundish at the base, under surface villous as well as the petioles, branches, peduncles, and calyx; leaflets connected beyond the middle, oval, obtuse, 3-nerved; peduncles 2-flowered, leaf-opposed; pedicels each with 3 bracteas at the base; calyx spathaceous, 5-toothed; petals oval; stamens all fertile; legumes flat, lanceolate, 5-6-seeded; flowers large, pale sulphur; one petal usually with a dark purple spot inside. *Fl.* July—August.—*W. & A. Prod.* i. 295.—*Roxb. Fl. Ind.* ii. 323.—*Rheede*, i. *t.* 35.——Malabar. Coromandel. Oude.

MEDICAL USES.—The native doctors administer the dried leaves and young flowers in dysenteric affections, and a decoction of the bark of the root is given in cases of liver and phlegmatic complaints, and also as a vermifuge. The bruised bark is also occasionally applied to tumours and wounds.—(*Ainslie. Rheede.*) The leaves of several species of Bauhinia are used in Bengal as demulcent or mucilaginous remedies in dysentery. The seeds are eaten, and are said to be tonic and aphrodisiac.—*Powell's Punj. Prod.*

(97) **Bauhinia Vahlii** (*W. & A.*) Do.

Mahwal, HIND. Adda, TEL.

DESCRIPTION.—Shrub, climbing to an immense extent; young shoots, petioles, peduncles, and tendrils covered with thick rusty-coloured tomentum; leaves roundish, deeply cordate at the base, upper side nearly glabrous, under tomentose; leaflets oval, obtuse, united to a little above the middle, 4-6 nerved; nerves covered with rusty tomentum; tendrils opposite, below the leaves, spiral; racemes terminal, corymbiform; pedicels elongated, and with the calyx densely villous; calyx ovate, splitting to the base of the limb into two reflexed segments; petals densely clothed on the back with silky hairs, the three upper a little larger than the others; fertile stamens 3, villous at the base; ovary densely villous, its stalk cohering on one side with the calyx tube; legumes pendulous, long, linear, compressed, 8-12 seeded; flowers largish, white, gradually becoming cream-coloured. *Fl.* March—April.—*W. & A. Prod.* i. 297. B. racemosa, *Vahl.*—*Roxb. Flor. Ind.* ii. 325.——Circars. Bengal.

ECONOMIC USES.—This is one of the largest of the Bauhinias, and a native of alpine districts. The large leaves are nearly a foot in diameter, and are collected in the northern districts of the Circars, and sold in the bazaars for various purposes, such as plates and packages. The seeds are eaten raw when ripe, tasting like cashew-nuts. The flowers hang down in elegant festoons, and the branches are very extensive, from 100 to 300 feet long, climbing over the highest trees. Ropes are made from the bark; the natives boil and then beat it, which makes it soft and pliable. It will, however, rot if kept too long in the water. The ropes have been occasionally used for suspension-bridges over the mountain-torrents in the Himalayan valleys.—*Royle, Fib. Plants. Roxb.*

(98) **Bauhinia variegata** (*Linn.*) Do.

Chovanna Mandaree, MAL. Sona, HIND.

DESCRIPTION.—Tree, 20-30 feet; unarmed; leaves roundish, upper side glabrous, under when young villous, cordate at the base; leaflets oval, obtuse, 5-nerved, united far beyond the middle; petals oblong, nearly sessile, the upper one somewhat larger and on a rather longer claw than the others; fertile stamens 5, all shortly united at the base; racemes axillary and terminal; calyx spathaceous, 5-toothed at the apex; legumes straight, 5-12 seeded. *Fl.* Feb.—March.—*W. & A. Prod.* i. 296.—*Rheede,* i. *t.* 32, 33.

The two varieties are:—

a—*B. purpurascens*—Rukhta-kanchun, Beedul, BENG.—four petals reddish and varied with purple; the fifth variegated with purple, brown, and yellow—B. purpurea, *Wall.*—B. variegata, *Roxb. Fl. Ind.* ii. 319.——Malabar. Coromandel.

b—*B. candida*—Kana-raj, BENG.—four petals whitish; the fifth variegated on the inner side, with yellow and green. *Roxb. Fl. Ind.* ii. 318.——Bengal. Malabar. Oude.

MEDICAL USES.—The bark is astringent, and used as a tonic in fevers. The natives reckon the dried buds astringent, and useful in diarrhœa and worms.—*Powell's Punj. Prod.*

ECONOMIC USES.—The buds are eaten as vegetables when prepared with animal food. The astringent bark is used for tanning and dyeing purposes.—*Roxb.*

(99) **Beesha Rheedii** (*Kunth*). N. O. GRAMINACEÆ.

Beesha, MAL. Bish-bansh, BENG.

DESCRIPTION.—Unarmed; leaves alternate, ovate-lanceolate, bifarious, smooth on both sides; sheaths villous, bearded at the mouth; pericarp a large, fleshy, conical-curved and pointed fruit, with a single oval seed in each. *Fl.* July—Sept.—*Roxb. Fl. Ind.* ii. 197.—Bambusa baccifera, *Kunth.*—*Roxb. Cor.* iii. *t.* 243.—*Rheede,* v. *t.* 60.——Peninsula. Chittagong mountains. Malabar.

ECONOMIC USES.—Indigenous to the mountains in Chittagong,

where it is called Pagu-tullu. It bears no thorns, and is, moreover, remarkable for its large pendulous pericarp. Pierard, quoted by Roxburgh, says that this bamboo is in common use in the country where it grows, for every purpose of building. "It grows in dry places chiefly on the sides of hills, where the upper stratum of the soil is sandy. The circumference near the base is 12-13 inches, the height from 50 to 70 feet, beautifully erect, and without the least flexure or inequality of surface, bare of branches, except near the extremity. Perishes after yielding its fruit. It yields more or less of the Tabasheer of a siliceous crystallisation; sometimes it is said the cavity is nearly filled with this, which the people called 'chuna, or lime.'" The natives make arrows and bows from the stems, and pens from the younger shoots.—(*Roxb.*) The native name is pronounced *Vay* or *Vaysha*. It is very common on the Travancore hills, growing also in the low country. The leaves are often put on verandahs and roofs of houses to keep away the white ants, and for this purpose the most effectual and simple remedy known where the plants are common.—*Pers. Obs.*

(100) **Berberis lycium** (*Royle*). N. O. Berberideæ.

Raisin Berberry, Eng.

Description.—Shrub, 6-8 feet; spines trifid or simple; leaves oval, cuneated or elliptical, mucronate, smooth, under surface, glaucous, entire or spinulosely toothed; racemes short, many-flowered, corymbose, shorter than the leaves; pedicels elongated, 1-flowered; berries purplish; flowers small, yellow. *Fl.* May—June.——Nepaul. Kumaon.

Medical Uses.—This plant is distinguished from other species by the very short racemes of its flowers. The fruit is oblong, purplish or pinkish, wrinkled and covered with bloom like that of the best raisins. Among many conflicting opinions of botanists it becomes difficult to identify the several described species of Berberis. It has now been definitively settled by Dr Royle that this is the *Lycium Indicum* of Dioscorides, over which much doubt has hung for a long period. The medicine it yields is of the highest antiquity, and has been known to the Hindoos from very early ages. The most celebrated part is the extract called Rusot, which is prepared by digesting in water pieces of the root, stem, and branches. This is frequently employed as a remedy in ophthalmia, especially useful after the acute symptoms have subsided. Some say that it is one of the best applications ever used in that complaint. The tincture, which is also prepared from the bark of the root, is recommended as preferable to the extract. It is very bitter, yielding a principle called *Berberine*. As a medicine it is reckoned exceedingly valuable, and is easily prepared where the plant is indigenous. According-ing to Dr O'Shaughnessy, the medicine is best administered as a febrifuge, promoting digestion and acting as a gentle but certain aperient. In ague and remittent fevers, it is peculiarly useful, and by some it is reckoned only second to quinine, externally either alone or with equal parts of alum and opium mixed up in water and applied round the eye. The *B. lycium* is found at a lower elevation (viz. at 3000 feet) than any of the other species, and therefore may be acclimated in the plains.

All the species of Berberry are supposed to possess similar properties in a greater or less degree. There has been much confusion in arranging them, but the following may perhaps be enumerated as distinct plants :—

B. aristata.—Spines very stiff and three parted; leaves oblong or oblong-lanceolate, nearly entire or toothed, sometimes deeply or coarsely veined; flowers in long loose slender racemes. ——Common in Northern India, distinguished by its slender pendulous or erect racemes of flowers, longer than the leaves, and not corymbose.

B. Sinensis.—Spines 3-5 or more; leaves lanceolate, very acute, much netted, entire, or regularly toothed; flowers numerous, in drooping racemes not much longer than the leaves.—— Found in Northern India and China.—Berries are said to be dark purple.

B. Wallichiana.—Spines long, slender, 3-parted; leaves oblong-lanceolate, deep green, sharp-pointed, finely serrated; flowers very numerous, in clusters shorter than the leaves.——Native of Nepaul at very high elevations.

B. Nepaulensis.—Leaves 3-5 pairs, ovate; leaflets spiny, toothed; racemes upright, slender, elongated; fruit bluish purple.—— Native of mountainous parts in Northern India, growing 10-12 feet high at 8000 feet elevations. Said to be one of the finest of the species. It differs very little from B. Leschenaultii.—(*W. & A. Prod.* i. 16.)—*Royle. Loudon. Indian Ann. of Med. Science.*

(101) **Berberis tinctoria** (*Lesch.*) Do.

Dyer's Berberry, Eng.

Description.—Shrub, 6-10 feet; leaves simple, oboval, entire, or with distant, small, spiny teeth, glaucous, with the principal veins and nerves prominent beneath, but not above; racemes stalked, longer than the leaves; pedicels slender; petals 6, distinctly biglandular; sepals 5, spines deeply divided into three sharp rigid segments; flowers yellow; berries 2-3 seeded. *Fl.* Jan.—April.—*W. & A. Prod.* i. 16.——Neilgherries. Pulney mountains.

Economic Uses.—This species of Berberry, found on the Neilgherries, serves, as the name implies, for dyeing a yellow colour. The roots contain 17 per cent of useful colouring matter. According to Leschenault, who had the wood analysed, it contained the yellow colouring principle in a greater state of purity than the common English Berberry. According to recent investigations, this species is identical with the *B. aristata*.—(*Dec.*) It ranges on the mountains of India from the Himalaya to the Neilgherries, and to Newera Ellia in Ceylon. It is a handsome and ornamental shrub, remarkable for its fine large compound racemes of flowers; the fruit is of an oblong shape and brownish-purple colour, with little or no bloom. It is very distinct from other species, and grows quickly. The root and wood are of a dark yellow colour, and form the yellow wood of Persian authors. In Nepaul the fruit of this species is dried like raisins.—*Wight. Loudon. Journ. Agri. Hort. Soc.*, iii. 272.

(102) **Bergera Kœnigii** (*Kœn.*) N. O. Aurantiaceæ.

Curry-leaf-tree, Eng. Kari-bepon, Karreya-pela, Mal. Carroova-pillay, Tam. Kari-vepa, Tel. Karay-paak, Hind. Bursunga, Beng.

Description.—Small tree with pinnate leaves; leaflets alternate, ovate, acuminate, pubescent, somewhat serrated; panicles corymbiform, terminal; calyx 5-cleft; petals 5, spreading; berry 1-celled, 1-seeded; flowers small, white. *Fl.* April—July.—*W. & A. Prod.* i. 94.—*Roxb. Fl. Ind.* ii. 376.—*Cor.* ii. *t.* 112.—*Rheede*, iv. *t.* 53.—Murraya Kœnigii, *Spreng.*——Circar mountains. Malabar. Cultivated in gardens.

Medical Uses.—The root is laxative, and both bark and roots are stimulant, and are used externally as remedies in eruptions, and in infusion to check vomitings in cholera. It is used for bites of poisonous animals, the tender leaves being boiled in milk, bruised, and applied as a poultice to the parts affected. The fresh leaves are eaten raw in dysentery. The pulp of the fruit gives out a kind of white juice, which blackens the skin like walnuts.—*Ainslie.*

Economic Uses.—The natives put the leaves of this tree in their curries, to which they impart an agreeable flavour. When rubbed together they emit a pleasant aromatic smell. They retain their flavour when dried, and are sold in that state in the bazaars. The wood is hard and durable, and is used for implements of husbandry. A yellow, clear, and transparent oil is procured from the seeds, known as the Limbolee oil.—*Roxb.*

(103) **Bignonia suberosa** (*Roxb.*) N. O. Bignoniaceæ.

Indian Cork-tree, Eng.

Description.—Tree, 40-50 feet; leaves opposite, supra-decompound; leaflets acuminated, sub-cordate, entire; panicles terminal, with horizontal ramifications, the first trichotomous, then dichotomous, with generally a simple flower in the fork; flowers numerous, large, pure white, fragrant. *Fl.* June—Aug. —*Roxb. Fl. Ind.* iii. 111.——Tanjore. Courtallum. Madras.

Economic Uses.—The wood is white, firm, and close-grained. The bark is very spongy, yielding an inferior kind of cork. The tree grows rapidly, is handsome and ornamental, and well adapted for avenues and plantations.—(*Roxb. Jury Reports, Mad. Exhib.*) The *B. xylocarpa* is a large but common tree in almost all the Madras forests, as well as in Mysore, Bengal, and Bombay. It grows rapidly. It is called Vadencarni in Tamil. The wood is brownish yellow, rather close-grained, takes a good polish, and is used for cabinet purposes.—*Bedd., Fl. Sylv., t.* 70.

(104) **Bixa Orellana** (*Linn.*) N. O. Bixineæ.

Arnotto-tree, Eng. Korungoomunga, Mal. Jafra, Tel. Kooragoomangjal, Tam. Gawpurgee, Hind.

Description.—Tree, 30 feet; leaves cordate-ovate, acuminated, entire or angular, smooth on both surfaces; sepals 5, orbicular; petals 5, capsule 2-valved, prickly on the outside; seeds 8-10 attached to each placenta, surrounded by a red pulp; corymbs terminal, panicled; peduncles 2-4 flowered; flowers pale peach-coloured, or white. *Fl.* May—Aug.—*W. & A. Prod.* i. 31.—*Roxb. Fl. Ind.* ii. 581.——Travancore. Bengal. Mysore.

Medical Uses.—The pulp surrounding the seeds is astringent and slightly purgative, and is esteemed a good antidote in dysentery and diseases of the kidneys.—(*Roxb.*) The seeds are cordial, astringent, and febrifugal, and the red pulp is a supposed antidote to the Mandioc poison.—*Lindley.*

Economic Uses.—A valuable dye known as the Arnotto dye is produced from the pulp surrounding the seeds of this plant. It is prepared by macerating the pods in boiling water, extracting the seeds, and leaving the pulp to subside; the fluid being subsequently thrown off. The residuum, with which oil is sometimes mixed, is placed in shallow vessels and dried in the shade. When properly made it should be of a bright yellow colour. It imparts a deep orange tinge to silk and cotton, and is used by the dyers for that purpose. The Spanish Americans mix it with their chocolate. In this country the dye prepared is of a pale rose-colour. The cloth is prepared by first being soaked in strong alum-water; the colour is then suspended in butter-milk, into which the cloth is dipped and charged with the colour. The dye is not very durable, and requires to be renewed from time to time; and that of the Indian variety is inferior to that of the West Indian plant. Mixed with lemon-juice and gum, it makes the paint with which the American Indians adorn their persons. The same people produce fire by the friction of two pieces of the wood. Cordage is made from the bark in the West Indies.

Several specimens of the Arnotto dye were sent to the Madras Exhibition. It is soluble in alkalies, by which means it is fixed to silk or wool. In Europe it is frequently used to impart a tinge to butter, cheese, oils, and varnish. The article is chiefly prepared and exported from South America to Europe. Dr Ure, in his 'Dictionary of Arts,' has given a long account of the process of manufacture in the West Indies, part of which is here subjoined. "The substance thus extracted is passed through sieves, in order to separate the remainder of the seeds, and the colour is allowed to subside. The precipitate is boiled in coppers till it be reduced to a consistent paste; it is then suffered to cool, and be dried in the shade. Instead of this long and painful labour, which occasions diseases by the putrefaction induced, and which affords a spoiled product, Leblond proposes simply to wash the seeds of Arnotto till they be entirely deprived of their colour, which lies wholly on their surface; to precipitate the colour by means of vinegar or lemon-juice, and to boil it up in the ordinary manner, or to drain it in bags, as is practised with Indigo.

"The experiments which Vauquelin made on the seeds of Arnotto imported by Leblond, confirmed the efficacy of the process which he proposed; and the dyers ascertained that the Arnotto obtained in this manner was worth at least four times more than that of commerce; that, moreover, it was more easily employed, that it required less solvents, that it gave less trouble in the copper, and furnished a purer colour."

The plant is cultivated in Mysore and the northern parts of India. There is a large importation, about 3,000,000 lb. per annum, for home consumption, chiefly from South America. In London the value is about a shilling a pound.—*Roxb. Simmonds. Ure.*

(105) **Blumea balsamifera** (*Dec.*) N. O. Compositæ.

Description.—Stem suffruticose at the base, branches woolly-villous; leaves oblong or elliptic-lanceolate, duplicato-dentate, villous above, silky-villous beneath, the veins wrinkled, lobes linear-lanceolate, appendiculate; corymb sub-panicled, divaricate; involucral scales linear, acute, hirsute; flowers small, yellow. *Fl.* Feb.—March.—*Dec. Prod.* v. p. 447.—Conyza balsamifera, *Linn.*—C. odorata, *Rumph.*—Baccharis salvia, *Lour.*——Concans. Assam.

Medical Uses.—This plant, which inhabits the Moluccas and Ceylon as well as India, possesses a strong camphoraceous odour and pungent taste. A warm infusion of the plant (*Horsf. As. Journ.* viii. 272) acts as a powerful sudorific, and is in very general use among the Javanese and Chinese as an expectorant. It has also been repeatedly employed in catarrhal affections. Loureiro (*Flor. Coch.*, p. 603) mentions its use in Cochin China as a stomachic, antispasmodic, and emmenagogue.—*Pharm. of India.*

(106) **Boehmeria nivea** (*Hook. & Arn.*) N. O. Urticaceæ.

China grass, Eng.

Description.—Perennial, herbaceous; leaves large, alternate, of equal shape, broadly ovate or elliptic-rounded, acuminate, cordate at the base, or more often shortly cuneate near the petiole, more seldom alternate or truncated at the base, crenato-serrate, snowy-tomentose beneath, scabrous above; stipules free; glomerules loosely cymose-panicled; fructiferous perigonium elliptic or oblong-compressed, hairy. *Hook. & Arn. Bot. Voy. Beech.* p. 214.—*Dec. Prod.* xvi. s. p. 206.—Urtica nivea, *Linn.*—*Hook. Journ. Bot.* 1851, *t.* 8.—*B. Candicans*, (var.)—Urtica candicans, *Burm.*—U. tenacissima, *Roxb.*—*Wight Icon. t.* 688.——Cultivated.

Economic Uses.—The fibres of the bark are second to none in strength and beauty. They are used throughout the East for making textile fabrics. The plant is very easy of cultivation, and of most luxuriant and rapid vegetation, throwing up numerous shoots, which may be cut and will be renewed three or four times in the course of the year. Its stem would become ligneous and covered with brown bark if suffered to attain its full growth, while it would throw out many branches; but the young shoots are those which are used, and on the stem being cut down numerous straight simple shoots spring up from one to eight feet, according to the season, quality of the soil, and other circumstances.—*Lankester, Veg. Subst.*

The Indo-Chinese prepare the Rheea fibre as follows: The plant is fit for cutting when the stems become of a brown colour for about six inches upwards from the root. In order to strip off the bark and fibre, the operator holds the stalk in both hands nearly in the middle, and, pressing the fore-finger and thumb of both hands firmly, gives it a peculiar twist, by which the inner pith is broken; and then, passing the fingers of his right and left hand alternately towards each end, the bark and fibre are completely separated from the stalk in two strands. The strands of bark and fibre are then made up into bundles of convenient size, tied at the smaller end with a shred of fibre, and put into clean water for a few hours, which probably deprives the plant of its tannin or colouring matter, the water becoming quite red in a short time. The cleaning process is as follows: The bundles are put on a hook fastened in a post by means of the tie at the smaller end, at a convenient height for the operator, who takes each strand of the larger end separately in his left hand, passes the thumb of his right hand quickly along the inner side, by which operation the outer bark is completely separated from the fibre, and the ribbon of fibre is then thoroughly cleaned by two or three scrapings with a small knife. This completes the operation, with some loss, however—say one-fifth; and if quickly dried in the sun, it might at once be made up for exportation; but the appearance of the fibre is much improved by exposure (immediately after cleaning) on the grass to a night's heavy dew in September or October, or a shower of rain during the rainy season. From its great value, if any other cheaper method of preparation could be discovered, it would undersell all other fibres.

(107) **Boerhavia diffusa** (*Linn.*) N. O. Nyctaginaceæ.

Spreading Hog-weed, Eng. Mookaretti, Tam. Ataka-Mamidi, Tel. Tameer-ama, Taludama, Mal. Tikri, Hind. Gada-poorna, Swhet-poorna, Beng.

Description.—Low creeping plant with many diffused stalks, about two feet long; flowers pale rose-coloured, much scattered on long branching peduncles from the axils and at the end of the branches; seeds brown, oblong, striated, very rough; leaves ovate, rather roundish, bright green above, whitish below; sometimes curled at the edges. *Fl.* All the year.—*Roxb. Fl. Ind.* i. 146.—*Rheede*, vii. *t.* 56.—*Wight Icon. t.* 874.——Coromandel. Travancore. India generally.

Medical Uses.—Of this troublesome weed, which is common in all parts of India, there are two varieties—one with white, the other with rose-coloured flowers. The root is given in powder as a laxative, and in infusion as a vermifuge. The taste is slightly bitter and nauseous. In Jamaica the leaves are given to hogs, whence the English name.—(*Ainslie.*) It has been found a good expectorant, and been prescribed in asthma with marked success, given in the form of powder, decoction, and infusion. Taken largely, it acts as an emetic.—*Pharm. of India.*

(108) **Borassus flabelliformis** (*Linn.*) N. O. PALMACEÆ.

Palmyra Palm, ENG. Pana, MAL. Pannei, TAM. Tadi, TEL. Talgachh, BENG. and HIND. Tala, SANS.

DESCRIPTION.—Trunk, 30-40 feet, everywhere marked with old cicatrices of fallen leaves; fronds composed of several folded linear-lanceolate divisions united as far as the centre; flowers male and female on different trees; drupe subglobular, flattened at the apex, filled with soft yellow pulp; nuts 3, perforated at the apex.—Lontarus domestica, *Rumph.*—*Roxb. Cor.* i. *t.* 71.—*Fl. Ind.* iii. 790.—*Rheede,* i. *t.* 9, 10.——Common in the Peninsula.

MEDICAL USES.—The saccharine juice obtained by excision from the spadix or young flowering-branch is, when freshly drawn before sunrise, of a pleasant sweet taste, and if taken in doses of a tumblerful every morning acts as a laxative. After fermentation has commenced, it becomes converted into arrack, one of the intoxicating drinks of the country. A useful stimulant application, called Toddy Poultice, is prepared by adding fresh drawn toddy to rice-flour till it has the consistence of a soft poultice; and this being subjected to a gentle fire, fermentation takes place. This, spread on a cloth and applied to the parts, acts as a valuable stimulant application to gangrenous ulcerations, carbuncles, and indolent ulcers. The light-brown cotton-like substance from the outside of the base of the fronds is employed as a styptic for arresting hæmorrhage from superficial wounds.—*Pharm. of India.*

ECONOMIC USES.—This palm is most extensively distributed over the continent of India, especially near the sea-coast. Sir W. Jones said that it was justly styled the king of its order among those which the Hindoos call grass-trees. Its uses are manifold, the best known among which is the fermented liquor called toddy, and this constitutes its chief value to the native inhabitants. The mode of procuring the vinous sap is as follows: The spadix or young flowering-branch is cut off near the top, and an earthen chatty or pitcher then tied on to the stump; into this the juice runs. Every morning it is emptied and replaced, the stump being again cut, the vessel placed as before, and so on, until the whole has been gradually exhausted and cut away. It is known in Tamil as the Pannungkhulloo. It is from this liquor that sugar is extracted, and by the same process as that described for procuring the toddy, except that the inside of the earthen vessel or receiver is powdered with chunam, which prevents any fermentation; the juice is then boiled down, and dried by exposure. Some few trees that from unknown causes do not flower in spring, put out their flowers in the cold season, and give a scanty supply; but in spring many are rendered artificially barren by breaking off the flowering-bud as it begins to form. These also flower in the winter season, and are called Basanti. They do not give above 2¼ maunds of juice, but this is of as much value as the 6 maunds which a tree gives in spring. Either the male or female will answer for the spring or winter crop, but the female alone will yield juice in the rainy season. When this is wanted, the fruit is allowed to form, and afterwards the point of the spadix or stem which supports the clusters is cut and allowed to bleed. This does not prevent a great many fruit on each cluster from coming to maturity. Palms managed thus are called Ghour. The fruit ripens in August, but many of the stems continue to bleed until October. A coleopterous insect often attacks the heart of this tree, and occasions it to languish. The remedy is to cut a hole about six inches long and two wide entirely through the middle of the stem, and four or five feet from the ground. The stem is found hollow, and a great deal of rubbish like sawdust falls out, but the palm soon recovers. The insect probably undergoes a change, and comes out by the hole. The coarse sugar is called Jaggery; and in Tamil, Karepootee. It is used for medicinal purposes, as well as for sweetening drinks. The pulpy matter surrounding the fresh seeds is cooling and pleasant to the taste, but after they ripen it becomes insipid. The stems when old become very hard, and are capable of taking a fine polish, being used for bows, &c. For house-building and various domestic purposes, the timber is the most generally used of the palm tribe. It is used chiefly for rafters, joists, and reapers, protected from moisture, and esteemed especially when of good age. For this purpose the trunk is split into 4 for rafters, into 8 for reapers, and these are dressed with an adze. From the structure of the fibres, it splits easily in the direction of its length, but supports a greater cross-strain than any other wood; iron nails, however, will rust rapidly in it. The fruits and fusiform roots are used as food by the poorer classes in the N. Circars; the leaves are used for writing on. They are also employed for thatching houses and making baskets, mats, umbrellas, and fans. Strong and durable fibres are produced from the petioles of the fronds.—*Roxb. Lind. Ainsl. Jury Rep. Mad. Exhib.*

(109) **Boswellia glabra** (*Roxb.*) N. O. Terebinthaceæ.

Koonthrekum, Mal. Googoola, Tel. Koondicrum, Tam.

Description.—Tall erect tree covered with greenish ash-coloured bark; leaves alternate, unequally pinnate, at the extremities of the branchlets; leaflets 6-10 pairs, opposite, broadly lanceolate, obtuse, serrated, glabrous; flowers numerous, on short pedicels, small, white; calyx small, 5-toothed; petals 5; capsule 3-angled, 3-celled, 3-valved; seeds solitary, surrounded by a membranaceous wing; racemes simple, terminal, fascicled, shorter than the leaves. *Fl.* March—April. —*W. & A. Prod.* i. 174.—*Roxb. Flor. Ind.* ii. 384.—*Cor.* iii. *t.* 207.——Coromandel mountains. Deccan.

Medical Uses.—This tree yields a fragrant resinous substance known as *Koondricum*. It is bitter and pungent, and is soluble in ether and spirits of wine. Resin exudes from wounds in the bark. It soon becomes hard and brittle, and is often used, when boiled with oil, as a substitute for pitch, and called Googul by the Telingies. Mixed with ghee, the native doctors prescribe it in gonorrhœa and other complaints. The resin is much burnt as an incense in the religious ceremonies of the Hindoos. Mixed with lime-juice or cocoa-nut oil, it is applied as a plaster in cutaneous affections, as well as in cases of ulcers and bad wounds.—(*Ainslie. Roxb.*) The resin both of this and the following species is employed as an incense in India, and both might be much more extensively collected than they are at present, as there is reason to believe that Central India alone furnishes the greatest portion of the Indian olibanum of commerce, as it is chiefly exported from Bombay.—(*Royle.*) There are extensive tracts of Googalam jungles in Goomsur and Cuttack provinces. The Khoonds and Woodias living in or near these jungles wound the trees in several places. The resin flows out, and is collected when sufficiently solid. The dammer collected from the decayed parts of the tree is of a dark colour. The Khoonds and Uryas make the leaves into the plates from off which they eat their food, and also roll up tobacco in them to smoke like a cheroot. In times of famine the above tribes live on a soup made from the fruit of the tree.—*Rep. Mad. Exhib.*

(110) **Boswellia thurifera** (*Roxb.*) Do.

Salai, Beng. Luban, Hind.

Description. — Large tree; leaves unequally pinnated; leaflets oblong, obtuse, serrated, pubescent; racemes axillary, single, shorter than the leaves; calyx 5-toothed; petals 5; flowers small, white; seeds solitary, with a winged membrane; capsule 3-angled. *Fl.* March—April.—*W. & A. Prod.* i. 174. —*Roxb. Fl. Ind.* ii. 383.—— Mountains of Coromandel. Belgaum.

Economic Uses.—This is a large tree, affording good timber. Colebrooke, in the Asiatic Researches, has identified the olibanum or frankincense of the ancients with the balsamic gum-resin which it produces. It is called Koondooroo, or Ghundurus, or Cundun, in

Bengal. For a long time this substance was supposed to have been produced by various species of junipers, and this opinion is held to this day by some; but it is known that the coniferæ, to which family the junipers belong, yield pure resin only, but not gum-resin. Of the present olibanum there are two varieties, one of which is far inferior to the other. The best is found in pieces as large as a walnut, of a high yellowish colour, inclining to red or brown, covered on the outside with a white powder, the whole becoming a whitish powder when pounded. It burns with a clear and steady light, not easily extinguished, and diffuses a pleasant fragrance. In taste it is slightly bitter, and not perfectly soluble in water or alcohol. It is seldom used in medicine, but has astringent and stimulant properties. The incense burnt in Roman Catholic churches is the produce of this tree.—*Colebr. in As. Res.*, ix. 377. *Roxb. Ainslie.*

Dr Royle says, "The Salai or Saleh of the Hindoos is common in Central India and Bundlecund, where I have seen it, especially about the Bisrumgunge Ghaut. It is probably also produced by the *B. glabra*, which has the same native name, and, though extending to a more northern latitude, is distributed over many of the same localities. It is common on the hills above Mohun Chowkee, where I have collected some very clear, pure, and fragrant resin, which burns rapidly away with a bright light, diffusing a pleasant odour."—(*Royle.*) The timber both of this and the preceding species is hard, heavy, and durable.—*Roxb.*

(111) **Bragantia Wallichii** (*R. Br.*) N. O. Aristolochiaceæ.

Alpam, Mal.

Description.—Shrub; leaves alternate, oblong, lanceolate; 3-nerved at the base; tube of the perianth smooth, lobes of the limb acutish; anther 9, 3-adelphous, united by threes; male pistil very short, stigmas, 9 radiating, united at the base, three of them bifid; fruit terete.—*W. & A. in Ed. Phil. Jour.* 1832.—*Wight Icon.* ii. *t.* 520.—*Rheede*, vi. t. 28——S. Concans. Wynaad. Travancore.

Medical Uses.—This is by no means a common plant, and would appear to be peculiar to the western coast. The whole plant, mixed with oil and reduced to an ointment, is said to be very efficacious in the treatment of psora or inveterate ulcers. Like other plants belonging to the same natural order, it is supposed to have virtues in the cure of snake-bites. The juice of the leaves, mixed with the Vussumboo root, the root itself rubbed up with lime-juice, and made into a poultice and externally applied, are the chief modes of administering it among the natives.

Bartolomeo, in his 'Voyage to the East Indies,' says, "The only

Malabar plant which I can with certainty call an antidote to poison is a shrub about three or four feet in height, named Alpam. The root is pounded, and administered in warm water to those who have been poisoned. A Malabar proverb says, 'Alpam agatta, Veszam poratta' "—As soon as the Alpam root enters the body, poison leaves it.—*Rheede. Bartolomeo, Voy. to East Indies. Wight & Arn. in Ed. Phil. Jour.* 1832.

(112) **Bridelia spinosa** (*Willd.*) N. O. Euphorbiaceæ.

Moolloo-vengay, Tam. Mooloo-vangay, Mal. Coraman, Tel. Sun, Duk.

Description.—Tree, 30-40 feet; bark scabrous; branches numerous, spreading; thorns large, few, chiefly on the large branches; leaves oblong, alternate, pointed, entire, with conspicuous parallel veins running from centre to circumference; spikes axillary or terminal; flowers aggregate, small, greenish yellow, males and females together. *Fl.* July—Oct.—*Roxb. Fl. Ind.* iii. 735.—Cluytia spinosa, *Roxb. Cor.* ii. *t.* 172.—*Wight Icon. t.* 1905.——Circars. Assam. Travancore.

Economic Uses.—The bark is a strong astringent, and the wood dark-coloured, hard, and durable. Cattle are fond of the leaves, which are said to free them from intestinal worms.—*Roxb.*

(113) **Bryonia callosa** (*Rottl.*) N. O. Cucurbitaceæ.

Toomutti, Tam. Boddama, Tel.

Description.—Climbing shrub, spreading; stem filiform, furrowed, rough with bristly hairs; leaves on long petioles, cordate, 3-5 lobed, roundish, toothed, scabrous, and hispid on the veins below; berries globose, largish, smooth; flowers yellow.—*Rottler ap. Ainslie,* ii. 428.——Coromandel.

Medical Uses.—The seeds, which are bitter-tasted, are mixed with oil, and employed as a vermifuge. They are also occasionally used by farriers in diseases of horses. They yield a fixed oil by boiling, which is used for lamps by the poorer classes.—*Ainslie.*

(114) **Bryonia epigæa** (*Rottl.*) Do.

Kolung Kovay, Tam. Akasagarooda, Tam. Rakus, Hind.

Description.—Climbing shrub; stem glabrous, often very flexuose at the joints; tendrils simple; leaves somewhat fleshy on longish petioles, cordate, usually 3-lobed, densely covered on both sides with short bristly hairs; lobes rounded, the lateral ones the broadest, and slightly 2-lobed, all remotely and slightly toothed; male flowers shortly racemose at the apex of a long thickish peduncle; calyx campanulate; females short peduncled, solitary, in the same or different axils from the males; berry ovate, rostrate, glabrous, few-seeded; seeds white, compressed.—*W. & A. Prod.* i. 346.—B. glabra, *Roxb. Fl. Ind.* iii. 725.——Coromandel.

MEDICAL USES.—The root of this species was once supposed to be the famous Calumba root, which it resembles in its medicinal qualities. It has a bitter sub-acid taste, and is marked on the outside with whitish circular rings. It is used as an external application, in conjunction with cummin-seeds, onions, and castor-oil, as a kind of liniment for chronic rheumatism. It has also other medicinal uses, and is esteemed of special value in dysenteric and long-standing venereal complaints. The root lives in the air without water, and will grow and send forth shoots in that position.—*Ainslie.*

The people of the Deccan regard it as a powerful internal and local remedy in snake-bites. It is used for similar purposes in Mysore.—*Pharm of India.*

(115) **Bryonia rostrata** (*Rottl.*) Do.

Appakovay, TAM.

DESCRIPTION.—Climbing; stem slender, hairy or pubescent; tendrils simple; leaves on longish petioles, roundish cordate, sinuate, toothed, pubescent; male flowers usually two together, pedicelled, on a slender peduncle, longer than the petiole; calyx campanulate; female solitary, very shortly peduncled, in the same axils with the male, being ovate, rostrate, longitudinally striated, hairy, 2-6 seeded; seeds black, compressed, with a thin margin.—*W. & A. Prod.* i. 346.—B. pilosa, *Roxb. Fl. Ind.* iii. 726.——Tranquebar.

MEDICAL USES.—The root, which is small and of a light-grey colour, is sweet and mucilaginous to the taste. It is administered internally in cases of piles, and, powdered, is sometimes given as a demulcent in humoral asthma. The leaves are eaten as greens in Southern India.—*Ainslie.*

(116) **Buchanania latifolia** (*Roxb.*) N. O. TEREBINTHACEÆ.

Moreda, Mowda, or Kat Mango Marum, TAM. Piyala, BENG. Chara puppoe, TEL. Peeyar Cheroonjie, HIND. Cala marum, MAL.

DESCRIPTION.—Tree, 30 feet; leaves alternate, entire, broadly oval or obovate, obtuse; calyx small, obtusely 5-cleft; petals 5, sessile recurved; branches of the panicles hirsute, terminal, and axillary, with the flowers crowded, assuming the appearance of a corymb at the tops of the branches; fruit a drupe with slightly fleshy-red sarcocarp; nut very hard, 2-valved, 1-celled; flowers small, greenish white. *Fl.* Feb.—March.—*W. & A. Prod.* i. 169.—*Roxb. Fl. Ind.* ii. 385.——Mountains of Coromandel and Malabar. Belgaum forests. Mysore.

Economic Uses.—The wood is used for various purposes. The kernels are a general substitute for almonds among the natives. They are much esteemed in confectionery, or roasted and eaten with milk. The bark is used in tanning. An oil is extracted from the seeds, of a pale straw colour, known as the Cheroonjie oil, and also a black varnish, similar to that obtained from the nuts of the *Semecarpus anacardium* and other trees of the same order. Another species, the *B. lancifolia* (*Roxb.*), grows in Chittagong, the tender unripe fruit of which is eaten by the natives in their curries.—(*Jury Rep. Roxb. Lindley.*) The *B. angustifolia* (Colah Mavuh in Tamil) is common in the Trichore forests. The bark is much used on the western coast for its adhesive properties, for which purpose it is frequently mixed with chunam. An oil exudes from the cut bark, used in lamps, and would probably serve as an excellent varnish.—*Pers. Obs.*

(117) **Butea frondosa** (*Roxb.*) N. O. Leguminosæ.

Bastard Teak, Eng. Porasum, Tam. Moduga, Tel. Palasie, Mal. Palas, Hind. Palas, Dhak, Beng.

Description.—Middle-sized tree; leaves pinnately trifoliolate; leaflets large, roundish ovate, rather velvety beneath; corolla papilionaceous; racemes simple, many-flowered, lax; calyx segments short, slightly acute, several times shorter than the tube; corolla densely pubescent; vexillum ovate, acute, recurved; keel and alæ incurved; legume flat, thin, with a large solitary seed at the apex; flowers in threes, bright scarlet. *Fl.* Dec.—Feb.—*W. & A. Prod.* i. 261.—*Roxb. Cor.* i. *t.* 21.—*Fl. Ind.* iii. 244.—Erythrina monosperma, *Lam.*——Malabar. Circars.

Medical Uses.—The seeds are reckoned an excellent vermifuge, especially with the Mohammedan doctors. English practitioners have also testified to their value in this respect. The seeds are first soaked in water, the testa removed, and the kernel then dried and pulverised. In large doses, however, this medicine is apt to produce vomiting; and, further, is apt to irritate the kidneys. The pounded seeds made into a paste have been found useful in ringworm. The inspissated juice obtained from the stem by incision is known as the Bengal Kino, and is an efficient substitute for the real kino. A similar exudation is yielded by the *B. superba* and *B. parviflora*. Both are employed medicinally by the natives, being possessed of some efficiency as astringents.—(*Pharm. of India.*) The flowers are used as a fomentation in dysuria. The seeds are considered warm purgatives, and are used in fevers, and also as anthelmintics. The juice is used in diarrhœa, pyrosis, and after parturition.—(*Powell's Punj. Prod.*) The Butea kino is one of the most valuable articles of the class to which it belongs. It appears to be one of the most useful kinds of gum, and might be supplied to any extent from the province of Pegu.—(*M'Clelland.*) The exudation of the Butea or Pulos kino, when exported to England a few years ago, was recognised as being "gummi rubrum astringens" of the old druggists. M. Guibert of Paris, to whom some of it had been sent, states his opinion in his work on drugs that it is the original kino, which had entirely disappeared from commerce, and was once so much valued as to be sold for nearly a guinea a-pound. Amherst province can furnish almost any quantity of the article, the tree which produces it being one of the most common denizens of its forests.—(*Mason.*) The true Pulos goond or Bengal kino is of brittle texture and ruby-red colour, freely soluble in the mouth, inodorous, of excessively astringent taste, soluble in water, the solution being of a deep-red colour, partially soluble in alcohol, giving a pale tincture. The juice is at first very fluid and red, then becomes paler and hardens. Its extraction takes place during the hot season. In the 'Dublin Pharmacopœia' the exudation is described as a variety of kino. The true kino, however, proceeds from a different source; but in chemical effects and medical properties both are identical. The Pulos kino is extremely rich in tannic and gallic acids, and contains, moreover, arabine and ulnine. From this composition, as might be expected, it exercises the most powerful astringent effects. In two or three grain doses it is an excellent remedy in many forms of chronic diarrhœa; and as an external astringent application it is quite unrivalled.—*O'Shaughnessy.*

Economic Uses.—This tree, when in flower, has a very striking appearance, from the gaudy appearance of its bright scarlet corollas. Peacock in his 'Greece in India' has remarked that the name of Pelassi has been derived from this plant. In modern times the name of Plassy, so celebrated in Indian history, is nothing more than Palas or Palasie, the Hindoostanee name for this beautiful tree. The natives are very fond of offering the flowers in their temples; and the women, by intertwining the rich scarlet blossoms in their hair, assume a very attractive and pleasing appearance. The natives in the North-Western Provinces employ the kino for precipitating their indigo, and in tanning; but in England it is objected to on account of the discoloration it imparts to leather. The lac insects are frequently found upon the smaller branches and petioles of the tree; but whether the natural juices of its bark contribute to improve the red colouring matter of the lac has not been determined. The expressed juice of the fresh flowers, and infusion of the dried flowers, yield a water-colour brighter than gamboge; they also yield a fine durable yellow lake in a large proportion. The wood of the tree is one of those burnt for gunpowder charcoal. Strong ropes are made from the fibre of the roots, used immediately after the bark has been stripped off.—*G. Don. Roxb. Ainslie.*

(118) **Butea superba** (*Roxb.*) Do.

Tiga-moduga, Tel.

Description.—Twining shrub with pinnated 3 foliolate leaves; leaflets roundish, velvety beneath; racemes simple, lax; pedicels about twice the length of the calyx; corolla papilionaceous; legumes flat, compressed, thin, clothed with rusty tomentum, with one solitary seed at the apex; calyx segments shortish, acuminate; vexillum ovate, acute; flowers large, bright scarlet. *Fl.* March.—*W. & A. Prod.* i. 261.—*Roxb. Cor.* i. *t.* 22.—*Fl. Ind.* iii. 247.——Travancore forests. Circar mountains.

Economic Uses.—The red juice which flows from fissures in the bark of this creeper is one of the kinds of East Indian kino, and is similar in most respects to that procured from the *B. frondosa.* The flowers are in like manner used for dyeing yellow, and for preparing a yellow pigment. Strong ropes are made from the roots of both species, used as cordage, and for agricultural purposes. The colour of the kino is ruby red, brittle and transparent, consisting of small round tears. It becomes opaque and dark-coloured after keeping. Exposed to heat, it ignites. It imparts a fine red colour to water, the interior only dissolving. In hot water the entire will dissolve. The exudation should be collected when fresh and only just hardening, as being then far more applicable to useful purposes than when after exposure to the air. It is soluble in alcohol, but far less than in water; also in ether slightly. It contains a large proportion of tannin, which might render it useful in the arts and in tanning leather, especially for thick hides.—*Solly in As. Researches. Ainslie. Royle.*

C

(119) **Cæsalpinia coriaria** (*Willd.*) N. O. LEGUMINOSÆ.

American Sumach, Divi-divi or Dibi-dibi, ENG.

DESCRIPTION.—Tree, 25-30 feet, unarmed; leaves bipinnate; pinnæ 6-7 pairs; leaflets 15-20 pairs, linear, obtuse; racemes panicled; pedicels shorter than the flowers; calyx cup-shaped at the base, 5-lobed; petals 5, unequal, upper one shorter than the rest; legume oblong, incurved laterally; flowers small, yellow. *Fl.* Dec.—Jan.——Cultivated in the Peninsula.

MEDICAL USES.—The powder of the dried pods has been recommended as an antiperiodic in cases of intermittent fever, the dose ranging from 40 to 60 grains. A decoction of the legume forms a good injection in bleeding piles.—(*Pharm. of India.*) The astringent pods are an excellent remedy for prolapsus ani in children. They are better if gathered before becoming ripe. The pods are admitted to English markets free of all duty. (For properties of divi-divi, see *Pharm. Journ.* v. 443; and *Journ. Agri. Hort. Soc. Beng.* vol. iv. *passim.*)

ECONOMIC USES.—This tree was introduced into India by Dr Wallich twenty-five years ago. It is properly a native of the sea-shore of St Domingo and of Curaçoa, but has now become so extensively distributed in this country, and promises to be so useful a tree, that it is well deserving of a place here. Its chief virtue resides in the pods, which are greatly employed for tanning purposes. These pods are said to contain about 50 per cent of tannin. The average yearly produce of pods from a single full-grown tree in the West Indies is 100 lb., which, deducting 25 lb. for seeds, leaves 75 lb. of tanning material. The pods form an article of export into Great Britain from the West Indies. By experiments it was ascertained that one part of divi-divi (which is the commercial name for the pod) is equal to four parts of bark for tanning purposes, and the process occupies about one-third of the time. The price of the pods ranges from £8 to £13 per ton. The pods are considered superior to any other material used in the tanneries of this country. When cured with this substance, leather resembles that tanned with oak-bark. The tree is easily propagated from seeds; indeed, they grow so fast and luxuriantly that large plantations might soon be raised with little outlay in the moist climate of the western coast.—(*Simmonds. Jury Rep. Mad. Exhib. Pers. obs.*) An oil is expressed from the seeds of the *C. digyna* which the natives use in lamps.

(120) Cæsalpinia sappan (*Linn.*) Do.

Sappan and Brasiletto, Eng. Patungha, Tam. Bukkum, Hind. and Beng. Tsiapangum, Mal. Bukkapu, Tel. Puttung, Duk.

Description.—Tree, 40 feet, armed; pinnæ 10-12 pair; leaflets 10-12 pair, unequal-sided, obliquely oval-oblong, emarginate, pale on the under side; terminal panicles; legumes compressed, glabrous, elliptic-obovate, obliquely truncated, cuspidate at the apex, 3-4 seeded; flowers yellow. *Fl.* March—May.—*W. & A. Prod.* i. 281.—*Roxb. Cor.* i. *t.* 16.—*Fl. Ind.* ii. 357.—*Rheede,* vi. *t.* 2.——Coromandel. Bengal.

Medical Uses.—The wood contains much tannic and gallic acids, and is a good substitute for logwood.—*Pharm. of India.*

Economic Uses.—The wood, which is the red wood of commerce, is extensively used in dyeing, and is exported for that purpose. It is an ingredient in the red dye on the Coromandel coast called the Chay-dye. Where a cheap red is required for cotton cloth, the wood is employed by the native dyers, but they cannot make it stand. The process of the Telinga dyers is as follows: The cotton cloth is well washed, to remove any remains of the quicklime, &c., used in bleaching; an infusion of half a pound of the powdered kadukai (*Terminalia chebula*) in a pint and a half of cold water, strained, is employed to prepare the cloth, which is done by wetting it twice in the same infusion, drying it between and after. The following day it is twice wetted in a strong solution of alum, and as often dried in the sun. Next day a decoction of the Sappan-wood is prepared as follows: Take 1 pound of Sappan-wood in powder, water 12 quarts; boil it till a third is consumed; divide the remaining 8 quarts into 3 parts, one of 4 and the other two of 2 quarts each; into the 4 quarts put the cloth, wet it well, wring it gently, and half-dry it; it is again wetted in one of the small portions, and, when half-dry, wetted for the third and last time in the other remaining portion of the decoction; dry in the shade, which finishes the process. In Paulghaut the tree is cultivated for the sake of the dye, which is used for colouring the mats made at that place. Much Sappan-wood is annually exported from Ceylon. The tree grows freely without any care, and is of the finest quality in Malabar and Mergui. It is largely shipped for the London market from Calcutta.—(*Roxb. Ainsl. Don. Simmonds.*) The export of Sappan-wood from Bombay in 1870-71 was 1085 cwt., valued at 4194 rupees. A custom prevails in Malabar among the Moplahs to plant, on the birth of a female child, 40 or 50 seeds of Sappan, and the trees which reach maturity in 10 or 12 years are her dowry when she is married.—*Rep. Mad. Exhib.*

(121) **Cæsalpinia sepiaria** (*Roxb.*) Do.

Mysore thorn, Eng. **Hyder ka jhar**, Hind. **Chillur**, Duk.

Description.—Scandent; branches and petioles armed with short, strong, sharp, recurved prickles; pinnæ of the leaves 6-10 pair; leaflets 8-12 pair, linear-oblong, obtuse; petioles pubescent; stipules broad, semi-sagittate; racemes axillary, solitary; calyx coloured, the segments soon reflexed; legumes linear-oblong, glabrous, with a long cuspidate point, 4-8 seeded. —*Roxb. Fl. Ind.* ii. 360.—*W. & A. Prod.* 282.—*Dec. Prod.* ii. 484.—*Wight Icon. t.* 37.

Economic Uses.—This species is indigenous to Mysore, but is now generally diffused throughout the country, and known as the Mysore thorn. Hyder Ali had it planted as a means of defence around his strongholds. It is employed as a fence in the Baghyan lands of the Dekkan, and possesses the twofold advantage of beauty and durability.

Immediately the shoot appears above ground, it separates into numerous lateral branches, which are strongly armed with recurved prickles. It is one of the best plants for a general enclosure. It is easily raised from seed, and grows vigorously. The hedge requires little care beyond occasionally trimming the side branches, and perhaps the introduction of a few dead stakes at intervals to steady and strengthen it.

(122) **Cajanus Indicus** (*Spreng.*) N. O. Leguminosæ.

Pigeon-pea, Eng. **Thovaray**, Tam. **Candaloo**, Tel. **Toor**, Hind. **Dal Urur**, Beng.

Description.—Shrub, 3-6 feet, softly pubescent; leaves pinnately trifoliolate; leaves oval, lanceolate, mucronate; calyx campanulate, somewhat bilabiate; lips nearly equal in length, upper one shortly bifid, lower one 3-partite; segments slightly curved upwards; apices recurved; corolla papilionaceous; petals equal in length; vexillum broad, bi-callous at the base; keel falcate; racemes axillary; pedicels slender, in pairs; legumes hirsutely pubescent; flowers yellow. *Fl.* Oct.—Nov. —*W. & A. Prod.* i. 256.——Peninsula. Bengal. Assam.

Of this shrub there are two varieties which differ by the colour of the vexillum alone.

a—Segapoo Thovaray, *Tam.*—Yerray candaloo, *Tel.*—Lal Toor, *Hind.*—Vexillum of a uniform yellow colour on both sides.—C. flavus, *Dec.*—Cytisus cajan, *Linn.*—*Roxb. Fl. Ind.* iii. 325.

b—Maenthoveray, *Tam.*—Conda Candaloo, *Tel.*—Paoud-ke-Toor, *Hind.*—Vexillum purplish, and veined on the outside, yellow on the inside.—C. bicolor, *Dec.*—Cytisus pseudo cajan, *Jacq.*—*Rheede, Mal.* vi. *t.* 13.

ECONOMIC USES.—The seeds are much esteemed by the natives, who hold them third in rank among their leguminous seeds, though they are apt to produce costiveness. Cattle are very fond of the tender parts of the plant, both green and dry. The dried stem makes excellent fuel, and is well adapted for producing fire by friction.—(*Roxb.*) That which is known as the small "Toor" ripens half as soon again as the larger one. Some varieties are remarkable for the gaudy colours of their orange and red-spotted flowers. The pulse is chiefly eaten mixed with rice, a mess known as kedjari. The best Toor is sown in alternate drills with *Sorghum vulgare*, which ripens first, and is cut while the Cajanus is yet small. It then remains two or three months longer, and is reaped at the end of the harvest. The stalks are strong and woody, and well adapted for making charcoal required in gunpowder manufacture.—*W. Elliott.*

(123) **Calamus fasciculatus** (*Roxb.*) N. O. PALMACEÆ.

Rattan-cane, ENG. Perambu, MAL. Paramboo, TAM. Buro-bet, BENG.

DESCRIPTION.—Stem scandent, elongated; fronds without tendrils; pinnæ aggregated into many distant fascicles, ensiform; prickles of the fronds straight, scattered, and confluent; spadix decompound, abortive ones whip-shaped; berries ovate. *Fl.* June—Aug.—*Roxb. Fl. Ind.* iii. 779.—*Mart. Palm.* 209.——Cuttack. Bengal.

ECONOMIC USES.—These plants, though arranged among the Palm tribe, hold a middle station between the Palms and Grasses, having the habit of the former, whereas their inflorescence resembles that of the latter. Canes and rattans, which are the stems of different species of Calamus, form considerable articles of commerce. They are exported from the valleys of the Himalaya into the plains, though the species yielding them are not well known. In some years from four to five millions have been exported from this country. The stems of this species, when divested of their sheaths, are about as thick as the forefinger, and are used as walking-sticks.—*Roxb. Royle.*

(124) **Calamus Rotang** (*Linn.*) Do.

Rattan-cane, ENG. Bet or Beta, BENG. and HIND. Bettam, TEL.

DESCRIPTION.—Stem scandent; fronds without tendrils, pinnæ somewhat equidistant, linear-lanceolate, acuminate; prickles of the sheaths frequent, compressed, straight, of the rachis straight and recurved, of the spathes and tendrils bent; spadix compound; male calyx 3-cleft, campanulate, a half shorter than the broad triangular segments of the corolla; berries ovate, sub-globose, size of a small cherry. *Fl.* June—Aug.—*Roxb. Fl. Ind.* iii. 777.—*Mart. Palm.* 208, *t.* 116, p. 8. ——Moist jungles in Bengal and the Peninsula.

ECONOMIC USES.—This yields the common rattan. It is the *Tsjeru tsjurel* of Rheede (*Mal.* xii. *t.* 64) and *C. Roxburghii* of Griffith, and is common in the S. Concans, as well as in Coromandel and Bengal. Though the several species yielding the rattans of commerce have not been distinctly identified, yet it is believed that this one is a stouter kind than the others. Some rattans grow to an immense length, climbing over the highest trees in the forest, even as long as 500 or 600 feet. Such are the dimensions given of the *C. extensus*, a native of Silhet. When fresh gathered, the stems are covered with green sheaths, but are divested of them while yet in a green state, and then dried. They are extensively used as props for plants, as well as for cables, ropes, wicker-work, baskets, chairs, and couches; and being very strong, and at the same time flexible, are admirably adapted for those purposes. Cordage and cables for vessels are sometimes made from the stems twisted together. In fact, their strength is exceedingly great when several are twisted in this way, and will answer all the purposes of the strongest cables. In China and Japan they are in great request. Marco Polo refers to their uses in those countries. Talking of a certain place in China, he says, "They do not employ hempen cordage, excepting for the masts and sails (standing and running rigging). They have canes of the length of fifteen paces, such as have been already described, which they split in their whole length into very thin pieces, and these, by twisting them together, they form into ropes three hundred paces long. So skilfully are they manufactured, that they are equal in strength to cordage made of hemp. With these ropes the vessels are tracked along the rivers, by means of ten or twelve horses to each, as well upwards against the current as in the opposite direction." Here he evidently refers to the rattan-canes, and not to bamboos, as supposed by some. The seeds are surrounded by a fleshy kind of substance, which is eaten as well as the young tender shoots, which are reckoned very delicate food. Of the species best known in India and the neighbouring countries the following may be enumerated: *C. rudentum* (Lour.), native of the Moluccas; *C. erectus* (Roxb.), indigenous to Silhet, where the poorer classes use the seeds as a substitute for betel-nut; *C. verus* (Lour.), Moluccas and Cochin China; *C. scipionum* (Lour.), which yields the so-called Malacca cane; *C. Royleanus*, a species found in Dheyra Dhoon; *C. draco* (Willd.), Sumatra and the Moluccas; *C. gracilis* and *tenuis*, both of Chittagong,—with several others. What are known as the Penang lawyers are yielded by a small Palm, the *Licuala acutifida.* —*Royle. Roxb.*

(125) **Callicarpa lanata** (*Linn.*) N. O. Verbenaceæ.

Caat comul, Tam. Bastra, Hind. Massandaree, Beng. Tonditeregam, Mal.

Description.—Shrub, or small tree; branches, peduncles, and leaves covered with a kind of woolly nap; leaves ovate; peduncles axillary, solitary; calyx 4-cleft; corolla monopetalous, funnel-shaped, 4-cleft; berry 1-celled, 4-seeded, convex on one side, concave on the other; margin slightly elevated; flowers purple. *Fl.* Feb.—March.—*Roxb. Fl. Ind.* i. 391.—C. cana, *Linn.*—C. tomentosa, *Lam.*—*Rheede,* iv. *t.* 60.—— Travancore. Neilgherries. Coromandel.

Economic Uses.—The bark, which is sub-aromatic and slightly bitter to the taste, is chewed by the Cingalese instead of betel-leaves. In Upper Hindoostan the root is employed in cutaneous complaints. It is one of the trees used for making charcoal. A fibre is procured from the inner bark called the Aroosha fibre in Chittagong, but not much value is attached to it.—*Ainslie. Royle. Jour. Agri. Hort. Soc.* vi. 186.

(126) **Calonyction speciosum** (*Choisy*). N. O. Convolvulaceæ.

Description.—Stem climbing to a great extent; leaves large, quite smooth, cordate, pointed; peduncles very long, 1-5 flowered; flowers very large, pure white, opening at sunset. *Fl.* June—Sept.—*Dec. Prod.* ix. 345.—*Choisy Conv.* p. 59.—Ipomæa bona nox, *Linn.*—I. grandiflora, *Roxb.*—— Common everywhere.

Medical Uses.—This species contains in its roots resin, fatty matter, volatile oil, albumen, starch, fibre, malic acid, and various salts. The bark of the root is used by the natives as a purgative.—*Long, Indig. Plants of Bengal.*

(127) **Calophyllum elatum** (*Bedd.*) N. O. GUTTIFERÆ.

Poonspar, ENG. Poon, Poongoo, MAL.

DESCRIPTION.—Large tree; young shoots, panicles, and outer sepals ferruginous; leaves elliptic, acuminate, attenuated at the base, very shining; panicles terminal and from the upper axils, large, many-flowered; sepals 4, two outer ones subrotund, small, two inner ones petaloid; petals 4; fruit ovoid, pointed, about the size of a thrush's egg. *Fl.* Jan.—Feb.—*Beddome Fl. Sylv. t.* 2.——Forests of the Western Ghauts. Coorg. Mysore. Travancore.

ECONOMIC USES.—This tree is never found in dry deciduous forests, but in the damp jungles of the western coast. It yields the Poonspar of commerce. The wood is scarcely known except as a spar; and some years ago a good specimen for that purpose would fetch a thousand rupees. It is reddish and coarse-grained.—*Beddome.*

(128) **Calophyllum inophyllum** (*Linn.*) Do.

Alexandrian Laurel, ENG. Ponna, MAL. Pinnay, TAM. Ponna, TEL. Sultan-champa, HIND. Oondee, DUK.

DESCRIPTION.—Tree, 50 feet; branches terete; leaves elliptical or oboval, obtuse or retuse, furnished with numerous parallel slender nerves; racemes longer than the leaves from the upper axils, or disposed in a terminal panicle; sepals 4; drupe spherical, 1-celled, 1-seeded; flowers white, very fragrant. *Fl.* June—Dec.—*W. & A. Prod.* i. 103. C. bintagor, *Roxb. Fl. Ind.* ii. 606.—*Rheede,* iv. *t.* 138.—*Wight Icon. t.* 77. ——Malabar. Peninsula.

MEDICAL USES.—A fixed oil is yielded by the kernels, held by the natives in high esteem as an external application in rheumatism. From the bark exudes a resinous substance, erroneously thought to be the *Tacamahaca* of the old pharmacologists. It resembles myrrh, and is a useful application to indolent ulcers.—(*Pharm. of India.*) The gum which flows from the wounded branches, being mixed with strips of the bark and leaves, is steeped in water, and the oil which rises to the surface is used as an application to sore eyes. Horsfield says that in Java the tree is supposed to possess diuretic properties.

ECONOMIC USES.—This tree is not less esteemed for its ornamental appearance than for the delicious fragrance of its flowers. A dark-green oil of a disagreeable odour is procured from the fresh seeds when subjected to pressure. It is more used as medicine than for domestic purposes; nor is it now exported from this country, except in small quantity to Ceylon. It is known as the Pinnay oil. The seeds, says Simmonds, or berries, contain nearly 60 per cent of a fixed oil, which is used for burning as well as for medicinal purposes. It is perfectly fluid at common temperatures, but begins to congeal when cooled below 50°. The Pinnay oil is one of those commonly used in Travancore, especially for lamps. It is manufactured in large quantities in that province, especially in the southern district. This tree flowers twice a-year, and is said to attain a great age.—*Lindley. Simmonds.*

(129) **Calophyllum spurium** (*Choisy*). Do.

Cheroo-pinnay, TAM. Tsirou-panna, MAL.

DESCRIPTION.—Tree; leaves cuneate-obovate, obtuse, or emarginate; young branches square; racemes lax, as long as the leaves, axillary near the ends of the branches; sepals 2; petals 2; drupe oblong, 1-celled; petals white.—*W. & A. Prod.* i. 103.—C. calaba, *Linn.*—*Rheede,* iv. *t.* 39.——Travancore. Malabar.

ECONOMIC USES.—This is a handsome-looking tree, somewhat similar to the former. The wood is hard and of a reddish colour. Fruit when ripe is red and sweet. It is eaten by the natives, and an oil is expressed from it used in lamps. It is called Pootunjee.—*Jury Rep. Mad. Exhib.*

(130) **Calotropis gigantea** (*R. Br.*) N. O. ASCLEPIADACEÆ.

Gigantic Swallow-wort, ENG. Yercum, TAM. Yerica, MAL. Nella-jilledoo, TEL. Akund, BENG. Mudar, Ark, HIND.

DESCRIPTION.—Shrub, 6-10 feet; leaves stem-clasping, decussate, oblong-ovate, wedge-shaped, bearded on the upper side at the base, smooth on the upper surface, clothed with woolly down on the under side; segments of corolla reflexed, with revolute edges; stamineous corona 5-leaved, shorter than the gynostegium; leaflets keel-formed, circinately recurved at the base, incurved and subtridentate at the apex; umbels sometimes compound, surrounded by involucral scales; follicles ventricose, smooth; seeds comose; flowers rose-colour and purple mixed. *Fl.* All the year.—*Dec. Prod.* viii. 535.—Asclepias gigantea, *Willd.*—*Roxb. Fl. Ind.* ii. 30.—Ericu,

Rheede, ii. *t.* 31.—*Wight Icon. t.* 1278.——Peninsula in waste places. Southern provinces.

a—Alba.—Shevet akund, *Beng.*—Belerica, *Mal.*—Tella jilledoo, *Tel.*—Vella-yercum, *Tam.*—Flowers white, cream-coloured, inodorous.

Medical Uses.—The only difference in the two varieties of this shrub consists in the colour of the flowers. It is commonly to be found in waste ground, among rubbish, ruins, and suchlike places. Of late years the plant has attracted much attention from the many and important uses to which its several properties can be applied. An acrid milky juice flows from every part of the shrub when wounded, and this the natives apply to medicinal purposes in many different ways, besides preparations of the plant itself in epilepsy, paralysis, bites of poisonous animals, and as a vermifuge. In almost all cutaneous affections, especially in leprosy, it is frequently employed, and much attention has lately been bestowed upon its virtues in the cure of the latter dreadful complaint. The root, bark, and inspissated juice are used as powerful alteratives and purgatives. Its activity is said to be owing to a principle called Mudarine, discovered by the late Dr Duncan of Edinburgh, which he found to possess the singular property of congealing by heat, and becoming again fluid on exposure to cold. It is obtained from the tincture of Mudar, the powdered root being macerated in cold rectified spirit. After recovering the spirit by distillation, the solution is allowed to cool. A granular resin is then deposited, which is allowed to dry, in order that it may concrete. If water be then applied, the coloured solution from which the resin was deposited dissolves, and the resin remains. This solution is called Mudarine. In taste it is very bitter, soluble in alcohol and cold water, but insoluble in sulphuric ether or olive-oil. By experiments made by Dr G. Playfair, the milky juice was found to be a very efficacious medicine in leprosy, lues, tænia, herpes, dropsy, rheumatism, hectic and intermittent fevers. By the Hindoos it is employed in typhus fever and syphilitic complaints with such success as to have earned the title of vegetable mercury. Dr Duncan considered that it agreed in every respect with ipecacuanha, and that from the facility of procuring it, might eventually supersede the latter medicine. The powdered bark is given in doses of 5-6 grains twice daily. It will occasionally produce nausea and vomiting, but such symptoms are removed by a dose of castor-oil. The root pulverised and made into an ointment is very efficacious in the treatment of old ulcers, so common in the western coast.

The milky juice mixed with common salt is given in toothache, and the juice of the young buds in ear-ache. The leaves warmed and moistened with oil are applied as a dry fomentation in abdominal pains, and, moreover, form a good rubefacient. They are fatal to cattle.—*Ainslie. Royle. Pharm. of India.*

Economic Uses.—Besides the various uses above enumerated, the root is used in the manufacture of gunpowder charcoal. With the powdered flour the natives adulterate Safflower. The silky floss which surrounds the seeds has been woven into shawls and handkerchiefs, and even paper, besides a soft kind of thread by the natives.

But in addition to its other uses, this plant is valuable from the fine strong fibres with which it abounds. To procure them, the straightest branches are cut and exposed to wither for at least twenty-four hours; on the second and third day they are slightly beaten; the skin is then peeled and the stringy substance between the bark and the wood taken out. They are then dried in the sun. This slow process is necessarily expensive, but if the bark is steeped in water, it becomes discoloured, and cutting will destroy it. Still the fibre is strong, and possessed of many of the properties of Europe flax. It can be spun into the finest thread for sowing or weaving cloth. It resists moisture for a long time. From recent experiments made by Dr Wight, its tenacity, compared with other Indian fibres, is as follows:—

	Breaking weights.
Yercum, Calotropis gigantea, . . .	552 lb.
Janapum, or Sunn, Crotalaria juncea, . .	407 "
Kattalay, Agave Americana, . . .	360 "
Cotton, Gossypium herbaceum, . . .	346 "
Marool, Sanseviera Zeylanica, . . .	316 "
Poolay-munja, Hibiscus cannabinus, . .	290 "
Coir, Cocos nucifera, ...	224 "

This fibre, however, is too valuable for ordinary cordage, and might fetch a high price in Europe. It is said by good judges to be better for cloth than cordage. It is much used in this country for bow-strings, ropes, bird-nets, and tiger-traps. It has never been cultivated as a cordage plant. It is widely diffused through the southern provinces of the Peninsula; while in the Bellary district and to the north it is replaced by the *C. procera*, which is equally abundant. In the 'Journal of the Society of Arts' it is stated "that Yercum, which much resembles Belgian flax, is well calculated for prime warp yarns, and worth £100 per ton." Royle says that it yields a kind of manna called Mudar-sugar. It has been tried to employ the viscid juice as a caoutchouc, and a great quantity was collected for that purpose. To prepare it, the juice was evaporated in a shallow dish, either in the sun or in the shade; when dry, it may be worked up in hot water with a wooden kneader, as this process removes the acridity of the gum. It becomes immediately flexible in hot water, but is said to become hard in cold water, and is soluble in oil of turpentine, takes impressions, and will no doubt prove a valuable product, either alone or mixed with other substances.

In experiments made in London, Petersburg hemp bore 160 lb. —brown hemp of Bombay and Jubbulpore hemp, 190 lb., which latter was also the strength of the Yercum. Its value in England might probably be reckoned at from £30 to £40 the ton.—*Ainslie. Royle. Report on Fibres. Jury Rep. Mad. Exhib.*

(131) **Calotropis procera** (*R. Br.*) Do.

DESCRIPTION.—Shrub, 6-10 feet; leaves ovate or oval, cordate at the base; segments of the corolla spreading, revolute at the margin; leaflets of the staminal corona equalling the gynostegium; umbels peduncled; follicles obovoid, downy; flowers pale purple. *Fl.* March—April.—*R. Br. in Hort. Kew,* ii. 78.—C. Wallichii, *Wight Contrib.* 53.—C. Hamiltonii, *do.* ——Deccan. Guzerat. Patna. Hindostan.

MEDICAL USES.—This species differs from the former in the segments of the corolla not being reflexed. It is a widely distributed plant, very abundant in the Bellary district, but quite unknown in the southern provinces. In uses, the two species are probably similar in every respect. Five grains of the bark of the root of this species mixed with very minute doses of arsenic, is internally administered in the form of a pill in leprosy with the best effect.—(*Wight.*) The bark of the root is diaphoretic and expectorant. It is used in European practice as a substitute for ipecacuanha, both as an emetic and cure for dysentery. The fresh juice is used as a rubefacient in rheumatism and chest-diseases, and the leaves as a cure for Guinea-worm.—(*Powell's Punj. Products.*) In the Peshawur valley the juice is employed in the preparation of catgut, and for raising blisters and discussing chronic tumours.—*Stewart's Punj. Plants. Pharm. of India.*

(132) **Calysaccion longifolium** (*Wight*). N. O. CLUSIACEÆ.

DESCRIPTION.—Large tree; leaves opposite, oblong, coriaceous; flowers polygamous, in clusters on the thick branches below the leaves, small, white, streaked with red; fruit oblong, falcate. *Fl.* March—April.—*J. Graham Cat.* 27.—Ochrocarpus longifolius, *Benth. and Hook.*—Mammea longifolia, *do.* —*Wight Ill.* i. 130.—*Icon. t.* 1999.——Concans. Kennary jungles. W. Mysore.

ECONOMIC USES.—The flower-buds are collected and sold in the bazaars for dyeing silk: they emit a fragrance not unlike that of violets, and are used as a perfume. The fruit is delicious to the taste. The native names in those districts where the tree abounds, are Woondy and Taringee for the male trees, and Poonag for the female ones.—*J. Graham, Cat.* *Cleghorn in Pharm. Journ.*, x. 597. *Seemann*, xii. 62.

(133) **Canarium commune** (*Linn.*) N. O. Terebinthaceæ.

Java Almond, Eng. Junglee-badam, Hind.

Description.—Tree, 50 feet; leaves unequally pinnate; leaflets 7-10 on long stalks, ovate-oblong, acute, or shortly acuminate, entire, glabrous; panicles terminal, divaricated; flowers 2-3 together, almost sessile at the extremity of the ultimate pedicels; drupe covered with a thin somewhat fleshy sarcocarp; calyx 3-lobed, externally silky; petals 3; nut very. hard, 3-angled; seed solitary; flowers white. *Fl.* March—May.—*W. & A. Prod.* i. 175.—Colophonia Mauritiana, *Dec.* Bursera paniculata, *Lam.*——Peninsula.

Medical Uses.—This is known as the Elemi tree. The resinous exudation from the tree is imported into England from Manilla. It is of a yellowish-white colour, and of a fragrant odour. This resinous gum has balsamic properties, and is used as an application to indolent ulcers, prepared in the form of an ointment. Dr Waitz ('Diseases of Children') speaks favourably of the kernels in emulsion, as a substitute for the European preparation (*Mistura Amygdalæ*), principally because the almonds imported from Europe are often spoilt by long keeping.—*Pharm. of India.*

Economic Uses.—This fine-looking tree is cultivated in the Moluccas for the sake of its fruit, which in taste is something like an almond. An oil is expressed from the nuts which in Java is used in lamps, and when fresh is mixed with food. Bread is also made from the nuts in the island of Celebes. If eaten fresh, or indulged in too freely, they are apt to bring on diarrhœa. Lindley says, "The bark yields an abundance of limpid oil with a pungent turpentine smell, congealing in a buttery camphoraceous substance; it has the same properties as balsam of copaiba." The resinous exudation is used for burning as a light in Amboyna.—(*Ainslie. Lindley, Flor. Med.*) Another species, the *C. Benghalense*, yields a very large quantity of pure, clear, amber-coloured resin, which soon becomes hard and brittle, and is not unlike copal; yet the natives set little or no value upon it. In the Calcutta Bazaar it sells at 2 to 3 rupees a maund of 80 lb. It is a native of Silhet and the adjacent mountainous countries, and flowers in May and June.—*Jury Rep. Mad. Exhib.*

(134) **Canarium strictum** (*Roxb.*) Do.

Black Dammer-tree, Eng. Thelly, Mal. Congilium-marum, Tam.

Description.—Large tree; young parts densely clothed with rusty-coloured pubescence; leaflets 9-15, stalked, ovate or ovate-lanceolate, acuminated, at length serrulate-ciliate, hairy. —*Roxb. Fl. Ind.* iii. 138.—*W. & A. Prod.* i. 195.—Tinnevelly. Malabar. Trichore forests. Pulney hills.

Economic Uses.—This is known in Malabar under the name of the black dammer-tree, in contradistinction to the white dammer-tree (*Vateria Malabarica*). It is common in the alpine forests about Courtallum in the Tinnevelly district, and is there rented for the sake of its dammer. The resin is transparent, and of a deep brownish-yellow or amber colour when held between the eye and the light, but when adhering to the tree it has a bright shining black appearance.—(*Wight, Ill.*, i. 134.) It is partially soluble in boiling alcohol, and completely so in oil of turpentine. Dr Bidie speaks of it as a substitute for Burgundy pitch.—*Pharm. of India.*

The following report upon the black dammer is given by Mr Broughton: "This well-known substance offers little chance of usefulness, in Europe at least, when the many resins are considered that are found in the market at a far less price. It is used in this country for many small purposes, as in the manufacture of bottling-wax, varnishes, &c. Its colour when in solution is pale, if compared with its dark tint when in mass. Thus, though insoluble in spirit, its solution in turpentine forms a tolerable varnish. When submitted to destructive distillation it yields about 78 per cent of oil, resembling that obtained from common colophony; but I fear in the majority of its possible applications it possesses few advantages over ordinary resin at 7s. 6d. per cwt. Major Beddome estimates the price of black dammer on the coast of Canara at 8 rupees per 25 lb. (or nearly ten times the price of resin in England). The number of substances suitable for varnishes have lately become very numerous in Europe. Common resin is now purified by a patent process, consisting of distillation with superheated steam, by which it is obtained nearly as transparent and colourless as glass, in such amount that a single firm turns out 60 tons per week."

(135) **Canavalia gladiata** (*Dec.*) N. O. Leguminosæ.

Sword-bean, Eng. Segapoo or Vellay Thumbetten, Tam. Yerra or Tellay Tumbetten-kaya, Tel. Suffaid or Lal Kudsumbal, Hind. Mekhun Shirn, Beng.

Description.—Perennial shrub, twining; leaves pinnately trifoliate; leaflets cordate-ovate, rather acute; calyx unequally bilabiate, upper lip largest, lower lip acutely 3-toothed;

corolla papilionaceous; vexillum bicallous at the base; keel falcate at a right angle, petals distinct; racemes axillary, many-flowered; flowers in pairs, or threes, purplish; legumes 5-10 times longer than broad.—*W. & A. Prod.* i. 253.—*Wight Icon. t.* 753.—Dolichos gladiatus, *Jacq.*—*Rheede,* viii. *t.* 44. ——Cultivated in the Peninsula.

Economic Uses.—Of this kind of bean there are several varieties, with seeds and flowers of different colours. The variety with large white seeds and flowers is considered the most wholesome, and is extensively used at the tables of Europeans, as well as by the natives. It is a common plant in hedges and thickets, but is cultivated for the sake of its esculent pods.—(*Roxb. Wight.*) *Canavalia obtusifolia,* Dec., common on the sea-shore, frequently entwined with the *Ipomœa pes capræ,* is also a useful plant, helping to bind the sand at the Adyar, the mouth of the Godavery, and between Quilon and Anjengo.—*Mad. Jour. of Sc.,* 1856, *pl.* 4.

(136) Canna Indica (*Linn.*) N. O. Marantaceæ.

Indian Shot, Eng. Kull-valei-munnie, Tam. Ukkil-bar-ki-Munker, Duk. Surbo-jaya, Beng. Katoo-bala, Mal. Krishna-tamarah, Tel.

Description.—Shrub, 2-3 feet; leaves large, ovate-lanceolate, stem-clasping; inner wing of the corolla trifid, segments lanceolate, straight; anther single, attached to the edge of the petal-like filament; style spathulate, growing to the tube of the corolla; capsule bristly, 3-celled, many-seeded; flowers bright scarlet or yellow. *Fl.* All the year.—*Roxb. Fl. Ind.* i. 1.—C. orientalis, *Roxb.*—*Rheede,* xi. *t.* 43.——Common everywhere.

Medical Uses.—The root is considered acrid and stimulant.—(*Fleming.*) When cattle have eaten any poisonous grass, which is generally discovered by the swelling of the abdomen, the natives administer to them the root of this plant, which they break up in small pieces, boil in rice-water with pepper, and give them to drink.

Economic Uses.—The leaves are large and tough, and are sometimes used for wrapping up goods. The seeds are black, hard, and shining, resembling shot, for which they are sometimes used. The natives make necklaces and other ornaments of them. They yield a beautiful purple dye, which is said not to be durable. In the West Indies the leaves are used to thatch houses. Nearly all the species contain starch in the root-stock, which renders them fit to be used as food after being cooked. From the root of one kind, *C. edulis,* a nutritious aliment (*Tous les mois*) is prepared; this is peculiarly fitted for invalids, not being liable to turn acid. To prepare it the starch is first separated by cutting the tubers in pieces, and putting them in water, which is poured off after a time, when the starch subsides.—*Lindley. Roxb.*

(137) Cannabis sativa (*Linn.*) N. O. CANNABINACEÆ.

Common hemp plant, ENG. Tsjeroo Cansjava, MAL. Gunja, TAM. Ganjah Chettoo, TEL. Ganjar, BENG.

DESCRIPTION.—Annual, 4-6 feet, covered all over with an extremely fine rough pubescence; stem erect, branched, green, angular; calyx 5-parted; leaves alternate or opposite, on long petioles, digitate, with linear-lanceolate, sharply-serrated leaflets, tapering to a long, smooth point; flowers in spikes, axillary, clustered, small, greenish white; males lax and drooping; females erect, leafy at the base. *Fl.* All the year. —*Roxb. Fl. Ind.* iii. 772.—*Rheede,* x. *t.* 60.——Hills north of India. Cultivated in the Peninsula.

MEDICAL USES.—The officinal part of the Indian hemp consists of the dried flowering-tops of the female plant, from which the resin has not been removed. This is called *Gunjah.* The resin itself, which exudes from the leaves, stem, and flowers, is called *Churrus.* And what is known as *Bhang* is the larger leaves and capsules without the stalks. The properties of Indian hemp are stimulant, sedative, and antispasmodic, often equalling opium in its effects. A good oil is procured from the seeds by pressure, which is used for the preparation of emulsions. Churrus has been employed by Dr O'Shaughnessy in tetanus with good results.—(*Pharm. of India.*) The anæsthetic effects of Indian hemp seem to equal that of the *Atropa Mandragora.* The Greeks and Romans were acquainted with it, but seem to have been ignorant of its narcotic and anæsthetic properties. Dr Royle suggests that the nepenthes of which Homer speaks may have been that Indian hemp, the "assuager of grief" (*Od.*, iv. 221), as having been given by Helen to Telemachus in the house of Menelaus. Helen is stated to have received the plant from Egyptian Thebes. The plant has long been known in Africa. "In Barbary," says Sir Joseph Banks, "bhang prepared from Indian hemp is always taken, if it can be procured, by criminals who are condemned to suffer amputation; and it is said to enable those miserables to bear the rough operations of an unfeeling executioner more than we Europeans can the keen knife of our most skilful surgeons." Dr Daniel states that it is smoked in large quantities by the natives of Congo, Angola, and South Africa. It does not appear that the Hindoos ever used it as an anæsthetic during surgical operations; but Hoa-tho, a Chinese physician who flourished about 230 B.C., is recorded to have done so. "If the malady was situated in parts on which the needle, the moxa, or liquid medicines could not act, he gave to the patient a preparation of hemp (Ma-yo), and at the end of some instants he became as insensible as if he had been drunk or deprived of life. Then, according to the case, he made openings and incisions, performed amputations, and removed the cause of mischief. After a certain number of days the patient found himself re-established, without having experienced the slightest pain during the operation." The experiments of scientific inquirers in modern days have rendered credible the above report. It produces exhilaration, inebriation with phantasms, confusion of intellect, followed by sleep. Mr Donovan and Dr Christison both testify to its producing numbness, and rendering obtuse the sense of touch and feeling. The *Diamba plant* of tropical Western Africa, called also Congo tobacco, is smoked by the native Africans to produce the pleasing excitement of intoxication! It is smoked from a large wooden pipe or reed called condo, or from a small calabash, or sometimes from common clay pipes. The liberated Africans and Creoles frequently meet at each other's houses; and on these occasions the pipe is handed about from mouth to mouth, and soon produces the desired effects—agreeable sensations, laughter, &c.; a continuance, however, causes temporary frenzy, and intense and maddening headache, accompanied by stupor. The plant is the *Cannabis sativa*, or common hemp, which on fertile soils, at Sierra Leone, grows 12 or 13 feet high, and 20 feet in circumference. The flowers, slowly dried and mixed with the seeds, are the parts preferred, and in this state the drug is called *maconie*. The leaflets are sometimes used; they are called *makiah*. A small plant in flower and seed will yield its owner ten shillings' worth of maconie.—(*Hooker's Journ. Bot.*, iii. 9.) The hemp is a plant of most powerful properties, as is evident from the numerous preparations of it employed in India; but no stronger evidence is needed to prove the influence of climate on vegetable productions than the fact that hemp grown in our cool and moist climate scarcely at all develops these properties.—*Paxton. O'Shaughnessy, Beng. Disp. Pereira, Elem. Met. Med. West. Rev.*, No. 29, 1859.

Economic Uses.—The earliest notice we have of the hemp plant is found in Herodotus (Book iv. c. 74-75), who says: "Hemp grows in Scythia; it is very like flax, only that it is a much taller and coarser plant. Some grows wild about the country; some is produced by cultivation. The Thracians make garments of it which closely resemble linen; so much so, that if a person has never seen hemp, he is sure to think they are linen; and if he has, unless he is very experienced in such matters, he will not know of which material they are. The Scythians take some of this hemp-seed, and, creeping under felt coverings, throw it upon the red-hot stones; immediately it smokes, and gives out such a vapour as no Grecian bath can excel." —(*Rawlinson's Trans.*, iii. 54.) The plant is here called Cannabis, the same word which we now use, and from which the English word canvas is derived. To the present day it grows in Northern Russia and Siberia, Tauria, the Caucasus, and Persia, and is found over the whole north of Europe. We next learn of it in Athenæus, who, quoting from an ancient historian, Moschion, the description of a ship built by Hiero, King of Syracuse, and which was superintended by the famous Archimedes, says, "for ropes he provided cordage from Spain, and hemp and pitch from the river Rhone." This was Hiero II., who flourished about 270 B.C. We next hear of it in Pliny, who describes the hemp plant as being well known to the Romans, who manufactured a kind of cordage from it. This author has minutely described, in the 19th book of his 'Natural History,' the mode of cultivating it, and its subsequent preparation in order to obtain the fibre. He further states that in those days it had some repute in medicine, especially the root and juice of the bark, but these uses are now obsolete or of little value. It is now cultivated everywhere in India, chiefly for the intoxicating property which resides in its leaves, and which is made into the drug called Bhang. Much attention has of late years been paid to its cultivation, and several able reports upon this subject have been drawn up. According to Captain Huddleston, in the 'Transactions of the Agri. Hort. Soc. of India' (viii. 260), "in the Himalaya there are two kinds; one is wild, of little or no value, but the other one is cultivated on high lands, selected for this purpose. The land is first cleared of the forest-trees: owing to the accumulation of decomposed vegetable matter, no manure is required for the first year; but after that, or in grounds which have not been cleared for the purpose, manure must be abundantly supplied to insure a good hemp crop. The plant flourishes best at elevations ranging from 4000 to 7000 feet. The seeds are put down about the end of May or beginning of June; and as soon as the young plants have risen up, the ground is carefully cleared of weeds and the plants thinned, with a distance between each of three or four inches. They are then left to grow, not being fit to cut before October or November."

The best hemp is procured from the male plants, and these latter are cut a month earlier than the female ones, and yield a tougher and better fibre. When the stalks are cut they are dried in the sun for several days. The seeds are then rubbed out between the hands, and this produces what is called Churrus, which is scraped off, and afterwards sold. The stalks being well dried are put up in bundles, and steeped for a fortnight in water, being kept well under by pressure, then taken out, beaten with mallets, and again dried. The fibre is now stripped off from the thickest end of the stalk, and then made up in twists for sale, and manufactured into bags and ropes.

It would appear that none of the hemp so cultivated is exported, only sufficient being grown for consumption among the inhabitants of the districts. Dr Roxburgh was the first who turned his attention to the cultivation of the plant in the plains; and found that to insure success the ground selected should be, if possible, of a low humid description, and that the rainy season was the best in which to sow the seeds, the intense heat of the sun being prejudicial to its favourable growth. Dr Royle and others consider that with ordinary care and judicious treatment the hemp plant can be successfully cultivated in the Indian plains, though the fibres yielded may not be of such fine quality as those grown in mountainous districts. When sown for the sake of its cordage, the plant should be sown thick, in order that the stem may run up to a considerable height without branching, whereby a longer fibre is obtained, and the evaporation is less from the exclusion of air and heat, rendering the fibre of a more soft and pliable nature. The natives, on the contrary, who cultivate the Cannabis solely for the Bhang, transplant it like rice, the plants being kept about eight or ten feet apart. This has the effect of inducing them to branch, and the heat naturally stimulating the secretion, the intoxicating properties are increased. Although the cultivation of the hemp plant has considerably decreased in this country of late years, yet it would appear that plants requiring so little care might be easily reared to any extent for the sake of their fibres, should the demand require it, even were they only for use in our own dominion, without the object of exportation. It has been shown in the 'Journal of the Asiatic Society' that the cost of hemp, as prepared by the natives in Dheyra Dhoon, would be about £6 or £7 per ton in Calcutta (preparation and carriage included); but were the cultivation increased and improved, the extra remuneration to the cultivators, with other contingent charges, would make the total cost at the Presidency about £17 per ton. With the introduction of railways this might be still further decreased. In point of strength and durability, as evinced by the samples produced, there is no doubt that good Himalayan hemp is superior to Russian hemp. At any rate, proof exists that it can be produced of a superior quality. On a specimen of Russian hemp being shown to a native cultivator, he remarked that were he to produce such an inferior article it would never find a sale.

The hemp plant, it is said, has the singular property of destroying caterpillars and other insects which prey upon vegetables, for which reason it is often the custom in Europe to encircle the beds with borders of the plant, which effectually keeps away all insects.

It is grown in almost all parts of Europe, especially in Russia, Italy, and England. Gunja has a strong aromatic and heavy odour, abounds in resin, and is sold in the form of flowering-stalks. Bhang is in the form of dried leaves, without stalk, of a dull-green colour, not much odour, and only slightly resinous: its intoxicating properties are much less. Gunja is smoked like tobacco. Bhang is not smoked, but pounded up with water into a pulp, so as to make a drink highly conducive to health, and people accustomed to it seldom get sick. In Scinde, a stimulating infusion made from the plant is much drunk among the upper classes, who imagine that it is an improver of the appetite. Gunja is frequently mixed with tobacco to render it more intoxicating. This is especially done by the Hottentots, who chop the hemp-leaves very fine, and smoke them together in this manner. Sometimes the leaves, powdered, are mixed with aromatics and thus taken as a beverage, producing much the same effects as opium, only more agreeable.—*Royle, Fib. Plants. Muller in Hooker's Journ. of Botany.*

(138) **Canthium parviflorum** (*Lam.*) N. O. CINCHONACEÆ.

Kanden-khara, MAL. Caray-cheddie, TAM. Ballusoo-kura, TEL.

DESCRIPTION.—Small shrub, usually with opposite horizontal thorns a little above the axils, sometimes unarmed; leaves opposite, ovate, often fascicled on the young shoots; racemes short, axillary, few-flowered on each side; drupe obovate, slightly emarginate, compressed, furrowed on each side; corolla with short tube, segments woolly inside or sometimes glabrous; nut 2-celled; seeds solitary; flowers small, yellow. *Fl.* April—May.—*W. & A. Prod.* i. 426.—*Roxb. Fl. Ind.* i. 534.—Webera tetrandra, *Willd.*——Southern Mahratta country. Travancore. Coromandel.

MEDICAL USES.—A decoction of the leaves, as well as of the root, is given in certain stages of flux; and the latter is supposed to have anthelmintic qualities. The bark and young shoots are used in dysentery.—*Ainslie.*

(139) **Capparis aphylla** (*Roxb.*) N. O. CAPPARIDACEÆ.

DESCRIPTION.—Shrubby; stipules thorny, nearly straight; leaves (on the young shoots only) linear-subulate, mucronate; flowers corymbose; corymbs nearly sessile, from the axils of the stipules; fruit globular, pointed. *Fl.* June—Aug.—*W. & A. Prod.* i. 27.—*Dec. Prod.* i. 246.——Waste places in the Deccan. Guzerat. Banks of the Jumna.

MEDICAL USES.—This plant, though used occasionally as food, is considered by the natives heating and aperient. It is reckoned useful in boils, eruptions, and swellings, and as an antidote to poisons; also in affections of the joints.—*Powell's Punj. Prod.*

ECONOMIC USES.—It has immense roots. The branches are commonly used for fuel, burning with a strong gaseous flame even when green, and are also used for brick-burning. The wood is very durable, bitter, and not liable to the attacks of white ants. On this latter account it is much used for rafters in the North-West Provinces. Ploughshares are also made of it. It is useful in turning. The bud is eaten as a pot-herb, and the fruit largely consumed by the natives, both green and ripe. In the former state it is generally steeped for fifteen days in salt and water, being put in the sun to ferment till it becomes acid, pepper and oil being then added. The ripe fruit is made into pickle with mustard or oil, to be eaten with bread.—*Stewart's Punj. Plants.*

The Capparidaceæ are chiefly tropical, yet are extensively found, too, in temperate climates. Species of *Polanisia* and *Gynandropsis* occur as high as 6000 feet in the Himalaya, but only during the moisture and equable temperature of the rainy months.—*Royle.*

(140) **Capsicum annuum** (*Linn.*) N. O. Solanaceæ.

Spanish pepper, Eng. Gach-murich, Beng. Mollaghai, Tam. Merapu-kai, Tel. Capoo Mologoo, Mal.

Description.—Small plant, 1-2 feet; stem herbaceous; calyx 5-toothed; corolla 5-cleft; leaves solitary, scattered, entire; peduncles extra-axillary, 1-flowered; fruit oblong, pendulous or erect, red, yellow, or variegated; flowers white. *Fl.* all the year.—*Roxb. Fl. Ind.* i. 573.——Cultivated in the Peninsula.

Medical Uses.—This is a native of South America. There are several varieties of it, distinguished by the shape of the fruit. Cayenne pepper is the produce of many of the smaller species of Capsicum, the fruits being dried and pounded small, and mixed with salt. They are considered wholesome for persons of phlegmatic temperament, being reckoned stimulating. When gathered and eaten fresh, they are excellent promoters of digestion in tropical countries. In Europe they are made into pickles, and otherwise used for seasoning food. There are two distinct principles in the pods, one of which is an ethereal oil, and which constitutes the real stimulating principle. The bruised berries are employed as powerful rubefacients, being reckoned preferable to sinapisms in sore throats. They are also given, with the best results, as a gargle. Mixed with Peruvian bark, they are given internally in typhus and intermittent fevers and dropsy. Chillies are a principal ingredient in all curries in India. By pouring hot vinegar upon the fruits, all the essential qualities are preserved, which cannot be effected by drying them, owing to their oleaginous properties. This Chilly vinegar is an excellent stomachic, imparting a fine flavour to fish and meats. A great quantity is exported to England, especially from the West Indies, the price of Chillies in London being from 15s. to 25s. the cwt. Of the different varieties the following are the best known: *C. baccatum* (Linn.), bird's-eye pepper; *C. fastigiatum* (Blume), cayenne pepper; *C. frutescens* (Linn.), Chilly pepper; *C. grossum* (Willd.), bell pepper (*Caffrie murich*, Hind.);

C. Nepalense, a variety growing in Nepaul, and to the taste far more pungent and acrid than any of the preceding species.

The cayenne pepper is prepared in the following manner in the West Indies: The ripe fruits are dried in the sun, and then in an oven, after bread is baked, in an earthen or stone pot, with flour between the strata of pods. When quite dry, they are cleaned from the flour, and beaten or ground to fine powder. To every ounce of this a pound of wheat-flour is added, and it is made into small cakes with leaven. These are baked again, that they may be as dry and hard as biscuit, and then are beaten into powder and sifted. It is then fit for use as a pepper, or for being packed in a compressed state, and so as to exclude air, for exportation.—*Lindley. Com. Prod. Mad. Pres.*

Chillies are employed, in combination with cinchona, in intermittents and lethargic affections, and also in atonic gout, dyspepsia accompanied with flatulence, tympanitis, and paralysis. Its most valuable application, however, appears to be in *Cynanche maligna* and *Scarlatina maligna*, used either as a gargle or administered internally.—*Lindley, E. B.*

(141) **Cardiospermum Halicacabum** (*Linn.*) N. O. Sapindaceæ.

Smooth-leaved heart pea, Eng. Palloolavum Ulinja, Mal. Moodacottan, Tam. Budda-kanka-rakoo or Nellagoolisienda, Tel. Shibjool or Nuphutkee, Beng.

Description.—Annual, climbing; stem, petioles, and leaves nearly glabrous; leaves biternate; leaflets stalked, oblong, much acuminated, coarsely cut and serrated; petals 4, each with an emarginate scale above the base, the two lower ones with their scales furnished with a glandular crest at their extremity, and ending in a yellow inflexed appendage beneath the apex; fruit a membranous bladdery capsule, 3-celled, 3-valved; seeds globose, with a 2-lobed aril at the base; flowers racemose; common peduncles with two opposite tendrils under the racemes; flowers small, white or pink, on long axillary peduncles. *Fl.* nearly all the year.—*W. & A. Prod.* i. 109.—*Wight Icon. t.* 508.—*Roxb. Fl. Ind.* ii. 292. —*Rheede,* viii. *t.* 28.——Common everywhere.

Medical Uses.—The root, which is diaphoretic and diuretic, is given in decoction as an aperient. It is mucilaginous, and slightly nauseous to the taste. On the Malabar coast the leaves are administered in pulmonic complaints, and, mixed with castor-oil, are internally employed in rheumatism and lumbago. The whole plant, boiled in oil, is rubbed over the body in bilious affections. In the Moluccas the leaves are cooked as a vegetable. The whole plant, says Rheede, rubbed up with water, is applied to rheumatism and stiffness of the limbs. The leaves, mixed with jaggery and boiled in oil, are a good specific in sore eyes.—(*Ainslie. Rheede.*) The whole plant, steeped in milk, is successfully applied to reduce swellings and hardened tumours.—*Pers. Obs.*

(142) **Careya arborea** (*Roxb.*) N. O. BARRINGTONIACEÆ.

Peloa, MAL. Kumbi, TEL. Poottatanni-marum, Ave-mavoo, TAM.

DESCRIPTION.—Large tree; leaves oval, serrulate, dentate; flowers several, large, greenish white; berry ovate, crowned with the segments of the calyx, 4-celled, many-seeded; calyx 4-parted; petals 4. *Fl.* March—April.—*W. & A. Prod.* i. 334.—*Roxb. Fl. Ind.* ii. 638.—*Rheede*, iii. *t.* 36.—*Wight Ill.* ii. 99, 100.——Mountains of Coromandel and Malabar.

ECONOMIC USES.—The fruit is about the size of an apple, and has a peculiar and unpleasant smell. The bark of the tree is made into a coarse kind of cordage, and used by matchlockmen as a slow match for their guns. The cabinetmakers of Monghyr use the wood for boxes. It takes a polish, is of a mahogany colour, well veined, and is not very heavy. It does not resist damp, and splits in the sun, but if kept dry is pretty durable. The timber was formerly used for making the drums of Sepoy corps. It is frequently employed for wooden hoops, being very flexible.—*Jury Rep. J. Grah. Cat. Martin's E. Indies.*

(143) **Carica papaya** (*Linn.*) N. O. PAPAYACEÆ.

Papaw-tree, ENG. Pappoia Umbbalay-marum, MAL. Pepeya, BENG. and HIND. Pappali-marum, TAM.

DESCRIPTION.—Tree, 20-30 feet, without branches; leaves alternate, palmate, 7-partite; segments oblong, acute, sinuated, the middle one 3-fid; fruit succulent, oblong, furrowed; calyx small, 5-toothed; corolla tubular in the male and 5-lobed in the female, divided nearly to the base into 5 segments; male flowers axillary in slightly-compound racemes or panicles, white female ones in short simple racemes, sometimes on a different tree; corolla longer than in the male, yellowish. *Fl.* July.—*W. & A. Prod.* i. 352.—*Wight Ill.* ii. *t.* 106, 107.—*Lindl. Fl. Med.* 107.—Papaya vulgaris, *Lam.*—P. carica, *Gœrtn.*—*Rheede Mal.* i. *t.* 15.——Domesticated in India.

MEDICAL USES.—This tree has several valuable medicinal properties. The milky juice is among the best vermifuges known. A single dose is sufficient for the cure. The natives in Travancore repeatedly use it for children. In the West Indies the powder of the seeds is used for the same purpose. The juice of the pulp of the fruit is used to destroy freckles on the skin caused by the sun's heat. —(*Wight. Lindley.*) Anthelmintic properties have also been assigned to the seeds. They are also believed among the natives to be powerfully emmenagogue.—*Pharm. of India.*

Economic Uses.—This remarkable tree was introduced from America, but is now found in most parts of the Peninsula. The fruit grows to a tolerably large size, and secretes a milky viscid juice, which has the extraordinary property of hastening the decay of muscular fibre, when the latter is exposed to its influence. A great deal has been written upon the various effects which this secretion produces upon animal substances, and there appears to be little doubt that the juice really possesses the wonderful virtues attributed to it. I have attempted to collect the most important remarks which have been written upon this subject, as I find there is still a tendency among scientific men to doubt the very peculiar properties of the juice. Humboldt thus writes (*Travels*, ii. 52, Bohn's ed.) concerning it: "I may be permitted to add the result of some experiments which I attempted to make on the juice of the Carica papaya during my stay in the valleys of Aragua, though I was then almost destitute of chemical tests. The juice has been since examined by Vauquelin, and this celebrated chemist has very clearly recognised the albumen and caseous matter; he compares the milky sap to a substance strongly animalised—to the blood of animals.

"The younger the fruit of the Carica, the more milk it yields. It is even found in the germen scarcely fecundated. In proportion as the fruit ripens the milk becomes less abundant and more aqueous. When nitric acid, diluted with four parts of water, is added drop by drop to the milk expressed from a very young fruit, a very extraordinary phenomenon appears. At the centre of each drop a gelatinous pellicle is formed, divided by greyish streaks. These streaks are simply the juice rendered more aqueous, owing to the contact of the acid having deprived it of the albumen. At the same time the centre of the pellicles becomes opaque, and of the colour of the yolk of an egg; they enlarge as if by the prolongation of divergent fibres. The whole liquid assumes at first the appearance of an agate with milky clouds, and it seems as if organic membranes were forming under the eye of the observer. When the coagulum extends to the whole mass, the yellow spots again disappear. By agitation it becomes granular, like soft cheese. The yellow colour reappears on adding a few more drops of nitric acid. After a few hours the yellow colour turns to brown. The coagulum of the Papaw-tree, when newly prepared, being thrown into water, softens, dissolves in part, and gives a yellowish tint to the fluid. The milk, placed in contact with water only, forms also membranes. In an instant a tremulous jelly is precipitated resembling starch. This phenomenon is particularly striking if the water employed be heated to 40° or 60°. The jelly condenses in proportion as more water is poured upon it. It preserves a long time its whiteness, only growing yellow by the contact of a few drops of nitric acid."

Browne, in his 'Natural History of Jamaica,' p. 360, states that "water impregnated with the milky juice of this tree is thought to make all sorts of meat washed in it tender; but eight or ten minutes' steeping, it is said, will make it so soft that it will drop in pieces from the spit before it is well roasted, or turn soon to rags in the boiling." This circumstance has been repeatedly confirmed, and, moreover, that old hogs and old poultry, which are fed upon the leaves and fruit, however tough the meat they afford might otherwise be, is thus rendered perfectly tender, and good if eaten as soon as killed, but that the flesh passes very soon into a state of putridity. In the third volume of the Wernerian Society's Memoirs there is a highly interesting paper on the properties of the juice of the Papaw-tree by Dr Holder, who witnessed its effects in the island of Barbadoes, and writes of them as known to all the inhabitants. The juice causes a separation of the muscular fibres. Nay, the very vapour of the tree serves this purpose; hence many people suspend the joints of meat, fowls, &c., in the upper part of the tree, in order to prepare them for the table. It is not known whether the power of hastening the decay of meat be attributable to the animal matter or fibrine contained in the juice of the Papaw. The resemblance between the juice of the Papaw-tree and animal matter is so close, that one would be tempted to suspect some imposition, were not the evidence that it is really the juice of the tree quite unquestionable.

The tree grows very quickly, and bears fruit in three years from first putting down the seed. The fruit itself is pleasant to the taste, and is much relished in this country both by natives and Europeans. In order to render meat tender, either flesh or fowl, the simplest operation is to hang the flesh under the tree for two or three hours, which is quite sufficient. I have repeatedly tried it, and can testify to the true result. Another way is to wrap the meat in the leaves and then to roast it. In a tropical climate like India, where meat requires to be cooked quickly, in order to provide against rapid decomposition (on which account it is often found very tough), there should be one of these trees in every garden.

Wight mentions (*Ill.* ii. 36) that the farmers in the isle of Barbadoes mix the milky juice with water, and give to horses in order (to use their expression) "to break down the blood;" and this is a remarkable fact, that the effects of this dissolving power in the fruit is not confined to muscular fibre, but acts on the circulating blood. The negroes in the West Indies employ the leaves to wash linen instead of soap. The natives in India both pickle and preserve the fruit for their curries. It is very palatable even raw.—*Humboldt. Don. Wight. Lindley. Pers. Obs.*

(144) **Carissa carandas** (*Linn.*) N. O. APOCYNACEÆ.

Keelay, MAL. Kalapa, TAM. Kurumchee, BENG. Kurunda, HIND. Wakay, TEL.

DESCRIPTION.—Shrub; leaves opposite, ovate, mucronate, nearly sessile, shining; calyx 5-toothed; corymbs terminal and axillary, many-flowered; spines always in pairs at the divisions of the branches, and at every other pair of leaves, strong and sharp, 2-forked; flowers pure white; berry black when ripe. *Fl.* Nearly all the year.—*Roxb. Cor.* i. *t.* 77.—*Wight Icon. t.* 426.——Common everywhere.

ECONOMIC USES.—This thorny shrub is very good for fences, the number and strength of the thorns rendering it impassable. The berries scarcely ripe are employed to make tarts, preserves, and pickles. They are universally eaten by the natives, and are pleasant-tasted. The shrub is found in jungles and uncultivated places.—*Roxb.*

Another species, the *C. diffusa*, a thorny shrub, bears a small black edible fruit. Native combs are made from the wood, which is also used in fences. The wood of a very old tree turns quite black, and acquires a strong fragrance. It is considered a valuable medicine, and is sold at a high price under the name of Ajar in the North-West Provinces.—*Powell's Punj. Prod.*

(145) **Carthamus tinctorius** (*Linn.*) N. O. ASTERACEÆ.

Bastard Saffron, or Safflower, ENG. Sendoorkum, TAM. Koosum, HIND. Koosumba, TEL. Kajeerah, BENG.

DESCRIPTION.—Annual, 1-2 feet; stem erect, cylindrical, branching near the summit; leaves oval, sessile, much acuminated, somewhat spiny; heads of flowers enclosed in a roundish spiny involucre: flowers large, deep orange. *Fl.* Nov.—Dec. —*Roxb. Fl. Ind.* iii. 409.——Peninsula (cultivated).

ECONOMIC USES.—The dried flowers, which are very like Saffron in appearance, have been employed to adulterate that drug. They contain a colouring principle called *Carthamite*, used by dyers, and constituting the basis of rouge. The flowers are used by the Chinese to give rose, scarlet, purple, and violet colours to their silks. They are thrown into an infusion of alkali and left to macerate. The colours are afterwards drawn out by the addition of lemon-juice in various proportions, or of any other vegetable acid. The flowers are imported to England from many parts of Europe, and from Egypt, for dyeing and painting. They are also used in cakes and toys; but if used too much they have purgative qualities. Poultry fatten on the seeds. An oil of a light-yellow colour is procured from the seeds.

It is used for lamps and for culinary purposes. The seeds contain about 28 per cent of oil. The dried florets yield a beautiful colouring matter which attaches itself without a mordant. It is chiefly used for colouring cotton, and produces various shades of pink, rose, crimson, scarlet, &c. In Bangalore silk is dyed with it, but the dye is fugitive, and will not bear washing. An alkaline extract precipitated by an acid will give a fine rose-colour to silks or cotton. The flower is gathered and rubbed down into powder, and sold in this state. When used for dyeing it is put into a cloth, and washed in cold water for a long time, to remove a yellow colouring matter. It is then boiled, and yields the pink dyeing liquid. The Chinese Safflower is considered superior to the Indian one. In Assam, Dacca, and Rajpootana, it is cultivated for exportation. About 300 tons are annually shipped from Calcutta, valued in England from £6 to £7, 10s. per cwt. That from Bombay is least esteemed. The mode of collecting the flowers and preparing the dye, as practised in Europe, where the plant is much cultivated, is as follows: The moment the florets which form the compound flowers begin to open, they are gathered in succession without waiting for the whole to expand, since, when allowed to remain till fully blown, the beauty of the colour is very much faded. As the flowers are collected they are dried in the shade. This work must be carefully performed; for if gathered in wet weather, or badly dried, the colour will be much deteriorated. These flowers contain two kinds of colouring matter—the one yellow, which is soluble in water; the other red, which being of a resinous nature, is insoluble in water, but soluble in alkaline carbonates. The first is never converted to any use, as it dyes only dull shades of colour; the other is a beautiful rose-red, capable of dyeing every shade, from the palest rose to a cherry-red. It is therefore requisite, before these flowers can be made available, to separate the valueless from the valuable colour; and since the former only is soluble in water, this operation is matter of little difficulty.

The flowers are tied in a sack and laid in a trough, through which a slender stream of water is constantly flowing; while, still further to promote the solution of the yellow colouring matter, a man in the trough treads the sack, and subjects every part to the action of the water. When this flows without receiving any yellow tinge in its passage, the washing is discontinued, and the Safflower, if not wanted for immediate use, is made into cakes, which are known in commerce under the name of Stripped Safflower. It is principally used for dyeing silk, producing poppy-red, bright orange, cherry, rose, or flesh colour, according to the alterative employed in combination. These are alum, potash, tartaric acid, or sulphuric acid. The fixed oil which the plant yields is used by the native practitioners in rheumatic and paralytic complaints. The seeds are reckoned laxative, and have been employed in dropsy, and the dried flowers in Jamaica are given in jaundice.—*Vegetable Substances. Jury Rept. Simmonds.*

(146) **Caryota urens** (*Linn.*) N. O. Palmaceæ.

Bastard Sago, Eng. Coonda-panna, Tam. Erimpana, Schunda-pana, Mal. Teeroogoo, Tel.

Description.—Trunk erect, 50-60 feet, slightly marked with the cicatrices of the fallen leaves; leaves pinnate; leaflets sub-alternate, sessile, obliquely præmorse, jagged with sharp points; spathe many-leaved; spadix pendulous, 6-16 feet long; branches covered with innumerable sessile flowers, regularly disposed in threes, one male on each side, and a single female between them; male calyx 3-leaved; petals 3, larger than the calyx, greenish outside; female flowers on the same spadix, with the calyx and corolla as in the male; berry roundish, 1-celled, size of a nutmeg, covered with thin yellow bark; nut solitary. *Fl.* Dec.—March.—*Roxb. Fl. Ind.* iii. 625.—*Rheede*, i. *t.* 11.——Malabar. Coromandel. Travancore.

Economic Uses.—Sugar and toddy-wine are both prepared from this palm, which is cultivated by the natives for those uses. It may be seen in its wild state in the jungles on the Malabar coast. Sago is prepared from the pith. The natives value it much from its yielding such a quantity of sap. The best tree will yield 100 pints of sap in twenty-four hours. This sago is made into bread, and boiled as a thick gruel. The seeds are used by Mahomedans as beads. A fibre is prepared from this palm used for fishing-lines and bow-strings, which is the Indian gut of the English market. It is strong and durable, and will resist for a long time the action of water, but is liable to snap if suddenly bent or knotted. In Ceylon the split trunks are used as rafters, and are found very hard and durable. The fibre of the leaf-stalks is made into ropes in that country, and used for tying wild elephants. The woolly substance found at the bottom of the leaves is employed occasionally for caulking ships. According to Buchanan, the trunks of this palm are the favourite food of elephants. The fruit, which is about the size of a plum, has a thin yellow rind, very acrid, and if applied to the tongue will produce a burning sensation, hence the specific name of the plant.—*Ainslie. Jury Rep. Royle.*

(147) **Casearia canziala** (*Wall.*) N. O. Samydaceæ.

Anavinga, Mal.

Description.—Large tree; leaves alternate, bifarious, ovate-oblong, serrulate, downy beneath, on short petioles; sepals 5, villous; corolla none; peduncles short, axillary, 1-flowered, surrounded at their base with villous involucres; flowers small, crowded into globular heads, pale green. *Fl.* March.—*Roxb. Fl. Ind.* ii. 420.—C. ovata, *Roxb.*——Goalpara. Banks of the Hoogly.

MEDICAL USES.—This tree is very bitter in all its parts; the leaves are used in medicated baths, and the pulp of the fruit is very diuretic.—(*Lindley.*) The *C. esculenta* (*Roxb.*), a native of the Circar mountains, has bitter purgative roots, much used by the mountaineers. The natives eat the leaves.—*Roxb.*

(148) **Cassia absus** (*Linn.*) N. O. LEGUMINOSÆ.

DESCRIPTION.—Biennial, all over clammy except the leaves; branches diffuse; leaves long-petioled; leaflets 2-pairs, obovate, obtuse, glabrous or slightly hairy on the under side; lower flowers axillary, solitary, upper ones forming a short raceme; pedicels short, with a bractea at their base, and minute bracteoles about the middle; stamens 5, all fertile; legume nearly straight, obliquely pointed, much compressed, sprinkled with rigid hairs, few-seeded; flowers small, yellow. *Fl.* All the year.—*W. & A. Prod.* i. 291.—Senna absus, *Roxb. Fl. Ind.* ii. 340.——Coromandel. Bengal.

MEDICAL USES.—A native of Egypt as well as of India. The seeds are very bitter, somewhat aromatic, and mucilaginous. They are regarded in Egypt as the best of remedies for ophthalmia.—(*Lindley.*) The seeds are small, black, and flat, with a projection at one end. An extract is made from them used to purify the blood. They are also employed in mucous disorders.—(*Powell's Punj. Prod.*) The mode of administering the seeds in cases of purulent ophthalmia is to reduce them to a fine powder, and introduce a small portion, a grain or more, beneath the eyelids. It is considered a dangerous application in catarrhal ophthalmia, as its application causes great pain.—*Pharm. of India.*

(149) **Cassia alata** (*Linn.*) Do.

Ringworm Shrub, ENG. Dadoo Murdun, BENG. Veleytie Aghatia, HIND. Wandukolli, Seemee Aghatie, TAM. Seema-avisee, Metta-tamara, TEL.

DESCRIPTION.—Shrub, 8-12 feet; branches spreading, irregularly angled, glabrous; leaflets 8-14 pairs, obovate-oblong, very obtuse, mucronate, glabrous on both sides, or nearly so, the lowest pair close to the branch, and at a distance from the next pair; petiole triangular, without glands; racemes terminal; legumes long, enlarged on each side with a broad crenulated wing, about 5 inches long and 1½ broad; flowers large, yellow. *Fl.* Sept.—Oct.—*W. & A. Prod.* i. 287.—*Wight Icon. t.* 253.—C. bracteata, *Linn.*—Senna alata, *Roxb. Fl. Ind.* i. 349.——Travancore. Cultivated in India.

Medical Uses.—The juice of the leaves mixed with lime-juice is used as a remedy for ringworm: the fresh leaves simply bruised and rubbed upon the parts will sometimes be found to remove the eruption. Roxburgh says the Hindoo doctors affirm that the plant is a cure in all poisonous bites, besides cutaneous affections. The plant is said to have been introduced from the West Indies. Its large yellow flowers give it a striking appearance when in blossom.—(*Ainslie. Roxb.*) The leaves taken internally act as an aperient. A tincture of the dried leaves operates in the same manner as senna; and an extract prepared from the fresh leaves is a good substitute for extract of colocynth.—*Pharm. of India.*

(150) **Cassia auriculata** (*Linn.*) Do.

Averie, Tam. Turwer, Hind. Tanghedu, Tel.

Description.—Shrub; young branches, petioles, and peduncles pubescent; leaflets 8-12 pairs, with a gland between each pair, oval, obtuse or retuse, mucronate, upper side glabrous, under slightly pubescent; racemes axillary, nearly as long as the leaves, many-flowered, approximated towards the ends of the branches; pedicels compressed; sepals slightly hairy; legumes compressed, straight; flowers 3-5 together, bright yellow. *Fl.* Oct.—Dec.—*W. & A. Prod.* i. 290.—Senna auriculata, *Roxb. Flor. Ind.* ii. 349.——Common in the Peninsula.

Medical Uses.—The smooth flattish seeds are pointed at one end, and vary in colour from brown to dull olive. The bark is highly astringent, and is employed in the place of oak-bark for gargles, enemas, &c., and has been found a most efficient substitute. Like as in other species, the seeds are a valued local application in that form of purulent ophthalmia known as "country sore eyes."—*Pharm. of India.*

Economic Uses.—A spirituous liquor is prepared in some parts of the country by adding the bruised bark to a solution of molasses, and allowing the mixture to ferment. The astringent bark is much used by the natives for tanning leather, and to dye it of a buff colour. Workers in iron employ the root in tempering iron with steel. Tooth-brushes are made from the branches.—*Ainslie. Roxb.*

(151) **Cassia lanceolata** (*Forsk.*) Do.

Indian or Tinnevelly Senna, Eng. Sona-pat, Beng. Soona-Mukhee, Hind. Nilaverie, Tam. Nela-ponna, Nela-tunghadoo, Tel.

Description.—Annual; stem erect, smooth; leaves narrow, equally pinnated; leaflets 4-8 pairs, lanceolate, nearly sessile, slightly mucronate, smooth above, rather downy beneath; petioles without glands; racemes axillary and terminal, erect, stalks longer than the leaves; petals bright yellow; legumes pendulous, oblong, membranous, about 1½ inch long, straight, tapering abruptly to the base, rounded at the apex, deep brown, many-seeded. *Fl.* Oct.—Dec.—*Lindl. Flor. Med.* 258. *Royle Ill. t.* 37.—*W. & A. Prod.* i. 288.—Senna officinalis, *Roxb. Fl. Ind.* ii. 346.——Tinnevelly. Guzerat.

Medical Uses.—Of this plant, Graham states that it is indigenous in Guzerat, and that by experiments made upon the leaves they were found to be equally efficacious with the best Egyptian or Italian Senna. They are far superior to the Senna brought to Bombay from Mocha, and may be obtained in any quantity. Lindley says the dried leaves form the finest Senna of commerce. Fine samples of the Tinnevelly Senna were sent to the Madras Exhibition, upon which the jurors reported very favourably. It is satisfactory to remark that Senna grown in the southern provinces of the Presidency is highly esteemed in Britain, and preferred by many to all other sorts, as being both cheaper and purer. As a purgative medicine, Senna is particularly valuable, if free from adulteration. Unfortunately leaves of other plants, even poisonous ones, are frequently mixed with the Senna-leaves, which is the cause of griping after being taken; this is not the case when pure Senna-leaves are employed, especially if the infusion be made with cold water. The concentrated infusion of Senna is prepared by druggists by pouring cold water on the leaves and letting it stand for 24 hours, carefully excluding the air. Senna contains a volatile oil and a principle called cathartine. Senna-leaves are worth from 10 to 15 rupees the cwt. at Bombay.—*Lindley. Simmonds.*

(152) **Cassia occidentalis** (*Linn.*) Do.

Payaverei, Tam. Payavera, Mal. Cashanda, Tel.

Description.—Annual; erect, branches glabrous; leaflets 3-5 pairs, without glands between them, ovate-lanceolate, very acute, glabrous on both sides; petiole with a large sessile gland near its tumid base; flowers longish-pedicelled, upper ones forming a terminal raceme, lower ones 3-5 together, on a very short axillary peduncle; legumes long when ripe, when dried surrounded with a tumid border nearly cylindrical; flowers yellow. *Fl.* All the year.—*W. & A. Prod.* i. 290.—Senna occidentalis, *Roxb. Fl. Ind.* ii. 343.——Common everywhere.

MEDICAL USES.—This is very nearly allied to *C. sophera;* the best distinction is the position of the seeds. It is a native of both Indies, and is found in this country everywhere among rubbish. The leaves, which are purgative, have a very unpleasant odour. In the West Indies the root is considered diuretic, and the leaves taken internally and applied externally, are given in cases of itch and other cutaneous diseases both to men and animals. The negroes apply the leaves smeared with grease to slight sores, as a plaster. The root is said by Martius to be beneficial in obstructions of the stomach, and in incipient dropsy.—*Wight. Lindley.*

(153) **Cassia sophera** (*Linn.*) Do.

Ponaverie, TAM. Pydee-tanghadu, TEL. Ponnam-taghera, MAL. Kulkashinda, BENG.

DESCRIPTION.—Annual; erect, branched, glabrous; leaflets 6-12 pairs, lanceolate or oblong-lanceolate, acute, with a single gland near the base of the petiole; racemes terminal or axillary, few-flowered; upper petal retuse; legumes long, linear, turgid; when immature and dried, compressed, glabrous, many-seeded; suture keeled; seeds horizontal with cellular partitions; flowers middle-sized, yellow. *Fl.* Nov.—Feb.—*W. & A. Prod.* i. 287. —Senna sophera, *Roxb. Fl. Ind.* ii. 347.—*Rheede,* ii. *t.* 52.—— Peninsula. Bengal. Assam.

MEDICAL USES.—The smell of this plant is heavy and disagreeable. The bark, when combined in the form of infusion, is given in diabetes, and the powdered seeds mixed with honey in the same. The bruised leaves and bark of the root, powdered and mixed with honey, are applied externally in ringworm and ulcers. Wight remarks, that "the legumes, when unripe and dried, appear quite flat, but when ripe and fresh are turgid and almost cylindrical; from not attending to which, this species has been split into many."—*Ainslie. Wight.*

(154) **Cassia tora** (*Linn.*) Do.

Tagara, MAL. Tageray, Tagashay, TAM. Tantipu, TEL. Chakoonda, BENG.

DESCRIPTION.—Annual, with spreading branches; leaflets 3-pairs, with a gland between the 1-2 lower pairs, but without any between the uppermost, cuneate-obovate, obtuse, glabrous or pubescent on the under side; flowers on long pedicels, upper ones forming a short terminal raceme, lower ones 1-2 together on a short axillary peduncle; upper petals obcordate; legumes very long, sharp-pointed, 4-sided, many-seeded, each suture two-grooved; flowers small, yellow. *Fl.* Oct.—Jan.—*W. & A. Prod.* i. 290.—Senna tora, *Roxb. Fl. Ind.* ii. 340, *var.* b.—C. tagera, *Lam.* (not *Linn.*)—Senna toroides, *Roxb.*—*Rheede Mal.* ii. *t.* 53.——Peninsula.

MEDICAL USES.—The leaves, which are mucilaginous and have a disagreeable odour, are given in decoction as aperients to children who suffer from fever while teething. Fried in castor-oil they are applied to ulcers: the seeds ground and mixed with buttermilk are used to allay irritation in itchy eruptions. The root rubbed with lime-juice is a good remedy for ringworm. The leaves are often employed for making warm poultices to hasten the suppuration of boils. The seeds are used in preparing a blue dye, generally fixed with lime-water. The leaves rubbed are applied to parts stung by bees.—(*Rheede. Ainslie.*) A warm remedy in gout, sciatica, and pains in the joints. The leaves are used to adulterate Senna, but are known by their wedge-shaped and ciliated margins. — *Powell's Punj. Prod.*

(155) **Cassyta filiformis** (*Linn.*) N. O. CASSYTHACEÆ.

Cottan, TAM. Kotan, DUK. Acataja-bulli, MAL. Akash-bullee, BENG. Pauneh-tiga, TEL.

DESCRIPTION.—Parasitic leafless plant; spikes lateral, ascending; calyx 3-leaved; segments very small, round; petals 3, larger than the calyx; flowers small, white, rather remote; bracteas 3-fold, embracing the fructification; fruit a drupe with a 1-seeded nut, round. *Fl.* Nov.—Dec.—*Roxb. Fl. Ind.* ii. 314.—Calodium Cochin-Chinese, *Lour.*—*Rheede,* vii. *t.* 44. ——Peninsula. Bengal. Cochin.

MEDICAL USES.—This leafless thread-like parasite is found twisting round the branches of trees in most parts of the Peninsula. It is put as a seasoning into buttermilk, and much used for this purpose by the Brahmins in Southern India. The whole plant pulverised and mixed with dry ginger and butter is used in the cleaning of inveterate ulcers. Mixed with gingely-oil it is employed in strengthening the roots of the hair. The juice of the plant mixed with sugar is occasionally applied to inflamed eyes.—*Rheede.*

(156) **Castanospermum Australe** (*Cunn.*) N. O. LEGUMINOSÆ.

Moreton Bay Chestnut, ENG.

DESCRIPTION.—Tree, 30-40 feet; leaves unequally pinnated, leaflets elliptical, ovate, acuminate, entire, smooth; flowers bright saffron-yellow, racemose; pods large, solitary, and pendulous, produced by 2-years-old wood, obtuse, rather inflated, containing 3-5 chestnut-like seeds. *Fl.* March—April.—*Hook. Bot. Misc.* i. *t.* 51, 52.——Cultivated.

ECONOMIC USES.—This elegant tree was first discovered in the forests near Moreton Bay, in Australia, and was introduced into India about thirty years ago. It grows rapidly from seed, and in its native woods attains a height of 100 feet. The shade afforded by the foliage is said to excel that of most Australian trees. The seeds are edible; when roasted they have the flavour of the Spanish chestnut, and travellers assert that Europeans who have subsisted on them have experienced no other unpleasant effect than a slight pain in the bowels, and that only when the seeds are eaten raw. They are, however, hard, astringent, and not better than acorns. The wood is used for staves for casks. There are several large trees in the Lalbagh at Bangalore.—*Hook. Bot. Misc. Cleghorn in Journ. Agri. Hort. Soc.* x. 116.

(157) **Casuarina muricata** (*Roxb.*) N. O. CASUARINACEÆ.

Casuarina, Tinian Pine, ENG. Chowk-marum, TAM. Serva-Chettoo, TEL.

DESCRIPTION.—Tree, 60 feet high; trunk straight, as in firs and pines; bark smooth, brown; branches scattered; leaves verticelled, slightly furrowed, jointed, joints ending in a cup, in which the next joint sits; stipules annular; male aments cylindric, terminating the leaves; scales 6 to 8 in a verticel, united at the base, pointed and woolly; flowers, as many as divisions in the verticel; corolla 2 opposite, boat-shaped, ciliate scales; filaments single; anthers 2-lobed. Female flowers on a different tree; aments oval, short, peduncled; scales 6 to 8 in a verticel, with a single flower between each; corolla none; germs oblong; style dividing into two long, recurved, garnet-coloured portions; stigmas simple; strobiles oval, size of a nutmeg, armed with the sharp points of the 2-valved capsule; seeds small, with a large, wedge-shaped, membranaceous wing. *Fl.* March—May.—C. litorea, *Rumph.*

Amb. iii. *t.* 57.—C. litoralis, *Salisb. Lam. Ill. t.* 746.—*Roxb. Fl. Ind.* iii. 519.

Economic Uses.—Native of the sand-hills, on the sea-side, in the province of Chittagong; and from thence sent by Dr Buchanan to the Botanic Garden, Calcutta, whence in the course of thirty years, from seed, it has been introduced all over Southern India, and grows well, with trunks 3½ feet in circumference 4 feet above ground. The timber, according to Wight, is, without exception, the strongest wood known for bearing cross strains. Its weight is a serious objection to its use for many purposes. A brown dye has been extracted from the bark by M. Jules Lepine of Pondicherry.—(*Jury. Rep. Mad. Exhib.*) It requires a light sandy soil. Its timber is the beefwood of commerce. Its growth resembles that of the larch fir. The ripe cones should be gathered before they open, and should be placed in a chatty in a dry place. After a few days the seed will be shed, and should be sown as soon as possible. The young plants, when 5 or 6 inches high, should be planted out in beds 9 inches apart; and when 2 or 3 feet high, which they ought to be in less than six months from the time of sowing, may be transplanted where required.—(*Best's Report to Bomb. Govt.* 1863.) This tree grows equally well near the coast, on the Mysore plateau, 3000 feet above the sea, and on the Neilgherries at 6000 feet, and may be propagated from seed to any extent. It grows rapidly, and, not casting much shade, would not injure crops growing near it. It is much grown for firewood, but is well adapted for rafters and building purposes. It forms very pretty avenues, especially in narrow roads.

(158) **Cathartocarpus fistula** (*Pers.*) N. O. Leguminosæ.

Pudding-pipe tree, Eng. Koannay, Tam. Choonnay, Mal. Rela, Tel. Amultas, Hind. Sonaloo, Beng.

Description.—Tree, middling size, with usually smooth bark; leaflets about 5 pairs, broadly ovate, obtuse or retuse, glabrous: petioles without glands; racemes terminal, long, lax, drooping; flowers on long pedicels; legumes cylindric, pendulous, glabrous, smooth, dark brown, nearly 2 feet in length: cells numerous, each containing 1 smooth, oval, shining seed, immersed in black pulp; flowers bright yellow, fragrant. *Fl.* May—June.—*W. & A. Prod.* i. 285.—Cassia fistula, *Linn.*—*Roxb. Fl. Ind.* ii. 333.——Peninsula.

Medical Uses.—The mucilaginous pulp which surrounds the seeds is considered a valuable laxative. It consists chiefly of sugar and gum. It enters into the composition of confection of senna. The pulp of Cassia is employed chiefly in the essence of coffee. It is gently aperient, and recommended to persons of dyspeptic habits. The flowers, which are fragrant, are given in decoction in certain stomachic affections, and the roots are said to be an excellent febrifuge. The bark and leaves rubbed up and mixed with oil are applied to pustules. Dr Irvine states that he found the root act as a strong purgative.—*Ainslie. Irvine's Top. of Ajmeer.*

ECONOMIC USES.—The bark is used for tanning, but not being very astringent is of no great value. The wood is close-grained, and when of large size is sufficient for the spars of native craft and other similar uses.—(*Ainslie.*) The *C. Roxburghii*, a beautiful tree, resembling the weeping-ash, and found on the Gingie hills, is of rare occurrence in the wild state. Its timber is hard, and handsomely marked.—*Roxb.*

(159) **Caturus spiciflorus** (*Linn.*) N. O. EUPHORBIACEÆ.

Watta-tali, MAL.

DESCRIPTION.—Shrub; leaves long-petioled, cordate, serrate; flowers axillary, spiked, pendulous, longer than the leaves; calyx 3-cleft; styles 3; capsule tricoccous.—*Roxb. Fl. Ind.* iii. 760.—Acalypha hispida, *Burm.*——Travancore.

MEDICAL USES.—The leaves, beaten up with green tobacco-leaf and infusion of rice, are usefully administered to inveterate ulcers.—(*Rheede.*) The flowers are spoken of as a specific in diarrhœa, either taken in decoction or conserve.—*Lindley.*

(160) **Cedrela toona** (*Roxb.*) N. O. CEDRELACEÆ.

Indian Mahogany, White Cedar, ENG. Toon-marum, TAM. Toona, HIND. Toon, BENG.

DESCRIPTION.—Tree, 60 feet; leaves abruptly pinnate; leaflets 6-12 pairs, ovate-lanceolate, acuminated, slightly undulated on the margins, quite entire or slightly and distinctly toothed, glabrous; calyx small, 5-cleft; petals 5, ciliated; panicles drooping, terminal; capsule oblong, 5-celled; dehiscent; flowers small, white, fragrant. *Fl.* May—June.—*W. & A. Prod.* i. 124.—*Roxb. Fl. Ind.* i. 635.—*Corom.* iii. *t.* 238.—*Wight Icon. t.* 161.——Peninsula. Bengal.

MEDICAL USES.—The bark is powerfully astringent, and has been found a good remedy in remittent and intermittent fevers, diarrhœa, and dysentery, and, though not bitter, is a fair substitute for Peruvian bark, particularly when united with powdered Bonduc nut. Powdered and applied externally it has been beneficially used in the treatment of ulcers. Rumphius states that an infusion of this bark in combination with the root of the *Acorus calamus* (*Vussamboo*) is given in Java in fevers and other complaints. Forster considered it especially useful in bilious fevers and inveterate diarrhœa arising from atony of the muscular fibre.—*Ainslie.*

ECONOMIC USES.—The wood of this tree is very like mahogany, but lighter, and not so close in the grain. It is much used for furniture and various other purposes. It is usually found in dry deciduous forests up to 4000 feet elevation. It is called *Suli* and *Mali* in the Salem district, *Kal Killingi* on the Neilgherry slopes, and *Sandaru Vembu* in Tinnevelly. It is often used as an avenue tree, especially in the Salem district, as it grows readily from seed. In Assam excellent boats are made from it. Nees von Esenbeck analysed the bark, which indicated the existence of a resinous astringent matter, a brown astringent gum, and a gummy brown extractive matter resembling ulmine. The flowers are used in Mysore for dyeing cotton a beautiful red.—(*Roxb. Bedd. Fl. Sylv. t.* 10.) The wood is dense, red, hard, close-grained, capable of high polish, not subjected to worms, nor liable to warp, and durable.—*Powell's Punj. Prod.*

(161) **Celastrus paniculata** (*Willd.*) N. O. CELASTRACEÆ.

Staff-tree, ENG. Valuluvy, TAM. Bavungie, TEL. Malkunganee, HIND.

DESCRIPTION.—Climbing shrub, unarmed; young shoots and flower-bearing branches pendulous; leaves alternate, broadly oval, or ovate, or obovate, usually with a sudden short acumination, slightly serrated, glabrous; racemes terminal, compound or supra-decompound, elongated, much longer than the uppermost leaves; petals 5; calyx 5-partite; lobes rounded, ciliated; capsule globose, 3-celled, 3-6 seeded; seeds with a complete arillus; flowers small, greenish. *Fl.* March—May.—*W. & A. Prod.* i. 158.—*Wight Icon. t.* 150.—*Roxb. Fl. Ind.* i. 621.—C. nutans, *Roxb. Fl. Ind.* i. 623.——Neilgherries. Hilly parts of the Concans. Dheyra Dhoon.

MEDICAL USES.—The seeds yield an empyreumatic oil (Oleum nigrum) used in lamps. It is said to be of a stimulant nature, and is used medicinally, having been found a successful remedy in beriberi. The seeds, owing to a resinous principle, have a very hot and biting taste. Royle says the oil is a stimulant and useful medicine. It is of a deep scarlet colour. It is administered in doses of a few drops daily in emulsion.—(*Royle. Malcolmson.*) The oil is principally used for horses; also for rheumatism and paralysis. It acts as a powerful diaphoretic and tonic. The oil is made by putting the seeds with benzoin, cloves, nutmegs, and mace into a perforated earthen pot, and then obtaining by distillation into another pot below a black empyreumatic oil.—*Powell's Punj. Prod.*

(162) **Celsia Coromandeliana** (*Vahl.*) N. O. Scrophulariaceæ.

Kukshima, Beng.

Description.—Herbaceous, pubescent, viscid; radical leaves lyrate, upper ones oblong-ovate or orbiculate, toothed; sepals 5, ovate or oblong, entire or serrated; racemes sub-panicled, peduncles longer than the calyx; flowers largish, yellow; filaments bearded with purple hairs. *Fl.* Dec.—Jan.—*Vahl. Symb.* iii. 79.—*Dec. Prod.* x. 246.—*Roxb. Fl. Ind.* iii. 100.—*Hook. Jour. Bot.* i. *t.* 129.——Waste places in the Deccan. Banks of rivers and still waters.

Medical Uses.—Often found as a common weed in gardens. The inspissated juice of the leaves has been prescribed in cases of acute and chronic dysentery with considerable success. Its action appears to be that of a sedative and astringent.—(*Pharm. of India.*) A species of this order possessing medicinal properties is the *Picrorrhiza kurroo* (*Royle Illust. t.* 71). Its root is very bitter, and is employed by the natives. Dr Irvine (*Mat. Med. Patna,* 38) assigns *Kootki* as its Hindustani name, and mentions its use as a tonic.

(163) **Celtis orientalis** (*Linn.*) N. O. Ulmaceæ.

Indian Nettle-tree, Eng. Mallam-toddali, Mal. Chakan Tubunna, Beng.

Description.—Small tree, 15 feet; leaves alternate, bifarious, short-petioled, ovate-cordate, acuminated, minutely serrated, scabrous above, villous underneath; flowers axillary, aggregated on short 2-cleft diverging peduncles; calyx 5-parted; male and female flowers generally on a separate tree; drupe small, succulent, black when ripe, nut wrinkled, 1-celled, 1-seeded; flowers very small, green. *Fl.* Nearly all the year.—*Wight Icon. t.* 602.—*Roxb. Fl. Ind.* ii. 65.—*Rheede,* iv. *t.* 40.——Coromandel. Bengal. Travancore.

Economic Uses.—This tree is common in most parts of India, and is in blossom the greater part of the year. It yields a gum resembling that of the cherry-tree. The inner bark, consisting of numerous reticulated fibres, forms a kind of natural cloth used by certain tribes in Assam. The leaves are used for polishing horns.—*Royle's Fibrous Plants of India,* 313. *Roxb.*

(164) **Cerbera odollam** (*Gærtn.*) N. O. APOCYNACEÆ.

Odallam, MAL. Caat-aralie, TAM.

DESCRIPTION.—Tree, 20 feet; leaves alternate, lanceolate, approximate, shining; calyx 5-cleft, segments revolute; corymbs terminal; segments of corolla sub-falcate; stigma large and conical, 2-cleft at the apex, resting on a saucer-shaped receptacle, the circumference fluted with 10 grooves; flowers large, white, fragrant; fruit a drupe as large as a mango. *Fl.* Nearly all the year.—*Roxb. Fl. Ind.* i. 692.—*Wight Icon.* ii. *t.* 441.—C. manghas, *Sims. Bot. Mag.* 43, *t.* 1844 (not *Linn.*)—*Rheede*, i. *t.* 39.——Salt swamps in Malabar.

ECONOMIC USES.—The wood is remarkably spongy and white. The fleshy drupe is harmless, but the nut is narcotic and even poisonous, and the bark is purgative. The trees are very common along the banks of the canals in Travancore, and may easily be known by their large green fruits like a mango. The natives in Travancore occasionally employ the fruit to kill dogs. To effect this it is first toasted and then covered with sugar or any sweet substance. The result is to loosen and destroy all the teeth, which are said to fall out after chewing the fleshy part of the drupe. In Java the leaves are used as a substitute for senna.—*Ainslie. Lindley. Beng. Disp.*

(165) **Chavica betle** (*Miq.*) N. O. PIPERACEÆ.

Betle-leaf Pepper, ENG. Vetta, MAL. Vettilee, TAM. Pan, BENG. Tamalapakoo, TEL.

DESCRIPTION.—Shrubby, scandent, rooting, branches striated; leaves membranaceous, or the adult ones coriaceous, shining above, glabrous on both sides; the inferior ones ovate, broadly cordate, equal-sided; slightly unequally cordate, or rounded at the base, 5-6-nerved; catkins peduncled; male ones long, slender, patulous or deflexed; female deflexed, shorter, long-peduncled.—*Wight Icon. t.* 1926.—Piper betle, *Linn.*—*Roxb. Fl. Ind.* i. 158.—*Rheede*, vii. *t.* 15.——Cultivated.

MEDICAL USES.—The leaves in conjunction with lime are masticated by all classes of natives, and for this purpose the plant is extensively cultivated. The juice of the leaves is regarded as a valuable stomachic. In catarrhal and pulmonary affection, especially of children, the leaves warmed and smeared with oil are applied in layers over the chest. They thus afford great relief to coughs and difficulty of breathing. A similar application has afforded marked relief in congestion and other affections of the liver. The leaves simply warmed and applied in layers to the breasts will arrest the secretion of milk. They are similarly employed as a resolvent to glandular swellings.—(*Pharm. of India.*) Dr Elliott of Colombo has observed several cases of cancer, which, from its peculiar characteristics, he has designated the Betle-chewer's cancer.

Economic Uses.—The leaf is chewed by the natives mixed with chunam and the nut of the Areca palm. It has been found wild in the island of Java, which is probably its native country. Marco Polo writes: "The natives of India in general are addicted to the custom of having continually in their mouths the leaf called 'tem-bul;' which they do partly from habit, and partly from the gratification it affords. Upon chewing it they spit out the saliva which it occasions. Persons of rank have the leaf prepared with camphor and other aromatic drugs, and also with a mixture of quicklime. I have been told that it is conducive to health. It is capable, however, of producing intoxicating effects, like some other species of Pepper, and should be used in moderation." In Travancore it is extensively cultivated, but only sufficient for home consumption. It is planted in rows, requires a moist situation and a rather rich soil. The leaves should not be plucked indiscriminately at all seasons, as this is apt to destroy the plant.—*Lindley. Ainslie.*

(166) **Chavica Roxburghii** (*Miq.*) Do.

Long Pepper, Eng. Tipilie, Tam. Pipuloo, Tel. Pipel, Peepla-mool, Hind. Cutta Terpali, Mal. Pipool, Beng.

Description.—Stem somewhat shrubby, the sterile ones decumbent, the floriferous ones ascending, dichotomously branched, at first slightly downy, afterwards glabrous; inferior leaves long-petioled, ovate, roundish, broadly cordate, acute or obtuse, 7-nerved; upper ones short-petioled; top ones sessile, embracing the stems, oblong, unequally cordate, 5-nerved, all thick, membranaceous; petioles and nerves beneath, especially near the base, finely downy, afterwards glabrous; male catkins filiform, cylindrical, with the peduncle as long as the leaves; female ones thicker, less than half that length, about the length of the peduncle.—*Wight Icon. t.* 1928.—Piper longum, *Linn.* —*Roxb. Fl. Ind.* i. 154.—*Rheede,* vii. *t.* 14.——Banks of watercourses. Circar mountains. South Concans. Bengal.

Medical Uses.—This plant is extensively cultivated; the female catkins dried form the long Pepper of the shops. "I have never," says Wight, "met with it except in gardens, and then only as single plants." It is readily propagated by cuttings. The stems are annual, but the roots live several years; and when cultivated, usually yield three or four crops, after which they seem to become exhausted, and require to be renewed by fresh planting. The berries of this species of Pepper are lodged in a pulpy matter like those of *P. nigrum*. They are at first green, becoming red when ripe. Being hotter when unripe, they are then gathered and dried in the sun, when they change to a dark-grey colour. The spikes are imported entire. The taste of the berries is pungent, though rather faint. On the Coromandel coast the natives prescribe the berries in an infusion mixed with honey for catarrhal affections. The roots are given by natives in palsy, tetanus, and apoplexy. These and the thickest parts of the stem are cut into small pieces and dried, and much used for medical purposes. The berries have nearly the same chemical composition and properties as the black Pepper, and are said to contain piperine.—(*Wight. Ainslie. Lindley.*) The root is in great repute among the natives. It is called *Peepla-mool* in the Taleef-Shereef, where it is described as bitter, stomachic, and producing digestion. In Travancore an infusion of the root is prescribed after parturition, with the view of causing expulsion of the placenta.—*Pharm. of India.*

(167) **Chickrassia tabularis** (*Ad. Juss.*) N. O. CEDRELACEÆ.

Chittagong wood, ENG. Aglay Marum, TAM. Chikrassee, BENG.

DESCRIPTION.—Tree; calyx short, 5-toothed; petals 5, erect; leaves abruptly pinnated; leaflets 5-8 pair, nearly opposite, obliquely ovate-oblong, unequal-sided, obtusely acuminated, quite entire, more or less conspicuous, hairy in the axils of the nerves beneath; panicles terminal, erect; capsule ovoid, 3-celled, 3-valved, dehiscent, septifragal; stamen-tube subcylindrical, rather shorter than the petals, striated, with 10 short antheriferous teeth; seeds numerous, expanding downwards into a wing, and imbricated in a double series across the cells; flowers large, greenish white. *Fl.* April—May.—*W. & A. Prod.* i. 123.—*Ill.* i. *t.* 76.—Swietenia chickrassia, *Roxb. Fl. Ind.* ii. 399.——Chittagong. Dindigul hills.

ECONOMIC USES.—The wood is one of those known as the Chittagong wood, and is very close-grained, light-coloured, and elegantly veined. It is employed much by cabinetmakers for furniture. The bark is powerfully astringent, though not bitter.—*Roxb. Jury Rep. Mad. Exhib.*

(168) **Chloroxylon swietenia** (*Dec.*) Do.

Satin-wood tree, ENG. Moodooda, Vum-maay, Kodawahporsh, TAM. Billo Billuda, TEL.

DESCRIPTION.—Tree; leaves abruptly pinnate; leaflets pale-coloured, small, numerous, alternate or nearly opposite, unequal-sided; calyx short, 5-partite; petals 5, shortly unguiculate; panicles terminal, branched; capsule oblong, 3-celled, 3-valved, dehiscing from the apex, septifragal; seeds about 4 in each cell, extending upwards into a wing; flowers small, greenish white. *Fl.* March—April.—*W. & A. Prod.* i. 123.—Swietenia chloroxylon, *Roxb. Cor.* i. *t.* 64.—*Fl. Ind.* ii. 400.——Circars. Mountainous districts of the Peninsula.

Economic Uses.—The wood, which is of a yellow or light-orange colour like box, is close-grained. It is durable, and will stand immersion in water. It is used for naves of wheels in the gun-carriage manufactory at Madras. Though not a tree of large size, planks of 12 or 15 inches broad may be obtained from it. It is very suitable for picture-frames, and if well varnished will preserve its handsome appearance for a long time. Satin-wood takes a fine polish, but is apt to split. It yields a wood oil.—*Roxb. Jury Rep. Mad. Exhib.*
At Paradenia, a bridge of a single arch 205 feet in span, chiefly constructed of Satin-wood, crosses the Mahawalliganga river. In point of size and durability it is by far the first of the timber-trees of Ceylon. All the forests round Batticaloa and Trincomalee are thickly set with this valuable tree. It grows to the height of 100 feet, with a rugged grey bark. Owing to the difficulty of carrying its heavy beams, the natives only cut it near the banks of rivers, down which it is floated to the coast, whence large quantities are exported to every part of the colony. The richly-coloured and feathery logs are used for cabinet-work, the more ordinary for building purposes, every house in the eastern provinces being floored and timbered with Satin-wood.—(*Tennent's Ceylon*, i. 43, 116.) The true mahogany-tree (*Swietenia Mahogani*) was introduced into India in 1866, and thrives exceedingly well in the lower provinces of Bengal. It was considered that its culture might be extended with great advantage in Lower Bengal, Assam, and Chittagong.

(169) **Chrysanthellum Indicum** (*Dec.*) N. O. Compositæ.

David's Flower, Eng.

Description.—Annual, herbaceous, very small, glabrous; branchlets somewhat naked, 1-headed at the apex; leaves of different shapes, radical ones oval, cuneate at the base, upper ones oblong-linear, 3-toothed at the apex; achænia somewhat compressed, very shortly emarginate at the apex, callous at the margin, at one place smooth and level, at another convex and striated; flowers bright yellow.—*Dec. Prod.* v. 631.——Sukanaghur.

MEDICAL USES.—This plant is considered by the natives heating and aperient, and useful in affections of the brain and calculus, and also to remove depression of spirits.—*(Powell's Punj. Prod.)* A plant of the same family, the *Chrysanthemum Roxburghii* (*Desv.*), is common in gardens throughout India. The flowers, when dried, form a tolerable substitute for chamomile. The root, when chewed, communicates a tingling sensation to the tongue as pellitory, and might be used as a substitute. The natives in the Deccan administer the plant, in conjunction with black pepper, in gonorrhœa.—*Dalz. Bomb. Flora. Pharm. of Ind.*

(170) **Cicca Disticha** (*Linn.*) N. O. EUPHORBIACEÆ.

Country Gooseberry, ENG. Arunelli, TAM. Nelli, MAL. Harfarcorie, HIND. Nubaree, BENG. Rassa useriki, TEL.

DESCRIPTION.—Small tree; calyx 4-parted; leaves pinnated, 1-2 feet long, often flower-bearing; leaflets numerous, alternate, stalked, nearly orbicular, 1-3 inches long; petioles round, smooth, sometimes ending in a short raceme of male flowers; racemes numerous, terminal, axillary, and from the old buds on the naked branches; flowers numerous, small, reddish, in globular heads; drupe 3-4 lobed, grooved, size of gooseberry *Fl.* May.—*Lindl. Flor. Med.*—*Roxb. Fl. Ind.* iii. 672.—Averrhoa acida, *Linn.*—*Rheede,* iii. *t.* 47, 48.——Cultivated in gardens.

MEDICAL USES.—The leaves are sudorific. The round succulent fruit is subacid, and is eaten raw, or pickled and preserved. The seeds are cathartic. The root is violently purgative, and a decoction of the leaves diaphoretic.—*Lindley.*

(171) **Cicendia hyssopifolia** (*Adans.*) N. O. GENTIANACEÆ.

Chota-chiretta, HIND. Chevukurti, Golimidi, Nella-gullie, TEL. Vallarugu, TAM. Kirota, BENG.

DESCRIPTION.—Annual, herbaceous; stem quadrangular, angles slightly winged; leaves opposite, decussate, linear-lanceolate, tapering at the base, embracing the stem with the short petioles, 3-nerved, paler below; calyx 5-cleft; segments margined, reflexed at the point, permanent, closely embracing the base of the mature capsule; corolla tubular, 5-cleft; segments spreading, oblique at the base, remaining attached to the capsule till the latter bursts; flowers 6-8 together in axillary whorls, sessile, white; capsule 2-valved, 1-celled;

seeds numerous, small, round, small white. *Fl.* July—Sept. —*W. & A.*—*Lindl. Flor. Med.* 520.—Gentiana hyssopifolia, *Linn.*—Exacum hyssopifolium, *Willd.*—*Roxb. Fl. Ind.* ii. 71. ——Moist uncultivated grounds. Coromandel. Banks of the Jumna.

Medical Uses.—The whole plant is very bitter. It is used as a tonic in recovery from fevers, and is a substitute for gentian. It is reckoned a good stomachic, and is administered either in powder or decoction.—*Wight. Lindley.*

(172) **Cicer arietinum** (*Linn.*) N. O. Leguminosæ.

Common Chick-pea, Bengal gram, Eng. Kadala, Mal. Kadalay, Tam. Sanagaloo, Tel. Chenna, Hind. Boot-kaley, Chuna, Beng.

Description.—Herbaceous, annual plant; calyx 5-lobed, scarcely gibbous, segment as long as the alæ of the corolla; leaves unequally pinnated; leaflets ovate, serrated, equal; stipules lanceolate, somewhat toothed; corolla papilionaceous; flowers axillary, bluish purple; legumes hairy. *Fl.* Sept.—Oct.—*W. & A. Prod.* i. 235.—*Roxb. Fl. Ind.* iii. 324.—*Wight Icon. t.* 20.——Cultivated.

Medical Uses.—This plant is employed by the natives as a refrigerant in fevers. In the Deccan it is used by the Portuguese in the treatment of dysmenorrhœa; the fresh plant is put into hot water, and the patient sits over the steam.—(*Pharm. of India.*) The free use of the vegetable, owing to the abundance of oxalic acid, is apt to do harm to persons liable to calculus, as it leads to the formation of oxalate of lime in the bladder. It is said to increase the biliary secretions. When roasted like coffee it is reckoned aphrodisial, and is also used in flatulency, dysuria, and catamenia. —*Powell's Punj. Prod. Christison in Mad. Journ. Sc.* No. 13.

Economic Uses.—In Mysore the natives spread a cloth over the young plants to catch the early dew; they then rinse it out in a vessel, when the extract becomes acid, and makes a pleasant beverage mixed with water. Dr Christie mentions that an acid (oxalic acid) exudes from all parts of the plant, which is collected by the ryots and used in their curries instead of vinegar. The seeds are eaten by the natives in curries, cakes, &c. They are very fattening to cattle. It is said that in Europe, when people walk through the fields where this plant grows, the leather of their shoes becomes spoiled by the acid.—*Lindley.*

(173) **Cinchona officinalis** (*Linn.*) N. O. Rubiaceæ.

Description.—Tree; leaves oblong, acuminated at both

ends, glabrous, shining, scrobiculate beneath at the axils of the nerves; limb of the corolla woolly; capsules ovate, twice longer than their breadth; stipules leafy, free, deciduous; flowers terminal, in corymbose panicles, tube red, petals snow-white above; bark ashy.—*Dec. Prod.* iv. 352.——Cultivated on mountain-lands.

Medical Uses.—Several species of Cinchona are now so extensively cultivated on the highlands of the North-West Provinces, the lower slopes of the Himalaya, and especially on the Neilgherry hills and Ceylon, and the bark has become of late years so important in a commercial point of view, that the plants amply deserve notice in this work.

It was not before 1859 that any successful results attended the introduction of the Cinchona into India. So far back as 1835 the Indian Government had been fully alive to the great importance of its introduction; but for various reasons the efforts were abortive. At last the purchase of quinine became so great, and had amounted annually to about £12,000, that it was determined to select a person to proceed purposely to the Cinchona countries in South America to bring some live plants for cultivation on the Neilgherry hills. Mr Clements Markham, being eminently qualified for the duty, was chosen. The experiment succeeded almost beyond expectation; and in 1860 a great number of plants and seeds had been sent to the hills, where their proper cultivation at once commenced, establishments being at the same time provided in Sikkim and Ceylon. The culture everywhere prospered. Vast numbers of plants have been raised from seeds and cuttings; and the yield of alkalies is now as great as, or greater than, in the native country of the plant. Early in 1867 there were nearly two million plants in the Government plantations on the Neilgherries, and the total area under actual cultivation was 677 acres. Besides this, private plantations have been formed in most of the habitable hill districts of the Peninsula, including Travancore; also at Darjeeling, at Kangra in the Punjaub, and on the Mahableshwar hills in Bombay.

The results of the cultivation of all the species of known value up to 1867 were communicated by Mr Markham in an interesting summary published in the appendix to the Pharmacopœia of India. (See Appendix B.) Since that time the cultivation and produce have continued steadily to increase. In a communication to the author, Mr Markham writes that a cheap Cinchona febrifuge medicine manufactured at the plantations on the Neilgherries is very nearly as efficacious as quinine, and the natives are taking to its use very readily. Five hundred and thirteen cases have been successfully treated in the hospitals with it. Eventually the plantations on the Neilgherries alone will yield 1300 lb. of this preparation annually, at about eight annas (= one shilling) per ounce.

The quantity used in the cases recently treated amounted to 43 grains each.

During the last five years the annual average consumption of English-made quinine in the Madras Presidency has been nearly 400 lb., and there will be a yearly increase. The cost of 400 lb. of quinine has been Rs. 16,400. The cost of the same quantity of the febrifuge preparation made at the Neilgherry plantations by Mr Broughton would be less than Rs. 4400, thereby effecting a saving of Rs. 12,000 a-year. For European quinine manufacture the bark of *C. officinalis* is admirably suited, as it is so rich in quinine. In addition, it is so easy to work, and the sulphate of quinine crystallises with greater readiness and purity. It is especially the bark for export to Europe, though perhaps in total yield the *C. succirubra* is the richest. After those two, perhaps, the *C. calisaya* is the most important at present. The following table shows at a glance the different species cultivated in India, their commercial names, and London market value :—

Species.	Botanical names.	Commercial names.	Value per lb. of dry bark in the London market.
1	C. succirubra	Red bark	2s. 6d. to 8s. 9d.
2	C. calisaya } C. frutex } C. Vera }	Yellow bark	2s. 10d. to 7s. 0d.
3	C. officinalis		
	A. Uritusinga	Original Loxa bark	2s. 10d. to 7s. 0d.
	B. Condaminea	Select crown bark	2s. 10d. to 7s. 0d.
	C. Crispa	Fine crown bark	2s. 10d. to 6s. 0d.
4	C. lancifolia	Pitayo bark	1s. 8d. to 2s. 10d.
5	C. nitida	Genuine grey bark	1s. 8d. to 2s. 9d.
6	C. sp. (no name)	Fine grey bark	1s. 8d. to 2s. 10d.
7	C. micrantha	Grey bark	1s. 8d. to 2s. 9d.
8	C. Perusiana	Finest grey bark	1s. 8d. to 2s. 10d.
9	C. Pahudiana	Unknown	Unknown

All the species are planted out on cleared forest-land or on grass-land, in both which places they thrive. They invariably grow best under full exposure to light and air; therefore, prior to being planted on forest-land, it is necessary to clear away the whole of the original forest. No diminution of water in the stream takes place by the felling of forest-trees; on the contrary, recent observations tend to prove that an increase of water takes place when the upper growth of trees is removed. It is usual to cover the outer bark of the trees with moss, as it prevents waste. By this simple discovery, the bulk of the bark is more than doubled, making the direct yield of alkaloid per acre fully thirty times the quantity that can be procured under any other treatment. Besides, mossing saves any damage that would otherwise be done to the plant. By mossing every twelve or eighteen months, the entire cellular bark of the stem can be removed easily and without injury.—*M'Ivor's Reports.*

The seeds begin to germinate about the sixteenth day after sowing, and from one ounce of seeds from 20,000 to 25,000 plants are obtained. No species can be successfully grown under the shade of other trees. The *C. calisaya* may require a certain degree of shade; but this can only be secured by placing the plants close together, so that they may shade each other, leaving the robust ultimately to destroy the weaker in the struggle for light and space. Neither can the different species be grown together, as the luxuriant-growing species injure and ultimately destroy the weaker. The total number of Cinchona plants propagated on the Neilgherries from May 1866 was nearly 1,123,645, exclusive of 100,757 distributed to the public.*—*Government Records. M'Ivor's Reports.*

The powerful tonic and astringent properties of quinine are well known. Quinia is procured from the bark, and is administered in every kind of fever. The properties and uses of all species are the same. The leaves have also been found to contain tonic and mildly anti-periodic properties. Various trials have been made with them; and it has been ascertained that although they will not supply a material for the extraction of quinine, yet they will prove very useful, when used fresh in decoction or infusion, for the cure of the fevers of the country. In mild uncomplicated cases it proved useful, like many other astringent tonics, but in no way comparable to quinine as an anti-periodic. But, besides in fevers, quinine is employed in croup, hooping-cough, ophthalmia, erysipelas, dysentery, and diarrhœa, and many other complaints. In fact, with the exception of opium, no single remedy has a wider range of therapeutic uses than quinine.—*Pharm. of India.*

It remains to add that the present species has variously been called *C. condaminea*, *C. uritusinga*, *C. academica*, and *C. lancifolia;* but Dr Hooker gives reasons for retaining Linnæus's original name of *C. officinalis*, the first change of which (because many species are truly officinal, and may be substituted the one for the other) being, he maintains, made on insufficient grounds.

(174) Cinnamomum iners (*Reinw.*) N. O. Lauraceæ.

Wild Cinnamon, Eng. Darchini, Hind. Kàt-carua, Mal. Cuddoo-lavanga, Can.

Description.—Small tree; leaves coriaceous, oval or oblong, nearly equally attenuated at both ends, usually 3-nerved, almost veinless, lateral nerves nearly reaching the apex, shining and glabrous above, glaucous beneath; panicles equalling

* For further information on Cinchona cultivation, &c., see Appendix B.

or exceeding the leaves, slender, peduncled, lax, branchlets 3-flowered, and with the flowers equalling the pedicel; lobes of the calyx falling off at the middle. *Fl.* Jan.—March.—*Dec. Prod.* xv. s. i. 20.—C. nitidum, *Hook. Exot. Fl.*—C. eucalyptoides, *Nees in Wall. Pl. As. Rar.*—C. Rauwolfii, *Blume.*—*Wight Icon. t.* 122.—*Rheede,* i. *t.* 57.——Peninsula. Concans. Malabar.

Medical Uses.—The seeds, bruised and mixed with honey or sugar, are given to children in dysentery and coughs, and combined with other ingredients in fevers. The leaves have a pleasant aromatic smell when bruised. It is supposed to have furnished the cassia of the ancients. The natives use the bark as a condiment in their curries. The tree is very common in the jungles on the western coast and Travancore forests.—(*J. Grah. Nimmo.*) The inner bark possesses, in the fresh state, a powerful aromatic odour and taste, and by careful preparation is capable of affording cassia lignea of good quality. The dried buds are employed by the natives in Travancore, with various combinations, in diarrhœa, dysentery, and coughs. They partake of the carminative properties of Cinnamon and Cassia. At the recommendation of Dr Æ. Ross, the Bombay Government now farms out these trees in North Canara, by means of which a very considerable addition has been made to the revenue. It may be used as a substitute for cinnamon, to which it can hardly be reckoned inferior.—*Pharm. of India.*

(175) **Cissampelos Pareira** (*Willd.*) N. O. Menispermaceæ.

Dukh-nirbisee, Hind.

Description.—Twining; stem pubescent; leaves cordate, usually obtuse or acute, rarely emarginate, sinus narrow or wide, upper side glabrous or slightly pubescent, under more or less pubescent, or even tomentose; petioles inserted at the margin; male racemes 3-4, shorter than the petioles; sepals orbicular, unguiculate; column of stamens longer than the entire and externally hairy cup-shaped corolla; female racemes usually in pairs, sometimes solitary and forked; in flower scarcely so long as, in fruit often longer than, the leaf; drupes hairy; flowers very small, yellowish. *Fl.* April—Aug.—*W. & A. Prod.* i. 14.—*Roxb. Fl. Ind.* iii. 842.——Common in hedges. Peninsula. Rajmahal. Nepaul.

Medical Uses.—The dried root is at first sweetish and aromatic, and afterwards becomes intensely bitter. It is employed as a mild tonic and diuretic.—*Pharm. of India.*

(176) **Citrullus Colocynthis** (*Schrad.*) N. O. CUCURBITACEÆ.

Colocynth or Bitter Apple, ENG. Peycommuttee, MAL. Paycoomuti, Varriecoomuttie, TAM. Putsa-kaya, TEL. Makhal, BENG. Indrawan, DUK.

DESCRIPTION.—Annual; stems scabrous; leaves smooth above, muricate beneath, with small white tubercles, many-cleft, obtuse-lobed; tendrils short; female flowers solitary; calyx, tube globose and hispid; fruits globose, glabrous, streaked; flowers yellow. *Fl.* July—September.—Cucumis colocynthis, *Linn.—W. & A. Prod.* i. 342.—*Roxb. Fl. Ind.* iii. 179.—*Wight Icon. t.* 498.——Peninsula. Lower India in sandy plantations.

MEDICAL USES.—The Colocynth plant is properly a native of Turkey, but has long been naturalised in India. The medullary part of the fruit, freed from the rinds and seeds, is alone made use of in medicine. It is very bitter to the taste. The seeds are perfectly bland and highly nutritious, and constitute an important article of food in Africa, especially at the Cape of Good Hope. The extract of Colocynth is one of the most powerful and useful of cathartics. The juice of the fruit when fresh, mixed with sugar, is given in dropsy, and is externally applied to discoloration of the skin. A bitter and poisonous principle called Colocynthine resides in the fruit, the incautious use of which has frequently proved fatal. An oil is extracted from the seeds, used in lamps. Before exportation to Europe, the rind is generally removed from the fruit. In medicine its chief uses are for constipation and the removal of visceral obstructions at the commencement of fevers and other inflammatory complaints.—*Ainslie. Lindley, Flor. Med.*

Sheep, goats, jackals, and rats eat Colocynth apples readily, and with no bad effects. They are often used as food for horses in Scindè, cut in pieces, boiled, and exposed to the cold winter nights. They are made into preserves with sugar, having previously been pierced all over with knives, and then boiled in six or seven waters, until all the bitterness disappears. The low Gypsy castes eat the kernel of the seed, freed from the seed-skin by a slight roasting.—*Stocks in Lond. Journ. Bot.* iii. 76.

(177) **Citrus aurantium** (*Linn.*) N. O. AURANTIACEÆ.

Sweet Orange, ENG. Kitchlee, TAM. Kichilie, TEL. Naringee, HIND. Kumlaneboo, BENG.

DESCRIPTION.—Tree, 20-25 feet; spines axillary, solitary; young shoots glabrous; leaves oval, elongated, acute, sometimes slightly toothed; petioles more or less dilated and winged; flowers white, large; fruit orange-coloured, roundish or ovoid, usually depressed, rarely terminated by a small knob; rind with convex vesicles of oil; pulp sweet. *Fl.* Feb. —*W. & A. Prod.* i. 97.—*Roxb. Fl. Ind.* iii. 392.——Circars. Aurungabad. Cultivated.

Medical Uses.—It has been remarked that the Orange is a rare instance of a plant having at once beautiful foliage, fragrant flowers, and nourishing fruit. India and China are the native countries of the Sweet Orange. Dr Royle found two plants having the character of the lemon and citron, growing wild in the forest at the base of the Himalaya. He has also stated that a kind of lime grows in the jungles at Rungpore. The Orange is indigenous in Silhet and on the slopes of the Neilgherry mountains.

There are several varieties cultivated in India. Those of Sautgur, near Vellore, are much esteemed. The Mandarin Orange has a large loose skin, and is found in the Northern Circars, where it is called *Cumbla nabla.* The large China Orange (*Burra chin*) is a fine smooth-skinned and sweet kind. Another species has the skin very rough, and is called the Caffrie Orange, a sweet and pleasant-tasted fruit. The common Orange of the country, called *Koda* in Hindoostanee and *Kitchlee* in Tamil, is of an indifferent flavour. The Hindoo Vytians think that Oranges are great purifiers of the blood and improve the appetite. The rind is well known as a useful carminative, and a valuable addition to bitter infusions in cases of dyspepsia. Oranges are used to form various perfumes and pomades, and the flowers distilled produce orange-water, used in cooking, medicine, and as a perfume; but the chief use of the Sweet Orange is for the dessert. Every part of the ripe fruit is used either in diet or medicine. It is invaluable in scurvy. The rind pulverised and added to magnesia and rhubarb affords a grateful tonic to the stomach in gout and dyspepsia. The roasted pulp is an excellent application to fœtid ulcers.—(*Ainslie. Royle.*) Dr Royle remarks: "So great a diversity of opinion being entertained regarding the different plants of the genus *Citrus*, whether they should constitute species or varieties, it becomes difficult to say what are such if only seen in a state of cultivation; but as some are still found wild, an opinion may be formed at least respecting those. In the valleys within the Himalaya I have seen two plants growing apparently wild—one called *Bijouree*, the other *Beharee nimboo*—the first having the characteristics of the citron, and the other, called also *Peharee ka guzee*, those of the lemon. Both, when transferred to gardens, retain their peculiar characters. Mr Saunders, who accompanied Captain Turner in his travels in Thibet, states that he found the wild Oranges delicious, and that many orange-trees and lime-trees were found at the foot of the hills approaching Buxendwar.—(*Turner's Thibet*, p. 20, 387.) *Citrus decumanus*, the shaddock or pumplemoose, does not appear indigenous to India, as its name, *Batavi nimboo*, or Batavian lime, denotes, as remarked by Dr Roxburgh, it being an exotic; and as it retains its characteristics even where it does not succeed as a fruit, it may also be reckoned as a distinct species. I feel therefore inclined to consider as distinct species the orange, lemon, lime, citron, and shaddock, without being able to say whether the sweet kinds should be considered varieties of the acid or ranked as distinct species."—(*Royle Him. Bot.*) The most full information on this difficult genus is contained in Risso's work on 'The Natural History of Orange-Trees,' lately translated by Lady Reid.

(178) **Citrus bergamia** (*Risso*). Do.

Bergamotte or Acid Lime, Eng. Eroomitchee-narracum, Mal. Elemitchum, Tam. Nemma Pundoo, Tel. Neemboo, Hind. Neboo, Beng.

Description.—Shrub or small tree; leaves oblong, more or less elongated, acute or obtuse, under side somewhat pale; petioles more or less winged or margined; flowers usually small, white; fruit pale yellow, pyriform or depressed; rind with vesicles of fragrant oil; pulp more or less acid. *Fl.* April—May.—*W. & A. Prod.* i. 98.—Citrus acida, *Roxb. Fl. Ind.* iii. 390.——Peninsula. Bengal.

Medical Uses.—Lime-juice is much used in medicine by native practitioners. They consider it to possess virtues in checking bilious vomiting, and to be refrigerant and antiseptic. It probably possesses all the virtues attributed to the lemon. An essence much used by perfumers is prepared from the flowers and fruit.—*Ainslie.*

(179) **Citrus limonum** (*Risso*). Do.

Lemon, Eng. Korna Neboo, Beng.

Description.—Small tree; young branches flexible; leaves oval-oblong, usually toothed; petioles simply margined; flowers white tinged with red, fragrant. *Fl.* March—May.—*W. & A. Prod.* i. 98.—C. medica, *Roxb. Fl. Ind.* iii. 392.——Foot of the Himalaya.

Medical Uses.—The useful parts of the Lemon are the juice and the rind of the fruit, and the volatile oil of the outer rind. The juice of Lemons is analogous to that of the orange, from which it only differs in containing more citric acid and less syrup. The quantity of the former is indeed so great that the acid has been named from the fruit, acid of Lemons, and is always prepared from it. The simple expressed juice will not keep, on account of the syrup, extractive, mucilage, and water, which cause it to ferment. The yellow peel is an elegant aromatic, and is frequently employed in stomachic tinctures and infusions, and yields by expression or distillation water, and essential oil, which is much used in perfumery. Fresh Lemon-juice is specific in the prevention and cure of scurvy, and is also a powerful and agreeable antiseptic. Citric acid is often used with great success for allaying vomiting; with this intention it is mixed with carbonate of potass, from which it expels the carbonic acid with effervescence. Lemon-juice, as well as lime-juice, is also an ingredient in many pleasant refrigerant drinks, which are of great use in allaying febrile heat and thirst. Lemon-juice, like other vegetable acids, is given to correct acidity in the stomach. By elevating the power of that organ it not only prevents the formation of an excess of acid, but is useful in the same way in bilious and remittent fevers, especially when combined with port-wine and cinchona bark. It is often employed internally to excite the nervous system after narcotic poisoning, but should not be used till all the poisonous substance has been removed from the stomach, otherwise its effects may prove the reverse. Slices of Lemon are applied with good effect to scorbutic and other sores.—*Don. Lindley.*

(180) **Citrus medica** (*Linn.*) Do.

Citron, Eng. Beg-poora, Beng. Leemoo, Hind.

Description.—Shrub; young branches rigid; leaves oblong, pointed; petioles simple; flowers white, tinged with red; fruit obovoid, deeply furrowed and wrinkled, terminated by a knob; pulp very slightly acid. *Fl.* April—June.—*W. & A. Prod.* i. 98.—*Roxb. Fl. Ind.* iii. 392.——Foot of the Himalaya. Cultivated in the Peninsula.

Economic Uses.—The Citron is supposed to be the same as the Median apple which was introduced into Greece and Italy from Persia and the warmer regions of Asia at an early period. It was cultivated in Judea, and the fruit may be seen as a device on Samaritan coins. To the present day the Jews make a conserve of the fruit, which is invariably used by them in the Feast of Tabernacles. The ancients attached medical virtues to the fruit, for Theophrastus in his history of plants says that it was an expellent of poisons. "The Median territory, and likewise Persia, have many other productions, and also the Persian or Median apple. Now, that tree has a leaf very like and almost exactly the same as that of the bay-tree, the arbutus, or the nut: and it has thorns like the prickly pear or black-thorn, smooth, but very sharp and strong; and the fruit is not good to eat, but is very fragrant, and so too are the leaves of the tree. And if any one puts one of the fruit among his clothes, it keeps them from the moth. And it is useful when any one has taken poison injurious to life; for when given in wine it produces a strong effect on the bowels, and draws out the poison. It is serviceable also in the way of making the breath sweet: for if any one boils the inner part of the fruit in broth or in anything else, it makes his breath smell sweet." Virgil, who has imitated this passage in his second Georgic, mentions also that the fruit was used in asthma:—

> "Media fert tristes succos, tardumque saporem
> Felicis mali: quo non præsentius ullum,
> Pocula si quando sævæ infecere novercæ,
> Miscueruntque herbas et non innoxia verba,
> Auxilium venit, ac membris agit atra venena,
> Ipsa ingens arbos, faciemque simillima lauro;
> Et, si non alium late jactaret odorem,
> Laurus erat: folia haud ullis labentia ventis:
> Flos ad prima tenax; animas et olentia Medi
> Ora fovent illo, et senibus medicantur anhelis."
>
> —*Georg.*, ii. 126-135.

There are three principal varieties now cultivated in Europe. The fruit itself is seldom eaten, but is generally preserved and made into confections. The outer rind yields a volatile oil. In China there is a large variety known as the fingered Citron, so called from its lobes separating into fingers of different shapes and sizes. The rind is very fragrant, from the quantity of aromatic oil which exists in it. On this account the Chinese place it on dishes in their apartments to perfume the air.—*G. Don.*

(181) **Cleistanthus patulus** (*Muller*). N. O. EUPHORBIACEÆ.

Jiguru, TEL.

DESCRIPTION.—Large tree; stipules small; leaves shortly petioled, ovate or oblong-ovate, acute or obtuse at the base, cuspidate, acuminate at the apex, entire, glabrous; flowers more or less sessile, axillary, sub-glomerate, and arranged in short axillary interrupted spikes; calycine segments oblong-ovate; petals shortly unguiculate, hairy at the back; bracts ciliated; ovary hairy; capsules tuberculated. *Fl.* March—July.—*Dec. Prod.* xv. *s.* 2, 505.—Cluytia patula, *Roxb.*—Bridelia patula, *Hook. at Arn. Bot. Beech.* 212.—Amanoa Indica, *Wight Icon. t.* 1911.—*Roxb. Cor. t.* 170.——Circar mountains. Courtallum.

ECONOMIC USES.—The timber of this tree, which is of a reddish colour, is hard and durable.—(*Roxb.*) It has been recommended for railway-sleepers, as well as other useful purposes.

(182) **Clerodendron infortunatum** (*Linn.*) N. O. VERBENACEÆ.

Peragu, MAL. Bockada, TEL. Bhant, BENG.

DESCRIPTION.—Under shrub, 2-3 feet; branchlets quadrangular; leaves long-petioled, rounded or ovate-cordate, the upper ones ovate, entire or dentate, strigose and hairy on both sides; panicle terminal, large, spreading, naked; flowers white, tinged with rose inside, the calyx increasing and turning red after the flower withers; drupe black within the increased calyx. *Fl.* Feb.—March.—*Linn. Fl. Zeyl.* 232.—*Dec. Prod.* xi. 667.—Volkameria infortunata, *Roxb.*—C. viscosum, *Vent.*—*Wight Icon. t.* 1471.—*Bot. Reg. t.* 629.—*Rheede*, ii. *t.* 25.——Peninsula. Belgaum. Bengal.

MEDICAL USES.—A cheap and efficient substitute for chiretta, as a tonic and anti-periodic. The fresh juice of the leaves is employed by the natives as a vermifuge, and also as a bitter tonic and febrifuge in malarious fevers, especially in those of children.—*Pharm. of India.*

(183) **Clerodendron serratum** (*Blume*). Do.

Tsjeru-teka, MAL. Chiru-dekku, TAM.

DESCRIPTION.—Shrub; young shoots four-sided; leaves opposite, 5-10 inches long, and broad in proportion, serrated; panicles terminal; flowers pale blue, with lower lip indigo-coloured. *Fl.* May—June.—*Wight Icon. t.* 1472.—Volkameria serrata, *Linn.*—*Roxb. Fl. Ind.* iii. 62.—*Rheede*, iv. *t.* 29.——Courtallum. Bombay. Cultivated in Travancore.

MEDICAL USES.—In the Northern Circars the root is known by the name of *Gunta-Bharinjie*, and is largely exported for medical purposes. It is used by the natives in febrile and catarrhal affections.—(*Pharm. of India.*) The leaves boiled with oil and butter are made into an ointment useful as an application in cephalalgia and ophthalmia. The seeds bruised and boiled in butter-milk are slightly aperient, and are occasionally administered in cases of dropsy.—*Ainslie. Rheede. J. Grah.*

(184) **Cleyera gymnanthera** (*W. & A.*) N. O. TERNSTRŒMIACEÆ.

DESCRIPTION.—Tree; leaves cuneate-obovate, obtuse or shortly and obtusely pointed, coriaceous, entire; peduncles twice as long as the petioles, 2-edged; anthers dotted with little points on the connectivum, without bristles; sepals five, with two persistent bracteoles at their base; petals five, distinct, alternating with the sepals; stamens distinct, adhering to the base of the petals; fruit baccate, 2-3 celled, seeds two in each cell; flowers yellowish. *Fl.* May—July.—*W. & A. Prod.* i. 87. *Wight's Neilgherry Plants*, i. 19.——Ootacamund.

Economic Uses.—This large tree is common about Ootacamund. The timber is of a reddish colour, and considered by the natives to be strong and durable.—*Wight.*

(185) **Clitorea Ternatea** (*Linn.*) N. O. Leguminosæ.

Shlongo Kuspi, Shunkoo-pushpa, Mal. Karka Kartun, Tam. Nulla-ghentana, Tel. Khagin, Hind. Upara-jita, Beng.

Description.—Climbing herbaceous plant; calyx 5-cleft; leaves unequally pinnated; leaflets 2-3 pairs, oval or ovate; stem pubescent, peduncles short, axillary, solitary, 1-flowered; bracteoles large, roundish; flowers resupinate; legumes slightly pubescent, 1-celled, many-seeded; flowers white or blue. *Fl.* All the year.—*W. & A. Prod.* i. 205.—*Roxb. Fl. Ind.* iii. 321. —*Rheede*, viii. *t.* 38.——Common in the Peninsula.

Medical Uses.—The powdered seeds are a useful purgative.* The root is used in croup: it sickens and occasions vomiting. It is also given as a laxative to children, and is also diuretic. Of the two varieties, that with the white flowers is said to be the best. Dr O'Shaughnessy states that he repeatedly tried the root in order to ascertain the truth of its alleged emetic effects, but the results were not satisfactory, and he could not recommend its use.—*Roxb. Beng. Disp.*

(186) **Cocculus villosus** (*Dec.*) N. O. Menispermaceæ.

Dier, Faridbuti, Hind. Doosra-tiga, Tel. Huyer, Beng.

Description.—Twining shrub; leaves on old branches, cordate-orbicular or hastate, 3-lobed, obtuse or retuse, mucronulate; on young shoots oblong, cordate or acute at the base, more or less downy; petals about equal to the filaments; racemes axillary, not half the length of the leaves, of *male* flowers branched and corymbose, of *female* simple and 1-3 flowered;

* In combination with cream of tartar, this forms a safe and efficient laxative. The alcoholic extract is also a useful preparation. The cost is trifling, as the seeds are easily procurable.

nuts of the drupe reniform, compressed; flowers small, greenish. *Fl.* Oct.—Dec.—*W. & A. Prod.* i. 13.—Menispermum villosum, *Lam.* (not *Roxb.*)—M. hirsutum, *Linn.*——Peninsula. Bengal.

MEDICAL USES.—A decoction of the fresh root mixed with pepper and goat's milk is given in rheumatism—dose, half a pint every morning. It is said to be laxative and sudorific. When under this treatment, the natives make a curry of the leaves, which they recommend to their patients. The leaves, when agitated in water, render it mucilaginous; this sweetened with sugar, and drank when fresh made to the extent of half a pint twice a-day, is given for the cure of gonorrhœa. If suffered to stand for a few minutes, the mucilaginous parts separate, contract, and float in the centre, leaving the water clear like Madeira wine, and almost tasteless.—*Roxb. Ainslie.*

(187) **Cochlospermum gossypium** (*Dec.*) N. O. TERNSTROEMIACEÆ.

Tanakoo-marum, TAM. Tschema-pungee Marum, MAL. Conda gongu-Chettu, TEL.

DESCRIPTION.—Tree, 50 feet; leaves palmately 5-lobed, lobes acuminated, quite entire, upper side becoming glabrous; under tomentose; sepals 5, oval-oblong, unequal, at length reflexed, the 2 exterior ones smaller; petals 5, emarginate, unequal-sided; capsules shortly obovate; seeds numerous, somewhat reniform; flowers large, yellow, panicled; peduncles somewhat jointed at the base. *Fl.* March—April. *W. & A. Prod.* i. 87. —Bombax gossipinum, *Linn.*—*Roxb. Fl. Ind.* iii. 169.—— Travancore. Coromandel. Hurdwar.

ECONOMIC USES.—The seeds are surrounded with a soft silky cotton, apparently of little value, except for stuffing pillows. The tree yields a gum called *Cuteera*, used as a substitute for Tragacanth in the North-West Provinces. This gummy substance exudes from every part of the tree, if broken. It is not uncommon in S. India, and is conspicuous when in blossom, from its large yellow flowers. —*Royle.*

(188) **Cocos nucifera** (*Linn.*) N. O. PALMACEÆ.

Cocoanut-palm, ENG. Taynga, TAM. Tenga, MAL. Narikadam, Tenkaia, TEL. Naril, HIND. Narikel, BENG.

DESCRIPTION.—Spathe axillary, cylindric, oblong, terete, bursting longitudinally; spadix erect, or nearly so, winding; male flowers numerous, approximate, sessile, above the female; calyx 3-sepalled; leaflets minute, broadly cordate, fleshy; petals

3; female flowers usually one (occasionally wanting) near the base of each ramification of the spadix; corolla 6-petalled.—*Roxb. Fl. Ind.* iii. 614.—*Rheede*, i. *t.* 1-4.——Shores of equinoctial Asia and its islands.

Medical Uses.—The freshly-prepared oil is of a pale-yellowish colour, and almost inodorous, but after a few days acquires a peculiar rancid odour and taste. It is much used for liniments and other external applications. It is often employed as a local application in baldness, and in loss of hair after fevers and debilitating diseases. It has been used as a substitute for cod-liver oil with good effect; but in such cases it was not the commercial oil in its crude state, but the oleine obtained by pressure, refined by being treated with alkalies, and then repeatedly washed with distilled water. Its prolonged use, however, is attended with disadvantage, inasmuch as it is apt to disturb the digestive organs, and induce diarrhœa. The expressed juice or milk of the fresh kernel has been successfully employed in debility, incipient phthisis, and cachexia. In large doses it proves aperient, and in some cases actively purgative, on which account it has been suggested as a substitute for castor-oil.—*Pharm. of India.*

Economic Uses.—The principal distribution of the Cocoa-palm lies within the intertropical regions of the Old and New Worlds, requiring a mean temperature of 72°. It is cultivated in great abundance in the Malabar and Coromandel coasts, Ceylon, the Laccadives, and everywhere in the islands of the Eastern Archipelago. It thrives best in low sandy situations, within the influence of the sea-breeze; and although it grows far inland on the continent, yet whenever found in places distant from the sea, the vigour of the palm is less than if cultivated in those maritime situations which nature has evidently determined should be its best and proper locality. Few if any products of the vegetable kingdom are so valuable to man in those countries where it is indigenous as the Cocoanut-palm, for there is scarcely a part of the plant which cannot be applied more or less to some use by the inhabitants of tropical climates. Of these uses, the chief are the oil from the nuts, the nuts themselves, the fibres, the leaves, the stem, and the toddy; but before detailing these separately, it may be as well to give a short account of the palm itself, its history, cultivation, &c. Many botanists have enumerated the manifold uses of the Cocoa-palm, and among them especially Kœmpfer and Loureiro have collected much valuable information. One of the earliest accounts is that by Marco Polo, whose description of the "Indian nuts," as he terms them, is remarkably accurate. When speaking of an island in the Indian Archipelago, he says: "The Indian nuts also grow here, of the size of a man's head, containing an edible substance that is sweet and pleasant to the taste, and white as milk. The cavity of this pulp is filled with a liquor clear as water, cool, and better flavoured and more delicate than wine or any other kind of drink whatever." Sir John Mandeville also mentions the "great nut of India;" and another ancient writer has said in a paper read before the Royal Society in 1688: "The Cocoanut-palm is alone sufficient to build, rig, and freight a ship with bread, wine, water, oil, vinegar, sugar, and other commodities. I have sailed," he adds, "in vessels where the bottom and the whole cargo hath been from the munificence of this palm-tree." Though there are several varieties enumerated by Rumphius, yet they have all been resolved into three species, of which one only is indigenous in the East, the other two being natives of Brazil. Fortunately so prolific a plant requires little care in its cultivation, and being essentially maritime, thrives best in those situations where other trees would perish or decay. In Ceylon, where greater care than elsewhere is bestowed upon its cultivation, it is considered best that they should not be planted too close together. The soil should first be carefully cleared from weeds. The nut should not be carelessly placed in the earth, but in a position favourable for germination, attention to which is somewhat important to the future perfection of the tree. The nut should be quite ripe before being deposited in the ground, and the hole may be dug with the slightest labour, it being sufficient to cover only two-thirds of the nut. In three or four months the nut begins to germinate. The usual time for planting on the western coast is before the rains; and, unless the nut is transplanted, no further watering is required in the hot season, the internal moisture of the nut being sufficient for the nourishment of the young plant for nearly a year. After that time the palm requires watering twice a-day until the fourth or fifth year, the roots being carefully heaped with earth to avoid too much exposure to the air. Beyond this no further care is requisite. From the fifth to the eighth year it begins to bear, according to the situation and soil, and continues bearing from seventy to eighty years. The tree is in its highest vigour from twenty-five to thirty years of age, and will attain the age of a hundred years. In the third year of its growth the fronds begin to fall, one new frond appearing at the end of every month. These fronds fall more frequently in hot than in rainy weather. Of these there are about 28, more or less, in a full-grown tree. On a single tree there are about 12 branches or spadices of nuts, one bearing the dry nuts called Baruta or Cotta-tenga in Malayalum, another spadix the ripe ones, called Maninga-tenga. Most of the young fruits fall off, only a few coming to perfection; but as from 10 to 15 nuts on an average are produced on one branch, a single tree may produce from 80 to 100 nuts every year. Of trees requiring so little attention, it may easily be imagined how much value is attached to their possession. In Travancore and on the Malabar coast, the natives draw their chief subsistence from the produce of this useful palm. The price of a full-grown tree varies from ½ rupee to 5 rupees, according to circumstances. A yearly tax to the Sircar is averaged at a few annas, so that the profit derived from a large plantation is very considerable. It will now be necessary to enumerate the various uses to which the several parts of the tree may be applied, and first among them may be mentioned,

The Oil.—This is procured by first extracting the kernel from its outer integument or shell, and boiling it in water. It is then pounded and subjected to strong pressure. This being boiled over a slow fire, the oil floats on the surface. This is skimmed off as it rises, and again boiled by itself. Fourteen or fifteen nuts will yield about two quarts of oil. A somewhat different practice obtains on the Malabar coast. The kernel is divided into half-pieces, which are laid on shelves, and underneath is placed a charcoal fire in order to dry them. After two or three days they are placed on mats, and kept in the sun to dry, after which they are put in a press. When the oil is well extracted by this method, a hundred nuts will yield about two gallons and a half of oil. This is the method usually resorted to when the oil is required for exportation; the former, when merely used for culinary purposes. Of late years the application of steam, especially to a press, for the purpose of procuring the oil, has been attended with the greatest advantages. Cocoanut-oil in India is used chiefly for culinary purposes, burning in lamps, &c., and in Europe for the manufacture of soap and candles. The oil becomes solid about 70°. It is said that its consumption in Europe is likely to decrease, owing partly to the new means of purifying tallow, whereby candles equally good as those made from Cocoanut-oil are produced. Great quantities of oil are shipped annually from Ceylon and the western coast, and in extraordinary seasons have realised in England £70 a-ton, or upwards: the average price is from £35 to £40 a-ton. That which is shipped from Cochin bears generally a higher price than that from Ceylon.

The *Copra*, which is the dried kernels, as also the *Poonac*, is occasionally sent to Europe by itself from Ceylon and Cochin. The *Poonac* is the refuse of the kernel after the oil has been expressed. It is very fattening to fowls and cattle, and forms the best manure to young Cocoanut-trees, as it returns to the soil many of the component parts which the tree has previously extracted for the formation of the fruits. For this reason it has been found worth while to transmit the *Poonac* to those localities where the Cocoanut-tree grows far inland, away from the saline soil of the coast. The Cocoa-palm abstracts from the soil chiefly silex and soda; and where these two salts are not in abundance, the trees do not thrive. Common salt applied to the roots will be found very beneficial as a manure to the young trees when cultivated at any distance from the sea.

Coir is the fibrous rind of the nuts, with which the latter are thickly covered. There are several ways of stripping the fibres from the husk. One is by placing a stake or iron spike in the ground, and by striking the nut on the point, the fibres are easily separated. The husks are first separated from the nuts, and then placed in salt or brackish water for about 12 or 18 months; they are then scraped and cleaned for use. There exists, however, no such necessity for steeping the husk so long in water, it having been found that a shorter time is sufficient for the purpose. In the Jury Report of the Madras Exhibition, we find: "It has lately been proved that the fibre from the husk of the ripe fruit is greatly improved in quality and appearance by beating, washing, and soaking, and that the old method of steeping in salt water for 18 months or 2 years is quite unnecessary, and that it produces a harsher and dirtier coir. The tannin which this substance contains prevents the fibre from rotting; but most of the coir of commerce is a dirty, harsh produce, very different from many of the clean and dyed samples exhibited, which are suited to a superior class of manufactures, as fine mats and furniture-brushes." Coir is applied to many uses—for stuffing couches and pillows, for cordage, saddles, &c. Large quantities are annually shipped to Europe, where it is manufactured into brushes, mats, and carpets, and even hats and bonnets; the latter attracted much attention at the Great Exhibition in London. The fibre is rather difficult to twist; still it is made into ropes for ordinary purposes in shipping. The character of Coir, says Royle, has long been established in the East, and is now well known in Europe as one of the best materials for cables, on account of its strength, lightness, and elasticity. These cables are further valuable, being durable, particularly when wetted with salt water.

Numerous instances have been related of ships furnished with cables of this light, buoyant, and elastic material, riding out a storm in security, while stronger-made though less elastic ropes of other vessels have snapped in two, and even when chain cables have given way. Indeed, until chain cables were so largely introduced, all the ships navigating the Indian seas were furnished with Coir cables. Coir cordage, in Dr Wight's experiments, broke at 224 lb. weight.

The mode of extracting the toddy is the same as that used in other palms (see *Borassus*). Spirit distilled from the toddy is called arrack. Good vinegar is also made from it, particularly at Mahè. One hundred gallons of toddy yield 25 of arrack. To procure the sugar or jaggery, the fresh toddy is boiled down over a slow fire, when the syrup is further evaporated to the brown coarse sugar. This jaggery is mixed with chunam for making a strong cement, enabling it to resist great heat and to take a fine polish. The toddy is called Tenna-kulloo, and Narillie in Dukhanie. If taken before sunrise it is very refreshing and delicious. The native doctors recommend it in consumption; and it is said that if regularly taken, it is good for delicate persons suffering from habitual constipation.

The water of the nuts is used by the bricklayers in preparing a fine whitewash, also in making the best and purest castor-oil, a certain portion of it being mixed with the water in which the seeds are boiled. The shell, when burnt, yields a black paint, which, in fine powder and mixed with chunam, is used for colouring walls of houses. The soft downy substance found at the bottom of the fronds is a good styptic for wounds, leech-bites, &c. It is called in *Tamil* Tennamarruttoo punjee, and in *Malayalum* Tennam-pooppa. The web-like substance which surrounds the Cocoa-palm at those parts where the branches expand is called Panaday in *Tamil*, Kon-jatty in *Malayalum*, and it is used by the toddy-drawers to strain the toddy through. In Ceylon it is manufactured into a coarse kind of cloth for bags and coverings, and from these bags, again, a coarse kind of paper is made. The Cocoanut cabbage is the terminal bud found at the summit of the tree; but to procure it the tree must be destroyed. It makes an excellent pickle, and may also be used as a vegetable.

In addition to the above uses, the leaves are employed for thatching houses, especially in Malabar, and the stems for rafters of houses, bridges, beams, small boats, and, where the wood is thick, is even used for picture-frames and articles of furniture. It is known in Europe as the porcupine-wood, and has a pretty mottled appearance. The nuts, dried and polished, are made into drinking cups, spoons, baskets, and a variety of fanciful ornaments. The midribs of the leaves are used for paddles.

The natives chew the roots as they do the areca-nut with the betle-leaf. Abundance of potash is yielded by the ashes of the leaves. Cocoanuts are occasionally fixed on stakes in the public roads in India for the purpose of giving light, for which they are well adapted from their fibrous covering without and oily substance within. Marine soap, or Cocoanut-oil soap, so useful for washing linen in salt water, is made of soda, Cocoanut-lard, and water. So great and so varied are the uses of the Cocoa-palm,—fully calculated to realise the old saying, "Be kind to your trees and they will be kind to you."*—*Royle's Fib. Plants. Simmonds. Lindley. Ainslie.*

(189) **Coffea Arabica** (*Linn.*) N. O. Cinchonaceæ.

Coffee, Eng. Capié-côttay, Tam. Bun, kahwa, Arab. Kawa, Mal. Kawa, Coffee, Hind.

Description.—Large erect bush, quite smooth in every part; leaves oblong-lanceolate, acuminate, shining on the upper side, wavy, deep green above, paler below; stipules subulate, undivided; peduncles axillary, short, clustered; corolla white, tubular, sweet-scented, with a spreading 5-cleft limb; anthers protruded; berries oval, deep purple, succulent, 2-seeded. *Bot. Mag. t.* 1303.—*Dec. Prod.* iv. 499.—*W. & A.*

* For further uses of the Cocoa-palm see Appendix C.

Prod. i. 435.—*Wight Icon. t.* 53.——Low mountains of Arabia. Neilgherries. Shevaroy hills.

MEDICAL USES.—The albumen of the seeds constitutes the aromatic Coffee of commerce, which, when dried and roasted, is an agreeable tonic and stimulant. It has the power of removing drowsiness and of retarding the access of sleep for some hours, and is prescribed medicinally in various derangements of the viscera and in nervous headaches. In small doses, a strong decoction of Coffee is capable of arresting diarrhœa. It is often given to disguise the taste of nauseous medicines, particularly quinine, senna, and Epsom salts. A strong decoction of Coffee (an ounce to a cup) has been found of great service in allaying the severity of a paroxysm of spasmodic asthma. In poisoning by *opium* or other narcotic poisons, a strong infusion of Coffee, without milk or sugar, is an effectual stimulant. It is also advantageously given in the depression after drunkenness.—*Lindley, Fl. Med. Waring, Ther.*

ECONOMIC USES.—The cultivation of this staple is now extending in a surprising manner, and becoming of much importance. It has been pursued with great success by private individuals, many Europeans having settled in Wynaad and Travancore, and other mountainous tracts on the western coast, for the purpose of its cultivation. The value of commercial Coffee depends upon the texture and form of the berry, the colour and flavour. A French chemist has ascertained that Coffee-grounds make an excellent manure, owing to the nitrogen and phosphoric acid they contain.

Bruce, in his 'Travels in Abyssinia,' states that the Coffee-plant is a native of Egypt. It is found in a wild state in the north of Kaffa, a district in the province of Navea; and it is not improbable that the plant takes its name from that place. The first writer who makes any reference to it is Rauwolf, who wrote a treatise on the plant, of whose stimulating properties he speaks in the highest terms. Towards the end of the fifteenth century the plant was introduced into Arabia, and from thence it was taken, in 1690, to Batavia, by Van Hoorn, then governor of Java. He cultivated it with much success at the latter place, and sent several plants to Amsterdam. In 1720 the plant was introduced into Martinique, and subsequently into the island of Bourbon and the Isle of France.

According to tradition, the Coffee-plant was introduced into Mysore by a Mohammedan pilgrim, named Baba Booden, who came and took up his abode on the uninhabited hills in the Nuggur division, named after him, and where he established a college, which still exists, endowed by Government. It is said that he brought seven Coffee-berries from Mocha, which he planted near to his hermitage, about which there are now to be seen some very old Coffee-trees. The Coffee-plant has been known there from time immemorial; but the earliest official account of it is in 1822, when the revenue was under contract.

It was estimated that in 1861 there were of Coffee-planters in Wynaad alone, and exclusive of Mysore, Coorg, &c., 75 separate properties, with a total acreage of 24,149, of which considerably more than one-third is in bearing. The quantity exported in ten years had risen from 35,000 to 165,000 cwts., a far greater proportion than that from Ceylon in the same time.

The genus *Coffea* includes fully fifty species, and, as at present constituted, occupies a very wide range. Africa, Asia, and America both North and South, claim indigenous species, but all confined to the warmer regions, either actually within the tropics or within a few degrees of either side. In Mexico, Brazil, and Peru, they abound. There are several from Africa, while India and her islands claim one-fourth of the whole number.—*Wight's Neilg. Plants*, i. 83.

(190) **Coldenia procumbens** (*Linn.*) N. O. Ehretiaceæ.

Seru-padi, Tam. Tripungki, Hind. Hamsa-padu, Tel.

Description.—Stems procumbent, hirsute; leaves short, petioled, obovate, unequally produced at the base above the petiole, folded, coarsely toothed, with adpressed villous hairs above, hirsute beneath; flowers axillary, solitary, sessile, small, white; nuts wrinkled, rough. *Fl.* Sept.—Dec.—*Linn. Spec.* 182.—*Dec. Prod.* ix. 558.——Common in rice-fields.

Medical Uses.—The dried plants, mixed with Fenugreek seeds and rubbed to a fine powder, are used to promote the suppuration of boils.—*Ainslie.*

(191) **Coleus aromaticus** (*Benth.*) N. O. Lamiaceæ.

Country Borage, Eng. Pathoor-choor, Beng.

Description. — Shrub, 2-3 feet; branches tomentosely pubescent, or hispid; leaves petiolate, broad, ovate, crenated, rounded at the base, or cuneate, very thick, hispid on both surfaces, or clothed with white villi, very fragrant, floral leaves hardly equal in length to the calyx; racemes simple; whorls 20-30 flowered or more; calyx tomentose; tube of corolla about twice as long as the calyx, defracted at the middle; throat dilated; lower lip a little dilated, boat-shaped; flowers smallish, pale blue, very aromatic. *Fl.* April.—*Dec. Prod.* xii. 72.—Plectranthus aromaticus, *Roxb. Fl. Ind.* iii. 22.——Common in gardens.

Medical Uses.—This plant, a native of the Moluccas, has a pleasant aromatic odour and pungent taste, and according to Loureiro is employed in Cochin China in asthma, chronic coughs, epilepsy, and other convulsive affections.—(*Lour. Flor. Coch.* 452.) It is a powerful aromatic carminative given to children in colic. It has, however, an intoxicating effect, a property remarked by Long in the Journ. of the Agric. Hort. Soc. of India, who also states that in Bengal the natives use it in colic and dyspepsia.—(*Long, ut supra*, x. 23. *Wight's Illustr.* ii.) Every part of the plant is delightfully fragrant. The leaves are frequently eaten, and mixed with various articles of food, drink, or medicine.—*Roxb. Pharm. of India.*

Another species, the *C. barbatus*, a native of the Peninsula, Guzerat, and Nepaul, is commonly cultivated in gardens of the natives at Bombay for the roots, which are pickled.—*J. Graham.*

(192) **Colocasia antiquorum** (*Schott.*) N. O. Araceæ.

Cocco, Eng. Chama, Tel. Kuchoo, Beng. Shema Kilangu, Tam.

Description.—Stemless; leaves peltate, ovate, repand, semibifid at the base; scape shorter than the petioles; spathe much longer than the spadix, cylindric, erect; club subcylindrical, length of the antheriferous part of the receptacle; anthers many-celled. *Fl.* Sept.—Nov.—*Roxb. Fl. Ind.* iii. 494. —*Wight Icon. t.* 786.—Arum colocasia, *Linn.*——Cultivated in the Peninsula. Tanjore in wet marshy grounds.

Medical Uses.—The pressed juice of the petioles is highly styptic, and is even said to arrest arterial hæmorrhage, the wound after application healing by first intention. The *C. macrorhiza* also possesses much acridity in the fresh state, and is employed by the natives as an external stimulant and rubefacient. The acrid principle is, however, very volatile, and by the application of heat, or simple drying, the roots become innocuous.—*Pharm. of India.*

Economic Uses.—There are two varieties cultivated in lower Bengal. They are planted about the beginning of the rainy season. Of the *Kala-kuchoo*, the leaves and petioles are eaten by the natives. Some varieties are seldom if ever eaten.

The *C. Indica* is cultivated in Bengal for its esculent stems and small pendulous tubers. There is one variety with dark-coloured petioles, but they seldom produce ripe seeds. The *C. nymphæfolia* is common in Malabar, where it forms part of the food of the inhabitants.—(*Roxb.*)

When the crop of *C. antiquorum*, says Dr Seemann (*Flora Vitiensis*), is gathered in, the tops of the tubers are cut off and at once replanted. The young leaves may be eaten like spinach; but, like the root, they require to be well cooked in order to destroy the acridity peculiar to Aroideous plants. A considerable number of varieties are known, some better adapted for puddings, some for bread, or simply for boiling or baking. The outer marks of distinction chiefly rest upon the different tinge observable in the corm, leaf, stalks, and ribs of the leaves—white, yellowish, purple.

(193) **Conocarpus acuminatus** (*Roxb.*) N. O. COMBRETACEÆ.

Pachi-man, TEL.

DESCRIPTION.—Large tree; limb of calyx 5-cleft; petals none; leaves without glands, nearly opposite, oval or oblong-lanceolate, entire, acute; when young, pubescent, adult ones glabrous; peduncles simple, with one head of flowers; flowers small, pale-greenish. *Fl.* Jan.—Feb.—*W. & A. Prod.* i. 316. —*Roxb. Fl. Ind.* ii. 443.—Anogeissus acuminatus, *Wall.*—— Circar mountains.

ECONOMIC USES.—The timber of this tree is very hard and durable, almost equalling teak, especially if kept dried, but decays if exposed to water. It is good for house-building, though it is difficult to procure straight logs of it.—*Roxb.*

(194) **Conocarpus latifolius** (*Roxb.*) Do.

Yella-maddi, Siri-maun, TEL. Vallay-naga, Veckeliè, TAM.

DESCRIPTION.—Tree; leaves alternate or nearly opposite, quite entire; limbs of calyx 5-cleft; petals none; leaves without glands, elliptical or obovate, obtuse, emarginate, glabrous; peduncles branched, bearing several heads of flowers sometimes thickly aggregated; fruit coriaceous, somewhat scaly, globular; seed solitary; flowers small, greenish pale. *Fl.* Jan. —Feb.—*W. & A. Prod.* i. 316.—*Wight Icon. t.* 994.—*Roxb. Fl. Ind.* ii. 442.—Anogeissus latifolius, *Wall.*——Valleys of the Concan rivers. Deccan hills. Dheyra Dhoon.

ECONOMIC USES.—This is a large tree found on the Circar mountains, and other parts of the Peninsula. The timber is good, and if kept dry is said to be very durable. It is especially esteemed for many economical purposes. Towards the centre it is of a chocolate colour. For house and ship building the natives reckon it superior to every other sort, except teak and perhaps one or two more.—(*Roxb.*)

The ashes of this tree are said to be in demand as an article of food among certain wild tribes, inhabitants of the forests about the Neilgherries. The demand for it has been attributed to the large proportion of pure carbonate of potash which it yields; the diet of the same people including a large quantity of tamarinds. The leaves are used for dying leather. The gum from the tree is extensively employed in printing on cloth.—*Powell's Punj. Prod.*

(195) **Corchorus capsularis** (*Linn.*) N. O. TILIACEÆ.

Capsular Corchorus, ENG. Ghinalita pat, BENG.

DESCRIPTION.—Annual, 5-10 feet; calyx deeply 5-cleft; petals 5; leaves alternate, oblong-acuminate, serrated, two lower serratures terminating in narrow filaments; peduncles short; flowers whitish-yellow in clusters opposite the leaves; capsules globose, truncated, wrinkled and muricated, 5-celled; seeds few in each cell, without transverse partitions; in addition to the 5 partite cells there are other 5 alternating, smaller and empty. *Fl.* June—July.—*W. & A. Prod.* i. 73. —*Wight Icon. t.* 311.—*Roxb. Flor. Ind.* ii. 581.—Peninsula. Bengal. Cultivated.

ECONOMIC USES.—Extensively cultivated for the sake of its fibres, especially in Bengal. The present species may be distinguished from all others by the capsules being globular instead of cylindrical. The cultivation and manufacture has been described in the excellent work of Dr Royle on the Fibrous Plants of India. According to his statement, the seeds are sown in April or May, when there is a probability of a small quantity of rain. In July or August the flowers have passed. When the plants are ripe, they being then from 3 to 12 feet in height, they are cut down close to the roots, when the tops are clipped off, and fifty or a hundred are tied together. Several of these bundles are placed in shallow water, with pressure above to cause them to sink. In this position they remain eight or ten days. When the bark separates, and the stalk and fibres become softened, they are taken up and untied; they are then broken off two feet from the bottom, the bark is held in both hands, and the stalks are taken off. The fibres are then exposed to the sun to be dried, and after being cleaned are considered fit for the market. These fibres are soft and silky, and may be used as a substitute for flax; but although the plant is one of rapid growth and easy culture, the fibres are very perishable, and it is owing to this circumstance that they lose much of their value. The attention of practical men has been turned to remedy so serious a defect in one of the most useful products of Bengal. Could the fibres be prepared without the lengthened immersion in water, whereby they are subsequently liable to rot and decay, the difficulty might be partially if not wholly overcome. So careful is the manufacturer obliged to be, that during the time the plants are in the water, he is forced to examine them daily in order to guard against undue decomposition;

and even after they are removed from the water, the lower part of the stem nearest the root, which the hand has previously held, are so contaminated that they are cut off as useless. These fragments, however, in themselves have their use: they are shipped off to America from Calcutta for the use of paper-making, preparing bags, and suchlike purposes, and even made into whisky. The great care of watching the immersed Jute until it almost putrefies, is to preserve the fine silky character so much valued in fibres intended for export. For consumption in this country such care is not taken, therefore the article is stronger and more durable. The trade is very considerable. Besides the gunny-bags made from the fibrous part or bark, the stems of the plant themselves are used for charcoal, for gunpowder, fences, basket-work, fuel.—*Royle.*

(196) **Corchorus olitorius** (*Linn.*) Do.

Jew's Mallow, Eng. Singin janascha, Hind. Blunjee Pat, Beng.

Description.—Annual, 5 - 6 feet, erect; leaves alternate, ovate-acuminated, serrated, the two lower serratures terminated by a slender filament; peduncles 1-2 flowered; calyx 5-sepalled; petals 5; capsules nearly cylindrical, 10-ribbed, 5-celled, 5-valved; seeds numerous, with nearly perfect transverse septa; flowers small, yellow. *Fl.* July—August.—*W. & A. Prod.* i. 73.—*Roxb. Fl. Ind.* ii. 581.—C. decem-angularis, *Roxb.*——Peninsula. Bengal. Cultivated.

Economic Uses.—Rauwolf says this plant is sown in great quantities in the neighbourhood of Aleppo as a pot-herb, the Jews boiling the leaves to eat with their meat. The leaves and tender shoots are also eaten by the natives. It is cultivated in Bengal for the fibres of its bark, which, like those of *C. capsularis*, are employed for making a coarse kind of cloth, known as gunny, as well as cordage for agricultural purposes, boats, and even paper. Roxburgh says there is a wild variety called *Bun pat* or Wild *pat*. An account of the manufacture of paper from this plant at Dinajepore, may be found in Dr Buchanan's survey of the lower provinces of the Bengal Presidency. This plant requires much longer steeping in water than hemp, a fortnight or three weeks being scarcely sufficient for its maceration. The fibre is long and fine, and might well be substituted for flax.—*Roxb. Royle.*

(197) **Cordia angustifolia** (*Roxb.*) N. O. Cordiaceæ.

Narrow-leaved Sepistan, Eng. Goond, Hind. Narroovalli, Tam. Nukkeru, Tel.

Description.—Tree, 12-15 feet; leaves nearly opposite, lanceolate, obtuse or emarginate, scabrous; **calyx campanulate, obscurely 4-toothed; corolla-tube longer than the calyx; limb 4-partite, with revolute edges; panicles terminal, corymbose; stamens 4; flowers small, white; drupe round, smooth, yellow; nut surrounded with mucilaginous pulp.** *Fl.* May.—*Roxb. Fl. Ind. ed. Car.* ii. 338.——Mysore. Bombay. Deccan.

Economic Uses.—This tree was originally brought to notice by Dr Buchanan, who found it in Mysore. A fibre is prepared from the bark which is made into ropes, and these are used in Malabar for dragging timber from the forests. It is very strong, and, by experiments made at Cannanore, supported a weight of more than 600 lb. The fruit is eatable. Dr Gibson mentions that the wood is very tough, and useful for poles of carriages, and suchlike purposes. A species of Cordia (*C. Macleodii*, Hooker) grows in the Godavery forests, called *Botka* in Telugu. It is a very beautiful wood, and would answer as a substitute for maple, for picture-frames and so on. It is abundant in the forests near Mahadeopur, but does not extend to the Circars. It is also indigenous to the Jubbulpoor forests, where it is called *Deyngan*. It is supposed to be the tree described by Griffiths as *Hemigymnia Macleodii.*—*Beddome's Cat. of Trees in Godavery Forests.*

(198) **Cordia latifolia** (*Roxb.*) Do.

Broad-leaved Sepistan, Eng. Buro buhooari, Beng. Bhokur, Buralesoora, Hind.

Description.—Tree, 12-25 feet; leaves roundish, cordate, entire, repand, 3-nerved, smooth above, scabrous beneath; calyx villous, campanulate, with an unequally-toothed mouth; corolla short, campanulate; segments five; panicles terminal and lateral; flowers numerous, small, white; drupe pale-straw colour, covered with whitish bloom; nut surrounded with soft clammy pulp. *Fl.* March—April.—*Roxb. Fl. Ind.* i. 581.—Guzerat. Silhet.

Medical Uses.—Young fruits are pickled, and also eaten as vegetables. There are two kinds of Sebesten fruit noticed by writers on Indian Materia Medica; the first with the pulp separable from the nut, the other a smaller fruit with the pulp adhering to the nut. The latter is the sweetest of the two. The tree under notice bears the large kind of fruit, which is about the size of a prune, the *C. myxa* producing the small ones. Lindley says that under the name of Sebesten plums, Sebestan, or Sepistans, two sorts of Indian fruit have been employed as pectoral medicines, for which their mucilaginous qualities, combined with some astringency, recommend them.

They are believed to have been the *Persea* of Dioscorides.—*Lindley, Fl. Med. Roxb. Colebr. in As. Res.*

(199) **Cordia myxa** (*Linn.*) Do.

Sepistan-plum, ENG. Vidi-marum, MAL. Vidi-marum, TAM. Lusora, HIND. Buhooari, BENG. Nakeru, TEL.

DESCRIPTION.—Tree, middling size; leaves oval, ovate, or obovate, repand, smooth above, rather scabrous beneath; calyx tubular, widening towards the mouth, torn as it were in 3-5 divisions; divisions of corolla revolute; drupes globular, smooth, yellow; panicles terminal and lateral; nut 4-celled, tetragonal, cordate at both ends, surrounded with transparent viscid pulp; flowers small, white. *Fl.* Feb.—March.—*Roxb. Fl. Ind. ed. Car.* ii. 332.—*Wight Icon. t.* 1378.—C. officinalis, or Sebestana domestica, *Lam.*—*Rheede*, iv. *t.* 37.——Both Peninsulas. Bengal. N. Circars.

MEDICAL USES.—The fruit was formerly known among medical writers as the Sebesten, and was occasionally sent to Europe as an article of Materia Medica. Horsfield mentions that the mucilage of the fruit is of a demulcent nature, useful in diseases of the chest and urethra, and also employed in Java as an astringent gargle. The seeds are a good remedy in ringworm, being powdered and mixed with oil, and so applied. The smell of the nuts when cut is heavy and disagreeable: the taste of the kernels is like that of fresh filberts. The wood is soft, and is said to have furnished the timber from which the Egyptian mummy-cases were made. It is one of those used for procuring fire by friction. Graham states that in Otaheite the leaves are used in dyeing. The bark is much used as a mild tonic in Java. —*Lindley. Ainslie.*

(200) **Corypha umbraculifera** (*Linn.*) N. O. PALMACEÆ.

Talipot or Fan Palm, ENG. Coddapana, MAL. Condapana, TAM. Talee, BENG. Sidalum, TEL.

DESCRIPTION.—Trunk 60-70 feet; leaves sublunate, palmate-pinnatifid, plaited; segments 40-50 pair; petioles armed; inflorescence pyramidal, equalling the trunk of the tree; calyx 3-toothed; petals 3; ovary 3-celled, 1-seeded.—*Roxb. Fl. Ind.* ii. 177.—*Rheede*, iii. *t.* 1-12 *incl.*——Ceylon. Malabar. Malay coast.

ECONOMIC USES.—This is the well-known Fan-palm of Ceylon. Its large broad fronds are used for thatching, and also for writing on with an iron style. Such records are said to resist the ravages of time. The seeds are used as beads by certain sects of Hindoos. The dried leaf is very strong, and is commonly used for umbrellas by all classes. It opens and shuts like a lady's fan, and is remarkably light. A kind of flour or sago is prepared from the pith of the trunk. Little bowls and other ornaments are made from the nuts, and when polished and coloured red, are easily passed off for genuine coral.—(*Roxb. Knox's Ceylon.*) The most majestic and wonderful of the palm tribe, says Sir E. Tennent (*Ceylon*, i. 109), is the Talipot, the stem of which sometimes attains the height of 100 feet; and each of its enormous fan-like leaves, when laid upon the ground, will form a semicircle of 16 feet in diameter, and cover an area of 200 superficial feet. The tree flowers but once and dies, and the natives firmly believe that the bursting of the spadix is accompanied by a loud explosion. The leaves alone are converted by the Singhalese to purposes of utility Of them they form coverings for their houses, and portable tents of a rude but effective character. But the most interesting use to which they are applied is a substitute for paper, both for books and ordinary purposes. In the preparation of *Olas*, which is the term applied to them when so employed, the leaves are taken whilst tender, and after separating the central ribs, they are cut into strips and boiled in spring-water. They are dried first in the shade and afterwards in the sun, then made into rolls and kept in store, or sent to the market for sale. Before they are fit for writing on they are subjected to a second process. A smooth plank of Areca palm is tied horizontally between two trees; each *Ola* is then damped, and a weight being attached to one end of it, it is drawn backwards and forwards across the edge of the wood till the surface becomes perfectly smooth and polished, and during the process, as the moisture dries up, it is necessary to renew it till the effect is complete. The smoothing of a single *Ola* will occupy from 15 to 20 minutes. Another palm is the *C. Taliera*, growing in Bengal, the leaves of which are used for writing on with an iron style, as well as for thatching roofs, being strong and durable. Hats and umbrellas are also made from them.—*Roxb.*

(201) * **Coscinium fenestratum** (*Colebr.*) N. O. MENISPERMACEÆ.

Tree Turmeric, ENG. Mara Munjel, TAM. Jar-ki-huldie, DUK. Mani-pussupoo, TEL.

DESCRIPTION.—Climbing plant with thick ligneous stem and branches; leaves alternate, petioled, cordate, entire, 5-7 nerved, smooth and shining above, very hoary below, acuminate or obtuse, 3-9 inches long, 2-6 broad; petioles downy, shorter than the leaves; flowers in small globular heads, numerous, sub-sessile, villous, of an obscure green; *female* umbels several

* Sir W. Hooker in Pharmaceutical Journal, xii. 185 (with fig.)

from the same bud, rising from the branches, on thick downy peduncles; the latter longer and thicker in fruit; calyx 6-leaved; 3 exterior sepals oval, downy outside; 3 interior ones longer; petals 6, filaments very downy; style recurved; berries round, villous, size of a large filbert; seed 1; flowers greenish. *Fl.* Nov.—Dec.—*Roxb. Fl. Ind.* iii. 809.—Menispermum fenestratum, *Gærtn.*——Aurungole Pass. Courtallum. Ceylon.

MEDICAL USES.—This plant, which has long been known in Ceylon, is considered in that country to be a valuable stomachic. The wood is of a deep yellow colour, and bitter to the taste. The root in infusion is used medicinally. This is sliced, and steeped in water for several hours, and then drunk. This is the plant alluded to by Ainslie (*Materia Indica*, ii. 183), where he says that the root, which is an inch in circumference, is commonly met with in the bazaars, being brought from the mountains for sale. It is employed in preparing certain cooling liniments for the head, as well as in the preparation of a yellow dye. But its chief value consists in its tonic properties, for which the wood and bark are employed.—*Lindley. Ainslie.*

(202) **Costus speciosus** (*Sm.*) N. O. ZINGIBERACEÆ.

Tsjana-kua, MAL. Bomma Kachica, TEL. Keoo, HIND. and BENG.

DESCRIPTION.—Height 3-4 feet, spirally ascending; leaves sub-sessile, spirally arranged, oblong, cuspidate, villous underneath; flowers large, pure white. *Fl.* July—Sept.—*Roxb. Fl. Ind. ed. Car.* i. 57.—*Wight Icon. t.* 2014.—C. Arabicus, *Linn.* —Amomum hirsutum, *Lam.*—*Rheede*, xi. *t.* 8.——Coromandel. Concans. Bengal.

ECONOMIC USES.—A very elegant plant, found chiefly near the banks of rivers and other moist and shady places. A kind of preserve is made from the roots, which the natives deem very wholesome. They are insipid.—*Roxb.*

(203) **Covellia glomerata** (*Miq.*) N. O. MORACEÆ.

DESCRIPTION.—Large tree; trunk crooked, thick, bark of a rusty-greenish colour, rough; leaves alternate, petioled, oblong or broad lanceolate, tapering equally to each end, entire, very slightly 3-nerved, smooth on both sides; racemes compound or panicled, issuing immediately from the trunk or large branches; fruit pedicelled, nearly as large as the common fig, clothed with soft down. *Dalz. Bomb. Fl.* 243.—*Miq. in Ann. Sc. Nat.* iii. *S.* i. 35.—Ficus glomerata, *Roxb.*——Western coast.

Medical Uses.—The bark is applied as an astringent to ulcers, and to remove the poison of wounds made by a tiger or cat. The root is used in dysentery. The fruit is edible, but inspid, and is usually found full of insects.—*Powell's Punj. Prod.*

(204) **Cratæva nurvala** (*Ham.*) N. O. Capparidaceæ.

Neer-vala, Mal. Mavilinghum, Tam. Maredoo, Tel. Tapia, Birmi, Hind.

Description.—Tree, 15-20 feet; leaves trifoliolate; leaflets ovate-lanceolate, acuminated, lateral ones unequal at the base; limb of the petals ovate-roundish; torus hemispherical, very ovoid; calyx 4-sepalled; petals 4, unguiculate; berry stipitate, pulpy inside; flowers greenish white, with red stamens; racemes terminal. *Fl.* Feb.—March.—*W. & A. Prod.* i. 23. —C. inermis, *Linn.*—*Rheede, Mal.* ii. *t.* 42.——Malabar. Mysore.

Medical Uses.—In the Society Islands, of which this tree is a native as well as of Malabar, it is planted in burial-grounds, being esteemed sacred to idols. The leaves are somewhat aromatic, slightly bitter, and considered stomachic. The root is said to possess alterative qualities. The juice of the bark is given in convulsions and flatulency, and, boiled in oil, is externally applied in rheumatism.—*Ainslie.*

Economic Uses.—The wood of *C. Roxburghii* is soft and easily cut, but tolerably tough, and is used for carving models, making writing-boards, and combs. At Jhelum the fruit is mixed with water to form a strong cement, and the rind as a mordant in dyeing. —(*Stewart's Punj. Plants.*) It grows well on the slopes of the Eastern Ghauts and those towards Salem, as also in the interior generally.

(205) **Crinum Asiaticum** (*Willd.*) N. O. Amaryllidaceæ.

Belutta pola-tali, Mal. Veshi Moonghee, Tam. Kesara-chettu, Tel. Vesha-mungaloo-pakoo, Tel. Sookh-dursun, Beng.

Description.—Stemless; leaves radical, linear, concave, 3-4 feet long, obtuse, pointed, margins smooth; umbels 6-16 flowered; flowers sub-sessile; roots bulbous, with a terminal fusiform portion, issuing from the crown, from which numerous fibrous roots proceed; flowers large, white, fragrant at night; corolla tube cylindrical, usually pale green, segments linear-lanceolate, margins broad, with a recurved process at the apex of each. *Fl.* Oct.—Dec.—*Roxb. Fl. Ind.* ii. 129.—C. defixum, *Bot. Mag.* 2208.—*Rheede, Mal.* xi. *t.* 38.——Both Concans.

MEDICAL USES.—The leaves, bruised and mixed with castor-oil, are useful in whitlows and local inflammations of the kind. In Upper India the juice of the leaves is given in ear-ache. In Java the plant is reckoned a good emetic, and it is also considered of efficacy in curing wounds made by poisoned arrows. The root, sliced and chewed, is emetic. The *C. toxicarium* is a variety indigenous to both Concans, and of which Dr O'Shaughnessy found by experiments the leaves to be equal as an emetic to the best ipecacuanha; but recommended its only being resorted to when the latter cannot be procured. The plant is found on the banks of rivers and in marshy places, and flowers nearly all the year.—*Roxb. J. Grah. Ainslie. O'Shaughnessy.*

(206) **Crotalaria juncea** (*Linn.*) N. O. LEGUMINOSÆ.

Sun-hemp plant, ENG. Wuckoo or Janupa nar, TAM. Shanamoo, TEL. Sunn, BENG.

DESCRIPTION.—Small plant, 4-8 feet, erect, branched, more or less clothed with shining silky pubescence or hairs; branches terete, striated; stipules and bracts setaceous; leaves from narrow linear to ovate-lanceolate, acute; calyx deeply 5-cleft, densely covered with rusty tomentum, the 3 lower segments usually cohering at the apex; racemes elongated, terminating every branch; flowers distant; legumes sessile, oblong, broader upwards, about twice the length of the calyx, tomentose and many-seeded; flowers yellow. *Fl.* Nov.—Jan.—*W. & A. Prod.* i. 185.—*Roxb. Fl. Ind.* iii. 259.—*Cor.* ii. *t.* 193.—C. Benghalensis, *Lam.*—C. tenuifolia, *Roxb.*—C. fenestrata, *Sims. Bot. Mag.*——Peninsula. Malabar. Bengal.

ECONOMIC USES.—This plant is extensively cultivated for the sake of its fibres in many parts of India, especially in Mysore and the Deccan. These are known by different names, according to the localities where they are prepared. In some places the fibre is known as the Madras hemp or Indian hemp, but this latter appellation is incorrect. It is the *Wuckoo-nar* of Travancore, the *Sunn* of Bengal, and so on. The mode of preparation differs from that of other fibres in one particular especially, the plant being pulled up by the roots, and not cut. After the seeds are beaten out, the stems are immersed in running water for five days or more, and the fibres are then separated by the fingers, which process makes it somewhat expensive to prepare. Dr Gibson asserts that the crops repay the labour bestowed on them, as the plant is suited for almost any soil. When properly prepared, the fibres are strong and much valued in the home markets. In this country they are used for fishing-nets, cordage, canvas, paper, gunny-bags, &c. &c.—the latter name being derived from the word *Goni*, the native name for the fibre on the Coromandel coast. In the 'Report on the Fibres of S. India' it is stated that the fibre makes excellent twine for nets, ropes, and various other similar articles. The fibres are much stronger if left in salt water. They will take tar easily, and with careful preparation the plant yields foss and hemp of excellent quality. It is greatly cultivated in Mysore, and also in Rajahmundry. In the latter district it is a dry crop, planted in November and cut in March. The yellow flowers resemble those of Spanish broom. It requires manure, but not too much moisture. Samples of the Sunn fibre were sent to the Great Exhibition, and also to the Madras Exhibition of 1855. On those forwarded to England Mr Dickson reported that these fibres will at all times command a market (when properly prepared) at £45 to £50 a-ton, for twine or common purposes; and when prepared in England with the patent liquid, they become so soft, fine, and white, as to bear comparison with flax, and to be superior to Russian flax for fine spinning. In the latter state it is valued at £80 a-ton. In several parts of India the price varies from R. 1 to Rs. 2-8 per maund; in Calcutta, about Rs. 5 per maund—and the prices both in the latter place and Bombay are gradually increasing. By experiments made on the strength of the fibre, it broke at 407 lb. in one instance. Large quantities are shipped for the English market. What is known as Jubbulpore hemp is the produce of *C. tenuifolia*, which, according to Wight, is a mere variety of *C. juncea*. Royle, however, and other botanists, think that it is a distinct plant. It is said to yield a very strong fibre, but probably not very different from the Sunn.—*Royle. Jury Reports. Report on Fibres of S. India.*

(207) **Croton tiglium** (*Linn.*) N. O. EUPHORBIACEÆ.

Croton-oil plant, ENG. Cadel-avanacu, Neervaula, MAL. Nervalum, TAM. Naypalum, TEL. Jumalghota, HIND. and DUK. Jypal, BENG.

DESCRIPTION.—Small tree with a few spreading branches; leaves alternate, ovate-oblong, smooth, acuminate, 3-5 nerved at the base, covered when young with minute stellate hairs; petioles channelled; calyx 5-cleft; petals 5, lanceolate, woolly; racemes erect, terminal; upper flowers male, lower ones female; seeds convex on one side, bluntly angular on the other, enveloped in a thin shell; flowers small, downy, greenish yellow.

Fl. April—June.—*Wight Icon. t.* 1914.—*Roxb. Fl. Ind.* iii. 682.—*Rheede,* ii. *t.* 33.——Coromandel. Travancore.

Medical Uses.—The seeds yield the well-known Croton-oil. They are the size of a sloe, and are considered one of the most drastic purgatives known. Ten or twenty seeds have been known to kill a horse by producing the most violent diarrhœa. The usual way to get the oil is first to roast the seeds and then compress them. The colour is brownish, or brownish yellow, soluble in fixed and volatile oils. So powerful is its action that a single drop of the oil applied to the tongue is considered sufficient to insure the full results, especially in incipient apoplexy, paralysis of the throat, or difficulty of breathing arising from these causes, even should the patient be insensible at the time. But this must be of the pure oil, for it is often adulterated with olive, castor, or purging nut oil. It is also employed in visceral obstruction, and occasionally in dropsy. The seeds mixed with honey and water are often applied to obstinate buboes in native practice. The expressed oil of the seed is a good remedy, externally applied, in rheumatism and indolent tumours. Rheede says that the leaves rubbed and soaked in water are also purgative, and when dried and powdered are a good application to snake-bites. If the leaves are chewed they inflame the mouth and lips, and cause them to swell, leaving a burning sensation. The mode of preparing the oil in Ceylon is by pulverising the seeds; the powder is then put into bags, placed between sheets of iron, left to stand for a fortnight and then filtered. Alcohol is then added to twice the weight of the residue. Much caution is requisite to avoid injury from the fumes which arise during the process. The wood, which is bitter-tasted, is gently emetic and powerfully sudorific.—(*Ainslie. Roxb. Lindley.*) The seeds of the *C. polyandrum* are reckoned a useful purgative. The natives mix them with water, administering two or three at a time, according to circumstances.—*Roxb. Lindley.*

(208) **Crozophora plicata** (*Ad. Juss.*) N. O. Do.

Souballi, Hind. Lingameriam chettu, Tel. Khoodi-okra, Beng.

Description.—Small annual, hoary; stems and branches round, dichotomous; leaves alternate, waved, toothed, broadly cordate, tapering to a stalk; flowers small, greenish white; male ones above the females; capsules scabrous. *Fl.* Nov.—Jan.—*Roxb. Fl. Ind.* iii. 681.—Croton plicatum, *Vahl.*——Common in the Peninsula. Behar.

Medical Uses.—This is commonly found in rice-fields, flowering during the cold weather. It is said to have virtues in leprous affections, the dry plant being made into a decoction to which is added a little mustard. A cloth moistened with the juice of the green capsules becomes blue after exposure to the air. This colouring matter might possibly be turned to good account.—*Roxb. Ainslie.*

(209) **Cryptostegia grandiflora** (*R. Br.*) N. O. Asclepiaceæ.

Palay, Mal.

Description.—Twining shrub; leaves opposite, elliptic, bluntly acuminated, shining above, minutely reticulated with brown beneath; calyx 5-parted, segments lanceolate with undulated margins; corolla funnel-shaped, tube furnished with five enclosed narrow bipartite scales inside, covering the anthers, being opposite them; stamens enclosed; stigmas globosely conical; corymbs trichotomous, terminal; flowers large, reddish purple; follicles divaricate, acutely triquetrous. *Fl.* All the year.—*Wight Icon. t.* 832.—Nerium grandiflorum, *Roxb. Fl. Ind.* ii. 10.——Malabar. Coromandel.

Economic Uses.—This plant yields a fine strong fibre resembling flax, and which may be spun into the finest yarn. A good specimen was exhibited at the Madras Exhibition. The milky juice has long been known to contain caoutchouc, which is often prepared for rubbing out pencil-marks, but it has not yet been collected for the purposes of commerce. Samples of a fair quality were sent to the Madras Exhibition.—*Jury Rep. Mad. Exhib.*

(210) **Cucumis utilissimus** (*Roxb.*) N. O. Cucurbitaceæ.

Field Cucumber, Eng. Kakrie, Hind. Kankoor kurktee, Beng. Doskai, Tel.

Description.—Trailing; stems scabrous; leaves broad-cordate, more or less 5-lobed; lobes rounded and toothed; *male* flowers crowded, *females* solitary; fruit short, oval, when young pubescent, when old glabrous, variegated; flowers yellow. *Fl.* Nearly all the year.—*W. & A. Prod.* i. 342.—*Roxb. Fl. Ind.* iii. 721.——Cultivated.

Economic Uses.—The fruit is pickled when half grown, and when ripe and hung up it will keep good for several months. The seeds contain much farinaceous matter mixed with a large proportion of mild oil. The meal is an article of diet with the natives, and the oil is used for lamps. Roxburgh has the following remarks upon this plant: "This appears to me to be by far the most useful species of *Cucumis* that I know: when little more than half grown, the fruits are oblong and a little downy—in this state they are pickled; when ripe, they are about as large as an ostrich's egg, smooth and yellow. When cut they have much the flavour of the Melon, and will keep for several months, if carefully gathered without being bruised, and hung up. They are also in this state eaten raw, and much used in curries by the natives. The seeds, like those of other Cucurbitaceous fruits, are nutritious; the natives dry and grind them into a meal, which they employ as an article of diet; they also express a bland oil from them, which they use in food and burn in their lamps. Experience as well as analogy proves these seeds to be highly nourishing, and well deserving of a more extensive culture than is bestowed on them at present. The powder of the toasted seeds mixed with sugar is said to be a powerful diuretic, and serviceable in promoting the passage of sand or gravel. As far as my observation and information go, this agriculture is chiefly confined to the Guntoor Circar, where the seeds form a considerable branch of commerce. They are mixed with those of *Holcus sorghum*, or some others of the large culmiferous tribe, and sown together: these plants run on the surface of the earth and help to shade them from the sun, so that they mutually help each other. The fruit, as I observed above, keeps well for several months if carefully gathered and suspended. This circumstance renders it an excellent article to carry to sea during long voyages."—(*Roxb.*) The *C. pseudocolocynthis* found on the slopes of the Western Himalaya is a good cathartic. It is called the Himalayan Colocynth.—(*Royle.*) The *C. momordica* is an article of diet, and a good substitute for the common Cucumber, which is also cultivated to a great extent in India.—(*Roxb.*) Two other plants of this natural order may be mentioned here—the *Cucurbita pepo*, the well-known Pumpkin, which is reputed to possess anthelmintic properties in its seeds useful in cases of Tænia. The fruit is very common in India, in which case the remedy, if really effectual, might be readily available. The other is the *C. maxima*, which would appear to possess similar properties, and to have been successfully applied in cases on record.—*Pharm. of India.*

(211) **Cuminum Cyminum** (*Linn.*) N. O. Umbelliferæ.

Cummin, Eng.

Description.—Herbaceous; leaves multifid, lobes linear-setaceous, acute; calycine teeth 5, unequal, persistent; petals with the point inflexed; umbel with 3-5 rays, involucre longer than the usually pubescent fruit; seeds slightly concave in front, convex on the back; flowers white.—*W. & A. Prod.* i. 373.—*Dec. Prod.* iv. 201.—*Roxb. Fl. Ind.* ii. 92.——Cultivated.

Medical Uses.—The seeds are met with in the bazaars throughout India, being much in use as a condiment. Their warm bitterish taste and aromatic odour reside in a volatile oil. Both seeds and oil possess carminative properties analogous to Coriander and Dill, and on this account are much valued by the natives.—*Pharm of India.*

(212) **Curculigo orchioides** (*Gærtn.*) N. O. HYPOXIDACEÆ.

Nelapanna, MAL. Nelapannay, TAM. Nala-tatta-gudda. TEL. Niahmooslie, HIND. Tamoolie, Telnoor Moodol, BENG.

DESCRIPTION.—Stemless; root tuberous, with many spreading fibres; leaves narrow-lanceolar, nerved, slender; petioles channelled, sheathing below; racemes solitary, axillary; flowers hermaphrodite, yellow. *Fl.* All the year.—*Roxb. Flor. Ind.* ii. 144.—*Cor.* i. *t.* 13.—*Rheede,* xii. *t.* 59.——Peninsula everywhere. Travancore.

MEDICAL USES.—The root is slightly bitter and aromatic, and mucilaginous to the taste, and is considered a demulcent. It is used in gonorrhœa, and also has tonic qualities. There are several species, or rather varieties, the *C. Malabarica* and *C. brevifolia,* but the same virtues attach to all. It grows in moist shady places. The apices of the leaves are viviparous, and will produce young plants, if allowed to rest on the ground for any length of time.—*Roxb. Ainslie.*

(213) **Curcuma angustifolia** (*Roxb.*) N. O. ZINGIBERACEÆ.

East Indian Arrowroot, ENG. Kooa, Kooghei, MAL. Kooa, TAM. Tikhur, HIND.

DESCRIPTION.—Bulbs oblong, with pale oblong pendulous tubers; leaves petioled, narrow lanceolate, most acute, striated with fine parallel veins; flowers longer than the bracts; petioles 6-10 inches long, lower half sheathing; spike radical, 4-6 inches long, crowned with an ovate purple tuft; flowers bright yellow, expanding at sunrise and fading at sunset. *Fl.* July.—*Roxb. Fl. Ind. ed. Car.* i. 31.——Nagpore. Travancore.

ECONOMIC USES.—An excellent kind of Arrowroot is prepared from the tubers of this species, especially in Travancore, where the plant grows in great abundance. This is a favourite article of diet among the natives. The flour, when finely powdered and boiled in milk, is an excellent diet for sick people or children. It is also much used for cakes, puddings, &c., though considered by some to produce constipation. In a commercial point of view the East Indian Arrowroot is below the West Indian starch, though similar in its qualities and uses. The exports of Arrowroot from Travancore average about 250 candies annually. In 1870-71 were exported from Bombay 3 cwt., and from Madras in 1869-70 3729 cwt., valued at 14,152 rupees. The mode of preparation is as follows: The tubers are first scraped on a rough stick, generally part of the stem of the common rattan, or any plant with rough prickles to serve the same purpose. Thus pulverised, the flour is thrown into a chatty of water, where it is kept for about two hours: all impurities being carefully removed from the surface. It is then taken out and again put into fresh water, and so on for the space of four or five days. The flour is ascertained to have lost its bitter taste when a yellowish tinge is communicated to the water, the whole being stirred up, again strained through a piece of coarse cloth and put in the sun to dry. It is then ready for use.—(*Roxb. Pers. Obs.*) The root of the *C. Amada* or Mango ginger is used as a carminative and stomachic, and a kind of Arrowroot is prepared from the tubers of the *C. leucorrhiza.*—*Roxb.*

(214) **Curcuma aromatica** (*Salisb.*) Do.

Wild Turmeric, ENG. Junglee-huldee, HIND. Bun-huldee, BENG.

DESCRIPTION.—Bulbs small, and, with the long palmate tubers, inwardly yellow; leaves 2-4 feet in length, broad lanceolate, sessile on their sheaths, sericeous underneath; the whole plant of a uniform green; spikes 6-12 inches long; flowers largish, pale rose-coloured, with a yellow tinge along the middle of the lip. *Fl.* March—May.—*Roxb. Fl. Ind. ed. Car.* i. 23.—*Wight Icon. t.* 2005.—Curcuma zedoaria, *Roxb.* ——Malabar. Bengal.

MEDICAL USES.—An ornamental and beautiful plant when in flower. It abounds in the Travancore forests. The natives use the root as a perfume and also medicinally, both when fresh and dried. They have an agreeable fragrant smell, are of a pale-yellow colour and aromatic taste. Roxburgh asserted that the roots of this species are not only the longer kinds of *Zedoary* sold in the shops, but identical with the shorter kind, the tubers having merely been cut previous to drying. The root possesses aromatic and tonic properties, and is less heating than ginger.—*Pereira. Roxb.*

(215) **Curcuma longa** (*Roxb.*) Do.

Long-rooted Turmeric, ENG. Mangella-kua, MAL. Munjel, TAM. Pasoopoo, TEL. Huldee, Pitras, HIND. Hurida, Huludee, BENG.

DESCRIPTION.—Leaves broad lanceolate, long-petioled; bulbs small, and with the palmate tubers inwardly of a deep orange-colour; flowers large, whitish, with a faint tinge of yellow, the tuft greenish white. *Fl.* July—Sept.—*Roxb. Fl. Ind. ed. Car.* i. 32.—*Rheede,* xi. *t.* 11.

MEDICAL USES.—Cultivated in most parts of India. According to Rumphius, the Javanese make an ointment with the pounded roots and rub it over their bodies as a preservation against cutaneous diseases. The root is considered a cordial and stomachic, and is prescribed by native doctors in diarrhœa. It is also an ingredient in curries. There is a wild sort which grows in Mysore. The natives consider Turmeric in powder an excellent application for cleaning foul ulcers. The root in its fresh state has rather an unpleasant smell, which goes off when it becomes dried; the colour is that of saffron, and the taste bitter. Mixed with juice of the Nelli-kai (*Emblica officinalis*), it is given in diabetes and jaundice. The juice of the fresh root is anthelmintic, and the burnt root mixed with margosa oil applied to soreness in the nasal organs. The root is applied by the Hindoos to recent wounds, bruises, and leech-bites. Roxburgh states that it is frequently planted, in the neighbourhood of Calcutta, on land where sugar-cane grew the preceding year, the soil being well ploughed and cleaned from weeds. It is raised in April and May. The cuttings or sets—viz., small portions of the fresh root—are planted on the tops of ridges prepared for the purpose, about 18 inches or 2 feet apart. One acre thus sown will yield about 2000 lb. weight of the fresh roots.—(*Ainslie. Roxb.*) Lindley says that the juice is a test for free alkalies. Turmeric is regarded in the East Indies as an important bitter, aromatic stimulant and tonic, and is employed in debilitated states of the stomach, intermittent fevers, and dropsy. The starch of the young tubers forms one of the East Indian arrowroots.—(*Royle.*) It is to be observed that the same tubers which yield starch when young yield Turmeric when old, the colour and aroma which gives its character to the latter appearing to be deposited in the cells at a later period of growth.—(*Lindley.*) Turmeric paper is unsized paper steeped in tincture of Turmeric and dried by exposure to the air. It is employed as a test for alkalies, which render it reddish or brownish.

(216) **Curcuma zedoaria** (*Roscoe*). Dō.

Long Zedoary, ENG. Katon-inschi-kua, MAL. Pulang Killungu, Capoor-kichlie, TAM. Kuchoora, Kichlie-gudda, TEL. Kuchoora, Kakhura, HIND. Shutee, BENG. Kutchoor, DUK.

DESCRIPTION.—Height 3-4 feet; bulbs and palmate tubers pale straw-coloured throughout; leaves broad lanceolate, with a dark-purple sheath down the middle; scape 5-6 inches long, distinct from the leafy stems; spike 4-5 inches long; flowers deep yellow and bright crimson tuft. *Fl.* April.—*Wight Icon. t.* 2005.—Curcuma zerumbet, *Roxb. Fl. Ind.* i. *ed. Car.* 20.—*Corom.* iii. *t.* 201.—*Rheede,* xi. *t.* 7.——Chittagong. Malabar.

MEDICAL USES.—According to Roxburgh this plant yields the *long Zedoary* of the shops, though Pereira states that the plant has not been well ascertained. The root is used medicinally by the natives. It is cut into small round pieces, about the third of an inch thick and two in circumference. The best comes from Ceylon, where it is considered tonic and carminative. According to Rheede it has virtues in nephritic complaints. The pulverised root is one of the ingredients in the red powder (*Abeer*) which the Hindoos use during the Hooly festival.—*Roxb. Pereira.*

(217) **Cuscuta reflexa** (*Roxb.*) N. O. Convolvulaceæ.

Description.—Stem funicular; flowers loosely racemose, each flower pedicelled; sepals acutish, ovate-oblong; corolla tubular, lobes minute, acute, externally reflexed; anthers sub-sessile at the throat of the corolla; scales inserted at the base, fimbriated; styles short; capsule baccate; flowers small, white. *Fl.* Feb.—March.—*Roxb. Fl. Ind.* i. *p.* 446.—*Dec. Prod.* ix. p. 454.—C. verrucosa, *Sweet Brit. Fl. Gard. t.* 6.—*Roxb. Cor. t.* 104.—*Hook Exot. Flor. t.* 150.——Peninsula. Silhet. Guzerat.

Medical Uses.—This plant is used by the natives to purify the blood, and is especially useful in bilious disorders. It is also used externally in cutaneous disorders. It is occasionally used in dyeing. —*Powell, Punj. Prod.*

(218) **Cycas circinalis** (*Linn.*) N. O. Cycadaceæ.

Wara-gudu, Tel. Todda-pana, Mal.

Description.—Trunk cylindrical, unbranched, surmounted with a terminal bud, consisting in the male of a cone composed of peltate scales; leaves pinnated, thorny, springing from the apex of the trunk. *Fl.* May.—*Roxb. Fl. Ind.* iii. 744.—*Rheede Mal.* iii. *t.* 13-21.——Malabar. S. Concans. Forests near Trichore.

Medical Uses.—The scales of the cone are a most useful narcotic medicine, and are commonly sold in the bazaars.—(*Suppl. to Pharm. of India.*) A gummy substance which exudes from the stem produces rapid suppuration in malignant ulcers.—(*Lindley.*) The fruit-bearing cone reduced to a poultice is applied to the loins for the removal of nephritic pains.—*Rheede.*

Economic Uses.—This is a singular-looking plant, very abundant in the forests of Malabar and Cochin. It is very fertile, and easily propagated both from nuts and branches. Its vitality is said by Rheede to be remarkable, insomuch that the tree, having been taken up and put down again a second time after one or two years, it will grow. A kind of sago is prepared from the nuts. In order to collect it the latter are dried in the sun for about a month, beaten in a mortar, and the kernel made into flour. It is much used by the poorer classes of natives and forest tribes. It, however, will not keep long.—*Simmonds.*

(219) **Cynodon dactylon** (*Pers.*) N. O. GRAMINACEÆ.

Huriallee Grass, ENG. Arugam-pilloo, TAM. Gericha, TEL. Doorba, BENG.

DESCRIPTION.—Culms creeping, with flower-bearing branchlets, erect, 6-12 inches high, smooth; leaves small; spikes 3-5, terminal, sessile, secund, 1-2 inches long; rachis waved; flowers alternate, single, disposed in two rows on the under side; calyx much smaller than the corolla; exterior valves boat-shaped, keel slightly ciliate. *Fl.* All the year.—Panicum dactylon, *Linn.*—*Roxb. Fl. Ind. ed. Car.* i. 292.—Agrostis linearis, *Retz.*—Both Peninsulas. Bengal.

ECONOMIC USES.—One of the commonest of Indian grasses, growing everywhere in great abundance. It forms the greater part of the food of cattle in this country. Respecting this grass Sir W. Jones observes (*As. Res.* iv. 242) that "it is the sweetest and most nutritious pasture for cattle." Its usefulness, added to its beauty, induced the Hindoos to celebrate it in their writings. The natives, too, eat the young leaves, and make a cooling drink from the roots. —(*Roxb.*) On account of its rooting stolons and close growth, when watered it is well adapted for turfing. From universal testimony it is the best of all our grasses for fattening and milk-producing powers.—*Stewart's Punj. Plants.*

(220) **Cynometra ramiflora** (*Linn.*) N. O. LEGUMINOSÆ.

Iripa, MAL.

DESCRIPTION.—Tree, 60 feet; leaves composed of 2-6 opposite leaflets; calyx tube very short, 4-partite, segment reflexed; petals 5, oblong-lanceolate; stamens distinct, inserted with the petals into a ring lining the calyx tube; peduncle solitary, few-flowered, springing from the branches among the leaves; flowers white.—*W. & A. Prod.* i. 293.—*Rheede Mal.* iv. *t.* 31.——Malabar.

MEDICAL USES.—The root is purgative. A lotion is made from the leaves boiled in cows' milk, which, mixed with honey, is applied externally in scabies, leprosy, and other cutaneous diseases. An oil is also prepared from the seeds used for the same purposes.—*Rheede.*

(221) **Cyperus bulbosus** (*Vahl.*) N. O. CYPERACEÆ.

Sheelandie, TAM. Pura-gaddi, TEL.

DESCRIPTION.—Culms 2-4 inches high, semi-terete, 3-cornered; root bulbous, tunicate, with bulbiferous fibres; spikelets linear-lanceolate, acuminate, 10-16 flowered, alternate in the apex of the culm, lower two double; scales ovate-lanceolate, acuminate; style trifid; seed oblong, 3-cornered, involucre with alternate leaflet; two lower ones longer than the spikes; leaves filiform, all radical, far-sheathing.—*Roxb. Fl. Ind. ed. Car.* i. 196.—*Wight Contrib.* p. 88.—C. jemenicus, *Roxb.*——Coromandel.

ECONOMIC USES.—This kind of sedge is found in sandy situations near the sea on the Coromandel coast, where it is known as the *Sheelandie arisee.* Roots are used as flour in times of scarcity, and eaten roasted or boiled: they have the taste of potatoes. *Puri gaddi* is the Telinga name of the plant, and *Puri dumpa* that of the root. The mode of preparing the flour is thus given by Roxburgh. The little bulbs are gently roasted or boiled, then rubbed between the hands in the folds of a cloth to take off the sheaths; this is all the preparation the natives adopt to make them a pleasant wholesome part of their diet, which they have frequent recourse to, particularly in times of scarcity. Some dry them in the sun, grind them into meal, and make bread of them; while others stew them in curries and other dishes. They are palatable, tasting like a roasted potato.—*Roxb.*

(222) **Cyperus hexastachyus** (*Rottl.*) Do.

Koray, TAM. Shaka-toonga, TEL. Kora, MAL. Moothoo, BENG.

DESCRIPTION.—Culms erect, 1-2 feet, triangular with rounded angles; leaves radical, sheathing, shorter than the culms; root tuberous, tubers irregular, size of filberts, rusty-coloured; umbels terminal, compound; involucre 3-leaved, unequal; spikes linear, sub-sessile. *Fl.* June—Aug.—*Roxb. Fl. Ind. ed. Car.* i. 201.—*Wight Contrib.* p. 81—C. rotundus, *Linn.*——Peninsula. Bengal.

MEDICAL USES.—The tubers are sold in the bazaars, and used by perfumers on account of their fragrance. In medicine they are used as tonic and stimulant, and have been employed in the treatment of cholera. In the fresh state, given in infusion as a demulcent in fevers, and also used in cases of dysentery and diarrhœa. It is perhaps the most common species in India of this extensive genus. It is found chiefly in sandy soils, but will grow almost anywhere. Hogs are very fond of the roots, and cattle eat the greens. It becomes a troublesome weed in the gardens, being difficult to extirpate. —(*Roxb. Ainslie.*) The roots are sweet, and slightly aromatic; the taste is bitter, resinous, and balsamic. Stimulant, diaphoretic, and diuretic properties are assigned them; and they are further described as astringent and vermifuge.—(*Bengal Disp.* p. 627. *Pharm. of India.*) The species *C. pertenuis* partakes of the same aromatic properties, and is also considered diaphoretic. Its delicate form, small and compound umbels, short slender leaves, readily distinguish this from the other Indian species. The roots, as well as being medicinal, are used for perfuming the hair.—*Roxb.*

D

(223) **Dæmia extensa** (*R. Br.*) N. O. Asclepiaceæ.

Vaylie-partie, Ootamunnie, Tam. Jutuga, Tel. Sagowania, Hind. Oobrun, Duk. Chagul-bantee, Beng.

Description.—Twining, shrubby; leaves roundish-cordate, acuminated, acute, auricled at the base, downy, glaucous beneath; stamineous corona double; outer one 10-parted, inner one 5-leaved; peduncles and pedicels elongated, filiform; margins of corolla ciliated; flowers in umbels, pale green, purplish inside; follicles ramentaceous. *Fl.* July—Dec.—*Wight's Contrib.* p. 59.—*Icon. t.* 596.—Cynanchum extensum, *Jacq. Icon.*—Asclepias echinata, *Roxb. Fl. Ind.* ii. 44.——Peninsula. Bengal. Himalaya.

Medical Uses.—In medicine the natives use the whole in infusion in pulmonary affections; if given in large doses it will cause nausea and vomiting. The juice of the leaves mixed with chunam is applied externally in rheumatic swellings of the limbs.—*Ainslie.*

Economic Uses.—A fibre is yielded by the stems which has been recommended as a fair substitute for flax. It is said to be very fine and strong.—*Jury Rep. Mad. Exhib.*

(224) **Dalbergia frondosa** (*Roxb.*) N. O. Leguminosæ.

Description.—Tree, 30 feet; bark smooth; leaves pinnate; leaflets about 5 pairs, alternate, cuneate-oval, emarginate, when very young silky; panicles axillary, pubescent; flowers secund, racemose along the alternate branches of the panicles, small, bluish white; calyx hairy; alæ as long as the vexillum, about twice as long as the keel; corolla papilionaceous; ovary very slightly pubescent; legume lanceolate, 1-4 seeded or less. *Fl.* May—June.—*W. & A. Prod.* i. 266.—*Roxb. Fl. Ind.* iii. 226.—*Wight Icon. t.* 266.——Courtallum. Travancore.

Medical Uses.—The bark in infusion is given internally in dyspepsia, and the leaves are rubbed over the body in cases of leprosy and other cutaneous diseases. An oil is procured from the seeds used in rheumatic affections, and a milk which exudes from the root is occasionally applied to ulcers.—*Roxb.*

(225) **Dalbergia latifolia** (*Roxb.*) Do.

Black-wood tree, ENG. Eettie, Corin-toweray, TAM. Eettie, MAL. Viroo-goodu-Chawa, TEL. Shwet-sal, BENG.

DESCRIPTION.—Tree, 40-50 feet; leaves pinnate; leaflets alternate 3-7, generally 5, orbicular, emarginate, above glabrous, beneath somewhat pubescent when young; panicles axillary, branched, and divaricating; corolla papilionaceous; calyx segments oblong; stamens united in a sheath open on the upper side; ovary stalked, 5-ovuled; legumes stalked, oblong-lanceolate, 1-seeded; flowers small, white, on short slender pedicels. *Fl.* April—July.—*W. & A. Prod.* i. 264.—*Roxb. Fl. Ind.* iii. 221.—*Cor.* ii. *t.* 113.—*Wight Icon. t.* 1156. ——Circar mountains. S. Concans. Travancore.

ECONOMIC USES.—A large tree, abundant in the forests of S. India and elsewhere, producing what is well known as the Black-wood. As a timber for furniture it is in great request. The planks, however, have a propensity to split longitudinally, when not well seasoned. An earthy deposit is frequently found embedded in the largest logs, which occasions a great defect in what would otherwise be fine planks. Some planks are four feet broad after the sapwood has been removed. Black-wood is one of the most valuable woods of S. India, and when well polished has much the appearance of rosewood, which name it frequently receives in commerce.—*Roxb. Pers. Obs.*

Black-wood is difficult to rear, from the ravages of insects on the sprouting seeds. It may, however, be successfully grown during heavy rains. The seed may also be sown in drills well supplied with the refuse of lamp-oil mills. The tree might be planted at distances of five yards, every alternate tree being afterwards removed. This tree also grows from suckers, but the wood does not turn out so well as that sown from seeds.—*Best's Report to Bomb. Govt.* 1863.

(226) **Dalbergia Oojeinensis** (*Roxb.*) Do.

DESCRIPTION.—Tree, 30 feet; leaves pinnately trifoliolate; leaflets ovate, roundish, rather villous, with undulated curved margins; pedicels 1-flowered, rising in fascicles, and as well as the calyx villous; flowers smallish, pale rose, fragrant. *Fl.* April—July.—*Roxb. Fl. Ind.* iii. 220.—Oujeinia dalbergioides, *Benth.*—*Wight Icon. t.* 391.——Nagpore. Godavery forests. Oude. Dheyra Dhoon.

Economic Uses.—This species yields a useful and valuable timber especially adapted for house-building.—(*Roxb.*) The wood in ripe trees is hard-veined and polishes well. It is used chiefly for cot posts and legs, as well as for combs and all small work, also makes handsome furniture. It is not liable to warp, nor is subject to worms. It is of slow growth, and attains full size in about thirty years.—(*Powell's Punj. Prod.*) A kino extracted from the bark is useful in bowel-complaints.—*Bedd. Flor. Sylv. t.* 36.

(227) **Dalbergia sissoo** (*Roxb.*) Do.

Tali, Shisham, Sissoo, Beng. and Hind. Sissu, Tel.

Description.—Tree, 50 feet; leaves pinnate; leaflets 3-5, alternate, orbicular or obcordate, with a short sudden acumination, slightly waved on the margin, when young pubescent; panicles axillary, composed of several short secund spikes; flowers almost quite sessile; stamens 9, united into a sheath open on the upper side; style very short; legumes stalked, linear-lanceolate, 3-seeded; flowers small, yellowish white. *Fl.* April—July.—*W. & A. Prod.* i. 264.—*Roxb. Fl. Ind.* iii. 223.——Coromandel. Guzerat. Bengal.

Economic Uses.—The timber is light and remarkably strong, of a light greyish-brown colour. It is good for ordinary economical purposes. It is much used in Bengal for knees and crooked timber in ship-building, as well as for gun-carriages and mail-carts. Its great durability combines to render it one of the most valuable timbers known. There are few trees which so much deserve attention, considering its rapid growth, beauty, and usefulness. It grows rapidly, is propagated and reared with facility, and early attains a good working condition of timber. Plantations have been recommended along the channels of the northern Annicuts.—(*Roxb. Jury Rep. Mad. Exhib.*) It attains its full size in fifty years. It is said to be proof against the attacks of white ants. The timber is very good for gun-carriages, and in some parts is largely used in dockyards. Also for saddles, boxes, and all furniture. A boat built from it is said to last twenty years. The raspings of the wood are said to be officinal, being considered alterative.—(*Stewart's Punj. Plants.*) Another species of *Dalbergia* yielding timber is the *D. sissoides*.—*Roxb.*

(228) **Daphne papyracea** (*Wall.*) N. O. Thymelæaceæ.

Nepaul Paper-shrub, Eng.

Description.—Tree, or small shrub; leaves lanceolate or oblong, veined, glabrous; fascicles terminal or lateral, sessile, bracteated; calyx funnel-shaped, pubescent, lobes ovate-oblong, shorter than the tube; ovary glabrous; flowers yellow. *Fl.* Jan.—Feb.—*Wall. Ap. Steud. Nom.*, ed. 2d, 483.—*Dec. Prod.* xiv. 537.—D. odora, *Don. Flor. Nep.* 68.—D. cannabina, *Wall. in As. Res.* xiii. 315.——Khasia. Silhet. Nepaul.

Economic Uses.—An excellent writing-paper is made from the inner bark, prepared like hemp. The process of making paper from this species is thus described in the 'Asiatic Researches:' After scraping the outer surface of the bark, what remains is boiled in water with a small quantity of oak-ashes. After the boiling it is washed and beat to a pulp on a stone. It is then spread on moulds or frames made of bamboo mats. The *Setburosa* or paper-shrub, says the same writer in the above journal, is found on the most exposed parts of the mountains, and those the most elevated and covered with snow throughout the province of Kumaon. In traversing the oak-forests between Bhumtah and Ramgur, and again from Almorah to Chimpanat and down towards the river, the paper-plant would appear to thrive luxuriantly only where the oak grows. The paper prepared from its bark is particularly suited for cartridges, being strong, tough, not liable to crack or break, however much bent or folded, proof against being moth-eaten, and not subject to damp from any change in the weather; besides, if drenched or left in water any considerable time, it will not rot. It is invariably used all over Kumaon, and is in great request in many parts of the plains, for the purpose of writing *misub-namahs* or genealogical records, deeds, &c., from its extraordinary durability. It is generally made about one yard square, and of three different qualities. The best sort is retailed at the rate of forty sheets for a rupee, and at wholesale eighty sheets. The second is retailed at the rate of fifty sheets for a rupee, and a hundred at wholesale. The third, of a much smaller size, is retailed at a hundred and forty sheets, and wholesale a hundred and sixty sheets to a hundred and seventy for a rupee. Specimens of the paper were sent by Colonel Sykes to the Great Exhibition. Dr Royle states that an engraver to whom it was sent to experiment upon, said that it afforded finer impressions than any English-made paper, and nearly as good as the fine Chinese paper, which is employed for what are called Indian paper proofs. Dr Campbell describes the paper as strong, and almost as durable as leather, and quite smooth enough to write on, and for office records incomparably better than any India paper. Many of the books in Nepaul written on this paper are of considerable age, and the art of making paper there seems to have been introduced about 500 years ago from China, and not from India.—*Murray in As. Res. Royle's Fibrous Plants.*

(229) **Datura alba** (*Nees, Ab. Esenb.*) N. O. SOLANACEÆ.

White-flowered Thorn-apple, ENG. Hummatoo, MAL. Vellay-oomatay, TAM. Dhootoora, BENG. Sada-dhatoora, HIND. Tella-oomatie, TEL.

DESCRIPTION.—Annual, 2-3 feet; leaves ovate, acuminated, repandly toothed, unequal at the base, and as well as the stem smooth; stamens enclosed; fruit prickly; corolla white; calyx 5-lobed. *Fl.* All the year.—*Wight Icon. t.* 852.—D. metel, *Roxb.*—*Rheede*, ii. *t.* 28.——Common everywhere.

MEDICAL USES.—This plant has probably in almost all respects the same properties as the *D. fastuosa.* It is a strong narcotic, though it is said not to be quite so virulently poisonous as the latter. The juice of the leaves boiled in oil is applied to cutaneous affections of the head. It is also used by Rajpoot mothers to smear their breasts, so as to poison their new-born female children. The seeds are employed in fevers about three at a dose, and are, with the leaves, applied externally in rheumatic and other swellings of the limbs.—*Roxb. Brown on Infanticide.*

The *D. fastuosa* is a variety with purple flowers. It is known for the intoxicating and narcotic properties of its fruit. The root in powder is given by Mohammedan doctors in cases of violent headaches and epilepsy. The inspissated juice of the leaves is used for the same purpose. The Hindoo doctors use the succulent leaves and fruit in preparing poultices, mixed with other ingredients, for repelling cutaneous tumours and for piles. They also assert that the seeds made into pills deaden the pain of the toothache when laid upon the decayed tooth. In Java the plant is considered anthelmintic, and is used externally in herpetic diseases. The Chinese employ the Datura seeds for stupefying and even poisoning those whom they are at enmity with—a practice resorted to also in India. This species is reckoned more poisonous than the white-flowered one. The leaves in oil are rubbed on the body in itch or rheumatic pains of the limbs. The seeds bruised are applied to boils and carbuncles. They are soporific, and very dangerous if incautiously used.—(*Rheede. Ainslie.*) It contains an alkaloid called Daturine, and is used as a narcotic anodyne and antispasmodic, especially in asthma and bronchitis, also in insanity and ophthalmia. —*Powell's Punj. Prod.*

(230) **Dendrocalamus strictus** (*Nees*). N. O. GRAMINACEÆ.

Male Bamboo, ENG. Sadanapa Vedroo, TEL.

DESCRIPTION.—Stems straight; thorns frequently wanting; inflorescence the same as in the common Bamboo; verticels sessile, globular, numerous, entirely surrounding the branchlets;

flowers hermaphrodite; corolla 2-valved; extreme valves pubescent, sharply pointed; pistil woolly. *Fl.* April—June.—*Roxb. Fl. Ind.* ii. 193.—*Corom.* i. *t.* 80.——Coromandel.

ECONOMIC USES.—This species of Bamboo has great strength and solidity, and is very straight, hence it is better suited for a variety of uses than the common Bamboo. The natives make great use of it for spears, shafts, and similar purposes. It is clearly a distinct species, growing in a drier situation than other Bamboos—(*Roxb.*) The natives assert that this species accomplishes the whole of its growth in two or three weeks during the rains; and some experiments made seem to indicate that in its natural habitats a very considerable proportion of the whole growth as to size, though not as to consistency, takes place within the first season. The new stems of the year are a much brighter green, and the sheaths remain on them. Single stems, as in several species, generally seed, and in such cases the stems die after the seeds ripen in June.—*Stewart's Punj. Plants.*

(231) **Dendrocalamus tulda** (*Nees*). Do.

Tulda Bans, BENG. Peka Bans, HIND.

DESCRIPTION.—Stems jointed, unarmed, smooth; leaves alternate, bifarious, sheathing, linear-lanceolate, broad, and sometimes cordate at the base; sheaths longer than the joints; panicles oblong, composed of numerous supra-decompound ramifications, only appearing when the plant is destitute of leaves; spikelets lanceolate, sessile, 4-8 flowered. *Fl.* May.—Bambusa tulda, *Roxb. Fl. Ind.* ii. 193.——Bengal.

ECONOMIC USES.—This is the common Bamboo of Bengal, and is there very abundant. It is much used for house-building, scaffolding, &c., and if soaked in water for some weeks previous to being used, lasts much longer and becomes stronger; besides, it prevents it being attacked by insects. It grows quickly. The tender shoots are eaten as pickles by the natives. There are two varieties, one called the *Peea-bans*, which is larger than the first, the joints being larger and thicker, and therefore better adapted for building. The other is the *Bashini-bans*, which has a larger cavity, and is much employed in basket-making. Another species, the *D. Ballcooa*, is also much prized for its strength and solidity, especially after having been immersed in water previous to using. Indeed this species is perhaps preferable to any other from its size.—*Roxb.*

(232) **Desmodium triflorum** (*Dec.*) N. O. LEGUMINOSÆ.

Koodaliya, BENG. Moonoodna-mooddoo, TEL. Kodaliya, HIND.

DESCRIPTION.—Stems procumbent, diffuse; leaves trifoliolate; leaflets orbicular, obovate or obcordate, more or less pubescent or hairy; peduncles axillary, solitary, fascicled, 1-3 flowered; calyx deeply divided; vexillum obovate, long-clawed; style bent acutely near the summit and tumid at the angle; legumes hispidly pubescent, 3-6 jointed, notched in the middle on the lower margins, even on the other; joints truncated at both ends; flowers small, blue. *Fl.* All the year.—*W. & A. Prod.* i. 229.—Hedysarum triflorum, *Linn.*—D. heterophyllum, *Dec.*—*Roxb. Fl. Ind.* iii. 353.—*Wight Icon.* i. *t.* 292.——Peninsula. Bengal.

Medical Uses.—This is a common and widely-distributed plant, springing up in all soils and situations, in India supplying the place of *Trifolium* and *Medicago* in Europe. There are several varieties. The natives apply the plant fresh gathered to abscesses and wounds that do not heal well.—*Wight.*

(233) **Dichrostachys cinerea** (*W. & A.*) Do.

Vadatara, Waratara, Tam. Vellitooroo Yeltoor, Tel. Vurtuli, Hind.

Description.—Shrub, 6-7 feet; thorns solitary; calyx 5-toothed; pinnæ 8-10 pair; leaflets ciliated, 12-15 pair; petioles pubescent; spikes axillary, usually solitary, cylindric, drooping, rather shorter than the leaves; corolla 5-cleft, petals scarcely cohering by their margins; flowers white or rose-coloured at the bottom, and yellow at the top; legumes thick, curved; joints 1-seeded. *Fl.* April—May.—*W. & A. Prod.* i. 271.—*Wight Icon. t.* 357.—Mimosa cinerea, *Linn.*—*Roxb. Fl. Ind.* ii. 561.—*Cor.* ii. *t.* 174.——Coromandel. Sterile plains in the Deccan.

Medical Uses.—The young shoots are bruised and applied to the eyes in cases of ophthalmia. The wood is very hard, like that of the *babool.* It is a striking plant when in flower, with its long, drooping, cylindric spikes of white and yellow flowers.—*Ainslie. Roxb.*

(234) **Dillenia pentagyna** (*Roxb.*) N. O. Dilleniaceæ.

Rai, Pinè, Nai-tek, Tam. Rawadarn, Chinna-kalinga, Tel.

Description. — Tree, 20 feet; leaves broadly lanceolate, sharply toothed or serrated, appearing after the flowers; peduncles from the axils of the scars of the former year's leaves, several together, 1-flowered; inner row of stamens longer than the others; styles 5; flowers gold-coloured, fragrant; seeds immersed in a gelatinous pulp; carpels joined into a ribbed baccate fruit. *Fl.* March—April.—*W. & A. Prod.* i. 5.—*Roxb. Cor.* i. *t.* 20.—*Fl. Ind.* ii. 652.—Colbertia Coromandeliana.——Malabar. Coromandel. S. Mahratta country. Assam.

Economic Uses.—A large timber-tree. The wood is close-grained, and used for a variety of purposes. In Assam it is used for canoes. The leaves are employed at Poona as a substratum for chuppered roofs.—(*Roxb.*) The Dillenias are found in great abundance in the Eastern Islands as well as in Australia. In fact, they have a large distribution; and two genera, *Tetracera* and *Delima*, being found in Travancore as well as Silhet, connect the flora of S. India with that of the Eastern Archipelago.—*Royle. Him. Bot.*

(235) **Dillenia speciosa** (*Thunb.*) Do.

Syalita, Mal. Uva-chitta, Tel. Chalita, Beng. Uva-maram, Tam.

Description.—Tree, 40 feet; leaves oblong, serrated, glabrous, appearing with the flowers; sepals and petals 5; peduncles solitary, terminal, 1-flowered; stamens all equal in length; styles and carpels about 20; seeds hairy; carpels joined into a spurious, many-celled, many-seeded berry, crowned by the radiant stigmas; flowers large, showy, with white petals and yellow anthers.—*W. & A. Prod.* i. 5.—*Wight Icon. t.* 823.—*Roxb. Fl. Ind.* ii. 650.—D. Indica, *Linn.*—*Rheede*, iii. *t.* 38-39.——Malabar. Bengal. Chittagong.

Medical Uses.—The fruit is eatable, and has a pleasant flavour though acid. Mixed with sugar and water, the juice is used as a cooling beverage in fevers and as a cough mixture. The bark and leaves are astringent, and are used medicinally. A good jelly is made in Assam from the outer rind of the fruit. The ripe fruit is slightly laxative, and apt to induce diarrhoea if too freely indulged in.—*Roxb. Royle.*

Economic Uses.—This tree yields good timber, and is especially valuable for its durability under water. It is used for making gun-stocks. The leaves, which are hard and rough, are used for polishing furniture and tinware, like others of the same family.—*Roxb.*

(236) **Dioscorea bulbifera** (*Linn.*) N. O. Dioscoreaceæ.

Katu-katsjil, Mal.

Description.—Leaves alternate, deeply cordate, acuminate,

7-nerved; the exterior nerves 2-cleft; transverse veins reticulated; stem bulbiferous; *male* spikes fascicled.—*Wight Icon. t.* 878.—*Rheede,* vii. *t.* 36.——Both Concans.

ECONOMIC USES.—The *Dioscoreas* are climbing and sarmentaceous plants. The roots are large, tuberous, and very rich in nutritious starch. The flowers and roots are eaten by the poorer classes: the latter are very bitter, but after undergoing the process of being covered over with ashes and steeped in cold water, they become eatable.—(*J. Graham.*) Several species yielding yams are eatable. Among the principal may be mentioned the *D. aculeata* (*Linn.*) The tubers are about 2 lb. or more in weight. They are dug up in the forests in the cold season, and sold in the bazaars. They are known as the Goa potato. The *D. globosa* (*Roxb.*) is much cultivated as yielding the best kind of yam, much esteemed both by Europeans and natives. The *D. triphylla* (*Linn.*), not eatable, for the tubers are dreadfully nauseous and intensely bitter even after being boiled. They are put into toddy to render it more potent, as they have intoxicating properties. A few slices are sufficient for the purpose.—*J. Graham.*

(237) **Dioscorea pentaphylla** (*Linn.*) Do.

Nureni-kelangu, MAL. Kanta-aloo, BENG.

DESCRIPTION.—Tubers oblong; stems herbaceous, twining, prickly; leaves digitate, downy; *male* flowers panicled, greenish white, fragrant; *female* ones spiked.—*Roxb. Fl. Ind.* iii. 806.—*Wight Icon. t.* 814.—*Rheede,* vii. *t.* 34, 35.——Concans.

ECONOMIC USES.—A common species in jungles on low hills, but never cultivated, so far as I have seen, says Dr Wight, which is remarkable, as I have always found the natives dig the tubers whenever they had an opportunity to dress and eat them. The male flowers are sold in the bazaars and eaten as greens, and are said to be wholesome. There are several other kinds of edible yams, among which may be mentioned the *D. fasciculata* (*Roxb.*), which is cultivated largely in the vicinity of Calcutta, where it is known as the *soosni-aloo;* a starch is also made from the tubers. Another kind is the *D. purpurea* (*Roxb.*), known as the Pondicherry sweet potato, which is an excellent kind of yam, but only found in a cultivated state.—(*Roxb. J. Grah.*) The roots of the *D. deltoidea* are used in Cashmere for washing the *pashm* or silk for shawls and woollen cloths.—*Powell's Punj. Prod.*

(238) **Diospyros melanoxylon** (*Roxb.*) N. O. EBENACEÆ.

Coromandel Ebony-tree, ENG. Tumballi, TAM. Toomida, TEL. Tindoo, HIND. Kiew, Kendoo, BENG.

DESCRIPTION.—Large tree; young shoots pubescent; leaves

nearly opposite, oblong or oblong-lanceolate, acute at the base, coriaceous, entire, obtuse, when young pubescent; calyx and corolla 5-cleft; *male* peduncles axillary, solitary, 3-6 flowered; stamens 12; hermaphrodite flowers rather larger than the male, nearly sessile; styles 3-4; berry round, yellow; flowers white; seeds 2-8 immersed in pulp. *Fl.* April—May.—*Roxb. Fl. Ind.* ii. 530.—*Cor.* i. *t.* 46.——Malabar. Coromandel. Orissa.

Medical Uses.—The bark is astringent, and, reduced to an impalpable powder, is applied to ulcerations, and mixed with black pepper is administered in dysentery.

Economic Uses.—The true Ebony of commerce is obtained from the *D. ebenum* (*Linn.*), a native of Ceylon, but in fact other species scarcely differing from one another yield this timber. The great peculiarity of Ebony-wood is its extreme heaviness and dark black colour. Some species have the wood variegated with white or brownish lines. Ebony was known and appreciated by the ancients as a valuable wood. Virgil said that it only came from India, though it is well known that Æthiopia was famous for it, a fact recorded by Pliny. Dioscorides said that Æthiopia's Ebony was the best. Herodotus wrote concerning the latter country, "It produces much gold, huge elephants, wild trees of all kinds, Ebony," &c.

This species yields a fine kind of Ebony. It is only the centre of the larger trees that is black and valuable, and the older the trees the better the quality. The outside wood is white and spongy, which decaying or destroyed by insects displays the central Ebony. It is much affected by the weather, on which account European cabinetmakers seldom use it except in veneer. The ripe fruit is eatable, but rather astringent. There is a slight export trade of Ebony from Madras. Other species which yield a kind of Ebony are *D. chloroxylon* (*Roxb.*), of which the wood is very hard and durable; the *D. cordifolia* (*Roxb.*), whose timber is used for many economical purposes.

Sir E. Tennent (*Ceylon*, i. 117) has some valuable remarks upon the different species of Ebony growing in that island. The Ebony (*D. ebenum*) grows in great abundance throughout all the flat country west of Trincomalee. It is a different species from the Ebony of the Mauritius (*D. reticulata*), and excels it and all others in the evenness and intensity of its colour. The centre of the trunk is the only portion which furnishes the extremely black part which is the Ebony of commerce; but the trees are of such magnitude that reduced logs of 2 feet in diameter, and varying from 10 to 15 feet in length, can readily be procured from the forests. There is another cabinet-wood of extreme beauty; it is a bastard species of Ebony (*D. ebenaster*), in which the prevailing black is stained with stripes of rich brown, approaching to yellow and pink. But its density is inconsiderable, and in durability it is far inferior to that of true Ebony.

The most valuable cabinet-wood of the island, resembling Rosewood, but much surpassing it in beauty and durability, has at all times been in the greatest repute in Ceylon; it is the *D. hirsuta*. It grows chiefly in the southern provinces, and especially in the forests at the foot of Adam's Peak, but here it has been so prodigally felled that it has become exceedingly rare. Wood of a large scantling is hardly procurable at any price, and it is only in a very few localities that even small sticks are now to be found. A reason assigned for this is, that the heart of the tree, neither of this species nor of *D. ebenaster*, is ever sound. The twisted portions, and especially the roots of the latter, yield veneers of unusual beauty, dark wavings and blotches, almost black, being gracefully disposed over a delicate fawn-coloured ground. The density is so great (nearly 60 lb. to a cubic foot) that it takes on excellent polish, and is in every way adapted for the manufacture of furniture. Notwithstanding its value, the tree is nearly eradicated; but as it is not peculiar to Ceylon, it may be restored by fresh importations from the S.E. coast of India, of which it is equally a native.

The *D. montana* (*Roxb.*) is a timber variegated with dark and white coloured veins. It is very hard and durable. The *D. tomentosa* (*Roxb.*) is a native of the northern parts of Bengal. The wood is black, hard, and heavy. Roxburgh compares this latter tree to a cypress, from its tall and elegant form. The leaves all fall off in the cold season. The *D. calycina* (*Bedd.*) has been found in the Tinnevelly district and southern provinces of Madura, being very abundant up to 3000 feet of elevation. It is called in those districts *Vellay Toveray*, and yields a valuable light-coloured wood much used in those parts.—*Bedd. Fl. Sylv. t.* 68.

(239) **Dipterocarpus lævis** (*Ham.*) N. O. Dipterocarpeæ.

Tilea gurjun, Beng.

Description.—Large tree; young branches compressed, two-edged; leaves ovate or oblong-ovate, retuse at the base, acute, shining on both sides, with numerous prominent veins; petioles glabrous; tube of enlarged calyx slightly ventricose, two segments expanded into wings when in fruit; capsule ovate, even; flowers white, tinged with red. *Fl.* March.—*W. & A. Prod.* i. 85.—Dipterocarpus turbinatus, *Roxb. Fl. Ind.* ii. 612.—*Cor.* iii. *t.* 213.——Chittagong. Tipperah.

Medical Uses.—This tree is famous over Eastern India and the Malay Islands on account of its yielding a thin liquid balsam commonly called Wood-oil, and known as the Gurjun balsam. A large notch is cut in the trunk of the tree near the ground, where fire is kept until the wound is charred, soon after which the liquid begins to ooze out. A small gutter is cut in the wood to conduct the fluid into a vessel placed to receive it. These operations are performed in the month of November to February; and should any of the trees become sickly the following season, a year's respite is given them. The average produce is 40 gallons in one season. Large quantities of this wood-oil is exported from Moulmein to Europe, where it has become a new drug in trade. It resembles in a remarkable degree the balsam of Copaiba, and has been used as a substitute for that medicine. It has a curious property, which is exhibited when it has been heated in a corked phial to about 266° Fahr.: it then becomes slightly turbid, and so gelatinous that the phial may be inverted even while hot without its contents being displaced; and on cooling, the solidification is still more complete. It is soluble in water, scarcely in ether, but freely in alcohol. Its price in the Calcutta bazaars varies from 3 to 5 rupees the maund. Dr Wight speaks from experience of the value of Gurjun oil mixed with dammer in preventing the white ants from attacking timber. A new species, the *D. indicus*, was discovered in South Canara in 1865.—*Beng. Disp. Pharm. Jour. Roxb.*

(240) **Dolichos sinensis** (*Linn.*) N. O. Leguminosæ.

Paru, Mal. Burbuti, Beng. Kara-mani, Tam. Lobia, Hind. Alsanda, Tel.

Description.—Twining annual, glabrous; leaves pinnately trifoliolate; leaflets ovate or oblong, acuminated; peduncles longer than the leaves; flowers in an oblong head or short raceme; calyx campanulate, 5-toothed; lowest one longer than the rest; legume nearly straight, cylindric, torulose, with a more or less recurved unguiculate beak, 6-12 seeded; seeds truncated at both ends; flowers largish, pale violet. *Fl.* June—Aug.—*W. & A. Prod.* i. 250.—*Roxb. Fl. Ind.* iii. 302.—*Rheede,* viii. *t.* 42.——Cultivated in the Peninsula.

Economic Uses.—Of this plant there are several varieties, differing in the colour of their flowers and seeds. It is cultivated for the seeds, which are much used by the natives in their food. Those with white seeds are most esteemed.—*Roxb.*

(241) **Dolichos uniflorus** (*Lam.*) Do.

Horse-gram plant, Eng. Koaltee, Hind. Koolthee, Beng. Kôlloo, Tam. Moothera, Mal. Woola-waloo, Tel.

Description.—Annual; stem erect; branches twining; young shoots and leaves covered with silk hairs; leaves pinnately trifoliolate; leaflets ovate, villous, pubescent when old; corolla papilionaceous; calyx deeply bilabiate; upper lip split at the apex; vexillum longer than the keel, ovate-oblong; alæ cohering with the keel at the base; flowers axillary, 1-3 together, sulphur-coloured; legumes compressed, linear, falcate, softly hairy, 6-seeded. *Fl.* Nov.—Dec.—*W. & A. Prod.* i. 248.—D. biflorus, *Roxb. Fl. Ind.* iii. 313 (not Lour.)——Coromandel. Deccan. Bengal. Cultivated in the Peninsula.

Economic Uses.—Of this there is a variety with jet-black seeds, those of the present plant being grey. Seeds of both are everywhere given in the Peninsula for feeding cattle. The natives also use them in curries. The gram plant has never been seen in a wild state. The best time to sow the seeds is at the end of the rainy season, and in a good soil in favourable years the produce will be sixty-fold.—*Roxb.*

(242) **Dracontium polyphyllum** (*Linn.*) N. O. Araceæ.

Purple-stalked Dragon, Eng. Caat-karnay, Tam. Junglee kandi, Duk. Adivie kanda, Tel.

Description.—Stalk 1 foot, smooth, purple-coloured, full of sharp variegated protuberances, with a tuft of leaves at the top; scape very short; petiole rooted; leaflets 3-parted; divisions pinnatifid; root irregular, knobbed, covered with a rugged skin; flower-stalk, rising from the root, about 3 inches high; spathe oblong, opening lengthwise; flowers closely arranged on a short thick style.—*Linn. Spec.* 1372.—*Bot. Reg. t.* 700.——Bombay. Concans.

Medical Uses.—In Japan a medicine is prepared from the acrid roots, esteemed a good emmenagogue. In the Society Islands the plant is cultivated for the sake of its roots, which, notwithstanding the taste being very acrid, are eaten in times of scarcity. Ainslie states that when properly prepared these roots possess antispasmodic virtues, and are also of repute in asthmatic affections, given in the quantity of from 12 to 15 grains per diem. They are used by the native doctors in hæmorrhoids. The plant is likewise a native of Guiana and Surinam; and in the former country is a remedy against the Labarri snake, which its spotted petioles resemble in colour. It is certainly a powerful stimulant. The spathe on first opening smells so powerfully that vomiting and fainting sometimes ensue from the stench. Graham states that it is a very common plant, the leaves opening in July, and the scape springing up at the commencement of the rains. There has existed some slight doubt as to whether the American and Indian species are identical.—*Ainslie. Miller. Lindley. J. Graham.*

(243) **Drosera peltata** (*Sm.*) N. O. DROSERACEÆ.

DESCRIPTION.—Herbaceous; stem erect, glabrous; leaves scattered, furnished with long reddish hairs, petioled, peltate, broadly lunate, with two longish horns pointing upwards; styles multifid, pencil-shaped; seeds oblong, testa not arilliform; sepals occasionally ciliated; capsule globose; seeds small, numerous; flowers yellow. *Fl.* Aug.—Sept.—*W. & A. Prod.* i. 34.——Neilgherries. Bababoodens.

ECONOMIC USES.—The viscous leaves of this plant close upon flies and other insects which happen to light upon them. A dye might be prepared from the plant, as Royle mentions the fact of the paper which contained his dried specimens being saturated with a red tinge. The leaves, bruised and mixed with salt and applied to the skin, are said to blister it. If mixed with milk they will curdle it. Cattle will not touch them. The sensitive irritability of the hairs of the leaves is a singular characteristic of the genus to which this plant belongs. Many of the other species yield a dye, but no one appears to have been made aware of these qualities.—*Royle. Lindley.*

E

(244) **Echaltium piscidium** (*Wight*). N. O. Apocynaceæ.

Description.—Perennial, climbing; leaves oblong, acuminated, shining; panicles terminal, shorter than the leaves; tube of corolla longer than the calyx; stamineous corona of five bifid villous segments; follicles swollen, oblong, obtuse; seeds membranaceous; flowers pale yellow. *Fl.* May—June. —*Dec. Prod.* viii. 416.—*Wight Icon. t.* 472—Nerium piscidium, *Roxb. Fl. Ind.* ii. 7.——Silhet.

Economic Uses.—The name of this creeper in Silhet, where the plant is indigenous, is Echalat; whence the origin of the generic name given by Dr Wight. The bark contains a quantity of fibrous matter, which the natives in Silhet use as a substitute for hemp. In steeping some of the young shoots in a fish-pond, to facilitate the removal of the bark and cleansing of the fibres, Dr Roxburgh found that it had the effect of killing nearly all the fish. Hence the specific name which he applied.—*Roxb. Royle Fib. Plant.*

(245) **Eclipta erecta** (*Linn.*) N. O. Asteraceæ.

Kaiantagarie, Kursalenkunnie, Tam. Goontagelinjeroo, Tel. Brinraj Bungrah, Hind. Keshooryia, Beng.

Description.—Stem prostrate or erect; leaves lanceolate, serrate, somewhat waved; flowers nearly sessile, alternate in pairs; corolla white. *Fl.* All the year.—*Wight Contrib.* p. 17. —E. prostrata, *Roxb. Fl. Ind.* iii. 438.—Cotula alba, *Linn.*—*Rheede Mal.* x. *t.* 41.——Common in wet clayey soils in the Peninsula.

Medical Uses.—This plant in its fresh state, ground up and mixed with gingely-oil, is applied externally in cases of elephantiasis. It has a peculiarly bitter taste and strong smell. Roxburgh considered the *E. erecta*, *prostrata*, and *punctata* to be the same species, varying in form from age, soil, and situation.—(*Roxb. Ainslie.*) The root has purgative and emetic properties assigned to it, and is also used in cases of liver, spleen, and dropsy.—*Pharm. of India.*

(246) **Ehretia buxifolia** (*Roxb.*) N. O. EHRETIACEÆ.

Cooruvingie, TAM. Bapana boory, TEL. Poluh, HIND.

DESCRIPTION.—Shrub or small tree; leaves alternate, fascicled, sessile, reflexed, cuneiform, very scabrous, shining; peduncles axillary, 2-6 flowered; pedicels very short; flowers small, white; calyx 5-parted, segments lanceolate; corolla campanulate, 5-6 cleft; berry succulent, red, quadrilocular; nuts 2. *Fl.* July—Aug.—*Roxb. Fl. Ind.* i. 598.—*Cor.* i. *t.* 57. ——Coromandel. Common on barren lands and in forests.

MEDICAL USES.—The root is used for purifying and altering the habit in cases of cachexia and venereal affections of long standing. By Mohammedan doctors it is considered an antidote to vegetable poisons.—*Ainslie. Lindley.*

(247) **Ehretia serrata** (*Roxb.*) Do.

Kala-oja, BENG.

DESCRIPTION.—Tree; leaves alternate, oblong, and broad lanceolate, acutely serrate, smooth; calyx 5-cleft; corolla 5-parted; panicles terminal, and from the exterior axils; flowers small, greenish white, fragrant, numerous, aggregate in somewhat remote sub-sessile fascicles; drupes round, pulpy, red when ripe. *Fl.* March—May.—*Roxb. Fl. Ind.* i. 596.——Bengal. Chittagong. Dheyrah Dhoon.

ECONOMIC USES.—The wood is tough, light, durable, and easily worked. Sword-handles are made from it. It is also considered good for gun-stocks. The tree is a native of Bhootan, as well as of the eastern parts of Bengal. It is also a common tree in Nepaul, where it is called *Nulshima.* It grows both on mountains and in valleys, blossoming profusely in the summer, and ripening its fruit during the rains. The latter are not touched by the natives. The flowers emit a powerful honey-like smell.—*Roxb. Wallich's Obs.*

(248) **Elœodendron Roxburghii** (*W. & A.*) N. O. CELASTRACEÆ.

Neerija, TEL.

DESCRIPTION.—Small tree; leaves opposite, elliptical or ovate, crenate-serrated, young ones glaucous; calyx 5-partite; petals 5, linear-oblong; peduncles axillary; cymes lax, dichotomous, divaricated, about half the length of the leaves, usually with a solitary flower in the forks; drupe 1-celled, obovoid; ut somewhat crustaceous and soft; flowers small, yellow. *Fl.* March—April.—*W. & A. Prod.* p. 157.—Nerija dichotoma, *Roxb. Fl. Ind.* i. 646.——Mountains of Coromandel. Courtallum.

MEDICAL USES.—The root is reported to be an excellent specific in snake-bites. The fresh bark of the roots rubbed with water is applied externally to remove almost any swelling. It is a very strong astringent.—*Roxb.*

(249) **Elephantopus scaber** (*Linn.*) N. O. ASTERACEÆ.

Anashovadi, MAL. and TAM. Shamdulun, BENG. Samdulun, HIND.

DESCRIPTION.—Stem dichotomous, ramous; leaves scabrous, radical ones crenate, cuneate, alternated at the base; cauline ones lanceolate; floral ones broad cordate, acuminate, canescent; flowers purple. *Fl.* Dec.—Feb.—*Wight Contrib.* p. 88; *Icon. t.* 1086.—*Roxb. Fl. Ind.* iii. 445.—*Rheede Mal.* x. *t.* 7.——Peninsula. Common in shady places.

MEDICAL USES.—According to Rheede, a decoction of the root and leaves is given in dysuria. In Travancore the natives boil the bruised leaves with rice, and give them internally in swellings of the body or pains of the stomach.—*Rheede.*

(250) **Elettaria cardamomum** (*Maton.*) N. O. ZINGIBERACEÆ.

Cardamom plant, ENG. Yalum, MAL. Aila-cheddie, TAM. Yaylakooloo, TEL. Eelachie, DUK. and HIND. Elachee, BENG.

DESCRIPTION.—Stem perennial, erect, jointed, 6-9 feet, enveloped in the sheaths of the leaves; leaves lanceolate, acuminate, sub-sessile, entire, 1-2 feet long; sheaths slightly villous; scapes several, flexuose, jointed, branched, 1-2 feet long; flowers alternate, short-stalked, solitary at each point of the racemes; calyx funnel-shaped, 3-toothed, finely striated; corolla tube as long as the calyx; limb double; exterior portion of 3 oblong, concave, nearly equal divisions; inner lip obovate, longer than the exterior divisions, curled at the margins; apex 3-lobed, marked in the centre with purple-violet stripes; capsule oval, somewhat 3-sided, 3-celled, 3-valved; seeds numerous, angular; flowers pale-greenish white.—Alpinia cardamomum, *Roxb. Fl. Ind.* i. 70.—*Cor.* iii. *t.* 226.—Amomum repens, *Roscoe.*—*Rheede Mal.* xi. *t.* 45.——Hilly parts of Travancore and Malabar. Wynaad. Coörg. Nuggur.

Medical Uses.—As cordial and stimulant the seeds are frequently used medicinally, but more frequently as correctives in conjunction with other medicines. A volatile oil is procured from them by distillation, which has a strong aromatic taste, soluble in alcohol. It loses its odour and taste by being kept too long. The natives chew the fruit with betle, and use it in decoction for bowel-complaints and to check vomiting. In infusion it is given in coughs.

Economic Uses.—Produces the Cardamoms of commerce. They are either cultivated or gathered wild. In the Travancore forests they are found at elevations of 3000 to 5000 feet. The mode of obtaining them is to clear the forests of trees, when the plants spontaneously grow up in the cleared ground. A similar mode has been mentioned by Roxburgh, who states that in Wynaad, before the commencement of the rains in June, the cultivators seek the shadiest and woodiest sides of the loftier hills. The trees are felled and the ground cleared of weeds, and in about three months the Cardamom plant springs up. In four years the shrub will have attained its full height, when the fruit is produced and gathered in the month of November, requiring no other preparation than drying in the sun. The plant continues to yield fruit till the seventh year, when the stem is cut down, new plants arising from the stumps. They may also be raised from seeds. Cardamoms are much esteemed as a condiment, and great quantities are annually shipped to Europe from Malabar and Travancore. In commerce there are three varieties, known as the *short*, *short-longs*, and *long-longs*. Of these the *short* are more coarsely ribbed, and of a brown colour, and are called the Malabar Cardamoms or Wynaad Cardamoms. They are reckoned the best of the three. The *long-longs* are more finely ribbed, and of a paler colour. Seeds are white and shrivelled. The *short-longs* merely differ from the latter in being shorter or less pointed. It is usual to mix the several kinds together when ready for exportation. Some care is required in the process of drying the seeds, as rain causes the seed-vessels to split, and otherwise injures them; and if kept too long in the sun their flavour becomes deteriorated. Malabar Cardamoms are worth in the London market from 2s. to 3s. per lb. In Travancore they are chiefly procured from the highlands overlooking the Dindigul, Madura, and Tinnevelly districts. In these mountains the cultivators make separate gardens for them, as they thrive better if a little care and attention be bestowed upon them. Cardamoms are a monopoly in the Travancore State, and cultivators come chiefly from the Company's country, obtaining about 200 or 210 rupees for every candy delivered over to the Government.—(*Ainslie. Pereira. Pers. Obs. Report of Prod. of Travancore.*) It is to be regretted, writes Major Beddome, that Cardamoms are not turned to more account. The plant grows spontaneously in many of our hill-tracts, and, with judicious management and some artificial planting, might be made to yield a very handsome revenue after a few years. In South Canara some Cardamom tracts within our reserves have been sold by the collector, on a lease of several years, for a very small sum, and the amount is credited to land revenue. In portions of the Annamallays, Madura, and Tinnevelley, our tracts are poached on by collectors under the Cochin and Travancore Governments; but in a great portion of these forests the Cardamoms simply rot in the jungles.—*Rep. to Mad. Govt.* 1870.

(251) **Eleusine coracana** (*Gærtn.*) N. O. Graminaceæ.

Mootamy, Tajetti-pullu, Mal. Kayvaru, Kelwaragoo, Tam. Tamida, Sodee, Tel. Murooa, Beng. Ragee, Nacheni, Hind.

Description.—Culms erect, 2-4 feet, a little compressed, smooth; leaves bifarious, large, smooth; mouths of sheaths bearded; calyx 3-6 flowered, glumes keeled, obtuse, with membranaceous margins; spikes 4-6 digitate, incurved, secund, 1-3 inches long, composed of two rows of sessile 3-4 flowered spikelets; rachis slightly waved; valves of corolla nearly equal; seeds globular, brown, a little wrinkled, covered with a thin aril. *Fl.* July—Sept.—*Roxb. Fl. Ind.* i. 342.—Cynosurus coracanus, *Linn.*—*Rheede*, xii. *t.* 78.——Cultivated.

Economic Uses.—This is the most prolific of cultivated grasses, forming the chief diet of the poorer classes in some parts of India, as Mysore, N. Circars, and slopes of the Ghauts. Roxburgh says he never saw it in a wild state. On the Coromandel coast it is known as the *Natchnee* grain, and is the *Raggee* of the Mohammedans. In Teloogoo the name of the grain is *Ponassa.* A fermented liquor is prepared from the seeds called Bojah in the Mahratta country.—(*Roxb.*) Ragi is perhaps the most productive of Indian cereals. Roxburgh adverts to the extraordinary fertility derived from two seeds which came up by accident in his garden. They yielded 81,000 corns. It is the staple grain of the Mysore country, where it is stored in pits, keeping sound for years.—(*W. Elliot.*) Another species, the *E. stricta*, is cultivated to a great extent. It differs from the preceding in having the spikes straight, being of a larger size, and more productive. The seeds are also heavier, which cause the spike to bend bown horizontally. All the millets prefer a light good soil, from which the water readily flows after the heavy rains. In a favourable season the farmers reckon on an increase of about a hundred and twenty fold. The variety known in Teloogoo as the *Maddi ruba-soloo* requires a richer soil than the others; and in good years, when the land fit for its cultivation can be procured, increases five hundred fold.—*Roxb.*

(252) **Embelia ribes** (*Burm.*) N. O. MYRSINACEÆ.

Vellal, TAM. Vishaul, MAL. Baberung, BENG.

DESCRIPTION.—Large climbing shrub; tender shoots and peduncles hoary; leaves alternate, oblong, entire, glabrous; panicles terminal, hoary; calyx and corolla 5-parted; stamens inserted in the middle of the petals; flowers numerous, very small, greenish yellow; tube of calyx concave; berries succulent, black. *Fl.* Feb.—March.—*Wight Icon. t.* 1207.—*Roxb. Fl. Ind.* i. 586.—E. ribesioides, *Linn.*——Peninsula. Silhet.

MEDICAL USES.—The natives in the vicinity of Silhet, where the plant grows abundantly, gather the berries, and when dry sell them to the small traders in black pepper, who fraudulently mix them with that spice, which they so resemble as to render it almost impossible to distinguish them by sight or by any other means, as they are withal somewhat spicy. Given in infusion, they are anthelmintic. They are also administered internally in piles. Their pungency is ascribed by Decandollo to the quantity of some peculiar quality of the resinous substance. Royle states they are cathartic. —*Don. Royle. Roxb.*

(253) **Emblica officinalis** (*Gærtn.*) N. O. EUPHORBIACEÆ.

Nellee, MAL. Nelle-kai, TAM. Amla, BENG. Amlika, Arooli, Aoongra, HIND. Asereki, TEL.

DESCRIPTION.—Tree; leaves alternate, bifarious, pinnate, flower-bearing; leaflets numerous, alternate, linear-obtuse, entire; petioles striated, round; calyx 6-parted; flowers in the *male* very numerous in the axils of the lower leaflets, and round the common petiole below the leaflets; in the *female* few, solitary, sessile, mixed with some males in the most exterior floriferous axils; stigmas 3; drupe globular, fleshy, smooth, 6-striated; nut obovate-triangular, 3-celled; seeds 2 in each cell; flowers small, greenish yellow. *Fl.* April—Nov. —*Wight Icon. t.* 1896.—Phyllanthus emblica, *Linn.*—*Roxb. Fl. Ind.* iii. 671.—*Rheede Mal.* i. *t.* 38.——Coromandel. Malabar. Deccan. Bengal.

MEDICAL USES.—The seeds are given internally as a cooling remedy in bilious affections and nausea, and in infusion make a good drink in fevers. They are also used in diabetes. Infusion of the leaves is applied to sore eyes. Bark of the root mixed with honey is applied to aphthous inflammations of the mouth. The bark of the tree itself is astringent, and is used for tanning purposes. It is medicinally used in diarrhœa. The fruit is occasionally pickled, or preserved in sugar. When dry it is said to be gently laxative. In the latter state the decoction is employed in fevers, and mixed with sugar and drunk in vertigo. The young leaves mixed with sour milk are given by the natives in dysentery. In Travancore the natives put the young branches into the wells to impart a pleasant flavour to the water, especially if it be impure from the accumulation of vegetable matter or other causes.—(*Ainslie. Rheede.*) Antiscorbutic virtues have been attributed to the fruits, which are known as the Emblic Myrobalans. The flowers are employed by the Hindoo doctors for their supposed refrigerant and aperient qualities. The bark partakes of the astringency of the fruit. Dr A. Ross prepared, by decoction and evaporation, from the root, an astringent extract equal to catechu both for medicine and the arts.—*Pharm. of India.*

Economic Uses.—This tree yields a valuable timber.

(254) **Embryopteris glutinifera** (*Roxb.*) N. O. Ebenaceæ.

Wild Mangosteen, Eng. Panitsjika marum, Mal. Panichekai toombika, Tam. Tumika, Tel. Gaub, Hind. Gab, Beng.

Description.—Tree, 25-30 feet; leaves alternate, linear-oblong, pointed, glabrous, shining, short-petioled; *male* peduncles axillary, solitary, 3-4 flowered; stamens 20; *females* 1-flowered, larger than the male; stamens 2-4, short; pistils 4; nut globular, size of a small apple, rusty-coloured, filled with pulpy juice and covered with a rusty farina; seeds 8; flowers white. *Fl.* March—April.—*Roxb. Fl. Ind.* ii. 533.—*Cor.* i. *t.* 70.—*Wight Icon. t.* 844.—*Rheede Mal.* iii. *t.* 41.——Peninsula. Travancore. Bengal.

Medical Uses.—The juice of the fruit is powerfully astringent, and is an excellent remedy in diarrhœa and dysentery. Dr Short mentions that it is used by the natives as a local application to bruises and sprains, as it tends to relieve the swelling.—*Pharm. of India.*

Economic Uses.—The fruit, though astringent, is eaten by the natives. The juice is used in Bengal for paying the bottom of boats. The unripe fruit contains a very large proportion of tannin. The infusion is used to steep fishing-nets in, to make them more durable. The Hindoo doctors apply the fresh juice of the fruit to wounds. On the Malabar coast it is much employed by carpenters as an excellent glue. The glutinous pulp surrounding the seeds is used by Europeans in binding books, as it is obnoxious to insects. The fruit also yields a concrete oil from boiling the seeds. They are first dried in the sun, then pounded and boiled; the oil collects on the surface, and becomes concrete during the cooling. It is of a yellowish colour.—*Roxb. Ainslie.*

(255) **Emilia sonchifolia** (*Dec.*) N. O. Asteraceæ.

Muel-schevi, Mal. Sadi-modi, Beng.

Description.—Annual; stem herbaceous, branching a little towards the top; leaves lyrate; stem clasping; flowers few, in terminal umbellets, cylindrical, peduncled; flowers small, bright purple. *Fl.* Nov.—Feb.—*Wight Contrib.* p. 24.—Cacalia sonchifolia, *Linn.*—*Rheede Mal.* x. *t.* 68.——Both Peninsulas. Common everywhere.

Medical Uses.—This plant is used in decoction on the Malabar coast as a febrifuge, and mixed with sugar the juice is given in bowel-complaints. The leaves are eaten raw in salads in China. In Travancore the pure juice of the leaves is poured drop by drop in the eyes for about ten minutes in cases of night-blindness. The natives consider the juice as cooling as rose-water, and prescribe it in inflammation of the eyes.—*Rheede. Ainslie. Pers. Ob.*

(256) **Entada pusætha** (*Dec.*) N. O. Leguminosæ.

Gila-gach, Beng. Parin-kaka Vully, Mal.

Description.—Climbing shrub; leaves bipinnated; pinnæ 2 pairs, sometimes only 1; leaflets 2-5 pairs, glabrous on both sides, oblong-ovate or ovate-emarginate; spikes solitary or in pairs, axillary; petals 5, connected at the base; stamens 10; legume more or less twisted, very large, 2-3 feet long, ligneous, with the sutures very thick; seeds nearly orbicular, 2 inches in diameter; flowers small, pale yellow. *Fl.* March—April.—*W. & A. Prod.* i. 267.—E. monostachya, *Dec.*—Mimosa scandens, *Linn.*—M. Entada, *Linn.*—*Rheede Mal.* viii. *t.* 32-34.—x. *t.* 77.——Travancore. Western Ghauts. N. Circars.

Medical Uses.—The seeds, which are of an immense size, are used by natives for washing the hair, and by the hill people as a febrifuge, and also said to be employed in pains of the loins and debility. In Java they are employed as emetic. When the plants are young, the spikes are frequently axillary on the young shoot, which has made some botanists suppose that there are two species in India.—*Wight. Rheede. Gibson.*

(257) **Epicarpurus orientalis** (*Blume*). N. O. MORACEÆ.

Sheora, BENG. Peerahi, TAM. Pukkie, TEL. Nuckchilnie, DUK. Seeura, HIND. Tinda-parua, MAL.

DESCRIPTION.—Tree; leaves alternate, short-petioled, obovate, cuspidate, acuminate, serrated towards the apex, very rough above; *male* flowers capitate, heads axillary, aggregated, short-peduncled; *females* axillary, 1-2 together, longish-pedicelled; fruit drupaceous, deep yellow, 1-seeded; cotyledons very unequal-sided; flowers small, greenish yellow. *Fl.* Jan.—Feb.—*Wight Icon.* vi. *t.* 1961.—Trophis aspera, *Willd.*—*Roxb. Fl. Ind.* iii. 761.—*Rheede Mal.* i. *t.* 48.——Concans. Coromandel. Bengal.

MEDICAL USES.—This is described by Dr Wight as a small, rigid, stunted-looking tree, common all over India, very suitable for hedges. The milky juice is applied to sand-cracks in the feet and excoriations of the skin. The plant is said to have astringent and antiseptic qualities. On the Malabar coast it is applied in decoction as a lotion to the body in fevers, and the root bruised is applied to boils. A fibre is procured from the stem, and pieces of the wood are frequently used by the natives as tooth-brushes.—*Ainslie. Rheede.*

(258) **Eriodendron anfractuosum** (*Dec.*) N. O. BOMBACEÆ.

Pania, Paniala, MAL. Elavum, TAM. ~~Poga~~, TEL. Huttian, HIND. Shwet-shimool, BENG.

DESCRIPTION.—Tree, 50-60 feet; trunk prickly at the base; branches growing out horizontally from the stem, three from one point; leaflets 5-8, quite entire, or serrulated towards the point, lanceolate, mucronate, glaucous beneath; petals 5, united at the base, filaments joined at the base, each bearing 2-3 versatile anfractuose anthers; style crowned with a 5-6 cleft stigma; capsule 5-celled, 5-valved; cells many-seeded; seeds embedded in silky cotton; flowers white, springing from the branches. *Fl.* Dec.—Jan.—*W. & A. Prod.* i. 61.—*Wight Icon.* *t.* 400.—Bombax pentandrum, *Linn.*—*Rheede Mal.* iii. *t.* 49-51.——Peninsula. Travancore.

ECONOMIC USES.—A solution of the gum of this tree is given in conjunction with spices in bowel-complaints. The cotton which is got from the pods is only of use for stuffing pillows and cushions. The texture is too loose to admit of its being used in the fabrication of cloth. The cotton from it, easily catching fire, is put in tinder-boxes, and employed in the preparation of fireworks. An oil is extracted from the seeds, of a dark-brown colour.—(*Jury Rep.*) Dr Macfadyen (*Flora of Jamaica*, i. 93) says of this tree, it is of rapid growth and is readily propagated by stakes placed in the ground. Perhaps no tree in the world has a more lofty or imposing appearance. Even the untutored children of Africa are so struck with the majesty of its appearance that they designate it the god-tree, and account it sacrilege to injure it with the axe. The large stems are hollowed out to form canoes. The wood is soft, and subject to the attacks of insects; but if steeped in strong lime-water it will last for several years, even when made into boards and shingles, and in situations exposed to the weather. The young leaves are sometimes dressed by the negroes as a substitute for okro.

(259) **Erythræa Roxburghii** (*Don*). N. O. Gentianaceæ.

Description.—Herbaceous; stem erect; lowermost leaves rosulate, obovate-oblong, obtuse; cymes 1-2 dichotomous, spreading; flowers lateral, ebracteate, star-like, pink. *Fl.* Jan.—Feb.—*Dec. Prod.* ix. 59.—Chironia centauroides, *Roxb.*—*Wight Icon. t.* 1325.——Bengal. Peninsula. Common in cultivated fields after the rains.

Medical Uses.—The whole plant is powerfully bitter, and is held in great repute as a tonic by the natives.—*Beng. Disp.* p. 461.

(260) **Erythrina Indica** (*Lam.*) N. O. Leguminosæ.

Indian Coral tree, Eng. Muruka-marum, Tam. Moolloo-moorikah, Mal. Palita-mundar, Beng. Furrud, Hind. Badide-chettu, Tel.

Description.—Tree, 10-30 feet, armed with prickles; petioles and leaves unarmed; leaves pinnately trifoliolate; leaflets glabrous, entire, the terminal ones broadly cordate; racemes terminal, horizontal; calyx spathaceous, contracted and 5-toothed at the apex; corolla papilionaceous; vexillum about three times shorter than the calyx, and four times longer than the alæ; petals of keel distinct; stamens monadelphous, with the sheath entire at the base, thence diadelphous with the tube split; legumes 6-8 seeded; flowers scarlet. *Fl.* Jan.—April.—*W. & A. Prod.* i. 260.—*Roxb. Fl. Ind.* iii. 249.—*Wight Icon. t.* 58.—*Rheede Mal.* vi. *t.* 7.—E. Corallodendron, *Linn.*——Coromandel. Concans. Bengal.

ECONOMIC USES.—This tree yields a light and soft wood called *Mootchie-wood*, much used for toys, sword-sheaths, and other light work. Leaves and bark are used in cases of fevers by the natives. The tree is much used in Malabar for the support of the betel vines; and from being armed with numerous prickles, it serves as an excellent hedge-plant to keep cattle from cultivated grounds.—*Wight.*

(261) **Eucalyptus globulus** (*Labill.*) N. O. MYRTACEÆ.

Australian or Blue-Gum tree, ENG.

DESCRIPTION.—Lofty tree; young shoots and foliage glaucous-white; leaves of the young trees opposite, sessile, and cordate, of the full-grown tree lanceolate or ovate-lanceolate, acuminate, falcate; veins rather conspicuous, oblique and anastomosing, the intra-marginal one at a distance from the edge; flowers large, axillary, solitary, or 2-3 together, closely sessile on the stem or on a peduncle not longer than thick; calyx tube broadly turbinate, thick, woody, and replete with oil-receptacles, more or less ribbed and rugose; border prominent; operculum thick, hard, and warty, depressed hemispherical; stamens inflected in the bud, raised above the calyx by the thick edge of the disk; anthers ovate, with parallel cells; fruit semi-globular, the broad flat-topped disk projecting above the calyx, the capsule nearly level with it; valves flat.—*Dec. Prod.* iii. 220.—*Hook. Fl. Tasm.* i. 133.—*Benth. Fl. Austr.* iii. 225. ——Cultivated on the Neilgherries and other high lands.

MEDICAL USES.—Several species of *Eucalyptus* have of late years become naturalised on the Neilgherries and other high lands of India. The red gum of Western Australia is the produce of several, especially of *E. resinifera.* In its medical properties it is nearly allied to kino. It has been introduced into British practice by Sir Ronald Martin, who found it very effectual in the treatment of chronic bowel-complaints, and especially in the chronic dysentery of Europeans. It is reckoned less directly astringent and more demulcent than catechu or kino. The dose is from five to ten grains in the form of powder or syrup.—(*Pharm. of India.*) Professor Wiesner of Vienna investigated the subject of *Eucalyptus kino*, as hitherto no reliable information on the subject existed. He adopts the name *kino*, because gums are mostly soluble in alcohol as well as in water. *Eucalyptus kino* contained from 15 to 17 per cent of water; it gave only a trace of ash, and no sugar was found on analysis. The physical properties nearly agree with those of ordinary kino: it forms dark red, more or less transparent grains: in thin fragments, under the microscope, quite transparent and amorphous. They sink in cold water. Water dissolves it more or less readily to a red, yellowish, or brownish liquid of astringent taste. Many of the species have hitherto not been known to yield any gum. The *E. kino* is applicable for tanning or dyeing. The value varies very much. The best is procured from *E. corymbosa*, *E. rostrata*, and *E. citriodora.*—(*Wiesner in Pharm. Jour.* Aug. 1871.) The species under consideration is easily acclimatised in the southern provinces of France, Corsica, Algiers, and Spain, being known in the last-named country as the fever-tree. An essential oil is obtained from the leaves by distillation, which has been named Eucalyptol. It has an agreeable, fragrant, aromatic odour, and a warm, bitter flavour. Large doses sometimes cause headache and fever, with accelerated respiration and thirst: upon anæmic persons it acts as a narcotic. The physiological action of the leaves is very similar.

In Australia the *E. globulus* is the popular remedy for fevers, and in Europe it has been used successfully in the treatment of diseases prevalent in marshy districts. M. Gubler quotes the testimony of several medical practitioners, who say that it produces marvellous results in cases of intermittent fevers, especially obstinate ones, where sulphate of quinine has failed. He also points out that in marshy districts near to Eucalyptus forests intermittent fevers are unknown, a result that he attributes either to the neutralisation of the effluvia by the aromatic emanations from the trees, or else to the sweetening of the stagnant waters by the leaves and pieces of bark that fall into them—such waters, according to travellers, being perfectly potable. Efforts are therefore being made to increase the number of Eucalyptus plantations in the marshy and insalubrious districts of Corsica and Algeria.

The tincture, infusion, and decoction of Eucalyptus are used for disinfecting the dressings of wounds. M. Marès has employed fresh young leaves as a local stimulant to small wounds slow to cicatrise. Dilute essence, infusion, and distilled water of the leaves are used as astringents and hæmostatics. The preparations are also used with success in purulent catarrhal affections of the urethra and vagina. The leaves, when masticated, perfume the breath and harden spongy and bleeding gums.—*Professor Gubler in Pharm. Jour.* March 1872.

ECONOMIC USES.—These trees have spread so rapidly on the Neilgherries and other high lands that they bid fair to become of the greatest importance as timber-trees, among which they rank very high, being especially rapid in their growth, and remarkably durable. They will succeed at low elevations, at 3000 or 4000 feet. The *E. rostrata*, known as the *Yarrah* of Western Australia, is particularly recommended for sleepers on railways, for piles in river-work, and in all purposes requiring strength and durability. It possesses the property of resisting the white ant and sea-worm (*Teredo navalis*), neither of which have been known to attack it, though constantly exposed to both. The specific gravity of *Yarrah* is about the same as teak. It is unsuited for cabinet-work, as it is extremely hard, and could not be worked to advantage. The *E. globulus* attained at Ootacamund 9 feet in girth in 18 years. The other species growing there are *E. gummifera* and *E. robusta*.—(*Cleghorn's Forests and Gardens of S. India. Govt. Reports.*) A valuable oil is yielded by several species of *Eucalyptus*, and now forms a considerable branch of trade in Australia. In his lecture on Forest Culture, Baron Von Mueller says it is possible to produce the oil at a price so cheap as to allow the article to be used in various branches of art—for instance, in the manufacture of scented soap, it having been ascertained that this oil surpasses any other in value for diluting the oils of roses, of orange-flowers, and other very costly oils, for which purpose it proves far more valuable than the oil of rosemary and other ethereal oils hitherto used. As this became known, such a demand arose that a thoughtful and enterprising citizen of Melbourne was able to export about 9000 lb. to England and 3000 lb. to foreign ports, though even now this oil is but very imperfectly known abroad. The average quantity now produced at his establishment for export is 700 lb. per month. Alcoholic extracts of the febrifugal foliage of *Eucalyptus globulus* and *E. amygdalina* have also been exported in quantity by the same gentleman to England, Germany, and America. Originally an opinion was entertained that all the Eucalyptus oils had great resemblance to each other; such, however, proved not to be the case when accurate experimental tests came to be applied. Thus, for instance, the oil, which in such rich percentage is obtained from *Eucalyptus amygdalina*, though excellent for diluting the most delicate essential oils, is of far less value as a solvent for resins in the fabrication of select varnishes. For this latter purpose the oil of one of the dwarf Eucalypts forming the Malee scrub, a species to which Dr Mueller gave, on account of its abundance of oil, the name *Eucalyptus oleosa*, nearly a quarter of a century ago, proved far the best. It is this Malee oil which is now coming into extensive adaptations for dissolving amber, Kauri resin, and various kinds of copal. Those Eucalypts are the most productive of oil from their leaves which have the largest number of pellucid dots in these organs. This is easily ascertained by viewing the leaves by transmitted light, when the transparent oil-glands will become apparent, even without the use of a magnifying lens. But there are still other reasons which have drawn the Eucalypts into extensive cultural use elsewhere—for instance, in Algeria, Spain, Portugal, Italy, the south of France, Greece, Egypt, Palestine, various uplands of India, the savannahs of North America, the llanos of South America, at Natal, and other places in South Africa, and even as near as New Zealand.* One of the advantages offered is the extraordinary facility and quickness with which the seeds are raised, scarcely any care being requisite in nursery-work—a seedling, moreover, being within a year, or even

* The seeds of *Eucalyptus rostrata* (red-gum tree) are available for all tropic countries, inasmuch as this species, which is almost incomparably valuable for its lasting wood, ranges naturally right through the hot zone of Australia.

less time, fit for final transplantation. Another advantage consists in the ease with which the transmit can be effected, in consequence of the minuteness of most kinds of Eucalyptus seeds,* there being, besides, no difficulty in packing on account of the natural dryness of these seeds. For curiosity's sake Dr Mueller had an ounce of the seed of several species counted, with the following results:—

Blue-gum tree 1 ounce—sifted fertile seed-grains, 10,112.
Stringy-bark tree (unsifted), 21,080.
Swamp-gum tree (unsifted), 28,264.
Peppermint Eucalypt (unsifted), 17,600.

According to this calculation, 161,792 plants could be raised from 1 lb. of seeds of the blue-gum tree. If only half the seeds of such grew, the number of seedlings would be enormous; and even if only the seedlings of one quarter of the seeds of 1 lb. finally were established, they would suffice, in the instance of the blue-gum tree, to cover 404 acres, assuming that we planted at the rate of 100 trees to the acre (allowing for thinning out).

It seems marvellous that trees of such colossal dimensions, counting among the most gigantic of the globe, should arise from a seed-grain so extremely minute.

The exportation of Eucalyptus seeds has already assumed some magnitude. The monthly mails convey occasionally quantities to the value of over £100; the total export during the last twelve years must have reached several, or perhaps many, thousand pounds sterling. For the initiation of this new resource, through his extensive correspondence abroad, Dr Mueller can lay much claim; and he believes that almost any quantity of Eucalyptus seed could be sold in the markets of London, Paris, Calcutta, San Francisco, Buenos Ayres, Valparaiso, and elsewhere, as it will be long before a sufficient local supply can be secured abroad from cultivated trees.—*Von Mueller on Forest Culture. Pharm. Jour.* Feb. 1872.

(262) **Eugenia acris** (*Wight*). N. O. Myrtaceæ.

The Pimento-tree, Eng.

Description.—Tree, 20-30 feet; young branches acutely 4-angled; leaves opposite, elliptic-oval, obtuse, very glabrous, upper side reticulated with elevated veins; peduncles compressed, axillary and terminal, trichotomous, corymbose, rather longer than the leaves; calyx limb 5-partite, segments roundish; berry globose, 1-4 seeded; flowers small, white. *Fl.* Jan.—March.—*W. & A. Prod.* i. 331.—E. pimenta, *Dec.*—Myrtus pimenta, *Linn.*——Courtallum. Travancore. Madras.

* The seeds of the West Australian red-gum tree (*Eucalyptus calophylla*) and the East Australian bloodwood-tree (*Eucalyptus corymbosa*) are comparatively large and heavy.

Economic Uses.—Introduced from America. The timber is hard, red, and heavy, capable of being polished and used for mill-cogs, and other purposes, where much friction is to be sustained. The bark is astringent and somewhat aromatic. The leaves are sweetly aromatic, astringent, and often used in sauce. The berries are used for culinary purposes.—*Lunan.*

(263) **Euonymus crenulatus** (*Wall.*) N. O. Celastraceæ.

Description.—Small tree; leaves elliptic, obtuse, crenulate-serrate towards the apex, coriaceous, deep shining green above; peduncles solitary, shorter than the leaves, 1-2 dichotomous, few-flowered; flowers 5-6 merous, petals orbicular; stamens very short; anthers opening transversely; margin of the torus free; style very short; stigma blunt, somewhat umbilicated; capsule turbinate, 5-celled, lobed at the apex; seed with a small aril.—*W. & A. Prod.* i. 161.—*Bedd. Flor. Sylv. t.* 144.——Neilgherries. Pulneys. Western Ghauts.

Economic Uses.—The wood is white, very hard and close-grained, and answers for wood-engraving, and about the best substitute for boxwood. The wood of the other species is similar.

(264) **Eupatorium Ayapana** (*Vent.*) N. O. Compositæ.

Description.—Small shrub; branchlets reddish; leaves opposite, lanceolate; flowers yellow.——Banks of the Jumna. Naturalised.

Medical Uses.—Properly indigenous to South America, though some botanists believe it to have been introduced into India from the Isle of France, and others that it is a native of the country. The leaves have a peculiar fragrant odour, and when first tasted slightly irritate the tongue, but afterwards the astringent quality is felt. When fresh bruised, they are advantageously applied to the cleansing of foul ulcers. The whole plant is aromatic, and is a good stimulant, tonic, and diaphoretic. In the Mauritius it is used in the form of infusion in dyspepsia and other affections of the bowels and lungs.—(*Bouton Med. Plants of Mauritius.*) As an antidote to snake-bites, it has been employed, both externally and internally, with apparent success.—(*Madras Quart. Med. Journ.* iv. 7.) A decoction of the leaves makes a good fomentation.—*Pharm. of India.*

(265) **Euphorbia antiquorum** (*Linn.*) N. O. Euphorbiaceæ.

Triangular Spurge, Eng. Schadida-calli, Mal. Shadray Kullie, Tam. Bonta-jammoodoo, Tel. Narashij, Seyard, Hind. Narsij, Beng.

Description.—Stems jointed, erect, ramous, 3-4 or more

angled; angles furnished with numerous protuberances, each armed with two short spreading stipulary spines; joints straight; peduncles solitary or in pairs, usually 3-flowered a little above the axils of the stipules; flowers greenish yellow. *Fl.* Dec.—Jan.—*Roxb. Fl. Ind.* ii. 468.—*Wight Icon. t.* 897 —*Rheede*, ii. *t.* 42.——Coromandel. Common in waste places in the Peninsula.

Medical Uses.—The juice which flows from the branches of this plant is corrosive. The natives use it externally in rheumatism; they also give it in toothache; and internally, when diluted, as a purgative in cases of obstinate constipation. This is easily distinguished from the allied species by the straight, not twisted stem, and the peduncles being few, one or two from each protuberance or bud, while in the others they are numerous. A plaster prepared from the roots and mixed with assafœtida is applied externally to the stomachs of children suffering from worms. The bark of the root is purgative, and the stem is given in decoction in gout.—(*Wight. Rheede. Ainslie.*) The resin has acrid, narcotic, drastic, and emetic qualities. It is used in dropsy, and as an errhine in chronic affections of the ears, eyes, or brain. It is a dangerous medicine. Mixed with cantharides, it forms gout-plaster.—*Lindley.*

(266) **Euphorbia Cattimandoo** (*W. Elliot*). Do.

Cattimandu, Tel.

Description.—Shrub or small tree; stem erect, 5-sided, with prominent repand angles; stipulary thorns paired, short, subulate; leaves sessile, succulent, deciduous, obovate, subcuneate, cuspidate, glabrous; peduncles crowded, 3-flowered, middle one usually sterile, and lateral one fertile, flowering after the fall of the leaf. *Fl.* March—June.—*Wight Icon. t.* 1993.——Vizagapatam.

Economic Uses.—This valuable plant was first brought to notice by the Hon. W. Elliot. I here transcribe from Dr Wight's 'Icones' the following notes, which were communicated to him by Mr Elliot: "The milk is obtained by cutting off the branches, when it flows freely. It is collected and boiled on the spot, at which time it is very elastic; but after being formed into cakes or cylinders, it becomes resinous or brittle, in which state it is sold in the bazaars, and employed as a cement for fixing knives into handles, and other similar purposes, which is effected by heating it. It is also employed medicinally, as an outward application in cases of rheumatism. The juice I sent you was, I think, boiled in water. It is much superior to what is sold in the bazaar; but it has not the valuable property, like gutta-percha, of being ductile at all times. It can be made to take any shape when first boiled, but, as far as we know, not afterwards, though some plan may be found for making it more pliant afterwards." In remarking upon the specimen sent him, Dr Wight states as follows: "Judging from the above-mentioned sample of the Cattimandoo now before me, I should suppose that, were it in the hands of men accustomed to work in such material, it would soon be turned to valuable account. I find, when exposed to the heat of a fire or lamp, it rapidly softens, and becomes as adhesive to the hands as shoemaker's wax; but when soaked for some time in warm water (150° to 180°), then it slowly softens, becomes pliable and plastic, and in that state takes any required form." Specimens of the gum were sent to the Great Exhibition in 1851, as well as to the Madras Exhibition. In the report of the jurors it was said that it may be applied to a variety of uses. It requires little or no preparation. The fresh juice is used as a vesicant. Articles may easily be moulded by the hand from it.—*Wight. Jury Rep.*

(267) **Euphorbia ligularia** (*Roxb.*) Do.

Munsa sij, BENG.

DESCRIPTION.—Tree, 20 feet; young shoots 5-sided, somewhat spirally disposed, and armed with large teeth, each of which supports a leaf, and a pair of short, black, stipulary thorns; leaves alternate about the ends of the branches, wedge-shaped, waved, fleshy; peduncles solitary between the serratures of the angles of the branchlets, 1-3 dichotomous, with a larger sessile flower in the forks; petals 5, fringed with a ragged margin inserted into the calyx; flowers greenish yellow. *Fl.* Feb.—March.—*Roxb. Fl. Ind.* ii. 465.——Peninsula. Bengal.

MEDICAL USES—The root mixed with black pepper is employed in cases of snake-bites, both internally and externally. The plant is sacred to Munsa, the goddess of serpents. Every part abounds with an acrid milky juice, employed to remove warts and cutaneous eruption.—(*Roxb.*) In July and August, on Tuesdays and Thursdays, the natives approach this tree with offerings of rice, milk, and sugar, praying to be delivered from snake-bites. However, they employ a surer means by mixing the root with black pepper as a remedy in bites. The native doctors purify arsenic by making a hole in the trunk of the tree, filling it up with solid arsenic, and after being covered with the bark of the same plant, the whole is exposed to a good fire, until the external parts of the trunk are completely charred, when the arsenic is taken out and becomes fit for use.—*Journ. of Agri. Hort. Soc. of India*, x. 37.

(268) **Euphorbia nivulia** (*Buch.*) Do.

Ellaculli, MAL. Elakullie, TAM. Akoo-jemmoodoo, TEL. Ptoon, HIND. Shij, BENG.

DESCRIPTION.—Tree; branches round; thorns stipulary; leaves sub-sessile, wedge-shaped; peduncles 3-flowered; flowers greenish yellow. *Fl.* March—April.—*Wight Icon. t.* 1862.—*Roxb. Fl. Ind.* ii. 467.—E. nereifolia, *Linn.*—*Rheede*, ii. *t.* 43.——Concans. Bengal. Coromandel.

MEDICAL USES.—The juice of the leaves of this plant is used internally as a purgative; mixed with Margosa oil it is applied externally in certain cases of rheumatism. On the western coast the bark of the root boiled in rice-water and arrack is given in dropsy. The leaves simply warmed in the fire will promote urine externally applied, while their juice warmed is a good remedy in ear-ache, and is occasionally rubbed over the eyes to remove dimness of sight.—(*Ainslie. Rheede.*) The pulp of the stem, mixed with green ginger, is given to persons who have been bitten by mad dogs, previous to the appearance of hydrophobia.—*Journ. of Agri.-Hort. Soc.* x. 37.

(269) **Euphorbia thymifolia** (*Linn.*) Do.

Chin-amaum-patchayarise, Sittra paladi, TAM. Biddarie-nanabeeam, TEL. Shewt-kherua, BENG.

DESCRIPTION.—Branches pressing flat on the earth, coloured, hairy; leaves opposite, obliquely ovate, serrate; flowers axillary, crowded on short peduncles, small, greenish; calyx and corolla each of four semilateral parts. *Fl.* Nearly all the year. —*Roxb. Fl. Ind.* ii. 473.——Peninsula. Bengal. Dry situations near woods.

MEDICAL USES.—The leaves and seeds are slightly aromatic and astringent. In a dried state they are given as a vermifuge. The leaves when carefully dried smell like tea.—*Ainslie.*

(270) **Euphorbia tirucalli** (*Linn.*) Do.

Milk-hedge or Indian Tree Spurge, ENG. Triucalli, MAL. and TAM. Lunka sij, BENG.

DESCRIPTION.—Tree unarmed, 20 feet; leaves alternate, remote, sessile, linear, smooth; flowers at the end of the twigs and in the divisions of the branchlets, crowded, subsessile, pale yellow; calyx campanulate, with 3-5 flat peltate horizontal segnents; capsule villous, 5-lobed, 3-celled; seeds solitary. *Fl.* June—Sept.—*Roxb. Fl. Ind.* ii. 470.—*Rheede,* ii. *t.* 44.——Coromandel. Malabar. Bengal.

Medical Uses.—The fresh acrid juice of this plant is used as a vesicatory. Rheede says that a decoction of the tender branches is given in colic, and the milky juice mixed with butter as a purgative, on the Malabar coast. It is used among the natives as a good manure. Goats will eat the plant notwithstanding its acrid juice. The bark and small branches are ingredients used in dyeing cotton a black colour. The root in decoction is administered internally in pains in the stomach. On the Coromandel coast it is frequently employed for hedges, and is known as the milk-hedge.—*Roxb.*

(271) **Euryale ferox** (*Salisb.*) N. O. Nymphæaceæ.

Machana, Hind.

Description.—Stemless floating plant; sepals 4; petals numerous in 4-7 series; leaves peltate, about 1-4 feet each way from orbicular to oval, entire, dark green above, with ferruginous veins, armed, with few slender prickles above, spinous beneath; petioles armed; calyx covered with recurved spines on the outside; carpel size of a pea; flowers bluish purple. *Fl.* Nearly all the year.—Anneslea spinosa, *Roxb. Fl. Ind.* ii. 573.——Chittagong. Lucknow.

Economic Uses.—The fibrous roots of this curious plant descend deep into the soil at the bottom of the water. If the water be shallow the peduncles are long enough to elevate the flower above the surface, but if deep they blossom under water. The petals of the flowers are very numerous, the exterior ones being large, and gradually lessening till they become very small. It is a native of sweet-water lakes and ponds in Chittagong and places eastward of Calcutta, where it is in blossom most part of the year. The seeds are farinaceous, and, after being heated in hot sand and husked, are eaten by the natives. Roxburgh states that the mode of preparation to fit them for the table is as follows: A quantity of sand is put into an earthen vessel, placed over a gentle fire: in the sand they put a quantity of the seed, agitate the vessel, or the sand, with an iron ladle. The seed swells to more than double its original size, when it becomes light, white, and spongy. During the operation the hard husk of the seed breaks in various parts, and then readily separates by rubbing between two boards, or striking it gently with a by-board. The Hindoo physicians consider these seeds to be possessed of powerful medical virtues, such as restraining seminal gleets, and invigorating the system.—(*Roxb.*) This plant was found by

Lord Valencia between Lucknow and the foot of the hills, and by Dr Roxburgh in the lakes of Tipperah and Chittagong. Dr Royle met with it in the jheels beyond Saharunpore, but it had no doubt been introduced there, as the names given it are synonymous with southern Nymphæa and purple Nelumbium. It is mentioned by Sir George Staunton as occurring in the province of Kianang, and by the Chinese missionaries it is said to have been introduced into China for three thousand years. It may, however, be one of those plants which belong equally to India and China.—*Royle Him. Bot.*

(272) **Evolvulus alsinoides** (*Linn.*) N. O. Convolvulaceæ.

Vistna-clandi, Mal. Vistnoo-krandie, Tam. Vistnoo-krandum, Tel.

Description.—Procumbent; stem, scarcely any; branches numerous, covered when young with long, soft, white hairs; leaves alternate, bifarious, sub-sessile, oblong, entire, hairy on both sides; peduncles axillary, solitary, longer than the leaves, pointed near the middle, 1-3 flowered, erect while in blossom, afterwards drooping; calyx of 5 segments, lanceolate; corolla campanulate; flowers small, blue with a white tube. *Fl.* Nov.—Jan.—*Roxb. Fl. Ind.* ii. 106.—E. hirsutus, *Lam.*—*Rheede,* xi. *t.* 64.——Peninsula. Bengal.

Medical Uses.—A widely-distributed plant. The leaves, stalks, and roots are used in medicine, and reputed to be excellent remedies in dysentery and fever.—*Ainslie.*

(273) **Exacum bicolor** (*Roxb.*) N. O. Gentianaceæ.

Description.—Small plant, 1-2 feet; stem and branches tetragonal; leaves sessile, sub-acute, ovate, 3-5 nerved, margins smooth; calyx 4-cleft; flowers axillary, solitary, on short pedicels; corolla white, having the segments tipped with blue. *Fl.* Aug.—Oct.—*Wight Icon. t.* 1321.—*Roxb. Fl. Ind.* i. 397. ——Neilgherries. Malabar. Cuttack. Salsette. By the margins of rivulets.

Medical Uses.—A valuable febrifuge. The dried stalks are sold at Mangalore and elsewhere in the Southern Peninsula under the name of *Country Kariyàt.* It possesses the tonic stomachic properties of Gentian, and may be advantageously substituted for it. The *E. tetragonum* is another species, possessing similar properties. It is common in the Himalaya, and the mountains and plains of Bengal and Central India as far south as Bombay. The whole plant is powerfully bitter, and, according to Royle, is called by the natives *Ooda (purple) Chiretta.* The *E. pedunculatum* is a third species, with similar virtues as a bitter tonic. It is common in the western districts of Mysore. Dr Wight recommends that the plants be gathered when the flowers begin to fade, and to be carefully dried in the shade. For administration it may be given in infusion and tincture of the same strength as those of Chiretta. Many other species occur in India, and are all worthy of trial where they are indigenous.—*Pharm. of India.*

(274) Excæcaria Agallocha (*Muller*). N. O. Euphorbiaceæ, *var.* Camettia.

Cametti, Mal.

Description.—Small tree or shrub; leaves ovate or elliptic; obtuse at the base, entire or crenate-serrulate; male spikes amentiform, dense-flowered, cylindric; female racemes shorter than the male spikes, and in separate branches, both axillary, solitary, or rarely twin; bracts destitute of distinct glands; male calyx sessile, covered by the bract, female sepals ovate, with one gland on both sides of the base inside; anthers long—exserted after flowering; capsule sulcately 3-lobed; flowers greenish. *Fl.* March—May.—*Dec. Prod.* xv. s. 2, p. 1221.—E. camettia, *Willd. Wight Icon. t.* 1865.—*Rheede,* v. *t.* 45. ——Salt marshes of the Peninsula. Travancore back-waters.

Medical Uses.—This shrub or small tree grows abundantly along the back-waters in Travancore and Cochin. It abounds in an acrid milky juice, and is known as the *Tiger's-milk tree.* The natives are afraid almost to cut the branches, for fear of the milk blistering the skin, or causing blindness should it by chance get into the eyes. The juice is applied with good effect to inveterate ulcers. The leaves are used also in decoction for this purpose. A good kind of caoutchouc may be prepared from the milk, which is worthy of attention.—*Rheede. Pers. Obs.*

(275) Excæcaria sebifera (*Muller*). Do.

China Tallow-tree, Eng.

Description.—Tree; leaves long-petioled, rhomb-ovate, entire, sharply acuminate at the apex, sub-membranaceous; racemes spiciform, terminal, at length far exceeding the leaves; bracts very broadly ovate, acute, many-flowered, many times shorter than the aggregated pedicels; male calyx 2-3 cleft, female 3-partite, 1-2 of the segments often cleft, and the calyx then becomes irregularly and spuriously 5-partite; stamens most frequently 2; styles connate below into a column, above recurved, spreading; capsules largish, globose-ellipsoid, subacute, thinly fleshy, long, black; seeds furnished under the skin with a thick, white, tallowy bed, forming a spurious aril.—*Muller in Dec. Prod.* xv. s. p. p. 1210.—Stillingia sebifera, *Michx.*—Sapium sebiferum, *Roxb.*—S. sinensis, *Baill. Euph.* p. 512. *t.* 7, fig. 26-30.——Cultivated.

Economic Uses.—A native of China, this useful tree has for some time been introduced into India. In northern China it forms a vast trade. At Shanghai it is equal to 2½ millions sterling, and by its produce the cultivators pay the revenue of whole districts. The tree now grows with great luxuriance in the Dhoons, and in the Kohistan of the N.W. Provinces and Punjaub, and there are now tens of thousands of trees in the Government plantations of Kowalghir, Hawal Bàgh, and Ayar Tolie, from which tons of seeds are available for distribution. For burning, the tallow is excellent, gives a bright, clear, inodorous flame, and without smoke. The tree fruits abundantly both in the Dhoons and in the plains, and grows with great rapidity. The tallow is separated by steaming the seeds in tubs with convex open wicker bottoms, placed over caldrons of boiling water. The seed-vessels are hard brownish husks, not unlike those of chestnuts, and each of them contains three round white kernels, having small stones within. It is the hard, white, oleaginous substance surrounding these stones which possesses most of the properties of tallow; but on stripping it off it does not soil the hands. From the shell and stone, or seed, oil is extracted, so that the fruit produces tallow for candles and oil for lamps. To obtain the extract the Chinese grind the fruit in a trunk of a tree which is hollowed out, shaped like a canoe, lined with iron, and firmly fixed in the ground. Lengthwise within this trunk there moves backwards and forwards a millstone, whose axis is fixed to a long pole laden with a heavy weight to increase the pressure, and suspended from a beam. After the seed has been pounded, it is thrown with a small quantity of water into a large iron vessel, exposed to fire, and reduced by heat into a thick consistent mass. It is next put into a case consisting of four or five broad iron hoops, piled one above the other, and lined with straw, and then pressed down with the feet as closely as possible till it fills the case. It is afterwards carried to the press.

Another, and perhaps more generally adopted process, is, merely to boil the bruised seed in water, and to collect the tallowy matter that floats to the surface. A certain quantity of some vegetable oil, occasionally in as great a proportion as 3 lb. to every 10 lb. procured from the tallow-tree, is mixed up with it.

It is not so consistent as tallow, and therefore, to promote the better cohesion of the material, the candles made of it are dipped in wax: this external coating hardens them, and preserves them from guttering. The combustion of these candles is described as being less perfect, yielding a thicker smoke, a dimmer light, and consuming much more rapidly than ours. Yet, animal tallow being very scarce in China, the vegetable production is there held in the highest estimation. The timber is white and close-grained, and well fitted for printing-blocks, while the leaves are valuable as a dye.—*Abel's Travels in China*, p. 177. *Lankester Veg. Subst.*

F

(276) **Feronia elephantum** (*Corr.*) N. O. Aurantiaceæ.

Elephant or Wood apple, Eng. Velanga marum, Mal. Velam marum, pitavoola, Tam. Velaga, Tel. Khoet, Hind. or Duk. Kuthbel, Beng.

Description.—Tree, 50-60 feet, armed with spines; leaves pinnated; leaflets 5-7, obovate, almost sessile; petioles winged, pointed; racemes lax, axillary or terminal; calyx 5-toothed; petals 5; style scarcely any; flowers small, pale pink with crimson anthers; fruit about the size of an apple with a hard greyish rind, 5-celled, many-seeded; seeds immersed in fleshy pulp. *Fl.* March.—*W. & A. Prod.* i. 96.—*Wight Icon. t.* 15.—*Roxb. Fl. Ind.* ii. 411.—*Cor.* ii. *t.* 141.——Coromandel. Travancore. Guzerat. Bengal.

Medical Uses.—A transparent gummy substance exudes from the stem when cut or broken which is called in Tamil *Velam pisnie.* It resembles much the true gum-arabic, and is used medicinally by the native Vytians, being reduced to powder and mixed with honey and then given in dysentery and diarrhœa. The leaves when bruised have a fragrant smell, like anise. The natives consider them as stomachic and carminative. They are also used by native practitioners as a gentle stomachic stimulant in the bowel-complaints of children. There is a variety of this tree, the properties of which are nearly the same as this. It is called *Cooti-Velam* in Tamil.—*Wight. Ainslie. Beng. Disp.*

Economic Uses.—The pulpy part of the fruit is edible. A jelly, much resembling black-currant jelly, only with a more astringent taste, is made from it. The wood is white, hard and durable, fine-grained, and would answer well for ornamental carving.—*Roxb.*

(277) **Ficus Bengalensis** (*Linn.*) N. O. Moraceæ.

Common Banyan-tree, Eng. Ala-marum, Tam. Bur, But, Beng. Marri, Tel. Peralu, Mal.

Description.—Tree; branches spreading very much; lower ones rooting; leaves alternate, ovate, bluntly acuminated, with parallel nerves, paler underneath, entire, downy when young, afterwards smooth; fruit-receptacles axillary, paired, sessile, as large as a middle-sized cherry, appearing and ripening in the hot season.—*Wight Icon. t.* 1989.—F. Indica, *Roxb. Fl. Ind.* iii. 539.—Urostigma Bengalense, *Miquel.*—*Rheede,* i. *t.* 28.——Common everywhere.

Medical Uses.—The seeds of the fruit are considered as cooling and tonic, being prescribed in the form of electuary. The white glutinous juice which flows from the stems is applied as a remedy in toothache, and also to the soles of the feet when cracked and inflamed. The bark given in infusion is said to be a tonic, and is also used in diabetes.—*Ainslie.*

Economic Uses.—There are several species as well as varieties of the Banyan-tree which throw out roots from their branches. The present one may perhaps be considered the best type of the family. It is remarkable, as every one knows, for the singular property of letting a gummy kind of rootlet fall from its branches. These on reaching the ground soon form a natural support to the larger branches of the parent tree, and several of these extending and increasing from year to year, forming a vast assemblage of pillar-like stems, cover a considerable area round the original trunk,—

> "Branching so broad and long that in the ground
> The bending twigs take root, and daughters grow
> About the mother tree, a pillared shade—
> High over-arched with echoing walks between."

Many instances are on record of the immense extent of some of these trees, which form so peculiar a feature in an Oriental landscape. One tree of the kind near Fort St David was computed to cover nearly 1700 yards. Colonel Sykes mentions one at Mhow with 68 stems descending from the branches, and capable of affording a shade under a vertical sun to 20,000 men. Roxburgh says that he has seen such trees fully 500 yards round the circumference of the branches and 100 feet high, the principal trunk being more than 25 feet to the branches, and 8 or 9 feet in diameter. Travellers in this country have described them large enough to shelter a regiment of cavalry, and how they have formed a natural canopy for public meetings and other assemblages. The ancients were acquainted with the tree, and both Strabo and Pliny have accurately described it. The wood is of no value, being light and porous. The Brahmins use the leaves as plates to eat off. Bird-lime is manufactured from the milky juice which abounds in every part of the tree. If the seeds drop into the axils of the leaves of the palmyra-tree, the roots grow downwards embracing the trunk in their descent, until by degrees they envelop every part except the top. In very old specimens the leaves and head of the palmyra are seen emerging from the trunk of the Banyan-tree, as if they grew from it. These the Hindoos regard with reverence, and call them holy marriages.—*Roxb.*

(278) **Ficus Benjamina** (*Linn.*) Do.

Oval-leaved Fig-tree, Eng. Itty alu, Mal. Tella barinka, Tel.

Description.—Tree; branches slender, flexuose, streaked and wrinkled; leaves petioled, ovate, entire, slenderly streaked across; fruit globular, scattered over the branchlets.—*Roxb. Fl. Ind.* iii. 550.—*Wight Icon. t.* 642, 668.—*Rheede,* i. *t.* 26. ——Peninsula. Malabar.

Medical Uses.—This is one of the most beautiful of the species. A decoction of the leaves mixed with oil is reckoned in Malabar a good application to ulcers.—(*Rheede.*) Another species growing in the Concans and Malabar, and called in Malayalum *Katù-alou,* is the *F. citrifolia.* Of this the bark of the root boiled in water is given as a wash in aphthous complaints. It is said to strengthen the gums, and also to be diuretic. A kind of balsam prepared from the bark is mixed with oil and applied to ulcerous affections of the ear, and in deafness. A bath made from the bark of root and stem is said by the natives to be very efficacious in the cure of leprosy, and mitigating pains in the limbs.—*Rheede.*

(279) **Ficus cunia** (*Buch.*) Do.

Perina teregam, Mal.

Description.—Fruit-receptacles turbinate, ribbed, pedicelled, size of a filbert, hairy, umbilicated, in pairs or threes on long procumbent, radical and cauline, compound, leafless branches, appearing all the year.—F. conglomerata, *Roxb. Fl. Ind.* iii. 561.—*Wight Icon. t.* 648.—*Rheede,* iii. *t.* 61.—— Concans. Malabar. Oude. Coromandel.

Medical Uses.—The rough leaves of this tree are used for polishing furniture. The fruit is administered in aphthous complaints; and also, boiled in milk, in visceral obstruction. A bath made both from the fruit and bark is reckoned a useful treatment in leprosy. —*Rheede.*

(280) **Ficus elastica** (*Roxb.*) Do.

Indian Caoutchouc-tree, Eng. Kusneer, Beng.

Description.—Tree, 30-40 feet; leaves from oval to oblong, pointed, thick, firm, and glossy; fruit in axillary pairs, sessile, oval, smooth, the size of an olive; stipules nearly as long as the leaves, smooth and rosy. *Fl.* March—April.—*Roxb. Fl. Ind.* iii. 541.—Stilpnophyllum elasticum, *Endl.*—*Wight Icon.*

t. 663.——Khassya mountains. Juntipoor hills. Cultivated in Malabar.

ECONOMIC USES.—This beautiful tree produces when wounded a quantity of milk which yields about one-third of its weight of Caoutchouc. This milk is used by the natives of Silhet to smear over the inside of baskets constructed of split rattan, which are then rendered water-tight. The milk is extracted by incisions made across the bark down to the wood, at a distance of about a foot from each other all round the trunk or branch up to the top of the tree; and the higher the incision, the more abundant the fluid is said to be. The tree requires a fortnight's rest before the operation is repeated. When the juice is exposed to the air, it separates spontaneously into a fine elastic substance and a fœtid whey-coloured liquid. Fifty ounces of pure milky juice taken from the tree in August yielded exactly 15½ oz. of clean-washed Caoutchouc. This substance is of the finest quality, and may be obtained in large quantities. It is perfectly soluble in the essential oil of Cajeput.

The tree is easily propagated by cuttings.—(*Roxb.*) Dr Royle (*Him. Bot.*, p. 338, 339, *note*) says: "I have been favoured with a letter from Professor Christison of Edinburgh, who obtained specimens of the East Indian Caoutchouc after it had been eight years in the country, and employed it in making a flexible tube for conveying coal-gas. Respecting it he says—'I can most decidedly state that, so far as my trials go, it is a far better article than is commonly thought, and quite fit for many most important economical uses.' The specimens have been submitted to experiment by M. Lierier the sculptor, so well known for his numerous experiments on any important applications of this substance. He pronounces the Indiarubber from Silhet, though carelessly collected, and so long ago as eleven years since, to be equal in elasticity to the best from South America, and superior to it from lightness of colour and freedom from smell. There can be little doubt, therefore, of its being an important and profitable article of commerce, since nearly 500 tons of Caoutchouc are now imported from other parts of the world; and its application and uses are so rapidly increasing that it is not possible at present for the supply to keep pace with the demand. It is hoped, therefore, that some enterprising individual will be induced carefully to collect—*i.e.*, keep clean—the juice of *Ficus elastica*. The tree is called *Kasmeer* by the inhabitants of Pundua and the Juntipoor mountains. It is also found near Durrunj in Assam, between the Burrampooter and the Bootan hills. The highest price of Caoutchouc can, however, only be obtained for that which is collected in the bottle form, or preferably in that of a cylinder of 1½ to 2½ inches in diameter, and 4 or 5 inches in length. Much useful information on the subject will be found in Roxburgh in his article *Urceola elastica*, and in his *Flora Indica*, iii. 541-5; also in an article on the same subject by Howison in the 5th vol. Trans. As. Soc. of Calcutta, and Falconer in Agri.-Hort. Soc. of India.—*Royle.*

(281) **Ficus excelsa** (*Vahl.*) Do.

Attimeralloo, MAL.

DESCRIPTION.—Tree; leaves alternate, bifarious, slightly scabrous beneath; fruit-receptacles axillary, solitary or paired, peduncled, somewhat turbinate, smooth, size of a cherry, yellow when ripe. *Fl.* June—July.—*Roxb. Fl. Ind.* iii. 552.—*Wight Icon. t.* 650.—*Rheede,* iii. *t.* 58.——Peninsula. Malabar.

MEDICAL USES.—Rheede states that at the pagoda at Vyekkam, a town on the back-water about twenty miles south-east of Cochin, one of these trees was growing in his time about fifty feet in circumference, and which was traditionally reported to be two thousand years old. A decoction is made from the root powerfully aperient in visceral obstructions. The bark of the root of the *F. nitida* and root itself, as well as the leaves, boiled in oil, are severally considered as good applications for wounds or bruises.—*Rheede.*

(282) **Ficus oppositifolia** (*Willd.*) Do.

DESCRIPTION.—Small tree; young shoots scabrous, and covered with short hair, fistulous and interrupted at the insertion of the leaves; leaves opposite, round or oblong, slightly serrate, glandular in the axils of the veins beneath, shining above, downy beneath; fruit axillary and peduncled, racemose on the naked woody branches, round, about the size of a large nutmeg, covered with short white hair, with several equidistant ridges.—*Roxb. Flor. Ind.* iii. 561.—*Cor. t.* 124. *Wight Icon. t.* 638.—Covellia oppositifolia, *Gaspar.*——Banks of rivulets in the Peninsula and Bengal.

MEDICAL USES.—The fruit, seeds, and bark are possessed of valuable emetic properties. The best form of administration appears to be the seed of the ripe fruit, dried and preserved from moisture in stoppered bottles. The bark is also a good anti-periodic and tonic. The *F. polycarpa* possesses the same medicinal properties.—*Pharm. of India.*

(283) **Ficus racemosa** (*Linn.*) Do.

Red-wooded Fig-tree, or Country Fig-tree, ENG. Atti-alu, MAL. Attie-marum, TAM. Maydi, TEL. Gooler, HIND.

DESCRIPTION.—Tree; leaves ovate, entire, pointed, veined;

fruit-receptacles on racemes, round, reddish, size of a small plum.—*Rheede*, i. *t* 25.——Concans. Malabar.

MEDICAL USES.—The root in decoction and bark of the tree are used in medicine. The latter is slightly astringent, and sometimes used in the form of a fine powder; and, in combination with Gingeley-oil, is applied in cancerous affections. The fruit is edible. A fluid which is yielded by incisions in the root is given as a tonic by native doctors. An infusion of the bark is given in diabetes; and the young leaves reduced to powder and mixed with honey in bilious affections.—*Ainslie. Rheede.*

(284) **Ficus religiosa** (*Linn.*) Do.

Poplar-leaved Fig-tree, ENG. Ashwuth, BENG. Pippul, HIND. Arasum-marum. TAM. Ray, Raghie, TEL. Arealu, MAL. Ani-peepul, DUK.

DESCRIPTION.—Tree; leaves long-petioled, ovate, cordate, narrow acuminate, acumen one-third the length of the leaf, entire, or repandly undulated towards the apex; fruit-receptacles axillary, paired, sessile, depressed, size of a small cherry, appearing in the hot season and ripening in the rainy season.—*Wight Icon.* vi. *t.* 1967.—*Roxb. Fl. Ind.* iii. 547.—Urostigma religiosum, *Miquel.*—*Rheede*, i. *t.* 27.——Common all over India.

MEDICAL USES.—The seeds are said to possess cooling and alterative qualities, and are prescribed in electuary and in powder. Leaves and young shoots are used as a purgative, and an infusion of the bark is given internally in scabies, though of doubtful efficacy.—*Ainslie. Wight.*

ECONOMIC USES.—Of this tree there are two nearly-allied species. The tree is commonly distributed over the country. It is much respected by the natives, who are very unwilling to cut it down at any time. It is frequently to be met with near pagodas, houses, and other buildings. The Hindoos venerate it from a superstitious belief that their deity Vishnoo was born among the branches. The petioles being very long and slender, the leaves tremble in the air like those of the aspen-tree. Silk-worms are very fond of the leaves. The Arabs use them in tanning. Birds are very fond of the fruit, and often drop the seeds in cracks of buildings, where they vegetate, and occasion great damage if not removed in time. The wood is light and of no use.—*Roxb. Wight.*

(285) **Ficus rubescens** (*Vahl.*) Do.

Valli-teragam, MAL. Buroni, TEL. Goori-shiora, BENG.

DESCRIPTION.—All rough and harsh; leaves alternate, short-petioled, stiff, membranaceous, roughish above and of a deep green, paler below, oblong-acute, acute at the base, serrated, entire or 3-lobed, of all shapes; fruit axillary, solitary, rarely twin, between turbinate and globose.—*Roxb. Fl. Ind.* iii. 532. —F. heterophylla, *Linn.*—*Wight Icon. t.* 659.—*Rheede,* iii. *t.* 62. ——Common in moist places in the Peninsula and Bengal.

MEDICAL USES.—The juice of the root of this shrub is internally administered in colic pains, and the juice of the leaves mixed with milk in dysentery. The bark of the root, which is very bitter, pulverised and mixed with Coriander seed, is considered a good remedy in coughs and asthma, and similar affections of the chest.—(*Rheede. Roxb.*) The *F. tsiela* appears to have similar virtues. From the bark of the root of the *F. infectoria* a peculiar kind of bow-string is made, and a red dye is prepared from the root used for dyeing cloths. Most of the species of *Ficus* have been removed to the new genus *Urostigma.*

(286) **Flacourtia cataphracta** (*Roxb.*) N. O. FLACOURTIACEÆ.

Talishaputrie, MAL. and TAM. Talishaputrie, TEL. Talisputrie, HIND. Paniyala, BENG.

DESCRIPTION.—Tree, armed with large multiple thorns; leaves oval-oblong, acuminated, serrated; racemes axillary, many-flowered; berry size of a small plum, purple, with very hard sharp-edged seeds; flowers small, greenish. *Fl.* Dec.—Jan.—*Roxb. Fl. Ind.* iii. 834.—*Dec. Prod.* i. 256.—*Rheede,* v. *t.* 38.——Warree country. Assam. Nepaul. Behar.

MEDICAL USES.—The fruit is edible. The leaves and young shoots, which are bitter and astringent, have the taste of rhubarb, and are considered stomachic, and are given in diarrhœa, dysentery, fevers, and even in consumption. An infusion of the bark is used in hoarseness.—*Ainslie. Lindley.*

ECONOMIC USES.—The wood is close-grained, hard, and durable. Another species, the *F. crenata,* is common on the Neilgherries and Shevaroys, and yields a first-rate timber. It is white, very hard, and dense.—*Bedd. Flor. Sylv. t.* 78.

(287) **Flacourtia sapida** (*Roxb.*) Do.

Booinch, BENG. Kanrègu, TEL.

DESCRIPTION.—Small tree or shrub; thorns scattered, naked; leaves serrated, elliptical, obtuse, older ones membranaceous; male flowers, stamens closely arranged on the dilated torus; female, stigmas 5-7, radiating, linear, furrowed above; peduncles axillary, many-flowered; flowers small, greenish. *Fl.* Dec.—Jan.—*W. & A. Prod.* i. 29.—*Roxb. Cor. t.* 69.——Peninsula. Bengal.

ECONOMIC USES.—This species has but few trifling points of difference between it and *F. Ramontchi*, the Mauritius plum. The fruit is eatable, but by no means good. The wood is hard and close-grained, and does not warp. The native inoculators for the small-pox use the thorns of this shrub for breaking the pustules of the small-pox on the ninth or tenth day.—*J. Grah. Wight. Long on Med. Plants of Bengal.*

(288) **Flacourtia sepiaria** (*Roxb.*) Do.

Courou moelli, MAL. Conrew, TEL. Sottacla, TAM. Jootay karoonday, DUK.

DESCRIPTION.—Shrub, 6 feet; thorns very numerous, patent, bearing both leaves and flowers; leaves obovate-oblong, older ones very rigid and coriaceous, serrate; peduncles axillary, solitary, 1-flowered; flowers small, green; berry very globular, size of a pea, succulent; seeds 4-8. *Fl.* April.—*W. & A. Prod.* i. 29.—*Roxb. Fl. Ind.* iii. 835.—*Cor.* i. *t.* 68.—*Rheede*, v. *t.* 39. ——Peninsula. Common everywhere.

MEDICAL USES.—The berries are eatable, and are sold in the bazaars. The plant makes good fences, from its numerous sharp thorns. An infusion of the leaves and roots is given in snake-bites, and the bark rubbed with oil and made into a liniment is used on the Malabar coast in cases of gout. The bark fried in oil is applied externally in rheumatism.—*Wight. Ainslie. Rheede.*

(289) **Fumaria parviflora** (*Dec.*) N. O. FUMARIACEÆ.

DESCRIPTION.—Annual; smooth; leaves linear, channelled; bracteas at first as long as the flower, afterwards as short as the fructiferous pedicel; petals 4, the lower one distinct, linear, the three upper united, the middle one spurred downwards; sepals minute; fruit globose, slightly pointed; flowers pale rose. *Fl.* Dec.—Jan.—*W. & A. Prod.* i. 18.—*Roxb. Flor. Ind.* iii. 217.—*Wight's Ill.* i. *t.* 11.——Neilgherries. Nepaul. Bombay. Bengal.

MEDICAL USES.—This plant has long been acclimatised in the East, and at the present day is considered, in conjunction with black pepper, an efficacious remedy in common agues.—(*Royle H. B.*) It is extensively employed as an anthelmintic, and to purify the blood in skin diseases. Also as a diuretic, diaphoretic, and aperient.—*Powell's Punj. Prod.*

G

(290) **Garcinia gambogia** (*Desrous*). N. O. CLUSIACEÆ.

DESCRIPTION.—Tree ; leaves lanceolate, deep green ; flowers terminal or axillary, sessile or sub-sessile, pedicelled, solitary or several together ; male, anthers numerous, on a short, thick androphore, oblong, 2-celled, dehiscing longitudinally, introrse ; female, staminodes surrounding the base of the ovary in several phalanges, each containing 2-3 sterile spathulate stamens ; stigmas 5-10-lobed, papillose, glandular ; ovary 6-10-celled ; fruit yellow or reddish, 6-10-furrowed, 6-10-seeded, nearly globular or ovate, furrows broad, with angular edges, the furrows not continued to the apex, which is smooth and depressed, and often nipple-shaped.—*Dec. Prod.* i. 561.—*W. & A. Prod.* i. 100.—G. Kydia, *W. & A. l. c.*—Cambogia gutta, *Linn.*—G. papilla, *Wight Icon. t.* 960.—*Bedd. Fl. Sylv. t.* 85.——Forests of the western coast.

ECONOMIC USES.—The pigment which exudes from the trunk is semi-transparent, very adhesive, and unsuitable as a paint. The acid rinds of the ripe fruit are eaten, and in Ceylon are dried, and eaten as a condiment in curries. The tree is called *Heela* on the Neilgherries. It yields an excellent, straight-grained, lemon-coloured, slightly elastic wood, and would answer for common furniture.—(*Beddome.*) The following report upon the gum-resin of this tree is given by Mr Broughton: "This Gamboge, though produced by a different tree to those which yield the Siam and Ceylon Gamboge, appears, nevertheless, exceedingly similar, and to be of fine quality. An estimation of the amount of colouring resin, which is the essential constituent, gave a yield of 76 per cent, the remainder consisting of gum and starch. The specimen I received was in small lumps, and differed thus in external appearance to the commercial specimens I have seen ; but in quality it can well compare with them. The yield of ordinary Gamboge in colouring resin varies from 40 to 75 per cent. Gamboge is used as a pigment in the manufacture of lacquer and in medicine. The price of the Canara gum is 1 rupee per lb. I believe the English wholesale price is £38 per cwt. As a commercial product, this Gamboge appears to promise well. I believe, some time ago, Dr Cleghorn was led to pay much attention to this substance."

(291) **Garcinia pedunculata** (*Roxb.*) Do.

Tikul or Tikoor, HIND.

DESCRIPTION.—Tree, 60 feet; leaves opposite, short-petioled, oblong or obovate-oblong, entire, smooth on both sides, with large parallel veins; flowers terminal, peduncled; male ones numerous, forming small trichotomous panicles on separate trees; females solitary; calyx of two opposite pairs of nearly equal sepals; petals 4, alternate with the segments of the calyx, and nearly of the same length; berry large, round, smooth, yellow when ripe; seeds 10, reniform, arillate. *Fl.* Jan.—March.—*Roxb. Fl. Ind.* ii. 625.—*Wight's Ill.* i. 125.—*Icon. t.* 114, 115. ——Rungpore.

ECONOMIC USES.—The fruit of this species of Garcinia ripens about April or May. It is very large, about 2 lb. weight, of a rich yellow colour when ripe, and exceedingly acid to the taste. Each seed is enclosed in its own proper aril, within which is generally found a soft yellow resin. The fleshy part of the fruit has a sharp, pleasant, acid taste. It is used by the natives in their curries, and for acidulating water. If cut into slices and dried it retains its qualities for years, and might possibly be used to advantage during long sea-voyages as a substitute for limes, or put into various messes where salt meat is employed.—*Roxb.*

One of the most delicious fruits, the Mangosteen, is produced by a tree of this order (*Garcinia mangostana*, Linn.), growing in the Eastern Archipelago. The white delicate pulp which surrounds the seeds has been aptly likened by Sir E. Tennent to "perfumed snow." The tree has been successfully grown and the fruit ripened at Courtallum; but it requires great care, and the fruit never acquires the size and flavour it has in its native country.—(*Pers. Obs.*) The fleshy pericarp is a valuable astringent. It contains tannin, resin, and a crystallisable principle. It has been successfully employed in the advanced stages of dysentery and in chronic diarrhœa. Dr Waitz (*Diseases of Children in Hot Climates*, p. 164) recommends a strong decoction as an external astringent application in dysentery. —*Pharm. of India.*

(292) **Garcinia pictoria** (*Roxb.*) Do.

Mysore Gamboge-tree, ENG. Mukki, TAM.

DESCRIPTION.—Tree, 60 feet; much branched; leaves opposite, short-petioled, oblong-ventricose, slightly acute, entire, smooth on both sides; hermaphrodite flowers axillary, solitary, sessile;

calyx segments obtuse, in two unequal pairs; petals 4, oval; berry oval, size of a large cherry, smooth, slightly marked with 4 lobes, and crowned with the sessile verrucose stigma; seeds 4, oblong, reniform; calyx and corolla of male flowers as in the female; flowers yellow. *Fl.* Feb.—*Wight Icon. t.* 102.—*Roxb. Fl. Ind.* ii. 627.—Hebradendron pictorium, *Christison.* ——Wynaad forests. Mysore.

Economic Uses.—The tree is found in the high mountain-lands of Wynaad, and attempts to cultivate it in the low country have failed. A good kind of Gamboge is procured from the tree. The bark, according to Roxburgh, is intermixed with many yellow specks, and through its substance, particularly on the inside, considerable masses of Gamboge are found. Samples which were sent to Dr R. from Tellicherry, even in a crude and unrefined state, he considered superior to most other kinds; and the specimens forwarded to the Madras Exhibition were also considered of an excellent quality. The tree is to be found in the greatest abundance along the whole line of Ghauts, and it is probable that if the attention of the trade were directed to these provinces it might become an important article of export. An oil is got from the seeds. The following particulars regarding it were furnished by Dr Oswald to the Madras Exhibition: It is procurable in moderate quantities by pounding the seeds in a stone mortar, and boiling the mass until the butter or oil rises to the surface. Two and a half measures of seeds should yield one seer and a half of butter. In the Nuggur division of Mysore it is sold at the rate of 1-4 As. per seer of 24 Rs. weight, or at £36, 6s. per ton; and is chiefly used as a lamp-oil by the better classes of natives, and by the poor as a substitute for ghee. The butter thus prepared does not appear to possess any of the purgative qualities of the Gamboge resin, but is considered an antiscorbutic ingredient in food. There has been some difference of opinion among botanists regarding the true definition of the species yielding the Mysore Gamboge; and also in what respect both the tree itself and its products differ with those from Ceylon and Siam. An excellent paper has been written by Dr Christison upon this subject. From the information which Dr C. has been able to collect regarding this Gamboge-tree, it would appear to constitute a genus distinct from the Ceylon plant, which latter Dr Graham (*Comp. Bot. Mag.*) has, from certain points of distinction in its botanical character, designated as the *Hebradendron Gambogioides.* The species under consideration is found on high lands in the Coorg and Mysore countries. Dr Cleghorn had an opportunity of personally examining the tree in its native forest, which is in the north-western parts of Mysore. He then remarked that its range of elevation was between 2000 and 3000 feet, and that he found it in greater abundance as he proceeded southward. It probably has an extensive range along the Western Ghauts. Regarding the quality of the specimens sent him, Dr Christison observed that they were all in a concrete state, of a tawny brownish yellow colour and glistening waxy lustre, exactly like fine Siam Gamboge, and showing its tendency to conchoidal fracture; free from odour, tasteless, and equal to the Siam Gamboge in being easily reducible to a fine emulsion in water. As a pigment it proved of an excellent quality, like that of Ceylon. It is in a great degree soluble in sulphuric ether, to which it communicates a fine orange colour, the solution yielding upon evaporation an orange-coloured resin. Upon analysis the composition proved to be essentially the same with that of Ceylon, but indicating more colouring matter, more resin, and less gum, than in the Gamboge of commerce. In its medicinal effects it would appear to excite the same influence on the animal body as common Gamboge, as it has undergone experiments both in England and in this country. The natives appear little acquainted with its uses, unless perhaps, as Dr Cleghorn ascertained, for colouring cloth in the low country. Dr Christison expressed his opinion that "it is probable this Gamboge might advantageously be applied to any use to which the Gamboge of Siam is habitually put." At all events it is an equally fine pigment, and as it can be obtained in almost unlimited quantity, it may be introduced equally into the European trade. Gamboge fetches in the London market from £5 to £11 per cwt.—*Dr Christison in Pharm. Journ. Dr Hunter's Indian Journ.*

(293) **Garcinia purpurea** (*Roxb.*) Do.

Mate Mangosteen, Eng.

Description.—Tree; branches drooping; leaves lanceolar, obtuse, shining, dark green; berry spherical, smooth, not furrowed, deep purple throughout.—*Roxb. Fl. Ind.* ii. 624.—*J. Grah. Cat.* p. 25.—*Wight Ill.* i. 125.——Concans. Ravines at Kandalla.

Medical Uses.—This differs, says Roxburgh, from every other species in the whole fruit, which is about the size of a small orange, being throughout of a deep purple colour, even the proper purple aril of the seeds. The seeds yield an oil known as the Kokum oil. It is of much use in cases of chapped skin, hands, and face, either scraped into hot water or powdered, the powder being rubbed on the face and hands. The fruit has an agreeable acid flavour, and is eaten by natives. Workers in iron use the acid juice as a mordant. A concrete oil is obtained from the seeds, which is well known and used at Goa for adulterating ghee. This oil is used by the natives as a healing application, and from its powerfully absorbing heat it might be usefully employed in such wounds or sores as are accompanied with inflammation. Kokum butter is a solid, firm, and friable substance, having a greasy feel. Its colour is pale yellow, and has a faint but not disagreeable odour. It is readily soluble in ether, and slightly so in rectified spirits—more in hot than in cold.—*Pharm. Journ. Roxb.*

(294) **Gardenia lucida** (*Roxb.*) N. O. CINCHONACEÆ.

DESCRIPTION.—Tree, unarmed, with resinous buds; leaves short-petioled, oblong or oval or obovate, obtuse or bluntly pointed, glabrous, shining, with simple parallel nerves and prominent veins; limb of calyx with 5 divisions, sprinkled on the inside with stoutish bristles; corolla hypocrateriform; tube long, striated; limb 5-partite, divisions as long as, or a little shorter than, the tube; berry drupaceous, even, oblong, crowned with the calyx; nut very hard, thick, and long, with two parietal receptacles; flowers somewhat terminal, solitary shortly pedicelled, large, pure white, fragrant. *Fl.* March—April.—*W. & A. Prod.* i. 395.—*Wight Icon. t.* 575.—*Roxb. Fl. Ind.* i. 707.——Circars. S. Mahratta country. Chittagong.

MEDICAL USES.—This is stated by Roxburgh to be in flower and fruit the greater part of the year. The total want of pubescence, structure of the stipules, length of the calyx, and sharpness of its divisions, distinguish this species from *G. gummifera*, which it most resembles. A fragrant resin, known in Canara and Mysore as the *Dikamali* resin, is procured from the tree, which is said to be useful in hospitals, keeping away flies from sores on account of its strong aroma. It is used by native farriers, and is certainly a substance worthy of attention.—(*Roxb. Jury Rep. Mad. Exhib.*) The *G. campanulata* is used as a cathartic and anthelmintic; and a yellow resin, similar to gum elemi, exudes from the buds and wounds in the bark of *G. gummifera*, which might be turned to good account. —*Roxb.*

(295) **Gendarussa vulgaris** (*Nees.*) N. O. ACANTHACEÆ.

Vada-kodi, MAL. Caroo-nochie, TAM. Kali-Thumbali, DUK. Nulla Vavali, TEL. Jugutmudun, BENG.

DESCRIPTION.—Shrub, 3-4 feet; leaves opposite, lanceolate, elongated; branches numerous, long, and straggling; flowers in whorls on terminal spikes; upper lip undivided; flowers pale, greenish white, sparingly stained with purple.—*Wigh Icon. t.* 468.—Justicia Gendarussa, *Roxb. Fl. Ind.* i. 128.—*Rheede,* ix. *t.* 42.——N. Concans. Travancore. Peninsula.

MEDICAL USES.—The leaves and tender stalks are prescribed in certain cases of chronic rheumatism; the bark of the young parts is generally of a dark-purple colour, whence it derives its Tamil name. In Java it is considered a good emetic. The leaves are scattered by the natives amongst their clothes to preserve them from insects. The same in infusion are given internally in fevers; and a bath in which these leaves are saturated is very efficacious in the same complaints. The juice of the leaves is administered in coughs to children, and the same mixed with oil as an embrocation in glandular swellings of the neck and throat; also, mixed with mustard-seed, is a good emetic. The natives put the leaves in a bag with some common salt, and warming them, reckon it a good remedy applied externally in diseases of the joints.—*Ainslie. Rheede.*

(296) **Girardinia heterophylla** (*Dalz.*) N. O. URTICACEÆ.

Neilgherry Nettle, ENG. Ana schorigenam, MAL.

DESCRIPTION.—Annual, erect; leaves broad-cordate, 7-lobed, lobes oblong, acute, coarsely serrated, clothed on both sides with fine whitish down, armed above with thin scattered prickles, thickly clothed beneath with the same; male and female flowers in distinct glomerate peduncled spikes; flowers small, green. *Fl.* Sept.—Nov.—*Dalz. Bomb. Flor.*, p. 238.—Urtica heterophylla, *Willd.* G. Leschenaultiana, *Decaisne.*—*Wight Icon. t.* 1976.—*Rheede,* ii. *t.* 41.——Common on the slopes of the Ghauts. Peninsula. Nepaul.

ECONOMIC USES.—If incautiously touched, this nettle will produce temporarily a most stinging pain. The plant succeeds well by cultivation. Its bark abounds in fine, white, glossy, silk-like, strong fibres. The Todawars on the Neilgherries separate the fibres by boiling the plant, and spin it into thin coarse thread: it produces a beautifully fine and soft flax-like fibre, which they use as a thread. The Malays simply steep the stems in water for ten or twelve days, after which they are so much softened that the outer fibrous portion is easily peeled off. Dr Dickson states that the Neilgherry nettle is the most extraordinary plant; it is almost all fine fibre, and the tow is very much like the fine wool of sheep, and no doubt will be largely used by wool-spinners.—*Wight. Royle.*

The following report upon the cultivation and preparation of the fibre was forwarded to the Madras Government by Mr M'Ivor, superintendent of the Horticultural Gardens at Ootacamund :—

Cultivation.—The Neilgherry nettle has been described as an annual plant; it has however proved, at least in cultivation, to be a perennial, continuing to throw out fresh shoots from the roots and stems with unabated vigour for a period of three or four years. The mode of cultivation, therefore, best suited to the plant, is to treat it

15

as a perennial by sowing the seeds in rows at fifteen inches apart, and cutting down the young shoots for the fibre twice a-year—viz., in July and January. The soil best suited to the growth of this plant is found in ravines which have received for years the deposit of alluvial soils washed down from the neighbouring slopes. In cutting off the first shoots from the seedling crop, about six inches of the stem is left above the ground; this forms "stools," from which fresh shoots for the succeeding crops are produced. After each cutting the earth is dug over between the rows to the depth of about eight inches; and where manure can be applied, it is very advantageous when dug into the soil between the rows with this operation. When the shoots have once begun to grow, no farther cultivation can be applied, as it is quite impossible to go in among the plants, owing to their stinging property. The plant is indigenous or growing wild all over the Neilgherries, at elevations varying from 4000 to 8000 feet, and this indicates the temperature best suited to the perfect development of the fibre.

Produce per acre.—From the crop of July an average produce of from 450 to 500 lb. of clean fibre per acre may be expected. Of this quantity about 120 lb. will be a very superior quality; this is obtained from the young and tender shoots, which should be placed by themselves during the operation of cutting. The crop of January will yield on an average 600 or 700 lb. per acre; but the fibre of this crop is all of a uniform and somewhat coarse quality, owing to shoots being matured by the setting in of the dry season in December. It might therefore be advantageous, where fine quality of fibre only was required, to cut the shoots more frequently—probably three or four times in the year—as only the finest quality of fibre is produced from young and tender shoots.

Preparation of the fibre.—Our experiments being limited, our treatment of the fibre has been necessarily very rude and imperfect, as in this respect only in extensive cultivation can efficient appliances be obtained.

The inner bark of the whole of the plant abounds in fibre, that of the young shoots being the finest and strongest, while that of the old stems is comparatively short and coarse, but still producing a fibre of very great strength and of a peculiar silky and woolly like appearance, and one which no doubt will prove very useful in manufactories.

For cutting down the crop fine weather is selected; and the shoots when cut are allowed to remain as they fall for two or three days, by which time they are sufficiently dry to have lost their stinging properties; they are, however, pliable enough to allow of the bark being easily pealed off the stems, and separated from the leaves. The bark thus taken from the stems is tied up in small bundles and dried in the sun, if the weather is fine; if wet, is dried in an open shed with a free circulation of air. When quite dry, the bark is slightly beaten with a wooden mallet, which causes the outer bark of that in which there is no fibre to break and fall off. The fibrous part of the bark is then wrapped up in small bundles, and boiled for about an hour in water to which a small quantity of wood-ashes has been added, in order to facilitate the separation of the woody matter from the fibre. The fibre is then removed out of the boiling water, and washed as rapidly as possible in a clear running stream, after which it is submitted to the usual bleaching process employed in the manufacture of fibre from flax or hemp.—*Report, April* 1862.

(297) **Gisekia pharnaceoides** (*Linn.*) N. O. PHYTOLACCACEÆ.

DESCRIPTION.—Herbaceous; leaves short-petioled, elliptic-lanceolate, very obtuse, scarcely mucronulate, pale green above, glaucous white beneath; cymes sub-sessile, shorter than the leaf, ball-shaped, simple, 5-10 flowered, somewhat loose; flowers nearly equalling the pedicel, pale green. *Fl.* All the year.—*Dec. Prod.* xiii., s. 2, p. 27.—*Wight Icon. t.* 1167.—*Roxb. Cor. t.* 183.——Common in pasture-grounds all over the country.

MEDICAL USES.—A powerful anthelmintic in cases of tænia. The fresh plant, including leaves, stalks, and capsules, is employed in doses of about an ounce, ground up in a mortar, with sufficient water to make a draught. This should be repeated three times at an interval of four days, the patient each time taking it after fasting for some hours.—*Lowther in Journ. of Agri.-Hort. Soc. of India.*, ix. p. 285.

(298) **Gloriosa superba** (*Linn.*) N. O. LILIACEÆ.

Mendoni, MAL. **Caateejan**, TAM. **Ulatchandul**, BENG. **Cariari**, HIND.

DESCRIPTION. — Climbing, with herbaceous stem; leaves cirriferous, ovate-lanceolate, inferior ones oblong; corolla 6-petalled; petals reflexed; flowers yellow and crimson mixed; capsule 3-celled, 3-valved. *Fl.* Aug.—Oct.—*Wight Icon.* vi. *t.* 2047.—*Roxb. Fl. Ind.* ii. 143.—Methonica superba, *Lam.*—*Rheede,* vii. *t.* 57.——Coromandel. Malabar. Concans. Bengal.

MEDICAL USES.—This splendid creeper, designated by Linnæus as "vere gloriosus flos," is commonly to be met with in the Travancore forests. Roxburgh says it is one of the most ornamental plants any country can boast of. The root of the plant is reckoned poisonous. The natives apply it in paste to the hands and feet of women in difficult parturition. A salt is procured from the root by repeated washing and grinding, throwing away the liquor, and washing the residuum carefully. The white powder so found is bitter to the taste. Mixed with honey it is given in gonorrhœa.—(*Lindley. Roxb.*) The native practitioners say it possesses nearly the same properties as the root of *Aconitum ferox*, hence its name of Country or Wild Aconite. Its taste is faintly bitter and acrid. It is farinaceous in structure. It is not poisonous in 12-grain doses, but, on the contrary, is alterative, tonic, and anti-periodic. It might be poisonous in larger quantities.—*Modern Sheriff in Suppl. to Pharm. of India.*

(299) **Gluta Travancorica** (*Bedd.*) N. O. Anacardiaceæ.

Shen-kurani, Tam.

Description.—Large tree; leaves crowded about the apex of the branches, alternate, entire, elliptic, attenuated at both ends, glabrous, petioles very short, ciliated, panicles terminal, and from the upper axils, crowded, canescent, shortly pubescent; calyx irregularly and slightly 5-toothed, splitting irregularly and caducous; bracts ovate, cymbiform; petals 5, imbricate; fruit depressed, transversely oblong, with a rough brownish rind.—*Bedd. Flor. Sylv. t.* 60.——Tinnevelly mountains and Travancore.

Economic Uses.—A valuable timber-tree. The wood is reddish, fine-grained, takes a good polish, and is well adapted for furniture. —*Beddome.*

(300) **Gmelina arborea** (*Roxb.*) N. O. Verbenaceæ.

Cumbulu, Mal. Joogani-chookur, Hind. Gumbaree, Beng. Tagoomooda, Tam. Goomadee, Tel.

Description.—Arboreous, unarmed; branchlets and young leaves covered with a greyish powdery tomentum; leaves long-petioled, cordate or somewhat produced and acute at the base, acuminate, the adult ones glabrous above, greyish tomentose beneath, with 2-4 glands at the base; panicles tomentose, axillary, and terminal; raceme-like cymules decussate, trichotomous, few-flowered; bracts lanceolate, deciduous; the acutely dentate calyx eglandulose; flowers large, sulphur-coloured, slightly tinged with red on the outside. *Fl.* April—May.—*Wight Icon. t.* 1470.—*Roxb. Fl. Ind.* iii. 84.—*Cor.* iii. *t.* 246.—*Rheede,* i. *t.* 41.——Coromandel. Neilgherries. Concans. Oude.

Economic Uses.—A small tree not unfrequent in the Paulghaut jungles, and generally distributed in Malabar. The light wood of this tree is used by natives for making the cylinders of their drums called *Dholucks*, also for making chairs, carriages, panels, &c., as it combines lightness with strength. It is common in the Ganjam and Vizagapatam districts. The wood is not readily attacked by insects. The shade is good. It grows rapidly, and the seeds may be planted in beds.—*Wight. Roxb.*

(301) **Gmelina Asiatica** (*Linn.*) Do.

Neelacoomil, TAM. Nelagoomadi, TEL.

DESCRIPTION.—Shrub; leaves opposite, petioled, ovate, tomentose underneath, with frequently a sharp short lobe on each side; spines axillary, opposite, horizontal, pubescent at the tip, the length of the petioles; flowers from the end of the tender twigs on peduncles; fruit a berried drupe size of a jujube, black, smooth; flowers large, bright sulphur. *Fl.* All the year.—*Roxb. Fl. Ind.* iii. 87.——Coromandel. Travancore.

MEDICAL USES.—The root is a demulcent and mucilaginous. Another species, the *G. parviflora*, has the power of rendering water mucilaginous, and is employed for the cure of the scalding of urine in gonorrhœa.—*Roxb.*

(302) **Gordonia obtusa** (*Wall.*) N. O. TERNSTRÆMIACEÆ.

DESCRIPTION.—Tree, middling size; leaves cuneate-oblong to elliptic-lanceolate, obtuse or with a blunt acumination, with shallow serratures, glabrous; petioles about 2 lines long; peduncles a little shorter than the petioles; petioles obcordate, slightly united at the base, silky on the outside, as are the bracts and calyx; stamens somewhat pentadelphous.—*W. & A. Prod.* p. 87.—G. parviflora, *Wight Ill.*—*Bedd. Fl. Sylv. t.* 73.

ECONOMIC USES.—A beautiful tree, common on the Neilgherries, Wynaad, and Western Ghauts of Madras, from 2500 to 7500 feet elevations. It is called Nagetta on the hills. The timber is white, with a straw tint, even-grained, and easy to work, and resembling beech. It is in general use for planks, doors, rafters, and beams, but liable to warp if not well seasoned.—*Beddome.*

(303) **Gossypium Indicum** (*Linn.*) N. O. MALVACEÆ.

Indian Cotton plant, ENG. Paratie, Van-paratie, TAM. Kapas, DUK. Puttie, TEL.

DESCRIPTION.—Herbaceous; stem more or less branched, 1½

foot; young parts velvety, often hairy, in the upper part sometimes of a reddish colour, frequently marked with black spots; leaves hairy, palmate, 3-5 lobed; lobes broad, rounded; petioles long, usually hispid and dotted; flowers axillary, generally solitary towards the extremities of the branches; petals yellow, with a purple spot near the claw; segment of involucel cordate at the base, margin dentate, sometimes entire; capsule ovate, pointed, 3-4 celled; seeds 5, clothed with greyish down under the short-staple white wool.—*Royle*. —G. herbaceum, *Linn.*—*Roxb. Fl. Ind.* iii. 184.—*Royle. Ill. Him. Bot. t.* 23, fig. 1.——Cultivated.

Economic Uses.—As flax is characteristic of Egypt, and the hemp of Europe, so cotton may truly be designated as belonging to India. Long before history can furnish any authentic account of this invaluable product, its uses must have been known to the inhabitants of this country, and their wants supplied from time immemorial, by the growth of a fleecy-like substance, covering the seeds of a plant, raised more perhaps by the bounty of Providence than the labour of mankind.

In Sanscrit, cotton is called *kurpas*, from whence is derived the Latin name *carbasus*, mentioned occasionally in Roman authors. This word subsequently came to mean sails for ships and tents. Herodotus says, talking of the products of India,—"And certain wild trees bear wool instead of fruit, that in beauty and quality exceeds that of sheep: and the Indians make their clothing from these trees" (iii. 106). And in the book of Esther (i. 6) the word *green* corresponds to the Hebrew *kurpas*, and is in the Vulgate translated *carbasinus*. The above shows from how early a period cotton was cultivated in this country. "The natives," says Royle (alluding to its manufacture in India), "of that country early attained excellence in the arts of spinning and weaving, employing only their fingers and the spinning-wheel for the former; but they seem to have exhausted their ingenuity when they invented the hand-loom for weaving, as they have for ages remained in a stationary condition."

It has sometimes been considered a subject of doubt whether the cotton was indigenous to America as well as Asia, but without sufficient reason, as it is mentioned by very early voyagers as forming the only clothing of the natives of Mexico; and, as stated by Humboldt, it is one of the plants whose cultivation among the Aztec tribes was as ancient as that of the Agave, the Maize, and the Quinoa (*Chenopodium*). If more evidence be required, it may be mentioned that Mr Brown has in his possession cotton not separated from the seeds, as well as cloth manufactured from it brought from the Peruvian tombs; and it may be added that the species now recognised as American differ in character from all known Indian species (*Royle*).

Cotton is not less valuable to the inhabitants of India than it is to European nations. It forms the clothing of the immense population of that country, besides being used by them in a thousand different ways for carpets, tents, screens, pillows, curtains, &c. The great demand for cotton in Europe has led of late years to the most important consideration of improvements in its cultivation. The labours and outlay which Government has expended in obtaining so important an object have happily been attended with the best results. The introduction of American seeds and experimental cultivation in various parts of India have been of the greatest benefit. They have been the means of producing a better article for the market, simplifying its mode of culture, and proving to the Ryots how, with a little care and attention, the article may be made to yield tenfold, and greatly increase its former value. To neither the soil nor the climate can the failure of Indian cotton be traced: the want of easy transit, however, from the interior to the coast, the ruinous effect of absurd fiscal regulations, and other influences, were at work to account for its failure. In 1834, Professor Royle drew attention to two circumstances: "I have no doubt that by the importation of foreign, and the selection of native seed—attention to the peculiarities not only of soil but also of climate, as regards the course of the seasons, and the temperature, dryness, and moisture of the atmosphere, as well as attention to the mode of cultivation, such as preparing the soil, sowing in lines so as to facilitate the circulation of air, weeding, ascertaining whether the mixture of other crops with the cotton be injurious or otherwise, pruning, picking the cotton as it ripens, and keeping it clean—great improvement must take place in the quality of the cotton. Experiments may at first be more expensive than the ordinary culture; the natives of India, when taught by example, would adopt the improved processes as regularly and as easily as the other; and as labour is nowhere cheaper, any extra outlay would be repaid fully as profitably as in countries where the best cottons are at present produced."

The experiments urged by so distinguished an authority were put in force in many parts of the country, and notwithstanding the great prejudice which existed to the introduction of novelty and other obstacles, the results have proved eminently successful. It has been urged that Indian cotton is valuable for qualities of its own, and especially that of wearing well. It is used for the same purposes as hemp and flax, hair and wool, are in England. There are, of course, a great many varieties in the market, whose value depends on the length, strength, and fineness as well as softness of the material, the chief distinction being the *long stapled* and the *short stapled*. Cotton was first imported into England from India in 1783, when about 114,133 lb. were received. In 1846, it has been calculated that the consumption of cotton for the last 30 years has increased at the compound ratio of 6 per cent, thereby doubling itself every twelve years. The chief parts of India where the cotton plant is cultivated are in Guzerat, especially in Surat and Broach, the principal cotton districts in the country; the southern Mahratta countries, including Dharwar, which is about a hundred miles from the seaport; the Concans, Canara, and Malabar. There has never been any great quantity exported from the Madras side, though it is cultivated in the Salem, Coimbatore, and Tinnevelly districts, having the port of Tuticorin on one coast, and of late years that of Cochin on the other, both increasing in importance as places of export. In the Bengal Presidency, Behar and Benares, and the Saugor and Nerbudda territories, are the districts where it is chiefly cultivated.

The present species and its varieties are by far the most generally cultivated in India. Dacca cotton is a variety chiefly found in Bengal, furnishing that exceedingly fine cotton, and employed in manufacturing the very delicate and beautiful muslins of that place, the chief difference being in the mode of spinning, not in any inherent virtue in the cotton or soil where it grows. The Berar cotton is another variety with which the N. Circar long-cloth is made. This district, since it has come under British rule, promises to be one of the most fertile and valuable cotton districts in the whole country.

Much diversity of opinion exists as to the best soil and climate adapted for the growth of the cotton plant; and considering that it grows at altitudes of 9000 feet, where Humboldt found it in the Andes, as well as at the level of the sea, in rich black soil and also on the sandy tracts of the sea-shore, it is superfluous to attempt specifying the particular amount of dryness or moisture absolutely requisite to insure perfection in the crop. It seems to be a favourite idea, however, that the neighbourhood of the sea-coast and islands are more favourable for the cultivation of the plant than places far inland, where the saline moisture of the sea-air cannot reach. But such is certainly not the case in Mexico and parts of Brazil, where the best districts for cotton-growing are far inland, removed from the influence of sea-air. Perhaps the different species of the plant may require different climates. However that may be, it is certain that they are found growing in every diversity of climate and soil, even on the Indian continent; while it is well known that the best and largest crops have invariably been obtained from island plantations, or those in the vicinity of the sea on the mainland.

A fine sort of cotton is grown in the eastern districts of Bengal for the most delicate manufactures; and a coarse kind is gathered in every part of the province from plants thinly interspersed in fields of pulse or grain. Captain Jenkins describes the cotton in Cachar as gathered from the Jaum cultivation: this consists in the jungle being burnt down after periods of from four to six years, the ground roughly hoed, and the seeds sown without further culture. Dr Buchanan Hamilton, in his statistical account of Dinagepore, gives a full account of the mode of cultivation in that district, where he says some cotton of bad quality is grown along with turmeric, and some by itself, which is sown in the beginning of May, and the produce collected from the middle of August to the middle of October, but the cultivation is miserable. A much better method, however, he adds, is practised in the south-east parts of the district, the cotton of which is finer than that imported from the west of India: The land is of the first quality, and the cotton is made to succeed rice, which is cut between August and the middle of September. The field is immediately ploughed until well broken, for which purpose it may require six double ploughings. After one-half of these has been given, it is manured with dung, or mud from ditches. Between the middle of October and the same time in November, the seed is sown broadcast; twenty measures of cotton and one of mustard. That of the cotton, before it is sown, is put into water for one-third of an hour, after which it is rubbed with a little dry earth to facilitate the sowing. About the beginning of February the mustard is ripe, when it is plucked and the field weeded. Between the 12th of April and 12th of June the cotton is collected as it ripens. The produce of a single acre is about 300 lb. of cotton, worth ten rupees; and as much mustard-seed, worth three rupees. A still greater quantity of cotton, Dr Hamilton continues, is reared on stiff clay-land, where the ground is also high and tanks numerous. If the soil is rich it gives a summer crop of rice in the same year, or at least produces the seedling rice that is to be transplanted. In the beginning of October the field is ploughed, and in the end of the month the cotton-seed is sown, mingled with *Sorisha* or *Lora* (species of *Sinapis* and *Eruca*); and some rows of flax and safflower are generally intermixed. About the end of January, or later, the oil-seeds are plucked, the field is hoed and manured with cow-dung and ashes, mud from tanks, and oil-cake; it is then watered once in from eight to twelve days. The cotton is gathered between the middle of April and the middle of June, and its produce may be from 360 to 500 lb. an acre.

In the most northern provinces of India the greatest care is bestowed on the cultivation. The seasons for sowing are about the middle of March and April, after the winter crops have been gathered in, and again about the commencement of the rainy season. The crops are commenced being gathered about the conclusion of the rains, and during October and November, after which the cold becomes considerable, and the rains again severe. About the beginning of February the cotton plants shoot forth new leaves, produce fresh flowers, and a second crop of cotton is produced, which is gathered during March and beginning of April. The same occurs with the cottons of Central India, one crop being collected after the rains and the other in February, and what is late in the beginning of March.

I venture to insert here the following interesting particulars about cotton manufacture: "The shrub *Perutti*, which produces the finer kind of cotton, requires in India little cultivation or care. When the cotton has been gathered it is thrown upon a floor and threshed, in order that it may be separated from the black seeds and husks which serve it as a covering. It is then put into bags or tied up in bales containing from 300 to 320 lb. of 16 oz. each. After it has been carded it is spun out into such delicate threads that a piece of cotton cloth 20 yards in length may almost be concealed in the hollows of both hands. Most of these pieces of cloth are twice washed; others remain as they come from the loom, and are dipped in cocoa-nut oil in order that they may be longer preserved. It is customary also to draw them through conjee or rice-water, that they may acquire more smoothness and body. This conjee is sometimes applied to cotton articles in so ingenious a manner that purchasers are often deceived, and imagine the cloth to be much stronger than it really is; for as soon as washed the conjee vanishes, and the cloth appears quite slight and thin.

"There are reckoned to be no less than 22 different kinds of cotton articles manufactured in India, without including muslin or coloured stuffs. The latter are not, as in Europe, printed by means of wooden blocks, but painted with a brush made of coir, which approaches near to horse-hair, becomes very elastic, and can be formed into any shape the painter chooses. The colours employed are indigo (*Indigofera tinctoria*), the stem and leaves of which plant yield that beautiful dark blue with which the Indian chintzes, coverlets, and other articles are painted, and which never loses the smallest shade of its beauty. Also curcuma or Indian saffron, a plant which dyes yellow; and lastly, gum-lac, together with some flowers, roots, and fruits which are used to dye red. With these few pigments, which are applied sometimes singly, sometimes mixed, the natives produce on their cotton cloths that admirable and beautiful painting which exceeds anything of the kind exhibited in Europe.

"No person in Turkey, Persia, or Europe has yet imitated the Betilla, a certain kind of white East Indian chintz made at Masulipatam, and known under the name of Organdi. The manufacture of this cloth, which was known in the time of Job, the painting of it, and the preparation of the colours, give employment in India to male and female, young and old. A great deal of cotton is brought from Arabia and Persia and mixed with that of India."—*Bart. Voy. to East Indies.*

The remaining uses of this valuable plant must now claim our attention. The seeds are bruised for their oil, which is very pure, and is largely manufactured at Marseilles from seeds brought from Egypt. These seeds are given as a fattening food to cattle. Cotton-seed cake is imported from the West Indies into England, being used as a valuable food for cattle. The produce of oil-cake and oil from cotton-seeds is, 2 gallons of oil to 1 cwt. of seeds, and 96 lb. of cake. A great quantity is shipped from China, chiefly from Shanghai, for the English market. It forms an invaluable manure for the farmer.—*Royle on Cotton Cultivation. Simmonds. Lindley. Roxb.*

(304) **Grangea Maderaspatana** (*Poir.*) N. O. COMPOSITÆ.

Mashiputri, TAM. Nelampata, MAL. Mustarû, TEL. Namuti, BENG.

DESCRIPTION.—Stems procumbent or diffuse, villous; leaves sinuately pinnatifid, lobes obtuse; peduncles terminal or leaf-opposed; heads of flowers sub-globose, solitary, yellow. *Fl.* Dec.—Jan. —*Dec. Prod.* v. 373.—*Wight Contrib.* p. 12.—Artemisia Maderaspatana, *Roxb.* — *Wight Icon. t.* 1097.—*Rheede,* x. *t.* 49. Rice-fields in the Peninsula.

MEDICAL USES.—The leaves are used medicinally as a stomachic. The Vytians also consider them to have deobstruent and antispasmodic properties. They are used also in the preparation of antiseptic and anodyne fomentations.—*Ainslie.*

(305) **Grewia oppositifolia** (*Buch.*) N. O. TILIACEÆ.

DESCRIPTION. — Tree; leaves bifarious, alternate, short-petioled, from ovate to rhomb-shaped, 3-nerved, serrate, serratures obtuse and glandular, rather harsh on both sides; peduncles leaf-opposed, solitary, longer than the petioles, 3-5 flowered; flowers large, yellowish; calyx 3-ribbed at the back; sepals 5, linear; petals lanceolate; drupe smooth, olive-coloured, fleshy; nut 1-celled. *Fl.* March—June.—*Roxb. Fl. Ind.* ii. 583.—*Wight Icon. t.* 82.——Kheree Pass. Dheyra Dhoon.

ECONOMIC USES.—The inner bark is used for cordage and coarse cloth. The former much used for agricultural purposes, and for rigging boats. A kind of paper is also made from it.—(*Royle.*) It attains its full size in about 15 years. The wood is straw-coloured, soft, elastic, and durable; and is well adapted for handles of axes and other tools, and cot-frames.—(*Powell's Punj. Prod.*) The chief value of the tree is on account of the leaves, which largely serve as fodder, and are said to increase the quantity of milk. The bark is made into sandals. A fair paper has been manufactured from the bark by Europeans in the Kangra valley.—(*Stewart's Punj. Plants.*) The timber of another species, the *G. elastica,* is highly esteemed for its strength and elasticity, and is much used for bows, buggy-shafts, and sticks. The berries have a pleasant acid taste, and are used for making sherbet.—*Royle.*

(306) **Grislea tomentosa** (*Roxb.*) N. O. LYTHRACEÆ.

Sirinjie, TEL. Dhaee-phool, BENG.

DESCRIPTION.—Shrub or small tree; branchlets pubescent;

leaves oppositc, entire, lanceolate, somewhate cordate at the base, sessile, under side hairy, smoothish above; petals usually 6, scarcely conspicuous; stamens declinate; capsule oblong; calyx tubular, sharply toothed; seeds numerous; peduncles axillary, many-flowered; flowers red. *Fl.* Dec.—April.—*W. & A. Prod.* i. 308.—*Roxb. Flor. Ind.* ii. 233.—*Cor.* i. *t.* 31. —Lythrum fruticosum, *Linn.*——Peninsula. Bengal. Oude. Dheyra Dhoon.

Economic Uses.—The petals are used as a red dye as well as in medicine. An infusion of the leaves is employed as a substitute for tea by the hill tribes near Ellichpoor, where the shrub grows. Dr Gibson remarks that it is a very common shrub throughout the forest of the Concan, and along the Ghauts. It has rather pretty red flowers, appearing from December to February; and in Candeish, where the plant grows abundantly, forms a considerable article of commerce inland as a dye.—(*Dr Gibson.*) There are two varieties of this tree, the white and black, distinguished by the colour of the bark, fruit, and shape of the leaves. The wood is light yellow, hard, smooth, and tough. It yields good material for ploughs, and attains its full size in 30 years.—(*Powell's Punj. Prod.*) In the Northern Circars, where it is known under the name of *godari* and *reyya manu*, the leaves are employed in dyeing leather. Sheep-skins steeped in an infusion of the dried leaves become a fine red, of which native slippers are made. The dried flowers are employed in Northern India, under the name of *dhouri*, in the process of dyeing with the Morinda bark, not so much for their colouring as their astringent properties. The shrub is abundant in the hilly tracts of the Northern Circars.—*Jury Rep. Mad. Exhib.*

(307) **Guazuma tomentosum** (*H. B. & Kth.*) N. O. Byttneriaceæ.

Bastard Cedar, Eng. Oodrick, Tel.

Description.—Tree, 40-60 feet; leaves alternate, ovate or oblong, unequal at the base, toothed, acuminate at the apex, stellately puberulous on the upper side, tomentose beneath; petals 5, yellow, with two purple awns at the apex; capsules 5-celled, many-seeded; seeds angular; peduncles axillary and terminal. *Fl.* Aug.—Sept.—*W. & A. Prod.* i. 64.—*Wight Ill. t.* 31.—G. ulmifolia, *Wall.*——Cultivated.

Medical Uses.—A decoction of the inner bark is very glutinous, and besides being employed to clarify sugar, is said to be of use in Elephantiasis; while the older bark is used as a sudorific, and is given in diseases of the chest and cutaneous complaints.—*Lindley.*

ECONOMIC USES.—This tree has been introduced from the West Indies, but is now common in India; it is not unlike the English elm, with leaves that droop hanging quite down whilst the petioles remain stiff and straight. The fruit is filled with mucilage, which is very agreeable to the taste. The wood is light and loose-grained, and is much used in making furniture, especially by coachmakers for panels. A fibre was prepared from the young shoots which was submitted to experiments by Dr Roxburgh, and found to be of considerable strength, breaking at 100 lb. when dry, and 140 lb. when wet.—(*Don. Royle Fib. Plants.*) It grows quickly, and is suited for avenues. In Coorg and the western forests it grows to a large size. Its leaves afford excellent fodder for cattle.

(308) **Guettarda speciosa** (*Linn.*) N. O. CINCHONACEÆ.

Puneer-marum, TAM. Ravapoo, MAL.

DESCRIPTION.—Tree; leaves ovate or obovate, often slightly cordate at the base, obtuse at the apex, pubescent on the under side; cymes peduncled, axillary, velvety, much shorter than the leaf; corolla hypocrateriform, with cylindrical tube; flowers 4-9 cleft; anthers sessile in the throat of the corolla; calyx limb deciduous; stamens 4-9; drupe depressed, marked by the traces of the calyx; cells of the nut curved, 1-seeded; flowers white, very fragrant. *Fl.* April—May.—*W. & A. Prod.* i. 422.—*Wight Icon.* i. *t.* 40.—*Roxb. Fl. Ind.* i. 686.—Nyctanthes hirsuta, *Linn.*—*Rheede*, iv. *t.* 47, 48.——Travancore. Coromandel in gardens.

ECONOMIC USES.—The flowers of this tree are exquisitely fragrant. They come out in the evening, and have all dropped on the ground by the morning. The natives in Travancore distil an odoriferous water from the corollas, which is very like rose-water. In order to procure it they spread a very thin muslin cloth over the tree in the evening, taking care that it comes well in contact with the flowers as much as possible. During the heavy dew at night the cloth becomes saturated, and imbibes the extract from the flowers. It is then wrung out in the morning. This extract is sold in the bazaars. —*Pers. Obs.*

(309) **Guilandina bonduc** (*Linn.*) N. O. LEGUMINOSÆ.

Kulunje, Caretti, MAL. Kalichikai, TAM. Getsakaia, TEL. Nata-caranja, HIND. Gutchka, DUK. Nata, BENG.

DESCRIPTION.—Climbing shrub; leaves abruptly bipinnated, more or less pubescent, 3-8 pair, with 1-2 small recurved prickles between them; leaflets oval or ovate; prickles solitary; flowers yellow; sepals 5, nearly equal; petals 5, sessile; flowers largish, sulphur-coloured, spicately racemose; legume ovate, 2-valved, 1-2 seeded, covered with straight prickles; seeds long, nearly globose. *Fl.* Aug.—Oct.—*W. & A. Prod.* i. 280.—G. bonducella, *Linn.*—Cæsalpinia bonduc, *Roxb. Fl. Ind.* ii. 362.—*Rheede,* ii. *t.* 22.——Coromandel. Travancore. Bombay. Bengal.

MEDICAL USES.—The kernels of the nuts are very bitter, and said by the native doctors to be powerfully tonic. They are given in cases of intermittent fevers mixed with spices in the form of powder. Pounded and mixed with castor-oil, they are applied externally in hydrocele. At Amboyna the seeds are considered as anthelmintic, and the root tonic in dyspepsia. In Cochin China the leaves are reckoned as deobstruent and emmenagogue, and the root astringent. The oil from the former is useful in convulsions, palsy, and similar complaints. In Scotland, where they are frequently thrown upon the sea-shore, they are known as Molucca beans. Piddington has detected in the nuts, oil, starch, sugar, and resin.—*Ainslie. Lour. Rumph.*

(310) **Guizotia oleifera** (*Dec.*) N. O. COMPOSITÆ.

Ramtil, BENG. Ramtilla, DUK. Kalatill, HIND. Valesuloo, TEL.

DESCRIPTION.—Annual, herbaceous, erect; leaves opposite, long lanceolate, coarsely serrated; peduncles elongated, sub-corymbose; flowers large, bright yellow. *Fl.* Nov.—Dec.—Verbesina sativa, *Roxb. Fl. Ind.* iii. 441.—Ramtilla oleifera, *Dec.*——Madras. Cultivated in the Deccan. Lower Bengal.

ECONOMIC USES.—Commonly cultivated in Mysore and the Deccan, for the sake of the oil yielded by its seeds. The Ramtil oil is sweet-tasted, and is used for the same purposes as the gingely-oil, though an inferior oil. The oil expressed from the larger seeds is the common lamp-oil of Upper India, and is very cheap. In Mysore the seed is sown in July or August after the first heavy rains, the fields being simply ploughed, neither weeding nor manure being required. In three months from the sowing, the crop is cut, and after being placed in the sun for a few days, the seeds are thrashed out with a stick. The produce is about two bushels an acre. In Mysore the price is about Rs. 3-8 a maund.—*Ainslie. Jury Rep. Mad. Exhib. Heyne's Tracts. Simmonds.*

(311) **Gynandropsis pentaphylla** (*Dec.*) N. O. CAPPARIDACEÆ.

Caat-kodokoo, Cara-vella, MAL. Kanala, Shada Hoorhooreeja, BENG. Nai-kadughoo, Nai Vaylla, TAM.

DESCRIPTION.—Annual, 1 foot; calyx sepals 4, spreading;

petals 4, open, not covering the stamens; stem more or less covered with glandular pubescence or hairs; middle leaves 5-foliolate, lower and floral leaves trifoliolate; leaflets obovate, puberulous, entire, or slightly serrulate; flowers white or flesh-coloured, with pink stamens and brown anthers; siliqua stalked. *Fl.* July—Aug.—*W. & A. Prod.* i. 21.—Cleome pentaphylla, *Linn.*—*Roxb. Fl. Ind.* iii. 126.—*Rheede,* ix. *t.* 24.——Common everywhere. Bengal. Nepaul.

MEDICAL USES.—The leaves bruised and applied to the skin act as a rubefacient, and produce abundant serous exudation, answering the purpose of a blister. The seeds are given internally, beaten to a paste, in fever and bilious affections; and the juice of leaves, beaten up with salt, in ear-ache. The whole plant made into an ointment with oil is applied to pustular eruptions of the skin, and simply boiled in oil is efficacious in cutaneous diseases, especially leprosy. —(*Rheede. Ainslie. Wight.*) Sir W. Jones remarked that its sensible qualities seemed to promise great antispasmodic virtues, it having a scent resembling Assafœtida. The seeds are used as a substitute for mustard, and yield a good oil.—*Pharm. of India.*

(312) **Gyrocarpus Asiaticus** (*Willd.*) N. O. COMBRETACEÆ.

Tanukoo, TEL.

DESCRIPTION.—Large tree; leaves crowded about the extremities of the branchlets, broad cordate, 3-nerved, often slightly lobed, above smooth, below downy, with two pits on the upper side of the base; petioles downy; panicles terminal, divisions 2-forked; hermaphrodite flowers solitary, sessile in the division of the panicle; calyx 5-sepalled, segments unequal, interior pairs large, wedge-shaped, 3-toothed, expanding into two long membranaceous wings; flowers small, yellow; capsule globular, wrinkled, 1-celled, 1-valved, size of a cherry, ending in two long lanceolate membranaceous wings. *Fl.* Dec.—Jan.—G. Jacquini, *Roxb. Fl. Ind.* i. 445.—*Cor.* i. *t.* 1.——Coromandel mountains. Banks of the Krishna.

ECONOMIC USES.—The wood of this tree is very light, and when procurable is preferred above all others in the construction of Catamarans. It is also used for making cowrie-boxes and toys, and takes paint and varnish well.—*Roxb.*

H

(313) **Hardwickia binata** (*Roxb.*) N. O. LEGUMINOSÆ.

Achà Karachi, Kat-udugu, TAM. Nar-yepi, TEL.

DESCRIPTION.—Tree, bark deeply cracked, branches spreading; leaves alternate, petioled, leaflets 1 pair, opposite, sessile, with a bristle between them, between semi-cordate and reniform, obtuse, entire, very smooth on both sides, 3-6 veined at the base, when young tinged with red, stipules small, cordate, caducous; panicles terminal and from the exterior axils; flowers pedicelled, scattered, small, bracts minute, caducous; calyx somewhat hoary outside, often dotted, yellowish within, filaments usually 10, rarely 6-8, anthers with or without an acute point between the lobes; style filiform, stigma large, peltate; legume lanceolate, 2-3 inches in length, 2-valved, striated lengthwise, opening at the apex; seed solitary in the apex of the legume.—*Roxb. Flor. Ind.* ii. 423.—*W. & A. Prod.* i. 284.—*Bedd. Flor. Sylv. t.* 26.——Banks of the Cauvery. Salem and Coimbatore districts. Western slopes of the Neilgherries. Mysore. Godavery forests. Bombay.

ECONOMIC USES.—This is a valuable tree, but cattle being very fond of its leaves, it is pollarded to a great extent. The timber is of a reddish colour, very hard, strong, and heavy, and of an excellent quality. It is a first-rate building and engineering timber. Its bark yields a strong fibre much used by the natives. It is easily raised from seed, and grows to 3500 feet elevation.—*Beddome.*

(314) **Hedyotis umbellata** (*Lam.*) N. O. CINCHONACEÆ.

Indian Madder, ENG. Saya or Emboorel cheddie, TAM. Chariveloo, TEL.

DESCRIPTION.—Small plant, suffruticose, erect or diffuse, slightly scabrous; calyx 4-parted; corolla rotate, 4-cleft; leaves opposite or verticillate, linear, paler on the under side, margins recurved; stipules ciliated with bristles; peduncles alternate, axillary, bearing a short raceme; partial peduncles 1-3 flowered; capsule globose with a wide dehiscence; flowers white.—*W. & A. Prod.* i. 413.—Oldenlandia umbellata, *Linn.*

—*Roxb. Cor.* i. *t.* 3.—*Fl. Ind.* i. 421.—— Coromandel. Concans. Cultivated in the Peninsula.

MEDICAL USES.—The leaves are considered expectorant. Dried and powdered they are mixed with flour and made into cakes, and given in asthmatic complaints and consumption, an ounce daily of decoction being the dose given.—*Ainslie.*

ECONOMIC USES.—This is much cultivated in sandy situations on the Coromandel coast, especially at Nellore, Masulipatam, and other places. The root, which is long and orange-coloured, gives the best and most durable red dye for cotton cloth. A purple and brown-orange dye is also procured from it. It is often called by the Tamulians the *Ramiseram Vayr,* from its growing plentifully on that island. Among Europeans it is known as the *Chay root.* Simmonds says the outer bark of the roots furnishes the colouring matter for the durable red for which the chintzes of India are famous. Chay root forms a considerable article of export from Ceylon. The wild plant there is considered preferable; the roots, which are shorter, yielding one-fourth part more colouring matter; and the right to dig it is farmed out. It grows spontaneously on light, dry, sandy ground on the sea-coast. The cultivated roots are slender, with a few lateral fibres, and from one to two feet long. The dye is said to have been tried in Europe, but not with much advantage. This red dye, similar to Munjeet, is used to a great extent in the southern parts of Hindostan by the native dyers. It is not held in very good estimation in Europe, but seems to deserve a better reputation than it at present possesses. Specimens of the dye were forwarded to the Madras Exhibition, upon which the Jurors reported as follows: The colouring matter resides entirely in the bark of the root; the inner portion is white and useless. The root is of great importance to the Indian dyer, yielding a red dye similar to Munjeet, which is used to a great extent in the southern parts of Hindostan. The celebrated red turbans of Madura are dyed with the Chay root, which is considered superior of its kind, but this is probably owing to some chemical effect which the water of the Vigay river has upon it, and not to any peculiar excellence of the dye itself. Wild Chay is considered to yield one-third more colouring matter than the cultivated root; this probably arises from too much watering, as much rain injures the quality of the root. Roots of two years' growth are preferred when procurable. It is currently reported that Chay root rapidly deteriorates by being kept in the hold of a ship, or indeed in any dark place.*—*Simmonds. Jury Rep. Mad. Exhib. Ainslie.*

(315) **Hemidesmus Indicus** (*R. Br.*) N. O. ASCLEPIACEÆ.

Country Sarsaparilla, ENG. Narooneendee, MAL. Nunnari, TAM. Soogundapala, TEL. Mugraboo, HIND. Unanto-mool, BENG.

DESCRIPTION.—Twining; stem glabrous; leaves from cordate

* For account of the cultivation and produce of the Chay root, see Appendix D.

to ovate, cuspidate, passing into narrow linear, acute, often oblong-lanceolate cymes, often sub-sessile, sometimes peduncled; scales of the corolla obtuse, cohering the whole length of the tube; follicles slender, straight; flowers on the outside, pale green, on the inside, dark blood-coloured. *Fl.* June—Aug.—*Wight Contrib.* p. 63.—*Icon. t.* p. 594.—Periploca Indica, *Willd.*—Asclepias pseudosarsa. *Var.* latifolia. *Roxb. Fl. Ind.* ii. 39.—*Rheede*, x. *t.* 34.——Coromandel. Bombay. Bengal. Very common in Travancore.

Medical Uses.—This root is an excellent substitute for sarsaparilla, and much used among the natives, being sold in the bazaars for this purpose. They employ it particularly for the thrush in children, giving about a drachm every morning and evening of the powder fried in butter. Dried and reduced to powder, and mixed with honey, it is reckoned a good specific in rheumatic pains and boils; and, in decoction with onions and cocoanut-oil, is internally recommended in hæmorrhoids, and simply bruised and mixed with water in diarrhœa. Ainslie states that the root is mucilaginous and slightly bitter, and is recommended by the Tamool doctors in cases of strangury and gravel, being pulverised and mixed with cow's milk; they also give it in decoction with cummin-seeds to purify the blood and correct the acrimony of the bile. A decoction of it is also prescribed by European practitioners in cutaneous diseases, scrofula, and venereal affections. Dr O'Shaughnessy repeatedly experimented upon the roots, and found their diuretic properties very remarkable. Two ounces infused in a pint of water, and allowed to cool, was the quantity usually employed daily; and by such doses the discharge of urine was generally trebled or quadrupled. It also acted as a diaphoretic and tonic, greatly increasing the appetite. Dr Pereira says the root is brownish externally, and has a peculiar aromatic odour, somewhat like that of sassafras. It has been employed as a cheap and efficacious substitute for sarsaparilla in cachectic diseases, increasing the appetite and improving the health. In some cases it has succeeded where sarsaparilla has failed, and in others failed where sarsaparilla proved successful.—*Ainslie. Roxb.*

(316) **Herpestis monniera** (*H. B. & Kth.*) N. O. Scrophulariaceæ.

Beami, Mal. Neerpirimie, Tam. Sambronichittoo, Tel. Shevet-chamni, Hind. Adha-birni, Beng.

Description.—Annual, creeping; leaves opposite, sessile, obovate, wedge-shaped or oblong, smooth, entire, fleshy, dotted with minute spots; peduncles axillary, alternate, solitary, shorter than the leaves, 1-flowered; flowers blue; calyx 5-cleft, exterior 3 segments larger than the others; corolla campanulate, 5-parted, divisions equal; capsule ovate, 2-celled, 2-valved; seeds numerous. *Fl.* Nearly all the year.—*Roxb. Fl. Ind.* i. 141.—*Cor.* ii. *t.* 178.—Gratiola monniera, *Linn.*—*Rheede*, x. *t.* 14.——Moist situations near streams or on the borders of tanks.

Medical Uses.—The root, stalks, and leaves are used by the Hindoos medicinally as diuretic and aperient. Roxburgh says that the expressed juice mixed with petroleum is rubbed on parts affected with rheumatism.—*Ainslie. Roxb.*

(317) **Hibiscus cannabinus** (*Linn.*) N. O. Malvaceæ.

Deckanee Hemp, Eng. Palungoo, Tam. Gongkura, Tel. Ambaree, Duk. Maesta-paut, Beng.

Description.—Stem herbaceous, prickly; leaves palmately 5-partite, glabrous, segments narrow lanceolated, acuminated, serrated; flowers almost sessile, axillary, solitary; leaves of the involucel about 9, subulate, prickly with rigid bristles, shorter than the undivided portion of the calyx; calyx divided beyond the middle, segments slightly prickly, 1-nerved; corolla spreading; fruit nearly globose, acuminated, very hairy; seeds few, glabrous; flowers pale sulphur, with a deep purple centre; carpels joined into a 5-celled, 5-valved capsule. *Fl.* June—July.—*W. & A. Prod.* i. 50.—*Roxb. Fl. Ind.* iii. 208.—*Cor.* ii. *t.* 190.——Negapatam. Cultivated in Western India.

Economic Uses.—The bark of this species is full of strong fibres which the inhabitants of the Malabar coast prepare and make into cordage, and it seems as if it might be worked into strong fine thread of any size. In Coimbatore it is called *Pooley-munjee*, and is cultivated in the cold season, though with sufficient moisture it will thrive all the year. A rich loose soil suits it best. It requires about three months from the time it is sown before it is fit to be pulled up for watering, which operation, with the subsequent dressing, is similar to that used in the preparation of the Sunn fibre. Dr Buchanan observed that it was sown by itself in fields where nothing else grew. It goes by various names in different parts of the country. The fibres are harsh, and more remarkable for strength than fineness, but might be improved by care. It is as much cultivated for the sake of its leaves as its fibres, which former are acidulous, and are eaten by the natives. In Dr Roxburgh's experiments a line broke at 115 lb., Sunn under the same circumstances at 160 lb. But in Professor Royle's experiments this broke at 190 lb., Sunn at 150 lb.

Dr Gibson states that in Bombay it is cut in November, and kept for a short time till ready for stripping the bark. The length of these fibres is usually from 5 to 10 feet.—(*Royle. Roxb.*) The bark of the *H. furcatus* yields a good strong white fibre. A line made from it broke at 89 lb. when dry, and at 92 lb. when wet. It is cut while the plant is flowering and steeped at once.—*Royle.*

(318) **Hibiscus Rosa sinensis** (*Linn.*) Do.

Shoe-flower plant, or China Rose, ENG. Schempariti, MAL. Sapatoo cheddie, TAM. Dasanie, TEL. Jasoon, DUK. Juva, BENG.

DESCRIPTION.—Shrub, 12-15 feet; stem arborescent, without prickles; leaves ovate, acuminated, coarsely toothed, and slightly cut towards the apex, entire at the base; pedicels axillary, as long as, or longer than, the leaves, jointed above their middle; involucel 6-7 leaved; calyx tubular, 5-cleft; flowers large, single or double, crimson, yellow, or white; seeds unknown. *Fl.* All the year.—*W. & A. Prod.* i. 49.—*Rheede,* ii. *t.* 16.—*Roxb. Fl. Ind.* iii. 194.——Peninsula. Cultivated in gardens.

MEDICAL USES.—The leaves are considered in Cochin China as emollient and slightly aperient. The flowers are used to tinge spirituous liquors, and the petals when rubbed on paper communicate a bluish-purple tint, which forms an excellent substitute for litmus-paper as a chemical test. The leaves are prescribed by the natives in smallpox, but are said to check the eruption too much.—(*Don. Ainslie.*) An infusion of the petals is given as a demulcent refrigerant drink in fevers.—*Pharm. of India.*

ECONOMIC USES.—In China they make these handsome flowers into garlands and festoons on all occasions of festivity, and even in their sepulchral rites. The petals of the flowers are used for blacking shoes, and the women also employ them to colour their hair and eyebrows black. They are also eaten by the natives as pickles.

(319) **Hibiscus subdariffa** (*Linn.*) Do.

Roselle, or Red Sorrel, ENG. Mesta, BENG. Polechee, MAL.

DESCRIPTION.—Annual, glabrous, 1-3 feet; lower leaves undivided, upper palmately 3-5 lobed, cuneate and entire at the base, lobes oblong-lanceolate, acuminated, toothed; flowers axillary, solitary on very short pedicels; involucel segments about 12; stems unarmed; capsule many-seeded; seeds smooth; flowers pale sulphur, with dark-brown eye. *Fl.* Oct.—Dec.—*W. & A. Prod.* i. 52.——Common in gardens.

ECONOMIC USES.—The fleshy calyx and capsule, freed from the seeds, make excellent tarts and jellies. A decoction of them sweetened and fermented is commonly called in the West Indies Sorrel-drink. The leaves are used in salads. *Sabdariffa* is the Turkish name for the plant. The stem is cut when in flower, and a fibre got from the bark which is rather fine and silky. In Rajahmundry they are planted for this purpose. The stems are left to rot in fresh water, but spoil if put in salt water. Excellent tow and hemp might be made from several species of Hibiscus, the staple being long, fibre uniform, silky, and fine. Cordage of greater compactness and density could therefore be made from them than from many of the coarser fibres. All plants of the kind should be sown thick, for the simple reason that they will grow tall and slender, thus giving a greater length of straight fibre yielding stem. No plant yielding fibres should be gathered for more than one or two days before being prepared, as the drying up of the sap stains the fibres, and the sooner the fibre is cleaned the stronger and whiter it will be; and newly-cleaned fibres must not be exposed to the sun, as they acquire a brown tinge. It must be recollected that all plants are usually in greatest vigour when in flower or fruit, and at that time they yield the greatest amount of fibre.—*Report on Fibres. Ainslie.*

(320) **Holarrhena antidysenterica** (*Wall.*) N. O. APOCYNACEÆ.

DESCRIPTION.—Shrub; leaves opposite, entire, elliptic, very obtuse at the base, acute or abruptly acuminated at the apex; calycine lobes lanceolate; corolla cup-shaped, tube dilated between the base and the middle, throat contracted; stamens inserted between the base and middle of the tube; cymes many-flowered, terminal; flowers puberulous, white; follicles a foot long. *Fl.* Feb.—May.—*Wight Icon. t.* 439.——Chittagong. Malabar. Peninsula.

MEDICAL USES.—The bark of this shrub was formerly imported into Europe under the names of *Conessi bark*, *Coduga pala*, *Corte de pala*, and *Tellicherry bark*. It has a bitter taste. It has astringent and tonic properties, but has obtained its chief repute as a remedy in dysentery. Cases have occurred of its having succeeded as a remedy in that complaint when *Ipecacuanha* and other remedies had failed. It has also been extensively employed as an anti-periodic. The seeds are also highly valued by the natives in dysenteric affections. They are narrow, elongated, about half an inch long, of a cinnamon-brown colour, convex on one side, and concave and marked with a longitudinal pale line on the other, easily broken, bitter to the taste, and of a heavy unpleasant odour. They are often confounded with the seeds of *Wrightia tinctoria*, to which they bear a general resemblance. An infusion of the toasted seeds is a gentle and safe astringent in bowel-complaints, and is given to allay the vomiting in cholera. — (*Ainslie.*) Anthelmintic virtues are also assigned to them. During the last cattle-plague epidemic in Bengal they were extensively employed, being regarded as possessing certain specific virtues.—(*Indian Med. Gazette. Pharm. of India.*) A variety of the above, the *H. pubescens*, is also an esteemed remedy for dysentery and bowel-complaints, the seeds being the parts used. The bark also possesses astringent, tonic properties, and is employed in fevers.—*Wight.*

(321) **Holigarna longifolia** (*Roxb.*) N. O. Anacardiaceæ.

Cattu Tsjeru, Mal.

Description.—Tree, 60 feet; leaves alternate, cuneate, oblong or acute; petioles usually with a soft, incurved, thorn-like, deciduous process on each side about the middle; panicles terminal and axillary; styles recurved; calyx 5-toothed; petals 5, oblong, spreading; stamens 5, shorter than the corolla; nut ovate, with a fleshy pericarp; flowers small, whitish. *Fl.* Jan.—Feb.—*W. & A. Prod.* i. 169.—*Roxb. Fl. Ind.* ii. 80.—*Cor.* iii. *t.* 282.—*Rheede,* iv. *t.* 9.——Travancore. Concans. Chittagong.

Economic Uses.—This is a tall tree found on the mountains of Malabar. The natives by incision extract an exceedingly acrid juice from the stem, which they use as varnish. The nut is about the size of an olive, containing between the laminæ numerous cells filled with black, rather thick, acrid fluid. The fruit is like a prune, at first glaucous and downy, when ripe dark blue and glabrous. The juice is succulent and glutinous. There is another variety with a round dark fruit. Small boats are made from the timber. The bark, when wounded, gives out tears acrid and glutinous. The juice of the fruit is used by painters, and also for fixing indelible colours figured on linen cloths.—*Don.*

(322) **Holostemma Rheedii** (*Spr.*) N. O. Asclepiaceæ.

Ada-kodien, Mal. Palla-gurgi, Tel.

Description.—Stems twining, perennial; leaves broad cordate, opposite; corolla subrotate, 5-cleft; stamineous corona inserted below the gynostegium, simple, annular, obsoletely 5-lobed; follicles ventricose, smooth; seeds comose; flowers largish, thick and fleshy, purplish green. *Fl.* Sept.—Oct.—*Wight Contrib.* p. 55.—*Icon. t.* 597.—Asclepias annularia,

Roxb. Fl. Ind. ii. 37.—*Rheede,* ix. *t.* 7.——Malabar. Covalum jungles near Trevandrum. Mysore. Circars.

Medical Uses.—The flowers of this creeper are remarkably pretty, and would answer well for trellis-work in gardens. The medical virtues of the plant are given by Rheede, who states that the root pulverised and applied to the eyes will remove dimness of vision. Mixed with other ingredients it is also used in ophthalmia—for, says that author, "vires hujus plantæ planè ophthalmicæ sunt." It has an extensive distribution, being found from the southernmost province to the base of the Himalaya. The plant yields a tolerable fibre, which is said to be in its best condition after the rains.—*Wight. Rheede. Pers. Obs.*

(323) **Homalonema aromaticum** (*Schott.*) N. O. Araceæ.

Description.—Perennial; caulescent leaves sub-sagittate, cordate, acuminate, lobes rounded and divaricate; spadix cylindric, obtuse, equalling the spathe, above male, below female with abortive stamens intermixed; anthers many-celled. *Fl.* Jan.—Feb.—*Wight Icon. t.* 805.—Calla aromatica, *Roxb. Fl. Ind.* iii. 513.——Chittagong.

Medical Uses.—A native of Chittagong: when cut it diffuses a pleasant aromatic scent. The natives hold the medical virtues of the root in high estimation.—*Roxb.*

(324) **Hopea parviflora** (*Beddome*). N. O. Dipterocarpeæ.

Irubogam, Mal.

Description.—Large tree; petioles, panicles, and calyx hairy; leaves short-petioled, glabrous, ovate to oblong, furnished with glands in the axils of the veins beneath; flowers secund, sub-sessile, numerous, very minute, fragrant; stamens 15, alternately single and in pairs; stigma 3-cleft.—*Bedd. Flor. Sylv. t.* 6.——Malabar and Canara, in moist and dry forests.

Economic Uses.—This tree grows to an elevation of 3500 feet. It is hitherto unknown commercially, but promises to be a very serviceable timber for gun-carriages and similar purposes, and especially for railway-sleepers. In south Canara it is much valued for temple buildings.—(*Beddome.*) It produces a gum, the uses of which are hitherto unknown. At the coast it costs about 10 rupees a maund. A considerable amount is annually available.

(325) **Hopea Wightiana** (*Wall.*) Do.

Kong or Kongoo, TAM.

DESCRIPTION.—Large tree; young branches and petioles densely pubescent; leaves ovate-oblong, rounded at the base and attenuated towards the apex into a very obtuse point, glabrous except on the rib above; panicles axillary, generally three together, shorter than, or as long as, the leaves; flowers pink, secund, bracteolate at the base of their very short pedicels; calyx glabrous; corolla hairy on the outside; stamens 15, alternately single and double; anthers terminated by a long bristle; fruit and calycine wings glabrous, bright crimson.—*W. & A. Prod.* i. 85.—*Ill. t.* 37.—*Bedd. Flor. Sylv. t.* 96.

VAR. *b. Glabra.*—Young petioles and branches glabrous.——Common in the western forests. Tinnevelly.

ECONOMIC USES.—The timber is very valuable, and similar to that of *H. parviflora.* The variety *b.* is the Kongoo of Tinnevelly, and is much used in that district.—*Beddome.*

(326) **Hoya pendula** (*W. & A.*) N. O. ASCLEPIACEÆ.

Nansjera-patsja, MAL.

DESCRIPTION.—Stem woody, twining; leaves fleshy, glabrous, from oblong-oval acute to broadly ovate, acuminate, revolute on the margins; peduncles somewhat longer than the petioles, pendulous, many-flowered; corolla downy inside; leaflets of stamineous corona oboval, very obtuse, depressed, having the inner angles short and truncate at the apex; stigma apiculated; flowers white, fragrant. *Fl.* March—May.—*Wight Contrib.* p. 36.—*Icon. t.* 474.—H. Rheedii, *W. & A.*—Asclepias pendula, *Roxb. Fl. Ind.* ii. 36.—*Rheede,* ix. *t.* 13.——Circar mountains. Malabar. Neilgherries.

MEDICAL USES.—This plant is emetic and alexipharmic. Rheede gives many uses for it when mixed with other ingredients. There are two varieties of the plant, differing in the shape of the leaves.—(*Rheede.*) The leaves of *H. viridiflora* are much employed by the natives as an application to boils and abscesses. The plant has the same emetic and expectorant virtues as *Dœmia extensa.*—*Pharm. of India.*

(327) **Hugonia mystax** (*Linn.*) N. O. HUGONIACEÆ.

Modera canni, MAL. Agoore, TAM.

DESCRIPTION.—Shrub, 10-15 feet; leaves alternate, or crowded at the ends of the branches, oval, glabrous, entire; sepals distinct, acute, unequal; petals 5, alternate with the sepals; styles 5, distinct; ovary roundish, 5-celled; fruit a drupe, enclosing 5 distinct one-seeded carpels; peduncles axillary, 1-flowered; spines circinate, opposite; flowers yellow. *Fl.* Feb.—May.—*W. & A. Prod.* i. 72.—*Wight Ill.* i. *t.* 32.—*Rheede,* ii. *t.* 19.——Travancore. Coromandel. Malabar.

MEDICAL USES.—This is a handsome shrub when in flower, commonly met with in Travancore. Its blossoms are of a beautiful golden-yellow colour. The bruised roots are used in reducing inflammatory tumours; also in the bites of serpents, and as a febrifuge and anthelmintic, especially for children. The bark of the root is employed as an antidote to poisons.—*Rheede.*

(328) **Hydnocarpus inebrians** (*Vahl.*) N. O. PANGIACEÆ.

Morotti, MAL. Maravuttie, TAM.

DESCRIPTION.—Tree, 50 feet; leaves glabrous, crenately serrated, alternate; sepals 5, two outer ones ovate, 3 inner ones larger, very concave; petals 5, fringed with soft white hairs; fruit globose, very hard, as large as an apple, crowned with the undivided portion of the stigma; seeds numerous; flowers small, white. *Fl.* Oct.—Feb.—*W. & A. Prod.* i. 30.—*Wight Ill.* i. *t.* 16.—*Icon. t.* 942.—*Rheede,* i. *t.* 36.——Common in Travancore. Malabar.

MEDICAL USES.—The fruit, if eaten, occasions giddiness, and is greedily devoured by fishes, but fish taken by these means are not fit to be eaten, occasioning vomiting and other violent symptoms. On the Malabar coast an oil is extracted from the seeds given in cutaneous diseases and ophthalmia, causing an excessive flow of tears.—(*Rheede.*) The seeds, the *Neeradimootoo* of Ainslie, have a nauseous smell and unctuous slightly acrid taste. The expressed oil is in much repute among the natives as a remedy in leprosy. The dose recommended by Ainslie is half a teaspoonful twice daily.—*Pharm. of India. Ainslie.*

ECONOMIC USES.—In Ceylon the seeds are used for poisoning fish. The tree is very common on the western coast. It is generally found overhanging tanks, and is usually laden with fruit which is excessively hard. The oil from the seeds is used as a sedative, and as a remedy in scabies and ulcers on the feet. The *H. alpinus*, common on the Neilgherries, is a good timber-tree, and much used for building purposes.—*Rheede. Wight.*

(329) **Hydnocarpus odoratus** (*Lindl.*) Do.

Chaulmoogra, BENG.

DESCRIPTION.—Large tree; leaves lanceolate, entire, acuminate; petals oblong; scales ciliated. *Male*, calyx 4-5 cleft. *Female*, peduncles 1-flowered, flowers larger than the males; styles 5, stigmas large, sagittate-cordate, and berry globular; seeds numerous, immersed in pulp; flowers large, pale yellow, fragrant. — *Wight Ill.* i. 37.—Gynocardia odorata, *Roxb.*—Chaulmoogra odorata, do.—*Roxb. Cor. t.* 299.——Assam. Silhet.

MEDICAL USES.—The seeds are used by the natives in Silhet in the cure of cutaneous disorders, especially leprosy. When freed from their integuments, they are beaten up with clarified butter into a soft mass, and in that state applied thrice a-day to the parts affected. —*Roxb.*

(330) **Hydrocotyle Asiatica** (*Linn.*) N. O. APIACEÆ.

Asiatic Penny-wort, ENG. Vullarei, TAM. Codagam, MAL. Babassa, TEL. Thulkuri, BENG.

DESCRIPTION.—Herbaceous; leaves attached by the margin, orbicular-reniform, equally crenated, 7-nerved, glabrous or slightly villous below when young; petioles and peduncles fascicled, sprinkled with soft hairs; umbels capitate, short-peduncled, few-flowered; calyx tube slightly compressed; petals ovate, acute, spreading; fruit orbicular, reticulated, with 4 ribs on each of the flat sides; flowers whitish or purplish red. *Fl.* July—Aug.—*W. & A. Prod.* i. 366.—*Roxb. Fl. Ind.* ii. 88.—*Wight Icon. t.* 565.—*Rheede*, x. *t.* 46.——Travancore.

MEDICAL USES.—A widely-distributed plant, growing in moist shady places near hedges or tanks. The leaves, which are bitter, are toasted and given in infusion to children in bowel-complaints and fevers. They are also applied to parts that have suffered from blows or bruises as anti-inflammatory. In Java, according to Horsfield, they are considered as diuretic. The plant is one of the remedies for leprosy on the Malabar coast, and one which is worthy of more attention than has hitherto been bestowed upon it.—(*Roxb. Rheede.*) In non-specific ulcerations and in skin diseases it is of value both as an internal and as a local remedy.—*Pharm. of India.*

(331) **Hydrolea Zeylanica** (*Vahl.*) N. O. HYDROLEACEÆ.

Kauchra Ishalangulya, BENG. Tajeru-vallel, MAL.

DESCRIPTION.—Annual, herbaceous; stems erect, variously bent towards the extremities; leaves short, lanceolate, rather obtuse, marked below with numerous prominent parallel veins; racemes axillary, spreading, few-flowered, and with the pedicels and calyx pubescent; pedicels 1-flowered, usually opposite to a small bracted leaf; flowers deep blue, with a white spot in the centre; calyx 5-parted, divisions lanceolate, thickly covered with glandular hairs; corolla wheel-shaped, tube short, 5-cleft, petals spreading, or even reflexed when fully open. *Fl.* Dec.—Jan.—*W. & A. in Bot. Mag.* ii. 103.—Nama zeylanica, *Linn.*—*Roxb. Fl. Ind.* ii. 73.—*Wight Icon. t.* 601.—*Rheede*, x. *t.* 28.——Marshy places in the Peninsula. Alwaye, near Cochin.

MEDICAL USES.—The leaves beaten into a pulp and applied as a poultice are considered efficacious in cleaning and healing bad ulcers, particularly those in which maggots have begun to breed.—*Wight.*

(332) **Hymenodyction excelsum** (*Wall.*) N. O. CINCHONACEÆ.

Pundaroo, TEL. Kala Buchnal, DUK.

DESCRIPTION.—Tree, 50 feet; leaves from oblong to roundish ovate, pubescent; stipules cordate; floral leaves oblong, coloured, bullate; panicles terminal and axillary; anthers nearly sessile in tube of the corolla; calyx 5-toothed; corolla infundibuliform, 5-parted; capsule 2-celled, many-seeded; seeds girded by a membranous reticulated border; flowers small, greenish; the lower pairs on two of the ramifications of the panicle are ornamented, each with a pair of coloured floral leaves. *Fl.* July—Aug.—*W. & A. Prod.* i. 392.—*Roxb. Fl. Ind.* ii. 149.—Cinchona excelsa, *Roxb. Cor.* ii. *t.* 106.—*Fl. Ind.* i. 529.—*Wight Icon.* p. 79, 1159.——Circars. Peninsula.

MEDICAL USES.—The two inner coats of the bark of this tree possess all the bitterness and astringency of Peruvian bark, and when fresh, in a stronger degree.—*Roxb.*

ECONOMIC USES.—The wood is fine and close-grained, of a pale mahogany colour, and is useful for many purposes.—(*Roxb.*) Another species, the *H. utile*, is common in the Palghaut jungles. The wood is also of mahogany colour, but is of a loose texture, soft, and hygrometric.—*Wight.*

(333) **Hyoscyamus niger** (*Linn.*) N. O. Solanaceæ.

Common Henbane, Eng.

Description.—Stem viscous, branched; leaves oblong, sinuately toothed, or sinuate-pinnatifid, viscously pubescent, lower ones petioled, the rest half stem-clasping, sub-decurrent; flowers sub-sessile, erect, arranged on simple, unilateral, recurved, leafy, terminal spikes, the corolla minutely reticulated with purple veins on a pale rose-coloured and yellowish ground, marked with a dark-purple throat. *Fl.* Feb.—March.—*Linn. Spec.* p. 257.—*Dec. Prod.* xiii. s. 1, p. 546.—H. agrestis, *Ait.*—*Sweet Fl. Gard.* i. *t.* 27.—*Bot. Mag. t.* 2394.——Rocky places in Northern India. Cultivated.

Medical Uses.—The medicinal properties of Henbane are too well known to require any detailed account in a work of this kind. One of its most valuable powers is that of dilating the pupil in diseases of the eye when applied locally. This plant is cultivated in India for medicinal purposes, and thrives well at moderate altitudes. In the Government gardens at Hewra, in the Deccan, from 150 to 200 lb. of the extract were annually supplied for the use of the Bombay army. Large supplies have also been prepared at Hoonsoor, in Mysore, and, on testing, proved equally efficacious with the European article. Henbane-seeds are met with in the native bazaars, but they are imported from Turkey. Another species (*H. insanus*) is a common plant in Beluchistan, where it is known by the name of *Kohl bung*, or *Mountain Hemp.* It has powerfully poisonous properties. It is smoked in small quantities, and also employed for criminal purposes.—(*Pharm. of India.* Stocks in *Hooker's Journ. Bot.* 1852, iv. 178.) Another plant of this order is the *Scopolia lurida* (Dunal), growing in Nepaul. The leaves, when bruised, emit a peculiar tobacco-like odour. A tincture prepared from them, in the proportion of one ounce to eight ounces of alcohol, was found to produce extreme dilatation of the pupil; and in two instances it induced blindness, which only disappeared when the medicine was discontinued.—*Gaz. Med. Nov.* 1843. *Braithwaite's Retrosp.* ix. 119.

I

(334) Ichnocarpus frutescens (*R. Br.*) N. O. APOCYNACEÆ.

Paal-vully, MAL. Shyama-luta, BENG. Nalla-tiga, TEL.

DESCRIPTION.—Twining; leaves oblong or broad lanceolate, deep green above, pale below, glabrous; calyx 5-cleft; corolla salver-shaped, throat hairy, segments twisted, hairy; panicles terminal; follicles long, linear; flowers greenish white. *Fl.* July—Aug.—*Wight Icon. t.* 430.—Echites frutescens, *Roxb. Fl. Ind.* ii. 12.—Apocynum frutescens, *Linn.*——Peninsula. Bengal. Travancore. Common in hedges.

MEDICAL USES.—This plant is occasionally used as a substitute for sarsaparilla. It has purgative and alterative qualities.—*Lindley.*

(335) Icica Indica (*W. & A.*) N. O. AMYRIDACEÆ.

Nayor, BENG.

DESCRIPTION.—Tree, 70 feet; young shoots, petioles, and calyx pubescent; leaves unequally pinnated; leaflets 7-11, petioled, oblong-lanceolate, more or less serrulated, from almost glabrous to densely pubescent; panicles axillary, solitary, lax, much shorter than the leaves; calyx small, 5-toothed; petals 5, recurved, sessile; stamens inserted with the petals and shorter than them; drupe globose, 1-3 celled; seeds bony, very hard, solitary in each cell, covered with an arilliform pulp; flowers small, whitish green. *Fl.* March—April.—*W. & A. Prod.* i. 177.—Bursera serrata, *Wall.*——Chittagong. Assam.

ECONOMIC USES.—The timber is close-grained and hard, is much esteemed, and used for furniture. It is as tough as oak, and much heavier.

(336) Indigofera aspalathoides (*Vahl.*) LEGUMINOSÆ.

Shevenar-Vaymboo, TAM. Manneli, MAL.

DESCRIPTION.—Shrubby, erect, young parts whitish, with

adpressed hairs; branches slender, spreading in every direction; leaves sessile, digitately 3-5 foliolate; leaflets narrow-cuneate, small, under side with a few scattered hairs; peduncles solitary, 1-flowered, about the length of the leaves; legumes cylindrical, pointed, straight, 4-6 seeded; flowers rose-coloured. *Fl.* Nearly all the year.—*W. & A. Prod.* i. 199.—*Wight Icon. t.* 332.—I. aspalathifolia, *Roxb. Fl. Ind.* iii. 337.—Aspalathus Indicus, *Linn.*—*Rheede,* ix. *t.* 37.——Peninsula. Common on waste lands.

Medical Uses.—The leaves, flowers, and tender shoots are said to be cooling and demulcent, and are employed in decoction in leprosy and cancerous affections. The root chewed is given in toothache and aphthæ. The whole plant rubbed up with butter is applied to reduce œdematous tumours. A preparation is made from the ashes of the burnt plant to clean dandruff from the hair. The leaves are applied to abscesses; and an oil is got from the root, used to anoint the head in erysipelas.—*Ainslie. Rheede.*

(337) **Indigofera enneaphylla** (*Linn.*) Do.

Cheppoo-neringie, Tam. Cherra-gaddaun, Tel.

Description.—Perennial, procumbent; young parts and leaves pubescent with white hairs; branches prostrate and edged; leaves pinnate, sessile, leaflets 3-5 pairs, obovate-oblong; racemes sessile, short, dense, many-flowered; legumes oval, pubescent, not winged; seeds 2, ovate and truncated at one end; flowers small, bright red. *Fl.* Nearly all the year. —*W. & A. Prod.* i. 199.—*Wight Icon. t.* 403.—*Roxb. Fl. Ind.* iii. 376.——Dindigul hills.

Medical Uses.—The juice is given as an antiscorbutic and alterative in certain affections. An infusion of the whole plant is diuretic, and as such is given in fevers and coughs.—*Ainslie.*

(338) **Indigofera tinctoria** (*Linn.*) Do.

Common Indigo, Eng. Ameri, Mal. Averie, Tam. Neelie, Tel. Neel, Beng. and Hind.

Description.—Shrub, 2-3 feet, erect, pubescent; branches terete, firm; leaves pinnated; leaflets 5-6 pairs, oblong-ovate, cuneate at the base, slightly decreasing in size towards the apex of the leaf; racemes shorter than the leaves, sessile, many-flowered; flowers small, approximated at the base of the raceme, more distant and deciduous towards the apex, greenish-rose colour; calyx 5-cleft, segments broad, acute; legumes approximated towards the base of the rachis, nearly cylindrical, slightly torulose, deflexed and curved upwards; seeds about 10, cylindrical, truncated at both ends. *Fl.* July—Aug.—*W. & A. Prod.* i. 202.—*Wight Icon. t.* 365.—*Roxb. Fl. Ind.* iii. 379.—I. Indica, *Lam.*—*Rheede,* i. 54.——Quilon. Concans. Cultivated in Bengal and elsewhere.

Medical Uses.—With regard to the medical properties of this plant, Ainslie states that the root is reckoned among those medicines which have the power of counteracting poisons, and that the leaf has virtues of an alterative nature, and is given in hepatitis in the form of a powder mixed with honey. The root is also given in decoction in calculus; and the leaves rubbed up in water and applied to the abdomen are efficacious in promoting urine. Indigo itself is frequently applied to reduce swellings of the body. Lunan states that the negroes in Jamaica use a strong infusion of the root mixed with rum to destroy vermin in the hair. Powdered indigo has been employed in epilepsy and erysipelas, and sprinkled on foul ulcers is said to cleanse them. The juice of the young branches mixed with honey is recommended for aphthæ of the mouth in children. The wild indigo, *I. paucifolia (Delile),* is considered an antidote to poisons of all kinds. The root boiled in milk is used as a purgative, and a decoction of the stem is considered of great efficacy in mercurial salivation used as a gargle.—*Ainslie. Beng. Disp. Lindley.*

Economic Uses.—According to Loureiro, the indigo plant is spontaneous in China and Cochin China, and is cultivated all over those vast empires. The ancients were acquainted with the dye which we call indigo, under the name of *Indicum.* Pliny knew that it was a preparation of a vegetable substance, but he was not acquainted with the plant, nor with the process of making the dye. Even at the close of the sixteenth century it was not known in England what plant produced it. The celebrated traveller Marco Polo thus mentions indigo as one of the products of Quilon, where the plant grows wild. "Indigo, also, of excellent quality and in large quantities, is made here. They procure it from a herbaceous plant, which is taken up by the root, and put into tubs of water, where it is suffered to remain till it rots, when they press out the juice. This, upon being exposed to the sun and evaporated, leaves a kind of paste, which is cut into small pieces of the form in which we see it brought to us." To the present day indigo is manufactured at Quilon, though probably some hundred years ago it was made in considerable quantities. The account given above is a tolerably correct one of the rude process of its manufacture. It is one of the most profitable articles of culture in Hindostan, chiefly because labour and land are cheaper than anywhere else, and partly because the raising of the plant and its manufacture may be carried on even without the aid of a house. It is chiefly cultivated in Bengal in the delta of the Ganges, on those districts lying between the Hooghly and the main stream of the former river. The ground is ploughed in October and November after the cessation of the rains, the seeds are sown in March and beginning of April. In July the plants are cut when in blossom, that being the time when there is the greatest abundance of dyeing matter. A fresh moist soil is the best, and about 12 lb. of seeds are used for an acre of land. The plants are destroyed by the periodical inundations, and so last only for a single year. When the plant is cut it is first steeped in a vat till it has become macerated and parted with its colouring matter, then the liquor is let off into another vat, in which it undergoes a peculiar process of beating to cause the fecula to separate from the water; the fecula is then let off into a third vat, where it remains some time, after which it is strained through cloth bags and evaporated in shallow wooden boxes placed in the shade. Before it is perfectly dry it is cut into small pieces an inch square; it is then packed up for sale. Indigo, however, is one of the most precarious of Indian crops, being liable to be destroyed by insects, as well as inundation of the rivers. It is generally divided into two classes—viz., the Bengal and Oude indigo. Madras indigo is not much inferior to that grown in Bengal.

In the Jury Report of the Madras Exhibition it is said, in former years the usual mode of extracting indigo, as practised in Southern India, was from the dry leaf, a process which will be found minutely described in the pages of Heyne and Roxburgh. But this is now almost entirely superseded by the better system of the *green leaf* manufacture, which is followed in all the indigo-growing districts of this Presidency, save the province of South Arcot. In the latter, the *dry leaf* process is still persevered in, but probably it is so only because of the distance to which the leaf has generally to be carried before it reaches the factory, and the consequent partial drying that takes place on the journey. Notwithstanding the importance of the traffic, the general manufacture is so indifferently conducted, or rather on so imperfect a system, that the value of the article produced is seriously diminished, and its currency injured as an article of trade. It is not that the quality of Madras indigo is inferior to the ordinary run of that of Bengal, but indigo is commonly manufactured over the Madras Presidency in driblets, one vat-owner often not producing enough to fill even a chest; and the consequence is, that no one can make a purchase of a quantity of indigo in the Madras market upon a sample, as is commonly done in Bengal,—that every parcel, and often the same chest, is of mixed qualities, and that the value of the dye becomes thereby disproportionately depreciated at home.

The best indigo comes from the district of Kishnagur, Jessore, Moorshedabad, and Tirhoot. Roxburgh stated that he extracted most beautiful light indigo from the *I. cœrulea*—(*Roxb.*), and in greater quantities than he ever procured from the common indigo plant.*—*Roxb. Simmonds. Jury Rep. Mad. Exhib.*

(339) **Inga dulcis** (*Willd.*) Do.

Manilla Tamarind, ENG. Coorookoo-pally, TAM. Sima chinta, TEL.

DESCRIPTION.—Tree, 30 feet; extreme branches pendulous, armed with short straight thorns; leaves bigeminate; leaflets oblong, very unequal-sided; petiole shorter than the leaflets; pinnæ and leaflets each one pair; flowers capitate, heads shortly peduncled, racemose, the racemes panicled; legumes turgid, much twisted; seeds glabrous, smooth, imbedded in a firm edible pulp; flowers small, yellowish-greenish. *Fl.* Jan.—Feb.—*W. & A. Prod.* i. 269.—*Wight Icon. t.* 198.—Mimosa dulcis, *Roxb. Cor.* i. *t.* 99.—*Flor. Ind.* ii. 556.——Cultivated. Madras.

ECONOMIC USES.—This tree makes an excellent hedge-plant, and is much used for that purpose on the Coromandel coast, especially at Madras. The sweet pulp in the legumes is reckoned wholesome. The timber is also said to be good.—(*Roxb. Pers. Obs.*) Isolated trees are found of 18 inches diameter. In general appearance it resembles the English hawthorn. The wood is hard. Roxburgh was of opinion that it was a native of the Philippines, but it appears that it had been imported thither from Mexico. It is now frequently met with, particularly towards the coast. It is easily raised from seeds, and the hedge it forms, being occasionally clipped, makes a neat and serviceable enclosure. *Inga* has been transferred to a new genus, *Pithecolobium*—(*Benth. Lond. Journ. Bot.* ii. 423); and another species, the *P. Saman*, a tree of rapid growth, from Central America, has recently been introduced and planted in the Cuddapah Codoor plantations. It was forwarded by Mr Thwaites from Ceylon, who considered it to be a tree of great value for railway fuel. It is known in Mexico as the Genisaro tree, and the specimen is described in Squier's 'Central America' as 90 feet high, with some of the branches quite horizontal, and 92 feet long, and 5 feet in diameter; the stem at 4 feet above the base 21 feet in circumference, and the head of the tree describing a circle of 348 feet.—*Beddome's Report to Government*, 1870.

(340) **Inga xylocarpa** (*Dec.*) Do.

Idou-moullou, MAL. Conda-tangheroo, TEL. Jamba, DUK.

DESCRIPTION.—Tree, 60 feet, unarmed; leaves conjugately

* For a detailed account of the process of planting and preparing Indigo, see Appendix E.

pinnated; leaflets 2-4 pairs, with an odd one on the outside below the pairs, ovate-oblong, acute; peduncles in pairs, axillary, long; flowers globose-capitate; legumes ovate-oblong, hatchet-shaped, woody, many-seeded; flowers small white. *Fl.* April—May.—*W. & A. Prod.* i. 269.—Mimosa xylocarpa, *Roxb. Cor. t.* 100.—*Fl. Ind.* ii. 543.——Coromandel. Hills of the Concans.

Economic Uses.—The wood of this tree is chocolate-coloured towards the centre. It is esteemed useful by the natives for its extreme hardness and durability, especially for plough-heads, as well as for knees and crooked timbers in shipbuilding.—*Roxb.*

(341) **Ionidium suffruticosum** (*Ging.*) N. O. Violaceæ.

Orala-tamaray, Tam. Oorelatamara, Mal. Pooroosharatanum, Tel. Ruttun-puruss, Duk. Noonbora, Beng.

Description.—Perennial; stem scarcely any; leaves alternate, sub-sessile, lanceolate, slightly serrate, smoothish; peduncles axillary, solitary, 1-flowered, shorter than the leaves, jointed above the middle, with 2 bracts at the joints; calyx 5-cleft; petals 5, two upper ones smallest, linear-oblong, two lateral ones sub-ovate, with long recurved apices, lower one largest, broad-cordate, supported on a claw; capsules round, 1-celled, 3-valved; seeds several; flowers small, rose-coloured. *Fl.* Nearly all the year.—*W. & A. Prod.* p. 32, 33.—*Wight Icon. t.* 308.—Viola suffruticosa, *Linn.*—*Roxb. Fl. Ind.* i. 649.—*Rheede,* ix. *t.* 60.——Peninsula. Travancore.

Medical Uses.—The root in infusion is diuretic, and is a remedy in gonorrhœa and affections of the urinary organs. The leaves and tender stalks are demulcent, and are used in decoction and electuary, and also employed, mixed with oil, as a cooling liniment for the head.—(*Ainslie.*) It may not be unworthy of remark that a species of this family of plants, the *I. parviflorum* (*Viola parviflora,* Linn.), is used as an undoubted specific in Elephantiasis in South America. It is there known as Cuichanchulli. For instances of its effects see Curtis (Comp. to) *Bot. Mag.* i. 278.

(342) **Ipomœa pes-capræ** (*Sweet.*) N. O. Convolvulaceæ.

Goat's-foot Creeper, Eng. Schovanna-adamboe, Mal. Chagul Khooree, Beng. Dopate-luta, Hind.

Description.—Perennial; creeping but never twining; leaves long-petioled, roundish, deeply 2-lobed, smooth; peduncles axillary, solitary, 2-flowered; sepals oblong, acute; seeds covered with a brownish pubescence; flowers large, reddish purple. *Fl.* Nearly all the year.—Convolvulus pes-capræ, *Linn.*—*Roxb. Fl. Ind.* i. 486.—C. bilobatus, *Roxb.*—C. Brasiliensis, *Linn.*—*Rheede,* xi. *t.* 57.——Peninsula. Common on sea-shores.

Medical Uses.—This plant is found on sandy beaches, where it is of great use in helping to bind the loose soil, and in time rendering it sufficiently stable to bear grass. Goats, horses, and rabbits eat it. The natives boil the leaves and apply them externally as an anodyne in cases of colic, and in decoction they use them in rheumatism. Another species, according to Ainslie (the *I. gemella*), has its leaves, which are mucilaginous to the taste, toasted and boiled with clarified butter, and thus reckoned of value in aphthæ.

(343) **Ipomœa turpethum** (*R. Br.*) Do.

Indian Jalap, Beng. Shevadie, Tam. Tella-tegada, Tel. Doodh-kulmee, Beng. Teoree, Beng.

Description.—Perennial, twining; stem angular, winged, glabrous or a little downy; leaves alternate, cordate, ovate, acuminated, sometimes entire or angularly sinuated or crenated; peduncles axillary, 1-4 flowered, bracteate at the apex; outer sepals the largest, ovate-roundish; corolla twice as long as the calyx, white; capsule 4-sided, 4-celled; seeds round, black, 1 in each cell; flowers white, with a tinge of cream colour. *Fl.* Nearly all the year.—Convolvulus turpethum, *Linn.*—*Roxb. Fl. Ind.* i. 476.——Malabar. Coromandel.

Medical Uses.—The bark of the root is employed by the natives as a purgative, which they use fresh rubbed up with milk. About 6 inches in length of the root is reckoned a dose. Cattle do not eat the plant. The root, being free from a nauseous taste and smell, possesses a decided superiority over jalap, for which it might be substituted. Turpethum is derived from its Arabic name. A resinous substance exudes from the root when wounded, which might probably be turned to some account; it is merely the milky juice of the fruits dried. Roxburgh has a long note upon this plant, wherein he communicates the following information on the subject of its medical virtues, as received from Dr Gordon of the Bengal establishment: "The drug which this plant yields is so excellent a substitute for jalap, and deserves so much the attention of practitioners, that I doubt not the following account will prove acceptable. It is a native of all parts of continental and probably of insular India also, as it is said to be found in the Society and Friendly Isles and the

New Hebrides. It thrives best in moist shady places on the sides of ditches, sending forth long climbing quadrangular stems, which in the rains are covered with abundance of large, white, bell-shaped flowers. Both root and stem are perennial. The roots are long, branchy, somewhat fleshy, and when fresh contain a milky juice which quickly hardens into a resinous substance, altogether soluble in spirits of wine. The milk has a taste at first sweetish, afterwards slightly acid; the dried root has scarcely any perceptible taste or smell. It abounds in woody fibres, whish, however, separate from the more resinous substance in pounding, and ought to be removed before the trituration is completed. It is, in fact, in the bark of the root that all the purgative matter exists. The older the plant the more woody is the bark of the root; and if attention be not paid in trituration to the removal of the woody fibres, the quality of the powder obtained must vary in strength accordingly. It is probably from this circumstance that its character for uncertainty of operation has arisen, which has occasioned its disuse in Europe. An extract which may be obtained in the proportion of one ounce to a pound of the dried root would not be liable to that objection. Both are given in rather larger proportion than jalap. Like it, the power and certainty of its operation are very much aided by the addition of cream of tartar to the powder, or of calomel to the extract. I have found the powder in this form to operate with a very small degree of tenesmus and very freely, producing three or four motions within two to four hours. It is considered by the natives as possessing peculiar hydragogue virtues, but I have used it also with decided advantage in the first stages of febrile affections."

According to the Raja Nirghaunta, the Teoree is dry and hot; a good remedy against worms; a remover of phlegm, swellings of the limbs, and diseases of the stomach. It also heals ulcers, and is useful in diseases of the skin. It is known to be one of the best purgatives.

The Bhavaprukasha has the following observation: "The white Teoree is cathartic; it is pungent; it increases wind, is hot and efficacious in removing cold and bile; it is useful in bilious fevers and complaints of the stomach. The black sort is somewhat less efficacious; it is a violent purgative, is good in faintings, and diminishes the heat of the body in fevers with delirium."—(*Ainslie. Roxb. Wallich's Obs.*) It should be here added that it has entirely fallen into disuse in European practice; and Sir W. O'Shaughnessy found it so uncertain in its operation, that he pronounced it as unworthy of a place in the pharmacopœia.—*Pharm. of India.*

(344) **Isonandra acuminata** (*Lindl.*) N. O. SAPOTACEÆ.

Indian Gutta-tree, ENG. Pauchoontee or Pashonti, MAL. Pauley or Pali, TAM.

DESCRIPTION.—Large tree, 80-90 feet; leaves fascicled at the extremities of the branches, somewhat coriaceous, dark green above, paler beneath, entire, long-petioled, oblong-obovate, tapering at the base, terminating in a sudden blunt acumination; flowers axillary, generally solitary, occasionally 2-3 together; calyx biserial,—*outer* deeply 3-cleft, segments broad, acute at the apex, leathery, valvate,—*inner* of 3 distinct sepals attached to the base of the outer calyx, alternate with its divisions, smaller, longer, equal, acuminated at the apex, of dirty white colour, imbricated in estivation; corolla deeply 6-cleft, occasionally 5-cleft, deciduous, tomentose at point of insertion at the stamens, colour darkish red; stamens 12-18, usually 16, inserted into the throat of the corolla, shorter than the corolla, sessile, extrorse, 2-celled, all perfect, alternate in two rows; ovary tomentose, superior, 6-celled, each cell with one ovule; style nearly 3 times the length of the ovary; stigma simple; fruit chartaceous, size of an almond; seed exalbuminous, erect; flowers dullish red. *Fl.* Jan.—April.—Bassia elliptica.—*Dalz. Bomb. Flor.—Dr Cleghorn's Report.* —— Wynaad. Coorg. Travancore forests. Annamallay mountains.

Economic Uses.—This tree, which promises to be of some importance among the vegetable products of the Peninsula, has only been discovered of late years. Although first actually noticed by Mr Lascelles in the Wynaad forests in 1850, yet the great attention paid to its locality and extensive distribution among the forests of the Western Ghauts by General Cullen, entitles the latter officer to an equal share in the merit of its discovery. "I feel bound to mention," says Dr Cleghorn, in his report to Government, "the continued exertions of General Cullen, who has done more to introduce this interesting tree and its useful product to public notice than any other individual." The tree has an extensive range, being found at the foot of the Ghauts as well as at elevations of about 3000 feet above the sea. It is so lofty a tree, and runs to such an immense height without giving off any branches, that the naked eye is unable to distinguish the forms of the leaves, and it is generally recognised by the fruit and flowers found fallen at the base. The bark is rusty, often whitish from the presence of numerous lichens; and a section of the trunk shows a reddish and sometimes mottled wood. The timber, when fully grown, is moderately hard, but does not appear to be much sought after by the natives. The exudation from the trunk, which has some similarity to the gutta-percha of commerce, is procured by tapping, and the quantity is not inconsiderable; but it would appear that the tree requires an interval of rest, of some hours, if not days, after frequent incision. "In five or six hours," says General Cullen, "upwards of $1\frac{1}{2}$ lb. (more than a catty) was collected from 4 or 5 incisions in one tree." Again he writes in the same month (April): "Incisions were made in forty places, at distances nearly 3 feet apart, along the whole trunk. The quantity produced was $2\frac{1}{2}$ dungalies (a dungaly is about half a gallon), the reeds were placed again, but in the evening no more milk was found; but the bark is thin, and the juice soon ceases to flow, although there is plenty of it in the tree." The gum when fresh is of a milky white colour, the larger lumps being of a dullish red. Specimens of the gum were forwarded to England, to be reported on by competent persons, and on an analysis of its properties, Messrs Teschemachar & Smith stated: "It is evident that this substance belongs to the class of the vegetable products of which caoutchouc and gutta-percha are types, and that it greatly resembles 'bird-lime' in its leading characteristics, but in a higher degree. It is evident that for waterproofing purposes it is (in its crude state) unfit; for although the coal-tar, oil of turpentine paste, might be applied to fabrics, as similar solutions of caoutchouc now are, and a material obtained impervious for a time to wet, yet, that owing to the capacity of this substance to combine with water, and become brittle in consequence at ordinary temperatures, such a waterproofed fabric would become useless very quickly. We do not, of course, in any way imply, that in the hands of some inventors this and other difficulties to its useful application may not be overcome. Although unfit for waterproof clothing, movable tarpauling, and its like, yet it might be usefully employed to waterproof fixed sheds, or temporary erections of little cost, covered with calico or cheap canvas; but there are already a numerous class of cheap varnishes equally adapted for such a purpose, so that, as a waterproofing material, it is but advisable for the present to look upon it as useless.

"Its perfume, when heated, might possibly render it of some value to the pastille and incense makers.

"Its bird-lime sticky quality might be made available by the gamekeeper and poacher in this country for taking vermin and small birds; we almost doubt whether a rabbit, hare, or pheasant, could free itself, if hair, feathers, or feet, came in contact with it. We think it might be useful and more legitimately employed by the trapper for taking the small fur-bearing animals; turpentine would cleanse the soiled furs. The only extensive and practical use, however, in this country, to which we at present think it may probably be with advantage applied, is as a subaqueous cement or glue. We beg to forward you some deal-wood glued together with this substance melted and applied hot, which we have now kept under water for several days, and two fragments of glasses which have been similarly treated. You will observe that the cement has hardened at the edges, but probably without injury to its cementing properties. We have no reason to think that it would not rot under water more rapidly than wood does, but experience must be the sole guide here. We have reason to think such a glue or cement would be readily tried, and if found good, employed by joiners and others, having been applied some time since to examine a glue, which after application resisted the action of water."

With regard to the wood, Mr Williams, assistant conservator of forests, reported as follows to Dr Cleghorn: "It is not unlike *saul* in the grain, and yet it takes after the character of some of the harder kinds of cedar and *kurbah*. As the wood is capable of receiving a good polish, I am inclined to think it ought to make good furniture. Its specific gravity, weighing the specimen piece in the hand, appears to be about 50 lb. to the cubic foot; and as the fibres possess both solidity and strength, I should say the wood ought to be useful in making doors and windows, &c., if not too readily destroyed by white ants; but I doubt whether it will be found capable of sustaining much weight, for the coalescing deposit is rather too pithy to make it useful as beams for terracing.

"The external surface with the bark peeled off exhibits hardness, and the fibres are greatly elongated and closely adhering; but in planing down a portion I find that the alburnum occupies much more space than is apparent outside, and renders the wood too pithy to answer for the more substantial parts in building."

It remains to add that the tree is very plentiful in those districts where it grows, and that it is found both on the eastern and western slopes of the Ghauts.—*Memorandum on the Indian Gutta-tree of western coast.*

(345) **Isora corylifolia** (*Schott and Endl.*) N. O. STERCULIACEÆ.

Isora murri, Valumpiri, MAL. Valimbiri, TAM. Valumbricaca, TEL. Maroori, HIND. Antumora, BENG.

DESCRIPTION.—Shrub, 12 feet; leaves broad, slightly cordate, roundish, obovate, suddenly and shortly acuminated, serrate, toothed, upper side scabrous, under tomentose; pedicels 2-4 together, forming an almost sessile, axillary corymb; petals reflexed; fruit cylindrical, spirally twisted, pubescent; flowers brick-coloured. *Fl.* Sept.—Nov.—*W. & A. Prod.* i. 60.—*Wight Icon. t.* 150.—Helicteres Isora, *Linn.—Roxb. Fl. Ind.* iii. 143.—*Rheede*, vi. *t.* 30.——Foot of the Himalaya. Peninsula. Travancore, at the base of the hills.

MEDICAL USES.—The leaves of this tree are very like the English hazel. The capsule has a singular appearance, being in the form of a screw. A liniment is prepared from the powder of it, applied to sore ears. It is mixed in preparation with castor-oil. The juice of the root is used in stomachic affections in Jamaica, as well as the leaves in certain cases of constipation. Seed-vessels used internally in bilious affections in combination with other medicines. Royle says that the natives of India, like those of Europe in former times, believing that external signs point out the properties possessed by plants, consider that the twisted fruit of this plant indicates that it is useful, and therefore prescribe it in pains of the bowels.

ECONOMIC USES.—This is a valuable plant from the fibrous qualities of its bark. These fibres have of late been much brought to notice, being well adapted for ropes and cordage. They are strong and white-coloured. In Travancore the fibre (known as the *kyvan nar*) is employed for making gunny-bags. The fibres are cleaned by soaking the plant in water and beating them out afterwards. The curtain-blinds of the verandahs of native houses are made from the fibre. It is one of the woods used by the natives for producing fire by friction.—*Ainslie. Report on Prod. of Travancore.*

J

(346) **Jambosa vulgaris** (*Dec.*) N. O. MYRTACEÆ.

Rose-Apple, ENG. Gulab-jamun, HIND.

DESCRIPTION.—Tree; leaves narrow-lanceolate, attenuated at the base, acuminated towards the apex; racemes cymose, terminal; flowers white; fruit globose.—*Dec. Prod.* iii. 286.—*W. & A. Prod.* i. 332.—Eugenia Jambos, *Linn.*—*Roxb. Fl. Ind.* ii. 494.—*Rheede Mal.* i. *t.* 17.——Cultivated.

ECONOMIC USES.—The fruit is about the size of a hen's egg, rose-coloured and white-fleshed, with the flavour of a ripe apricot. The tree grows rapidly and shoots up from the stump with vigour, yielding much firewood. In a communication to the Agri.-Hort. Soc. of Bengal (May 1848), Colonel Ouseley observes: "I have just made a discovery that promises well in places where roses do not thrive, if the rose-apple ripens well; most excellent rose-water can be distilled from the fruit, taking the seed out first. I had it distilled *four* times, and it proved equal to the best rose-water, to the great surprise of the distiller."

(347) **Janipha Manihot** (*Kth.*) N. O. EUPHORBIACEÆ.

Bitter Cassava, Tapioca, or Mandioc plant, ENG. Maravullie, TAM. Maracheenie, MAL.

DESCRIPTION. — Stems white, crooked, 6 - 7 feet, smooth, covered with protuberances from the fallen leaves; branches crooked; leaves palmate, divided nearly to their base into 5 lanceolate, entire lobes, attenuated at both extremities, dark green above, glaucous beneath; midrib prominent below, of a yellowish-red colour; panicles axillary and terminal, 4 - 5 inches long; male flowers smaller than the female; calyx purplish on the outside, brownish within, segments 5, spreading, divided nearly to the base; female flowers deeply 5-parted, with lanceolate-ovate segments; root oblong, tuberous; capsule ovate, triangular, tricoccous; seeds elliptical, black, shining; flowers small, reddish. *Fl.* April—May.—*Lindley Fl. Med.* p.

185. — Jatropha Manihot, *Linn.* — Manihot utilissima, *Pohl.* ——Cultivated in Travancore.

Economic Uses.—A native of South America, but now cultivated in lower India to a great extent, especially in Travancore. It yields the *Tapioca* of commerce. The following account of the preparation of this substance is given by Ainslie: "An amylum or starch is first to be obtained from the fresh roots, which starch, to form it into Tapioca, must be sprinkled with a little water and then boiled in steam; it is in this way converted into viscid irregular masses, which must be dried in the sun till they have become quite hard, and then they may be broken into small grains for use." Tapioca is a light and nourishing food, and affords a good diet for the sick. The poisonous substance which resides in the root is said to be hydrocyanic acid. It can only be expelled by roasting, when the starch becomes fit for food. This starch being formed into granules by the action of heat, constitutes the Tapioca of commerce. *Cassava* flour is obtained by immersing the grated starch in water, when the flour is self-deposited, and afterwards washed thoroughly and dried in the sun. Cassava is said to be very nourishing, one acre being equal in its nutritive qualities to six acres of wheat. Recently much attention has been paid to the cultivation of the plant, for the purpose of exportation to Europe from the West Indies, it having been found to be a most profitable article of commerce, and one requiring little or no care in its cultivation, the plant thriving on the most barren soil. This is equally the case in Travancore, where the cultivator has merely to clear away the low brushwood and plant it, when it will spring up luxuriantly on the most rocky and exposed situations, either in the vicinity of the sea or inland. Simmonds says on the subject—"The experimental researches of Dr Shier have led him to believe that the green bitter cassava will give one-fifth its weight of starch. If this be the case the return per acre would, under favourable circumstances, when the land is properly worked, be enormous. On an estate at Essequibo, an acre of cassava, grown in fine permeable soil, yielded 25 tons of green cassava. Such a return as this per acre would enable our West India colonies to inundate Great Britain with food, and at a rate which would make flour to be considered a luxury." If more attention were paid to its cultivation in India, a similar profitable return might be anticipated. The poorer classes in Travancore use it as food, especially when rice becomes scarce and dear; and nearly one-half the population of several of the southern districts live on Tapioca in the months of July, August, and September. They reduce the root to powder for conjee, and cook the raw root for curries.

It is from the juice of this plant that the Red Indians in South America prepare the most deadly *mandioc poison* with which they tip their arrows. This is procured by distillation, and it is said that thirty drops will cause the death of a human being in six hours.

Cases are not unfrequent of children being poisoned in the country by incautiously eating the roots before they have undergone the necessary preparations.

An extract is made from the concentrated juice of the root called *Cassareep*, the poisonous principle being destroyed during the course of evaporation. It is used in the West Indies for flavouring soups and other dishes. It is a powerful antiseptic. In Jamaica the scrapings from the fresh roots are applied to bad ulcers.—*Ainslie. Simmonds. Pereira. Rep. on Prod. of Travancore. Pers. Obs.*

(348) **Jasminum angustifolium** (*Vahl.*) N. O. Jasminaceæ.

Katu-pitsjegam-mulla, Mal. Caat-mallica, Tam. Adevie-mallie, Tel. Ban-mallica, Hind.

Description.—Twining; leaves opposite, ovate or oblong, finely pointed, smooth, of a shining deep green; flowers terminal, generally by threes; calycine segments acute; segments of corolla 8-9, lanceolate; berries single, ovate; flowers large, white with a faint tinge of red, star-shaped, fragrant. *Fl.* March—May.—*Roxb. Fl. Ind.* i. 96.—*Wight Icon. t.* 698-700. —Nyctanthes angustifolia, *Linn.*—*Rheede*, vi. *t.* 53.——Coromandel forests. Travancore.

Medical Uses.—This species being constantly covered with leaves of a bright shining green, renders it particularly well adapted for screening windows, and covering arbours in warm climates. The bitter root ground small and mixed with lime-juice and *vassamboo* root is considered a good remedy in ringworm.—(*Roxb. Ainslie.*) The *J. revolutum* contains an essential oil of an aromatic flavour, and is used as a perfume. The root is said to be useful in ringworm.—*Powell's Punj. Prod.*

(349) **Jasminum sambac** (*Ait.*) Do.

Tsjeregam-mulla, Mal. Pun-mullika, Mal. Kôdy-mulli, Tam. Boondoc-mallie, Tel. But-moogra, Beng.

Description.—Twining shrub; leaves opposite, cordate, ovate or oblong, waved, sometimes scolloped, pointed, smooth, downy on the veins on the under side; calyx segments 5-9; flowers terminal, generally in small trichotomous umbellets, white. *Fl.* March—May.—*Roxb. Fl. Ind.* i. 88.—*Wight Icon. t.* 704.—Nyctanthes Sambac, *Linn.*——Common everywhere.

Medical Uses.—Of this there are two other varieties: the double-flowered Jasmin, called *Bela* in Bengal—the *Nulla mulla* of Rheede

(vi. *t.* 50); and the *Buro-bel* and *Kadda mulla* of Rheede (vi. *t.* 51). The plant is common in every forest in the Peninsula, and is generally cultivated in gardens. The leaves if boiled in oil exude a balsam which is used for anointing the head in eye-complaints. It is said to strengthen the vision. An oil is also expressed from the roots used medicinally. The flowers, commonly known as the *Moogree* flowers, are sacred to Vishnoo.—(*Rheede.*) The flowers possess considerable power as a lactifuge, and are effectual in arresting the secretion of milk in the puerperal state, in cases of threatened abscess. For this purpose about two or three handfuls of the flowers bruised and unmoistened are applied to each breast, and renewed once or twice a-day. The secretion is sometimes arrested in about twenty-four hours, though it generally requires two or even three days.—*Pharm. of India.*

(350) **Jatropha curcas** (*Linn.*) N. O. Euphorbiaceæ.

Angular-leaved Physic-nut, Eng. Caat-amunak, Tam. Caak-avanakoo, Mal. Nepalam, Adivie amida, Tel. Bag-bherenda, Hind. Erundi, Duk. Bagh-Dharanda, Beng.

Description.—Small tree or shrub; leaves scattered, broad-cordate, 5-angled, smooth; panicles terminal, or from the exterior axils, cymose, many-flowered; male flowers at the extremities of the ramification on short articulated pedicels, the female ones in their divisions, with pedicels not articulated; calyx 5-leaved; corolla 5-petalled, campanulate, somewhat hairy; styles 3, short; flowers small, green; ovary oblong, smooth. *Fl.* Nearly all the year.—*Roxb. Fl. Ind.* iii. 686.——Domesticated in India. Coromandel. Travancore.

Medical Uses.—The seeds are purgative, occasionally exciting vomiting. It is said that they may be safely eaten if first deprived of their outer teguments. They consist of a fixed oil, and an acid poisonous principle. The leaves are reckoned as discutient and rubefacient; and the milky juice of the plant is said to possess a healing and detergent quality, and to dye linen black. A fixed or expressed oil is prepared from the seeds useful in cutaneous diseases and chronic rheumatism applied externally; also for burning in lamps. The Chinese boil the oil with oxide of iron, and use the preparation for varnishing boxes, &c. It is frequently used as a hedge-plant, as cattle will not touch the leaves. The juice of the plant is of a very tenacious nature, and if blown, forms large bubbles, probably owing to the presence of caoutchouc. The leaves warmed and rubbed with castor-oil are applied by the natives to inflammations when suppuration is wished for. The oil has been imported to England as a substitute for linseed-oil. It is of a pale colour, and can be cheaply supplied in any part of the country. It differs from castor and croton oil in its slight solubility in alcohol; but mixed with castor-oil its solubility is increased. According to Dr Christison, 12 or 15 drops are equal to one ounce of castor-oil. The juice of the plant has been applied externally in hæmorrhoids. A decoction of the leaves is used in the Cape Verd Islands to excite secretion of milk in women.—*Simmonds. Ainslie. Beng. Disp.*

(351) **Jatropha glandulifera** (*Roxb.*) Do.

Addaley, TAM. Nela-amida, TEL.

DESCRIPTION.—Small plant, 1 foot, erect, pubescent; leaves 5-3 cleft, serrated, smooth, glaucous, almost veinless; petioles sub-villose, longer than the leaves, with glandular hairs; petals of female flowers ovate, the length of the calyx; capsule muricated, as large as a hazel nut; seed size of a pea; flowers small, greenish yellow. *Fl.* All the year.—*Roxb. Fl. Ind.* iii. 688.—J. glauca, *Vahl. ?*——Panderpore in the Deccan. On bunds of tanks; Northern Circars.

MEDICAL USES.—An oil is expressed from the seeds which, from its stimulating property, is reckoned useful externally applied in cases of chronic rheumatism and paralytic affections. The plant exudes a pale thin juice, which the Hindoos employ for removing films from the eyes.—*Roxb. Ainslie.*

ECONOMIC USES.—In 1862, Dr Thompson, civil surgeon, of Malda, submitted to the Agri.-Hort. Society specimens of cloth dyed with a green vegetable dye prepared from the leaves, it is believed, of this species. He wrote as follows: One maund of the dried leaves will dye 1280 yards of cloth of a fine apple-green colour. The supply is cheap and unlimited, and the cultivation is easily extended from cuttings or seed, requiring little care or watching, as no animal will eat it. The plant is doubly valuable from the seeds yielding a fine, clear, limpid oil for burning purposes. It takes half an hour to dye a whole *than* of cloth. For preparing the oil the seeds should be collected as the capsule begins to split or change colour from green to brown; the latter should then be thrown down on a mat, and covered over with another mat, and on a few hours' exposure to a bright sun the seeds will have separated from the shell, for if allowed to remain on the shrub till quite ripe, the capsule bursts, and the seeds are scattered and lost.

(352) **Jussiæa villosa** (*Lam.*) N. O. ONAGRACEÆ.

Carambu, MAL. Lal-bunlunga, BENG.

DESCRIPTION.—Perennial, herbaceous, 1½ foot, erect, more or less pubescent or villous; leaves from broadly lanceolate to linear acuminate, tapering at the base into a short petiole; flowers almost sessile; calyx lobes 4 or 5, broadly lanceolate or ovate, 3-5 nerved, much shorter than the roundish-ovate petals; capsule nearly cylindrical, elongated, tapering at the base into a short pedicel; flowers largish, yellow. *Fl.* Oct.—Nov.—*W. & A. Prod.* i. 336.—J. suffruticosa, *Linn.*—J. exaltata, *Roxb. Fl. Ind.* ii. 401.—*Rheede,* ii. *t.* 50.——Peninsula. Bengal.

Medical Uses.—There are two varieties given by Wight of this plant. According to Rheede, the plant, ground small, and steeped in butter-milk, is considered good in dysentery; also in decoction as a vermifuge and purgative.—*Ainslie.*

K

(353) **Kœmpferia galanga** (*Linn.*) N. O. ZINGIBERACEÆ.

Katsjulum, MAL. Katsjolum, TAM. Chundra Moola, Kumula, BENG.

DESCRIPTION.—Rhizome biennial, tuberous; stem none; leaves stalked, spreading flat on the surface of the earth, round, ovate-cordate, margins membranaceous and waved, upper surface smooth, somewhat woolly towards the base; flowers fascicled, 6-12 within the sheath of the leaves, expanding in succession, pure white with a purple spot on the centre of each of the divisions of the inner series; bracts 3 to each flower, linear, acute, half the length of the tube of the corolla; calyx the length of the bracts; tube of corolla long, filiform, limbs double, both series 3-parted. *Fl.* Oct.—Nov. —*Wight Icon. t.* 899.—*Roxb. Fl. Ind.* i. 15.——Peninsula. Bengal. Much cultivated in gardens.

MEDICAL USES.—This plant is said to be very common on the mountainous districts beyond Chittagong, and is brought by the mountaineers for sale to the markets in Bengal, where the inhabitants use it as an ingredient in their betel. The root is fragrant, and used medicinally by the natives as well as for perfumes. Reduced to powder and mixed with honey it is given in coughs and pectoral affections. Boiled in oil it is externally applied in stoppages of the nasal organs.—*Rheede. Roxb.*

(354) **Kœmpferia rotunda** (*Linn.*) Do.

Melan-kua, MAL. Bhuchampa, BENG.

DESCRIPTION.—Leaves oblong, coloured; spikes radical, appearing before the leaves, which are oblong, waved, and usually stained underneath; upper segments of the inner series of the corolla lanceolate, acute, lower ones divided into two broad obcordate lobes; flowers near, fragrant, sessile, purplish white; scapes embraced by a few common sheaths, very short, greenish purple; calyx above, 1-leafed, as long as the tube of the corolla, somewhat gibbous; apex generally two-toothed, and of a dotted purplish colour. *Fl.* March—April. —*Roxb. Fl. Ind.* i. 16.—*Wight Icon. t.* 2029.—K. longa, *Redout.*—*Rheede*, xi. *t.* 9.——Native place unknown.

MEDICAL USES.—This species is much cultivated in gardens for the beauty and fragrance of its flowers. When in flower the plant is destitute of leaves. The whole plant, according to Rheede, is first reduced to a powder, and then used as an ointment. It is in this state reckoned very useful in healing wounds, and taken internally will remove coagulated blood or any purulent matters. The root is useful in anasarcous swellings. It has a hot, ginger-like taste.—*Ainslie. Roxb. Rheede.*

(355) **Kandelia Rheedii** (*W. & A.*) N. O. RHIZOPHORACEÆ.

Tsjeron-kandel, MAL.

DESCRIPTION.—Shrub; leaves quite entire, linear-oblong, obtuse, 2-3 chotomous, 4-9 flowered; inflorescence axillary; calyx tube campanulate, segments linear, persistent; petals as many as the segments of the calyx, membranaceous, cleft to below the middle into numerous capillary segments; fruit oblong, longer than the tube of the calyx; germinating embryo subulate-clavate, acute; flowers largish, white and green.—*W. & A. Prod.* i. 311.—*Wight Ill. t.* 89.—Rhizophora Candel, *Linn.*—*Rheede*, vi. *t.* 35.——Malabar. Sunderbunds. Deltas on Coromandel coast.

MEDICAL USES.—This species of mangrove is common on the back-waters in Travancore. The bark mixed with dried ginger or long pepper and rose-water is said to be a cure for diabetes.—(*Rheede.*) It is also used for tanning purposes at Cochin.—*Pers. Obs.*

(356) **Kydia calycina** (*Roxb.*) N. O. BYTTNERIACEÆ.

DESCRIPTION.—Tree; leaves alternate, 5-nerved, somewhat 5-lobed; calyx campanulate; capsule 3-valved, 3-celled, perfect cells 1-seeded, involucels of fertile flowers usually 4-leaved, longer than the calyx, spathulate, enlarging with the fruit; filaments united their whole length into a tube; style elongated, stigmas projecting; male involucel 4-6 leaved shorter than the calyx, lanceolate, blunt; filaments united about half their length, free above; petals in both obliquely cordate, clawed, emarginate, ciliate; flowers white or pale yellowish. *Fl.* Aug.—Dec.—*W. & A. Prod.* i. 70.—*Roxb. Cor.* iii. *t.* 215.—*Fl. Ind.* iii. 189.—*Wight Icon. t.* 879, 880.——Valleys of the Circar mountains. Mysore. Slopes of the Neilgherries.

ECONOMIC USES.—The bark is mucilaginous, and is employed in the northern provinces to clarify sugar.—*Royle.*

L

(357) **Lablab vulgaris** (*Savi.*) N. O. Leguminosæ.

Chota-sim, Hind. Bun-shim, Beng. Anapa-anoomooloo, Tel. Avarei, Mutcheh, Tam.

Description.—Twining; leaves pinnately trifoliolate; leaflets entire; racemes axillary, elongated; pedicels short; corolla papilionaceous; calyx bi-bracteolate, campanulate, tubular 4-cleft; legume broadly scimitar-shaped, gibbous below the apex, and ending abruptly in a straight or recurved cuspidate point; seeds longitudinally oval, of various colours; flowers red, purple, or white. *Fl.* Nov.—Feb.—*W. & A. Prod.* i. 250. *Wight Icon. t.* 57-203.—*Roxb. Fl. Ind.* iii. 305.—Dolichos lablab, *Linn.*——Peninsula. Bengal. Cultivated.

Economic Uses.—There are several varieties differing in the colour of their seeds and forms of their legumes, some of which are cultivated, and others are not. Of one variety which is cultivated on the Coromandel coast, Roxburgh states that it will yield in a good soil about forty-fold. The seeds bear a low price comparatively, and are much eaten by the poorer classes, particularly when rice is dear. They are not palatable, but are reckoned wholesome substantial food. Cattle are fed with the seeds, and greedily eat the straw. Another variety, which has white flowers, is cultivated in gardens and supported on poles, often forming arbours about the doors of native houses. The pods are eaten, but not the seeds. The pulse of the best kind is imported from Madras to Ceylon.—(*Roxb.*) The different kinds are distinguished by the colours of their flowers, which vary from white to red and purple, and by the size and shape of the pods, which exhibit every degree of curvature, one kind being designated as the *Bugh-nak* (tiger's claw), from its rounded form. The same diversity occurring in the seeds has given rise to the many specific varieties, or even species, which after all may well be reduced to the present form of Lablab.—*W. Elliott.*

(358) **Lagenaria vulgaris** (*Ser.*) N. O. Cucurbitaceæ.

White Pumpkin, Bottle-gourd, Eng. Hunea-kuddoo, Duk. Shora-Kai, Tam. Bella-schora, Mal. Lavoo, Beng. Anapa-kai, Tel.

Description.—Stem climbing softly pubescent; calyx campanulate; petals rising from within the margin of the calyx; tendrils 3-4 cleft; leaves cordate, nearly entire or lobed, lobes obtuse, or somewhat acute, glaucous; flowers fascicled, white; petals very patent; fruit pubescent, at length nearly glabrous and very smooth; seeds numerous, flesh-white, edible; fruit bottle-shaped, yellow when ripe. *Fl.* July—Sept.—*W. & A. Prod.* i. 341.—Cucurbita lagenaria, *Linn. sp.*—*Roxb. Fl. Ind.* iii. 718.—*Rheede,* viii. *t.* i. 4, 5.——Cultivated.

Medical Uses.—The pulp of the fruit is often used in poultices; it is bitter and slightly purgative, and may be used as a substitute for colocynth. A decoction of the leaves mixed with sugar is given in jaundice.

Economic Uses.—The fruit is known as the bottle-gourd. The poorer classes eat it, boiled with vinegar, or fill the shells with rice and meat, thus making a kind of pudding of it. In Jamaica, and many other places within the tropics, the shells are used for holding water or palm-wine, and so serve as bottles. The hard shell, when dry, is used for faqueers' bottles, and a variety of it is employed in making the stringed instrument known as the *Sitar*, as well as buoys for swimming across rivers and transporting baggage. There is one kind, the fleshy part of which is poisonous.—*Royle. Don.*

(359) **Lagerstrœmia microcarpa** (*R. W.*) N. O. Lythraceæ.

Ventek, Veveyla, Tam.

Description.—Large tree; leaves from elliptic to ovate, often attenuated or acute at the base, obtusely pointed at the apex, glabrous above, pale beneath, often very finely downy; panicles axillary and terminal, glabrous or hoary, with minute pubescence; flowers very numerous, white; calyx white outside, with hoary pubescence; six outer stamens longer than the others; capsule scarcely an inch long.—*Wight Icon. t.* 109.—*Bedd. Flor. Sylv. t.* 30.——Western forests, but not on the eastern side.

Economic Uses.—A handsome tree, abundant in all the western forests of the Madras Presidency, flowering in the hot weather. The wood is light-coloured, straight, and elastic. It is very much used for building purposes, and also in dockyards. It makes capital coffee-cases, but if left in the forests exposed will soon decay, and be rapidly attacked by white ants.—*Beddome.*

(360) **Lagerstrœmia parviflora** (*Roxb.*) Do.

Chinangee, Tel.

Description.—Tree; branches quadrangular; leaves opposite,

entire, from oblong or oval and obtuse to ovate and acute, pale beneath; peduncles axillary, 3-6 flowered; calyx 6-cleft, even; petals 6, flattish, shortly unguiculate; the six outer stamens longer than the rest; capsule oblong, 3-4 celled; flowers small, white, fragrant. *Fl.* May—June.—*W. & A. Prod.* i. 308.—*Wight Icon. t.* 69.—*Roxb. Fl. Ind.* ii. 505.—*Cor.* i. 66.——Circars. Courtallum. Neilgherries. Bengal.

Economic Uses.—Of this large tree there are two varieties, one which has the under sides of the leaves downy, and the other having them glabrous. The wood is very hard, and is reputed to be an excellent timber. It is light brown, close-grained, straight, and elastic. It is used for building, boat-timber, ploughs, and axe-handles.—*Beddome Flor. Sylv. t.* 31.

(361) **Lagerstrœmia reginæ** (*Roxb.*) Do.

Kadali, Tam. Adamboe, Mal. Jarool, Beng.

Description.—Tree; petals 6, orbicular, waved, shortly unguiculate; leaves opposite, entire, oblong, glabrous; panicles terminal; calyx 6-cleft, longitudinally furrowed and plaited; capsule 3-6 valved, 3-6 celled; seeds numerous; flowers purple or rose-coloured. *Fl.* April—July.—*W. & A. Prod.* i. 308.—*Wight Icon. t.* 413.—*Roxb. Cor.* i. *t.* 65.—*Rheede,* iv. *t.* 20-21.—*Bedd. Flor. Sylv. t.* 29.——Circars. Courtallum. Travancore.

Economic Uses.—This is without exception, when in blossom, one of the most showy trees of the Indian forests. It is now commonly cultivated in gardens on the western coast, where the moist damp climâte is most suitable for its growth, and the full development of the rich rose-coloured blossoms. In the forests near the banks of rivers it grows to an enormous size, some having purple flowers, and forming a most beautiful and striking appearance. The timber is reddish, tough, and very durable under water, though it soon decays under ground. It is much used for building and boats. In the Madras gun-carriage manufactory it is used for light and heavy field-checks, felloes, and cart-naves, framing and boards of waggons, timbers and ammunition-box boards. In Burmah, according to Dr Brandis, it is more in use than any other timber except teak, and is there used for a vast variety of purposes.—*Beddome.*

(362) **Lawsonia alba** (*Lam.*) Do.

Henna, Broad Egyptian Privet, Eng. Maroodanie, Tam. Goounta Chettoo, Tel. Mayndie, Hind. Mailanschi, Ponta-letsche, Mal.

Description.—Shrub, 6-10 feet; calyx 4-partite; petals 4,

unguiculate, alternate with the lobes of the calyx, obovate, spreading ; stamens in pairs alternating with the petals ; leaves opposite, oval-lanceolate, quite entire, glabrous ; flowers panicled ; ovary sessile, 4-celled ; capsule globose, 3-4 celled ; seeds numerous ; flowers white or pale greenish. *Fl.* Nearly all the year.—*W. & A. Prod.* i. 307.—*Wight Ill. t.* 94.—L. spinosa, *Linn.*—L. inermis, *Roxb.*—*Rheede,* i. *t.* 40.——Peninsula. Bengal.

MEDICAL USES.—The powdered leaves beaten up with catechu, and made into paste, are much used by Mohammedan women to dye their nails and skin a reddish-orange. The colour will last for three or four weeks before requiring renewal. The plant is supposed to possess vulnerary and astringent properties. The flowers have a strong smell, from which, as well as from the leaves and young shoots, the natives prepare a kind of extract which they reckon useful in leprosy. The leaves are also used externally applied in cutaneous affections. In Barbary the natives use them for staining the tail and mane of their horses red. The plant is often employed for making garden hedges. The old plants become somewhat thorny, but the species called *spinosa,* says Roxburgh, is nothing more, probably, than the same plant growing in a dry sterile soil, the branchlets becoming then short and rigid, with sharp thorny points.—*Ainslie. Roxb.*

(363) **Lebidieropsis orbiculata** (*Muller*). N. O. EUPHORBIACEÆ.
var. Collina.

Wodisha, TEL. Wodagû marum, TAM.

DESCRIPTION.—Tree ; leaves elliptic or obovate, round-obtuse, obtuse or slightly cordate at the base, pubescent on the rib below ; flowers subsessile, softly grey hairy white ; sepals oblong triangular ovate ; petals very minute glabrous, irregularly rhomboid above ; capsules glabrous ; seeds globose. *Fl.* —March—May.—*Dec. Prod.* xv. s. 2, p. 509.—Cluytia collina, *Roxb.*—Bridelia collina, *Hook. et Arn. Bot. Beech.* p. 211.—C. patula et retusa, *Wall.*——Circars. Orissa. Concans.

ECONOMIC USES.—The wood is of a reddish colour, very hard and durable, much used in Rajahmandry and the Northern Circars. The bark or outer crust of the capsules is said to be very poisonous.—*Roxb.*

(364) **Leea macrophylla** (*Roxb.*) N. O. VITACEÆ.

Toolsoo-moodryia, BENG.

DESCRIPTION.—Herbaceous, 4 feet ; stems angular ; leaves

simple, stalked, dentato-serrate, broad-cordate or lobed, posterior lobes overlapping each other; calyx 5-cleft; petals 5; cymes trichotomous, terminal; flowers numerous, small, white; berries depressed, obscurely 6 or more lobed, when ripe black and succulent. *Fl.* June—Aug.—*Roxb. Fl. Ind.* i. 653.—*Wight Icon. t.* 1154.——Bengal. Both Concans. Palghaut.

Medical Uses.—The root is astringent and mucilaginous, and is a reputed remedy for ringworm.—*Roxb. J. Grah.*

(365) **Leucas linifolia** (*Spreng*). N. O. Labiatæ.

Description. — Herbaceous, erect, slightly pubescent or tomentose; leaves oblong-linear, entire or remotely serrated; verticils dense, subequal, many-flowered; bracts linear, hoary; calyx elongated above, mouth very oblique, lower teeth very short, upper longest; flowers white. *Fl.* Dec.—Jan.—*Dec. Prod.* xii. 533.—Phlomis zeylanica, *Roxb. Jacq. Ic. rar.* i. *t.* 111. ——Bengal. Peninsula.

Medical Uses.—The Cinghalese attribute miraculous curative powers to this plant. The leaves are bruised, and a teaspoonful of the juice given, which is snuffed up by the nostrils, and used by the natives in the North-West Provinces as a remedy in snake-bites. The fresh juice is also employed in headache and colds.—(*Long. Ind. Plants of Bengal.*) The juice of the leaves of the *L. aspera* is applied successfully in psora and other chronic eruptions.—*Pharm. of India.*

(366) **Limonia acidissima** (*Linn.*) N. O. Aurantiaceæ.

Tsjeru Caat-naregam, Mal.

Description.—Shrub, 6-10 feet; leaves pinnate, with 2-3 pairs of leaflets and an odd one; leaflets oblong, retuse, crenated; spines solitary; petioles broadly-winged; flowers corymbose; corymbs umbelliform, 2-3 together from the axils of the fallen leaves; petals 4; fruit globose, size of a nutmeg, yellowish, but red when perfectly ripe; flowers small, white, fragrant. *Fl.* March—May.—*W. & A. Prod.* i. 92.—L. crenulata, *Roxb. Cor.* i. 86.—*Rheede,* iv. *t.* 14.——Coromandel. Malabar. Hurdwar. Assam.

Medical Uses.—The pulp of this fruit is flesh-coloured, is very acid, and is used by the inhabitants of Java instead of soap. The leaves are good in epilepsy. The root is purgative, sudorific, and used in colic pains. The dried fruits are tonic, and said to resist contagious air from small-pox, malignant and pestilential fevers, and considered an excellent antidote to various poisons, on which account they are much sought for, especially by the Arabs and other merchants on the western coast, where they form an article of commerce. —*Gibson. Rheede.*

(367) **Linum usitatissimum** (*Linn.*) N. O. LINACEÆ.

Common Flax, ENG. Alleeveray, TAM. Musina, BENG. Tisi, HIND. Ulsee, DUK.

DESCRIPTION.—Annual, erect, glabrous; leaves alternate, lanceolate or linear, acute, entire; panicles corymbose; sepals ovate, acute or mucronate, with scarious or membranaceous margins; petals slightly crenated, three times larger than the calyx; stamens alternate with the petals, having their filaments united together near their basis; capsule roundish, pointed at the apex, 5-celled, each cell divided into two partitions, containing a single seed; seeds oval, smooth, brown or white, mucilaginous outside, with oily and farinaceous kernels; flowers blue. *Fl.* Dec.—Feb.—*W. & A. Prod.* i. 134.—*Roxb. Fl. Ind.* ii. 100.——Neilgherries. Cultivated in Northern India.

MEDICAL USES.—An oil is expressed from the seeds without heat. As the oil made in India has not the full drying properties of that prepared in Europe, a considerable quantity of the seeds is imported. This arises from the Indian seeds being mixed with those of mustard, with which they are grown, the mixture deteriorating the quality of the oil. The oil-cake made from the seeds after the expression of the oil is very fattening food for cattle. Linseed-meal is the cake coarsely pulverised, and is used for making emollient poultices. European practitioners in this country consider linseed a valuable demulcent, according to Ainslie, and is useful in diarrhœa, catarrh, dysentery, and visceral obstructions. A decoction of the seeds forms an excellent enema in abrasion of the intestines. The meal of the seeds is used for cataplasms; the oil mixed with lime-water (*carron oil*) has been a favourable application to burns and scalds. Linseed-oil is one of the chief ingredients in oil varnishes and painters' inks; by boiling with litharge its drying properties are much improved. The inferior seeds which are not sufficiently good for oil are boiled and made into a flax-seed jelly, esteemed an excellent nutriment for stock. Linseed contains 1-5th of mucilage, 1-6th of fixed oil. The former resides entirely in the skin, and is separated by infusion or decoction, the latter by expression.—*Simmonds. Ainslie.*

Economic Uses.—The native country of the flax-plant is unknown, though it has been considered as indigenous to Central Asia, from whence it has spread to Europe, as well as to the surrounding Oriental countries. For centuries it has been cultivated in India, though, strange to say, for its seeds alone; whereas in Europe it is chiefly sown for the sake of its fibres. The best flax comes from Russia, Belgium, and of late years from Ireland, where it has been cultivated with the greatest success. Much attention has lately been directed to the sowing of the flax-plant in India for the sake of the fibres; and although the experiments hitherto made have not in every case met with that success which was anticipated, yet there seems little reason to doubt that when the causes of the failure are well ascertained, and the apparent difficulties overcome, that flax will be as profitably cultivated on the continent of India as it is in Europe; while European cultivators must eventually supersede the ryots, whose obstinate prejudice to the introduction of novelty is fatal to any improvement at their hands.

As their object is solely to plant for the seeds alone, they generally mix the latter with other crops, usually mustard, a system which could never be persisted in when the object is for fibres. Among those parts of India where flax has best succeeded may be mentioned the Saugor and Nerbudda territories, Burdwan and Jubbulpore. In the former districts especially the rich soil and temperate climate are peculiarly favourable for its growth. In the Punjaub also its cultivation has been attended with the most successful results, as appears from the report of Dr Jamieson, who says: "For some years I have been cultivating flax on a small scale, from seeds procured from Russia, and its fibres have been pronounced by parties in Calcutta of a very superior description. There is nothing to prevent this country from supplying both flax and hemp on a vast scale. In the Punjaub thousands of acres are available; and from the means of producing both flax and hemp, this part of India will always be able to compete with other countries." In the Madras Presidency it has been grown with the best results on the Neilgherries and Shevaroy Hills, near Salem; and it would probably succeed equally well wherever the temperature is low, accompanied with considerable moisture in the atmosphere. The chief reason of the failures of the crops in Bengal and Behar was owing to the want of sufficient moisture after the cessation of the rains during the growth of the plant. In the Bombay Presidency it has been grown for the seeds alone. In India the time of sowing is the autumn. The soil should be of that character which retains its moisture, though not in an excessive degree. If not rich, manure must be amply supplied, and the plant kept free from all weeds. The best seeds procurable should be selected, of which the Dutch and American are reckoned superior for this country. Dr Roxburgh was the first who attempted the cultivation of flax in India. In the early part of this century he had an experimental farm in the neighbourhood of

Calcutta. Since his day the improvements which have taken place, resulting from extended observation and experience, have of course been very great, and specimens of flax which have been sent from Calcutta to the United Kingdom have been valued at rates varying from £30 to £60 a-ton.

The following information on the mode of the culture of flax in India is selected from a report made by Mr Denreef, a Belgian farmer, whose practical experience in this country enabled him to be a correct judge, and whose report is printed entire in the Journal of the Agri-Horticultural Society of Bengal. Such portions of land as are annually renewed by the overflowing of the Ganges, or which are fresh and rich, are the best adapted for the cultivation of flax.

After the earth has been turned up twice or thrice with the Indian plough, it must be rolled; because without the aid of the roller the large clods cannot be reduced, and the land rendered fine enough to receive the seed. The employment of the roller, both before and after sowing, hardens the surface of the earth, by which the moisture of the soil is better preserved, and more sheltered from the heat of the sun. About and near Calcutta, where manure can be obtained in great abundance for the trouble of collecting it, flax may be produced of as good a quality as in any part of Europe.

Manure is the mainspring of cultivation. It would certainly be the better, if the earth be well manured, to sow first of all either *Sunn* (Indian hemp), or hemp, or rice, or any other rainy-season crop; and when this has been reaped, then to sow the flax. The tillage of the land by means of the spade (mamoty) used by the natives (a method which is far preferable to the labour of the plough), with a little manure and watering at proper seasons, will yield double the produce obtainable from land tilled without manure and irrigation.

The proper time to sow the flax in India is from the beginning of October until the 20th of November, according to the state of the soil. The culture must be performed, if possible, some time before the soil. The flax which I have sown in November was generally much finer and much longer than that sown in the former month, which I attributed to the greater fall of dew during the time it was growing. The quantity of country seed required to the Bengal beega is twenty seers, but only fifteen seers of the foreign seed, because it is much smaller and produces larger stalks. The latter should be preferred; it is not only more productive in flax, but, owing to the tenderness of its stalks, it can be dressed much more easily.

The flax must be pulled up by the roots before it is ripe, and while the outer bark is in a state of fusibility. This is easily known by the lower part of the stalks becoming yellow; the fusion or disappearing of the outer bark is effected during the steeping, which may be fixed according to the temperature; say, in December at six days, in January five, in February four days, and less time during the hot season. The steeping is made a day after the pulling, when the seed is separated, and then the stalks are loosely bound in small sheaves, in the same way as the *Sunn*. The Indians understand this business very well, but in taking the flax out of the water it should be handled softly and with great care, on account of the tenderness of its fibres. When it is newly taken out, it should be left on the side of the steeping-pit for four hours, or until the draining of its water has ceased. It is then spread out with the root-ends even turned once, and when dry it is fit for dressing or to be stapled.

To save the seed, the capsules, after they are separated from the stalks, should be put in heaps to ferment from twenty-four to thirty hours, and then dried slowly in the sun to acquire their ripeness.

When flax is cultivated for the seed alone, the country flax should be preferred. Six seers per beega are sufficient for the sowing. It should be sown very early in October, and taken up, a little before perfect ripeness, by its roots, separately, when it is mixed with mustard seeds: the flax seed, being intended for the purpose of drying oil, is greatly injured by being mixed with mustard seed, by which mixture its drying qualities are much deteriorated.

The oil which is procured from the seeds, and known as Linseed oil, is obtained in two ways—either cold drawn, when it is of a pale colour, or by the application of heat at a temperature of not less than 200°. This latter is of a deeper yellow or brownish colour, and is disagreeable in its odour. One bushel of East Indian seeds will yield 14¾ lb. of oil; of English seeds, from 10 to 12 lb. Nearly 100,000 quarters of seeds are annually exported to Great Britain for the sake of the oil they contain. Great quantities are also shipped from Bombay, where the plant is cultivated for the sake of its seeds alone. The export of linseed from Bombay, says Dr Royle, is now estimated at an annual value of four lacs of rupees.—*Simmonds. Ainslie. Lindley.*

(368) **Lobelia nicotianæfolia** (*Heyne*). N. O. Lobeliaceæ.

Dawul, Deonul, Boke-nul, Mahr.

Description.—Stem erect; leaves subsessile, oblong, lanceolate, denticulate, narrowed at the base, acuminated; racemes many-flowered; bracts leafy; pedicels slightly longer than the bract, bibracteolate in the middle; sepals lanceolate serrated; corolla pubescent, lateral lobes long-linear, centre ones lanceolate; two lower anthers penicillate at the apex; flowers purple. —*Dec. Prod.* vii. 381.—*Drury Handb.* ii. 109.—*Wight Illustr. t.* 135.——Neilgherries. Canara.

Medical Uses.—The seeds of this plant, which is found on the mountain-ranges of the Peninsula and Ceylon, are extremely acrid. An infusion of the leaves is used by the natives as an antispasmodic. —*Pharm. of India.*

(369) **Luffa acutangula** (*Roxb.*) N. O. Cucurbitaceæ.

Torooi, Hind. Jhingo, Beng. Beer-kai, Tel. Peechenggah, Mal. Peekun-kai, Tam.

Description.—Climbing; stems glabrous; leaves 5-angled or 5-lobed; male racemes long peduncled; stamens distinct; calyx segments of the female flowers covered with glands; fruit (about 1 foot long and 2-3 inches thick) clavate, obtuse, or shortly pointed, pretty smooth, 10-angled, the angles sharp and smooth; seeds (black) irregularly pitted, 2-lobed at the base; flowers large, yellow. *Fl.* Nearly all the year.—*W. & A. Prod.* i. 343.—*Roxb. Fl. Ind.* iii. 713.—Cucumis acutangulus, *Linn.*—*Rheede*, viii. *t.* 7.——Peninsula. Hedges and waste lands. Cultivated.

Economic Uses.—The half-grown fruit is one of the best native vegetables in India. The natives use it much in their curries. Peeled, boiled, and dressed with butter, pepper, and salt, it is little inferior to boiled peas.—*Roxb.*

(370) **Luffa amara** (*Roxb.*) Do.

Kerula, Hind. Sendu-beer-kai, Tel. Tito-dhoondhool, Beng.

Description.—Climbing; stems slender; leaves a little scabrous, roundish-cordate, slightly 5-7 lobed; calyx 5-toothed; petals 5, distinct; male racemes long peduncled; fruit oblong, tapering towards each end, acutely 10-angled; seeds blackish grey, marked with elevated minute black dots; margin turned, 2-lobed at the base; flowers large, yellow. *Fl.* Aug.—Oct.—*W. & A. Prod.* i. 343.—*Roxb. Fl. Ind.* iii. 715.——Peninsula. Bengal.

Medical Uses.—This is bitter in every part. The fruit is violently cathartic and emetic, and the juice of the young roasted fruit is applied by the natives to their temples in cases of headache. The seeds in substance or infusion are used as emeto-cathartic.—(*Roxb.*) Dr Green states that the plant is not only a grateful bitter tonic, but a powerful diuretic when given in infusion in doses of from one to two fluid ounces three or four times a-day, two drachms of the fresh stalks being put to one pint of boiling water. Combined with nitro-hydrochloric acid, he found it useful in dropsy supervening on enlargement of the spleen and liver from malarious poison.—(*Pharm. of India.*) The *L. pentandra* is edible. In the Peshawur valley the seeds are given, mixed with black pepper in warm water, as emetic or cathartic.—*Stewart Punj. Plants.*

(371) **Lumnitzera racemosa** (*Willd.*) N. O. COMBRETACEÆ.

Káda Kandel, MAL.

DESCRIPTION.—Tree; calyx 5-cleft; segments rounded; petals 5, acute, inserted on the calyx and longer than it; leaves alternate, cuneate-obovate, alternated at the base into a short petiole, glabrous, thick and somewhat fleshy; spikes axillary, 5 stamens longer than the other alternating ones, and about the length of the petals; drupe clove-shaped, ovate-oblong, bluntly angled, crowned with the calyx; nut linear-oblong angled, 1-seeded; flowers small white.—*W. & A. Prod.* i. 316.—Petaloma alternifolia, *Roxb.*—Bruguiera Madagascariensis, *Dec.*—*Rheede*, vi. *t.* 37.——Salt-marshes in the S. provinces and Malabar. S. Concans. Sunderbunds.

ECONOMIC USES.—The timber is very strong and durable, and is used as fuel in Calcutta, where it is brought in great quantities from the Sunderbunds. It grows in the backwater in Cochin among species of Rhizophora.—*Roxb.* *Wight.*

M

(372) **Maba buxifolia** (*Pers.*) N. O. Ebenaceæ.

Erumbelie, Tam. Pishanna, Tel.

Description.—Shrub or small tree; leaves alternate, oval, entire, smooth; male flowers axillary in the lower leaves, 3-fold, sessile, white; calyx 3-cleft; corolla 3-cleft, hairy; stamens 6, short, inserted round a semi-globose receptacle; female flowers axillary, sessile, white or yellowish, very small; style 1; berry round, smooth, pulpy, size of a pea; seeds 2, flat on one side. *Fl.* March—June.—*Wight Icon. t.* 763.—Ferreola buxifolia, *Roxb. Cor.* i. *t.* 45.——Circar Mountains.

Economic Uses.—The berries are edible, and agreeable to the taste. The wood is dark-coloured, very hard and durable, and useful for various economical purposes.—*Roxb.*

(373) **Macaranga Indica** (*R. W.*) N. O. Euphorbiaceæ.

Vuttathamaray, Tam. Putta-thamara, Mal.

Description. — Tree; leaves stipuled, peltate; stipules paired, broad-ovate, cuspidate; male flowers panicled, glomerate; bracts petioled, glandulose; calyx 3-parted, pubescent; stamens 6-8; female panicles axillary; flowers solitary or paired, pedicelled, bracteate; style 1; ovary 1-celled; calyx 4-parted; capsule covered with resinous points, flowers greenish. *Fl.* Dec.—Jan.—*Wight Icon. t.* 1883.——Neilgherries. Travancore.

Economic Uses. — A gummy substance exudes from the cut branches and base of the petioles. It is of a light crimson colour, and has been used for taking impressions of leaves, coins, and medallions. When the gum is pure and carefully prepared the impressions are as sharp as those of sulphur without its brittleness. This substance is very little known. The *M. tomentosa* is also to be found in Travancore, and a similar gum exudes from both species. The leaves afford a good manure for rice-fields, and are much used for that purpose. Coffee-trees thrive well if planted under the shade of these trees, as the fallen leaves, which are large, enrich the soil.—*Jury Rep. Mad. Exhib. Pers. Obs.*

(374) **Mallotus Philippensis** (*Muller*). Do.

Ponnagam, Mal. Capilapodi, Tam. Vassuntagunda, Tel. Kamal, Hind. Toong, Beng.

Description.—Small tree or under-shrub; younger branchlets, petioles, and inflorescences rusty-tomentose; leaves rhomb-ovate, acuminate, acute at the base, entire or slightly toothed, clothed with scarlet tomentum beneath, glabrous above; spikes of either sex axillary and terminal, rusty-tomentose; male bracts 3-flowered, female 1-flowered; bracts triangular-ovate, acute; segments of the female calyx ovate-lanceolate; stamens 12-15; ovary densely scarlet; capsules slightly 3-cornered, globose, covered with scarlet dust. *Dec. Prod.* xv. s. 2, p. 980.—Rottlera tinctoria, *Roxb.*——Common almost everywhere.

Medical Uses.—The mealy powder covering the capsules yields a dye called *Kamila* dye, which is used as a vermifuge, and whose action, according to Dr Royle, depends on the minute stellate hairs found in the powder. Kamila is the powder rubbed off the capsules, and which is also found, though in smaller quantities, on the leaves and stalks of the plant. The powder is of a rich red colour, and has a heavy odour.

Economic Uses.—The dye is used all over India, especially for silk, to which it imparts a fine yellow colour. It is rarely used for cotton. When the capsules are ripe in February or March they are gathered; the red powder is carefully brushed off and collected for sale, no preparation being necessary. This substance is scarcely acted on by water, and has no particular taste. To spirit it gives a rich deep orange, inclining to red. Neither spirit nor alkaline solution dissolves it, for the minute grains of powder are seen adhering to the sides of the vessels if shaken, about the size of small grains of sand. Alum added to the alkaline infusion renders the colour more bright and permanent. The Hindoo silk-dyers use the following method:—Four parts of powder, one of powdered alum, two of salts of soda (sold in the bazaars), rubbed well together with a small quantity of oil of sesamum. When well mixed it is boiled in water proportionate to the silk to be dyed, and kept boiling smartly, according to the shade required, turning the silk frequently to render the colour uniform. Of the dye which is called *Cupela-Rung* in Hindustanee, the jurors at the Madras Exhibition reported as follows:—"The tree is widely spread over the Madras Presidency, and large supplies of the dye might be easily obtained. The colouring matter does not require a mordant, all that is necessary being to mix it with water containing about half its weight of carbonate of soda. On silk the colour is a rich flame or orange tint of great beauty and extreme stability;" and "the fact that the material supplied by commerce contains between 70 and 80 per cent of real colouring matter ought to induce the silk-dyers of this country to turn their attention to it."*—*Roxb. Jury Rep. Mad. Exhib.*

(375) **Malva rotundifolia** (*Linn.*) N. O. MALVACEÆ.

DESCRIPTION.—Annual; stems herbaceous, spreading; leaves cordate, roundish, shortly and obtusely lobed, crenated; petioles elongated, sometimes with a line of hairs on their upper side; pedicels several, unequal, axillary, 1-flowered; bracteoles 3; carpels much wrinkled; flowers middle-sized, pale purple. *Fl.* Feb.—March.—*W. & A. Prod.* i. 45.—*Dec. Prod.* i. 433. ——Peninsula.

MEDICAL USES.—The mucilaginous and emollient leaves are used for poultices, and also as an external application in cutaneous diseases. The natives reckon them useful in piles, and also in ulcerations of the bladder.—*Powell Punj. Prod.*

(376) **Mangifera Indica** (*Linn.*) N. O. TEREBINTHACEÆ.

Common Mango, ENG. Am, BENG. and HIND. Mamadichitoo, TEL. Mava, MAL. Mam-marum, TAM.

DESCRIPTION.—Tree; leaves alternate, lanceolate, acuminated, glabrous; calyx 5-cleft; petals 5; panicles terminal, much branched, pubescent, erect; drupe obliquely-oblong or somewhat reniform; seed solitary; flowers small, greenish-yellowish. *Fl.* Jan.—March.—*W. & A. Prod.* i. 170.—*Roxb. Fl. Ind.* i. 641.—*Rheede*, iv. *t.* 1, 2.——Common everywhere.

MEDICAL USES.—The kernel of the fruit is used in India as well as in Brazil as an anthelmintic. Dr Kirkpatrick states having used it in this character in doses of 20 to 30 grains, and found it most effectual in expelling lumbrici. It contains a large proportion of gallic acid, and has been successfully administered in bleeding piles and menorrhagia.—(*Pharm. of India.*) As the fruit contains much acid and turpentine, it acts as a diaphoretic and refrigerant. —(*Powell Punj. Prod.*) From wounds in the bark issues a soft reddish-brown gum-resin, hardening by age, and much resembling bdellium. Burnt in the flame of a candle, it emits a smell like that of cashew-nuts when roasting. It softens in the mouth and adheres to the teeth, and in taste is somewhat pungent and bitter. It dis-

* For a careful report on the colouring matter, see Anderson in Ed. Phil. Jour., April 1858; and for its vermifuge properties, see Indian Annals of Medical Science. Also a valuable paper by D. Hanbury in the Pharm. Journal.

solves entirely in spirit, and partly so in water. Mixed with lime-juice or oil, it is used externally in scabies and cutaneous affections. The bark of the tree is administered in infusion in menorrhagia and leucorrhœa; and the resinous juice, mixed with white of egg and a little opium, is considered a good specific on the Malabar coast for diarrhœa and dysentery.—*Ainslie.*

ECONOMIC USES.—The Mango is well known as the most delicious of Indian fruits. It is esteemed very wholesome, and when unripe is much used in tarts, preserves, and pickles. There are many varieties, all more or more less having a peculiar turpentine flavour, though the best kinds are generally free from it. The kernels of the nut seemingly contain much nourishment, but are only used in times of scarcity and famine, when they are boiled and eaten by the poorer classes. In the pulp of the fruit there is sugar, gum, and citric acid; gallic acid has also been procured from the seed, and also stearic acid. Interesting experiments were made some time ago, by a French chemist, upon the process of procuring the gallic acid, which he stated might be used in the preparation of ink instead of galls. Whenever the fruit is cut with a knife, a blue stain is seen on the blade, which is due to the presence of gallic acid. The timber is soft, of a dull-grey colour, porous, soon decaying if exposed to wet, but useful for common purposes. In large old trees the wood acquires a light chocolate colour towards the centre of the trunk and larger branches, and is then hard, close-grained and somewhat durable. The Mango-tree is best propagated by grafting, though it will readily grow from seeds. In the latter case the seed must be sown soon after it is taken from the fruit, but the produce is so inferior that it is hardly worth the trouble bestowed upon it. The wood, burnt with sandal-wood, is one of those used by the Hindoos for burning corpses, and is reckoned sacred for this purpose. The natives use the leaves as tooth-brushes, and the stalks instead of betel for chewing: powdered and calcined, they employ the latter also to take away warts.—*Roxb. Journ. of As. Soc.*

(377) **Manisuris granularis** (*Linn.*) N. O. GRAMINACEÆ.

Trinpali, HIND.

DESCRIPTION.—Height 1-2 feet; culm very resinous, sub-erect, hairy; spikes terminal and axillary, several together, 1 inch in length; leaves numerous, very hairy, stiff, sharp; rachis jointed, much waved; flowers male and hermaphrodite, 4-10 of each sort. *Fl.* Oct.—Dec.—*Roxb. Fl. Ind.* i. 352.—*Cor.* ii. *t.* 118.—Peltophorus granularis, *Beauv.*——Peninsula. Behar.

MEDICAL USES.—This plant is medicinal, and is administered internally, in conjunction with sweet-oil, in cases of spleen and liver-complaints.—*Ainslie.*

(378) **Maranta dichotoma** (*Wall.*) N. O. MARANTACEÆ.

Mookto-patee, Pattee patee or Madarpatee, BENG.

DESCRIPTION.—Stems straight, 3-6 feet, very smooth polished; branches numerous, dichotomous, spreading, jointed at every division; leaves alternate, petioled, ovate-cordate, smooth, entire, acute, with fine parallel veins; petioles sheathing; racemes terminal, usually solitary, jointed, a little flexuose; flowers in pairs on a common pedicel, from the alternate joints of the rachis; calyx 3-leaved; border of corolla double, exterior of 3 equal, recurved segments, interior of 5 unequal ones far extending above the rest; flowers large, white. *Fl.* April—May.—*Roxb. Fl. Ind.* i. 2.—Phrynium dichotomum, *Roxb.*——Coromandel. Bengal.

ECONOMIC USES.—The split stems are very tough, and from them are made the Calcutta mats called *Sital-pati*, which signifies a cool mat. The stems are 4 feet long, thin as paper, shining and striated in the inside.—*Colebrooke In. As. Res. Roxb.*

(379) **Marsdenia tenacissima** (*R. W.*) N. O. ASCLEPIACEÆ.

DESCRIPTION.—Twining; corolla salver-shaped; leaves opposite, cordate, acuminate, tomentose on both surfaces; cymes large; segments of corolla broad, obtuse; leaflets of corona broad, truncate, nearly entire at the apex, or bifurcate; flowers greenish yellow. *Fl.* April.—*Wight Contrib.* p. 41.—*Icon. t.* 590.—Asclepias tenacissima, *Roxb. Fl. Ind.* ii. 51.—*Cor.* iii. *t.* 240.——Rajmahal. Chittagong. Mysore.

ECONOMIC USES.—The bark of the young shoots yields a large portion of beautiful fine silky fibres, with which the mountaineers of Rajmahal make their bowstrings, on account of their great strength and durability. These fibres are much stronger than hemp, and even than those of the *Sanseveria Zeylanica.* A line of this substance broke with 248 lb. when dry, and 343 lb. when wet. Wight considers this species not to be a native of the Peninsula. The specimens in the Madras herbarium are—the one from the missionary's garden; the other (*A. echinata*) was sent to Klein by Heyne, but is not the plant of Roxburgh. The milk exuding from wounds made in the stem thickens into an elastic substance, acting like caoutchouc on black-lead marks.—(*Roxb. Wight.*) Another species, the *M. tinctoria*, is cultivated in Northern India, being a native of Silhet and Burmah. The leaves yield more and superior indigo to the *Indigofera tinctoria*, on which account it has been recommended for more extensive cultivation.—*Roxb. Wight.*

(380) **Melanthesa rhamnoides** (*Retz.*) N. O. EUPHORBIACEÆ.

Pavala-poola, TAM. Surasaruni, HIND.

DESCRIPTION.—Shrub; leaves oval, rounded at the apex, acute at the base, glabrous; peduncles axillary, the inferior ones paired, male, upper ones solitary, female, about the length of the petiole; fruit embraced by the short calyx; berries globose, bright red, mealy when ripe; flowers small, greenish. *Fl.* Nearly all the year.—*Wight Icon. t.* 1898.—P. Vitis Idœa.—*Roxb. Fl. Ind.* iii. 665.——Coromandel coast.

MEDICAL USES.—The bright-red fruits give this shrub a rather lively and attractive appearance. The leaves are used by Hindoo practitioners in discussing tumours, especially carbuncles, applied warm with castor-oil. In Behar the dried leaves are smoked as tobacco when the uvula and tonsils are swollen. The bark of the root mixed with long-pepper and ginger is drunk as a tonic.—*Rheede. Ainslie. Wight.*

(381) **Melia azedarach** (*Linn.*) N. O. MELIACEÆ.

Common Bead-tree or Persian Lilac, ENG. Malay-vaymboo, TAM. Turuka vepa, TEL. Mullay vaempoo, MAL.

DESCRIPTION.—Tree, 40 feet; petals 5, nearly glabrous; calyx small, 5-cleft; stamen tube 10-cleft; leaves alternate, bipinnate, deciduous; leaflets about 5 together, obliquely ovate-lanceolate, serrated, finely acuminated, glabrous; peduncles axillary, simple below, above panicled, branched, and many-flowered; flowers smallish, white externally, lilac at the top, fragrant; fruit size of a cherry, pale yellow when ripe; nut 5-celled; cells 1-seeded. *Fl.* March.—*W. & A. Prod.* i. 117.—*Wight Icon. t.* 160.——Common in the Deccan. Concans. N. India.

MEDICAL USES.—The pulp surrounding the seeds is said to be poisonous, and, mixed with grease, is reputed to kill dogs. This, however, is doubtful The root, which is nauseous and bitter, is used in North America as an anthelmintic. A valuable oil is procured from them.—(*Ainslie. Lindley.*) Melia azederach has been considered poisonous from the time of Avicenna; but it is only in larger doses that its fruit can be considered as such. Loureiro recognises the utility of *azedarach* in worm cases, and Blume states that both it and *M. azadirachta* are employed in Java as anthelmintics. A decoction of the leaves is said to be astringent and stomachic, and also to be injurious to insects, and employed with success against porrigo.—*Royle.*

ECONOMIC USES.—The mature wood is hard and handsomely marked, and might be used for many economical purposes. The tree has been naturalised in the south of Europe.—*Jury Rep. Mad. Exhib.*

(382) **Melia composita** (*Willd.*) Do.

Mullay-vaymboo, TAM.

DESCRIPTION.—Large tree; young shoots, petioles, and panicles very mealy; leaves bi-pinnate, alternate; pinnæ about 3 pair; leaflets 3-7 pair to each pinnæ, ovate, acuminate, crenulated, glabrous, 2-3 inches long; panicles axillary, scarcely half the length of the leaves; flowers numerous, small, whitish, inodorous; calyx and petals mealy; stigma large, with a 5-pointed apex; drupe ovate, size of a large olive, smooth, and yellowish green when ripe.—*W. & A. Prod.* 117.—Melia robusta, *Roxb.*—M. superba, do.—*Bedd. Flor. Sylv. t.* 12.——Malabar. Canara. Mysore.

ECONOMIC USES.—A handsome tree, with smooth dark-brown bark. The timber is often used by planters for building purposes, and it is desirable to be introduced into Madras for avenues, as it grows quickly, especially from seeds. It is said that white ants will not attack it.—*Beddome.*

(383) **Memecylon tinctorium** (*Koen.*) N. O. MELASTOMACEÆ.

Kashawa, MAL. Alli chettu, TEL. Kayampoovoocheddi, Casau-cheddy, Casha-marum, TAM.

DESCRIPTION.—Shrub, 10-12 feet; calyx with a hemispherical or sub-globose tube; petals 4; branches terete; leaves shortly-petioled, ovate or oblong, 1-nerved; peduncles axillary, and below the leaves on the elder branches bearing a more or less compound corymb of pedicellate flowers; stamens shortish; style about the length of the stamens; fruit globose, crowned with the 4-toothed limb of the calyx; fruit 1-2 seeded; flowers bluish purple. *Fl.* April—May.—*W. & A. Prod.* i. 319.—M. tinctorium, *Willd.*—M. edule, *Roxb. Cor.* i. *t.* 82.—*Rheede,* v. *t.* 19.——Travancore. Malabar. Coromandel.

Medical Uses.—A lotion is made from the leaves, used by the natives as an eye-wash; and the root in decoction is considered very beneficial in excessive menstrual discharge.

Economic Uses.—The pulp of the fruit when ripe is eaten by the natives. It is rather astringent. The leaves are used in dyeing, affording a delicate yellow lake. The shrub is very common, and highly ornamental in gardens, when in flower the stem being crowded with the beautiful sessile purple florets. The leaves are used by the mat-makers in conjunction with kadukai (*myrobalan nuts*) and vuttang-cuttay (*sappan wood*) in imparting a deep-red tinge to the mats. They are also good for dyeing cloths red.—(*Ainslie. Pers. Obs.*) The native names for the blue flowers of this shrub are *Alli, Cassa,* and *Vassa Casa,* the first being its northern or Telugu, the latter its Tamil, designation. The native dyers employ it as an adjunct to chayroot for bringing out the colour, in preference to alum, which injures the thread. By itself it gives an evanescent yellow. It is very cheap, costing 1 anna the marcal.—*Jury Rep. Mad. Exhib.* 1857.

(384) **Mesua ferrea** (*Linn.*) N. O. Clusiaceæ.

Belutta-champagam, Mal. Nagkushur, Beng.

Description.—Tree, 40 feet; sepals 4, unequal; petals 4, alternate with the sepals; leaves oblong-lanceolate, acuminated, glaucous beneath, upper side shining, midrib and margins coloured; flowers stalked, axillary, large, white, fragrant; fruit about the size of a small apple, 1-celled, 1-4 seeded. *Fl.* March—April.—*W. & A. Prod.* i. 102.—*Wight Icon. t.* 117. —*Roxb. Fl. Ind.* ii. 605.—*Rheede,* iii. *t.* 53.——Courtallum hills.

Medical Uses.—The dried flowers are said to possess stimulant properties, but are probably of little importance in medicine. The expressed oil of the seeds is much employed by the natives in North Canara as an embrocation in rheumatism. The bark and roots are also an excellent bitter tonic in infusion or decoction.—*Pharm. of India.*

Economic Uses.—This tree is much cultivated in Java as well as in Malabar for the beauty and fragrance of its flowers. When dried they are mixed with other aromatics, such as the white sandal-wood, and used for perfuming ointment. The fruit is reddish and wrinkled when ripe, with a rind like that of the chestnut, which latter it much resembles both in size, shape, substance, and taste. The tree bears fruit in six years from the planting of the seed, and continues to bear during three centuries. It is planted near houses, and affords an excellent shade. The bark, wood, and roots are bitter and sweet-scented. The blossoms are found in a dried state in the bazaars, and are called *Naghesur;* they are used medicinally, and are much esteemed for their fragrance, on which latter account the Burmese grandees stuff their pillows with the dried anthers. Round the base, or rather at the bottom of the tender fruits, a tenacious and glutinous resin exudes with a sharp aromatic smell.—*Roxb. Ainslie.*

(385) **Michelia champaca** (*Linn.*) N. O. MAGNOLIACEÆ.

Chempacam, MAL. Chumpaka or Chumpa, BENG.

DESCRIPTION.—Tree, 30-40 feet; petals numerous, disposed in several rows; leaves alternate, entire, lanceolate, acuminated, glabrous; flowers on short peduncles, axillary; spathe of one leaf; carpels 2-valved; seeds several; flowers large, yellow, fragrant. *Fl.* Nearly all the year.—*W. & A. Prod.* i. 6.—*Roxb. Fl. Ind.* ii. 656.—*Wight Ill.* i. 13.——Cultivated in Bengal. Gardens in the Peninsula.

MEDICAL USES.—The bitter aromatic bark has been successfully employed in the Mauritius in the treatment of low intermittent fevers. The bark of the root is red, bitter, and very acid, and when pulverised is reckoned emmenagogue. The flowers beaten up with oil are applied to fetid discharges from the nostrils. All parts of the tree are said to be powerfully stimulant.—*Lindley. Roxb. Pharm. of India.*

ECONOMIC USES.—This tree is highly venerated by the Hindoos, and is dedicated to Vishnoo. It is celebrated for the exquisite perfume of its flowers. Sir W. Jones states that their fragrance is so strong that bees will seldom, if ever, alight upon them. The natives adorn their heads with them, the rich orange colour of the flowers contrasting strongly with their dark black hair. The fruit is said to be edible. The name *Champaca* is derived from Ciampa, an island between Cambogia and Cochin-China, where the tree grows. The wood is light, but is used for making drums. The seeds are said to destroy vermin.—(*Roxb. Don.*) Another species is the *M. nilagirica,* the timber of which is used in house-building. It is of a handsome mottled colour, and has been tried at Bombay for ships.—*Wight. J. Grah.*

(386) **Mimusops elengi** (*Linn.*) N. O. SAPOTACEÆ.

Elengee, MAL. Maghadam, TAM. Poghada, TEL. Bholseri, DUK. Mulsari, HIND. Bukul, BENG.

DESCRIPTION.—Tree, middling size; leaves alternate, oval-lanceolate or oblong, acuminated, glabrous; pedicels shorter than the petioles, many together, 1-flowered; calyx 8-cleft, in a double series, segments lanceolate, 4 exterior ones larger and permanent; corolla-tube very short, fleshy, segments in a double series, exterior ones 16, spreading, interior ones 8, generally contorted, and converging, lanceolate, and slightly torn at the extremities; berry oval, smooth, yellow when ripe, usually 1-celled; seeds solitary, oblong; flowers white, fragrant. *Fl.* March—April.—*Roxb. Fl. Ind.* ii. 236.—*Cor.* i. *t.* 14.—*Wight Icon.* *t.* 1586.—*Rheede,* i. *t.* 20.——Peninsula. Bengal. Silhet.

MEDICAL USES.—According to Horsfield, the bark possesses astringent tonic properties, and has proved useful in fevers. A decoction of the bark forms a good gargle in salivation. A water distilled from the flowers is used by the natives in Southern India, both as a stimulant medicine and as a perfume.—*Pharm. of India.*

ECONOMIC USES.—This tree has an ornamental appearance. The flowers, which appear twice a-year, are somewhat fragrant and powerfully aromatic. The natives distil an odoriferous water from them. The fruit is edible. The seeds yield an abundance of oil, in request for painters. If the leaves are put in the flame of a candle, they will make a smart crackling noise. The tree is much cultivated in the gardens of the natives, especially round the mausoleums of the Mohammedans. Dr Roxburgh said he only once found it in a wild state. It was on the mountains of the Rajahmundry district.—*Roxb.*

(387) **Mimusops hexandra** (*Roxb.*) Do.

Pallœ, TAM. Palla, TEL.

DESCRIPTION.—Tree; leaves alternate, cuneiform or obcordate, deeply emarginate, glabrous and shining on both surfaces; calyx 6-cleft, with 3-interior and 3-exterior segments; corolla tube very short, interior segments 6, the exterior 12; pedicels 1-6 together, nearly as long as the smooth petioles, 1-flowering; berry size and shape of an olive, yellow when ripe; flowers small, whitish. *Fl.* March—April.—*Roxb. Fl. Ind.* ii. 238.—*Cor.* i. *t.* 15.—*Wight Icon.* *t.* 1587.——Mountains of the Circars. Bombay.

ECONOMIC USES.—The wood is much used in Guzerat for a variety of purposes, such as sugar-mill beams and well-frames. It is also much used by washermen to beetle their cloths on, being remarkably heavy and tough. The fruit is eatable.—*Roxb. Dr Gibson.*

(388) **Mimusops Kanki** (*Linn.*) Do.

Manilkara, MAL.

DESCRIPTION.—Tree; leaves alternate, obovate, very blunt,

silvery or hoary beneath, crowded at the ends of the branches; flowers fascicled, hexandrous; fruit oval, drooping; flowers yellowish white, tinged with rose. *Fl.* March—April.—*Roxb. Fl. Ind.* ii. 238.—*Rheede*, iv. *t.* 35.——Malabar.

MEDICAL USES.—The bark is astringent, and yields a kind of gummy fluid. The leaves ground and mixed with the root of Curcuma and ginger are used as cataplasm for tumours. The tree is extensively cultivated in China and Malabar on account of its acid and esculent fruit, which is said to increase the appetite. The leaves boiled in gingely oil and added to the pulverised barks are reckoned a good remedy in Beriberi.—(*Rheede. Hooker.*) The seeds yield an oil which is applied to the eyes in ophthalmia, and also internally as an anthelmintic.—*Powell's Punj. Prod.*

(389) **Mollugo cerviana** (*Ser.*) N. O. CARYOPHYLLACEÆ.

Parpadagum, TAM. Parpatakum, TEL. Ghimashak, BENG.

DESCRIPTION.—Small plant half a foot; stems straightish, ascending, terete; leaves opposite, or alternate by abortion, linear, verticillate, very narrow, bluntish, glaucous; calyx 5-parted; petals none; peduncles elongated, bearing 3 umbellate flowers; stamens usually 5, or less by abortion; capsule 3-valved, 3-celled, many-seeded; calyx white on the inside. —*W. & A. Prod.* i. 44.—Pharnaceum cerviana, *Linn.*—— Peninsula.

MEDICAL USES.—This plant mixed with oil is made into an ointment for scabies and other cutaneous diseases. The young shoots and flowers are given in infusion as a mild diaphoretic in fever cases. —*Ainslie.*

(390) **Mollugo spergula** (*Linn.*) Do.

Toora, TAM. Chatarashi, TEL. Ghimi Shak, BENG.

DESCRIPTION.—Small plant; stem very straggling and branched; leaves more or less succulent, oblong or obovate, mucronate, alternated towards their base; pedicels 1-flowered, several together, forming a simple sessile umbel; stamens 3-5 or 10; petals narrow, cleft to the middle, or none; seeds rough with numerous tubercles; flowers small, white. *Fl.* Nearly all the year.—*W. & A. Prod.* i. 44.—M. verticillata, *Roxb. Fl. Ind.* i. 360 (not *Linn.*)—Pharnaceum mollugo, *Linn.*—*Roxb. Fl. Ind.* ii. 102.—*Rheede*, x. *t.* 24.——Peninsula. Bengal.

Medical Uses.—The bitter leaves are esteemed by the natives as stomachic, aperient, and antiseptic, and are given in infusion, and are considered especially efficacious in suppressed lochia. Moistened with castor-oil and applied warm, they are said to be a good remedy in ear-ache.—*Ainslie.*

(391) **Momordica Charantia** (*Linn.*) N. O. Cucurbitaceæ.

Kurula, Beng. Pandipasel, Mal. Pava-kai, Tam.

Description.—Climbing; stems more or less hairy; leaves palmately 5-lobed, sinuate, toothed, when young more or less villous on the under side, particularly on the nerves; peduncles slender, with a reniform bracteole, *male* ones with the bracteole about the middle, *female* with it near the base; fruit oblong or ovate, more or less tubercled or muricated; seeds with a thick notched margin and red aril; flowers middle-sized, pale yellow. *Fl.* Aug.—Oct.—*W. & A. Prod.* i. 348.—*Roxb. Fl. Ind.* iii. 707.—*Wight Icon.* ii. *t.* 504.—M. muricata, *Willd.*—*Rheede Mal.* viii. *t.* 9, 10.——Cultivated everywhere in the Peninsula.

Medical Uses.—There are two chief varieties differing in the forms of the fruit, the one having the fruit longer and more oblong, the other with the fruit smaller, more ovate, muricated, and tubercled. There are besides these many intermediate gradations. The fruit is bitter but wholesome, and is eaten in curries by the natives. It requires, however, to be steeped in salt water before being cooked. That of the smaller variety is most esteemed. The whole plant mixed with cinnamon, long-pepper, rice, and marothy oil (*Hydnocarpus inebrians*), is administered in the form of an ointment in psora, scabies, and other cutaneous diseases. The juice of the leaves mixed with warm water is reckoned anthelmintic. The whole plant pulverised is a good specific externally applied in leprosy and malignant ulcers.—*Rheede. Dr Gibson. Wight.*

(392) **Momordica dioica** (*Roxb.*) Do.

Erimapasel, Mal. Paloopaghel, Tam. Agakara, Tel.

Description.—Climbing, diœcious; root tuberous; stems glabrous; leaves long-petioled, cordate at the base, from entire to 3-4 lobed, toothed, upper side slightly scabrous, under smooth or nearly so; peduncles slender, with entire bracteoles, *male* with the bracteole close to the flower, and concealing the lower part, *female* one small near the base; fruit ovate, muricated; seeds oval, surrounded with a large red aril; flowers large, yellow. *Fl.* Sept.—Nov.—*W. & A. Prod.* i. 348.—*Wight Icon. t.* 505, 506.—*Rheede,* viii. *t.* 12.——Peninsula.

Medical Uses.—Of this species there are several varieties, differing chiefly in the forms of the leaves. The young green fruits and tuberous roots of the female plants are eaten by the natives. They sometimes weigh from 2 to 3 lb. Rheede says that this plant is truly cephalic, for mixed with cocoanut, pepper, red sandal, and other ingredients, and applied in the form of liniment, it stops all pains in the head. The root, which is mucilaginous to the taste, is prescribed by Hindoo practitioners in the form of electuary in hœmorrhoids.—*Ainslie. Rheede.*

(393) **Morinda citrifolia** (*Linn.*) N. O. Cinchonaceæ.

Indian Mulberry, Eng. Manja-pavattay, Noona, Tam. Cada pilva, Mal. Molagha, Maddichettoo, Tel. Al, Atchy, Hind.

Description.—Small tree; leaves opposite, oval, alternated at both ends, shining; capituli shortly peduncled, leaf opposed; branchlets 4-angled; corolla long-infundibuliform 5 (occasionally 4-7) cleft; anthers half hid in the tube; style the length of the tube; berries concrete into an obtuse ovate shining fruit; flowers white. *Fl.* Nearly all the year.—*W. & A. Prod.* i. 419.—*Roxb. Fl. Ind.* i. 541.—*Rheede,* i. *t.* 52.——Coromandel. Cultivated in Kandeish, Berar, and the Deccan. Bombay.

Medical Uses.—The fruit is used among the Cochin-Chinese as a deobstruent and emmenagogue. The expressed juice of the leaves is externally applied in gout; and applied fresh to wounds and ulcers, are said to accelerate their cure with great efficacy. By a chemical process, a kind of salt is extracted from the leaves, reckoned useful in cleaning bad and inveterate ulcers.—*Wight. Ainslie. Rheede.*

Economic Uses.—A scarlet dye is procured from the root, used for handkerchiefs, turbans, &c. The colouring matter resides chiefly in the bark of the roots. The small pieces, which are best, are worth from 4 to 5 rupees a maund. It is exported in large quantities from Malabar to Guzerat and the northern part of Hindoostan. Dr Gibson says they are partly dug up the second year, and are in perfection the third. The wood is of a deep yellow colour, and useful for ordinary purposes. The natives use it for their wooden slippers. The *M. tinctoria* (Roxb.) is considered to be the same species in its wild state. It is common in most parts of India. The green fruits are eaten by the natives in their curries. The wood is hard, very durable, variegated red and white, and employed for gun-stocks in preference to any other wood. This latter is the *Tagaroo* of the Teloogoos.—(*Roxb. Simmonds.*) The *M. tomentosa* (*Munjenatie* in Malayalim) is common in Travancore. A dye is procured from the interior of the wood in older trees. The timber, which is yellow, will take an excellent polish, and is useful for various economical purposes.—*Pers. Obs.*

(394) **Morinda umbellata** (*Linn.*) Do.

Noona-marum, TAM. Chota-Alka, DUK. Mooloogboodoo, TEL.

DESCRIPTION.—Climbing, glabrous; corolla short infundibuliform; leaves from oblong-lanceolate to cuneate oblong, pointed; stipules membranaceous, united in a truncated sheath; peduncles terminal, 3-7 in a sessile terminal umbel about half the length of the leaves; capituli globose; calyx margin entire; limb 4 (occasionally 5) cleft; filaments short, inserted into the bottom of the dilated part of the tube among many hairs; anthers exerted; flowers white. *Fl.* March.—*W. & A. Prod.* i. 420.—M. scandens, *Roxb. Fl. Ind.* i. 548.—*Rheede,* vii. *t.* 27.——Courtallum. Travancore. Malabar.

ECONOMIC USES.—The root yields a dye of permanent yellow; and with the addition of sappan-wood a red dye is prepared from the same in Cochin China. Simmonds says that the colours dyed with it are for the most part exceedingly brilliant, and the colouring matter far more permanent than many other red colours are. With improved management it would probably rival that of madder. This will apply to the various species of the Indian mulberry plant. In this species the number of stamens varies in the same head of flowers, but there are usually only four.—*Wight. Simmonds. Ainslie. Lour.*

(395) **Moringa pterygosperma** (*Gærtn.*) N. O. MORINGACEÆ.

Horse-radish tree, ENG. Mooringhy, TAM. Mooraga, TEL. Moongay, DUK. Sujna, HIND. Shajina, BENG. Mooringeh, MAL.

DESCRIPTION.—Tree, 30-35 feet; leaves 2-3 pinnate with an odd leaflet; calyx 5-cleft; petals 5, nearly equal, the upper one ascending; filaments hairy at the base; racemes panicled; 5 stamens without anthers; seeds numerous, 3-angled, the angles expanding into wings; flowers white. *Fl.* Jan.—July. —*W. & A. Prod.* i. 178.—Guilandina Moringa, *Linn. sp.*—Hyperanthera Moringa, *Vahl.*—*Roxb. Fl. Ind.* ii. 368.—*Rheede,* vi. *t.* 11.——Common in gardens in the Peninsula.

MEDICAL USES.—The native practitioners prescribe the fresh root as a stimulant in paralysis and intermittent fevers. They also use it in epilepsy and hysteria, and reckon it a valuable rubefacient in palsy and chronic rheumatism. In Java the roots have been reported beneficial in dropsy. The same virtues have been ascribed to the horse-radish of Europe, a syrup made with an infusion of which the celebrated Dr Cullen found efficacious in removing hoarseness. The root has a pungent odour and a heavy aromatic taste. Dr Wight suggested that it would greatly increase the activity of sinapisms. An oil is prepared from the seeds which is used externally for pains in the limbs, gout, and rheumatism. In the West Indies it is used as a salad oil, because it does not congeal or turn rancid. The leaves, bark, and root, according to Rheede, are antispasmodic. The juice of the leaves mixed with pepper is applied over the eyes in vertigo; and mixed with common salt is given to children in flatulency. It is also used to hasten suppuration in boils. The bark, rubbed up in rice-water mixed with cummin-seed, is a cure for gumboils and toothache. The leaves simply warmed are applied in hydrocele, and also good for ulcers and guinea-worm. A gum resembling tragacanth exudes from this tree if an incision be made in the bark. It is used, in headache, mixed with milk and externally rubbed on the temples. It is also locally applied to buboes and venereal pains in the limbs. In Jamaica the wood is employed for dyeing a blue colour.—*Ainslie. Rheede.*

Economic Uses.—The root of this tree is much like the English horse-radish. The long legumes are well known as a vegetable so often used both by Europeans and natives in curries. The seeds were formerly known as the *Ben nuts*, from which the oil of *Ben* was extracted. It is chiefly used by perfumers and watchmakers. Both leaves and flowers are eaten by the natives.—*Wight. Lindley.*

(396) **Mucuna gigantea** (*Dec.*) N. O. Leguminosæ.

Kakavalli, Mal.

Description.—Climbing, perennial; leaflets ovate, acute, adult ones glabrous; flowers almost umbellate, at the apex of long pendulous peduncles; pedicels long, slender; 3 lower segments of the calyx short, tooth-like, the other very short; legumes linear-oblong, deeply furrowed along the sutures, not plaited, armed with stiff, stinging hairs, 3-6 seeded; seeds oval; flowers large, sulphur-coloured. *Fl.* Aug.—Dec.—*W. & A. Prod.* i. 254.—Carpopogon giganteum, *Roxb.*—*Rheede,* viii. *t.* 36.——Malabar. Coromandel. Concans.

Medical Uses.—Rheede states that the virtues of this plant in rheumatism are very conspicuous. The bark, pulverised and mixed with dried ginger and other ingredients, rubbed over the parts affected, is one of the best modes of administering it.—*Rheede.*

(397) **Mucuna prurita** (*Hook.*) Do.

Cowhage, Eng. Naicorma, Mal. Poonaykalie, Tam. Peeliadagoo kaila, Tel. Kiwach, Hind. Kanchkoorie, Duk. Alkushee, Beng.

Description.—Annual, twining; branches pubescent or slightly hairy; leaves pinnately trifoliolate; leaflets ovate, upper side glabrous, under sprinkled with adpressed silvery hairs; racemes shorter than the leaves, drooping; pedicels shorter than the calyx; calyx cleft to the middle, white with adpressed hairs, segments broad-lanceolate; corolla papilionaceous; vexillum cordate, incumbent on the alæ, alæ oblong-linear, sometimes slightly cohering, keel straight below, slightly falcate in the upper part, terminated by an acute beak; legume slightly curved like an S, densely clothed with rigid stinging hairs, 6-seeded; flowers large, dark purple. *Fl.* Dec.—Feb.—*W. & A. Prod.* i. 255.—Carpopogon pruriens, *Roxb.*—*Rheede,* viii. *t.* 35.——Peninsula. Bengal. Dheyra Dhoon.

Medical Uses.—The root in infusion is administered in cholera, and a syrup thickened with the hairs till it is of the consistence of honey is prescribed by European practitioners as a good anthelmintic; but the natives do not use the stinging hairs of the pods for this purpose. There is no doubt, Ainslie observes, but that it is simply by these mechanical means that the hairs act in worm cases. Neither the tincture nor decoction has the same effect. If the pods are incautiously touched, they will cause an intolerable itching in the fingers. In the West Indies a decoction of the root is reckoned a powerful diuretic and cleanser of the kidneys, and is also made into an ointment for elephantiasis. The leaves are applied to ulcers, and the beans reckoned aphrodisiac. A vinous infusion of the pods (12 to a quart) is said to be a certain remedy for the dropsy.—*Ainslie. Rheede.*

Economic Uses.—The seeds of many species are edible, and reckoned equal to the English bean. Among these may be enumerated the *M. monosperma* (Dec.), known as the Negro Bean, a favourite vegetable with Brahmins; the *M. nivea* is also cultivated, the tender fleshy pods of which, when stripped of their exterior skin, make a most excellent vegetable for the table, scarcely inferior to the garden-bean of Europe. The present species is a native of both Indies. The seed is said to absorb the poison of scorpions, and to remain on the sting until all is removed.—*Powell's Punj. Prod. Roxb.*

(398) **Musa paradisiaca** (*Linn.*) N. O. MUSACEÆ.

Common Plantain, ENG. Vala, MAL. Valie, TAM. Komarettie, TEL. Kayla, HIND. Kach Kula, BENG. Maoz, DUK.

DESCRIPTION.—Herbaceous; stem simple, thickly clothed with the sheathing petioles of the leaves; leaves forming a tuft on the apex of the stem; spike of flowers compound, rising from the apex of the stem, each division enclosed in a large spathe with male flowers at the base, female or hermaphrodite ones at the upper end; perianth with 6 superior divisions, 5 of which are grown together into a tube, slit at the back, the 6th is small and concave; style short; fruit oblong, fleshy, obscurely 3-5 cornered, with numerous seeds buried in pulp; flowers yellowish whitish. *Fl.* All the year. M. sapientum, *Roxb. Fl. Ind.* i. 663.—*Cor.* iii. 275.—*Rheede*, i. *t.* 12-14.——Cultivated everywhere. Chittagong.

MEDICAL USES.—The tender leaves are in common use for dressing blistered surfaces. For this purpose a piece of the leaf, of the required size, smeared with any bland vegetable oil, is applied to the denuded surface, and kept on the place by means of a bandage. The blistered surface is generally found to heal after four or five days. For the first two days the upper smooth surface of the leaf is placed next the skin, and subsequently the under side, until the healing process is complete. This is considered better than the usual mode of treatment with spermacetti ointment. Dr Van Someren occasionally employed the plaintain leaf as a substitute for gutta-percha tissue in the water-dressing of wounds and ulcers, and found it answer very well. A piece of fresh plantain leaf forms a cool and pleasant shade for the eyes in the various forms of ophthalmia so common in the East. The preserved fruit, which resembles dried figs, is a nourishing and antiscorbutic article of diet for long voyages. In this state they will keep for a long time.—(*Pharm. of India.*) Long, in his History of Jamaica, says that on thrusting a knife into the body of the plant the astringent lumped water that issues out is given with great success to persons subject to spitting blood, and in fluxes.

ECONOMIC USES.—This extensively cultivated plant is common to both Indies. The ancients were acquainted with the fruit; and the name of *Pala*, which is used in Pliny's description of it, is identical with the word *Vala*, which is the Malayalum name to the present day. Probably all the cultivated varieties in this country have sprung from a single species, of which the original, according to Dr Roxburgh, was grown from seeds procured from Chittagong. A wild variety, probably the *M. superba*, which is found in the Dindigul valleys, I have often met with on the mountains in Travancore, at high elevations.

In the Himalaya it is cultivated at 5000 feet, and may be found wild on the Neilgherries at 7000 feet. It is cultivated in Syria as far as latitude 34°, but, Humboldt says, ceases to bear fruit at a height of 3000 feet, where the mean annual temperature is 68°, and where, probably, the heat of summer is deficient. Lindley enumerates ten species of Musa, some of which grow to the height of 25 or 30 feet, but the Chinese species (*M. Chinensis* or *Cavendishii*) does not exceed 4 or 5 feet in height. The specific name of the plant under consideration was given by botanists in allusion to an old notion that it was the forbidden fruit of Scripture. It has also been supposed to be what was intended by the grapes, one branch of which was borne upon a pole between two men that the spies of Moses brought out of the Promised Land. The plantain is considered very nutritious and wholesome, either dressed or raw; and no fruit is so easily cultivated in tropical countries. There is hardly a cottage in India that has not its grove of plantains. The natives live almost upon them; and the stems of the plantain, laden with their branches of fruit, are invariably placed at the entrance of their houses during their marriage or other festivals, appropriate emblems of plenty and fertility. Its succulent roots and large leaves are well adapted for keeping the ground moist, even in the hottest months. The best soil for its cultivation is newly-cleared forest-land where there is much decayed vegetation. Additional manure will greatly affect the increase and flavour of the fruit. Some of the varieties are far inferior to the rest; the Guindy plantains are the best known in Madras, which, though small, are of delicious flavour. The plant must be cut down immediately after the fruit is gathered; new shoots spring up from the old stems; and in this way it will grow on springing up and bearing for twenty years or more. In America and the Society Isles the fruit is preserved as an article of trade. A meal is prepared from the fruit, by stripping off the skins, slicing the core, and, when thoroughly dried in the sun, powdering and sifting it. It is much used in the West Indies for infants and invalids, and is said to be especially nourishing. Regarding its nutritive qualities, Professor Johnston published the following information in the 'Journal of the Agricultural Society of Scotland:' "We find the plantain *fruit* to approach most nearly in composition and nutritive value to the potato, and the plantain *meal* to those of rice. Thus, the fruit of the plantain gives 37 per cent, and the raw potato 25 per cent of dry matter. In regard to its value as a food for man in our northern climates, there is no reason to believe that it is unfit to sustain life and health; and as to warmer or tropical climates, this conclusion is of more weight. The only chemical writer who has previously made personal observations upon this point (M. Boussingault) says, 'I have not sufficient data to determine the nutritive value of the banana, but I have reason to believe that it is superior to that of potato. I have given as rations to men employed at hard labour about 6½ lb. of half-ripe bananas and 2 ounces of salt meat.' Of these green bananas he elsewhere states that 38 per cent consisted of husk, and that the internal eatable part lost 56 per cent of water by drying in the sun. The composition of the ash of the plantain also bears a close resemblance to that of potato. Both contain much alkaline matter, potash, and soda salts; and in both there is nearly the same percentage of phosphoric acid and magnesia. In so far, therefore, as the supply of those mineral ingredients is concerned, by which the body is supported as necessarily as by the organic food, there is no reason to doubt the banana, equally with the potato, is fitted to sustain the strength of the animal body."

Dried plantains form an article of commerce at Bombay and other parts of the Peninsula. They are merely cut in slices and dried in the sun, and being full of saccharine matter, make a good preserve for the table. Exports from the former place to the extent of 267 cwt., valued at rupees 1456, were shipped in 1850–51. The juice of the unripe fruit and lymph of the stamens are slightly astringent. In the West Indies the latter has been used as a kind of marking ink.

All the species of Musa are remarkable for the number of the spiral vessels they contain, and one species (*M. textilis*) yields a fine kind of flax, with which a very delicate kind of cloth is fabricated. The plantain fibre is an excellent substitute for hemp in linen thread. The fine grass cloth, ship's cordage and ropes, which are made and used in the South Sea fisheries, are made from it. The outer layers of the sheathing foot-stalks yield the thickest and strongest fibres. It is considered that there would be no difficulty in obtaining from this plant alone any required quantity of fibre, of admitted valuable quality, which might be exported to Europe. It can be used with no less facility and advantage in the manufacture of paper. A profitable export made of plantain and aloe fibre has been established on the western coast. The best mode of preparing the fibre is thus given by Dr Hunter:—

"Take the upright stem and the central stalk of the leaves; if the outer ones are old, stained, or withered, reject them; strip off the different layers, and proceed to clean them, in shade if possible, soon after the tree has been cut down. Lay a leaf-stalk on a long flat board with the inner surface uppermost, scrape the pulp off with a blunt piece of hoop-iron fixed in a grove in a long piece of wood. (An old iron spoon makes a very good scraper.) When the inner side, which has the thickest layer of pulp, has been cleaned, turn over the leaf and scrape the back of it. When a good bundle of fibres has been thus partially cleaned and piled up, wash it briskly in a large quantity of water, rubbing it all well and shaking it about in the water, so as to get rid of all the pulp and sap as quick as possible. Boiling the fibres in an alkaline ley (potash or soda dissolved in water), or washing with Europe soap, gets rid of the sap quickly. The common country soap, which is made with quick-lime, is too corrosive to be depended upon. After washing the fibres thoroughly, spread them out in very thin layers, or hang them up in the wind to dry. Do not expose the fibres to the sun when damp, as this communicates a brownish-yellow tinge to them, which cannot be easily removed by bleaching. Leaving the fibres out at night in the dew bleaches them, but it is at the expense of part of their strength. All vegetable substances are apt to rot if kept long in a damp state."

In the Jury Reports of the Madras Exhibition it is stated: "It yields a fine white silky fibre of considerable length, especially lighter than hemp, flax, and aloe fibre, by one-fourth or one-fifth, and possessing considerable strength. There are numerous varieties of the plantain, which yield fibres of different qualities, viz. :—

Rustaley, superior table plantain.
Poovaley, or small Guindy variety.
Payvaley, a pale ash-coloured sweet fruit.
Monden, 3-sided coarse fruit.
Shevaley, large red fruit.
Putchay Laden, or long curved green fruit.

"These varieties, as might be expected, yield fibres of very different quality. This plant has a particular tendency to rot, and to become stiff, brittle, and discoloured, by steeping in the green state; and it has been ascertained by trial that the strength is in proportion to the cleanness of the fibre. If it has been well cleaned, and all the sap quickly removed, it bears immersion in water as well as most other fibres, and is about the same strength as Russian hemp. The coarse large-fruited plantains yield the strongest and thickest fibres; the smaller kinds yield fine fibres, suited for weaving, and if carefully prepared, these have a glossy appearance like silk. This gloss, however, can only be got by cleaning rapidly, and before the sap has time to stain the fibre; it is soon lost if the plant be steeped in water."

In Dr Royle's experiments on its strength, some prepared at Madras broke at 190 lb., that from Singapore at 390 lb., a 12-thread rope broke at 864 lb.; proving that it is of great strength, and applicable to cordage and rough canvas. Perhaps its value in the European markets might be £50, or at any rate £35 a-ton the coarser fibres, if sent in sufficient quantity and in a proper state. Respecting the manufacture of paper from the plantain fibres, the subjoined information is selected from Dr Royle's memorandum :—

"Among cultivated plants there is probably nothing so well calculated to yield a large supply of material, fit for making paper of almost every quality, as the plantain, so extensively cultivated in all tropical countries on account of its fruit, and of which the fibre-yielding stems are applied to no useful purpose. As the fruit already pays the expenses of the culture, this fibre could be afforded at a cheap rate, as from the nature of the plant consisting almost only of water and fibre, the latter might easily be separated. One planter calculates that it could be afforded for £9, 13s. 4d. per ton. Some very useful and tough kinds of paper have been made in India from the fibres of the plantain, and some of finer quality from the same material both in France and in the country."

Plantains and bananas are mere varieties of the same plant.—*Roxb. Royle, Fib. Plants. Simmonds. Indian Journal of Arts and Sciences.*

(399) **Myrica sapida** (*Wall.*) N. O. Myricaceæ.

Description.—Tree; leaves lanceolate, acuminate or obtuse at the apex, quite entire, glabrous, coriaceous; aments cylindric, alternate, remote, with a pubescent rachis; male flowers with an ovate puberulous bract; stamens 3-5, longer than the bract; anthers glabrous; female flowers with a pear-shaped granular fruit; nut very hard, attenuated at both ends.—*Wall. Tent. Flor. Nep.* p. 59, *t.* 45.——Khasia hills. Slopes of the Himalaya.

Medical Uses.—The bark, called *Kaephul* in Hindostani, forms an export to Patna and the low country, where it enjoys much repute as an aromatic stimulant, and is used as rubifacient and sternutatory. Dr Irvine (*Med. Top. of Ajmere*) states that he found kaephul and ginger mixed the best substance with which to rub cholera patients, to promote reaction.—*Pharm. of India.*

(400) **Myriophyllum verticillatum** (*Linn.*) N. O. Halorageæ.

Poonatsoo, Tel. పూనాచు

Description.—Small aquatic plant, consisting of filiform roots, and jointed shoots and stems, some creeping, some floating below the water; leaves sessile, verticillate, oblong, linear-lanceolate; *male* flowers axillary, sessile, 1-4 in the verticel, smaller than the *female;* spathe 1-flowered; corolla 3-petalled, petals reflected; *female* flowers on a distinct plant, axillary, generally solitary; capsule apparently siliquose, 1-celled, 3-5 seeded; flowers small, yellow. *Fl.* Aug.—Dec.—*Roxb. H. B.* p. 12.——Bengal.

Economic Uses.—When the male flowers are ready to expand, the murexed spathe bursts, the flowers are then quickly detached, and swim remote from the parent plant on the surface of the water in search of the female flowers, resting on the extremities of the reflected leaflets of the perianth and petals of the corolla. The sugar-refiners use the herb while moist to cover the surface of their sugar, as clay is used in the West Indies. Two or three days suffice for the use.—*Roxb.*

(401) **Myristica Malabarica** (*Lam.*) N. O. MYRISTICACEÆ.

Malabar Nutmeg, ENG.

DESCRIPTION.—Tree; leaves narrow-oblong or elliptic-lanceolate, acute at both ends or obtuse, quite glabrous, glaucous beneath; in *male*, inflorescence axillary, dichotomously cymose, many-flowered, longer than the petiole; *female* few-flowered, alabastrum globose, pubescent externally, bract very broad, embracing the base; fruit oblong, tawny, hairy; aril lacunose; lobes twisted and folded into a cone at the top.—*Dec. Prod.* xiv. 194.—*Hook. & Thoms. Flor. Ind.* i. 163.—*Rheede, Mal. t.* 5.——Forests of Malabar and Travancore.

MEDICAL USES.—This tree yields a kind of nutmeg larger than the common nutmeg, and possessing but little fragrance or aromatic taste. When bruised and subjected to boiling, it yields a quantity of yellowish concrete oil, which has been employed as an efficacious application to bad and indolent ulcers, allaying pain, cleansing the surface, and establishing healthy action. For this purpose it requires to be melted down with a small quantity of any bland oil. It may be found serviceable as an embrocation in rheumatism.—*Pharm. of India.*

(402) **Myristica moschata** (*Thunb.*) Do.

Nutmeg-tree, ENG. Jadikaé, TAM.

DESCRIPTION.—Tree; leaves ovate, elliptic, acute at the base, acuminate at the apex, lateral nerves on both sides, 8-9; peduncles supra-axillary, *males* few-flowered, *females* 1-flowered; pedicels nearly equalling the peduncle; bracteole under the flower broadly ovate, scale-shaped; flower nodding; perigonium ovoid, half 3-cleft, nearly equalling the pedicel, strigose externately with adpressed hairs; anthers 9-12; fruit ovoid-globose, drooping; aril laciniated, red, aromatic, covering the seed.—*Dec. Prod.* xiv. 189.—M. fragrans, *Houtt. Hist. Nat.* ii. part 3, p. 233.—*Blume Rumphia*, p. 180, *t.* 55.—M. officinalis, *Linn. Hook. Exot. Bot. t.* 155, 156.—*Rumph. Amb. t.* 4.——Cultivated.

20

Medical Uses.—A volatile oil resides in the kernel of the fruit. It is stimulant and carminative, and in larger doses narcotic. It is used in atonic diarrhœa and some forms of dyspepsia, but is chiefly used as an addition to other remedies. It is used largely as a condiment. Oil of nutmeg is a useful application in rheumatism, paralysis, and sprains, diluted with a bland oil. Mace, the false aril investing the shell of the kernel as met with in commerce, is of a pale cinnamon yellow, and an odcur and taste analogous to those of nutmegs. It yields by distillation a volatile oil, which, in composition, effects, and uses, is similar to that of nutmegs. It is chiefly used as a condiment.—*Pharm. of India.*

Economic Uses.—Indigenous to the Indian Archipelago, but has long been successfully cultivated in the warm moist climate of the western coast of India. The tree begins to bear at eight years old; it is in its prime at twenty-five years, and continues to bear fruit till sixty or older. The mace is dried in the sun, but the nutmegs are smoked by slow fires of wood for three months before they are fit for exportation. The refuse nuts are ground down, and by steaming and pressure afford a brown fluid, which cools into the so-called "nutmeg soap."—(*T. Oxley.*) In 1870–71 about 7 cwt. of nutmegs were exported from Bombay, and 30 cwt. from Madras, valued respectively at Rs. 575 and Rs. 3012.—*Trade Reports.*

N

(403) **Naregamia alata** (*W. & A.*) N. O. Meliaceæ.

Nela-naregam, Mal.

Description. — Small shrub, glabrous; calyx small, cup-shaped, 5-cleft; petals 5, very long, strap-shaped, distinct, free; filaments united into a long slender tube that is inflated and globular at the apex, the mouth with 10 very slight anther-bearing crenatures; leaves trifoliolate; leaflets cuneate-obovate, quite entire, sessile; petiole margined; flowers on long axillary solitary peduncles, white; capsule slightly membranaceous, 3-cornered, 3-valved; seeds 2. *Fl.* April—May.—*W. & A. Prod.* i. 116.—*Wight Icon. t.* 90.—*Rheede,* x. 22.——Travancore.

Medical Uses.—This is a pretty little plant, and will flower freely when introduced in gardens. It grows wild in the Travancore forests. The root and leaves are used in rheumatism, and the juice of the plant mixed with cocoanut-oil is used in cases of psora.—*Rheede. Pers. Obs.*

(404) **Nauclea Cadamba** (*Roxb.*) N. O. Cinchonaceæ.

Vella Cadamba, Tam. Rudrakshakamba, Tel. Cuddum, Hind. Kudum, Beng.

Description. — Large tree with a perfectly straight erect trunk; leaves opposite, between bifarious and decussate, oval, smooth, entire; petioles smooth; peduncles terminal, solitary; heads of flowers globose; calyx 5-partite; capsules 4-sided, 4-celled; seeds numerous, not winged; flowers small, orange-coloured, fragrant. *Fl.* April—May.—*Roxb. Fl. Ind.* i. 516.——Bengal. Wynaad. Malabar on river banks.

Economic Uses.—This is a large and ornamental tree. It is common about Calcutta, and is planted for the extensive shade it yields. The wood is of a yellow colour, and is used for various kinds of furniture.—*Roxb. Jury Rep.*

(405) **Nauclea cordifolia** (*Roxb.*) Do.

Manja cadamba, TAM. Dadnga, TEL. Kelikudum, BENG.

DESCRIPTION.—Tree 40-50 feet; leaves opposite, decussate, cordate, roundish, pubescent on the upper side, tomentose on the under; general peduncles axillary, 1-3 together, partial one shorter than the general, rather longer than the globose head of flowers; calyx 5-partite, segments clavate; corolla pubescent, lobes spreading; capsule 2-celled; seeds 6, winged at the extremities; flowers small, yellow. *Fl.* Nov.—Dec.—*W. & A. Prod.* i. 391.—*Roxb. Fl. Ind.* i. 514.—*Cor.* i. *t.* 53. ——Coromandel mountains. Concans. Hurdwar. Bengal. Travancore.

ECONOMIC USES.—The wood is exceedingly beautiful, and like that of the box-tree. It is very close-grained, and is procured from 1 to 2 feet in diameter. It is good especially for furniture, being light and durable. If, however, exposed to wet, it soon decays. In Bombay the carpenters use it for planking.—*Roxb. Jury Rep. Mad. Exhib.*

(406) **Nauclea parvifolia** (*Roxb.*) Do.

Bota-cadamie, TEL. Neer-cadamba, TAM.

DESCRIPTION.—Tree 30-40 feet, glabrous except in the axils of the nerves on the under side of the leaves; branches brachiate; leaves opposite, ovate or oval, bluntish; general peduncles opposite, terminal, bearing a pair of small deciduous leaves, partial ones scarcely so long as the globose head of flowers; limb of calyx very short, and almost truncated; lobes of corolla spreading; capsule containing 2 cocci splitting at the inner angle; flowers small, yellow. *Fl.* April—Aug.—*W. & A. Prod.* i. 391.—*Roxb. Fl. Ind.* i. 513.—*Cor.* i. *t.* 52.—*Wight Ill.* ii. 123.—N. orientalis, *Linn.*——Coromandel. Concans. Bengal.

ECONOMIC USES.—The wood of this tree is of light chestnut colour, fine and close grained. It is useful for many purposes, but if exposed to wet it soon rots. It is used in Malabar for flooring, planks, packing-boxes, and similar purposes.—*Roxb. Jury Rep. Mad. Exhib.*

(407) **Nelumbium speciosum** (*Willd.*) N. O. NELUMBIACEÆ.

Egyptian or Pythagorean Bean, ENG. Tamaray, TAM. Tamara, Bem-tamara, MAL. Yerra-tamaray, TEL. Lalkamal; Kungwel; Kamal; Padam; Ambuj, HIND. Pudmapodoo; Komol; Pongbuj, BENG. Kung-evelka, DUK.

DESCRIPTION.—Aquatic; leaves orbicular, attached by their centre, glabrous, under surface pale, margins somewhat waved; peduncles longer than the petioles, erect; root-stock horizontal, fleshy, sending out many fibres from the under-surface; petioles long, rising above the surface of the water, scabrous with acute tubercles; corolla polypetalous; connectivum produced beyond the cells of the anthers into a clavafe appendage; nuts loose in the hollows of the torus, 1-2 seeded; flowers large, white or rose-coloured. *Fl.* nearly all the year.—*W. & A. Prod.* i. 16.—*Wight Ill.* i. *t.* 9.——*Roxb. Fl. Ind.* ii. 647.—Nymphæa Nelumbo, *Linn.*—*Rheede*, xi. *t.* 30, 31.——Common in tanks in the Peninsula and other parts of India.

ECONOMIC USES.—It is universally believed that this is the sacred *Egyptian Lotus*, which originally found its way from India, where it was indigenous, and the fruit was known as the *Pythagorean* bean. If this be the case, it is a singular fact that, while the plant still survives in its native country, it has died out after the lapse of centuries in Egypt, for the real Lotus is no longer found on the waters of the Nile. Up to the 17th century it was commonly believed to be peculiar to Lower Egypt, but no one had ever met with it there. Herodotus has alluded to the plant, and indeed accurately describes it. He called it the "Lily of the Nile," but this must not be confounded with several species of the Nymphæa tribe which are found in the Nile to the present day. Of the Lotus he says,—"There are also other lilies, like roses, that grow in the river, the fruit of which is contained in a separate pod, that springs up from the root in form very like a wasp's nest; in this there are many berries fit to be eaten, of the size of an olive stone, and they are eaten both fresh and dried." It grew abundantly in all the lakes and canals. Strabo and particularly Theophrastus have both mentioned the sacred plant of Egypt, and the latter has most minutely described it, but the *savans* who accompanied Napoleon in his expedition to that country looked in vain for it. It has long ago disappeared. The most remarkable part of the plant is the structure of the seed-receptacle, which has been aptly compared to a pomegranate cut in half, or, as Herodotus says, like a wasp's nest. When ripe, the seeds are loose each in their separate cell, and if shaken make a noise like a rattle. Unlike the Nymphæa, the stems, petioles, and flower-stems of the

Lotus are raised above the water, a peculiarity which may serve to distinguish it, where so many errors have been made in the specification of the two genera. In this country as well as in China and Ceylon the flowers are held especially sacred. The roots and seeds were eaten by the Egyptians in the time of Herodotus, as they are now in India. It is also cultivated for the purpose. The mode of sowing the seeds is by first enclosing them in balls of clay and then throwing them into the water. The same method was adopted by the early Egyptians. Sir J. Staunton remarked that the leaf from its structure growing entirely round the stalk has the advantage of defending both flowers and fruit arising from its centre from contact with the water. The stem never fails to ascend with the water from whatever depth, where its leaf expands, rests upon it, and often rises above it. There are several varieties with white or rose-coloured flowers, and with or without a prickly stem. When the tanks are dry the roots are embedded in the mud, but on the appearance of the rain they burst out again, and the surface of the water, as if by a miracle, becomes covered with the large broad leaves. As a modern writer has observed, "There is no plant in the world which possesses so much interest in an historical point of view as the Lotus. The emblem of sanctity amongst the priests of an extinct religion four thousand years ago, it is now no longer known in the countries where once it was held sacred, and has sought refuge in the gardens and conservatories of the far-off lands of the west, of which the votaries of Isis never dreamt." Dr Roxburgh says that the tender shoots of the roots between the joints are eaten by the natives either simply boiled or in their curries. The seeds are eaten either raw, roasted, or boiled. The leaves and flower-stalks abound in spiral tubes, which are extracted with great care by gently breaking the stems and drawing apart the ends; with these filaments are prepared those wicks which are burnt by the Hindoos in the lamps placed before the shrines of their gods. The leaves are used as substitutes for plates; and in China the seeds and slices of the root are served up in summer with ice, and the roots are laid up in salt and vinegar for the winter.—*Roxb.* *Loudon.*

(408) **Nerium odorum** (*Ait.*) N. O. Apocynaceæ.

Sweet-scented Oleander, Eng. Tsjovanna Aralee, Mal. Aralee, Tam. Ghenneru, Tel. Kaneer, Duk. Kaner, Hind. Lal-kharubee, Beng.

Description.—Shrub, 6-8 feet; calyx 5-cleft; corolla salver-shaped, throat crowned by lacerated segments, segments of the limb twisted, unequal-sided; leaves linear lanceolate, 3 in a whorl, veiny beneath, with revolute edges; peduncles terminal; flowers pale-red, fragrant; follicles cylindrical. *Fl.* June—Aug.—*Roxb. Fl. Ind.* ii. 2.—*Rheede,* ix. *t.* 1-2.——Near banks of rivers. Common in gardens.

Medical Uses.—There are two or three varieties with deep red, white, rose-coloured, single and double flowers. The bark of the root is used externally as a powerful repellent, and made into a paste is applied in cases of ringworm. The root itself taken internally acts as a poison.—(*Ainslie.*) The root contains a yellow poisonous resin, tannic acid, wax, and sugar, but no alcaloid or volatile poison. The same poison resides in the bark and flowers. It is very soluble in carbonate of soda, and, though not volatile, is carried off mechanically when the plant is distilled with water. It is used in leprosy, eruptions of the skin, and boils.—*Powell's Punj. Plants.*

(409) **Nicotiana Tabacum** (*Linn.*) N. O. Solanaceæ.

Tobacco plant, Eng.

Description.—Herbaceous, pubescent, glutinous, stem erect, tapering, branched above; leaves oblong-lanceolate, acuminate, sessile, lower ones decurrent, half stem-clasping; flowers pedicelled bracteate; segments of the oblong calyx lanceolate, acute, unequal; corolla outwardly downy, throat somewhat inflated, segments of the much-spreading limb acute; capsule the length of the calyx, or slightly longer.—*Dec. Prod.* xiii. pt. 1, p. 557.—*Lam. Ill. t.* 113.—*Woodv. Med. Bot.* i. *t.* 60.——Cultivated.

Medical Uses.—The juice of tobacco-leaves is powerfully sedative and antispasmodic. It is used medicinally in dropsy and similar affections. As a local application it has been employed for relieving pain in rheumatic affections and skin diseases. Tobacco-smoking is sometimes effectually resorted to in asthma, spasmodic coughs, and nervous irritability. Poultices of tobacco-leaves have been successfully applied to the spine in tetanus.—*Pharm. of India.*

Economic Uses.—The tobacco plant has long been cultivated in India for the purpose of its leaves being manufactured into cheroots. Many acres of land are planted with it in the Salem and Trichinopoly districts, especially in the latter. Its cultivation also extends to the northern parts of the Deccan, and, in fact, wherever the locality may be favourable for its proper development. In a paper forwarded to the Agri.-Hort. Soc. of Madras in May 1862, Dr Shortt gives the following account of its cultivation at Chingleput:—It is a cultivation of four months. The seeds are sown into seed-beds late in the month of December, and the tobacco is gathered early in April. The beds are square, and receive the seeds sometimes before and sometimes after being irrigated. The beds are carefully prepared by free digging and turning up of the soil, when it is manured with equal portions of wood-ashes and dung-heap rubbish. Land in the mean time is prepared by the soil being freely ploughed, manured, and the earth drawn out into small, narrow, parallel trenches, about a foot wide, with intervening ridges of the same breadth. When the seedlings have attained between 3 and 5 inches in height, and have put out three or four leaves, which they do in about twenty days, they are ready for being transplanted. The trenches are previously filled with water, and the seedlings planted on the top of the ridges, at the distance of 15 inches from each other, and for the first three or four days irrigated daily, after which irrigation is practised every second day throughout their growth. About the fifteenth or twentieth day after transplantation the weeds are scraped out of the land either with a cocoanut-shell or an iron scraper. In about a fortnight after this the soil is loosened and weeds exterminated. Advantage is taken of this opportunity to complete the stand of plants by filling up the vacancies caused by the failure or accidental destruction of plants. Irrigation is practised as usual. At the commencement of the third month, a second hoeing or loosening of the soil and extermination of the weed is practised; and some two or three days after that, the side-shoots, which have begun to show themselves in the axilla of the leaves, are removed by being broken off. And about the end of the third month, when the stand of plants has attained between 2 and 3 feet in height, the tops of the bushes and all superfluous leaves are pinched off, leaving to each plant some ten or fifteen of the best-formed leaves. The plants throughout their growth are subject to attacks from insects of the caterpillar kind; these should be looked for daily, the first thing in the morning, when they should be picked out and destroyed. When the plants have become ripe, which they do at the end of the fourth month, the leaves become speckled, and will frequently crack between the fingers. At this period, should the plants have grown well and luxuriantly, the average size of the leaf is 25 to 30 inches in length, and 5 to 7 inches in breadth. The plants are then cut down (leaving a couple of inches of the stem in the ground), and allowed to be on the field to dry. In the evening they are gathered and stacked into a heap in some open place for the night; the next day the ground is spread over with palmyra leaves and straw of the varagoo (*Panicum miliaceum*) to the height of 6 or 8 inches; and on this the plants are stacked, and covered over with straw and palm leaves, and pressed with stones for five or six days, when the weights, straw, &c. are removed, the tobacco-plants taken up and hung in the shade by their stalks for a few days till the stalks become dry, when they are taken down and placed in a small close room, and covered as before with palm-leaves and straw, and pressed down by weights. Should the plants have become too dry and brittle, a few of the stalks are cut out and boiled with a sufficient quantity of water, to which a cake of Palmyra sugar or jaggery is added, and the fluid or decoction sprinkled on the tobacco previous to stacking the second time. The stack is turned upside down once in three or four days. When this has been done several times, the leaves are stripped off the stalks and tied into bundles, each containing from sixty to seventy leaves; these are again stacked in bundles, and have weights placed over them, after being covered with straw, &c. The bundles are rearranged once in three or four days for some two or three weeks, when the tobacco is considered cured and fit for use, and is removed. The produce of one cawnie of land is about 350 *thooks* of tobacco; a *thook* is equivalent to 3 lb. 10 oz. The attendant expenses are—

	Rs.	As.	P.
For ploughing the land, ...	14	0	0
Watering, weeding, &c., ...	15	0	0
Land-rent, ...	5	0	0
Total, ...	34	0	0

The value of the produce of one cawnie—viz., 350 thooks of tobacco—is valued at 150 rupees, from which if 34 rupees be deducted, and allowing 16 rupees for contingent expenses, a clear profit of 100 rupees goes to the cultivator. The seeds are so extremely minute and numerous that one pound suffices for planting a cawnie of land, and the price of the seed is eight annas a-pound. When the tobacco-stalks are cut down, the stumps left in the soil soon throw out fresh shoots; these, if carefully weeded and watered, thrive well. The produce thus obtained will realise one-third of the value of the original crop. The tobacco from the second crop is greatly inferior to the first in quantity and quality, consequently it deteriorates in value in the market.

(410) **Notonia grandiflora** (*Dec.*) N. O. Compositæ.

Description.—Shrubby; stem thick, round, marked with scars of fallen leaves; leaves oblong or obovate, quite entire; corymb few-headed; pedicels much longer than the capitulum; flowers terminal, pale yellow. *Fl.* Dec.—Jan.—*Dec. Prod.* vi. 442.—*Wight Contrib.* 24.—N. corymbosa, *Dec.*—*Wight Icon. t.* 484.——South Travancore. Neilgherries. High rocky places in the Deccan.

Medical Uses.—This plant is asserted by Dr Gibson to be a remedy in hydrophobia. The mode of administration is as follows: About four ounces of the freshly-gathered stems, infused in a pint of cold water for a night, yield in the morning, when subjected to pressure, a quantity of viscid greenish juice, which being mixed with the water is taken at a draught. In the evening a further quantity of juice made up into boluses with flour is taken. These medicines are to be repeated for three successive days.—*Pharm. of India.*

(411) **Nyctanthes arbor tristis** (*Linn.*) N. O. Jasminaceæ.

Munja-pumerum, Mal. Singahar, Beng. Hursinghar, Hind. Pagala-mully, Tam.

Description.—Tree, 15-20 feet, young shoots 4-sided; leaves opposite, short-petioled, cordate, or oblong, pointed, entire or coarsely serrate, scabrous; panicles terminal, composed of smaller 6-flowered terminal umbellets; calyx campanulate, slightly 5-notched, downy; corolla tube cylindric, as long as the calyx, segments 5-7; involucel of 4 inverse-cordate, opposite, sessile leaflets; flowers numerous; tube orange-coloured; border white, fragrant. *Fl.* Nearly all the year.—*Roxb. Fl. Ind.* i. 86.—*Rheede,* i. *t.* 21.——Cultivated in gardens.

Economic Uses.—The flowers of this plant shed a delicious fragrance in gardens where they grow, only during the night. It is at sunset that they open, and before the morning the ground is covered with the fallen corollas. The native women collect them, and, stringing them on threads, wear them as necklaces or twine them in their hair. The orange-coloured tubes dye a beautiful buff or orange colour, with the various shades between them, according to the preparation and mode of conducting the operation; but no way has yet been discovered of rendering the colour durable. Simmonds mentions the bark of this tree among other yielding tanning substances.—(*Roxb. Lindley.*) This tree is extremely common along the foot of the mountains which skirt the Deyra Dhoon, and may be seen for several hundred feet above Rajpore in the ascent to Mussoorie. Dr Wallich found it in a wild state near the banks of the Irrawaddy, on the hills near Prome. This affords a very satisfactory instance of the extensive distribution of the same species along the base of the mountains, even when separated by 12° of latitude, or from 18° to 30°.—*Royle. Him. Bot.*

(412) **Nymphæa edulis** (*Dec.*) N. O. Nymphæaceæ.

Koteka, Tel. Chhota-sundhi, Beng.

Description.—Aquatic; leaves oval, quite entire, downy underneath, margin sometimes slightly waved; petiole attached a little within the margin; petals 10-15; stamens 30, in a double series; stigmas 10-15, rayed; flowers white; connectivum not prolonged; seeds numerous. *Fl.* Nearly all the year.—*W. & A. Prod.* i. 447.—N. esculenta, *Roxb. Fl. Ind.* ii. 578.——Bengal. Circars.

Economic Uses.—The tubers are much sought after by the

natives, both as an article of food and medicine. The capsule and seeds are either pickled or put into curries, or ground and mixed with flour to make cakes. The flowers are nearly three inches in diameter.—*Roxb.*

(413) **Nymphæa rubra** (*Roxb.*) Do.

Red-flowered Water-Lily, ENG. Yerra Kulwa, TEL. Rukhta-chunduna, HIND. Buro-rukto-kumbal, BENG.

DESCRIPTION.—Aquatic; sepals 4; petals numerous; leaves peltate, sharply toothed, downy but not spotted beneath; lobes diverging; connectivum not prolonged; petioles inserted very near the margin of the leaf; flowers deep red; torus bottle-shaped; carpels numerous, many-seeded; stigma 10-20, rayed. *Fl.* March—Aug.—*W. & A. Prod.* i. 17.—*Wight Ill.* i. 10.—*Roxb. Fl. Ind.* ii. 576.——Peninsula in tanks and ditches. Tanjore.

ECONOMIC USES.—The roots and seeds are eaten by the natives; and the capsules and seeds together are prepared in different ways, sometimes pickled, or put into curries, or made into cakes. A kind of starch and arrowroot is made from the underground stems and roots, and both are used as aliments as well as in medicine. In Bengal there is a small rose-coloured variety with fewer stamens. This is a beautiful flower, yet neither common nor so gaudy as the Egyptian Lotus.—*Roxb.*

O

(414) **Ocimum Basilicum** (*Linn.*) N. O. Lamiaceæ.

Sweet Basil, Eng. Tirnoot-patchie, Tam. Vepoodipatsa, Tel. Subzeh, Duk. Kala-tulsee, Pashana Cheddee, Hind. Babooitulsee, Beng.

Description.—Herbaceous, erect, glabrous; leaves petiolate, ovate or oblong, narrowed at the base, slightly toothed; petioles ciliated; racemes simple; calyxes longer than the pedicels; upper teeth ovate, concave, shortly acuminated; whorls about 6, rarely 10-flowered; flowers small, white. *Fl.* Nearly all the year.—*Wight Icon. t.* 868.—O. pilosum, *Benth.* and *Willd.* —*Roxb. Fl. Ind.* iii. 16.——Peninsula. Bengal. Oude. Travancore.

The varieties are :—

a *O. anisatum, Benth.*

More erect and less pilose; leaves larger, thicker, and slightly toothed; corollas usually villous.—O. basilicum, *Linn.*—*Roxb. Fl. Ind.* iii. 17.—*Rheede,* x. *t.* 87.

b *O. glabratum, Benth.*

Erect; petioles and calyxes sparingly ciliated; leaves scarcely toothed; racemes elongated, simple.—O. integerrimum, *Willd.*—O. caryophyllatum, *Roxb. Fl. Ind.* iii. 16.—Goolaltulsee, *Beng.*——Patna.

c *O. thyrsiflorum, Benth.*

Erect, glabrous; petioles and calyxes hardly ciliated; raceme thyrsoid; branched flowers pale-pink.—*Roxb. Fl. Ind.* iii. 15.—*Wight Icon. t.* 868.

Medical Uses.—The whole plant is aromatic and fragrant. The seeds are cooling and mucilaginous, and are said to be very nourishing and demulcent. An infusion is given as a remedy in gonorrhœa, catarrh, dysentery, and chronic diarrhœa. The juice of the leaves is squeezed in the ear in ear-ache. Dr Fleming states that the seeds are a favourite medicine with Hindoo women for relieving the after-pains of parturition. In Europe the leaves and small branches or leafy tops are gathered for culinary purposes, and used in highly-seasoned dishes. Sometimes they are introduced into salad and soups.—(*Don. Ainslie.*) The juice of the leaves of *O. villosum*, mixed with ginger and black pepper, is given during the cold stages of intermittent fever. It is also prescribed to allay vomiting arising from irritation produced by worms.—(*Long Indig. Plants of Bengal.*) The seeds steeped in water swell and form a pleasant jelly, useful as a diaphoretic and demulcent.—*Powell's Panj. Prod.*

(415) **Ocimum sanctum** (*Linn.*) Do.

Holy basil, ENG. Toolasee, TAM. Toolsee, DUK. Niella-tirtova, Khrishna toolsee, MAL. Kala-toolsie, HIND. Kalo-tulsee, BENG.

DESCRIPTION.—Stems and petioles pilose; leaves petiolate, oval, obtuse, toothed, pubescent; floral leaves sessile, shorter than the pedicels; racemes slender, simple or branched at the base; calyx shorter than the pedicels, smoothish, upper-tooth obovate, concave; corolla hardly exceeding the calyx; flowers pale purple. *Fl.* Nearly all the year.—*Roxb. Fl. Ind.* iii. 14. —O. hirsutum, *Benth.*—*Rheede,* x. *t.* 85.——Cultivated in gardens and near pagodahs.

MEDICAL USES.—The whole plant is of a dark purple colour, and has a grateful smell. The root is given in decoction in fevers, and the juice of the leaves in catarrhal affections in children. Also an excellent remedy, mixed with lime-juice, in cutaneous affections and ringworm. The leaves, dried and pulverised, are used by natives in Bengal as snuff in the endemic affection of the nasal cavities called *Peenash;* it is said to be an effectual means of dislodging the maggots.—*Pharm. of India.*

(416) **Odina wodier** (*Roxb.*) N. O. ANACARDIACEÆ.

Woodian, TAM. Waddi gampina, TEL. Cushmulla, HIND. Jiwul, BENG. Wodier Marum, MAL.

DESCRIPTION.—Large tree; leaves alternate about the ends of the branches, unequally pinnated; leaflets 3-4 pair, opposite, almost sessile, oblong-obovate, acuminated, glabrous, entire, paler below; calyx shortly 4-lobed, segments rounded; petals 5, oblong, spreading; drupe uniform, very hard, 1-celled; seeds solitary, of the same shape as the nut; racemes terminal, fascicled; flowers small, greenish yellowish, externally purplish. *Fl.* Feb.—March.—*W. & A. Prod.* i. 171.—*Wight Icon.* i. *t.* 60.—*Roxb. Fl. Ind.* ii. 293.—*Royle Ill. t.* 31, *f.* 2.—*Rheede,* iv. *t.* 32.——Coromandel mountains. Bengal. Travancore.

MEDICAL USES.—A gum which exudes from the tree is beaten up with cocoanut-milk and applied to sprains and bruises, and the pulverised bark, when boiled in or mixed with oil, is put to bad ulcers and wounds. The leaves boiled in oil are externally applied to bruises.—(*Ainslie. Wight.*) The bark, which is very astringent, is employed in the form of decoction as a lotion in impetiginous eruptions and obstinate ulcerations. It also forms an excellent astringent gargle.—*Pharm. of India.*

ECONOMIC USES.—This tree, says Dr Wight, is one of the most commonly cultivated and best known in the Peninsula, where, though far from being ornamental or useful, its quickness of growth from cuttings recommends it. The tree is planted in avenues, but yields no shade in the hot weather, being without leaves till June. The wood of the old trees is close-grained, of a deep reddish mahogany colour towards the centre. The coloured part is serviceable and looks well. It is useful for ordinary work, especially for sheaths of swords, knives, &c. The bark is full of fibrous materials.—*Wight. Jury Rep. Mad. Exhib.*

(417) **Olea dioica** (*Roxb.*) N. O. OLEACEÆ.

Indian olive, ENG. Kara-vetti, MAL.

DESCRIPTION.—Tree; leaves opposite, oblong, remotely and acutely serrate, acuminate, smooth, on short petioles; panicles axillary and opposite below the leaves; *male* flowers numerous; calyx 4-toothed; corolla tube very short, border 4-cleft; *female* flowers on a separate tree; calyx as in the male; corolla none; drupe nearly round, 1-celled, 1-seeded; flowers small, white. *Fl.* March—April.—*Roxb. Fl. Ind.* i. 106.—*Rheede*, iv. *t.* 54.——Chittagong. Silhet. Malabar.

ECONOMIC USES.—The fruit in size and colour is much like the English sloe. The timber of the tree is reckoned excellent, and is much used by the natives.—(*Wall.*) The *O. robusta*, indigenous to Silhet, furnishes the natives in that country with a hard and durable wood.—*Roxb.*

(418) **Ophelia elegans** (*R. W.*) N. O. GENTIANACEÆ.

DESCRIPTION. — Shrub, erect, ramous above, obsoletely 4-sided; leaves sessile, narrow, ovate-lanceolate, tapering to a slender point, 3-nerved, lateral nerves close to the margin; branches ascending, slender, bearing at each point lateral few-flowered cymes, forming together a large, many-flowered, leafy panicle; calyx lobes narrow-lanceolate, acute, about two-thirds the length of the corolla; lobes of the corolla obovate-cuspidate; foveæ bound with longish coarse hairs; flowers pale blue. *Fl.* Aug.—Sept.—*Wight Icon. t.* 1331.——Pulney Hills. Northern Circars.

Medical Uses.—A very handsome species, says Dr Wight, when in full flower, forming as it does a rich panicle of light-blue flowers streaked with deeper-coloured veins. It seems very distinct from all other species. The stems are used as a bitter and febrifuge in the northern Circars, and are there in great request. It closely resembles the *O. chiretta*, which is brought from the slopes of the Himalaya, and which is there reckoned useful as a tonic in intermittent fevers. Of the present species the stalks are tied up in bundles about a foot long and 3 or 4 inches in thickness. The native name in the districts where it grows is *Salaras* or *Salajit.* It is exported to a considerable extent, and is easily procured in the bazaars, where the plant is indigenous. The Honourable W. Elliot was the first to bring this new species of gentian to notice.—*Ind. Annals of Med. Science. Jury Rep. Mad. Exhib. Wight.*

(419) **Ophelia multiflora** (*Dalz.*) Do.

Description.—Stem quadrangular, 4-winged, ascending, densely leafy; leaves round, ovate, stem-clasping, 5-nerved, mucronulate, glabrous, decussate; cymes many-flowered; calyx divisions lanceolate-acuminate; corolla white, 4-divided, segments ovate-elliptic, their rounded pits surrounded by long fringes; filaments united at the very base.—*Dalz. Bomb. Flor.* 156.—*Hook. Journ. Bot.* ii. 135.——Mahableshwar.

Medical Uses.—This is used in Bombay as an excellent substitute for chiretta. The dried root occurs in pieces of 2 inches in length, of the diameter of a quill, giving off two or three rootlets, covered with a whitish-brown epidermis, wrinkled longitudinally, white internally, and brittle. Dr Broughton considers that its medicinal action and uses are similar to those of gentian and chiretta, for which it may be advantageously substituted. The dried plant also appears to be used for the same purposes.—*Pharm. of India.*

(420) **Ophiorrhiza munghos** (*Linn.*) N. O. Cinchonaceæ.

Description.—Perennial 1-½ foot; stem when old suffruticose; leaves opposite, elliptic-lanceolate, acuminated at both ends, glabrous, very thin, unequal in size; calyx tube turbinate, limb 5-cleft; corolla tube infundibuliform, short, hairy within, limb 5-lobed; stamens enclosed; capsule compressed, crowned with the calycine segments, 2-celled, 2-valved; seeds numerous, somewhat hexagonal; cymes peduncled, terminal, branched; flowers nearly sessile, white. *Fl.* Aug.—Sept.—*W. & A. Prod.* i. 404.—*Roxb. Fl. Ind.* i. 701.——Dindigul. Courtallum. Travancore.

Medical Uses.—There are several varieties slightly differing in the disposition of their form of inflorescence. Dr Wallich found the plant growing in the forests of the valleys of Nepaul, though he was not quite sure whether those he gathered did not belong to a distinct species. The Malays, according to Kœmpfer, called the root "earth-galls," from its intense bitterness. The root is very bitter, and reported to be a powerful alexipharmic. The plant in Ceylon is accounted a good specific in snake-bites; the parts used are the leaves, root, and bark made into decoction and administered in doses of ½ oz. Roxburgh doubted the good qualities ascribed to it.——*Ainslie. Roxb.*

(421) **Ophioxylon serpentinum** (*Linn.*) N. O. Apocynaceæ.

Tsjovanna-amelpodi, Mal. Chivan-amelpodi, Tam. Patal-ganni, Tel. Chota-chand, Hind. Chandra, Beng.

Description.—Twining; calyx 5-cleft; corolla funnel-shaped, with long tube, thick in the middle, 5-cleft, limb oblique; anthers almost sessile inserted in the middle of the tube; leaves 3-4-5 in a whorl, cuneate-oblong, acute, sometimes drooping; pedicels and calyxes red; drupe black, size of a pea, twin or solitary by abortion; nut wrinkled, 1-seeded; flowers white, with the tube pale rose-lilac. *Fl.* All the year.—*Roxb. Fl. Ind.* i. 694.—*Wight Icon. t.* 849.—*Rheede,* vi. *t.* 47.——Peninsula. Bengal. Malabar.

Medical Uses.—Few shrubs, says Sir W. Jones, in the world are more elegant, especially when the vivid carmine of the perianth is contrasted, not only with the milk-white corolla, but with the rich green berries, which at the same time embellish the fascicles. Rheede says it is always bearing, the berries and flowers appearing together at all times. The root is used internally in various disorders both as a febrifuge and for the bites of poisonous animals, such as snakes and scorpions, the dose being a pint of the decoction every twenty-four hours; the powder being also applied to the parts. The juice is also expressed and dropped into the eye for the same purpose. It is also administered to promote delivery in tedious cases, acting upon the uterine system in the same manner as ergot of rye.—*Roxb. Wight.*

(422) **Oryza sativa** (*Linn.*) N. O. Graminaceæ.

Common Rice-plant, Eng. Payera, Mal. Nelloo, Tam. Dhan, Beng. Pusuel, Hind. Oori. cheni, Tel.

Description. — Annual; culms numerous, jointed, round and smooth; leaves sheathing, long, scabrous outside; panicles terminal; rachis common and partial, angular, hispid; flowers simple, pedicelled; calyx glume 2-valved, 1-flowered, the larger valve ending in a long, hispid, coloured awn; corolla 2-valved, growing to the seed.—*Roxb. Fl. Ind.* ii. 200.—— Circars. Cultivated everywhere.

Medical Uses.—A decoction of rice makes an excellent demulcent refrigerant drink in febrile and inflammatory diseases, dysuria, and affections requiring these remedies. Rice poultices are constantly used in hospital practice, forming an excellent substitute for linseed-meal.

Economic Uses. — The rice-plant is extensively cultivated in almost all the countries of the East under the equator, requiring a summer temperature of at least 73°, humidity and heat being the indispensable conditions of its growth. It is grown in Japan, China, the Philippines, Ceylon, Siam, both shores of the Red Sea, Egypt, and Madagascar, and from these countries it has emigrated to the coasts of Western Africa and America. The wild rice-plant, from which all the cultivated varieties have sprung, is found in and on the borders of lakes in the Circars; and also in the back-waters of Travancore, near Allepey, and other places. This wild rice is never cultivated, though it is gathered and eaten by the richer classes in the Rajahmundry districts, who boil it in steam and consider it a great dainty. It sells at a high price. It is white, palatable, and wholesome. A coarse kind of confection is made from it which is sold in most bazaars. Rice, although the commonest and cheapest kind of food in the Peninsula, is far from being so universally used among the natives of India as people are apt to imagine. Great numbers in that country do not eat it. In all the North-Western Provinces wheat is the principal crop, and the natives have rather a contempt for the rice-eating districts. Still it constitutes one of the most important articles of food, not only in India, but especially in America and China. It is grown now in Italy, Spain, and even slightly in Germany. "A rice-field," said Adam Smith, "produces a much greater quantity of food than the most fertile corn-field. Two crops in the year, from 30 to 60 bushels each, are said to be the ordinary produce of an acre." Dr Roxburgh, however, states that two crops in the year from the same land do not yield much more than a single crop would; but owing to the liability of the seasons to fail, the cultivators rear as much as possible for the first crop. This is reaped in the rainy season when the straw cannot be preserved; and as rice-straw is almost the only food which the cattle have in many districts, there is an absolute necessity for sowing the second crop for fodder. Dr Roxburgh's statement, that he never saw or heard of a farmer manuring in the smallest degree a rice-field, is only applicable to those districts where the soil is sufficiently rich to yield those large crops which he speaks of. In Travancore and Tinnevelly, and perhaps other districts, the farmers invariably manure the rice-fields with leaves of trees, ashes, and cow-dung. The most fertile soil for rice-sowing is land periodically inundated in the neighbourhood of large rivers, where the plant can receive much fertilising matter from the overflowing of the streams. Yet this is not sufficient for the perfect maturity and wellbeing of the plant, for it requires rain also, the showers falling on the plant being absolutely requisite to insure the full development of the flowers and seeds. Rice-seed is usually first sown thick, and then transplanted about forty days afterwards; the fields must be kept constantly supplied with water; the usual time for planting-out to the reaping season is about two months. This is, however, not the case with all kinds; some are sown broadcast in the same place where it is intended the seeds should ripen. In this latter case the sowing should commence about fifteen days before the rains set in. There are several ways of watering the rice-crops. It is generally believed that the plants cannot have too much water (provided they be not quite submerged), except for a few days before the seeds become ripe, when a drier state is requisite to perfect the maturity and improve the quality of the grain. Of the many varieties (and there are about forty or fifty in the Peninsula, although Moon has enumerated one hundred and sixty-one growing in Ceylon) some require more water than others. The time of sowing depends of course upon the season, varying on either coast according to the setting in of the periodical rains. When the rice-stalks are once cut they are immediately carried off the fields, when they are stacked and left for two or three days. The farmers then proceed to thrash the grain out either by manual labour or by the help of cattle. The mode of separating the husk from the grain is by beating it with the rice-stamper. This work is usually performed by women. Of late years the process of rice-cleaning has been greatly simplified among Europeans by the introduction of machinery, which is usually resorted to in Ceylon. Although there is no actual rotation of crops so called in rice-lands, yet during the intervals of the seasons the natives frequently sow the land with other grains, such as horse-gram, sesamum, and different kinds of peas, &c., and the stubbles of these latter are used as manure for the succeeding crops of rice. Hill-rice is sown on dry and rather elevated lands which cannot be flooded, and these crops, therefore, must depend entirely upon the annual rains. This rice is called *Modun* in Malabar, and is of no great value. On the Himalaya it grows at considerable elevations, even on the slopes of the mountains. But this is sown in places within the influence of the periodical rains, and the moisture arising from the heated valleys is very favourable to its growth. Some of the Himalayan rice (*O. Nepalensis*) which was reared without irrigation was displayed at the Great Exhibition 1850.

Specimens of wild paddy were forwarded to the Agri.-Hort. Soc. of India by Mr Terry from Tumlook, where it grows in any quantity in marshy salt-water land. It grows in similar situations all over Madras.

Rice in the husk, which we call paddy, is *Nelloo* in Tamil, *Dhan* in Dukhanie, *Oodloo* or *Urloo* in Teloogoo. The husk-seed is *Arisee* in Tamil, *Chawul* in Hindustanee and Dukhanie, *Beum* in Teloogoo, *Arie* in Malayalum. The two great crops of rice in Southern India are the Caar and Soombah crops, the last of which is also called the Peshanum crop, and is reaped in February and March; and the Hindoo doctors assert that the produce of the different crops have different effects when medicinally prescribed. The produce of the Peshanum crop is more appreciated for this latter purpose. On the other hand, the Caar crop, which is reaped in October, is reckoned inferior. In the Circars the cultivators divide the numerous varieties into two orders—the Poonas or the early sort, and the Pedda worloo, the late or great crop. Dr Roxburgh has given ample information upon this subject. Rice is composed almost entirely of fecula, and on this account, although valuable for exportation, yet is not so nourishing as wheat or other cereal grains, owing to the absence of gluten. It is light, wholesome, and very easy of digestion, but cannot be baked into bread. Rice may be kept a very long period in the rough. After being cleaned, if it be of a good quality and well milled, it will keep a considerable time in European climates. Mustiness, however, is apt to accumulate on it, which should be carefully washed off if it has been long kept. Rough rice may remain under water twenty-four hours without injury if dried soon after. Rice-glue is made by mixing rice-flour with cold water and then boiling the mixture. This conjee is used in the process of papermaking, and also by weavers in dressing and preparing thread for the loom, and generally used by mechanics whenever strong adhesion may be required. There is a great percentage of starch in rice, more so perhaps than in wheat, sometimes as much as 85 per cent. In manufacturing rice-starch on a large scale, Patna rice yields 80 per cent of marketable starch. The following is Jones's patent process for its manufacture, as given in the 'Pharmaceutical Journal:' "100 lb. of rice are macerated for twenty-four hours in 50 gal. of the alkaline solution, and afterwards washed with cold water, drained and ground. To 100 gallons of the alkaline solution are then to be added 100 lb. of ground rice, and the mixture stirred repeatedly during twenty-four hours, and then allowed to stand for about seventy hours to settle or deposit. The alkaline solution is to be drawn off, and to the deposit cold water is to be added, for the double purpose of washing out the alkali and for drawing off the starch from the other matters. The mixture is to be well stirred up, and then allowed to rest about an hour for the fibre to fall down. The liquor holding the starch in suspension is to be drawn off and allowed to stand for about seventy hours for the starch to deposit. The waste liquor is now to be removed, and the starch stirred up, blued (if thought necessary), drained, dried, and finished in the usual way." Among other kinds the Patna rice is justly celebrated, but perhaps the most fertile province for rice-growing is Arracan, from whence great quantities of the grain are shipped to Europe from the port of Akyab, the importance of which is yearly increasing.—*Roxb. Ainslie. Simmonds.*

(423) **Oxalis corniculata** (*Linn.*) N. O. Oxalidaceæ.

Yellow Wood-sorrel, Eng. Pooliaray, Tam. Poolichinta, Tel. Umbuti, Duk. Amrool, Hind.

Description. — Stems decumbent, branched, radicating, leafy; stipules united to the base of the petioles; leaves palmately 3-foliolate; leaflets obcordate, pubescent; peduncles 2-5, but mostly 2-flowered; stamens monadelphous; sepals pubescent; petals emarginate; pistils as long as the longer stamens; capsule many-seeded, densely pubescent; flowers yellow. *Fl.* Nearly all the year.—*W. & A. Prod.* i. 142.—*Roxb. Fl. Ind.* ii. 457.—*Wight Icon.* i. *t.* 18.——Common everywhere. Base of the Himalaya.

Medical Uses.—The leaves, stalks, and flowers are used by the Hindoos as cooling medicines, especially in dysentery.—(*Ainslie.*) It contains salts of oxalic acid, and acts as a refrigerant in fevers, as well as an antiscorbutic. Its juice may be used to remove ink-spots, as it rapidly dissolves most compounds of iron. It is used externally to remove warts, and fibres over the cornea.—(*Powell's Punj. Prod.*) The *O. sensitiva* is reckoned tonic in Java.—*Ainslie.*

P

(424) **Pæderia fœtida** (*Linn.*) N. O. CINCHONACEÆ.

Gundhalee, HIND. Gundo-bhadulee, BENG.

DESCRIPTION.—Climbing; leaves opposite, oblong or lanceolate, cordate at the base, glabrous; panicles axillary and opposite, or terminal; flowers sessile along the ultimate divisions; berry ovate, somewhat compressed, 2-celled, 2-seeded; calyx 5-toothed; corolla infundibuliform, hairy inside, 5-lobed; stamens almost sessile on the middle of the tube; flowers small, white. *Fl.* Dec.—Jan.—*W. & A. Prod.* i. 424.—*Roxb. Fl. Ind.* i. 683.——Peninsula. Bengal.

MEDICAL USES.—The whole plant when bruised has a fetid smell. The roots are used as emetic by the Hindoos.—*Roxb.*

ECONOMIC USES.—The very beautiful fibre obtained from the stalk has recently been attracting much attention in England.

(425) **Pandanus odoratissimus** (*Linn. Fil.*) N. O. PANDANACEÆ.

Caldera bush, Fragrant Screw-pine, ENG. Thalay, TAM. Kaida, or Thala, MAL. Mogheli, TEL. Keori, BENG.

DESCRIPTION.—Large shrub, 10 feet or more, bushy; roots issuing from lower parts of the stem or larger branches; leaves confluent, stem clasping, closely imbricated in 3 spiral rows round the extremities of the branches, tapering to a fine triangular point, smooth, shining, margin and back armed with sharp spines—those on the margin point towards the apex, those below in various ways; flowers male and female in terminal racemes on different plants; in female flowers no other corolla or calyx than the termination of the 3 rows of leaves forming 3 imbricated fascicles of white floral leaves, standing at equal distance round the base of the young fruit; fruit something in appearance like a pine-apple, orange-coloured, composed of numerous drupes, detached when ripe, and covered with a deeper orange-coloured skin, interior filled with rich-looking yellow pulp, intermixed with strong fibres; seed 1, oblong, smooth; flowers small, fragrant. *Fl.* June—Sept.—*Roxb. Cor.* i. *t.* 94-96.—*Fl. Ind.* iii. 738.—*Rheede,* ii. *t.* 8.—— Peninsula, near bank of streams and water-courses.

Economic Uses.—This large and singular-looking bush is very common along the banks of the canals and back-waters in Travancore, in which places it is planted to bind the soil. The flowers are seldom visible, but the large red fruit, much like a pine-apple, is very attractive. The flowers are very fragrant, and from them is made an oil known as the *Keora-oil.* The perfume is extracted chiefly from the male flowers. The floral leaves themselves are eaten either raw or boiled. The lower pulpy part of the drupes is eaten by the natives in times of scarcity. The fusiform roots are used by the basket-makers to tie their work with, and also, by reason of their soft and spongy nature, for corks. There are manufactures at Cuddalore and other places, where mats, baskets, and hats are made from these roots, and a coarse brush for whitewashing houses: when beaten out with a mallet they open out like a soft brush. Matting and packing-bags are made from them in the Mauritius and China. The leaves, which abound in toughish fibres, are used for matting, cordage, and thatch. They are said to be good for paper-making also. The natives make with them a fine kind of mat to sleep on, which they stain red and yellow. Also used for making common umbrellas. In some districts the fibres are used for making the larger kinds of hunting-nets, and drag-ropes of fishing-nets. In Tinnevelly they are mixed with flax in small quantities for the manufacture of *gunny* and ropes, but they are not sold in their pure state. It is the farina of the male flowers which is used as a perfume. In Arabia and India people bestrew their heads with it, as Europeans do with perfumed powder.—(*Ainslie. Roxb. Jury Rep. Mad. Exhib.*) A species of *Pandanus* is used in most parts of the Mauritius for its leaves, which are employed for the purpose of package-bags for the transportation of coffee, sugar, and grain from one place to another, and for exportation. The preparation of the leaves for working into matting is simple and short. As soon as gathered, the spines on their edges and dorsal nerve are stripped off and the leaf divided into strips of the breadth proper for the use they are required for.—*Col. Hardwicke.*

(426) Panicum Italicum (*Linn.*) N. O. Graminaceæ.

Italian Millet, Eng. Tenney, Tam. Tenna, Mal. Rawla, Duk. Kangoo Kungnee, Beng. Râla, Kora, Hind. Cora, Tel.

Description.—Culms erect, 3-5 feet, round, smooth; roots issuing from the lower joints; margins of leaves hispid;

mouths of the sheaths bearded; spikes nodding; spikelets scattered; pedicels 2-4 flowered, with smooth intermediate bristles; seeds ovate.—*Roxb. Fl. Ind.* i. 302.—Setaria Italica, *Beauv.*——Cultivated.

Economic Uses.—This is considered by the natives one of the most delicious of cultivated grains. The Brahmins—indeed all classes of natives—particularly esteem it, and use the seeds for cakes, porridge, &c. It is good for pastry—scarcely inferior, says Ainslie, to wheat; and when boiled with milk, makes a pleasant light diet for invalids. It is cultivated in many parts of India, requiring a dry light soil. The seed-time for the first crop is in June and July; for the second, between September and February. There are several kinds of millet cultivated in the Peninsula, among which the most celebrated are *P. miliaceum* (*Willd.*) and *P. frumentaceum* (*Roxb.*), of which there are several varieties.—*Roxb. Ainslie.*

(427) **Papaver somniferum** (*Linn.*) N. O. Papaveraceæ.

Opium Poppy, Eng. Casa casa, Tam. Cassa cassa, Tel. Post, Hind. Pasto, Beng.

Description.—Herbaceous, 2-3 feet; sepals 2, deciduous; petals 4; stem smooth, glaucous; leaves amplexicaul, repand, cut and toothed, teeth somewhat obtuse; capsules obovate or glabrous; peduncles drooping; seeds numerous; flowers red, white, or purplish. *Fl.* Feb.—March.—*W. & A. Prod.* i. 17. —*Roxb. Fl. Ind.* ii. 571.——Cultivated in high lands in Northern India. Neilgherries. Mysore.

Medical Uses.—According to Dioscorides and Pliny, opium was formerly obtained from the Black Poppy; now it is principally taken from the White Poppy, the capsules being chiefly received from Asia Minor, India, and Egypt. The former gives a very active opium, which may also be procured from the common Red Poppies of our gardens. Liquid opium extracted from the Poppies contains from 20 to 53 per cent of water. The value of opium consists in the quantity of the alkaloid morphine which it contains. Morphine is obtained in crystals from opium, treated with alcohol and ammonia, nearly all the narcotine being separated. The proportions of morphine vary from 12.35 to 14.78 per cent. The opium of commerce has been gradually deteriorating. That from Smyrna is reputed the best, and contains ordinarily only 3 to 6 per cent of morphine. The very best opium contains only from 8 to 9 per cent. —(*Guibourt Journ. de Pharmacie.*) The Poppy is cultivated both in Europe and Asia for its flowers and seeds. The half-ripe capsules wounded yield the juice which concretes into opium. From the dried capsules, the decoction, syrup, and extract of Poppies are prepared. Dr Pereira considered that the capsules are more active if gathered before becoming ripe; when full grown, and just when the first change of colour is perceptible, is the best time to collect them. In Great Britain, although attempts have been made to extract good opium from the plant cultivated there, yet it would appear that the results, although satisfactory, are not such as to render the manufacture profitable. In Turkey, Persia, and Egypt it is extensively cultivated for the purpose of obtaining the opium. In Greece the seeds were used as fruit from the earliest times. All the parts of the Poppy abound in a narcotic milky juice, which is partially extracted, together with a quantity of mucilage, by decoction. The heads or capsules possess anodyne properties: they are chiefly employed, boiled in water, as fomentations to inflamed or ulcerated surfaces, and the syrup prepared from them with inspissated decoction is used as an anodyne for children and to allay cough, &c. The milky juice of the Poppy in its more perfect state, which is the case in warm climates only, is extracted by incisions made in the capsules and inspissated, and in this state forms the opium of commerce.

The white variety is the one invariably cultivated in India. The Poppy-plant requires a rich soil, plenty of manuring, and frequent irrigation. The cultivation is simple enough if these three requisites be attended to. The lands in the neighbourhood of streams or other supplies of water are usually chosen for the purpose. The whole quantity of land under Poppy cultivation in India in 1840 did not exceed 50,000 acres, and perhaps about as many persons were employed. The chief Poppy-growing districts are Behar, Patna, and Malwah. In the latter district it is grown at different elevations, from 2000 to 7000 feet, requiring a moderate temperature, as the plant will not thrive in the plains. The Malwah opium, according to Dr Royle, is the produce of the *P. glabrum*, which differs from the Bengal opium in quality and appearance. The following mode of extracting the opium is given in the 'Bengal Dispensatory:'—"Early in February and March the bleeding process commences. Three small lancet-shaped pieces of iron are bound together with cotton, about one-twelfth of an inch of the blade alone protruding, so that no discretion as to the depth of the wound to be inflicted shall be left to the operator; and this is drawn sharply up from the top of the stalk at the base to the summit of the pod. The sets of people are so arranged that each plant is bled all over once every three or four days, the bleedings being three or four times repeated on each plant. This operation always begins to be performed about three or four o'clock in the afternoon, the hottest part of the day. The juice appears almost immediately on the wound being inflicted, in the shape of a thick gummy milk, which is thickly covered with a brownish pellicle. The exudation is greatest over night, when the incisions are washed and kept open by the dew. The opium thus derived is scraped off next morning with a blunt iron tool, resembling a cleaver in miniature. Here the work of adulteration begins; the scraper being passed heavily over the seed-pod so as to carry with it a considerable portion of the beard or pubescence, which contaminates the drug and increases its apparent quantity. The work of scraping begins at dawn, and must be continued till ten o'clock. During this time a workman will collect seven or eight ounces of what is called *chick.* The drug is next thrown into an earthen vessel, and covered over or drowned in linseed-oil, at the rate of two parts of oil to one of chick, so as to prevent evaporation. This is the second process of adulteration—the ryot desiring to sell the drug as much drenched with oil as possible, the retailers at the same time refusing to purchase that which is thinner than half-dried glue. One acre of well-cultivated ground will yield from 70 to 100 lb. of chick. The price of chick varies from 3 to 6 rupees a lb., so that an acre will yield from 200 to 600 rupees' worth of opium at one crop. Three pounds of chick will produce about two pounds of opium, from a third to a fifth of the weight being lost in evaporation. It now passes into the hands of the Bunniah, who prepares it and brings it to market. From 25 to 50 lb. having been collected, it is tied up in parcels in double bags of sheeting-cloth, which are suspended from the ceilings so as to avoid air and light, while the spare linseed-oil is allowed to drop through. This operation is completed in a week or ten days, but the bags are allowed to remain for a month or six weeks, during which period the last of the oil that can be separated comes away; the rest probably absorbs oxygen and becomes thicker, as in paint. This process occupies from April to June or July, when rain begins. The bags are next taken down and their contents carefully emptied into large vats, from 10 to 15 feet in diameter, and 6 or 8 inches thick. Here it is mixed together and worked up with the hands five or six hours, until it has acquired a uniform colour and consistence throughout, and become tough and capable of being formed into masses. This process is peculiar to Malwah. It is now made up into balls of from 8 to 10 oz. each, these being thrown as formed into a basket full of the chaff of the seeds-pod. It is next spread out on ground previously covered with leaves and stalks of the Poppy. Here it remains for a week or so, when it is turned over and left further to consolidate until hard enough to bear packing. .It is ready for weighing in October or November, and is then sent to market. It is next packed in chests of 150 cakes, the total cost of the drug at the place of production being about 14 rupees per chest, including all expenses. About 20,000 chests are annually sent from Malwah, at a prime cost charge of 2 lacs and 80,000 rupees."

The opium produced in Malwah differs from Bengal opium in quality and appearance as much as Turkey opium does; while the latter yields 6½ per cent of morphia, the Malwah yields 6 per cent; the Bengal half as much; but some specimen of Bareilly opium no less than 8½ per cent of morphia. Several causes combine to produce important effects in the quality of the drug. Among these, locality and the atmosphere exercise a considerable influence. The dew, it is said, has the effect of facilitating the flow of juice, and, though increasing it in quantity, renders it of a darker colour, and more liquid than otherwise. A dry state of the atmosphere, accompanied by strong winds, is a favourable condition for elaborating the juice in the capsules, and this is well known not only to the cultivators, but to the chemists, who are aware how the chemical nature of the drug is deteriorated, or otherwise altered, by the effect of soil, climate, &c., the proportions of narcotine and morphia becoming changed under certain conditions.

It is in the difference of their chemical constituents that Bengal opium differs so much from Turkey opium, the former possessing a much greater quantity of narcotine. Two kinds of opium are found in commerce, the Turkey and East Indian: the former solid, compact, and transparent, somewhat brittle, of a dark-brown colour; the latter has much less consistence, being sometimes not thicker than tar, and always ductile. In colour it is more dark, nauseous, but less bitter. It is cheaper, and not so strong as the Turkey. It is often adulterated with oil of sesamum, even cow-dung, the aqueous extract of the capsules, gum-arabic, tragacanth, aloes, and other articles.

Indian opium is acknowledged to be the best, owing to the care taken in its cultivation and preparation. Good opium is not perfectly soluble in water; when it is soluble in water it is of an inferior kind. Good opium is very inflammable, and burns with a clear flame; inferior kinds are not inflammable. Opium is fatal to plants, acting as a poison to vegetable as well as animal substances. It is still an open question whether it can be called stimulant or sedative. It is believed that the practice of taking opium in England is more on the increase than heretofore. It enters into the composition of many quack medicines. It is the most powerful ingredient in "Godfrey's cordial," and is also employed in other soothing medicines, such as "Battley's sedative liquor," "Jeremy's sedative solution," &c. It is always necessary on the new purchase of opium for medicinal purposes to ascertain previously both the presence as well as the amount of morphia, some specimens being occasionally found on analysis to be perfectly destitute of that principle. The following test is given in the new 'Edinburgh Pharmacopœia:' "A solution from 100 grs. of fine opium macerated 24 hours, in *f.* ℥ii. of water, filtered and strongly squeezed in a cloth, if treated with a cold solution of ℥*gs.* of carbonate of soda in two waters, yields a precipitate which weighs when dry at least 10 grs., and dissolved entirely in solution of oxalic acid."

The stimulant effects of opium are most apparent from small doses, which increase the energy of the mind, the frequency of the pulse, &c. These effects are succeeded by languor and lassitude. In excessive doses it proves a violent and fatal poison. By habit, the effects of opium on the body are remarkably diminished. The habitual use of this drug produces the same effects as habitual dram-drinking—big tumours, paralysis, stupidity, and general emaciation. In disease it is chiefly employed to mitigate pain, procure sleep, and to check diarrhœa and other excessive discharges. It is also used with good effect in intermittent and other fevers. Combined with calomel it is employed in cases of inflammation from local causes, such as wounds, fractures, &c. It is also employed in smallpox, dysentery, and cholera, and many other complaints. It is taken in various ways in different countries. The Chinese both smoke and swallow it. In Turkey it is chiefly taken in pills, being sometimes mixed with syrup to render it more palatable. In England the drug is administered either in its solid state, made into pills, or as a tincture in the shape of laudanum. The natives in India take it in pills, or dissolved in water. They sometimes put the seeds into sweet cakes, which are eaten by the higher ranks of Hindoos at their festivals. In Upper India an intoxicating liquor is prepared by heating the capsules of the Poppy with jaggery and water. The native practitioners consider it to be injurious in typhus fever, but they administer it in intermittents, lockjaw, and in certain stages of dysentery; externally they recommend it in conjunction with ginger, arrack, aloes, benzoin, and bdellium, in rheumatic affections. They however consider, after all, that it merely is efficacious in giving temporary relief. The oil of the seeds is almost as good as olive-oil for culinary purposes. It is also used for lamps, and is much prized by artists. At Bhopaul the oil is sold at the rate of 4-8 rupees per maund of 25 lb., or £40, 6s. a-ton. By mere exposure of the oil to the heat of the sun in shallow vessels, it is rendered perfectly colourless. The seeds are not narcotic, nor in any way deleterious, but are eaten freely by birds. It is well known that the opium trade is one of the monopolies of Government. Great quantities are annually shipped to China, although the importation is strictly prohibited by the Chinese Government. A chest contains about 140 lb. According to Mr Thornton, the production of opium in Bengal has increased within the last ten years cent per cent. But it is not to China alone that there is so large an export trade from this country; the drug is now consumed in almost every country in the world. It is sent both from Bombay and Bengal to China. Foreign opium is only admitted at a heavy duty.*—*Roxb. Royle. Bengal Dispensatory. Ainslie. Simmonds. Lindley.*

(428) **Papyrus pangorei** (*Nees*). N. O. Cyperaceæ.

Madoorkati, Beng.

Description.—Root, perennial; culms 3-6 feet, naked,

* For an excellent account of the cultivation and manufacture of opium, see Pharm. Journ., vol. xi. p. 205.

obsoletely 3-sided, smooth; leaves consisting of 2 or 3 sheaths embracing the base of the culms; umbels decompound; umbellets sub-sessile; involucre about 4-leaved, one or two longer than the umbel; spikelets alternate, many-flowered; seeds elliptically triangular. *Fl.* Aug.—Sept.—*Roxb. Fl. Ind.* i. 208. —*Wight Contrib.* p. 88.—Cyperus tegetum, *Roxb.*——Peninsula. Bengal. Common in ditches and borders of tanks.

ECONOMIC USES.—The mats so common at Calcutta, and which are used for the floors of rooms, are made from this grass. When green, they are split into three or four pieces, which on drying contract sufficiently to bring the margins in contact or to overlap each other. In this state they are woven.—*Roxb.*

(429) **Paratropia venulosa** (*Wall.*) N. O. ARALIACEÆ.

Unjala, MAL. Dain, HIND.

DESCRIPTION.—Tree; leaves digitate; leaflets 5-7, long-petioled, elliptic, shortly and suddenly pointed, quite entire, coriaceous, with the veins prominent; thyrses numerous at the end of the branches; flowers pedicelled and umbelled, numerous; berry 5-celled.—*W. & A. Prod.* i. 377.—Arabia digitata, *Roxb.*—*Rheede,* vii. *t.* 28.——Circars. Courtallum hills. Malabar.

ECONOMIC USES.—A valuable oil is procured from sections in the trunk.

(430) **Paritium tiliaceum** (*St Hil.*) N. O. MALVACEÆ.

Bola, BENG. Parootte, MAL.

DESCRIPTION.—Small tree; leaves crenulated, sometimes quite entire, roundish-cordate with a sudden acumination, 7-11 nerved, upper side glabrous, under hoary with pubescence; involucel 10-lobed, shorter than the calyx; capsule 5-celled, 5-valved; cells many-seeded; flowers large, sulphur with a blood-coloured eye. *Fl.* All the year.—*W. & A. Prod.* i. 52.—*Wight Icon. t.* 7.—Hibiscus tiliaceus, *Linn.*—*Rheede,* i. *t.* 30.——Malabar and Travancore.

ECONOMIC USES.—This species is common to both Indies. Forster states that the bark is sucked in times of scarcity when bread-fruit fails in the West Indies. It abounds in mucilage. The fibres of the inner bark are used in the South Sea Islands. They are stronger when tarred. A line when tarred and tanned broke at 62 lb., when white at 41 lb. After a hundred and sixteen days maceration their strength was much diminished. Ropes, cords, and whips are made from these fibres. Fine mats are made from them in Otaheite.—*Royle.*

(431) **Pavetta Indica** (*Linn.*) N. O. Cinchonaceæ.

Pavuttay, Tam. Paputta and Nooni-papoota, Tel. Kookoora-choora, Beng. Cancra, Hind. Malleamothe, Mal.

Description. — Shrub, 3-4 feet; calyx-tube ovate, limb 4-toothed, teeth minute, acute; corolla hypocrateriform, lobes 4 (occasionally 5), 2-3 times shorter than the tube, oval, obtuse; leaves opposite, oval-oblong, acuminated, tapering at the base, petioled; corymbs terminal and from the upper axils, their primary ramifications opposite; stamens 4 (occasionally 5); style twice the length of the corolla, glabrous; flowers white; drupe globose, crowned with the calyx, 2-celled, cells 1-seeded. *Fl.* April—May.—*W. & A. Prod.* i. 431.—*Wight Icon. t.* 148.—P. alba, *Vahl.*—Ixora Pavetta, *Roxb.*—*Rheede,* v. *t.* 10.——Coromandel. Malabar. Bengal. Chittagong. Silhet.

Medical Uses.—The bitter root has aperient qualities, and is prescribed by native doctors in visceral obstructions. The fruit is made into pickles. The leaves are used for manuring fields. Boiled in water, a fomentation is made from them for hæmorrhoid pains. The root pulverised and mixed with ginger and rice-water is given in dropsy.—*Ainslie. Rheede.*

(432) **Pavia Indica** (*Colebr.*) N. O. Sapindaceæ.

Indian Horse-Chestnut, Eng.

Description.—Large tree; leaves opposite, long-petioled; leaflets 7-9, spreading, petiolate, broad-lanceolate, serrated, sub-acuminate, somewhat glaucous above; terminal leaflets larger; flowers numerous in terminal thyrsoid, somewhat lax panicles at the extremities of the branches; calyx downy, somewhat angular, upper lip 3-toothed, under lip 2-toothed, lips erect; petals 5, unequal, oval or obovate, clawed, very downy on the back, fifth petal often wanting; colour white, the two superior and narrow ones red and yellow at the base, lateral ones blush-coloured; ovary oblong, downy.—*Colebr. MS.*—*Curtis Bot. Mag. t.* 173.——Kumaon. Himalaya.

Economic Uses.—This is a species of Æsculus, known as the Indian Horse-Chestnut, called by the hill-people *Kunour* or *Pangla*, and is found on mountains at elevations of from 8000 to 10,000 feet in Kumaon, Gurwhal, and Sirmore, also near the sources of the Ganges, and in Kunawur. It is a lofty and not less ornamental tree than the common horse-chestnut. The bulky seeds of this species contain a large proportion of fecula, though combined with some bitter principle, and is eaten in the Himalaya as those of the horse-chestnut have been in other parts of the world in times of famine. The bark of the latter, from its astringent properties, being employed as a tonic and febrifuge, it is worthy of inquiry whether the Himalayan species of Pavia is possessed of any of the same properties.—*Royle.*

It is not a little remarkable that although this handsome Æsculus was distributed by Dr Wallich in 1828, it was never noticed by any author until the appearance of Victor Jacquemont's work (*Plantæ rariores quas in India Orientali collegit V. Jacquemont,* 1844). The native country of the English horse-chestnut is still unknown, though this species of Pavia is very nearly allied to it, distinguished merely by its unarmed fruit.

Of the species under notice the wood is soft, but strong, of a white colour, veined and fine-grained, polishes well, and is used for building and cabinet purposes.—*Balfour.*

(433) **Pavonia odorata** (*Willd.*) N. O. Malvaceæ.

Peramootie, Tam. Mootoo-polagum, Tel.

Description.—Shrub, 2-3 feet; calyx 5-cleft; involucel 12-leaved, ciliated, longer than the calyx; stems viscidly hairy; leaves cordate, roundish-ovate, upper one 3-lobed, toothed, more or less hairy and viscid, lower ones sometimes entire; pedicels axillary, 1-flowered; carpels 5, 2-valved, 1-seeded, not prickly; flowers rose-coloured. *Fl.* Nearly all the year.—*W. & A. Prod.* i. 47.—*Roxb. Fl. Ind.* iii. 214.——Dindigul hills. Vendalore. Coromandel.

Medical Uses.—The root is used in infusion as a diet-drink among the Hindoos in fevers. It is thick as a quill and light-coloured.—*Wight.*

(434) **Pedalium murex** (*Linn.*) N. O. Pedaliaceæ.

Ana-neringie, Tam. Kaka-mooloo, Mal. Yea-nugapulleroo, Tel. Burra-ghokeroo, Hind. and Duk.

Description.—Small plant, 1-2 feet; calyx 5-parted, upper

segments shortest; corolla with a 3-cornered tube and 5-lobed limb, sub-labiate; stamens 4; leaves opposite, obovate, obtuse, regularly toothed, truncate, smooth; flowers yellow on short pedicels; drupe armed with sharp spines, and containing a 2-celled, 4-winged nut; cells 2-seeded; seeds arillate; flowers axillary, solitary, yellow. *Fl.* Aug.—Nov.—*Roxb. Fl. Ind.* iii. 114.—*Burm. Ind. t.* 45, *f.* 2.—*Rheede*, x. *t.* 72.——Shores of Coromandel. Cape Comorin. Bombay.

Medical Uses.—The whole plant has an odour of musk. If the leaves when fresh are stirred in water they render it mucilaginous, and this is given as a drink in gonorrhœa. The effect, however, goes off in ten or twelve hours, leaving the liquid in its former state. The seeds are administered as a decoction for the same purpose. They are diuretic, and are used in dropsy. The leafy stems are used in thickening butter-milk, to which they give a rich appearance. The plant is common about Cape Comorin on the sea-shores.—*Ainslie.*

(435) **Peganum Harmala** (*Linn.*) N. O. Zygophyllaceæ.

Description.—Herbaceous; calyx 5-partite; stamens 15, shorter than the petals, some abortive; anthers linear; style simple; stigma trigonal; leaves multifid, lobes linear; flowers terminal, white; capsule 3-celled, 3-furrowed, many-seeded. —*Dec. Prod.* i. 712.—*Dalz. Bomb. Flor.* p. 45.——Indapore. Bejapore. Punjaub.

Medical Uses.—The plant has a strong disagreeable odour and bitter taste. The seeds are stimulant, emmenagogue, and anthelmintic. Mild narcotic properties have been assigned to them.—*Pharm. of India.*

(436) **Penicillaria spicata** (*Willd.*) N. O. Graminaceæ.

Kumboo, Tam. Bujura, Beng. Pedda-gantee, Tel.

Description.—Culms erect, with roots from the lowermost joints or two, round, smooth, 3-6 feet, nearly as thick as the little finger; leaves alternate, sheathing, broad and long, mouths of the sheaths bearded; spikes terminal, cylindric, erect, 6-9 inches long; pedicels generally 2-flowered, occasionally 1-4 flowered; flowers surrounded with many woolly, hispid, purple bristles or involucres; calyx 2-flowered, one hermaphrodite, the other male, 2-valved, exterior valvelet minute, interior one nearly as long as the corolla, retuse, both awnless; corolla of the hermaphrodite flower 2-valved, of the male 1-valved; stigma 2-cleft, feathery; seed pearl-coloured, smooth. *Fl.* Sept.—Nov.—*Roxb. Fl. Ind.* i. 283.—Holcus spicatus, *Linn.*—Panicum spicatum, *Delile.*——Cultivated.

ECONOMIC USES.—This species is much cultivated over the higher lands on the coast of Coromandel. The soil it likes is one that is loose and rich; in such it yields upwards of a hundred-fold. The same ground will yield a second crop of this or some other sort of dry grain from October to January. Cattle are fond of the straw; and the grain is a very essential article of diet among the natives of the Northern Circars. The grain is called *Gantiloo* in Teloogoo.—*Roxb.*

(437) **Pentaptera Arjuna** (*Roxb.*) N. O. COMBRETACEÆ.

Cahua, HIND. Arjoon, BENG.

DESCRIPTION.—Tree, 50 feet; leaves nearly opposite, petioled, oblong, acute, glabrous, entire, bi-glandular; spikes usually tern, panicled; drupe furnished with 6-7 thick coriaceous wings; flowers small, greenish white. *Fl.* April—May.—*Roxb. Flor. Ind.* ii. 438.—Terminalia Arjuna, *W. & A. Prod.* i. 314, *ann.*——Bengal. Surat jungles.

MEDICAL USES.—The bark is in great repute among the natives as a tonic taken internally, and a vulnerary externally applied. It is sold by most druggists in the bazaars.—(*Roxb. Dr Gibson.*) It is useful in bilious affections, and as an antidote to poisons. The fruit is tonic and deobstruent. The juice of the leaves is given in ear-ache.—*Powell's Punj. Prod.*

ECONOMIC USES.—The heart-wood is dark, heavy, and strong, but splits on exposure to the sun, and is liable to the attacks of white ants.—*Powell's Punj. Prod.*

(438) **Pharbitis Nil** (*Choisy*). N. O. CONVOLVULACEÆ.

Neel kalmee, BENG.

DESCRIPTION.—Annual, twining, hairy; leaves alternate, cordate, 3-lobed, intermediate lobe dilated at the base, downy; peduncles axillary, 2-3 flowered, usually longer than the petioles; sepals ovate-lanceolate, hispid at the base; flowers pale blue, expanding in the morning and closing during the day. *Fl.* July—Sept.—Convolvulus Nil, *Linn.* —Ipomœa Nil, *Roth.*—*Roxb. Fl. Ind.* i. 501.——Common in most parts of India.

Medical Uses.—The seeds are sold in the bazaars, under the name of *Kala-dana*, as an effectual and safe cathartic. Thirty to forty grains of the seeds, previously roasted gently and pulverised, make a sufficient dose for an adult.—(*Roxb.*) Dr O'Shaughnessy remarks that in 10-grain doses it produces all the effects of jalap with certainty and speed; the taste is scarcely perceptible. Four pods sell for one rupee. We have thus a remedy of unparalleled cheapness, perfectly equal to jalap as a cathartic, superior to it in portability and flavour, occurring in all parts of India.—(*Beng. Disp.*) The seeds are black, angular, a quarter of an inch or more in length, weighing about half a grain each, of a sweetish and subsequently rather acrid taste and heavy smell. Dr G. Bidie prepared a resin from the seeds called *Pharbitisin*, which is a safe and efficient purgative. The seeds of another species of *Pharbitis* is sold in the bazaars of Bengal and the Upper Provinces by the name of *Shapussundo*. Each capsule contains three seeds of a brownish-red colour, and studded with minute hairs. When soaked in water they swell and yield a mucilage. In doses of from a scruple to half a drachm of the sun-dried powdered seed, it acts as a gentle and safe aperient. It is at the same time considered to exercise a beneficial influence, as an alterative, in skin diseases. They are probably the seeds of *Ipomœa cymosa* and *I. sepiaria*, which have their seeds covered with short brown hairs. Both species are widely diffused throughout India. These are sometimes called *Lal-dana* (Red seed), in contradistinction to *Kala-dana* (Black seed).—*Pharm. of India.*

(439) **Phaseolus Mungo** (*Linn.*) N. O. Leguminosæ.

Green Gram, Eng. Moong, Hind. Kali-moong, Kherooya, Bulat, Beng. Pucha-payaroo, Siroo-payaru, Tam. Woothooloo, Pessaloo. Tel.

Description.—Annual, nearly erect, hairy; leaves pinnately trifoliolate; leaflets broadly ovate or rhomboid, entire; peduncles at first shorter, afterwards longer than the petioles; racemes axillary; corolla papilionaceous; flowers in a kind of cylindrical head; keel twisted to the left with a short spur near the base on the left; legume horizontal, cylindrical, slender, hairy, 6-15 seeded; seeds striated; flowers greenish yellow. *Fl.* Dec.—Jan.—*W. & A. Prod.* i. 245.—*Roxb. Fl. Ind.* iii. 292.—P. Max.—*Roxb. Fl. Ind.* iii. 295.—*Rheede*, viii. *t.* 50.——Cultivated.

Economic Uses.—This is extensively cultivated by the natives, to whom the pulse is of great importance, especially in times of famine.

There are several varieties, one of which has dark-coloured seeds, and is called Black gram. Large quantities are annually exported from Madras, and shipped chiefly for Pegu, Bengal, Bombay, Mauritius, and other places.—(*Comm. Prod. Mad. Pres. Roxb.*) It is sometimes sown in alternate drills with the great millet (*Sorghum*) or spiked millet, and in rice cultivation a crop is generally taken off the same land when it has become dry. It is sown in the cold weather, and reaped in the hot season, after a period varying from seventy-five to ninety days. So large a proportion of the pulse crops does it form that these are collectively called *Payaroo*, hence the word is synonymous with our *pulse*. The black variety, *P. Max*, (Roxb.), is less esteemed, and is sown earlier, requiring more moisture. The flour of the green variety is an excellent variety for soap, leaving the skin soft and smooth, and is an invariable concomitant of the Hindoo bath.—(*W. Elliott.*) The tuberous roots of the *P. rostratus* (Wall.) are eaten by the natives.—*J. Graham.*

(440) Phaseolus Roxburghii (W. & A.) Do.

Mash-kulay, BENG. Minoomooloo, TEL. Moong Thikeree, HIND. Oalandoo, TAM.

DESCRIPTION.—Annual, diffuse; leaves pinnately trifoliolate, hairy; leaflets ovate, acuminated, slightly repand, but not lobed; peduncles erect, shorter than the petioles; flowers somewhat capitate; keel twisted to the left with a very long horn near the base on the left side; legumes very hairy, cylindrical, few-seeded, nearly erect; seeds smooth, somewhat truncated at both ends; flowers yellow. *Fl.* Dec.—Jan. —*W. & A. Prod.* i. 246.—P. radiatus, *Roxb. Fl. Ind.* iii. 296 (not Linn.)——Circars. Travancore. Malabar.

ECONOMIC USES.—There are two other varieties, with black and green seeds respectively. This is the most esteemed of all the leguminous plants, and the pulse bears the highest price. Of the meal the natives make bread for many of their religious ceremonies. Its produce is about thirty-fold. Cattle are very fond of the straw. The root is said by Dr Royle to contain a narcotic principle.—(*Roxb.*) Mixed with grain it is reckoned strengthening for horses. An average seed is the origin of the most common weights used by Hindoo goldsmiths. The unit is the *retti* or seed of the *Abrus precatorius*, from five to ten of which make a *masha*, or about 17 grains Troy.—*W. Elliott.*

(441) Phaseolus trilobus (*Ait.*) Do.

Mooganee, BENG. Pilli-pessara, TEL. Triangguli, HIND.

DESCRIPTION.—Herbaceous, procumbent, diffuse; petioles

elongated; leaves pinnately trifoliolate; leaves much shorter than the petioles, roundish and entire, 3-lobed, middle lobe obovate, narrower towards the base; peduncles elongated, ascending; flowers few, small, capitate, yellow; legume cylindrical, glabrous, or slightly hairy. *Fl.* Dec.—Jan.—*W. & A. Prod.* i. 246.—*Wight Icon. t.* 94.—*Roxb. Fl. Ind.* iii. 298.—Dolichos trilobus, *Dec.*——Common in the Deccan and Bengal.

ECONOMIC USES.—There are several varieties. The plant is cultivated for its seeds, which are eaten by the poorer classes. It affords good fodder. Ainslie states that the plant in Behar is given by the Vytians in decoction in cases of irregular fever.—*Roxb. Ainslie.*

(442) **Phœnix farinifera** (*Roxb.*) N. O. PALMACEÆ.

Chiruta-ita, TEL. Eentha, MAL. Eethie, TAM.

DESCRIPTION.—Shrub, 2-3 feet; leaves pinnate; leaflets long, narrow, pointed; spathe axillary, 1-valved; spadix erect, much ramified; branches simple, spreading; *male* flowers, calyx 3-toothed; petals 3; stamens 6; *female* flowers, petals 3; berry-black, shining. *Fl.* Jan.—Feb.—*Roxb. Fl. Ind.* iii. 785.—*Cor.* i. *t.* 74.——Sandy situations and plains in the Deccan. Travancore.

ECONOMIC USES.—The sweet pulp of the seeds of this dwarf species of date-palm is eaten by the natives. The leaflets are made into mats and the petioles into baskets. A large quantity of farinaceous substance, which is found in the small stem, is used as food in times of scarcity. In order to separate it from the numerous white fibres in which it is enclosed, the stem is split into six or eight pieces, dried, beaten in mortars, and then sifted; this is then boiled to a thick gruel. It is not so nutritive as common sago, and it has a bitter taste. A better preparation might make it more deserving of attention.—(*Roxb.*) The *Phœnix paludosa* (*Roxb.*), an elegant-looking palm, is characteristic of the Sunderbunds. It is easily recognised by its flat solitary pinnæ, and the shape of its fruit, which is sessile, on thick knobs pointing downwards, first yellow, then red, lastly black-purple, oval. The trunks of the smaller trees serve for walking-sticks, and the natives have an idea that snakes get out of the way of any person having such a staff. The larger ones serve for rafters to houses and the leaves for thatch. It is an elegant palm, and well adapted for bank scenery.—*Roxb.*

(443) Phœnix sylvestris (*Roxb.*) Do.

Wild-date, Eng. **Khajoor,** Beng. **Estchum-pannay,** Tam. **Esta,** Tel. **Seyndie,** Hind.

Description.—Height 30-40 feet; fronds 10-15 feet long; petioles compressed towards the apex with a few short spines at the base; pinnæ numerous, densely fascicled, ensiform, rigid; *male* spadix 2-3 feet long; spathe of the same length, separating into 2 valves; spikes numerous towards the apex of the peduncle, 4-6 inches long, slender, very flexuose; calyx cup-shaped, 3-toothed; petals longer than the calyx, ridged and furrowed on the inside; *female* spikes 1½ feet long, not bearing flowers throughout, the lower 4-6 inches; flowers distant; petals 3, very broad; style recurved; fruit scattered on long pendulous spikes, roundish. *Fl.* March.—*Roxb. Fl. Ind.* iii. 787.—Elate sylvestris, *Linn.*—*Rheede*, iii. 22-25.——Common all over India.

Economic Uses.—This tree yields Palm-wine. But free extraction destroys the appearance and fertility of the tree, the fruit of those that have been cut for drawing off the juice being very small. The mode of drawing off the juice is, by removing the lower leaves and their sheaths, and cutting a notch into the pith of the tree near the top, whence it issues, and is conducted by a small channel made of a bit of the Palmyra palm-leaf into a pot suspended to receive it. On the coast of Coromandel this palm-juice is either drunk fresh from the tree, or boiled down into sugar, or fermented for distillation, when it gives out a large portion of ardent spirit, commonly called *Paria-arak* on the coast of Coromandel. There, as well as in Guzerat, and especially in Bengal, the *Khajûr* is the only tree whose sap is much employed for boiling down to sugar, mixed more or less with the juice of the sugar-cane. At the age of from seven to ten years, when the trunk of the trees will be about 4 feet in height, they begin to yield juice, and continue productive for twenty or twenty-five years. It is extracted from November till February, during which period each tree is reckoned to yield from 120 to 240 pints of juice, which averages 180 pints. Every 12 pints or pounds is boiled down to one of *Goor* or *Jagari*, and 4 of this yield 1 of good powdered sugar, so that the average produce of each tree is about 7 or 8 lb. of sugar annually. This date-sugar is not so much esteemed as cane-sugar, and sells for about one-fourth less.

A further description is given in Martin's 'East Indies,' where he says, "A tree is fit for being cut when ten years old, and lasts about twenty years more, during which time, every other year, a notch is cut into the stem just under the new leaves that annually shoot from the extremity. The notches are made alternately on opposite sides of the stem. The upper cut is horizontal, the lower slopes gradually inward from a point at the bottom until it meets the upper, and a leaf at this point collects into a pot the juice that exudes. The season commences about the beginning of October, and lasts until about the end of April. After the first commencement, so long as the cut bleeds, a very thin slice is daily taken from the surface. In from two to seven days the bleeding stops, the tree is allowed an equal number of days' rest, and is then cut again, giving daily 2 seers of juice. The juice when fresh is very sweet, with somewhat the flavour of the water contained in a young cocoanut. This is slightly bitter and astringent, but at the same time has somewhat of a nauseous smell. Owing to the coolness of the season, it does not readily ferment. It is therefore collected in large pots; a little ($\frac{1}{16}$) old fermented juice is added, and it is exposed to the sun for about three hours, when the process is complete. A tree gives annually about 64 seers of juice, or bleeds about thirty-two days. No sugar is made from the juice; ½ seer or a pint of the fermented juice makes some people drunk, and few can stand double the quantity. Mats for sleeping on are made of the leaves, and are reckoned the best used in the districts, and also baskets from the leaf-stalks, &c." The latter are twisted into ropes, and employed for drawing water from wells in Bellary and other places. The natives chew the fruit in the same manner as they do the areca-nut with the betel-leaf and chunam.—*Roxb. Royle. Fib. Plants. Martin's East Indies. Simmonds.*

(444) Phyllanthus multiflorus (*Willd.*) N. O. Euphorbiaceæ.

Poola vayr puttay, Tam. Nella-pooroogoodoo, Tel. Katou niruri, Mal.

Description.—Shrubby; primary branches virgate, young shoots pubescent; floriferous branchlets angular; leaves nearly oval, obtuse, bifarious; flowers axillary, aggregated, several males and usually 1-female; *male* flowers purplish; berries 8-12 seeded, dark, purple, or black, soft and pulpy, sweet-tasted. *Fl.* Nearly all the year.—Anisonema multiflora. *R. W.*—*Wight Icon. t.* 1899.—*Roxb. Fl. Ind.* iii. 664. *Rheede,* x. *t.* 27.——Coromandel. Concans. Bengal.

Medical Uses.—A common shrub near water, climbing if it has the support of bushes. The root, which is sold in the bazaars, is about a foot long and 2 inches thick, dark outside and sweetish-tasted. It is considered alterative and attenuant, and is given in decoction, about four ounces or more twice daily. The bark is used for dyeing a reddish brown.—*Ainslie. Wight.*

(445) **Phyllanthus niruri** (*Linn.*) Do.

Kirjaneilie, MAL. Sada hajur-muni, BENG. Kilanelly, TAM. Neela-oosbireker, TEL. Bheen ounlah, DUK.

DESCRIPTION.—Annual, erect, ramous; branches herbaceous, ascending; floriferous branchlets filiform; leaves elliptic, mucronate, entire, glabrous; flowers axillary; *male* flowers minute, two or three with one longer pedicelled; *female* in each axil, terminating in three transverse anthers; capsule globose, glabrous, 3-angled, with 2 seeds in each cell; seed triangular; flowers minute, greenish. *Fl.* Nearly all the year.—*Wight Icon. t.* 1894.—*Roxb. Fl. Ind.* iii. 659.—*Rheede,* x. *t.* 15.——Peninsula. Travancore. Bengal.

MEDICAL USES.—The root, leaves, and young shoots are used medicinally as deobstruent and diuretic; the two first in powder or decoction in jaundice or bilious complaints, the latter in infusion in dysentery. The leaves, which are bitter, are a good stomachic. The fresh root is given in jaundice. Half an ounce rubbed up in a cup of milk and given morning and evening will complete the cure in a few days without any sensible operation of the medicine. The juice of the stem mixed with oil is employed in ophthalmia. The leaves and root pulverised and made into poultice with rice-water are said to lessen œdematous swelling and ulcers.—(*Roxb. Ainslie. Rheede.*) The *P. urinaria* (Linn.) is said to be powerfully diuretic, from whence its specific name.—(*Ainslie.*) The fresh leaves of the *P. simplex* (Retz) bruised and mixed with butter-milk are used by the natives to cure itch in children.—*Roxb.*

(446) **Pinus Deodara** (*Roxb.*) N. O. CONIFERÆ.

Deodar Pine, ENG.

DESCRIPTION.—Large tree, coma pyramidal, large, branches verticillate, lower ones somewhat hanging down, upper ones spreading, all pendulous at the apex; leaves spreading or pendulous at the top of the shortened branchlets, somewhat 30-fasciculately collected, shortish, straight, stiffish, somewhat quadrangular, sides slightly compressed, green, bluntishly mucronate at the apex; male aments solitary, erect, oblong, acute; antheriferous bracts stalked, ovate above, rounded and denticulate at the apex; cones solitary, erect on a short branchlet or on a 2-cleft branchlet twin, oval or oval-oblong, very obtuse, not umbilicate; scales numerous, imbricated, somewhat woody; bracts small, much shorter than the scale;

nuts obovate, narrowed at the base, shorter than the obovate-triangular wing.—*Roxb. Fl. Ind.* iii. p. 651.—*Dec. Prod.* xvi. *s. post,* p. 408.—Cedrus deodara, *Loudon* (*cum. fig.*)—Abies deodara, *Lindl.*——Himalaya.

Medical Uses.—This species of pine yields a coarse fluid kind of turpentine (*Kelon ka tel,* Hind.), esteemed by the natives as an application to ulcers and skin diseases, as well as in the treatment of leprosy. Dr Gibson regards it as very effectual in this latter disease when given in large doses. It always acts as a diaphoretic, but is found very variable in its action,—in some cases a drachm causing vomiting; in others half an ounce inducing only slight nausea.—(*Johnst. in Calc. Med. Phys. Trans.,* i. 41.) Dr Royle states that the leaves and twigs of the deodar are brought down to the plains, being much employed in native medicine.

Another species is the *P. longifolia* (Roxb.), which grows at elevations on the Himalaya from 2000 to 6000 feet. It is known by the native names *Cheersullah, Sarul,* and *Thansa.* The natives of Upper India obtain from it both tar and turpentine. The former is said to be equal to that obtained by a more refined process in Europe, and the turpentine is stated merely to require attention to render it equal to the imported article.—(*Journ. As. Soc. Beng.* ii. 249). Dr Cleghorn has furnished some valuable remarks on the manufacture of tar from this tree as well as from *P. excelsa.* He considers it fully equal to Swedish tar.—*Agri. Hort. Soc. of India,* 1865, xiv. p. i. App. p. 7.

Economic Uses.—The Deodar pine is highly valued for its timber, large quantities of which are annually felled for the railways and government purposes. Large forests of it exist on the Himalaya slopes, and especially in the Punjaub, along the banks of the Ravee, Beas, and other rivers. In the Chenab forests, too, they are plentiful. The *P. excelsa,* a tree in nowise inferior to the Deodar, grows in the same regions. The range within which the Deodar is found growing spontaneously extends from about 3000 to 9000 feet above the sea, though it rarely occurs so low as 3000 feet, and grows at a disadvantage at the highest elevation. Previous to the establishment of the Forest Conservancy, vast quantities of these valuable timber-trees were recklessly destroyed, and it has been found desirable to form plantations for fresh plants, which, in the Punjaub especially, have been carried out on a large scale. According to the Conservator's report (Feb. 1867) on the forests of the Chenab and Ravee divisions, there were only remaining of first-class deodars 17,500—viz., 12,000 in Chenab, and 5500 in the Ravee division. This diminution of the numbers formerly known to exist caused the Government to limit the number to be felled annually, and rules for this object are now strictly observed. Prices for good Deodar in the Punjaub, increasing in the case of logs under 20 feet in length, averaged from about eight annas in 1850 to one rupee per cubic foot in 1866. For the greater lengths, from 20 to 30 feet, which are very scarce, the rate of eleven annas has now risen at Lahore to Rs. 2, 8 ; at Attock the price is one rupee per cubic foot.—*Govt. Reports, July* 1866.

In Joonsar Bawur, situated between the native states under the Simla agency and the Rajah of Gurwhal's country, there are several fine Deodar forests which were inspected by Dr Brandis in 1863, and reported upon by him. He found one beautiful forest of pure Deodar, which seemed to spring up with great vigour wherever it had a chance, and thousands upon thousands of young seedlings coming up as thick as corn in a field. In the Kotee forest the Deodar growth was perfectly extraordinary. Two of the old stumps, which were of huge size, though imperfect, showed that the trees in the twenty-one years of their life had attained a diameter of timber of 12 and 13 inches respectively. In another forest, in Lokan, there were counted in one spot, in about 4 acres, between 200 and 250 first-class trees of 6 feet girth, none of them under 100 feet in height, while many must have approached 200 feet. The estimated contents of these nine forests of Joonsar Bawur were 34,000 first-class and 37,000 second-class Deodars. The above will give some idea of the resources of these forests. These are exclusive of the *P. excelsa* (*Cheel*), which also abounds there, and the *Cheer* or *P. longifolia*. In Major Pearson's report upon the localities at the head of the Jumna river he states—"It would be difficult adequately to describe the enormous seas of *Cheer* forest which line its banks. The trees must be numbered by hundreds of thousands, many of them of a huge size. The same exists on the left bank of the Tonse, but higher up the river the Cheel (*P. excelsa*) takes the place of the Cheer, but the latter may be considered the chief tree. I believe, from inquiries, that if 15,000 or 20,000 logs can be got down to the river, there would be no difficulty in sawing up a lakh of sleepers per annum in these forests."—(*Major Pearson's Report to Secy. to Govt.*, *5th Dec.* 1869.) It may be interesting to mention here that the first conifer found in Southern India (*Podocarpus*) was discovered by Major Beddome in 1870 abundant on the Tinnevelly Hills.

(447) **Piper nigrum** (*Linn.*) N. O. Piperaceæ.

Black-pepper vine, Eng. Molago-codi, Mal. Molagoo-vully, Tam. Choca, Duk. Moloovoo-kodi, Tel. Kala-mirch, Hind. Gol-murich, Beng.

Description.—Stem shrubby, climbing, rooting, round; leaves coriaceous, glabrous, pale glaucous beneath, adult ones revolute on the margins, the lower ones roundish-ovate, about equal-sided, slightly cordate or truncated at the base, 7-9 nerved, upper ones ovate-elliptic or elliptic, usually unequal-sided, acutely acuminate, 7-5 nerved; catkins hermaphrodite or female, filiform, pendulous, shortly peduncled, shorter than the leaves; berries globose, red when ripe; floriferous calycule in the hermaphrodite, 4-lobed. *Wight Icon.* 1934.—*Roxb. Fl. Ind.* i. 150.—*Rheede,* vii. *t.* 12.——Malabar forests. N. Circars.

Medical Uses.—Pepper contains an acrid soft resin, volatile oil, piperin, gum, bassorine, malic and tartaric acids, &c.; the odour being probably due to the volatile oil, and the pungent taste to the resin. The berries medicinally used are given as stimulant and stomachic, and when toasted have been employed successfully in stopping vomiting in cases of cholera. The root is used as a tonic, stimulant, and cordial. A liniment is also prepared with them of use in chronic rheumatism. The watery infusion has been of use as a gargle in relaxation of the uvula. As a seasoner of food, pepper is well known for its excellent stomachic qualities. An infusion of the seeds is given as an antidote to arsenic, and the juice of the leaves boiled in oil externally in scabies. Pepper in over-doses acts as a poison, by over-exerting the inflammation of the stomach, and its acting powerfully on the nervous system. It is known to be a poison to hogs. The distilled oil has very little acrimony. A tincture made in rectified spirit is extremely hot and fiery. Pepper has been successfully used in vertigo, and paralytic and arthritic disorders.—*Lindley. Ainslie.*

Economic Uses.—The black-pepper vine is indigenous to the forests of Malabar and Travancore. For centuries pepper has been an article of exportation to European countries from the western coast of India. It was an article of the greatest luxury to the Romans during the Empire, and is frequently alluded to by historians. Pliny states its price in the Roman market as being 4s. 9d. a-lb. in English money. Persius gives it the epithet *sacrum*, as it were a thing to set a store by, so much was it esteemed. Even in later ages, so valuable an article of commerce was it considered, that when Attila was besieging Rome in the fifth century, he particularly named among other things in the ransom for the city about 3000 lb. of pepper. Although a product of many countries in the East, that which comes from Malabar is acknowledged to be the best.

Its cultivation is very simple, and is effected by cuttings or suckers put down before the commencement of the rains in June. The soil should be rich, but if too much moisture be allowed to accumulate near the roots, the young plants are apt to rot. In three years the vine begins to bear. They are planted chiefly in hilly districts, but thrive well enough in the low country in the moist climate of Malabar. They are usually planted at the base of trees which have rough or prickly bark, such as the jack, the erythrina, cashewnut, mango-tree, and others of similar description. They will climb about 20 or 30 feet, but are purposely kept lower than that. During their growth it is requisite to remove all suckers, and the vine should be pruned, thinned, and kept clean of weeds. After the berries have been gathered they are dried on mats in the sun, turning from red to black. They must be plucked before they are quite ripe, and if too early they will spoil. White-pepper is the same fruit freed from its outer skin, the ripe berries being macerated in water for the purpose. In this latter state they are smaller, of greyish-white colour, and have a less aromatic or pungent taste. The pepper-vine is very common in the hilly districts of Travancore, especially in the Cottayam, Meenachel, and Chenganacherry districts, where at an average calculation about 5000 candies are produced annually. It is one of the Sircar monopolies.

The greatest quantity of pepper comes from Sumatra. The duty on pepper in England is 6d. per lb., the wholesale price being 4d. per lb. White-pepper varies from ninepence to one shilling per lb. It may not be irrelevant here to notice the *P. trioicum* (*Roxb.*), which both Dr Wight and Miquel consider to be the original type of the *P. nigrum*, and from which it is scarcely distinct as a species. The question will be set at rest by future botanists. The species in question was first discovered by Dr Roxburgh growing wild in the hills north of Samulcottah, where it is called in Teloogoo the *Murial-tiga*. It was growing plentifully about every valley among the hills, delighting in a moist rich soil, and well shaded by trees; the flowers appearing in September and October, and the berries ripening in March. Dr R. commenced a large plantation, and in 1789 it contained about 40,000 or 50,000 pepper-vines, occupying about 50 acres of land. The produce was great, about 1000 vines yielding from 500 to 1000 lb. of berries. He discovered that the pepper of the female vines did not ripen properly, but dropped while green, and that when dried it had not the pungency of the common pepper; whereas the pepper of those plants which had the hermaphrodite and female flowers mixed on the same ament was exceedingly pungent, and was reckoned by the merchants equal to the best Malabar pepper.—*Roxb. Simmonds. Wight. Ainslie.*

(448) **Pistia stratiotes** (*Linn.*) N. O. Pistiaceæ.

Kodda-pail, Mal. Agasatamaray, Tam. Antarei-tamara, Tel. Unter-ghungha, Duk. Toka-pana, Hind.

Description.—Stemless, floating; roots numerous, fibrous; leaves subsessile, wedge-shaped at the base, elliptic or obovate, alternated at the base, glaucous on the upper surface, radiate-veined, about 20, spreading out, central leaves smaller than the outer ones, inner ones erect, tomentose; fibres long, terminated by other plants; flowers axillary, solitary, erect, on short peduncles, white. *Fl.* April.—*Roxb. Fl. Ind.* iii. 131.—*Rheede*, xi. *t.* 32.——Tanks and ditches everywhere.

Medical Uses.—This plant is common throughout the country. Adanson affirms in his History of Senegal that the primary root is fixed strongly in the bank. It was suggested by Jacquin that perhaps the young plant may be fixed at first and break loose afterwards. The plant is cooling and demulcent, and is given in dysuria. The leaves are made into poultices and applied to hæmorrhoids. In Jamaica, according to Browne, it impregnates the water in hot dry weather with its particles to such a degree as to give rise to the bloody flux. The leaves mixed with rice and cocoa-nut milk are given in dysentery, and with rose-water and sugar in coughs and asthma. The root is laxative and emollient.—*Rheede. Ainslie.*

(449) **Plantago Isphagula** (*Roxb.*) N. O. Plantaginaceæ.

Ispagool, Hind.

Description.—Annual; stem short, if any, branches ascending, 2-3 inches long; leaves alternate, linear-lanceolate, 3-nerved, somewhat woolly, channelled towards the base, stem-clasping, 6-8 inches long; peduncles axillary, solitary, erect, slightly villous, the length of the leaves; spikes solitary, terminal; flowers numerous, imbricated, small, dull white; bracts 1-flowered, with green keel and membranaceous sides; calyx 4-leaved, with membranaceous margins; corolla 4-cleft, segments ovate, acute; capsule ovate, 2-celled; seeds solitary. *Fl.* Nov.—Jan.—*Roxb. Flor. Ind.* i. 404.——Cultivated.

Medical Uses.—From the seeds a mucilaginous drink is prepared, and often prescribed as an emollient. They are also employed by native practitioners in medicine, and are to be met with in the Indian bazaars under the name of Ispagool.—(*Roxb.*) The seeds are of a very cooling nature, and are used medicinally in catarrh, blennorhæa, and affections of the kidneys. They are also deservedly recommended in chronic diarrhœa, two teaspoonfuls being given twice a-day with a little powdered sugar-candy.—(*Ainslie.*) The seeds are convex on the outside, concave within. This medicine has been especially recommended by the late Mr Twining ('Diseases of Bengal,' i. 212) for the chronic diarrhœa of Europeans long resident in India. This remedy sometimes cures the protracted diarrhœa of European and native children when all other remedies have failed.—*Pharm. of India.*

(450) **Plumbago rosea** (*Linn.*) N. O. Plumbaginaceæ.

Rose-coloured Leadwort, Eng. Schettie codivalie or Choovonda-coduvalie, Mal. Shencodie vaylie, Tam. Yerracithra moolum, Tel. Lal-chitra, Duk. Rukto chita, Beng.

Description.—Shrubby, perennial, stems jointed, smooth,

flexuous; branches nearly bifarious; leaves alternate, ovate, waved, smooth, entire; petioles short, stem-clasping, channelled; raceme axillary and terminal, smooth; flowers bright red. *Fl.* March—July.—*Roxb. Fl. Ind.* i. 463.—*Rheede,* xii. *t.* 9.—— Peninsula. Common in gardens.

Medical Uses.—The root when bruised is acrid and stimulating; and when mixed with oil is used externally in rheumatic and paralytic affections. It is also given internally for the same complaints. In Java it is used for the purpose of blistering, exciting great inflammation, and producing less effusion than cantharides. Also a good remedy in ulcers, cutaneous diseases, rheumatism, and leprosy. The leaves made into plasters are said by the natives to be a good application to buboes and incipient abscesses.—(*Ainslie. Horsfield.*) Taken internally, it is an acrid stimulant, and in large doses acts as an acro-narcotic poison, in which character it is not unfrequently employed by the natives in Bengal. Its action is apparently directed to the uterine system, and according to Dr Allan Webb is one of the articles used among the natives for procuring abortion. The Javanese apply the root topically for the cure of toothache.—*Pharm. of India.*

(451) **Plumbago Zeylanica** (*Linn.*) Do.

Tumba-codivælie, Mal. Chitramoolum or Kodivaylie, Tam. Chitturmal, Duk. Chita, Hind. Chitra, Beng.

Description.—Perennial, shrubby; stems jointed, smooth, flexuous; branches nearly bifarious; leaves alternative, ovate, waved, smooth, entire; racemes axillary and terminal, covered with much glutinous hair; outer bract much larger than the lateral ones, glutinous; flowers pure white. *Fl.* Nearly all the year.—*Roxb. Fl. Ind.* i. 463.—*Rheede,* x. *t.* 8.——Courtallum. Travancore. Concans. Bengal.

Medical Uses.—The fresh bark bruised is made into a paste, mixed with rice-conjee and applied to buboes. It acts as a vesicatory. Wight says the natives believe that the root, reduced to powder and administered during pregnancy, will cause abortion.—(*Ainslie. Wight.*) It appears to possess the properties of the preceding species, but is milder in its operation. A tincture of the root-bark has been employed as an antiperiodic. Dr Oswald states that he has employed it in the treatment of intermittents with good effect. It acts as a powerful sudorific. The activity of both species resides in a peculiar crystalline principle known as *Plumbagin.*—(*Pharm. of India.*) The root used in combination with *Bishtali* is applied in cases of enlarged spleen, and as a tonic in dyspepsia. In the Sandwich Islands it is employed to stain the skin permanently black.—*Ag. Hort. Journ. of India.*

(452) Pogostemon Patchouli (*Pellet*). N. O. Lamiaceæ.

Cottam, Mal. Kottum, Tam. Pucha-pat or Patchouli, Beng.

Description. — Suffruticose, 2-3 feet, pubescent; stems ascending; leaves petioled, rhombo-ovate, slightly obtuse, crenato-dentate; spikes terminal and axillary, densely crowded with flowers interrupted at the base; calyx hirsute; segments lanceolate; filaments bearded; flowers white, with red stamens and yellow anthers.—*Hooker's Journ. of Bot.* i. 329.—*Benth. in Dec. Prod.* xii. 153.—*Rheede,* x. *t.* 77.——Silhet.

Economic Uses.—The true identification of this plant was long a matter of discussion among botanists, but the subject has been set at rest by Sir W. Hooker, who managed to raise the plant in the Botanic Gardens at Kew, and which flowered there in 1849. It appears to be a native of Silhet, Penang, and the Malay Peninsula; but the dried flowering-spikes and leaves of the plant, which are used, are sold in every bazaar in Hindostan. From the few scattered notices of this celebrated perfume, it would appear that it is exported in great quantities to Europe, and sold in all perfumers' shops. The odour is most powerful, more so perhaps than that derived from any other plant. In its pure state it has a kind of musty odour analogous to Lycopodium, or, as some say, smelling of "old coats." Chinese or Indian ink is scented by some admixture of it. Its introduction into Europe as a perfume was singular enough, accounted for in the following manner:—

A few years ago, real Indian shawls bore an extravagant price, and purchasers distinguished them by their odour—in fact, they were perfumed with Patchouly. The French manufacturers had for some time successfully imitated the Indian fabric, but could not impart the odour. At length they discovered the secret, and began to import this plant to perfume articles of their make, and thus palm off home-spun shawls as real Indian ones. From this origin the perfumers have brought it into use. The leaves powdered and put into muslin bags prevent cloths from being attacked by moths.

Dr Wallich states that a native friend of his told him that the leaf is largely imported by Mogul merchants; that it is used as an ingredient in tobacco for smoking, and for scenting the hair of women; and that the essential oil is in common use among the superior classes of the natives, for imparting the peculiar fragrance of the leaf to clothes. It is exported in great quantities from Penang. The Arab merchants buy it chiefly, employing it for stuffing mattresses and pillows, asserting that it is very efficacious in preventing contagion and prolonging life. For these purposes no other preparation is required, save simply drying the plant in the sun, taking care not to dry it too much, lest the leaves become too brittle for packing. In Bengal it has cost Rs. 11-8 per maund, but the price varies. It has been sold as low as Rs. 6. The drug has been exported from China to New York, and from thence to England. The volatile oil is procured by distillation. The *Sachets de Patchouli*, which are sold in the shops, consist of the herb, coarsely powdered, mixed with cotton root and folded in paper. These are placed in drawers and cupboards to drive away moth and insects. The *P. Heyneanum* (*Benth.*) is probably merely a variety, with larger spikes and more drooping in habit. This plant is figured in Wallich, *Pl. As. Res.* i. *t.* 31. J. Graham states that it is found wild in the Concans. Rheede's synonym probably is the *P. Heyneanum*, which the natives use for perfuming purposes.—*Hooker's Journ. of Bot. Pharm. Journ.* viii. 574, and ix. 282. *Wallich in Med. Phys. Soc. Trans. Plant As. Rar. Simmonds.*

(453) **Poinciana elata** (*Linn.*) N. O. LEGUMINOSÆ.

Sooncaishla, TEL. **Pade rarrayan**, TAM. **Neerangi**, CAN.

DESCRIPTION.—Arboreous, unarmed; leaflets linear, obtuse; flower-buds obovate-oblong, acute; calyx more or less pubescent or shortly villous, particularly on the inside; sepals coriaceous, equal, lanceolate, acute; æstivation valvular; petals fringed; ovary villous; legume flat-compressed, several-seeded. —*Linn. sp.* p. 554.—*Dec. Prod.* ii. 484.—*W. & A. Prod.* i. 282.——Coromandel and Malabar.

ECONOMIC USES.—This tree has been extensively and successfully used as a protection for the footings of rivers and channel banks, where it is not wanted to spread laterally and cause obstructions. It should be planted in cuttings in December. It grows quickly, and its wood may be used for basket-boats. The tree gives a good shade, and for this purpose is planted on roadsides. The leaves are much used for manuring indigo-fields in Cuddapah; and though the trees are greatly stripped for this purpose, they quickly grow again in great abundance.—*Captain Best's Report to Bomb. Govt.* 1863.

(454) **Poinciana pulcherrima** (*Linn.*) Do.

Barbadoes Flowerfence, ENG. Tsetti mandarum, MAL. Myle konney, Komri, TAM. Khurish churin, HIND. Krishna choora, BENG. Reyla, TEL.

DESCRIPTION.—Shrub, 8-10 feet, armed; sepals 5, obtuse, unequal, lower one vaulted; æstivation imbricative; leaves bipinnate; leaflets obovate-oblong, retuse or emarginate; calyx glabrous on both sides; petals 5, fringed on long claws, the upper one shaped differently from the others; racemes terminal, corymbiform; style very long; legume 2-valved, several-seeded; flowers orange, variegated with crimson. *Fl.* nearly all the year.—*W. & A. Prod.* i. 282.—*Roxb. Fl. Ind.* ii. 355.—*Rheede,* vi. *t.* i.——Peninsula. Common in gardens.

MEDICAL USES.—All parts of this plant are thought to be powerfully emmenagogue. The roots are acid and tonic, and are even said to be poisonous. A decoction of the leaves and flowers has been employed with success in fevers in the West Indies. The wood makes good charcoal. The leaves are said to be purgative, and have been used as a substitute for senna. The seeds in powder are employed as a remedy in colic pains.—*Ainslie. Lindley. Macfadyen. Browne's Hist. of Jamaica.*

(455) **Polanisia icosandra** (*W. & A.*) N. O. CAPPARIDACEÆ.

Nayavaylie or Nahi Kuddaghoo, TAM. Kat-kuddaghoo, MAL. Hoorhoorya, HIND.

DESCRIPTION.—Small plant, 2-3 feet; stem covered with viscid glandular hairs; leaves 3-5 foliolate; leaflets obovate-cuneate or oblong, pubescent, scarcely longer than the petiole; siliqua terete, striated, rough with glandular hairs, sessile, accuminated; flowers small, yellow. *Fl.* Nearly all the year.—*W. & A. Prod.* i. 22.—*Wight Icon. t.* 2.—P. viscosa, *Dec.*—Cleome icosandra, *Linn.*——Peninsula. Bengal.

MEDICAL USES.—This plant has an acrid taste, something like mustard, and is eaten by the natives among other herbs as a salad. The seeds are pungent, and are considered anthelmintic and carminative. The leaves bruised and applied to the skin act as a sinapism. The root is used as a vermifuge in the United States. The leaves boiled in ghee are applied to recent wounds, and the juice to ulcers. The seeds are occasionally given internally in fevers and diarrhœa.—(*Ainslie. Lindley.*) It is curious to observe, remarks Dr Royle, that the seeds of *P. viscosa,* as well as of *P. chelidonii,* having a considerable degree of pungency, are used by the natives as an addition to their curries in the same way that mustard is, belonging to a family to which the *Capparideæ* are most closely allied through *Cleome.*

(456) **Polyalthia cerasoides** (*Dun.*) N. O. ANONACEÆ.

Dudugu, Chilka dudugu, TEL.

DESCRIPTION.—Tree; leaves oblong or lanceolate, acute, pubescent beneath; flower-bearing shoots almost abortive,

lateral ones leafless; peduncles solitary, terminal, with one or two bracteas at their base; calycine lobes nearly as long as the corolla; petals equal, oval, oblong, thick; carpels globose, dark red, size of a cherry, on stalks nearly twice their length. *Fl.* June—Aug.—*Dec. Prod.* i. 93.—Guatteria cerasoides, *W. & A. Prod.* p. 10.—Uvaria cerasoides, *Roxb.*——Dry forests of Central India.

ECONOMIC USES.—A moderate-sized tree. The timber is whitish, close-grained, and of considerable value, much used in the central provinces and Bombay Presidency. It is used in carpentry and for naval purposes, such as boats and small spars. It is common in all the dry forests near the foot of all the mountains on the western side of the Madras Presidency and in the Salem and Godavery forests.—*Beddome Flor. Sylv. t.* 1.

(457) **Polygala crotalaroides** (*Buch.*) N. O. POLYGALACEÆ.

DESCRIPTION.—Stems branching from the base, shrubby, decumbent, hairy; leaves obovate, cuneate at the base, petioled; racemes 8-10 flowered, wings ovate-oblong; capsules sub-orbiculate, ciliate; bracts persistent, acute.—*Dec. Prod.* i. 327.—*Wall. Pl. As. Rar.*——Mussooree. Common on the Himalaya.

MEDICAL USES.—This plant was sent to Dr Royle by Major Colvin of the Bengal army, informing him that the root was employed by the hill-people as a cure in the bites of snakes. Dr Royle took occasion to remark that the above is a remarkable instance of the same properties being ascribed to plants of the same genus in widely distant parts of the world, and it is a striking illustration of the utility which may attend investigations into the medical properties of plants connected by botanical analogies. *Polygala senega*, now employed as a stimulant and diuretic, is employed in South America as a cure against the bites of venomous reptiles.—(*Royle Him. Bot.*) Both the present species, as well as another, the *P. telephoides* (Willd.), are used medicinally in catarrhal affections by the natives of the localities they respectively inhabit. —*Pharm of India.*

(458) **Polygonum barbatum** (*Linn.*) N. O. POLYGONACEÆ.

Velutta-modela-mucu, MAL. **Aat-alarie**, TAM. **Kunda-mallier**, TEL.

DESCRIPTION.—Stems several, erect, slender, smooth, 3-4 feet, joints slightly swelled; leaves lanceolar, smooth; racemes terminal, long, short peduncled; fascicles remote;

flowers rose-coloured, numerous; seeds triangular. *Fl.* Aug.—Sept.—*Roxb. Fl. Ind.* ii. 289.—*Wight Icon. t.* 1798.——Peninsula. Bengal. Malabar.

MEDICAL USES.—The leaves are used in infusion, in colic. The seeds are carminative. Cattle eat the plant greedily.—*Ainslie. Roxb.*

(459) **Pongamia glabra** (*Vent.*) N. O. LEGUMINOSÆ.

Indian Beech, ENG. Pongam, MAL. Poongu marum, TAM. Kanoogoo, TEL. Kurung, HIND. Kurunja, BENG.

DESCRIPTION.—Tree; leaves unequally pinnated; leaflets opposite, 2-3 pairs, ovate, acuminated, glabrous; racemes axillary, many-flowered, about half the length of the leaves; pedicels in pairs; vexillum with 2 callosities at the base of the limb and decurrent along the claw; legume oblong, nearly sessile, thick and somewhat woody, with a short recurved beak, tumid along both sutures; calyx cup-shaped, red; corolla papilionaceous, white. *Fl.* April—May.—*W. & A. Prod.* i. 262.—*Wight Icon. t.* 59.—Robinia mitis, *Linn.*—Dalbergia arborea, *Willd.*—*Rheede,* vi. *t.* 3.——Coromandel. Concans. Travancore. Bengal.

MEDICAL USES.—The seeds yield by expression a fixed oil, which the natives use externally in eruptive diseases.—(*Roxb.*) It holds a high place as an application in scabies, herpes, and other cutaneous diseases. Dr Gibson asserts that he knows no article of the vegetable kingdom possessed of more marked properties in such cases than the above. The oil is much used as an embrocation in rheumatism. Dr Crosse (*Journ. Agri.-Hort. Soc.*, 1858, x. pt. ii. p. 223) has made some valuable remarks on the physical characters and properties of this oil.—*Pharm. of India.*

ECONOMIC USES.—The wood, which is light, white, and firm, is used for many economical purposes. The oil is used in lamps among the poorer classes. The leaves are eaten by cattle, and are valuable as a strong manure, especially for the sugar-cane.—*Roxb.*

(460) **Portulaca oleracea** (*Linn.*) N. O. PORTULACACEÆ.

Common Purslane, ENG. Puropoo keray, Corie keeray, TAM. Karie cheera, MAL. Lonia, HIND. Buro-looniya, BENG. Pedda pail kuru, TEL.

DESCRIPTION.—Annual, herbaceous, diffuse; leaves scattered, entire, cuneiform, fleshy, axils and joints naked; flowers sessile; petals 5, small, yellow; capsule 1-celled; seeds numerous. *Fl.* Aug.—Sept.—*W. & A. Prod.* i. 356.—*Roxb. Fl. Ind.* ii. 463.—*Rheede,* x. *t.* 36.——Common everywhere.

Medical Uses.—This plant is common to both Indies, and there are varieties in Europe and America. In Jamaica it is given as a cooling medicine in fevers. Bruised and applied to the temples it allays heat, and such pains as occasion want of rest and sleep. —(*Ainslie.*) It acts as a refrigerant and alterative in scurvy and liver-diseases. The seeds are said to be used as a vermifuge, and to be useful in mucous disorders and dyspnœa. The native doctors use the plant in inflammations of the stomach, and internally in spitting of blood.—*Powell's Punj. Prod.*

(461) **Portulaca quadrifida** (*Linn.*) Do.

Passelie keeray, Tam. Cholee, Duk. Sun pail kura, Tel. Neelacheera, Mal.

Description.—Annual, diffuse, creeping; joints and axils hairy; leaves oblong, fleshy, entire, flat; flowers terminal, nearly sessile, surrounded by four leaves, small, yellow; petals 4; stamens 8-12. *Fl.* Aug.—Sept.—*W. & A. Prod.* i. 356.—*Roxb. Fl. Ind.* ii. 464.—*Rheede,* x. *t.* 31.——Peninsula.

Medical Uses.—According to Roxburgh, this species is reckoned unwholesome and apt to produce stupefaction. The fresh leaves bruised are applied externally in erysipelas, and an infusion of them as a diuretic in dysuria; also internally in hæmorrhage. Wight says that he could perceive no difference between the two varieties, except that, according to Roxburgh's statement, the flowers of the *P. quadrifida* expand at noon and continue open till sunset; but that *P. meridiana* is much used as a pot-herb, and that its flowers open at noon and shut at two.—*Wight. Roxb.*

(462) **Premna latifolia** (*Roxb.*) N. O. Verbenaceæ.

Pedda-nella-kura, Tel.

Description.—Tree; leaves round, cordate, entire, smooth; corymbs axillary and terminal; throat of corolla woolly; flowers dirty yellow; drupe size of a pea, erect, wrinkled, 4-celled.—*Roxb. Fl. Ind.* iii. 76.—*Wight Icon. t.* 869.——Coromandel.

Economic Uses.—The wood is white and firm, and is used for many economical purposes. The leaves have a strong but not disagreeable odour, and are eaten by the natives in their curries. The leaves of the *P. esculenta*, a native of Chittagong, are used medicinally by the people of that country.—*Roxb.*

(463) **Premna tomentosa** (*Willd.*) Do.

DESCRIPTION.—Small tree; branchlets, young leaves, and cymes everywhere tomentose; leaves petioled, ovate or ovate-oblong, long-acuminate, entire, venoso-rugous, stellato-pubescent on both sides, sparingly above, copiously beneath; panicles large, terminal, many-flowered, compact; flowers small, white.—*Wight Icon. t.* 1468.——Circar mountains. Travancore.

ECONOMIC USES.—A common shrub, or small tree, flowering during the hot season. The leaves have a pale yellowish-green pubescence, with which all the young parts are clothed. The wood is hard and close-grained, of a brownish-yellow colour, well fitted for ornamental purposes.—*Wight. Jury Rep. Mad. Exhib.*

(464) **Prosopis spicigera** (*Linn.*) N. O. LEGUMINOSÆ.

Parumbay, TAM. Chamee, TEL. Shumee, BENG.

DESCRIPTION.—Somewhat arboreous, armed with scattered prickles, occasionally wanting; leaves rarely simply pinnated, usually bipinnate with 1-2 pair of pinnæ; leaflets 7-10 pair, oblong, linear, obtuse, glabrous; spikes axillary, several together, elongated, filiform; legumes cylindric, filled with mealy pulp; calyx 5-toothed; petals 5, distinct; flowers small, yellow. *Fl.* Dec.—Feb.—*W. & A. Prod.* i. 271.—*Roxb. Cor.* i. *t.* 63.—Adenanthera aculeata.—*Roxb.*——Coromandel. Guzerat. Delhi.

ECONOMIC USES.—In Mysore this tree attains a large size. The timber is strong, hard, straight-grained, and easily worked. The pods contain a great quantity of mealy sweetish substance, which the natives eat.—(*Roxb. Jury Rep. Mad. Exhib.*) It is common throughout the Madras Presidency. The timber is dark red, close-grained, hard, and durable, superior to teak in strength, and is much used for building and other purposes. It is of very slow growth.—*Bedd. Flor. Sylv. t.* 56.

(465) **Psidium pomiferum** (*Linn.*) N. O. MYRTACEÆ.

Red Guava, ENG. Lal-peyara, BENG. Malacka pela, MAL. Lal-sufriam, HIND.

DESCRIPTION.—Arborescent; branchlets 4-angled; leaves opposite, quite entire, oval or oblong-lanceolate, pubescent beneath; calyx 5-cleft; petals 5; peduncles 3 or many-flowered; fruit globose; flowers white, fragrant. *Fl.* Dec.—Jan.—*W. & A. Prod.* i. 328.—*Roxb. Fl. Ind.* ii. 480.—*Rheede,* iii. *t.* 35.——Malabar. Cultivated in gardens.

MEDICAL USES.—This is a larger tree than the white guava. Many people think the fruit inferior to the latter. The fruit is somewhat astringent; this is probably improved by proper cultivation. The root and young leaves are astringent, and are esteemed useful in strengthening the stomach.—(*Don.*) During the cholera epidemic at the Mauritius a decoction of the leaves, according to M. Bouton, was frequently used for arresting the vomiting and diarrhœa.—*Bout. Med. Plants of Mauritius.*

(466) **Psidium pyriferum** (*Linn.*) Do.

White Guava, ENG. Pela, MAL. Peyara, BENG. Soopaeriam, HIND. Jam, DUK.

DESCRIPTION.—Arborescent; branchlets 4-angled; leaves opposite, elliptical, quite entire, slightly acute, marked by the prominent nerves, densely pubescent beneath; peduncles axillary; pedicels 1-flowered; fruit turbinate, crowned with the calyx; petals 5; flowers white, fragrant. *Fl.* Nov.—Dec.—*W. & A. Prod.* i. 328.—*Roxb. Fl. Ind.* ii. 480.—*Rheede,* iii. *t.* 34.——Malabar. Cultivated in gardens.

MEDICAL USES.—The bark, especially of the root, is much valued as an astringent. Dr Waitz employed it with much success in chronic diarrhœa of children. He administered it in the form of decoction, in doses of one or more teaspoonfuls three or four times daily. He also found the decoction useful as a local application in the prolapsus ani of children.—*Waitz Dis. of Child. in Hot Climates. Pharm. of India.*

ECONOMIC USES.—The white guava is the best. The pulp of the fruit is sweet, and very grateful to the palate. It is used as a dessert fruit, and preserved in sugar—and guava jelly makes an excellent conserve. The wood is hard and tough.

(467) **Psoralea corylifolia** (*Linn.*) N. O. LEGUMINOSÆ.

Kaurkoal, MAL. Karpoogum, TAM. Hakooch, BENG. Bapunga, TEL. Bawchan, DUK.

DESCRIPTION.—Herbaceous, erect, 2 feet; leaves simple, roundish-ovate, repand-toothed; racemes dense, spike-like, usually short, on long axillary solitary peduncles, pedicels much shorter than the calyx, about 3 together from each bractea; sepals 5; legume the length of the calyx, 1-seeded, indehiscent; flowers violaceous or pale flesh-coloured. *Fl.* July—Aug.—*W. & A. Prod.* i. 198.—*Roxb. Fl. Ind.* iii. 387.—*Burm. Ind. t.* 49.——Peninsula. Bengal.

USES, &c.—The seeds, which are somewhat ovate and of a dark-brown colour, have an aromatic and slightly bitter taste. The natives prescribe them as stomachic and deobstruent, and also use them in cases of leprosy and other cutaneous affections.—*Ainslie.*

(468) **Pterocarpus marsupium** (*Roxb.*) Do.

Red Sanders, ENG. Karinthagara, MAL. Vengay, TAM. Peet-shola, HIND. Yegi, TEL.

DESCRIPTION.—Tree, 40-80 feet; leaves unequally pinnated; leaflets 5-7, alternate, elliptical, usually deeply emarginate, glabrous; panicles terminal; calyx 5-cleft; corolla papilionaceous; petals long-clawed, waved or curled on the margins; stamens combined into a sheath, split down to the base on one side, and half-way down the other; legume long-stalked, surrounded by a membranaceous wing, 1 or rarely 2-seeded; flowers pale yellow. *Fl.* Aug.—Sept.—*W. & A. Prod.* i. 266. —*Roxb. Fl. Ind.* iii. 234.—*Cor.* ii. *t.* 116.—P. bilobus, *Don's Mill.* ii. 376.—*Rheede,* vi. *t.* 25.——Neilgherries. Concans. Travancore.

MEDICAL USES.—A reddish gum-resin exudes from the bark of this tree known as one of the gum *Kinos** of commerce. It becomes very brittle on hardening, and is very astringent. It is exported in considerable quantities from Malabar. Its properties are similar to those of catechu, but being milder in its operation, is better adapted for children and delicate females.—*Pharm. of India.*

ECONOMIC USES.—The wood is employed for house-building purposes, and is little inferior to teak.—(*Roxb. Ainslie. Dr Gibson.*) The timber is dark-coloured. Mr Rohde asserts it is the best timber for exposed Venetian-blinds and weather-boards. It is attacked by the *Teredo navalis* when used for ships' bottoms, and is apt to warp if sawn green.—*Bedd. Flor. Sylv. t.* 21.

The tree is singularly local in its distribution, being found only in quantity on the gravelly slopes of the rocky hills in North Arcot and Cuddapah, and the southern parts of Kurnool. It is now comparatively rare in the first of these districts. Some years ago two officers of the forest department made various attempts to raise the

* The origin of E. I. Kino was long unknown; the history of the discovery will be found in an interesting paper by Dr Royle. See Pharm. Jour. iv. 510, and v. 498.

Red Sanders in the Cuddapah district, but there was no result; the curious flat-winged seed appears to have been planted too deep. The seeds are washed down in the north-east monsoon, and are partially covered with sand in the rocky nullahs. The stem is valued for house-posts beyond any other, being impervious to white ants. The smaller portions are carved into images, &c. The leaves are the favourite food of cattle and goats, and are much in demand. The wood is extremely hard, finely grained, and of a garnet-red colour, which deepens on exposure. It is employed to dye a permanent reddish-brown colour. It communicates a deep red to alcohol and ether, but gives no tinge to water. In the cold season, large heaps of short billets (2 feet to 3 feet) or gnarled roots may be seen on the Madras beach, where it is sold by weight, and being heavy is used as dunnage. The North-West line traverses the native habitat, and the supply has been diminishing. The seigniorage in Cuddapah was raised from 1 rupee to 6 rupees per cartload, to prevent its extermination. As the value of a post is not less than 2½ rupees, and there are often 26 in a cart, the value of the cartload is often 50 rupees. Price of the roots keeps steadily at £3, 10s., sometimes £4 per ton.—(*Conservator of Forest's Report to Madras Government*, 1867.) A very large tree, affording excellent shade and timber. The latter is of a dark-brown, and dyes yellow. It cannot be used for lintels of doors, windows, &c., as it discolours the white-wash. It grows luxuriantly on the Eastern Ghauts, on the hills between Vellore and Salem, and on the Malabar and Canara Ghauts, where large quantities of the Kino it yields are collected and sent to England. The tree is very plentiful in the forests of Cuddapah and North Arcot. It is indispensable for cart-building, and eagerly sought after for that purpose. It is considered unlucky to use it for house-building. The estimated number in the Cuddapah forests is about 50,000 trees.—*Cleghorn's Forests of India.*

(469) **Pterocarpus santalinus** (*Linn.*) Do.

Red Sandal-wood, Eng. Ooruttah chundanum, Mal. Segapoo shandanum, Tam. Kuchandanum, Tel. Lalchundend, Duk. Rukhto chandun, Hind. Ruckta chandana, Beng.

Description. — Tree, 60 feet or more; leaves unequally pinnated; calyx 5-cleft; corolla papilionaceous; leaflets 3, roundish, retuse; racemes axillary, simple or branched; petals long-clawed, waved or curled on the margins; stamens triadelphous (5, 4, and 1); legume 1-seeded, slightly membranaceous, waved; flowers yellow, streaked with red.—*W. & A. Prod.* i. 266.—*Roxb. Fl. Ind.* iii. 234.——Coromandel. Cuddapah. North Arcot. Godavery forests.

Medical Uses.—The wood is dark red with black veins, close,

capable of good polish, and sinking in water. It is known in commerce as the *Red Sandal-wood*,* which is used chiefly by dyers and colour manufacturers. Also employed to colour several officinal preparations, such as the compound tincture of lavender. This deep-red colouring matter is apparently of a resinous nature. It forms beautifully-coloured precipitates with many metallic solutions. It also yields a kind of dragon's-blood. The wood powdered and mixed with oil is used for bathing and purifying the skin. Also given internally in hæmorrhages in powders ground up with milk; and externally, is mixed with honey in case of scabies. Also in certain cases of ophthalmia and sore eyes, beaten up into a paste and applied to the eyes.—*Roxb. Ainslie. Lindley.*

(470) **Pterospermum rubiginosum** (*Heyne*). N. O. Sterculiaceæ.

Kara-toveray, Tam.

Description.—Large tree; young branches covered with rusty tomentum; leaves very obliquely ovate, very unequal-sided, quite entire, acuminate, upper side covered with fugacious rusty down, at length glabrous, under side softly downy with close brown tomentum; stipules downy, with a broad concave base and 1-2 filiform teeth; peduncles axillary, 1-flowered, 2-3 times longer than the petioles, furnished at the base with a few bracts resembling the stipules; flower-bud angled, stellately downy on the outside; flowers white, sepals and petals narrow-linear, connective of the anthers produced into a terminal point; stigma obscurely 5-lobed; capsule ovate, pointed, 5-angled, downy.—*W. & A. Prod.* i. 68.—*Bedd. Flor Sylv. t.* 106.——Southern Peninsula.

Economic Uses.—This tree is common in Tinnevelly, Wynaad, the Annamullays and western forests. The timber is excellent. In Tinnevelly the wood is much used for building and other purposes. —*Beddome.*

(471) **Ptychotis ajowan** (*Dec.*) N. O. Apiaceæ.

Bishops-weed Seed, Eng. Ajwan, Hind. Womum, Tam. Boro-joan, Beng.

Description.—Annual; stem erect, dichotomous; calyx 5-toothed; leaves few, cut into numerous linear or filiform segments, the uppermost simply pinnate; umbel 7-9 rayed;

* Large quantities of Red Sandal-wood are exported from Madras, the billets being brought in from the low hills near Pulicat; in Royle's 'Materia Medica' the station is erroneously printed Paulghaut, where the tree does not occur.

involucel few-leaved; leaflets linear, entire; fruit strongly ribbed, covered with small blunt tubercles; flowers white. *Fl.* Dec.—Jan.—*W. & A. Prod.* i. 368.—*Wight Icon. t.* 566.—Ligusticum ajowan, *Flem.*—*Roxb. Fl. Ind.* ii. 91.——Cultivated all over India.

MEDICAL USES.—The seeds have an aromatic smell and a warm pungent taste; they are much used by the natives for medicinal and culinary purposes. They are small plants of the Umbelliferous order, and are to be met with in every market of India.—(*Roxb.*) The virtues of the seeds reside in a volatile oil. They are stimulant, carminative, and antispasmodic; and are of much value in atonic dyspepsia and diarrhœa. The preparation known as omum-water is a valuable carminative, useful in disguising the taste of nauseous drugs, and obviating their tendency to cause griping. The fruits of the *Ptychotis Roxburghianum* are valued by the natives as a stomachic and carminative. They partake of the properties of the former, but in aroma are undoubtedly inferior.—(*Pharm. of India.*) The wild plant is said to be poisonous. It probably contains apiol, an oily liquid used as a substitute for quinine.—*Powell's Punj. Prod.*

(472) **Pueraria tuberosa** (*Dec.*) N. O. LEGUMINOSÆ.

Daree, Goomodee, TEL.

DESCRIPTION.—Twining shrub; root tuberous, very large; leaves trifoliolate, leaflets roundish, pubescent above, beneath silky-villous; racemes simple or branched, the length of the leaves; flowers in threes; legume very hairy, linear, pointed, 2-6 seeded, much contracted between the seeds; flowers blue. *Fl.* March—April.—*W. & A. Prod.* i. 205.—*Wight Icon. t.* 412.—Hedysarum tuberosum, *Roxb. Fl. Ind.* iii. 363.——Circars. Malabar hills.

MEDICAL USES.—A rare species, according to Roxburgh; a native of valleys far up amongst the mountains. Its leaves are deciduous about the beginning of the cold season. Cataplasms are made from the large tuberous roots, used by the natives to reduce swellings in the joints.—*Roxb.*

(473) **Punica granatum** (*Linn.*) N. O. MYRTACEÆ.

Pomegranate-tree, ENG. Madalum or Magilam, TAM. Madala, MAL. Dadima, TEL. Anar, Darim, HIND. Dalim or Darim, BENG.

DESCRIPTION.—Tree, 15-20 feet; leaves opposite, oblong-lanceolate; calyx 5-cleft; petals 5; fruit globose, crowned by the tubular limb of the calyx; seeds numerous, covered with a pellucid pulp; flowers nearly sessile, scarlet. *Fl.* Nearly all the year.—*W. & A. Prod.* i. 327.—*Wight Ill.* ii. 99.—*Roxb. Fl. Ind.* ii. 499.——Cultivated.

MEDICAL USES.—The pomegranate, according to Pliny, is a native of Carthage, as its name would denote. It is now common in Barbary, France, and Southern Europe, and has become naturalised in this as well as many other countries of the East, to which it has migrated. Royle states that it may be seen growing wild in the Himalaya. The rind of the fruit and the flowers are the parts used medicinally. They are both powerfully astringent, and are employed successfully as gargles in diarrhœa and similar diseases. The pulp is sub-acid, quenching thirst, and gently laxative. The bark of the root is a remedy for tape-worm given in decoction. It sickens the stomach, but seldom fails to destroy the worm. All parts of the plant are rich in tannic acid, and act as astringents and anthelmintics. Besides the above uses, it is used as a local application for relaxed sore-throat and cancer of the uterus.—*Ainslie. Powell's Punj. Prod. Royle.*

ECONOMIC USES.—The Jews employ the fruit in their religious ceremonies. The bark was formerly employed in dyeing leather, the yellow morocco of Tunis being still tinted with an extract from it. The flowers also were used to dye cloth a light red. The tree is easily propagated by cuttings. The longevity of the tree is said to be remarkable, some at Versailles being nearly two hundred years old. There are several varieties, those with the yellow flowers being most rare.—*Don. Royle.*

(474) **Putranjiva Roxburghii** (*Wall.*) N. O. EUPHORBIACEÆ.

Wild Olive, ENG. Kuduru-juvee, TEL. Pongolam, MAL.

DESCRIPTION.—Tree; branchlets and petioles pubescent; leaves elliptic, unequal-sided at the base, serrately denticulate; glomerules of male flowers numerous; segments of male calyx densely ciliate-pubescent, sparingly puberulous at the back; ovary tawny-silky; fruit oblong-ellipsoid, clothed with thick, pale, rusty hairs; flowers small, yellowish white.—*Fl.* March—April.—*Wall. Tent. Flor. Nep.* p. 61.—*Dec. Prod.* xv. s. 2, p. 443.—*Wight Icon. t.* 1876.—Nageia Putranjiva, *Roxb.*——Coromandel mountains. Oude. Palghaut. Concans.

ECONOMIC USES.—This is an ornamental tree, and worthy of being planted in gardens. The wood is white, close-grained, and very hard. It is used for house-building and agricultural implements. The leaves are used as fodder, and the fruits are made into necklaces by the Brahmins.—*Roxb. Ainslie.*

Q

(475) **Quisqualis Indica** (*Linn.*) N. O. Combretaceæ.

Rangoon Creeper, Eng.

Description. — Shrub, with scandent branches; young branches densely pubescent; leaves opposite, ovate, quite entire, rounded or slightly cordate at the base, when young more or less villous or pubescent, afterwards almost glabrous; bracts ovate-rhomboid, acuminated, slightly hairy, particularly on the margin; spikes axillary and terminal; flowers lax, red; calycine tube slender; stamens 10, protruded, inserted into the throat of the calyx, alternately shorter; style filiform, exserted; drupe dry, 5-furrowed, acutely 5-angled; seed solitary, pendulous, 5-angled.—*Dec. Prod.* iii. 23.—*W. & A. Prod.* i. 318.—*Roxb. Fl. Ind.* ii. 426.—*Rumph. Amb.* v. *t.* 38.—*Bot. Mag.* 1820, *t.* 492.——Cultivated in gardens.

Medical Uses.—This is a native of Burmah and the Malayan Archipelago, but thrives well in most parts of India. The oval or oblong fruits are about an inch in length, pointed at either extremity, and shortly pentagonal. In the Moluccas the seeds have long been in repute as an anthelmintic. In cases of lumbrici, four or five of these seeds, bruised and given in electuary with honey or jam, suffice for the expulsion of entozoa in children.—(*Calc. Med. Phys. Trans.* vii. 488.) The shrub is known as the *Liane Vermifuge* in the Mauritius.—(*Pharm. of India.*) The Chinese use the nuts for worms. They are boiled or roasted, and the kernels or the water in which they are boiled used, and from 6 to 12 a dose, taken three times every other day.—*Dr Iver.*

R

(476) **Randia dumetorum** (*Lam.*) N. O. Cinchonaceæ.

Marukarung, Tam. Mangha, Tel. Myn, Hind.

Description.—Shrub, 6-10 feet, armed; spines opposite; leaves almost sessile, oval, cuneate at the base, when young, slightly pubescent; flowers axillary, solitary, terminal on the young shoots, on short pedicels; calyx campanulate, 5-parted; lobes oblong; corolla hirsute on the outside; tube with a ring of dense hairs inside near the base; fruit usually globose, sometimes oblong, crowned with the limb of the calyx, 2-celled, many-seeded; flowers white. *Fl.* April.—*W. & A. Prod.* i. 396.—*Wight Icon. t.* 580.—Gardenia dumetorum, *Retz.* —*Roxb. Cor.* ii. *t.* 136.——Coromandel. Mahableshwar.

Medical Uses.—The fruit is used as an emetic. The bark of the root in infusion is used in the southern provinces as a nauseating medicine.—*Roxb.* The fruit is about the size of a crab-apple. It has a peculiar sweetish sickly smell: it is very commonly used as an emetic by the poorer classes in Mysore, and is said to be safe and speedy in its action. The dose is one ripe fruit, well bruised, which may be repeated if necessary.—(*Dr Bidie in Pharm. of India.*) It is also used externally as an anodyne in rheumatism.—*Stewart's Punj. Plants.*

Economic Uses.—According to Dr Wight, the habit of this plant is extremely variable, as it grows in a poor or rich soil. The size of the fruit varies from that of a small cherry to as large as a walnut. The shrub is employed for fences in the places of its natural growth. The fruit bruised and thrown into ponds where fish are, they are soon intoxicated and seen floating. Fishermen frequently adopt this plan to catch fish; nor are the latter less wholesome to eat afterwards.—*Roxb.*

(477) **Rhinacanthus communis** (*Nees.*) N. O. Acanthaceæ.

Nagamully, Tam. Pul-colli, Peelcolue, Mal. Nargamollay, Tel. Palek-joohie, Hind. Jooi-pona, Beng.

Description.—Shrub, 4-5 feet; stem erect, green, shrubby; young shoots jointed; leaves opposite, broad lanceolate, short-petioled, a little downy below, entire; panicles corymbiform, axillary and terminal, trichotomous; peduncles and pedicels short, round, a little downy; corolla with a long slender compressed tube, under lip broad, 3-cleft, upper one erect, linear, sides reflected, apex bifid; flowers small, white. *Fl.* March—April.—*Wight Icon. t.* 464.—*Roxb. Fl. Ind.* i. 120. —Justicia nasuta, *Linn.*—*Rheede,* ix. *t.* 69.——Travancore. Mahableshwar.

MEDICAL USES.—The fresh root and leaves bruised and mixed with lime-juice are reckoned a useful remedy in ringworm and other cutaneous affections.—(*Ainslie. Roxb.*) Royle speaks of the seeds being very efficacious in ringworm.—*Illustr.* i. 298.

(478) **Rhododendron arboreum** (*Smith*). N. O. RHODORACEÆ.

DESCRIPTION.—Tree; leaves very coriaceous, lanceolate, acute, cordate at the base, or attenuated into the thick petiole, shining green above, glabrous below, silvery or rusty-pubescent; flowers densely capitate; calyx none; corolla campanulate, white, rose, or blood-coloured; ovary 7-10 celled. *Fl.* March—April.—*Dec. Prod.* vii. 720.—*Wight Ill.* ii. *t.* 140.—*Spicil.* ii. *t.* 131.——Neilgherries and other lofty mountain-ranges.

ECONOMIC USES.—The flowers have a sweetish-sour taste, and make a good sub-acid jelly. Hoffmeister notes that a snuff made from the bark of the tree is excellent. Madden says the young leaves are poisonous to cattle.—*Stewart Punj. Plants.*

(479) **Rhodomyrtus tomentosa** (*R. W.*) N. O. MYRTACEÆ.

Hill Gooseberry, ENG.

DESCRIPTION.—Small tree; branches downy; leaves opposite, entire, ovate, 3-nerved, the lateral nerves near the margin, upper side when young downy, under hoary and tomentose; peduncles 1-3 flowered, bearing two ovate bracteoles under the flower; calyx downy, 5-cleft; petals slightly downy outside; berry 3-celled; seeds compressed, forming two rows in each cell.—*W. & A. Prod.* i. 328.—Myrtus tomentosa, *Ait.*—*Dec. Prod.* iii. 240.——Neilgherries.

ECONOMIC USES.—This tree is common on every part of the Neilgherries. The fruit much resembles the gooseberry when ripe, and is very palatable. An excellent jelly is made from the berries, very similar to apple-jelly in taste and appearance. The tree equally abounds in Ceylon, Malacca, and China, in all of which places they eat and preserve the fruit.—*Wight.*

(480) **Ricinus communis** (*Linn.*) N. O. Euphorbiaceæ.

Castor-oil plant, Eng. Sittamunak or Valluk, Tam. Citavanakoo, Avanak, or Pandiavanak, Mal. Sittamindi or Amidum, Tel. Erundie, Duk. Arend, Hind. Bherenda, Beng.

Description.—Height 8-10 feet; root perennial; stem round, thick, jointed, channelled, glaucous, purplish-red colour upwards; leaves alternate, large, deeply divided into seven segments, on long, tapering, purplish stalks; spikes glaucous, springing from the divisions of the branches; the *males* from the lower part of the spike, the *females* from the upper; capsules prickly; seeds oval, shining, black dotted with grey. *Fl.* Nearly all the year.—*Roxb. Fl. Ind.* iii. 689.—*Rheede,* ii. *t.* 32.——Cultivated.

Medical Uses.—There are two varieties of the Castor-oil plant which are known respectively as *fructibus majoribus and minoribus.* The oil of the former differs from the medicinal Castor-oil in having a heavy disagreeable smell, probably owing to the seeds being toasted previous to boiling, for the purpose of extracting the oil. The colour, too, is darker, and the nature is more gross. The real Castor-oil used in medicine is from the small-seeded variety. The lamp-oil of the former, like the Castor-oil, is of a purgative nature, but chiefly employed for lamps and in horse-medicine. The mode of preparation is given in the report on the fixed vegetable oils sent to the Madras Exhibition as follows: "The seeds having been partially roasted over a charcoal fire, both to coagulate the albumen and to liquefy the oil, are then pounded and boiled in water until the oil rises to the surface. The roasting process, however, gives it a deeper red colour and an empyreumatic odour. The price of this oil varies in different parts of the country from Rs. 1-10-0 to 3-13-6 per maund of 25 lb." Castor-oil was known in very early times to the Egyptians, and is mentioned in the second book of Herodotus. The plant is supposed to be indigenous to Barbary. In hot countries it is a perennial, in cold ones an annual or biennial plant. The skin of the seeds consists of three coverings, and it was for a long time believed even by Humboldt that the embryo of the seeds was the seat of the purgative principle alone, and that if that part were removed the seeds might safely be eaten. It has now, however, been proved, that although the active principle may exist in a greater quantity in the embryo, yet that it is found more or less throughout the entire seed. The use of the oil depends in a great degree upon several circumstances, such as the mode of extraction, the maturity or otherwise of the seeds in the plant from whence they are procured, and so on. Other seeds, too, are frequently mixed with them. The application of heat was formerly resorted to in the extraction of the oil, and is still occasionally used, though quite unnecessary. The following is the process given by Ainslie for making a fine kind of Castor-oil for domestic purposes: "Take five seers of the small Castor-oil nuts and soak them for one night in cold water; next morning strain the water off and put the nuts into more water, and boil them in it for two hours, then strain off. The nuts are then to be dried in the sun for three days, after which to be well bruised in a mortar. Add to the nuts thus bruised ten measures of water, and put on to boil, stirring it all the time until all the oil appears at the top; then carefully strained off and being allowed to cool, it will be fit for use. The quantity of nuts mentioned in the above recipe should yield one bottle of oil. If cocoa-nut water be used instead of common water, the oil has a paler and finer colour."

Another way of preparing the oil is given in the report of the Juries on the fixed vegetable oils sent to the Madras Exhibition. "The fresh seeds, after having been sifted and cleaned from dust, stones, and extraneous matters, are slightly crushed between two rollers, freed by hand from husks and coloured grains, and enclosed in clean gunny. They then receive a slight pressure in an oblong mould, which gives a uniform shape and density to the packets of seed. The 'Bricks,' as they are technically called, are then placed alternately with plates of sheet-iron in the ordinary screw or hydraulic press. The oil thus procured is received in clean tin pans, and water in the proportion of a pint to a gallon of oil being added, the whole is boiled until the water has evaporated: the mucilage will be found to have subsided and encrusted at the bottom of the pan, whilst the albumen, solidified by the heat, forms a white layer between the oil and the water. Great care must be taken on removing the pan from the fire the instant the whole of the water has evaporated, which may be known by the bubbles having ceased; for if allowed to remain longer, the oil, which has hitherto been of the temperature of boiling water or 212°, *suddenly* rises to that of oil or nearly 600°, thereby heightening the colour and communicating an empyreumatic taste and odour. The oil is then filtered through blanket, flannel, or American drill, and put into cans for exportation. It is usually of a light straw colour, sometimes approaching to a greenish tinge. The cleaned seeds yield from 47 to 50 per cent of oil, worth in England from 4d. to 6d. per lb."

In France the fresh seeds are bruised and then put into a cold press. The oil thus expressed is allowed to stand some time to permit the albumen, mucilage, &c., to subside, or it is filtered to separate them more rapidly. The produce is equal to one-third of the seeds employed, and the oil possesses all its natural qualities. The oils made in France and Italy are much weaker than those procured from tropical countries. Another mode of obtaining the oil is to macerate the bruised seeds in cold alcohol, by which 6 oz. of oil are procured from every pound of the seeds. Castor-oil is soluble in pure sulphuric ether and alcohol. It also combines easily with alkaline leys, by which is formed a test of its purity. It is one of the best ways of overcoming the repulsive taste by mixing the oil with an alkaline ley, which alters the appearance of the oil, but does not destroy its purgative powers. Other ways of rendering the oil less unpleasant are by using lime-juice, orange-peel, coffee, gin, or an emulsion of the yolk of egg. Castor-oil is a mild laxative medicine, and among the Hindoos is used as a remedy in cutaneous affections externally applied. It is particularly recommended in rheumatism, lumbago, and habitual constipation, piles, and other diseases of the rectum. Alone or mixed with turpentine it is efficacious in expelling worms. Air should always be excluded to prevent rancidity, although when rancid it may be purified by calcined magnesia. The bark of the root is a powerful purgative, and when made into a ball about the size of a lime, in conjunction with chillies and tobacco-leaves, is an excellent remedy for gripes in horses. In Jamaica the oil is considered a valuable external remedy in cramps, pains arising from cold. The leaves heated and applied to the breasts, and kept on for 12 or 24 hours, will not fail to bring milk after child-birth. The same applied to the abdomen will promote the menstrual discharge. The seeds are used by the dyers to mix with colours and render them permanent. The leaves are a favourite food of some silk-worms.—*Ainslie. Simmonds. Lindley. Jury Rep. Mad. Exhib.*

(481) **Rosa Damascena** (*Miller*). N. O. Rosaceæ.

Damask Rose, Eng.

Description. — Shrubby; prickles numerous, unequal, strong, dilated at the base; leaflets 5-7, ovate, stiffish; flower-bud oblong, sepals deflexed in flower, tube elongated, often dilated at the top, sepals spreading, not inflexed; fruit ovate, pulpy; calyx and peduncles glandulosely hispid, viscous.—*Dec. Prod.* ii. 620.—*Lindl. Ros.* 62.——Cultivated at Ghazeepore.

Economic Uses.—The roses of Ghazeepore are planted formally in large fields, occupying many hundred acres of the adjacent country.

The first process which the roses undergo is that of distillation. They are put into the alembic with nearly double their weight of water. The *Goolābee pānee* (rose-water) thus obtained is poured into large shallow vessels, which are exposed uncovered to the open air during the night. The narnes, or jars, are skimmed occasionally; the essential oil floating on the surface being the precious concentration of aroma so highly prized by the worshippers of the rose. It takes 200,000 flowers to produce the weight of a rupee in atta. This small quantity, when pure and unadulterated with sandal-oil, sells upon the spot at 100 rupees (£10)—an enormous price, which, it is said, does not yield very large profits. A civilian having made the experiment, found that the rent of land producing the above-named quantity of atta, and the purchase of utensils alone, came to £5; to this sum the hire of labourers remained still to be added, to say nothing of the risk of an unproductive season.

The oil produced by the above-mentioned process is not always of the same colour, being sometimes green, sometimes bright amber, and frequently of a reddish hue. When skimmed, the produce is carefully bottled, each vessel being hermetically sealed with wax, and the bottles are then exposed to the strongest heat of the sun during several days.

Rose-water which has been skimmed is reckoned inferior to that which retains its essential oil, and is sold at Ghazeepore at a lower price; though, according to the opinion of many persons, there is scarcely, if any, perceptible difference in the quality. A seer (a full quart) of the best may be obtained for eight annas (about 1s.) Rose-water enters into almost every part of the domestic economy of the natives of India; it is used for ablutions, in medicine, and in cookery. Before the abolition of nuzzurs (presents), it made a part of the offering of persons who were not rich enough to load the trays with gifts of greater value. It is poured over the hands after meals, and at the festival of the Hoolee all the guests are profusely sprinkled with it. Europeans suffering under attacks of prickly heat find the use of rose-water a great alleviation. Natives take it internally for all sorts of complaints: they consider it to be the sovereignest thing on earth for an inward bruise, and eau-de-Cologne cannot be more popular in France than the *Goolābee pānee* in India. Rose-water also, when bottled, is exposed to the sun for a fortnight at least.—*Journ. of Asiat. Soc.* 1839.

(482) **Rostellaria procumbens** (*Nees.*) N. O. Acanthaceæ.

Nereipoottie, Tam. Nakapootta chittoo, Tel.

Description.—Shrub, 7-8 feet; stem spreading, jointed, 5-striated, often rooting at the joints; leaves linear-lanceolate, opposite, sub-sessile, entire, a little downy; spikes terminal, erect, 4-sided; flowers opposite, decussate, rose-coloured; upper divisions of calyx very minute; tube of corolla short, upper lip erect, 2-cleft, under lip broad, 3-parted; capsule 4-seeded, seeds 2 in each cell. *Fl.* Nearly all the year.—*Wight Icon. t.* 1539.—*Roxb. Fl. Ind.* i. 132.—Justicia procumbens, *Linn.*——Peninsula.

Medical Uses.—This shrub is very common on pasture-ground on the Coromandel coast. The juice of the leaves squeezed into the eyes is a remedy in ophthalmia.—*Ainslie. Roxb.*

(483) **Rubia cordifolia** (*Linn.*) N. O. Cinchonaceæ.

Bengal Madder, Eng. Manjittee or Sawil codie, Tam. Mandastie, Tel. Munjith, aroona, Beng. Poout, Mal. Munjittee, Hind.

Description.—Herbaceous; stem rough, with prickles on the angles, rarely smooth; leaves in fours, long-petioled, oblong or ovate, acute, more or less cordate, 3-7 nerved, margins, middle nerve, and petioles rough with minute prickles; calyx tube ovate-globose; panicles in the upper axils peduncled, trichotomous; bracts opposite, not forming an involucre; flowers usually 5-cleft, whitish; berries red or black.—*W. & A. Prod.* i. 442.—R. Munjista, *Roxb. Fl. Ind.* i. 374.—*Wight Icon. t.* 187.——Neilgherries. Dindigul.

Medical Uses.—An infusion made from the root is prescribed by native doctors as a grateful deobstruent drink in cases of scanty lochial discharge.—*Ainslie.*

Economic Uses.—There are varieties of this plant with glabrous, hairy, narrower or broader leaves, and disposed 8 in a whorl. The plant yields a red dye. The plant would appear to be chiefly produced in Kuchar, and the root is in great demand in the adjacent countries for dyeing coarse cloths and stuffs red: the Nepaulese barter it for rock-salt and borax. The fibres of the root are exported to Europe, but have not been used medicinally except as above related. Its use as a dye-stuff is increasing yearly, and it is well worth the attention of dyers. It is cultivated in Assam, Nepaul, Bombay, and other parts of this country. The price in the London market ranges from 20 to 30 shillings the cwt. — *Simmonds. Ainslie.*

(484) **Rungia repens** (*Nees*). N. O. Acanthaceæ.

Kadaga saleh, Tam.

Description. — Shrub, 2 feet; stems creeping, diffuse, smooth, jointed, sometimes rooting at the joints; leaves opposite, lanceolate, on short petioles, entire, acuminated; bracts in four rows, ovate, nerveless; margin broad, silvery, sub-ciliate; calyx with two minute separate bracts; spikes axillary; flowers pale rose. *Fl.* Nearly all the year.—

Wight Icon. t. 465.—*Roxb. Cor.* ii. *t.* 152.—*Fl. Ind.* i. 132.—Justicia repens, *Linn.*——Peninsula.

Medical Uses.—The leaves resemble those of the Thyme in appearance and taste; the fresh leaves, bruised and mixed with Castor-oil, are given as an application in *tinea capitis.* The whole plant dried and pulverised is given in doses of from 4 to 12 drachms in fevers and coughs, and is also considered a vermifuge. —*Ainslie.*

S

(485) **Saccharum munja** (*Roxb.*) N. O. Graminaceæ.

Munja, Hind.

Description.—Culms straight, 8-12 feet, smooth; leaves channelled, long, linear, white-nerved, hispid at the base inside; panicles large, oblong, spreading; ramifications verticilled; flowers hermaphrodite; corolla 2-valved.—*Roxb. Fl. Ind.* i. 246.——Benares.

Economic Uses.—The leaves twisted into ropes are used for Persian wheels, tying up cattle, and as tow-ropes by the boatmen at Benares. On the Indus the boatmen always use them for rigging their vessels. Their strength is very great, as proved by being used to drag their largest boats against the full force of the stream. It is not injured by the action of fresh water. The reed grows abundantly on the banks of the river. The upper leaves, about a foot or so in length, are preferred and collected; and having been made up into bundles, are so kept for use.—(*Royle.*) The natives make pens of the culms of the *S. fuscum* (Roxb.), and use them for a screen and light fences. The *S. procerum* (Roxb.) is used for the same purposes.—*Roxb.*

(486) **Saccharum officinarum** (*Linn.*) Do.

Common Sugar-cane, Eng. Karimba, Mal. Karoomboo, Tam. Cherukoo bodi, Tel. Ook, Beng. Uch, Hind.

Description.—Culm 6-12 feet; panicles terminal, spreading, erect, oblong, 1-3 feet long, of a grey colour from the large quantity of long soft hairs surrounding the flowers, ramifications alternate, very ramous, expanding; flowers hermaphrodite in pairs, one sessile the other pedicelled; calyx 2-leaved, smooth; corolla 1-valved, membranaceous, rose-coloured. *Fl.* July—Sept.—*Roxb. Fl. Ind.* i. 237.——Cultivated in most parts of India.

Economic Uses.—There is every reason to believe that sugar was manufactured from the cane in India in very early ages, and that the Greek word *Sakcharon* was employed for this identical product, and not for Tabasheer as formerly supposed. From the Arab *Sukkur*, the Persian *Shukkar*, and Sanscrit *Sarkara*, our word sugar is evidently derived. Herodotus certainly alludes to sugar in his fourth book, when he talks of "honey made by the hand of confectioners;" and he is the earliest writer who mentions it. Theophrastus talks of honey made from canes; but Dioscorides, who flourished in the reign of Nero, was the first Greek writer who used the word Sakcharon. He says, "There is a sort of concreted honey which is called sugar found upon canes in India and Arabia Felix; it is a consistence like salt, and is brittle between the teeth like salt." Pliny also speaks of sugar brought from this country. It was certainly an article of commerce at the commencement of the Christian era, though the early Greek and Roman writers seem to have been imperfectly acquainted with its origin. Its first appearance in Europe is not exactly known, though it was introduced by the Saracens into Sicily, and was known at Venice in 990 A.D. From Sicily it soon spread to all countries of the Old World.

The sugar-cane is now cultivated over most parts of India, the estimated annual produce of sugar being about a million tons. In a report upon the sugar cultivation made by desire of the E. I. Company some years ago, it was stated that the three following kinds were cultivated :—

1st, The *Kajooli*, or purple-coloured cane. This grows on dry lands in Bengal. It yields a sweet and rich juice of a darkish colour, but sparingly, and is hard to press.

2d, The *Pooree*, or light-coloured cane. This is deeper yellow when ripe. It grows on richer soil than the former, but the juice is less rich, and of a softer nature.

3d, The *Kulloor*, or white cane. This grows in moist swampy lands where the other two will not succeed. It yields a less strong sugar than the former, and has a more watery juice. It is more cultivated than the others.

According to Dr Buchanan, there are four kinds known in Mysore—namely, the *Restali*, the native sugar of Mysore, and the *Puttaputti*, from which alone the natives extract sugar, and which yields the best Jaggery. The two others are the *Maracabo* and *Cuttaycabo*.

The season of planting is soon after the commencement of the rains, in whatever districts the cane may be cultivated, the chief requisites being frequent ploughing of the soil, much manuring, careful removal of weeds; and in those varieties requiring much moisture the land must occasionally be artificially watered. Dr Roxburgh has given the following account of the cultivation of the Pooree or common yellow cane in the Rajamundry Circars :—

"The land is first well ploughed during the month of April and beginning of May. The field is then flooded from the river if there is not sufficient rain. The upper part of the cane is then cut into two lengths of one or two joints each (the lower part of the same canes are employed to make sugar from); these are placed over the wet fields, at about fifteen or eighteen inches asunder in rows, the rows about four feet from one another, and trod under the soft wet surface with the foot. In six days after the planting the field is again flooded, if there has not been rain. In about eight days more the shoots appear; the land is soon after slightly hoed and weeded. A month after the planting, some rotten chaff or other such manure is scattered about the young plants. Every ten or fifteen days, if there be not sufficient rain, the field is watered. Two months from the planting some stronger manure is strewed about the plants; and every fifteen or twenty days the field is slightly hoed, and the weeds rooted out.

"During the wet season, drains must be made to carry off the superabundant water. By August or September the cane will be from three to five feet high. In each shoot, the produce of every cutting, which may contain from three to six canes, a straight bamboo is struck into the earth, in the centre; to this the canes are tied by their leaves. In this country the leaves are never stripped from the cane, but as they wither are tied round them. This must impede the free circulation of air, which may be conceived hurtful. In January—viz., between nine and ten months from the time they were planted—the cane, when stripped of its leaves and the useless top cut off, will be about as thick as a good stout walking-cane, and from four to six feet long: they then begin to cut the cane, express the juice, and boil the sugar, which is with the natives here a very simple process,—a small mill turned by cattle squeezes the cane, and one boiler boils it."

Either a too wet or too dry season is injurious to the sugar-cane; in the former case the quantity of saccharine juice is much diminished. The crops suffer much from the depredations of wild animals, particularly elephants, wild hogs, jackals, besides caterpillars and worms. White ants are also very destructive. As a remedy against the attacks of the ants, the following recipe has been proposed:—

Assafœtida, 8 chittacks.
Mustard-seed cake, 8 seers.
Putrid fish, 4 seers.
Bruised butch-root, 2 seers; or muddur, 2 seers.

Mix the above together in a large vessel, with water sufficient to make them into the thickness of curds; then steep each slip of cane in it for half an hour before planting; and lastly, water the lines three times previous to setting the cane, by irrigating the water-course with water mixed up with bruised butch-root, or muddur if the former be not procurable.

A very effectual mode of destroying the white ant is by mixing a small quantity of arsenic with a few ounces of burned bread, pulverised flour, or oatmeal, moistened with molasses, and placing pieces of the dough thus made, each about the size of a turkey's egg, on a flat board, and covered over with a wooden bowl, in several parts of the plantations. The ants soon take possession of these, and the poison has continuous effect, for the ants which die are eaten by those which succeed them. They are said to be driven from a soil by frequently hoeing it. They are found to prevail most upon newly broken up lands.

In Central India, the penetration of the white ants into the interior of the sets, and the consequent destruction of the latter, is prevented by dipping each end into buttermilk, assafœtida, and powdered mustard-seed, mixed into a thick compound.—*Simmonds*.

There are different processes for separating the sugar from the cane-juice, in different countries. The following is the method which obtains in the East Indies: "The liquor, after being strained so as to separate the coarser feculencies, is boiled down, in a range of open boilers heated by a long flue, into a thick inspissate juice, the scum which rises during the operation being removed. When it is sufficiently evaporated, it is removed into earthern pots to cool, and in these it becomes a dark-coloured, soft, viscid mass, called *goor* or *jaggery*. Sometimes a little quicklime is added to the juice before boiling, which, by partly clarifying it, renders it capable of being formed into cakes or lumps. In general, however, if intended for subsequent clarification, the juice is merely boiled down, and sold in pots, in a granular honey-like state, to the boilers or refiners. These separate much of the molasses or uncrystallisable part of the juice, by putting the *goor* into a coarse cloth and subjecting it to pressure. The sugar, which in this state is called *shuckar* or *khand*, is further purified by boiling it with water, with the addition of an alkaline solution and a quantity of milk. When this has been continued until scum no longer rises upon the liquor, it is evaporated, and sometimes strained, and afterwards transferred to earthen pots or jars, wide at the top, but coming to a point at the bottom, which is perforated with a small hole, that, at the commencement of the operation, is stopped with the stem of a plantain-leaf. After it has been left for a few days to granulate, the holes in the pots are unstopped, and the molasses drain off into vessels placed to receive it." The sugar is rendered still purer and whiter by covering it with the moist leaves of some succulent aquatic plant,* the moisture from which drains slowly through the sugar and carries with it the dark-coloured molasses. After several days the leaves are removed, and the upper part of the sugar, which has been most purified, is taken away and dried in the sun. Fresh leaves are then added, by which another layer of sugar is whitened in like manner; and the operation is repeated until the whole mass is refined. The sugar thus prepared is called *chenee*, and is that which is commonly sent to England.

In regard to quantity and the purity of its sugar, the cane is preferred to any other plant containing saccharine juice. Six to eight lb. of the latter yield 1 lb. of raw sugar; and when properly

* *Vallisneria spiralis* and *Hydrilla verticillata* are employed by sugar-refiners for this purpose.

ripe, 16 to 20 bandy-loads of canes ought to yield a hogshead of sugar. Sugar when simply sucked from the cane is highly nutritious. In the West Indies immense quantities of the cane are consumed in this way; and it has often been remarked how singularly the condition of the negroes becomes changed during the cane harvest, when they become far more plump and healthy than they are at other seasons. The alimentary properties of sugar are much lessened by crystallisation. The common brown sugar is more nutritious than what has been refined. To persons disposed to dyspepsia and bilious habits, sugar in excess becomes more hurtful than otherwise; and, as Dr Prout observes, "the derangement or partial suspension of the power of converting the saccharine principle in man into the albuminous or oleaginous not only constitutes a formidable species of dyspepsia, but the unassimilated saccharine matter in passing through the kidneys gives occasion to the disease termed diabetes." Now in the blood of a person in perfect health scarcely any sugar exists, whereas during the disease above named it will be found abundantly in the system. Sugar, therefore, whether in the shape of fruit or in whatever form, should be entirely avoided by persons in that condition, and only taken in moderation by persons suffering from bilious habits.

Sugar when concentrated is highly antiseptic, and from a knowledge of its possessing this principle, it is frequently employed in the preservation of vegetable, animal, and medicinal substances. Dried fruits are often preserved a longer time by reason of the sugar contained in them. In cases of poisoning by copper, arsenic, or corrosive sublimate, sugar has been successfully employed as an antidote; and white sugar finely pulverised is occasionally sprinkled upon ulcers with unhealthy granulations. The Hindoos set a great value upon sugar, and in medicine it is considered by them as nutritious, pectoral, and anthelmintic.

The average annual quantity of cane-sugar imported into the markets of the civilised world at the present time may be taken at 1,500,000 tons, exclusive of what is made for consumption in the several countries where the canes grow, and this would probably amount to another million.—*Simmonds. Lindley.*

(487) Saccharum sara (*Roxb.*) Do.

Penreed Grass, ENG. Shur or saro, BENG.

DESCRIPTION.—Culms perennial, erect, 6-16 feet, smooth, very strong; lower leaves 4-8 feet long, narrow, upper ones shorter, broader, tapering from the base to a fine acumination, concave above, with hispid margin; sheaths 12-18 inches long, with a tuft of hair above their mouths on the inside; panicles dense, open when in flower, condensed when in seed;

ramification decompound, the inferior ones alternate, superior ones sub-verticilled, generally with their sharp angles armed with stiff bristles and covered with white silky hairs; flowers paired, one sessile, the other pedicelled; calyx 2-valved, clothed with long silky hairs; corolla 3-valved, fringed.—*Roxb. Fl. Ind.* i. 244.——Bengal.

Economic Uses.—Ropes made from the leaves are employed by the boatmen about Allahabad and Mirzapore as tow-lines. These ropes are reckoned very strong and durable, even when exposed to the action of water. They are first beaten to a rough fibre and then twisted into ropes. The pens made from these reeds are exported to a small amount from Madras, and are sent chiefly to Bombay.—(*Royle. Comm. Prod. Mad. Pres.*) The leaves are made into mats, and bundles of the stems are used for floating heavy timber on rivers. The stems are made into blinds, chairs, and basket-work, and are laid down on sandy roads in default of macadamising. The tops, just before flowering, are reckoned good fodder for increasing the supply of milk; and in the southern parts of the Punjaub the delicate part of the pith, in the upper part of the stem, is eaten by the poor. When burnt, its smoke is considered beneficial applied to burns and scalds.—*Stewart's Punj. Plants.*

(488) Saccharum spontaneum (*Linn.*) Do.

Thatch Grass, Eng. Belloogaddy, Tel. Kagara, Hind. Kash, Beng.

Description.—Root perennial; culms annual, erect, leafy, round; leaves sheathing, remarkably long and narrow, margins hispid; mouths of the sheaths woolly; panicles terminal, spreading, erect, 1-2 feet long, composed of verticilled, filiform, simple ramifications (except the lower verticil or two), spiked as racemes; flowers paired, one pedicelled and the other sessile; calyx 2-leaved, margins ciliate, surrounded with soft silvery hairs; corolla 1-valved, ciliate, membranaceous; stigma feathery, purple.—*Roxb. Fl. Ind.* i. 235. ——Peninsula. Bengal.

Economic Uses.—The leaves of this species make good mats for various purposes, and are also used for thatching houses. Buffaloes are fed on the grass. It grows on the banks of rivers, in hedges, and on moist uncultivated lands. The immense quantity of long bright silver-coloured wool which surrounds the base of the flowers gives this species a most conspicuous and gaudy appearance. On the banks of the Irrawady this tall grass is very abundant, and forms a striking object in the landscape.—*Roxb.*

(489) **Salicornia brachiata** (*Roxb.*) N. O. CHENOPODIACEÆ.

Quoiloo, TEL.

DESCRIPTION.—Perennial; stems erect; branches numerous, decussate; joints clubbed; spikes cylindrical; flowers greenish, conspicuous, 3-fold, opposite. *Fl.* All the year.—*Roxb. Fl. Ind.* i. 84.—*Wight Icon. t.* 738.——Coromandel. Sunderbunds.

ECONOMIC USES.—This plant grows plentifully on low wet ground, generally such as is overflowed by the spring-tides. It yields a Barilla for soap and glass. This species grows so abundantly on the coasts of India, that by incineration the plant might supply Barilla enough for the whole world. The *sejjie muttie* of the bazaars, a coarse kind of Barilla, is a mineral product, obtained from Monghir and other parts of Bengal.—(*Royle. Roxb.*) Sir W. O'Shaughnessy expresses a doubt whether Indian prepared Barilla could compete in point of cheapness with that manufactured in Europe. Another species, the *S. Indica* (Willd.), yields a similar Barilla for soap and glass. It abounds on the western coast, but is not so frequently met with in the south. It is pickled by the natives.—*Roxb.*

(490) **Salix tetrasperma** (*Roxb.*) N. O. SALICACEÆ.

DESCRIPTION.—Small tree; leaves alternate, lanceolate, entire; stipules leafy; catkins lateral, peduncled, male long, lax, and few-flowered, female cylindric, rather dense, elongated; peduncle 3-6-leaved; scales oblong, spathulate, puberulous; capsule long-pedicelled, ovoid, glabrous. *Fl.*—March—July.—*Roxb. Flor. Ind.* iii. 753.—*Dec. Prod.* xvi. s. 2. p. 192.—S. ichnostachya, *R. W.*—*Wight Icon. t.* 1953.—*Roxb. Cor.* i. *t.* 97.——Rivulets on the Ghauts and similar places in the Peninsula. Neilgherries. Khasia hills. Oude.

MEDICAL USES.—The bark is stated to be valuable as a febrifuge.—(*Dalz. Bomb. Flor.*) Under the Hindustani names of *Khilaf* and *Bed-i-musk* is included *Salix caprea* (Linn.), the flowers of which yield, on distillation, an aromatic water which has valuable stimulant properties assigned to it, and is held in high repute in a variety of diseases. The ashes of the wood are also prescribed in hæmoptysis.—*Journ. Agri.-Hort. Soc. Punj.* Feb. 1852, p. 161.

(491) **Salsola Indica** (*Willd.*) N. O. CHENOPODIACEÆ.

Yella-kura, TEL.

DESCRIPTION.—Stems perennial, erect, branching out into

many diffuse, alternate ramifications; leaves scattered round the branchlets, erect, approximate, sessile, linear, semi-cylindric, coloured in the older plants; spikes terminal, erect, compound or panicled, leafy; flowers minute, greenish, aggregate in the axils of the floral leaves; calyx 5-cleft; segments concave within, with a slightly membranaceous margin. *Fl.* Nearly all the year.—*Roxb. Fl. Ind.* ii. 62.—*Wight Icon. t.* 1797.——Coast of Coromandel. Salsette. Sunderbunds.

ECONOMIC USES.—The leaves are eaten by the natives where the plant grows, and considered very wholesome. This species is found in moist situations on the sea-coast.—(*Roxb.*) An impure soda is described by Irvine (*Mat. Med. of Patna*), under the name of *Kharsuji*, imported from Scinde, employed in the manufacture of soap and glass, and applied locally to tumours with the view of causing their resolution. This is the plant named as yielding this. —*Pharm. of India.*

(492) **Salsola nudiflora** (*Willd*). Do.

Rawa-kada, TEL.

DESCRIPTION.—Stems perennial, many, spreading close upon the ground, and often rooting; extremities of the branches ascending, young parts smooth and coloured reddish; leaves alternate, sessile, linear, fleshy; spikes terminal, erect, very long, compound, leafless; flowers very small, greenish, numerous, fascicled. *Fl.* Nearly all the year.—*Roxb. Fl. Ind.* ii. 60.——Shores of Coromandel. Sunderbunds. Travancore.

ECONOMIC USES.—This species yields a kind of Barilla used for making soap and glass. It is common in salt barren land near the sea. The natives gather it for fuel, but do not appear to eat it, from its very saline taste.—*Roxb.*

(493) **Salvadora Persica** (*Linn.*) N. O. SALVADORACEÆ.

Ooghai, TAM. Ghoonia, Pedda-warago-wenki, TEL.

DESCRIPTION.—Tree, 15-20 feet; bark very scabrous; branches numerous, spreading, pendulous at their extremities; leaves opposite, petioled, oval or oblong, entire, very smooth, shining on both surfaces, veinless; panicles terminal, and from the exterior axils; flowers small, numerous, greenish yellow;

berry minute, smooth, red, juicy, 1-seeded; calyx 4-toothed, corolla 1-petalled. *Fl.* Nearly all the year.—*Roxb. Fl. Ind.* i. 389.—*Cor.* i. 26—S. Indica, *R. W.*—*Wight Icon. t.* 161.—Rivina paniculata, *Linn.*——Circars, near the sea. Both Concans.

Medical Uses.—This is not a common tree. The bark is recommended by the Vytians in decoction in cases of low fevers, and as a tonic and stimulant in amenorrhœa. The bark of the root, which is very acrid, when fresh bruised acts as a vesicatory. The berries are aromatic, and taste like garden-cress. It grows equally well in any soil, and produces flower and fruit all the year round.—*Roxb. Ainslie.*

In Dr Imlach's Report on snake-bites in Scinde (*Bombay Med. Trans.* iii. N. S. p. 80), several cases are mentioned in which the fruit of this tree was administered internally with good effect. It is likewise said to be a favourite purgative. Roxburgh considered that the tree promised to be valuable as a medicinal agent. The *S. oleoides* (Decaisne in Jacq. Voy. Bot. *t.* 144) partakes, though in a less degree, of the properties of this species. It is known by the name of *Miswak* or tooth-brush tree, from the fact of the younger branches being in common use among the natives of Northern India for the purpose of cleansing and strengthening the gums.—(*Pharm. of India.*) The fruit is sweetish, and much eaten. Aphrodisiac qualities have been attributed to it. It is often dried and kept like currants. Pieces of the wood are carried to long distances for sale, as it is much favoured for tooth-sticks by the Mohammedans, who use theirs for numbers of times, the Hindoos only once. The employment of it is said to be good for digestion, and speedily to cure bleeding gums.—(*Stewart's Punj. Plants.*) In Scinde and the northern parts of India it grows to be a very large tree. Dr Royle considered it to be the mustard-tree of Scripture, and Sir Emerson Tennent was of the same opinion. He says the *Salvadora Persica* was the mustard-tree alluded to by our Saviour. The Greek term *Sinapis* (Matt. xiii. 31) is the name given to mustard, for which the Arabic equivalent is Chandul or Khandul. The same name is applied at the present day to a tree which grows freely in the neighbourhood of Jerusalem, and generally throughout Palestine, the seeds of which have an aromatic pungency, which enables them to be used instead of the ordinary mustard (*Sinapis nigra*); besides which, its structure presents all the essentials to sustain the illustrations sought to be established in the parable, some of which are wanting or dubious in the common plant. It has a very small seed; it may be sown in a garden; it grows into a "herb," and eventually becomes a "tree," so that the birds of the air come and lodge in the branches thereof. The Khandul grows abundantly in Syria, Egypt, Arabia, on the Indus, and throughout the north-west of India.—*Tennent's Ceylon*, i. 51, note.

(494) **Salvia plebeia** (*R. Br.*) N. O. Labiatæ.

Description.—Stem herbaceous, erect, branched, pubescent; leaves petioled, oblong, wrinkled; verticels lax, about 6-flowered, racemose; racemes paniculate; calyx campanulate, upper lip quite entire, teeth of the lower lip obtuse; corolla scarcely longer than the calyx; flowers purple. *Fl.* Nov.—Jan.—*R. Br. Prod.* p. 501.—*Dalz. Bomb. Flor.* p. 209.—S. brachiata, *Roxb.*——Hindostan. Oude. Silhet. Bengal. Kandalla.

Medical Uses.—The seeds are officinal. They are much used by the Hindoos as mustard, and in gonorrhœa and menorrhagia. The stalks of another species, the *Salvia lanuta* (Roxb.), are peeled and eaten, and the roots used in coughs, the seeds as an emetic, and the leaves applied in cases of guinea-worm. The latter are also made into poultices and applied to wounds. The seeds are administered internally for hæmorrhoids, and at Lahore in colic and dysentery, and externally to boils.—*Stewart's Punj. Plants.*

(495) **Samadera Indica** (*Gærtn.*) N. O. Simarubaceæ.

Karinghota, Mal.

Description.—Tree, 30-35 feet; leaves alternate, oblong, elliptical, very long; calycine segments 4-5 each, marked with an external gland; petals 5, longer than the calyx; flower-bearing peduncles longer than the leaves, pendulous, compressed, axillary or terminal, divided at the apex into a small umbel; drupe with a thick pericarp; flowers yellowish white. *Fl.* Dec.—Feb.—*W. & A. Prod.* i. 151.—Niota tetrapetala, *Wall.* (not *Lam.*)—*Rheede*, vi. *t.* 18.——Concans. Balghotty, in Cochin. Travancore.

Medical Uses.—This tree grows abundantly in Travancore and Cochin, and is propagated easily from seeds. The bark has febrifugal properties, and is used by the natives for this purpose. An oil is extracted from the kernels of the fruit which is extensively used in rheumatism on the western coast, and is procurable in the bazaars. In erysipelas the leaves bruised are externally applied.—(*Rheede. Pers. Obs.*) The seeds are strung together and tied round children's necks as a preventive of asthma and affections of the chest. The following directions for the use of *Karinghota* bark are given in the 'Technologist:' *Decoction as a febrifuge*—Take 6 oz. of rasped wood, three pints of water, boil over a slow fire until reduced to one pint, and strain. *Dose*—Two ounces to be taken three times a-day.

It may be given in all stages of fever. When taken during a febrile paroxysm, it should be given in three-ounce doses. It abates the severity of the symptoms, shortens the paroxysm, and hastens the cure. Sometimes nausea and vomiting occur after taking the dose. This will rather favour the recovery of the patient than otherwise. In such cases the dose should be lessened to one ounce, and repeated at greater intervals, or it may be given during the paroxysm only. In recent cases the fever is generally speedily subdued by the decoction.

An infusion of the wood may at all times be used as a general tonic, and is a perfect substitute for the infusion of Quassia in the following form: Take two drachms of the rasped wood, one pint of boiling water; infuse for two hours in a covered vessel, and strain. *Dose*—One ounce as a bitter tonic to improve the appetite and invigorate the system. It is of a light lemon colour, and a good vehicle for the administration of Iron, Iodide of Potash, &c.—(*Technologist.*) Among plants of this order may be mentioned here the *Brucea* (Nima) *Quassioides* (Ham.), which grows in Himalaya, the root of which, according to Royle (*Illustr.* p. 158), is as bitter as the Quassia of the West Indies. The bark is imported into Bengal from the hills, and is sold under the name of *Bharangi.* It partakes of the bitterness of the root.—*Pharm. of India.*

ECONOMIC USES.—The wood is light but durable, and is used for shoes and other articles. It takes a good polish.

(496) **Sanseviera Zeylanica** (*Willd.*) N. O. LILIACEÆ.

Bowstring Hemp, ENG. **Marool,** TAM. **Moorgalie,** DUK. **Chaga, Sága,** TEL.

DESCRIPTION. — Stemless; roots perennial; leaves radical, exterior ones shorter, spreading, and more broad, interior ones nearly erect, 1-4 feet long, semi-cylindric, grooved on the upper side, sharply acuminated at the apex, somewhat striated, smooth; scapes rising from the centre of the leaves, 1-2 feet long, erect, with four or five alternate sheaths between the raceme or flower-bearing part and the base; racemes erect, about as long as, or longer than, the scape below the flowers, striated, smooth; flowers greenish white, erect, fascicled, 4-6 together; pedicels short, 1-flowered; corolla 1-petalled, funnel-shaped; calyx none. *Fl.* Aug.—Sept.—*Roxb. Fl. Ind.* ii. 161. —*Cor.* ii. 184.—S. Roxburghiana, *Schult.*——Bengal. Peninsula. Dindigul hills.

ECONOMIC USES.—This species is probably not different from the *S. Roxburghiana,* though some botanists have separated the two species. The present one is well known for the excellent fibres it yields. It is easily propagated by cuttings, and thrives in almost any soil, throwing up abundance of fresh root-shoots, and thus extending itself in every direction.

The method of preparing the fibres usually adopted by the natives is to steep the leaves, which are 3 or 4 feet long, in water for several days, in order that the pulpy part may rot. The fibres are then easily separated, but putting them in water is apt to discolour them. In other cases they are first beaten to separate the fibres more easily, and placed on a board and scraped with a piece of rough stick or iron till all the pulp is removed. For every 40 lb. of the fresh leaves, Dr Roxburgh obtained about 11 lb. of the clean fibre; and he reckoned that two crops might be easily calculated upon where they are planted for the sake of these fibres. In 1831 the plant was discovered in the neighbourhood of Cuttack by the Rev. Mr Garrow, and its fine qualities brought to light, as will be seen by the following notice quoted by Dr Royle: "In the course of a short time afterwards he discovered a short species of Aloe, growing wildly and profusely in all the moist woods of the neighbourhood, which the natives called *Moorgabbee*. On experiment, this plant produced a most beautiful fibre, as soft and as fine as human hair, but possessing, notwithstanding, extraordinary strength and tenacity. He derived a great quantity of flax from this plant, which, when portioned off in hanks, bore a strict resemblance to raw silk; indeed, side by side, the difference could not be distinguished. It was this article that first induced the writer to turn his attention to the manufacture of cloth. He engaged two native weavers to construct a narrow loom for this purpose. They at first found some difficulty in the undertaking, but in the course of four or five days they produced as fine a piece of cloth as was ever beheld."

The Moorva fibre is very soft, silky, and pliant, especially if well prepared, more resembling that of the pine-apple than any other. The fibres are used for ropes, twine, thread, bowstrings, and cord. They are considered valuable for the manufacture of paper, and are used for that purpose at Trichinopoly. Regarding the comparative strength of the Moorva fibre, Dr Roxburgh had a line 4 feet long, which bore a weight of 120 lb., a cord of similar size, made of Russian hemp, breaking at 105 lb. In other experiments the fibre in an untwisted state bore 280 lb., and Agave fibre only 270 lb.

This is certainly a plant deserving every attention for the sake of its fibre. Its easy propagation, its general distribution over the country, the simple process of preparing the fibre, and the variety of uses to which it can be applied, whether for rope, paper, cloth, or other purpose, render it valuable in every way.—*Royle Fib. Plants. Roxb. Ainslie.*

(497) **Santalum album.** (*Linn.*) N. O. SANTALACEÆ.

Sandal-wood, ENG. Chandanum, TAM. Tsjandana-marum, MAL. Chandanum, TEL. Sundel, DUK. Chundoie, HIND.

DESCRIPTION.—Tree, 20-25 feet; branches numerous, much dividing and spreading, and forming nearly spherical heads; leaves opposite on short petioles, oblong, smooth, entire, glaucous below; thyrse axillary and terminal, shorter than the leaves; pedicels opposite, lower pair of each thyrse usually 3-flowered; flowers numerous, small, first straw-coloured, afterwards deep ferruginous purple, inodorous; calyx campanulate, 4-cleft; corolla none; berry round, smooth, black when ripe, succulent, crowned with the calyx, 1-celled; nut solitary. *Fl.* Nearly all the year.—*Roxb. Fl. Ind.* i. 442.—— Border of Wynaad. Peninsula. Mysore.

MEDICAL USES.—The wood ground up with water to the consistence of paste is a common application among the natives to erysipelatous and local inflammations, to the temples in fevers, and to allay heat in cutaneous diseases. In remittent fevers it acts as a diaphoretic. It yields by distillation a pale-yellow volatile oil, which is stated to be a remedy in gonorrhœa, and from the use of which the most satisfactory results have arisen. It has been reckoned superior to Copaiba and Cubebs, and has succeeded where these latter have failed.*—*Pharm. of India.*

ECONOMIC USES.—This tree yields the Sandal-wood of commerce, which is usually cut into billets and disposed of in that state. It is burnt to perfume temples and dwelling-houses. Reduced to powder, it is taken in cocoa-nut water, and the natives use it in bathing to cool the body. The Mohammedans express a precious oil from the moist yellow part of the wood, which they value as a perfume. The same tree yields both the white and yellow Sandal-wood, the last being the inner part of the tree, and is very hard and fragrant, especially near the root. Large quantities of Sandal-wood oil are annually exported from Madras.—*J. Graham, Comm. Prod. Mad. Pres.*

In Mysore an experimental attempt has been made to cultivate the Sandal-wood tree. The revenue derived from its sale forms the principal item of forest revenue in Mysore. In 1866-67, 74,598 rupees were realised, the value of stock being 156,321 rupees. The natural habitats of the tree, it is said, have been reduced with the spread of cultivation. An increased production of the tree, either by cultivation or by aiding its natural growth and regeneration,

* For the mode of extraction of this oil, see Appendix F. For the growth and management of the Sandal-wood tree, see Buchanan's Jour., *passim*.

would therefore be most useful, and would produce a largely-expanding revenue. The tree is said to attain the age of maturity in about twenty-five years.—(*Govt. Letter to Comm. of Mysore*, Sept. 1867.) Though found all over Mysore, it grows very unequally in different parts of the country. The tree attains its greatest bulk and height in talooks with a moderately heavy rainfall, but the perfume of the wood grown in such localities is not so strong as of that grown in more arid spots, especially where the soil is red and stony. It will thrive among rocks where the soil is good; and trees in such places, though small, are generally fuller of oil. The bark and sapwood have no smell, but the heartwood and roots are highly scented, and rich in oil. The heartwood is hard and heavy. The best parts are used for carving boxes, album-covers, desks, and other useful and ornamental articles. The roots (which are richest in oil) and chips go to the still; while Hindoos who can afford it, show their wealth and respect for their departed relatives by adding sticks of Sandal-wood to the funeral pyre. The wood, either in powder or rubbed up into a paste, is used by all Brahmins in the pigments used in their distinguishing caste-marks. The oil forms the basis of many scents, and is sometimes used for disguising with its scent articles which, being really carved from common wood, are passed off as if made from the true Sandal-wood. The greatest portion of the wood sold yearly in Mysore goes to Bombay.—(*Van Someren's Report on Mysore Forests*, 1869-70.) A fine quality is said to grow at the foot of the Annamullays. A large revenue from the sale of the wood from the forests of South Canara and others on the western coast is realised; this amounted to 3½ lakhs in eight years. Great attention is here paid to the preparation and classification of the billets and roots, and also the distillation of the oil from the chips, which operation is carried on in South Canara by Mr Cadell. Reproduction of the tree by planting is attended with great difficulty. —*Conservator's Report to Mad. Govt.* 1867.

(498) **Sapindus detergens** (*Roxb.*) N. O. SAPINDACEÆ.

Reetha, HIND. and BENG.

DESCRIPTION.—Tree, 20 feet; bark smooth, ash-coloured; leaves alternate, about the ends of the branchlets alternately pinnate; leaflets 4-6 pairs, obliquely lanceolate, oblong, smooth on both sides; petioles flexuose, smooth; panicles terminal, and from the exterior axils, diffuse, with compound ramifications; calyx 5-cleft; petals 5, equal, regular; drupes solitary, 1-celled, sub-globular, very smooth, yellow, with a large margin round the base on the outside; flowers small, white. *Fl.* March—April.—*Roxb. Fl. Ind.* ii. 280.——Bengal.

ECONOMIC USES. — The Hindoos use the pulp of the fruit for washing linen. Several of the species are used for the same purpose instead of soap, owing to the presence of the vegetable principle called *saponine*. The root and bark, too, of many species are said to be saponaceous.—*Roxb. Royle.*

(499) **Sapindus emarginatus** (*Vahl*). Do.

Soapnut-tree, ENG. Poovandie or ponnanga, TAM. Ritah, DUK. Konkoodoo, TEL. Buro-reetha, BENG. Rarak, MAL. Aratavala, CAN.

DESCRIPTION.—Tree, middling size; petiole pubescent; leaves abruptly pinnate; leaflets 2-3 pairs, oblong, retuse or emarginate, entire, upper side glabrous, under very downy; racemes in terminal panicles; calyx segments 5, oblong; petals 5, oval, outside densely hairy, margin very woolly, with a small woolly appendage on each side about the middle, inside nearly glabrous, or with a few scattered hairs about the middle; ovary densely hairy; fruit 1-4, generally 3-lobed, lobes very hairy on the inside at the insertion of the seeds; flowers small, white. *Fl.* Oct.—Nov.—*W. & A. Prod.* i. 111.—*Wight Ill.* i. *t.* 51.—*Roxb. Fl. Ind.* ii. 279.——Bengal. Northern Circars. Mysore. Bombay. Annamullays.

MEDIÇAL USES.—The capsule is considered by the Vytians to be expectorant, and is prescribed in humoral asthma. It also has a detergent quality when bruised, forming suds if agitated in hot water. The natives use this as a soap for washing the hair, silk, &c. The seeds are said to be applied to the mouth of persons in epileptic fits with success. Dr Wight had never seen the tree in the Peninsula, and remarks that it is only distinguishable from *S. detergens* (Roxb.) by the leaflets being glabrous on both sides, and from four to six pair.—*Ainslie. Wight.*

ECONOMIC USES.—The wood is yellow, hard, and prettily grained, and is used for ordinary work, but not very durable.—(*Beddome Flor. Sylv. t.* 154.) The wood of the *S. rubiginosus* (Roxb.) is useful for various purposes, being strong and durable. It is of a chocolate colour towards the middle. The leaves resemble those of the ash, and are very soft to the touch.—*J. Graham. Roxb.*

(500) **Sarcostemma brevistigma** (*R. W.*) N. O. ASCLEPIACEÆ.

Tiga tshomoodoo, TEL. Bramee, Shomluta, BENG.

DESCRIPTION.—Twining; leafless; umbels terminal or terminating the short lateral branches; calyx and pedicels glabrous; outer stamineous corona 10-plicate, 10-crenate; leaflets of inner corona gibbous on the back, equal to the gynostegium; flowers small, white. *Fl.* June—Aug.—*W. & A. Contrib.* p. 59.—*Wight Icon. t.* 595.—Asclepias acida, *Roxb. Fl. Ind.* ii. 31.——Coromandel.

Economic Uses.—Bundles of this plant put into the trough of the well from which a sugar-cane field is watered, together with a bag of common salt, will extirpate white ants; and the water so impregnated will destroy the ants without injuring the sugar-cane. The plant yields a quantity of milky juice, but of such a mild nature that travellers will often suck the tender shoots to allay thirst.—*Roxb. Gibson.*

(501) **Sarcostigma Kleinii** (*W. & A.*) N. O. Hernandiaceæ.

Description.—Climbing shrub, branched; leaves alternate, short-petioled, oblong-oval, acuminate, coriaceous, glabrous; racemes usually paired, axillary, very long, interrupted; flowers forming numerous sessile fascicles, without pedicels; fruit an oval somewhat flattened nut, about an inch long and half an inch broad.—*Wight Icon. t.* 1854.——Travancore.

Medical Uses.—This plant yields a highly-esteemed medicinal oil (*Adul* or *Odul*), much used on the western coast for rheumatism. —*Jury Rep.*

(502) **Schleichera trijuga** (*Willd.*) N. O. Sapindaceæ.

Poo-marum, Tam. May, Roatangha, Tel. Poovum, Mal.

Description.—Tree, 50 feet; leaves abruptly pinnate; leaflets opposite, about 3 pairs, oblong or broadly lanceolate, quite entire, nearly glabrous; calyx 5-cleft; petals none; racemes axillary or below the leaves round the base of the young shoots, solitary, simple or compound; drupe globose, pointed, with a dry pericarp; seeds 1-2, rarely 3, covered with a pulpy aril; flowers small, greenish. *Fl.* Feb.—March.—*W. & A. Prod.* i. 114.—*Roxb. Fl. Ind.* ii. 277.——Coromandel. Common on the Ghauts. Travancore.

Medical Uses.—The bark is astringent; powdered and rubbed up with oil, the natives use it as a remedy in itch.—*Roxb.*

Economic Uses.—Lamp-oil is expressed from the seeds in Malabar, and the fruit is eaten by the natives. The wood is hard, and is employed for various useful purposes.—*J. Graham.*

(503) **Schmidelia serrata** (*Dec.*) Do.

Taualikœ, TEL. Rakhal-phul, HIND.

DESCRIPTION.—Tree, 12 feet; leaves trifoliate; leaflets stalked, ovate or oblong, acute, serrated, younger ones glabrous, or pubescent beneath and on the nerves, older ones with a glandular tuft of hairs in the axils of the nerves; calyx 5-parted, segments unequal; petals 4, cuneate, with a scale bearing a tuft of hairs above the unguis; racemes axillary, solitary, simple; flowers white; ovary hairy, 2-lobed; fruit baccate. *Fl.* Aug.—Oct.—*W. & A. Prod.* i. 110.—Ornitrophe serrata, *Roxb. Cor.* i. *t.* 61.—*Fl. Ind.* ii. 266.—(Var.) ——Coromandel. Bengal.

MEDICAL USES.—There are several varieties of this species, which have apparently given rise to some difference of opinion among botanists. The fruit is small and red, and is eaten when ripe by the natives. The root is astringent, and is given by the Telinga doctors in diarrhœa.—*Roxb.*

(504) **Schrebera swietenioides** (*Roxb.*) N. O. BIGNONIACEÆ.

Weaver's-beam tree, ENG. Mogalinga marum, TAM. Muccadi-chettoo, TEL.

DESCRIPTION.—Large tree; leaves nearly opposite, imparipinnate, about a foot long, leaflets 3-4 pairs, opposite, obliquely-ovate or cordate, entire, pointed, smooth on both sides, the lower ones largest; calyx tubular, bilabiate; corolla salver-shaped, with cylindrical tube, and three times larger than the calyx; segments 5-7, curved, truncated; capsule large, pear-shaped, scabrous, very hard, 2-celled, opening from the apex; seeds 4 in each cell, compressed, and with a long membranaceous wing; panicles terminal, trichotomous; flowers small, white and brown variegated, very fragrant at night. *Fl.* March—April.—*Roxb. Fl. Ind.* i. 109.—*Cor.* ii. *t.* 101.——Circar mountains.

ECONOMIC USES.—A large timber-tree. The wood is of a grey colour, close-grained, hard, and durable. It is used for a great variety of purposes, being less liable to warp than most other woods. It is employed by weavers chiefly for the beams of the loom, not being liable to bend or warp.—*Roxb.*

(505) **Scindapsus officinalis** (*Schott*). N. O. Araceæ.

Attie-tippilie, Tam. Guj-pippul, Beng. Auna tippilie, Mal.

Description.—Perennial, epiphytic, stems rooting; leaves alternate, sub-bifarious, oblong-cordate, entire, smooth on both sides; petioles sheathing, channelled; peduncles terminal, solitary, smooth, erect when in flower; spathe sub-cylindric, greenish without, pale yellow within; apex filiform; spadix sub-cylindric, equalling the spathes, pale greenish, dotted with the dark-coloured stigmas; berries seeded, arillate at the base. *Fl.* July—Aug.—*Wight Icon. t.* 778.—Pothos officinalis, *Roxb. Fl. Ind.* i. 431.——Bengal. Calicut.

Medical Uses.—At Midnapore this plant is cultivated for its fruit, which is cut into transverse pieces, dried, and used medicinally. —(*Roxb.*) It is reputed to have stimulant, diaphoretic, and anthelmintic virtues.—*Pharm. of India.*

(506) **Semecarpus Anacardium** (*Linn.*) N. O. Anacardiaceæ.

Marking-nut, Eng. Shayng-cottay, Tam. Kampira, Mal. Neela jeedie, Jeedighenzaloo, Tel. Bheela, Hind. Bhilawa, Duk.

Description.—Tree, 50 feet; leaves entire, cuneate-obovate, rounded at the apex, whitish beneath, but not downy; calyx flat, 5-cleft; petals 5, sessile, spreading; flowers panicled, terminal, branched; fruit sessile, cordate-ovate, with a slight notch on one side under the apex; flowers small, green. *Fl.* May—July.—*W. & A. Prod.* i. 168.—*Wight Icon. t.* 558.—*Roxb. Cor.* i. *t.* 12.—*Fl. Ind.* ii. 83.——Concans. Coromandel. Courtallum. Guzerat. Bengal. Travancore.

Medical Uses.—The receptacle of the fruit when ripe is yellow, about the size of the nut, which is black The latter contains the black, corrosive, resinous juice so well known. This juice is employed by the natives to remove rheumatic pains, aches, and sprains; in tender constitutions it often produces inflammation and swelling. It is employed by the Telinga physicians in the cure of almost every kind of venereal complaint. It is also given in small doses in leprous and scrofulous affections. An oil is also prepared from the kernels, used externally in rheumatism and sprains; undiluted it acts as a blister. The juice of the nut should always be cautiously handled. —(*Ainslie. Roxb.*) Bhilawa is the nut of a large forest-tree, which is common throughout India. The acrid viscid oil which the nut contains is used as an escharotic and counter-irritant. It leaves a mark for life. It creates great pain, and often very intractable sores; but ignorant natives, unacquainted with the blisters of Europe, have a greater dread of them than of the Bhilawa. It is given medicinally in small doses, and is considered a stimulant and narcotic, and is much used in the *Musalehs* of elephants. Given in large doses, it renders these animals furious. The farina of the anthers of the flowers is very narcotic and irritating; people of a peculiar habit accidentally sleeping under the tree when in blossom, or even going near the flowers, are stupefied, and have their faces and limbs swollen. The use of the Bhilawa as a counter-irritant frequently causes the whole body and face to swell with erythematous inflammation and much constitutional disturbance. The mature corolla and receptacle are fleshy and of a sweetish-sour taste, and are eaten roasted.—*Irvine Med. Tap. of Ajmere.*

ECONOMIC USES.—The wood of the tree is of no use, not only on account of its softness, but also because it contains much acrid juice, which renders it dangerous to cut down and work upon. The kernels are rarely eaten. The green fruit, well pounded into a pulp, makes good bird-lime. The juice is in general use for marking cotton cloths; the colour is improved and prevented from running by the mixture of a little quicklime and water. The juice is not soluble in water, and only diffusible in spirits of wine. It sinks in expressed oils, but unites perfectly with them.—*Roxb.*

(507) **Sesamum Indicum** (*Linn.*) N. O. PEDALIACEÆ.

Gingely-oil plant, ENG. Yelloo cheddie, TAM. Noowooloo, TEL. Bareek-till, DUK. Schit-eloo, MAL. Til, BENG.

DESCRIPTION.—Annual, 2-3 feet; leaves ovate-oblong, entire; calyx 5-parted; corolla with a short tube and campanulate throat; flowers axillary, solitary; corolla dirty white or pale red; capsule oblong, tetragonal, 4-celled; seeds numerous. *Fl.* July.—*Roxb. Fl. Ind.* iii. 100.—S. orientale, *Linn.*—*Rheede,* ix. *t.* 54, 55.——Cultivated.

MEDICAL USES.—This is extensively cultivated in India for the sake of the oil of its seeds, known as *Til* or *Gingely-oil.* This is reckoned quite equal to olive-oil for medicinal purposes, especially in the treatment of wounds and ulcers. A piece of common country cloth dipped in pure sesamum-oil is superior to any other simple dressing for ulcers, especially during the hot season of the year. The seeds have powerful emmenagogue properties assigned them. The leaves abound with thick viscid mucilage, and an infusion of them is used in parts of North America, in all affections requiring demulcents. One or two full-sized fresh leaves, infused in half a pint of cold water, will soon render it sufficiently viscid for the purpose. If the dried leaves be used, hot water should be substituted for the cold.

The leaves also serve for the preparation of emollient poultices.—*U. S. disp.* p. 714. *Pharm. of India.*

Economic Uses.—The oil known as the *Gingely-oil* is expressed from the seeds, and is one of the most valuable of Indian vegetable oils. It will keep for many years without becoming rancid either in smell or taste; after a time it becomes so mild as to be used as a substitute for sweet-oil in salads. In Japan, where they have no butter, they use the oil for frying fish and other things; also as a varnish, and medicinally as a resolvent and emollient. The plant is cultivated to a great extent in every part of the Peninsula. The following mode of preparation is given in the Jury Reports of the Madras Exhibition: "The method sometimes adopted is that of throwing the fresh seeds, without any cleansing process, into the common mill, and expressing in the usual way. The oil thus becomes mixed with a large portion of the colouring matter of the epidermis of the seed, and is neither so pleasant to the eye nor so agreeable to the taste as that obtained by first repeatedly washing the seeds in cold water, or by boiling them for a short time, until the whole of the reddish-brown colouring matter is removed, and the seeds have become perfectly white. They are then dried in the sun, and the oil expressed as usual. This process yields 40 to 44 per cent of a very pale, straw-coloured, sweet-smelling oil, and excellent substitute for olive-oil."

There are two varieties of seeds known in commerce, one white and the other black: the plant bearing white seeds is not so common as the other one. The *Kala-til*, or black seed, must not be confounded with that of the *Guizotia oleifera*, to which the same name is applied. It is said that the fragrance of the oil is much weaker when the plant has been sown in too moist a soil. The plant has a very general distribution, and the oil is procured and used in Egypt, China, Cashmere, and the West Indies. In the Rajahmundry district, the seed is sown in the month of March, after the rice crop, and is irrigated twice, once at sowing and once afterwards. The seed which is black is called first-sort gingely, from the fact of its yielding the largest percentage of oil, ripens in May, and sells at the rate of 60 rupees per candy of 500 lb. The oil obtained from both varieties sells at the same price—viz., 2-14-0 to 3 rupees per maund of 25 lb., according to quality.

Second-sort gingely is sown in June, and produces a red seed. The plant, although a little larger, resembles in most respects the former: it has, however, a somewhat longer leaf, and the flower differs a shade or two in colour. A candy of 500 lb. of this seed sells at 57-8-0 rupees. The price of the oil is the same as that of gingely. "The fix or expressed oil, besides being eaten by the natives, is used medicinally. It possesses such qualities as fairly entitle it to introduction into Europe; and if divested of its mucilage, it might perhaps compete with oil of olives, at least for medicinal purposes, and could be raised in any quantity in the

British Indian Presidencies. It is sufficiently free from smell to admit of being made the medium for extracting the perfume of the jasmine, the tuberose narcissus, camomile, and of the yellow rose. The process is managed by adding one weight of flowers to three weights of oil in a bottle, which being corked is exposed to the rays of the sun for forty days, when the oil is supposed to be sufficiently impregnated for use. This oil, under the name of gingely-oil, is used in India to adulterate oil of almonds."

The seeds are toasted and ground into meal, and so eaten by the Hindoos. It is externally used in rheumatism, also in the process of dyeing silk a pale-orange colour.

Sesamum-seeds contain about 45 per cent of oil; the Ramtil seeds only 34 per cent. The price of the oil varies in different districts, but the average price is from 3 to 4 rupees a maund. In England its value is about £47, 10s. a ton.—*Jury Rep. Mad. Exhib. Simmonds. Roxb. Ainslie.*

(508) **Sesbania Ægyptiaca** (*Pers.*) N. O. Leguminosæ.

Carum chembai, Tam. Kedangu, Mal. Suiminta, Tel. Byojainti, Beng. Jait, Hind.

Description.—Small tree, unarmed; leaves abruptly pinnate, about three times longer than broad; leaflets 10-18 pairs, oblong-linear, obtuse, slightly mucronate; racemes axillary, lax, pendulous, about the length of the leaves, 3-12 flowered; legumes linear, slender, much contracted between the seeds, twisting when ripe; calyx 5-cleft; corolla papilionaceous; keel obtuse; petals distinct at the base; flowers yellow. *Fl.* Nearly all the year.—*W. & A. Prod.* i. 214.—*Wight Icon. t.* 32.—Æschynomene Sesban, *Linn.*—*Roxb. Fl. Ind.* iii. 332. —Coronilla Sesban, *Willd.*——Peninsula. Bengal.

Medical Uses.—There are two varieties, one the *S. bicolor*, which has leaflets 15-18 pairs, flowers orange, and vexillum purple on the outside; and the other, *S. concolor*, leaflets 10-12 pairs, vexillum yellow-speckled, with black dots and lines.

The leaves are much used by the natives as poultices to promote suppuration.—*Wight.*

Economic Uses.—The wood makes excellent charcoal in the manufacture of gunpowder. In the plains of the Deccan the tree is cultivated and used as a substitute for Bamboos.—*Gibson. Roxb.*

(509) **Sethia indica** (*Dec.*) N. O. Erythroxylaceæ.

Red Cedar, Eng. Tevadarum, Semmanatty, Tam. Dewadar, Duk. Adevi gerenta, Tel.

Description.—Small tree; petals 5; leaves alternate,

obovate or oblong, obtuse, cuneate at the base, feather-nerved, reticulated with veins, under side pale; pedicels axillary, 1-3, about twice as long as the petiole, 1-flowered; calyx 5-lobed; styles combined nearly to the apex, longer than the stamens; drupes oblong, triangular, 3-celled, 2 of the cells small, abortive, and without seeds; flowers small, greenish. *Fl.* July—December.—*W. & A. Prod.* i. 106.—*Wight Ill.* i. *t.* 48. —Erythroxylon monogynum, *Roxb. Cor.* i. *t.* 88; *Fl. Ind.* ii. 449.——Circars. Travancore mountains. Mysore. Malabar.

Medical Uses.—The young leaves and tender shoots are reckoned refrigerant. Bruised and mixed with gingely-oil, they are applied as a liniment to the head. The bark is occasionally administered in infusion as a tonic.—*Ainslie. Lindley.*

Economic Uses.—The timber is flesh-coloured, and is considered excellent for the size of the tree. The wood is so fragrant as to be used in Mysore instead of sandal-wood. An empyreumatic oil of a reddish-brown colour is procured from it.—*Jury Rep. Mad. Exhib.*

(510) **Shorea laccifera** (*W. & A.*) N. O. Dipteraceæ.

Talura, Tam. Jallari, Tel.

Description.—Large tree; leaves coriaceous, oblong, obtuse or emarginate, and often emarginate at the base; panicles numerous from the axils of the fallen leaves; branches and pedicels glabrous; stamens 15; anther-bristle very long; flowers yellow. *Fl.* March—April.—*W. & A. Prod.* i. 84.—*Wight Icon. t.* 164.—Shorea Talura, *Roxb.*——Cuddapah. Wynaad. Mysore. Palghaut forests.

Economic Uses.—The timber is very useful for house-building, panels of doors, and various other purposes. It has a ready sale in the Cuddapah district, and is largely imported into Madras. A species of lac is procured from the tree.—*Bedd. Flor. Sylv. t.* 6.

(511) **Shorea robusta** (*Roxb.*) Do.

Sal, Hind. and Beng.

Description.—Tree, 100-150 feet; calyx 5-sepalled, afterwards enlarging into long wings; petals 5, twisted in the bud, rather silky outside; leaves cordate-oblong, entire, on short petioles; calyx pubescent as well as the branches of the panicles; panicles terminal and axillary; ovary 3-celled; cells 2-seeded; seeds single; flowers yellow. *Fl.* March—

April.—*Roxb. Cor.* iii. *t.* 212; *Fl. Ind.* ii. 615.—*Bedd. Flor. Sylv. t.* 4.—— Foot of the Himalaya. Godavery forests. Goomsur. Orissa.

MEDICAL USES.—A resin exudes from this tree known as the *Dammer* in the bazaars in Bengal. The colour ranges from pale amber to dark brown. It is devoid of taste or smell, sparingly soluble in alcohol, entirely so in ether, and perfectly in turpentine and the fixed oils. It unites with the fixed oils and forms plasters. The superior kinds are efficient substitutes for the pine-resins of the European pharmacopœias.—(*Beng. Disp.* p. 221.) The resin is applied medicinally to ulcers and chilblains, acting as a stimulant. Sulphuric acid dissolves and gives it a red colour. Two parts of colourless dammer and two and a half parts of oil of turpentine make the best varnish for lithographic drawings.—*Jury Rep. Mad. Exhib. Powell's Punj. Prod.*

ECONOMIC USES.—The wood of this tree is in very general use in Bengal for beams, rafters, gun-carriages, and for various other economical purposes. It is close-grained and heavy, but does not appear to be very durable, and on that account inferior to teak; but in strength it surpasses the latter, and deserves to be considered the second-best timber-tree in India. It yields a large quantity of resin-dammer known as the *Ral* or *Dhooma*, which is extensively used as a substitute for pitch in the marine yard. It is also burnt for incense in Hindoo temples. Royle observed these trees forming extensive forests of themselves, frequently unmixed with any other tree.—(*Roxb. Royle.*) All attempts to grow it from seed have failed. The timber is used in Madras in the gun-carriage manufactory, also for house-building and ships, but it warps in planks. It lasts a long time under water, and is unequalled for sleepers, and is proof against white ants.

The Sàl tree of Hindustan extends in a nearly unbroken belt of forest along the Terai, from the Ganges at Hurdwar to the Brahmaputra. The seed has the utmost susceptibility of germination, with a vitality so limited in duration, that it will not survive many days unplanted. The Sàl seed ripens at the commencement of the rains, and after the first shower falls actually sprouting from the tree. In consequence, young plants come up in the utmost profusion, often so thick as to choke each other. They form patches of forest, literally impenetrable. — (*Falconer.*) The most important and accessible of Sàl forests are in the district of Goomsur and in the zemindary of Bodogoda, both of which are traversed by rivers which admit of rafting timber to the coast during the freshes. The tree grows remarkably tall and straight. Thousands of young trees are removed to form posts for native houses and telegraph poles; others of a larger size are useful for public works and officers' houses; and if sawn longitudinally, they give excellent half-round sleepers. On measurement, the straight stump shoot of two years' growth was found to be twelve feet high and three inches in diameter at the base.—(*Cleghorn's Forests of S. India.*) Captain Wood has considered the question of the growth of Sàl wood in the Oude forests, and has arrived at the conclusion that at sixty-five years of age a tree reaches the second-class dimensions, and that it requires thirty-three years more of growth to reach the first-class size. Dr Brandis had before assumed fifty and eighty years as the ages of second and first class trees respectively.—(*Forest Reports in Oude,* 1867-68, *by Captain Wood.*) The Sàl is very abundant about Russelcondah. Many tracts of forest are here composed almost entirely of Sàl, it growing thick and to the exclusion of every other tree. There is no timber equal to it for engineering purposes. It is durable under water, and quite proof against white ants.—*Beddome's Reports,* 1864.

(512) **Shorea Tumbugaia** (*Roxb.*) Do.

Tembagum, MAL. Tumbugai, TAM.

DESCRIPTION. — Large tree; leaves long-petioled, ovate-cordate; panicles terminal; stamens about 100, with bearded anthers; sepals enlarging into wings; flowers yellow. *Fl.* March—April.—*Roxb. Flor. Ind.* ii. 617.—Vatica Tumbugaia, *W. & A. Prod.* i. 84.—*Bedd. Flor. Sylv. t.* 5.—*Wight Icon. t.* 27.——Palghaut forests. Cuddapah. North Arcot.

ECONOMIC USES.—Yields a valuable timber. It is largely used in house-building, and is exported to Madras for that purpose. A dammer exudes from the trunk.—*Roxb. Beddome.*

(513) **Sida acuta** (*Burm.*) N. O. MALVACEÆ.

Malay-taynghie or Arrooa-manopoudoo, TAM. Kureta, BENG. Vishaboddee, TEL. Tsjeru-parua, MAL.

DESCRIPTION.—Shrub, 4-6 feet; calyx 5-cleft, without involucel; leaves narrow lanceolate, acuminated, slightly sprinkled with bristly hairs on the nerves beneath, coarsely simple serrated; pedicels axillary, solitary, not shorter than the petioles, jointed about the middle, sometimes arranged in a short, axillary, almost leafless branch; carpels 5-9, birostrate; flowers yellow. *Fl.* Aug.—Dec.—*W. & A. Prod.* i. 57.—*Wight Icon. t.* 95.—S. lanceolata, *Retz.*—*Rheede,* x. *t.* 53.——Peninsula. Bengal.

MEDICAL USES.—The root is bitter, and is given in infusion, in conjunction with ginger, in intermittent fevers. The Hindoos consider it a valuable stomachic, and a useful remedy in chronic bowel-complaints. The leaves made warm and moistened with gingely-oil are employed to hasten suppuration. The juice of the leaves mixed with honey is given in dysentery and pains in the chest.—(*Ainslie.*) The roots of the *S. retusa* are held in great repute by the natives in the treatment of rheumatism.—*Pharm of India.*

(514) **Sida rhomboidea** (*Roxb.*) Do.

Swet-baryala, Beng. Sufed-bariyala, Hind.

Description.—Shrub; leaves rhomboid-lanceolate, serrated, under side hoary, with short tomentum; pedicels more than half the length of the leaf, jointed at the very base, axillary, solitary, usually collected into leafy corymbs at the extremity of the branches; carpels 8-11, slightly bicuspidate; flowers smallish, pale yellow. *Fl.* Aug.—Dec.—*W. & A. Prod.* i. 57. —*Roxb. Fl. Ind.* iii. 176.——Negapatam. Coromandel. Assam. Cultivated.

Economic Uses.—The bark yields abundant delicate flaxy fibres. A line, after exposure to wet and the sun for ten days, bore 400 lb. The *S. rhombifolia* (*Roxb.*) is a native of Bengal, and also yields fibres. The Secretary to the Chamber of Commerce at Dundee, writing to Madras, says: "Of all the likely plants I have seen, the *Sida rhomboidea* appears to be the best, and I sincerely trust India will send us plenty of it. Do use every exertion to have it cultivated, and sent home as a regular mercantile article, and I see no reason why we should not use as much of it as we do now of jute." It grows luxuriantly in Assam. From the length of its staple, its similarity to silk, and great strength, it would fetch a high price in England. A line only half an inch in circumference, after exposure to wet and sun for ten days, sustained a weight of 400 lb.—*Hannay's Report to Agri.-Hort. Soc. Beng.* 1862.

(515) **Sinapis juncea** (*Linn.*) N. O. Brassicaceæ.

Indian Mustard, Eng. Rai, Beng. Kudaghoo, Tam. Kaduja, Mal.

Description.—Herbaceous; lower leaves ovate-lanceolate, deeply serrated, upper ones lanceolate, attenuated at the base, quite entire; branches fascicled; siliqua somewhat erect, upper joint valveless, awl-shaped, destitute of seeds; flowers yellow. —*W. & A. Prod.* i. 20.—*Dec. Prod.* i. 218.——Cultivated all over India.

Medical Uses.—The seeds, which are of a brown colour, possess properties similar to those of the black and white mustard, for which they may be employed as an efficient substitute, especially in the preparation of mustard-poultices. If previously deprived of their fixed oil by expression, their activity is increased. By long keeping they lose much of their pungency, hence fresh seeds should be employed.—(*Pharm. of India.*) The seeds are much used as a condiment. This as well as other species—the *S. glauca*, *S. dichotoma*, and *S. ramosa*—are extensively cultivated for the oil yielded by the seeds, as well as for dietetical purposes. Mustard-oil is reckoned the best for invigorating the body. It is used as a rubefacient.—(*Jury Rep. Mad. Exhib.*) To this order belongs the Rape (*Brassica napus*), which is cultivated extensively, and whose seeds are exported (*vide* Appendix). The oil which the seeds yield is known as the Colza oil. It is used in the manufacture of soap as well as in lamps. It has very little smell, if properly prepared, is of a yellow colour, and of rather a sweet taste. It has the advantage of remaining limpid at a much lower temperature than most oils, which causes it to be preferred for street lamps.—*Veg. Subst.*

(516) **Smilax glabra** (*Roxb.*) N. O. SMILACEÆ.

DESCRIPTION.—Scandent; stem and branches unarmed, terete, smooth; leaves lanceolate, acuminate, rotund at the base, 3-nerved, nerves smooth, glaucous beneath; umbels axillary, simple sessile, solitary; calycine segments broad, obcordate; anthers sessile; roots tuberous.—*Roxb. Flor. Ind.* iii. 792.—Silhet.

MEDICAL USES.—The large tuberous roots known by the name of *Hurina-shuk China* are used by the natives in Silhet and the Garrow country in the treatment of syphilitic affections. The roots of *S. lanceæfolia* (Roxb.) are likewise employed in rheumatism. Roxburgh states that the roots of both these species so closely resemble China root (the produce of *Smilax China*), that they can hardly be distinguished from it. The *S. ovalifolia* is another species growing in the low jungles of the Peninsula, but after several trials it has been found worthless as a medicine.—*Pharm. of India.*

(517) **Solanum Indicum** (*Linn.*) N. O. SOLANACEÆ.

Indian Nightshade, ENG. Moollie, TAM. Tella mulaka, TEL. Kolsi, DUK. Cheruchunda, MAL. Byakoor, BENG.

DESCRIPTION.—Shrub, armed; prickles of stem compressed, recurved; leaves solitary or twin, oblong or ovate, tomentose, discoloured, sinuately lobed, unequal at the base, prickly on both surfaces; racemes interfoliaceous; calyx prickly, segments reflexed; berries globose; corolla deeply 5-cleft, blue; berries orange yellow. *Fl.* Nearly all the year.—*Wight Icon. t.* 346—*Roxb. Fl. Ind.* i. 570.—*Rheede,* ii. *t.* 36.——All over India.

Medical Uses.—The root is used by Indian doctors in cases of dysuria and ischuria, in the form of decoction. It is said to possess strong exciting qualities, if taken internally, and is employed in difficult parturition. It is also used in toothache. There are varieties of the plant, differing chiefly in the shape of the leaves. —*Ainslie.*

(518) **Solanum Jacquini** (*Willd.*) Do.

Cundunghatrie, Tam. Van-kuda or Nella Mollunga, Tel. Kootsya, Hind. Chudra Kanta-karee, Beng.

Description.—Procumbent, diffuse, prickly; leaves sinuately pinnatifid, prickly on both surfaces, with naked margins; racemes simple, which, as well as the calyx, are prickly; corolla bluish purple. *Fl.* All the year.—*Wight Icon. t.* 1401. ——Coromandel. Travancore.

The varieties are—

a. Fruit larger, plant less armed. S. diffusum.—*Roxb. Fl. Ind.* i. 568.—S. xanthocarpum, *Willd.*——Coromandel. Deccan.

b. Fruit smaller; plant strongly armed. S. Jacquini, *Willd.* —*Roxb. Fl. Ind.* i. 569.—Kanta-karee. Flowers bright blue.——Bengal.

Medical Uses.—The fruit is bitter and sub-acid, considered an expectorant by the natives, and given by them in coughs and consumptive complaints; also in decoction in humoral asthma. In the West Indies the juice of the berry is used in cases of sore throat. The fruits are much esteemed by the natives, who eat them in their curries. For this purpose the plant is cultivated in the Circars.—(*Ainslie. Roxb.*) This plant has diuretic properties assigned to it, and is largely employed in catarrhal and febrile diseases. The stems, flowers, and fruit are bitter and carminative, and are prescribed in cases of burning feet, attended with a vesicular watery eruption.—(*Calc. Med. Phys. Trans.* ii. 406. Fumigations with the burning seeds are in great repute in the cure of toothache. It acts as a powerful sialagogue, and by these means probably relief is obtained.—*Pharm. of India.*

(519) **Solanum melongena** (*Linn.*) Do.

The Brinjal or Egg-plant, Eng. Valoothala, Mal. Valoothalay, Tam. Wankai, Tel.

Description.—Perennial; stem clothed with stellate tomentum; leaves ovate, unequal at the base, angularly sinuated, downy; flowering peduncles solitary, reflexed; calyx prickly, campanulate; segments linear-lanceolate; corolla violaceous, 6-9 cleft, marked by a yellow star inside; fruit oval, smooth. *Fl.* Nearly all the year.

The varieties are—

a. Stem, leaves, and calyxes unarmed or nearly so. Solanum ovigerum, *Dun. Rom.* and *Sch.*—S. Melongena, *Linn. Willd. Roxb. Fl. Ind.* i. 566, *Beng.*—Brinjal, Egg-plant, *Eng.*—Bangan, *Hind.*—Wankai, *Tel.*——All over India. *Fl.* largish, violet.

b. Stem, leaves, and calyxes more or less aculeate. Solanum esculentum, *Dun.*—S. Melongena, *Linn. suppl.*—S. insanum, *Linn. Willd.* (not *Roxb.*)—S. longum, *Roxb. Fl. Ind.* i. 567.—Neelavaloothana, *Rheede*, x. *t.* 74.—Kooli-begoon, *Beng.*—Long Brinjal. *Fl.* largish, bright bluish purple.

The fruit of each of these varieties is either ovate-oblong or oblong, violet or white; or globular (larger and smaller), violet; or more and less globular, white, or white-striped on a violet ground.

Economic Uses.—The Brinjal is universally cultivated in India as an esculent vegetable, belonging to an order of plants remarkable for their poisonous as well as harmless qualities. On this subject Dr Lindley has well remarked: "The leaves of all are narcotic and exciting, but in different degrees,—from the *Atropa Belladonna*, which causes vertigo, convulsions, and vomiting—the well-known Tobacco, which will frequently produce the first and last of these symptoms—the Henbane, and Stramonium, down to some of the Solanum tribe, the leaves of which are used as kitchen herbs. It is in the fruit that the greatest diversity of character exists. *Atropa Belladonna*, *Solanum nigrum*, and others, are highly dangerous poisons; Stramonium, Henbane, and Physalis are narcotic; the fruit of *Physalis Alkekengi* is diuretic, that of *Capsicum* is pungent, and even acrid; some species of *Physalis* are sub-acid, and so wholesome as to be eaten with impunity (*e. g.*, the well-known Tepariga) and finally, the Egg-plant (*Solanum Melongena*, Brinjal), and all the Tomato tribe of *Solanum*, yield fruits which are common articles of cookery. It is stated that the poisonous species derive their properties from the presence of a pulpy matter which surrounds the seeds; and that the wholesome kinds are destitute of this, the pulp consisting only of what botanists call the sarcocarp—that is to say, the centre of the rind, in a more or less succulent state. It must also be remembered that if the fruit of the Egg-plant is eatable, it only becomes so after undergoing a peculiar process, by which all its bitter acrid matter is removed, and that the Tomato is always exposed to heat before it is eaten."

(520) **Solanum trilobatum** (*Linn.*) Do.

Toodavullay, TAM. Moondla moosteh, Oochinta Kura, TEL.

DESCRIPTION.—Climbing shrub; stem armed with numerous very sharp recurved prickles; leaves remote, panduriformly 3-5 lobed, smooth on both sides; petioles and veins armed; peduncles prickly, leaf opposed, solitary, few-flowered, terminal, and axillary; corolla deeply 5-cleft, bluish purple; berries small, globose, red, drooping. *Fl.* Nearly all the year.—*Wight Icon. t.* 854.—*Roxb. Fl. Ind.* i. 571.——Deccan. Cape Comorin.

MEDICAL USES.—The root, leaves, and tender shoots are all used medicinally—the two first in decoction or powder in consumptive complaints. The leaves are eaten by the Hindoos. The berries and flowers are given internally in decoction for coughs.—*Ainslie.*

(521) **Sonneratia acida** (*Linn.*) N. O. LYTHRACEÆ.

Blatti, MAL. Orchaka, BENG.

DESCRIPTION.—Small tree; leaves opposite, oval-oblong, quite entire, thick, veinless; branchlets drooping, 4-angled; calyx campanulate; petals 6, narrow lanceolate; fruit a berry, nearly globose, many-celled; seeds numerous, surrounded with a fleshy pulp, curved; flowers in threes or sometimes solitary, large, purple. *Fl.* April—May.—*W. & A. Prod.* i. 327.—*Wight Icon. t.* 340.—*Roxb. Fl. Ind.* ii. 506.—*Rheede,* iii. *t.* 40. ——Malabar. Sunderbunds. Delta of Indus.

ECONOMIC USES.—It is said that the wood of this tree is the best substitute for coal in steamers. The tree grows in great quantities in the delta of the river Indus. It grows also in Malabar on the banks of tidal backwaters. The natives eat the fruit mixed with other food; it is said to be cooling.—(*Graham.*) These trees send out the most curious, long, spindle-shaped excrescences four or five feet above the surface. They are firm in their texture, nearly devoid of fibrous structure, and take a moderate polish when cut with a sharp instrument. For lining insect-boxes and making setting-boards they have no equal in the world. The finest pin passes in with delightful ease and smoothness, and there is no risk of the insects becoming disengaged. With a fine saw they may be formed into little boards, and then smoothed with a sharp case-knife. Some of them are two feet long, and three and a half inches wide. The natives in Ceylon call them *Kirilinow*, the latter syllable signifying "root."—*Templeton Trans. Ent. Soc.* iii. 302.—*Tenn. Ceyl.* i. 86, *note.*

(522) **Sorghum saccharatum** (*Pers.*) N. O. Graminaceæ.

Chinese Sugar-cane, Eng.

Description.—Erect; panicles verticillate, rays nodding; calyx hairy; spikelets sessile, entirely or interruptedly villous, shining, at length glabrate; pedicels scarcely equally their own floret.—*Pers. Hort. Gram.* iv. *t.* 4.—Andropogon saccharatum, *Roxb.*——Cultivated.

Economic Uses.—In the districts in Northern India where this grass is cultivated it is used as a valuable fodder for cattle. It can be cut down two or three times a-year, and will sprout again. As a forage-plant it is said to be unsurpassed, and is attracting much attention in France and the United States. The juice affords sugar, alcohol, and a liquor-like cider. It is planted in drills about three or four feet apart. The stocks grow about two feet apart. It sends up new shoots after being cut, so that three crops per year proceed from one plant. It makes a fifth to a fourth of its bulk in good syrup. When the seed becomes quite ripe the fodder is pulled, and the seed-heads cut. The yield of fodder per acre is 1000 to 1300, the yield of seed 2536 bushels. On the first trial, 70 average canes passed once through the rollers gave 38 gallons 1 quart of juice, and a second time 2 gallons of juice—the 40 gallons 1 quart so obtained yielding 8 gallons of syrup.—*Powell's Punj. Prod.*

(523) **Sorghum vulgare** (*Pers.*) Do.

Great Millet, Eng. Jonna, Tel. Cholum, Tam. Jowari, Beng.

Description.—Culms erect; panicles contracted, dense, hermaphrodite; calyxes hairy; corolla 3-valved, awned.—*Roxb. Fl. Ind.* i. 269.—Holcus sorghum, *Linn.*—Andropogon sorghum, *Roxb.*——Cultivated.

ECONOMIC USES.—This species is cultivated for its grain, which is much used as food. The produce in good soil is often upwards of a hundred-fold. Cattle are very fond of the straw; the latter is also a substitute for forage for horses when gram is not obtainable. The *S. bicolor* (Willd.) is also used for the same purposes.—(*J. Grah. Roxb.*) There are several varieties, one called the Black, the other the White Cholam. The word Coromandel given to the eastern coast of the Peninsula is merely a corruption of the word *Chola-mandala*, *i.e.*, the Land of Millet—as *Malyala* or Malabar is the Land of Mountains.—(*Bart. Voy.*) Cholum is the staple dry grain of India, and indeed of all tropical countries of Asia and Africa. It is largely cultivated in Europe as well as the United States, and its range is probably not less extensive than that of wheat. It forms the principal article of food among the agricultural classes on table-lands, as rice does of those of the lower country.—*W. Elliott.*

(524) **Soymida febrifuga** (*Juss.*) N. O. CEDRELACEÆ.

Red wood-tree, ENG. Shem-marum, Woond-marum, TAM. Soimida, TEL. Rohana, HIND. Rohun, BENG.

DESCRIPTION.—Tree, 60 feet; petals 5-shortly, unguiculate; calyx 5-toothed; leaves abruptly pinnate; leaflets opposite, 3-6 pair, oval-oblong, obtuse; panicles terminal or axillary from the upper leaves; capsules 5-celled; seeds numerous, winged; flowers small, greenish white. *Fl.* March—April.—*W. & A. Prod.* i. 122.—Swietenia febrifuga, *Roxb. Cor.* i. *t.* 17; *Fl. Ind.* ii. 398.——Central and Southern Provinces. Guzerat.

MEDICAL USES.—The bark has a bitter and astringent taste, but not nauseous or disagreeable, and may be used in the same way as Peruvian bark. The bark is a good tonic in intermittent fevers, but if taken in too large quantities is apt to derange the nervous system, occasioning vertigo and stupor. The virtues of the bark are extracted by water both in infusion and decoction; but the tincture is perhaps the most valuable of all its preparations, when the bark is as good as a stomachic.—*Ainslie. Roxb.*

ECONOMIC USES.—The wood of this tree is of a dull-red colour, remarkably hard and heavy; it is reckoned by the natives the most durable of woods, on which account it is greatly used in their temples for wood-work. The bark is internally of a light-red colour; a decoction of it dyes brown of various shades according as the cloth is prepared.—*Roxb.*

(525) **Spathodea Rheedii** (*Spreng.*) N. O. BIGNONIACEÆ.

Woody, TEL. Nir pongelion, MAL.

DESCRIPTION.—Small tree; leaves unequally pinnate, downy;

leaflets 3-7 pairs, roundish; racemes terminal, erect; calyx spathaceous; flowers pure white, with a long tube and plaited border; pod about a foot long, linear, twisted, pendulous. *Fl.* May—June.—*Wight Icon. t.* 1339.—Bignonia spathacea, *Roxb. Cor.* ii. *t.* 144; *Fl. Ind.* iii. 103.—*Rheede,* vi. *t.* 29.——Bombay. Khandalla Ghauts. Malabar.

Economic Uses.—Nets are made from the fibres of the branches and roots; and a red decoction prepared from the root, the fishermen say, preserves the nets. The timber is light-coloured, strong, and serviceable, and much used by the natives for agricultural and building purposes.—(*Beddome.*) The wood of the *S. Roxburghii* (Heterophragma) is also used for various economical purposes. It is remarkable for its serrated leaves.—*Roxb.*

(526) **Spermacoce hispida** (*Linn.*) N. O. Cinchonaceæ.

Shaggy Button-weed, Eng. Nuttee choorie, Tam. Thartavel, Mal. Madana, Tel.

Description.—Plant, 1½ foot, herbaceous, diffuse, hairy; leaves from obovate-oblong to roundish, somewhat mucronate, flattish or waved; bristles of stipules longer than the hirsute sheath; flowers axillary, 1-4 together, sessile; tube of corolla rather wide; fruit hirsute or villous, oval, crowned with the 4-calycine teeth; flowers small, purplish. *Fl.* Nearly all the year.—*W. & A. Prod.* i. 438.—*Roxb. Fl. Ind.* i. 373.—S. scabra, *Willd.*—*Rheede,* ix. *t.* 76.——Peninsula. Travancore. Bengal.

Medical Uses.—The root, which is not unlike Sarsaparilla in taste, is employed for similar purposes—viz., as an alterative and purifier of the blood. It is given in decoction.—*Ainslie.*

(527) **Sphæranthus hirtus** (*Burm.*) N. O. Asteraceæ.

Kottang-Karundie, Tam. Adaca majyen, Mal. Bodatarum, Tel. Moondie, Duk. Chagul-nudie, Beng.

Description.—Small plant with herbaceous stem; leaves lanceolate, serrate, alternate; peduncles curled; flowers solitary, terminal, sub-globular, purplish red. *Fl.* Nearly all the year.—*Wight Icon. t.* 1094.—S. mollis, *Roxb. Fl. Ind.* iii. 446. —*Rheede, Mal.* x. *t.* 43.——Peninsula. Common on the banks of rice-fields.

Medical Uses.—The seeds are considered as anthelmintic, and are prescribed in powders. The root powdered is stomachic; and the bark of the same, ground small and mixed with whey, is a valuable remedy for piles. In Java the plant is reckoned a useful diuretic.—(*Ainslie.*) The flowers are employed in cutaneous diseases and in purifying the blood. The roots are reckoned anthelmintic.—*Powell's Punj. Prod.*

(528) **Spinifex squarrosus** (*Linn.*) N. O. GRAMINACEÆ.

Water-pink, ENG.

DESCRIPTION.—Frutescent; culms large, glaucous, fasciculate-leafy at the knots; leaves convolute, recurved, spreading, stiff, pointed; sheaths woolly at the mouth, the rest striated, and with the spikelets and leaves glabrous; male axils flower-bearing; bracts of the capitules fascicled, very large, involucres mucronate.—*Linn. Mant.* 300.—*Drury Handb. Ind. Fl.* iii. 591.—*Rheede, Mal.* xii. *t.* 75.——Sandy shores of the Peninsula on both coasts.

ECONOMIC USES.—This is one of the sand-binding plants common on the shores of the Peninsula and Ceylon. They perform an important function in the fertilisation of dry sandy tracts. The seeds are contained in a circular head, composed of a series of spine-like divisions, which radiate from the stalk in all directions, making the diameter of the whole about 8 to 9 inches. When the seeds are mature and ready for dispersion, these heads become detached from the plant, and are carried by the winds with great velocity along the sands, over the surface of which they are impelled on their elastic spines. One of these balls may be followed by the eye for miles as it hurriés along the level shore, dropping its seeds as it rolls, which speedily germinate and take root where they fall. The globular heads are so buoyant as to float lightly on water, and the uppermost spines acting as sails, they are thus carried across narrow estuaries to continue the process of embanking on newly-formed sandbars.—*Tennent's Ceylon*, i. 49.

(529) **Spondias mangifera** (*Pers.*) N. O. ANACARDIACEÆ.

Hog-plum or Wild Mango, ENG. Caat maavu, TAM. Adivie mamadie, Amatum, TEL. Ambalam, MAL. Junglie-am, DUK. Amna, BENG.

DESCRIPTION.—Large tree; calyx small, 5-cleft; petals 5, spreading; leaves alternate, unequally pinnated; leaflets 4-5 pairs, ovate or elliptic-oblong, oblique at the base, entire, glabrous; panicles axillary and terminal, diffuse; drupe fleshy, oval, yellow; nut oblong, woody, outwardly fibrous, 5-celled, very hard; flowers small, white. *Fl.* March.—*W. & A. Prod.*

i. 173.—*Roxb. Fl. Ind.* ii. 451.—*Rheede*, i. *t.* 50.——Bengal. Peninsula. Travancore.

ECONOMIC USES.—The fruit is eaten when ripe. It is of a yellowish-green colour. Before ripening it makes excellent pickles. A mild insipid gum exudes from the bark. This is collected and sold in the bazaars as Gum-Arabic, which it greatly resembles.—*Wight.*

(530) **Sterculia fœtida** (*Linn.*) N. O. STERCULIACEÆ.

Kudrapdukku, Peenaree-marum, TAM. Jungle-baddam, BENG.

DESCRIPTION.—Tree; leaves compound, peltate; leaflets 7-9, oblong-lanceolate, acuminated, young ones slightly pubescent; flowers panicled; calyx deeply divided, segments lanceolate, slightly velvety within; carpels oblong, many-seeded; flowers brownish, tinged with red at the base, very fetid. *Fl.* March. —*W. & A. Prod.* i. 63.—*Roxb. Fl. Ind.* iii. 154.—*Wight Icon. t.* 181, 364.——Peninsula. Bengal. Travancore.

MEDICAL USES.—The leaves and bark are aperient, repellent, diuretic, and diaphoretic. The seeds are oily, and if swallowed incautiously they bring on nausea and vertigo. Horsfield says a decoction of the capsule is mucilaginous and astringent. The seeds if roasted are edible.—*Ainslie.*

ECONOMIC USES.—This tree has a most unpleasant smell when bruised and cut. The wood is pale, lasting, and does not split; it is therefore suitable for the turner, and if well varnished makes handsome vases. It is a most useful tree, and furnishes some of the masts known as *Poon-spars.*—*J. Grah. Roxb.*

(531) **Sterculia guttata** (*Roxb.*) Do.

Pee marum, TAM. Ramenapoo-marum, MAL.

DESCRIPTION.—Tree, 70 feet; leaves between broadly and oblong ovate, entire, obtuse, or with sudden acumination, prominently nerved and veined beneath; young leaves densely pubescent; racemes somewhat fascicled; pedicels short; calyx deeply 5-cleft, tomentose; segments lanceolate, distinct; flowers yellow. *Fl.* Dec.—*W. & A. Prod.* i. 62.—*Wight Icon.* ii. *t.* 487.—*Roxb. Fl. Ind.* iii. 148.—*Rheede*, iv. *t.* 61.—— Peninsula.

ECONOMIC USES.—The root is aromatic. The bark of the young parts of this tree is converted by the natives of the western coast into a flaxy substance, of which they make a sort of clothing and cordage, the inner bark being very tough and pliable. The bark is not used till the tenth year; the tree is felled, branches lopped, trunk cut into pieces of 6 feet long, a perpendicular incision made in each, the bark opened, taken off entire, chopped, washed, and dried in the sun. In this state it is used for clothing. The fibres of the bark are well adapted for cordage.—*Royle.*

(532) **Sterculia urens** (*Roxb.*) Do.

Kavalee, TEL. Vellay Bootalli, TAM. Bulee, HIND.

DESCRIPTION.—Tree; leaves palmately 5-lobed, soft, velvety beneath, lobes acuminate, entire; calyx campanulate; panicles terminal; carpels ovate, hispid, with rigid bristly hairs, pubescent within; seeds several in each carpel; flowers small, yellow. *Fl.* Feb.—March.—*W. & A. Prod.* i. 63.—*Roxb. Fl. Ind.* iii. 145.—*Cor.* i. *t.* 24.——Courtallum. Concans.

ECONOMIC USES.—The wood is soft and spongy. It is used to make Hindoo guitars. The bark is very astringent, and tinges the saliva reddish. The seeds are roasted and eaten. The bark yields a gum resembling Tragacanth, and was formerly used as a substitute for it. A kind of coffee may be made from the seeds.—*Gibson. Roxb.*

(533) **Sterculia villosa** (*Roxb.*) Do.

Odul or Oadal, TAM.

DESCRIPTION.—Tree; leaves deeply and palmately 5-7 lobed, under side soft, velvety, lobes acuminated, deeply toothed; calyx 5-partite, patent; carpels coriaceous, rough, with stellate pubescence; flowers small, pale yellow, scarlet. *Fl.* March.—*W. & A. Prod.* i. 63.—*Roxb. Fl. Ind.* iii. 153. ——Peninsula. Assam.

ECONOMIC USES.—Bags and ropes are made of the fibrous bark. The bark is easily stripped off the whole length of the tree; finer ropes are made from the inner bark, not injured by wet, and, besides, being strong and durable.—(*Royle.*) It is the common rope used by all elephant-hunters in the Himalaya, as well as in the Annamallay forests. In Deyra Dhoon good paper has been made from it. The seeds of the *S. Balanghas* are wholesome, and when roasted are nearly as palatable as chestnuts.—(*Roxb.*) In Amboyna the pericarp is burnt to make a pigment called Cassoumba.—*Hooker.*

(534) **Stereospermum chelonoides** (*Dec.*) N. O. BIGNONIACEÆ.

Padrie-marum, MAL. Pompadyra Marum, TAM. Tagada, Kalighootroo, TEL.

DESCRIPTION.—Large tree; leaves impari-pinnate; leaflets about four pairs, ovate to oblong, entire, downy while young, lower pair the smallest; calyx spathaceous; panicles large, terminal, with decussate ramification, smaller ones dichotomous, with a sessile flower in the fork; corolla bilabiate; follicles pendulous, very long, with sharp edges and variously curved; flowers large, yellowish, tinged with orange and brown. *Fl.* May—July.—*Roxb. Fl. Ind.* iii. 106.—*Rheede,* vi. *t.* 26.—*Wight Icon. t.* 1341.—*Bedd. t.* 72.——Coromandel. Forests in Malabar. Silhet.

ECONOMIC USES.—The beautiful flowers of this tree are offered by the Hindoos as acceptable to their deities, and are often brought to their temples for this purpose. When immersed in water, they give it an agreeable odour. The wood is high-coloured, hard, and durable, and much used by the inhabitants of the hills where it abounds.—(*Roxb.*) The wood of the *S. suaveolens* (Roxb.) is strong and elastic, and is said to be good for making bows.—*Jury Rep. Mad. Exhib.*

(535) **Strychnos colubrina** (*Linn.*) N. O. LOGANIACEÆ.

Snakewood-tree, ENG. Modira-caniram, MAL. Nagamusadi, TEL. Koochila-luta, BENG.

DESCRIPTION.—Climbing shrub; calyx 5-parted; corolla tubular, with a 5-parted spreading limb; leaves opposite, from oval to oblong, bluntly acuminate, 3-nerved; berries globose, pulpy, many-seeded; tendrils lateral, simple; corymbs terminal, composed of 2-3 pairs of villous branches; flowers small, greenish yellow; berry as large as an orange; rind yellowish.—*Wight Icon. t.* 434.—*Roxb. Fl. Ind.* i. 577.—*Rheede,* viii. *t.* 24.——Malabar.

MEDICAL USES.—This species yields the real, or at least one sort of *Lignum Colubrinum.* The wood is esteemed by the Telinga doctors as an infallible remedy in the bite of the *Naga* snake, as well as for that of every other venomous serpent. It is applied both externally and internally. It is also given in substance for the cure of intermittent fevers. The tree is called by the Telingas *Nagamusadi* or *Tansoopaum.* The latter word in their language means the *Cobra-de-Capella,* or *Coluber-naga* of Linnæus. *Tansoo* means dancing, and *paum* a serpent, this sort being famous for erecting its head, and moving it from side to side at the sound of music. In Java the plant is used in intermittent fevers, as an anthelmintic, and externally in cutaneous diseases, especially for alleviating the pain attending the swelling in the confluent small-pox. An excellent bitter tincture is prepared from it by the Malays. Some say it has purgative qualities, the part used being the root, which is woody, and covered with iron-coloured bark.—(*Ainslie. Roxb.*) From the fact of the wood containing strychnia, it should be used very cautiously. In the present state of our information, *Lignum Colubrinum* must be looked upon as a dangerous remedy.—*Pharm. of India.*

(536) **Strychnos nux vomica** (*Linn.*) Do.

Vomit-nut, or Poison-nut, ENG. Yettie-marum, TAM. Cariram, MAL. Mooshti-ganga, Musadi, TEL. Coochla, DUK.

DESCRIPTION.—Tree, middling-sized; leaves short-petioled, opposite, smooth, shining, 3-5 nerved, oval; calyx 5-parted, permanent; corolla tubular, funnel-shaped; flowers small, greenish white; filaments, scarcely any, inserted over the bottom of the divisions of the corolla, style the length of the tube of the corolla; fruit round, smooth, very variable in size, orange-coloured when ripe, many-seeded, pulpy. *Fl.* Dec.—Jan.—*Roxb. Flor. Ind.* i. 575.—*Cor.* i. *t.* 4.—*Rheede,* i. *t.* 37.——Peninsula.

MEDICAL USES.—The wood of this tree, being hard and durable, is used for many purposes. It is exceedingly bitter, particularly that of the root, which is used in the cure of intermittent fevers and the bites of venomous snakes. The seeds are employed in the distillation of country spirits, to render them more intoxicating. The pulp of the fruit is harmless. Birds eat it greedily. *Nux vomica* is one of the narcotico-acrid class of poisons, and seems to act directly upon the spinal cord. Mr Duprey has ascertained that by numerous experiments the fruit of *Feuillea cordifolia* is a powerful antidote against this and other vegetable poisons. It has for a long time been known as a powerful medicine, and is employed in a variety of diseases. It has been effectually used in paralysis, as it acts upon the spinal marrow without affecting the brain. It is also given in partial or general palsies, and various kinds of local and general debility. *Strychnine* is a preparation of *N. vomica.* The Vytians say that the seeds will produce mental derangement, or death itself, if an overdose be taken. The nut, when finely pounded and mixed with margosa-oil, is considered tonic and astringent given in minute doses. The seeds are given in leprosy, paralysis, and bites of venomous serpents, and are used by the lower class of natives as a stimulant, like opium, in very small doses. A decoction of the leaves is employed externally in paralysis and rheumatic swelling of the joints.—(*Ainslie.*) Professor Christison considers it probable that the bark might be advantageously substituted for the seed in the preparation of strychnia. It forms the principal ingredient in the chief of the medicated oils commonly in use among the natives as local applications to leprous, syphilitic, and other obstinate eruptions.—(*Pharm. of India.*) In 1870-71 were exported from Bombay 2568 cwt. of seeds, valued at Rs. 10,966; and from Madras, in 1869-70, 4805 cwt., valued at Rs.12,262.—*Trade Reports.*

(537) **Strychnos potatorum** (*Linn.*) Do.

Clearing-nut tree, Eng. Tettan-cottay marum, Tam. Tettamparel marum, Mal. Tsilla ghenjaloo, Induga, Tel. Ner mullie, Beng. and Hind.

Description.—Tree; calyx 5-parted; corolla funnel-shaped; leaves opposite, from ovate to oval, glabrous, pointed; bark deeply cracked; corymbs form the tops of the old shoots round the base of the new ones, bearing in ternary order many small, greenish-yellow, fragrant flowers; berry shining, black when ripe, 1-seeded. *Fl.* April—May.—*Roxb. Fl. Ind.* i. 576.—*Cor.* i. *t.* 5.——Mountains and forests of the Peninsula.

Medical Uses.—The pulverised fruit is reckoned emetic by the natives, and the seeds in the same form mixed with honey are applied to boils to hasten suppuration, and also with milk are given in sore eyes to strengthen them. The seeds are devoid of all poisonous properties, and are used as a remedy in diabetes and gonorrhœa.—*Ainslie. Roxb. Pharm. of India.*

Economic Uses.—The wood is hard and durable, and used for many economical purposes. The pulp of the fruit, when ripe, is eaten by the natives. The ripe seeds are dried, and sold in the bazaars to clear muddy water. One of the seeds is well rubbed for a minute or two round the inside of the chatty or vessel containing the water, which is then left to settle; in a short time the impurities fall to the bottom, leaving the water clear and perfectly wholesome. They are easier to be obtained than alum, and are probably less hurtful to the constitution. In this process the gelatinous matter of the seed at first mixes with the water, but afterwards combines with the lime salts, and both become insoluble, and are precipitated, carrying with them the matters held in suspension. It is said that almonds used in a similar way will clear water.—(*Powell's Punj. Prod.*) Considering by how simple a process muddy water may be freed from all impurities by the use of the "clearing-nut," it may be remarked what advantage might be taken of this fact by troops marching in India during the rainy season, when clear water is scarce.—*Pharm. of India.*

(538) **Stylocoryne Webera** (*A. Rich.*) N. O. CINCHONACEÆ.

Cupi, MAL. Commi, TEL.

DESCRIPTION.—Shrub, glabrous; leaves lanceolate-oblong, shining; corymbs trichotomous, terminal; calyx 5-cleft; tube of corolla short, twice the length of the calyx-tube, widened and bearded at the mouth, segments of limb recurved, villous at the base along the middle, about twice as long as the tube; berry 2-celled; cells 4-8 seeded; flowers small, white afterwards, cream-coloured, fragrant. *Fl.* March—May.—*W. & A. Prod.* i. 401.—*Wight Icon. t.* 309, 584.—Webera corymbosa, *Willd.*—*Roxb. Fl. Ind.* i. 696.—*Rheede,* ii. *t.* 23.——Coromandel. Malabar. Concans.

ECONOMIC USES.—The young shoots are frequently covered with a resinous exudation. The wood is hard and prettily marked, and is much esteemed by the natives.

(539) **Symplocos racemosa** (*Roxb.*) N. O. STYRACACEÆ.

DESCRIPTION.—Tree; leaves oblong-lanceolate, acuminate, acute at the base, quite glabrous, sub-denticulate, shining above; racemes simple, axillary, nearly equalling the petiole, hairy; sepals and bracteoles ovate, obtuse, ciliated; ovary free at the apex; flowers small, yellow. *Fl.* Dec.—*Roxb. Flor. Ind.* ii. 539.—*Dec. Prod.* viii. 255.—S. theæfolia, *Don. Prod. Flor. Nep.* 145.——Bengal. Western Ghauts.

ECONOMIC USES.—This tree grows in the Kotah jungles. The bark is used to dye red, and is exported for that purpose.—*Fleming.*

(540) **Syzygium Jambolanum** (*Dec.*) N. O. MYRTACEÆ.

Nawel, TAM. Periu-njara, MAL. Jamoon, HIND. Kallajam, BENG. Naredoo, TEL.

DESCRIPTION.—Tree; leaves oval or oblong, more or less acuminated or obtuse, feather-nerved, coriaceous; cymes panicled, lax, usually lateral on the former year's branches, occasionally axillary or terminal; calyx shortly turbinate, truncated; berry olive-shaped, often oblique; flowers small, white. *Fl.* March.—*W. & A. Prod.* i. 329.—*Wight Icon. t.*

535, 553.—Eugenia Jambolana, *Lam.*—*Wight Ill.* ii. 16.—*Roxb. Fl. Ind.* ii. 484.—S. caryophyllifolium, *Dec.*—*Rheede,* v. *t.* 29.——Peninsula. Bengal. Tinnevelly.

Medical Uses.—The bark possesses astringent properties, and in the form of decoction is much used in Bengal in chronic dysentery. A syrup prepared with the juice of the ripe fruit is a pleasant stomachic, and acts as an efficient astringent in chronic diarrhœa.—*Pharm. of India.*

Economic Uses.—The timber is fine, hard, and close-grained. The bark dyes excellent durable browns of various shades according to the mordaunt employed, or the strength of the decoction.—(*Roxb. Wight.*) The tree attains its full size in 40 years. The wood is dark red, slightly liable to warp, but not subject to worms. It is used for agricultural implements.—(*Balfour.*) It does not rot in water, and thence is used in Ajmere to line wells.—(*Fleming.*) A communication was made to the Agri. Hort. Soc. of Beng. (Jan. 1864), stating that with the fruit called Jamoon the writer had made in Rampore Bauleah a wine, that for its qualities and taste was almost similar to the wine made from the grape. The wine was very cheap, as from two maunds of the fruit collected about one maund of wine was made, which cost altogether three rupees.

T

(541) **Tacca pinnatifida** (*Forsk.*) N. O. TACCACEÆ.

Carachunay, TAM. Kunda, DUK. Cunda, TEL.

DESCRIPTION.—Root tuberous, perennial, very large, round and smoothish, with a few fibres issuing from the surface; leaves radical, 3-parted, divisions 2-3 partite, and alternately pinnatifid, margins waved; petioles slightly grooved, 1-3 feet long; scapes radical, round, smooth, slightly grooved, and striped with darker and paler green; umbels consisting of 10-40 long-pedicelled, drooping, greenish flowers, intermixed with as many long drooping bracts; involucel 6-12 leaved; leaflets lanceolate, recurved, beautifully marked with pale-purple veins; calyx globose, fleshy, 6-cleft, segments incurved, green, with purplish margins; corolla none. *Fl.* June —August.—*Roxb. Fl. Ind.* ii. 172.——Concans. Parell hills, Bombay.

ECONOMIC USES.—The root is intensely bitter when raw, but yielding a great quantity of white fecula, of which good flour for confectionery is made. In the South Sea Islands, where every kind of grain disappears, its place is partly supplied by these fleshy tubers. The fecula much resembles arrowroot, and is very nutritive. It possesses a considerable degree of acrimony, and requires frequent washing in cold water previous to being dressed. In Travancore, where the root grows to a large size, and is called *Chanay kalungoo*, it is much eaten by the natives, who mix some agreeable acids with it to subdue its natural pungency.—*Roxb. Ainslie.*

(542) **Tamarindus Indica** (*Linn.*) N. O. LEGUMINOSÆ.

Tamarind or Indian Date, ENG. Poolie, TAM. Balam Poolie, MAL. Chinta-chettu, TEL. Umbli, HIND. or DUK. Hoonise, CAN.

DESCRIPTION.—Tree, 80 feet; calyx limb bilabiate, reflexed; petals 3, alternate with the segments of the upper lip of the calyx; seven short stamens all sterile, the others longer, fertile; leaves abruptly pinnated; leaflets numerous; legumes linear, more or less curved, 1-celled, many-seeded; seeds compressed, bluntly 4-angled; flowers in racemes with straw-coloured calyx, and yellow petals streaked with red, purple filaments and brown anthers. *Fl.* May—June.—*W. & A. Prod.* i. 285.—*Roxb. Fl. Ind.* iii. 215.—*Rheede*, i. 23.——Peninsula. Bengal.

Medical Uses.—The pulp of the pods is used both in food and in medicine. It has a pleasant juice, which contains a larger proportion of acid with the saccharine matter than is usually found in acid fruit. Tamarinds are preserved in two ways: first, by throwing hot sugar from the boiler on the ripe pulp; but a better way is to put alternate layers of tamarinds and powdered sugar into a stone jar. By this means they preserve their colour, and taste better. They contain sugar, mucilage, citric acid, tartaric and malic acids. In medicine, the pulp taken in quantity of half an ounce or more proves gently laxative and stomachic, and at the same time quenches the thirst. It increases the action of the sweet purgatives cassia and manna, and weakens that of resinous cathartics. The seed is sometimes given by the Vytians in cases of dysentery, and also as a tonic, and in the form of an electuary. In times of scarcity the poor eat the tamarind-stones. After being roasted and soaked for a few hours in water, the dark outer skin comes off, and they are then boiled or fried. In Ceylon, a confection prepared with the flowers is supposed to have virtues in obstructions of the liver and spleen. A decoction of the acid leaves of the tree is employed externally in cases requiring repellent fomentation. They are also used for preparing collyria, and taken internally are supposed a remedy in jaundice. The natives have a prejudice against sleeping under the tree, and the acid damp does certainly affect the cloth of tents if they are pitched under them for any length of time. Many plants do not grow under its shade, but it is a mistake to suppose that this applies to all herbs and shrubs. In sore-throat the pulp has been found beneficial as a powerful cleanser. The gum reduced to fine powder is applied to ulcers; the leaves in infusion to country sore eyes and foul ulcers. The stones, pulverised and made into thick paste with water, have the property when applied to the skin of promoting suppuration in indolent boils.—*Ainslie. Thornton. Don.*

Economic Uses.—The timber is heavy, firm, and hard, and is converted to many useful purposes in building. An infusion of the leaves is used in Bengal in preparing a fine fixed yellow dye, to give those silks a green colour which have been previously dyed with indigo. Used also simply as a red dye for woollen stuffs. In S. India a strong infusion of the fruit mixed with sea-salt is used by silversmiths in preparing a mixture for cleaning and brightening silver. The pulverised seeds boiled into a paste with thin glue form one of the strongest wood-cements. The tree is one of those preferred for making charcoal for gunpowder.—(*Lindley. Roxb.*) The tree is of slow growth, but is longer-lived than most trees. The timber is used for mills and the teeth of wheels, and whenever very hard timber is requisite. It is much prized as fuel for bricks. Its seeds should be sown where it is to remain, and it may be planted in avenues alternately with short-lived trees of quicker growth. From the liability of this tree to become hollow in the centre, it is extremely difficult to get a tamarind-plank of any width.—(*Best's Report to Bomb. Govt.*, 1863.) There is a considerable export trade of tamarinds from Bombay and Madras. In 1869-70 were exported from the latter Presidency 10,071 cwt., valued at Rs. 33,009; and from the former 6232 cwt., valued at Rs. 26,209.—*Trade Reports.*

(543) **Tamarix Gallica** (*Linn.*) N. O. TAMARICACEÆ.

Indian Tamarix, ENG. Jahoo, BENG.

DESCRIPTION.—Shrub, 6 feet; sepals 5; petals 5; young branches glabrous; leaves amplexicaul, glabrous; torus 10-toothed, leaves ovate, acute, with white edges; spikes elongated, straight, panicled; capsules attenuated; flowers small, rose-coloured. *Fl.* July—Aug.—*W. & A. Prod.* i. 40.—*Wight Ill.* i. *t.* 24, *f.* 1.—T. Indica, *Roxb. Fl. Ind.* ii. 100. ——Coromandel. Banks of the Indus and Ganges.

MEDICAL USES.—The twigs of this shrub are considered astringent, and are valuable for the galls which are formed on the plant, and which are used for dyeing and in medicine. The ashes of the shrub, when it grows near the sea, are remarkable for containing a quantity of sulphate of soda, and cannot be used as a ley for washing, as they coagulate soap. When grown in sweet soil they are free from soda. —(*Royle. Wight.*) The late Dr Stocks spoke highly of the astringent properties of the Tamarix Gall, and from personal experience recommended a strong infusion of them as a local application to foul ulcers and buboes. By the natives they are administered internally in dysentery and diarrhœa. The *T. orientalis* (Vahl.) also yields galls, but of smaller size; they are likewise employed as an astringent. The bark is bitter, astringent, and probably tonic.—*Pharm. of India.*

(544) **Tectona grandis** (*Linn.*) N. O. VERBENACEÆ.

Teak-tree, ENG. Theka or Tekka, MAL. Thaikoo marum, TAM. Teka, TEL. Segoon, BENG.

DESCRIPTION.—Large tree, with an ash-coloured and scaly bark; young shoots 4-sided, channelled; leaves opposite, oval, scabrous above, whitish and downy beneath; panicles terminal, large, cross-armed, divisions dichotomous, with a sessile fertile flower in each cleft, the whole covered with a coloured farina; peduncles quadrangular, sides deeply channelled; flowers numerous, small, white; calyx and corolla 5-6 cleft; stamens often six; ovary round, hairy, 4-celled; cells 1-seeded; nut very hard. *Fl.* June—Aug.—*Roxb. Cor.* i. *t.* 6.—*Fl. Ind.* i. 600.—*Rheede*, iv. *t.* 27.——Banks of the Taptee and Godavery. Malabar. Concans. Bundlecund.

MEDICAL USES.—Endlicher states that the flowers are diuretic, an observation confirmed by Dalzell (*Bomb. Flor.* p. 319), who saw a striking instance of the effect of fresh teak-seeds applied to the umbilicus in a case of infantile suppression of urine.

ECONOMIC USES.—The Teak is perhaps the most useful of all the timber-trees of the Indian Peninsula. Its strength and durability are well known. For house-building it is the best of woods when it can be procured, owing to its resisting the attacks of white ants from the oily nature of the wood. It is, however, an expensive kind of timber, and except in those countries where it is plentiful, the price is too great to allow of its being used for ordinary purposes. Great quantities are used on the western coast for shipbuilding, for which it is superior to any other kinds of wood. The Malabar Teak is reckoned better than any other. It grows best by the sides of rivers; and though not extensively distributed, is found in detached clumps rather than scattered among other trees. In the mountains of Bundlecund it is a very moderate-sized tree. Extensive forests of Teak are found in Pegu and the banks of the Irrawaddy. The tree requires sixty to eighty years to reach a proper age and maturity to fit it for shipbuilding. After the best straight timber has been taken, the crooked pieces, called *shin-logs*, are used for many useful purposes. Teak does not injure iron, and is not liable to shrink in width.

Much valuable information respecting Teak may be found in Dr Falconer's Report upon the Teak-forests of the Tenasserim Provinces. Among other remarks, he states: "Malabar Teak is by common consent ranked higher for shipbuilding than Tenasserim or Pegu timber. The cause of its greater durability and power of resisting dry-rot appears to depend chiefly on its more oily or resinous quality, and the greater density arising from its slow growth on the sides of hills. The Teak in favourable ground shoots up rapidly during the first eight or ten years. I have cut down a young tree measuring 25 feet in height with a slender stem of 11 inches in girth near the base, which showed 8 concentric rings, indicating 8 years of age. After this the growth is much slower, and the tree does not attain the timber size of 6 to 8 feet in girth under from 80 to 100 years, varying greatly according to situation, soil, and exposure. The seeds ought to be collected off the trees before shedding in the month of January, when fully ripe, and sown in narrow raised beds, carefully prepared as nurseries early in March. The plan of sowing which has proved so successful with Mr Conolly at Nelumboor in Malabar, ought to be adopted in preference to all others, as it is founded upon experience; viz., steeping the nuts in water for thirty-six hours, then sowing them in holes 4 inches apart, about half an inch under the surface, and covering the beds with straw and grass litter, so as to prevent evaporation. The beds thus prepared to be gently watered every evening, so as to keep the soil constantly moist around the nuts, which will sprout in from four to eight weeks—that is to say, such of them as are capable of germination. Mr Conolly's memorandum states a shorter period, probably caused by the preliminary steeping. In order to guard against accident from over-soaking at the outset, in the Tenasserim nurseries half of the nuts might be sown dry. A little experience would soon indicate which plan was the best.

"In selecting the nuts, the largest and best-formed to be chosen, and for every 1000 seedlings required, 30,000 or 40,000 nuts ought to be put in the ground, so as to allow a wide margin for failures in germination, and for the selection of good plants. Where two or three stems sprout from the same nut, such plants ought to be rejected, if the nursery is well filled, or the superfluous shoots lopped off, leaving only one to grow. If the sowing has been well managed, the plants will have attained from 4 to 6 inches early in the rains, when they ought at once to be transplanted into the holes prepared for their reception. Repeated transplantations are injurious to the vigour of a seedling, besides being additionally expensive."

Again, in the reports made to Government regarding the Madras and Bombay forests it is stated: "The principal forest districts are those of Malabar, Canara, Travancore, and Goojerat on the western coast of the Peninsula of Hindostan. There are also in the neighbourhood of Rajahmundry, on the eastern side of the Peninsula, extensive forests which stretch inland in a westerly direction towards the territories of the Nizam." Mr Monro, formerly Resident in Travancore, says: "The Teak-tree shoots up for the first seven or eight years remarkably fast, till it attains the height of 12 or 15 feet, after which its growth is uncommonly slow; and it does not attain the rise of the sixth-class log even in the most favourable situation till it is about 35 or 40 years old; a fifth class takes about 50 years, a fourth about 60, a third about 70 or 80, a second about 90, and first class takes about 100 to 120 years." The Teak which grows on the sides and tops of mountains is far superior to that which grows in the black heavy soil of the low grounds; and though it takes a longer time to attain the same dimensions as the other, yet in strength and durability it is generally superior.

The difference in the qualities of Malabar and Burmah Teak arises from differences of soil, exposure, and humidity. A Teak-tree in Burmah 10 years old has a girth of 18 inches at 6 feet from the ground, while one in Bombay will require 20 years to reach this size. Quality depends much on the comparative rate of growth; and the slower this is, as a general rule, the denser and finer-grained is the timber. Thus Teak grown in Burmah weighs generally 42 lb. to the cubic foot, while that grown on the western coast of India rises as high as 55 lb., and the difference in strength varies from 190 to 289. In Malabar the price has risen gradually from 20 rupees to 45 rupees per candy of 12½ cubic feet in 1864.—(*Conserv. of Forests Report to Bomb. Govt.*, 1865.) There are two practical lessons to be learnt with regard to sowing and the selection of the seed: First, Teak-seed should be gathered and sown when it is ripe, as then, the juices not having dried up, the germination will be more speedy; second, the seed should always be taken from young and healthy trees. Teak-forests may be divided into high Teak-forests, as in the Dangs and North Canara, and scrubby Teak-forests, as they exist in the Concan. Although the same plants, the growth is materially altered by soil, climate, and forest operations. The former is felled every 80 to 120 years; the scrub is cut down every 15 years, the roots remaining in the ground and sending forth fresh shoots to form a new coppice. The Teak takes up from the soil a quantity of silica, hence sandstone and granite soils are the favourite places for the tree. To this large secretion of silica must be attributed the strength and durability of the timber. The vertical range of the Teak-tree is from the sea-level up to 3000 feet, but it always avoids exposed situations. The tree blossoms in the rains, and by the end of August is the proper time to commence cutting down the tree, when the cambium will have been expended, as otherwise it would render the timber liable to the attacks of certain insects which subsist on this fluid.—*Dalzell's Natural History of the Teak-tree.*

The Annamullay mountains yield the finest Teak in the Madras Presidency. The Teak-forests are at an elevation of from 2000 to 3000 feet. Some portions of the Cochin forests are still untouched, and the Teak-trees there are superb: trees have been measured 20 feet in circumference.

Captain Harris gives the following description of the method of preparing the timber: "On the opening of the season the tree is sawed through above the roots, and left in that state for a time to absorb the sap, then felled to the ground and trimmed into shape; here it may be left one or two seasons, or is at once dragged by elephants to the banks of rivers, and finally floated down to the sea on the first rise of its waters. In Malabar the timber merchants who purchase the trees have them felled and conveyed to the adjacent streams, down which they are taken to the markets on the coast, where an inland duty of 5 per cent is levied. From this depot the Bombay or foreign merchant exports it at an enormous profit to the coast dealer, who then pays an additional 3 per cent, or in all a duty of 8 per cent per candy, on its leaving the coast." This duty is levied on an assessment of the article on the average of

$9\frac{2}{3}$ rupees the candy—the first-class timber being assessed at 12 rupees, the second at 9 rupees, and the third class at 8 rupees the candy.

From the tender leaves a purple colour is extracted which is used as a dye for silk and cotton cloths.—*Roxb.* *Dr Falconer's Reports.* *Reports on Madras and Bombay Forests in Government Selections.**

(545) **Terminalia angustifolia** (*Jacq.*) N. O. COMBRETACEÆ.

DESCRIPTION.—Tree, 30-40 feet; calyx campanulate, 5-cleft; petals none; leaves alternate, linear-lanceolate, attenuated at both ends, crowded at the ends of the branches, under side and petioles pubescent or hairy; drupe compressed, 2-winged, gibbous on one side; stamens in 2 rows; seed almond-like; flowers spiked, small, green, odoriferous. *Fl.* March—April.—*W. & A. Prod.* i. 312.——Peninsula.

ECONOMIC USES.—This tree produces one kind of benzoin. It is procured by wounding the tree; and is composed of large white and light-brown pieces easily broken between the hands. When gently dried it forms a white powder, formerly in great request as a cosmetic. It has a most agreeable scent. But the most striking ingredient of this resin is the *Benzoic acid.* In the churches in Mauritius this benzoin is used as incense. The fruit is used like that of *T. chebula.*—*Royle.*

(546) **Terminalia Bellerica** (*Roxb.*) Do.

Belleric Myrobalen, ENG. Tani-kai, TAM. Tani, MAL. Bahura, BENG. Teandee, Tadi, TEL.

DESCRIPTION.—Tree, 100 feet; leaves about the extremities of the branchlets, long-petioled, obovate, quite entire, glabrous; spikes axillary, solitary, almost as long as the leaves; bisexual flowers sessile; male shortly pedicellate; drupe obovate, obscurely 5-angled, fleshy, covered with greyish silky down; flowers fetid, small, greyish green. *Fl.* March—April.—*W. & A. Prod.* i. 313.—*Wight Ill.* i. *t.* 91.—*Roxb. Fl. Ind.* ii. 431.—*Cor.* ii. *t.* 198.—*Rheede, Mal.* iv. *t.* 10.——Peninsula. Bengal.

MEDICAL USES.—A quantity of insipid gum, resembling Gum-Arabic, issues from the trunk when wounded; soluble in water, but inflammable, and will burn like a candle. The kernel of the nut is said to intoxicate if eaten in any great quantity. Mixed with

* For mode of seasoning Teak, see Appendix F.

honey it is used in ophthalmia. The fruit in its dried state is larger than a gall-nut, but not so regular in shape. It is astringent in taste, and is tonic and attenuant.—(*Ainslie. Roxb.*) It is also used in dropsy, diarrhœa, piles, and leprosy, as well as for coughs. In large doses it becomes a narcotic poison. The produce of a single tree will sometimes sell for 2000 rupees. The fruit ripens about October, and consists of a nut enclosed in a thin exterior rind. It is used as an aperient, and also forms a dingy yellow dye. The fruit is exported by traders from the plains, who generally contract for each tree according to the produce it bears. A single nut sometimes sells for a rupee.—(*Barnes in Powell's Punj. Prod.*) These fruits are procurable at a nominal cost throughout India; and when other aperients are not available, may safely be resorted to. Their astringency renders them valuable in the arts, as well as a substitute for galls for lotions, injections, and so on. Twining (*Diseases of Bengal*) gives a case of enlargement of the spleen where this medicine was used with the best effects.—*Pharm. of India.*

ECONOMIC USES.—The wood is white and durable, good for working purposes, large chests, and shipbuilding.—*Roxb.*

(547) Terminalia Catappa (*Linn.*) Do.

Indian Almond, ENG. Nattoo vadamcottay, TAM. Adamarum, MAL. Vadam, TEL. Bādāmia-hindie, DUK. Badam, BENG.

DESCRIPTION.—Tree, 50 feet; leaves about the extremities of the branchlets, short-petioled, obovate, cuneate or slightly cordate at the base, a little repand, with a large gland beneath on either side the midrib near the base; racemes axillary, solitary, simple, shorter than the leaves; drupe compressed, oval, with elevated margins, convex on both sides; flowers small, dull white, with a hairy glandular disk at the bottom of the calyx. *Fl.* March—April.—*W. & A. Prod.* i. 313.—*Rheede,* iv. *t.* 3, 4.—T. Catappa, *Roxb. Fl. Ind.* ii. 430.—*Wight Icon. t.* 172. ——Cultivated.

MEDICAL USES.—The bark is astringent. The kernels, known as country almonds, might probably be used as a substitute for the officinal almond. They yield upwards of fifty per cent of pure bland oil. After being kept for some time, this oil deposits a large proportion of stearine.—(*Journ. of Agri. Hort. Soc. of India,* ii. 539.) The oil which is expressed from the seeds is edible and pleasant-tasted. To extract it, the fruit is gathered and allowed to dry in the sun for a few days, when the kernels are cleaned, and bruised in a mill. Six seers of almonds will produce 3 pucka seers of oil. The colour is a deep straw. It is very like Europe almond-oil both in taste and smell, but becomes turbid by keeping. It only requires care and attention in its preparation to render it of greater commercial value and importance.—*Ainslie. Pharm. of India.*

ECONOMIC USES.—The tree is handsome and ornamental, and answers well for avenues. The timber is light but lasting, and is useful for many purposes. The bark and leaves yield a black pigment, with which the natives dye their teeth and make Indian ink. The levers of Pakottahs are usually made of the timber of this tree. Tussah-silk worms feed on the leaves. Rheede says the tree bears fruit three times a-year on the Malabar coast. It is a native of the Moluccas.—*Roxb. Ainslie.*

(548) **Terminalia Chebula** (*Retz.*) Do.

Kadukai-marum, TAM. Kodorka-marum, MAL. Karakaia, TEL. Huldah, DUK. Hur or Hara, HIND. Haree-tukee, BENG. Atala, CAN.

DESCRIPTION.—Tree, 40-50 feet; leaves nearly opposite, shortly petioled, ovate-oblong, obtuse or cordate at the base, quite entire, when young clothed with glossy silky hairs, particularly above, adult ones glabrous, sometimes glaucous, upper surface inconspicuously dotted, under closely reticulated with purplish veins; glands one on each side at the apex of the petiole; spikes terminal, often panicled; drupes oval, glabrous; nut irregularly and obscurely 5-furrowed; flowers small, whitish, fetid. *Fl.* March—April.—*W. & A. Prod.* i. 313.—*Roxb. Fl. Ind.* ii. 433.—*Cor.* ii. *t.* 197.—T. reticulata, *Roth.*——Peninsula. Bengal.

MEDICAL USES.—The Kadukai (*gall-nuts*) well rubbed with an equal proportion of catechu is used in aphthous complaints, and considered a valuable remedy. The unripe dried fruits, which are the Indian or black myrobolan (Kooroovillah-kadukai, *Tam. and Mal.*) of old writers, and which are sold in the Northern Provinces in Bengal, are recommended as purgative by the natives.—(*Ainslie.*) The gall-like excrescences found on the leaves, caused by the deposited ova of some insect, are held in great repute as an astringent by the natives. They are very efficacious remedies in infantile diarrhœa, the dose for a child under a year old being one grain every three hours. It has been administered in many instances with the greatest benefit.—(*Pharm. of India.*) The price and supposed efficacy of the fruit increase with the size; one weighing six tolahs would cost about 20 rupees. It acts internally as aperient, externally as an astringent applicatiốn to ulcers and skin diseases.—*Powell's Punj. Prod.*

ECONOMIC USES.—The outer coat of the fruit of this tree mixed with sulphate of iron makes a very durable ink. The galls are found on the leaves, and are produced by insects puncturing the tender leaves. With them and alum the best and most durable yellow is dyed, and in conjunction with ferruginous mud, black is procured from them. The fruit is very astringent, and on that account much used by the Hindoos in their arts and manufactures. The timber is good, of a yellowish-brown colour. It is used for agricultural purposes and for building. It attains its full size in thirty years.—*Roxb.*

(549) **Terminalia coriacea** (*W. & A.*) Do.

Kara-maradoo, TAM. Mutti, CAN.

DESCRIPTION.—Tree; bark deeply cracked; leaves nearly opposite, short-petioled, coriaceous, oval, cordate at the base, hard above, hoary and soft beneath, 1-2 sessile glands at or near the base of the midrib; spikes panicled; nut hoary; flowers small, dull yellow. *Fl.* July.—*W. & A. Prod.* i. 315.—Pentaptera coriacea, *Roxb. Fl. Ind.* ii. 438.——Coromandel mountains.

ECONOMIC USES.—A large tree, yielding strong, hard, and heavy timber. It is much used for making the solid wheels of buffalo-carts and for railway-sleepers.

(550) **Terminalia glabra** (*W. & A.*) Do.

Tella-madoo, TEL.

DESCRIPTION.—Tree; bark smooth; leaves nearly opposite, narrow-oblong, obtuse or acute at the apex, glabrous on both sides, often reddish beneath, with some nearly sessile glands near the base of the mid-rib; spikes terminal; drupe ovate, with 5-7 equal longitudinal wings. *Fl.* May—April.—*W. & A. Prod.* i. 314.—Pentaptera glabra, *Roxb. Fl. Ind.* ii. 440.——Peninsula. Silhet. Monghyr.

ECONOMIC USES.—A valuable timber-tree, with a large and lofty trunk.—(*Roxb.*) It is very suitable for strong framings, and very durable. It is procurable 25-30 feet in length, 15 inches in diameter, will season in 12 to 15 months in planks, and is not touched by white ants.—(*Jury Rep. Mad. Exhib.*) The *T. paniculata* (W. & A.) is a fine stout timber-tree. The wood is improved by being kept under water for some time. The bark contains tannin. It grows in Malabar and the Concan valleys.—*Roxb.*

(551) **Terminalia tomentosa** (*W. & A.*) Do.

Nella-madoo, TEL. Aanis, HIND. Peea-sal or Usan, BENG.

DESCRIPTION.—Tree; bark deeply cracked; leaves nearly

opposite, linear-oblong, somewhat cordate at the base, pubescent, but finally glabrous above, tomentose or pubescent beneath, with thick-stalked turbinate glands on the mid-rib near the base; fruit glabrous; spikes disposed in a brachiate panicle; flowers small, greenish white. *Fl.* April—June.—*W. & A. Prod.* i. 314.—*Wight Icon. t.* 195.—Pentaptera tomentosa, *Roxb. Fl. Ind.* ii. 440.——Concan. Oude. Monghyr.

Medical Uses.—The bark is astringent, and in the form of decoction is useful internally in atonic diarrhœa, and locally as an application to indolent ulcers. The dose of the decoction (two ounces of the bruised bark to a pint of water) is two ounces thrice daily.—*Pharm. of India.*

Economic Uses.—The timber is valuable, and is much used for making shafts of gigs, and other things where toughness of fibre is required. The bark is astringent and used for dyeing black.—(*Roxb.*) The bark, in addition to yielding a black dye, is so charged with calcareous matter, that its ashes, when burnt, afford a substitute for the lime which the natives in Ceylon chew with their betel.—(*Tennent's Ceylon,* i. 99.) It yields a gum used as an incense and cosmetic. It costs 27 to 30 rupees the maund. The trees are plentiful in the Kurnool forests.

(552) **Tetranthera monopetala** (*Roxb.*) N. O. Lauraceæ.

Narra mamady, Tel. Buro kookoorchitta, Beng.

Description.—Tree, middling size; leaves alternate, short-petioled, oblong, entire, smooth on the upper surface, pubescent beneath; flowers male and female; peduncles axillary, numerous, short; flowers small, yellowish green. *Fl.* May—June.—*Roxb. Cor.* ii. *t.* 148.—*Fl. Ind.* iii. 821.——Peninsula. Bengal. Oude.

Medical Uses.—The bark is mildly astringent, and has balsamic properties. It is used by the hill people in diarrhœa, and is also applied to wounds and bruises. The leaves are given to silk-worms. They have a smell of cinnamon if bruised.—(*Ainslie. J. Graham.*) The berries yield an oil, which is used for ointment as well as for candles. The wood is aromatic.—*Powell's Punj. Prod.*

(553) **Thalictrum foliolosum** (*Dec.*) N. O. Ranunculaceæ.

Description.—Herbaceous, erect, branched; leaves large, supra-decompound, leaflets very numerous, small, oval, cut and lobed; petioles auricular at the base; sepals oblong, obtuse, 5-7 nerved, pale green or brownish purple; stamens numerous; filaments filiform; anthers mucronate; panicles much branched, leafless; bracts small; achenia few, oval-oblong, acute at both ends, narrowly ribbed; flowers yellowish. *Fl.* Aug.—Sept.—*Dec. Prod.* i. 12.—*Hook. & Thoms. Fl. Ind.* i. 16.—*Royle Ill.* 51.——Khasia mountains.

MEDICAL USES.—The root is called by the hill people where it grows *Pila jari* (*i. e.*, yellow-root), and it is exported from the Kumaon mountains under the name of *Momeeree*. It is yellow internally, and contains a yellow bitter extractive, which yields to alcohol and water. It combines tonic and aperient qualities, and has been found useful in convalescence after acute diseases, in mild forms of intermittent fevers and atonic dyspepsia. The 'Bengal Dispensatory' gives the dose of the powdered root from five to ten grains; and of the extract, prepared like extract of gentian, from two to three grains thrice daily.—(*Beng. Disp. Royle. Pharm. of India.*) Another species, the *T. majus*, is used as a substitute for rhubarb.

(554) Thea viridis (*Linn.*) N. O. TERNSTRŒMIACEÆ.

China Tea-plant, ENG.

DESCRIPTION.—Shrubby; leaves lanceolate, flat, serrated, three times longer than broad; sepals 5-6; petals 6-9; flowers axillary, solitary, erect, white; fruit nodding, dehiscent; capsule tricoccous.—*Dec. Prod.* i. 530.—*Sim's Bot. Mag. t.* 998. ——Cultivated.

ECONOMIC USES.—The first attempt to introduce the cultivation of the tea-plant in India was in 1830, at which time it was discovered to be indigenous to the country of Assam. From the similarity in point of climate between that country and China, it was considered a desirable measure by the Government to promote its cultivation in the district, from whence it soon extended to the neighbouring countries of Cachar and Silhet, and subsequently to the hill districts of the North-Western Provinces of India and the Punjaub.

In the latter country experiments were soon in full operation. Extensive nurseries and plantations were laid out under the direction of Government in Kumaon, Gurwhal, and in the Dehra Dhoon. The progress was at first slow, but no doubt existed as to the favourable results of the future, and the first crop of tea was obtained in 1843. The Chinamen who had been located there to assist in the work asserted that the tea-plant of Kumaon was the genuine cultivated Chinese plant, and superior to the indigenous tea of Assam. Specimens of the tea sent to London were pronounced to be fine-flavoured and strong, and superior for the most part to Chinese tea imported for mercantile purposes. It was at this time that Dr William Jameson was appointed to the charge of the Government tea-plantations in the hill districts of the North-Western Provinces. Encouraged by his success in Kumaon, that officer resolved to introduce the plant into the Punjaub, and with that view selected the Kangra valley, choosing at first two sites for nurseries at the respective elevations of 2900 and 3300 feet above the level of the sea. The experiment was justified by the most satisfactory results. In 1869 there were nineteen plantations in the Kangra valley, including one in the Mundee territory and one in the Koolloo valley. Of these the area actually under tea cultivation comprised 2635 acres, the gross aggregate produce in the season of 1868 amounting to 241,332 lb. of tea. The average produce per acre was 91.6 lb. of tea, and the average price realised by sale Rs. 1-1-3 (2s. 2d.) per lb.

The first desiderata in selecting the site for a tea-plantation are soil and climate, the best mode of cultivation, system of manufacture, and cost of production. Small plantations are far preferable to large ones. It was owing to the too rapid formation of extensive and therefore unmanageable estates, that led to so many failures in Assam. A rich loamy soil is the best suited for tea; but, *cæteris paribus*, the various soils suitable for cereals are also suited for tea. The great object is to insure deep soil, free from rocks and stones. A tolerably moist climate, such as may be found at elevations of from 2500 to 5000 feet above the level of the sea, are most suitable, and in localities free from all influence of hot winds in summer.

The following mode of cultivation, as adopted in the Kangra district, is given in Major Paske's Report, 1869, p. 14, 15: "On most of the plantations a system of high cultivation is adopted. The ground is well prepared by deep digging and manuring, the seed carefully sown, and only healthy seedlings planted out. Twice in the year the soil is turned up with the hoe, grass and weeds removed, and manure given. Top-pruning of the plants is attended to, buds and blossoms are picked off, and no seeds are allowed to ripen. Under a good system of high cultivation, an acre of tea-bushes might be made to produce 250 lb. of tea. . . . The flashes or new shoots come on four or five times between April and October, and the pickings take place when these new shoots are 3 or 4 inches long. . . . The cost of production varies on different plantations, according to their condition and the care and skill displayed in their management. On a plantation where tea is manufactured at an average of 190 lb. or 200 lb. per acre, the cost of production and manufacture may be set down at about, or a trifle under, 8 annas (1s.) per lb."—*Selections from Records of Punj. Govt.*, No. V., 1869.

The estimated number of seedlings for 1 acre is about 4000. This allows for the young plant being planted about 4½ feet apart. The custom of putting a number of plants in one and the same pit, so as to form a bush rapidly, is not desirable, as the growth of one plant interferes with the other. It has been calculated that if properly planted, and the work carried on energetically, the Kohistan of the Punjaub and North-Western Provinces in forty years might raise tea in quantity to equal the whole export trade of China—as with good cultivation on good land, 300 lb. of tea per acre may readily be obtained. Tea has been proved to be a hardy plant, and its cultivation very profitable. The plantations give employment to thousands of men, women, and children, especially in the Punjaub, and by indirect means insures the comfort and welfare of the population in those districts where they are located.

During 1867-8, 21,588 lb. of various teas were prepared in the Kumaon plantations. The manufacture of black tea in that year appears to have had small demand, whereas green tea met with a ready sale. The fact is, it is only the better classes of natives who consume it, and then the market in India is necessarily limited. The demand in the countries beyond the Indus is considerable, and it appears that the consumption in Russia alone amounts to £60,000,000.—(*Dr Jameson's Report.*) There is no regular price in the markets of the North-Western Provinces for Indian teas. By private sales the prices obtained are: Souchong from Rs. 2 to 1-12; Bohea, 12 annas; Green, Rs. 2; Hyson, 12 annas. A considerable export trade takes place to Cabool and Bokhara, nearly 8000 lb. having been sent there during six months.

Of late years much attention has been paid to the cultivation of tea on the Neilgherry hills at elevations ranging from 5000 to 7000 feet, as well as in other mountainous districts. In fact, the increasing cultivation of this useful product in the hill districts of India is attracting that attention it deserves.*

(555) **Theobroma Cacao** (*Linn.*) N. O. Byttneriaceæ.

Cacao or Chocolate tree, Eng.

Description.—Small tree; leaves quite entire, ovate-oblong, acuminate, quite glabrous; sepals 5; petals 5, forked at the base, produced into a spathulate ligula; urceolus of stamens exserting 5 little horns, and between them 5 bi-antheriferous filaments opposite the petals; style filiform; capsule 5-celled, without valves; seeds nestling in buttery pulp.—*Dec. Prod.* i. 484.—Cacao sativa, *Lam.* i. *t.* 635.——Cultivated.

Medical Uses.—A concrete oil is obtained by expression and heat from the ground seeds. It is of the consistence of tallow, and its odour resembles that of chocolate. The taste is agreeable, and

* The fullest information regarding the Tea-planting operations in Cachar, Darjeeling, and Assam, may be found in the Prize Essays published in the 14th vol. of the Journal of the Agri.-Hort. Soc. of India, and also in the Records of Government, and Dr Jameson's several valuable reports. See also Appendix G.

it does not become rancid from exposure to the air. It is chiefly used as an emollient.—*Pharm. of India.*

ECONOMIC USES.—The Cacao plant has been long introduced into India from tropical America. In cultivation it requires shade, and the young plants especially must be well supplied with water. Under favourable circumstances the yield of fruit is very considerable. The trees are raised from seed, and come into full bearing when five or six years old. The tree seldom grows above the height of 20 feet. The flowers spring from the trunk and larger branches. The seeds are oval, and covered with a husk of a reddish-brown colour. A tree in full bearing is said to yield annually 150 lb. of seed, but the number of nuts in the pods varies considerably. These nuts, when separated from the pulp in which they are surrounded, laid on mats and dried in the sun, and then ground and roasted, constitute the Cocoa of commerce. Chocolate is the same made into a paste and flavoured.—(*Oliver's Kew Guide.*) The Cacao-seeds were made use of by the Mexicans previous to the arrival of the Spaniards, boiled with maize and roughly bruised between two stones, and eaten seasoned with capsicum and honey.—(*Macfadyen's Jamaica.*) The process at present used by Europeans does not greatly differ from the above; more care is taken in grinding the seeds after they are roasted, so as to convert them into a perfectly smooth paste. Cloves and cinnamon are much used as flavouring ingredients, but the principal one is vanilla. The thorough mixture of these substances having been effected, the whole is put while hot into tin moulds, where it hardens in cooling; and in this form, if kept from the air, will keep good for a considerable time. The seeds of the Cacao were made use of as money in Mexico in the time of the Aztec kings, and this use of them is still continued, the smaller seeds being used for the purpose.—*Lankester Veg. Subst.*

(556) **Thespesia populnea** (*Lam.*) N. O. MALVACEÆ.

Portia tree, ENG. Porsung or Pooarasoo, TAM. Parspippu, HIND. Poresh, BENG. Ghengheravie, TEL. Parish, DUK. Boogooi, CAN.

DESCRIPTION.—Tree; leaves roundish-cordate, acuminated, quite entire, 5-7 nerved, sprinkled beneath with small rusty scales; calyx truncated; involucel 3-leaved; capsule 5-celled, coriaceous; cells about 4-seeded; flowers yellow, with a dark blood-coloured eye. *Fl.* Nearly all the year.—*W. & A. Prod.* i. 54.—*Wight Icon. t.* 8.—Hibiscus populneus, *Linn.—Roxb. Fl. Ind.* iii. 190.—*Rheede,* i. *t.* 29.——Travancore. Courtallum. Bengal.

MEDICAL USES.—The capsule is filled with a yellow pigment like liquid gamboge, which is a good external application in scabies and other cutaneous diseases, the juice being simply applied to the parts affected. The bark boiled in water is used as a wash for the same purposes with the best effect. The bark in decoction is given as an alterative internally. The Cingalese dye yellow with the capsules. —*Ainslie. Pers. Obs.*

Economic Uses.—The wood is used for making rollers, and other purposes where closeness of grain is required. It is also an excellent wood for gun-stocks. The tree is remarkable for its easy and rapid growth from cuttings. It is frequently used on this account as a tree for roadside avenues. Its wood makes pretty furniture, and is much used for the ribs of the roofs of the cabin-boats at Cochin.—*Ainslie. J. Grah.*

(557) Thevetia nereifolia (*Juss.*) N. O. Apocynaceæ.

Exile tree, Eng.

Description.—Tree, 12 feet; leaves linear, entire, almost veinless, glabrous; calyx 5-cleft; segments ovate-lanceolate, acute, three times shorter than the tube of the corolla; peduncles extra-axillary at the tops of the branches, 1-flowered; corolla funnel-shaped, tube hairy inside; flowers yellow, fragrant; drupe half orbicular, truncated at the apex, 2-celled; cells bipartite. *Fl.* Nearly all the year.——Domesticated in India.

Medical Uses.—This pretty shrub is a native of South America and the West Indies, but has long been naturalised in India. An oil is extracted from the kernels of nuts. It is of a clear bright yellow colour, but its uses and properties are as yet undetermined. The milk of the tree is highly venomous. Its bitter and cathartic bark is reported to be a powerful febrifuge, two grains only being affirmed to be equal to an ordinary dose of cinchona. —*Lindley. Jury Rep. Mad. Exhib.*

(558) Tiaridium Indicum (*Lehm.*) N. O. Ehretiaceæ.

Indian Turnsole, Eng. Tayl-kodukhoo, Tam. Benapatsja, Mal. Tayl-munnie, Tel. Hatee-shooro, Beng.

Description.—Annual, 1 foot; stem hairy; leaves generally alternate, petioled, cordate, wrinkled, curled at the margins; spikes leaf-opposed, solitary, peduncled, longer than the leaves; flowers sessile, minute, in 2 rows on the upper sides of the spikes; corolla longer than the calyx, tube gibbous; flowers small, lilac-bluish. *Fl.* April—Nov.—*Roxb. Fl. Ind.* i. 454.—Heliotropium Indicum, *Linn.*—*Rheede,* x. *t.* 48.——Travancore. Chittagong.

MEDICAL USES.—This is commonly to be met with in rubbish and out-of-the-way corners, in rich and rank soils. The plant is astringent. The juice of the leaves is applied to gum-boils and pimples on the face, and also in certain cases of ophthalmia. In Jamaica it is used to clean and consolidate wounds and ulcers, and boiled with castor-oil it is of use in the stings or bites of poisonous animals. It is said by Martius to allay inflammation with undoubted advantage.—*Ainslie. Lindley. Browne's History of Jamaica.*

(559) **Tiliacora acuminata** (*Miers*). N. O. MENISPERMACEÆ.

Tiga-mushadi, TEL. Baga-luta, HIND. Tilia-kora, BENG. Vully-caniram, MAL.

DESCRIPTION.—Twining shrub; leaves ovate, acuminated, acute or truncate, or slightly cordate at the base, glabrous; racemes axillary, usually about half the length of the leaf; pedicels in the males, one or two from each bractea, 2-3 flowered, in the females solitary, 1-flowered; petals much shorter than the filaments; flowers small, cream-coloured, fragrant; drupes numerous. *Fl.* April—July.—*W. & A. Prod.* i. 12.—*Hook. & Thoms. Fl. Ind.* i. p. 187.—Menispermum acuminatum, *Lam.*—M. polycarpum, *Roxb. Fl. Ind.* iii. 816.—*Rheede,* vii. *t.* 3.——Peninsula. Bengal. Common in hedges. Negapatam.

MEDICAL USES.—One of the many plants used as an antidote to snake-bites. It is administered by being rubbed between two stones and mixed with water. It is used in elephantiasis, and a decoction of the leaves is applied externally in ulcers and pustular eruptions.—*Roxb. Rheede.*

(560) **Tinospora cordifolia** (*Miers*). Do.

Sheendie Codie, TAM. Citamerdoo, MAL. Goolbayl, DUK. Gurcha, HIND. Tippatingay, TEL. Guluncha, BENG.

DESCRIPTION.—Twining shrub; bark corky, slightly tubercled; leaves alternate, roundish-cordate, with a broad sinus, shortly and sharply pointed, glabrous; racemes axillary or lateral, of male flowers longer than the leaves, pedicels several together, of female ones scarcely so long as the leaves; pedicels solitary; petals unguiculate; unguis linear, slightly margined upwards; limb triangular, ovate, reflexed; drupes 2-3, globose; flowers small, yellowish. *Fl.* April—July.—*Hook. & Thoms. Fl. Ind.* i. 184.—*W. & A. Prod.* i. 12.

—*Wight Icon.* ii. *t.* 485.—Cocculus cordifolius, *Dec.*—Menispermum cordifolium, *Willd.*—*Rheede,* vii. *t.* 21.——Peninsula. Bengal. Assam.

Medical Uses.—What is known as *Guluncha* extract is procured from the stems of this plant. It is a well-known specific in the bites of poisonous insects, as well as in fevers and rheumatism. The leaves beaten up and mixed with honey are applied externally to ulcers, and with oil to the head as a remedy in colds. In decoction they are given as a tonic in gout. The native practitioners use this plant extensively in a great variety of diseases, especially in fevers, jaundice, and visceral obstructions. The parts chiefly used are the roots, stem, and leaves, from which a decoction called Pachuna is prepared. The extract called Paho is procured also from the stem, and is reputed of much value in urinary affections.

Dr Wight states that from 15 to 20 grains of the powdered root constitute a good emetic, a fact also recorded by Ainslie, who especially remarks that it is a successful remedy in snake-bites, administered in the above dose about three times a-day, at an interval of twenty minutes between each dose. The bitterness of the extract varies according to the season when the plant is gathered, which should be during the hot weather. The young leaves bruised and mixed with milk are used as a liniment in erysipelas. It is stated in the 'Bengal Dispensatory' that in experiments made at the college hospital, the Guluncha was found to be a very useful tonic. The decoction or cold infusion was of great utility in chronic rheumatism and secondary venereal affections. Its action is decidedly diuretic and tonic in a high degree.—(*Bengal Disp. Roxb. Trans. Med. and Phys. Soc., Calcutta. Ainslie.*) The *T. crispa* (Miers), and some other allied species inhabiting various parts of India, possess the bitterness, and probably the tonic properties, of Guluncha.—*Pharm. of India.*

(561) **Toddalia aculeata** (*Pers.*) N. O. Xanthoxylaceæ.

Moolacarnay-marum, Tam. Conda-cashinda, Tel. Kaka-toddali, Mal.

Description.—Shrub, 6 feet; stem and branches prickly; leaflets sessile, from oblong to broad-lanceolate, crenulate, glabrous; midrib beneath, and petioles prickly or occasionally unarmed; racemes simple or compound; fruit 5-furrowed, with 3-5 perfect cells; petals 5, spreading; leaves alternate, digitately trifoliate; flowers small, white, fragrant.—*W. & W. Prod.* i. 149.—*Rheede,* v. *t.* 41.——Coromandel. Malabar. Concans.

Medical Uses.—This is a very common bush on the Coromandel

coast, frequently found in hedges and under trees. All the parts are reckoned febrifugal. The bark of the root is given in remittent jungle fevers. The fresh leaves are eaten raw in stomach complaints. The ripe berries are as pungent as pepper, and make excellent pickles. The whole plant is reckoned a valuable stimulant, and has a strong pungent taste, especially the root. A liniment good in rheumatism is made from the root and green fruit fried in oil.—(*Rheede. Roxb.*) It is apparently a remedy of some value in constitutional debility, and in convalescence after febrile and other exhausting diseases. Under the name of *Lopez root* it formerly had some celebrity in Europe as a remedy for diarrhœa. Dr Bidie states the whole plant possesses active, stimulant, carminative, and tonic properties, and that he knows of no single remedy in which all these three qualities are so happily combined.—*Pharm. of India.*—*Guibourt Hist. des Drogues. Simpl.* ii. 530.—*Murray Appar. Medic.*, ed. 1792, vi. 164.

(562) **Tragia cannabina** (*Linn.*) N. O. Euphorbiaceæ.

Sirroo-canchorie, Tam. Kanch koorie, Duk. Trinuadoolagondie, Tel.

Description.—Annual; stem twining, hispid; leaves hairy, stinging, 3-parted, lanceolate, petioled; peduncles lateral, solitary, 1-flowered, the length of the leaves; flowers small, yellowish. *Fl.* Aug.—Sept.—*Roxb. Fl. Ind.* iii. 575.—— Coromandel. Bengal. Travancore.

Medical Uses.—The hairs of this plant sting like the common nettle. The root is considered diaphoretic, and is prescribed in decoction as an alterative; also in infusion in ardent fevers.—*Ainslie.*

(563) **Tragia involucrata** (*Linn.*) Do.

Canchoorie, Tam. Doolaghondi, Tel. Schorigenam, Mal. Bichitee, Beng.

Description.—Annual, twining; leaves oblong-lanceolate, acute, sharply serrated, alternate, closely covered with stinging hairs; *female* bracts 5-leaved, pinnated; flowers axillary in small clusters, several together on the same footstalk, upper ones male, under ones female; flowers small, greenish. *Fl.* Nearly all the year.—*Roxb. Fl.* iii. 576.—*Rheede*, ii. *t.* 39.—— Peninsula. Bengal. Malabar.

Medical Uses.—The root is used medicinally as an alterative in old venereal complaints. The juice of the same mixed with cow's milk and sugar is given as a drink in fevers and itch. The root in decoction is administered internally against suppression of urine.—*Ainslie. Rheede.*

(564) **Trapa bispinosa** (*Roxb.*) N. O. HALORAGACEÆ.

Panee phul, HIND. **Singhara,** BENG. **Karim pola,** MAL.

DESCRIPTION.—Herbaceous, floating; upper leaves and petioles tomentose beneath, lower leaves opposite, others alternate, floating leaves rather quadrate, serrulately toothed; calyx villous, limb 4-partite; petals 4; crown of the ovary 8-furrowed, the margins curled; fruit 2-horned; horns opposite, conical, very sharp, barbed backwards; petioles furnished with a large bladder in the middle; ovary 2-celled, surrounded by a cap-shaped crown; flowers smallish, white. *Fl.* May—June.—*W. & A. Prod.* i. 337.—*Roxb. Fl. Ind.* i. 428. —*Cor.* iii. 234.—*Rheede,* xi. *t.* 33.——Peninsula. Bengal.

ECONOMIC USES.—The seeds contain a great quantity of fecula, and are eaten by the natives. In Guzerat they form an important article of food. During the Hooly festival a red dye is made from the fruit, mixed with a yellow dye from the flowers of the *Butea frondosa*. Col. Sleeman has given the following interesting account of this plant in his travels in the North-Western Provinces :—

Here, as in most other parts of India, the tank gets spoiled by the water-chestnut (*Singhara*), which is everywhere as regularly planted and cultivated in fields under a large surface of water as wheat or barley is on the dry plains. It is cultivated by a class of men called Dheemurs, who are everywhere fishermen and palankeen-bearers; and they keep boats for the planting, weeding, and gathering the Singhara. The holdings or tenements of each cultivator are marked out carefully on the surface of the water by long bamboos stuck up in it; and they pay so much the acre for the portion they till. The long straws of the plants reach up to the surface of the water, upon which float their green leaves; and their pure white flowers expand beautifully among them in the latter part of the afternoon. The nut grows under the water after the flowers decay, and is of a triangular shape, and covered with a tough brown integument adhering strongly to the kernel, which is white, esculent, and of a fine cartilaginous texture. The people are very fond of these nuts, and they are carried often upon bullocks' backs two or three hundred miles to market. They ripen in the latter end of the rains, or in September, and are eatable till the end of November. The rent paid for an ordinary tank by the cultivator is about one hundred rupees a-year. I have known two hundred rupees to be paid for a very large one, and even three hundred, or thirty pounds a-year. But the mud increases so rapidly from this cultivation, that it soon destroys all reservoirs in which it is permitted; and where it is thought desirable to keep up the tank for the sake of the water, it should be carefully prohibited.—(*Roxb.*

Col. Sleeman's Rambles.) In Cashmere, miles of the lakes and marshes are covered with this plant. Moorcroft states that in the valley it furnishes almost the only food for at least 30,000 people for five months of the year; and that, from the Woolar lake, 96 to 100,000 ass-loads are taken annually.—*Stewart's Punj. Plants.*

(565) Trianthema decandra (*Linn.*) N. O. Portulacaceæ.

Vallay-Sharunnay, Tam. Tella Ghalijeroo, Tel. Gada buni, Beng. Bhees Khupra, Duk.

Description.—Annual; stems diffuse, prostrate, glabrous or pubescent on the upper side; leaves opposite, elliptic, obtuse or acute, petioled, entire, one of each pair a little larger than the other; petioles dilated at the margins; flowers several, pedicelled on a short peduncle; sepals membranaceous on the margin; stamens 10-12; style bipartite; capsule 4-seeded, with a spurious dissepiment, lid slightly 2-lobed at the apex, nearly closed below, nut-like, and containing 2 seeds; flowers small, greenish white. *Fl.* Nearly all the year.—*W. & A. Prod.* i. 355.—*Wight Icon. t.* 296.—*Roxb. Fl. Ind.* ii. 44.——Bengal. Peninsula.

Medical Uses.—The root is light brown outside, and white within. It is aperient, and said to be useful in hepatitis and asthma. The bark of the root in decoction is also given as an aperient.—*Ainslie.*

(566) Trianthema obcordata (*Roxb.*) Do.

Sharunnay, Tam. Ghelijehroo, Tel. Nasurjanghi, Duk. Sabuni, Beng.

Description.—Perennial; stems diffuse, prostrate, slightly pubescent on the upper side; leaves, one of each pair larger and obovate or obcordate, the other smaller and oblong; flowers solitary, sessile, nearly concealed within the broad sheath of the petioles; stamens 15-20; capsule 6-8 seeded, lid concave, with 2 spreading teeth, nearly enclosed at the bottom, including 1 seed; flowers small, greenish white. *Fl.* Nearly all the year.—*W. & A. Prod.* i. 355.—*Wight Icon. t.* 288.—*Roxb. Fl. Ind.* ii. 445.——Coromandel. Bengal.

Medical Uses.—The root, which is bitter and nauseous, is given in powder in combination with ginger as a cathartic; when taken fresh it is somewhat sweet. The leaves and tender tops are eaten by the natives.—(*Roxb. Ainslie.*) A common weed in waste ground, eaten in times of scarcity, but apt to produce diarrhœa and paralysis. The plant is officinal, being considered astringent in abdominal diseases.—*Stewart's Punj. Plants.*

(567) **Tribulus lanuginosus** (*Linn.*) N. O. ZYGOPHYLLACEÆ.

Nerinjie, TAM. Neringil, MAL. Gokoroo, DUK. Palleroo, TEL. Gokhoor, BENG.

DESCRIPTION.—Trailing; leaves opposite, abruptly pinnated; leaflets about 5-6 pair, nearly equal, with a close-pressed villous pubescence; peduncles shorter than the leaf; flowers axillary; calyx deeply 5-partite; petals 5, broad, obtuse; fruit 5-coccous, cocci each with 2 prickles; flowers solitary, bright yellow, sweet-scented. *Fl.* All the year.—*W. & A. Prod.* i. 145.—*Roxb. Fl. Ind.* ii. 401.—*Wight Icon.* i. *t.* 98.——Coromandel. Deccan. Bengal. Travancore.

MEDICAL USES.—There is a variety common in the southern parts of the Peninsula with red flowers called in Tamil *Yerra-Pulleroo*, whose leaves have the smell of cloves. Of the present one the leaves and root are said by the natives to possess diuretic qualities; and are prescribed in decoction. The seeds powdered are given in infusion to increase the urinary discharge, and are also used in dropsy and gonorrhœa.—(*Ainslie.*) The herb is said to be astringent and vermifuge, and the seeds cordial.—*Powell's Punj. Prod.*

(568) **Trichodesma Indicum** (*R. Br.*) N. O. BORAGINACEÆ.

DESCRIPTION.—Diffuse or erect; stem shortly villous; leaves usually opposite, narrow-lanceolate, half-stem-clasping, sessile; pedicels opposite-flowered or lateral 1-flowered; calyx villous, acutely auricled at the base, lobes increased by a subulate point; limb of the corolla spreading, reflexed; flowers pale blue.—*R. Br. Prod.* p. 496.—*Dec. Prod.* x. 172.—Borago Indica, *Linn.*—*Pluk. Alm. t.* 76. fig. 3.——Peninsula. Deccan.

MEDICAL USES.—This plant is held in repute in cases of snake-bites. A case of recovery under its use is given in Spry's 'Modern India' (vol. i.) The natives in the Deccan employ the leaves for making emollient poultices.—(*Pharm. of India.*) In the Punjaub it is used for purifying the blood, and as a diuretic.—*Powell's Punj. Prod.*

(569) **Trichosanthes cucumerina** (*Linn.*) N. O. CUCURBITACEÆ.

Podavalam, MAL. Pepoodel or Poodel, TAM. Chaynd-potla, TEL. Bunputol, BENG.

DESCRIPTION.—Annual, climbing; leaves broadly cordate, 3-7 angled, toothed or serrated, pubescent or glabrous; tendrils 3-cleft; *male* flowers disposed in something like umbels; *female* ones solitary on short peduncles, often from the same axils as the males; fruit ovate, pointed; petals 5, ciliated; calyx 5-cleft; flowers small, white. *Fl.* Aug.—Dec.—*W. & A. Prod.* i. 350.—*Roxb. Fl. Ind.* iii. 702.—*Rheede, Mal.* viii. *t.* 15. ——Peninsula. Bengal.

MEDICAL USES.—The seeds are reputed good in disorders of the stomach on the Malabar coast. The unripe fruit is very bitter, but is eaten by the natives in their curries. The tender shoots and dried capsules are very bitter and aperient, and are reckoned among the laxative medicines by the Hindoos. They are used in infusion. In decoction with sugar they are given to assist digestion. The seeds are anti-febrile and anthelmintic. The juice of the leaves expressed is emetic, and that of the root drank in the quantity of 2 oz. for a dose is very purgative. The stalk in decoction is expectorant.

One species, the *T. cordata* (Roxb.), is found on the banks of the Megna, where the inhabitants use the root as a substitute for Columba-root. It has been sent to England as the real Columba of Mozambique.—(*Ainslie. Rheede. Roxb.*) The *T. dioica* (Roxb.) is cultivated as an article of food. An alcoholic extract of the unripe fruit is described as a powerful and safe cathartic, in doses of from 3 to 5 grains, repeated every third hour as long as may be necessary. —(*Beng. Disp.*) The plant is a wholesome bitter, which imparts a tone to the system after protracted illness. It has also been employed as a febrifuge and tonic. The old Hindoo physicians used it in leprosy.—*Pharm. of India.*

(570) **Trichosanthes palmata** (*Roxb.*) Do.

Ancoruthay, TAM. Abuva, TEL.

DESCRIPTION.—Climbing; leaves palmately lobed, toothed; tendrils 3-cleft; *male* flowers racemose; *female* ones solitary in the same axils as the male, or occasionally racemose; calyx 5-cleft; segments deeply toothed or serrated; corolla fringed, 5-petalled; fruit globose; flowers large, white. *Fl.* Aug.—Sept.—*W. & A. Prod.* i. 350.—*Roxb. Fl. Ind.* iii. 704.—— Bengal. Peninsula.

MEDICAL USES.—The fruit mixed with cocoa-nut oil is a specific in ear-ache; but it is not eatable, being considered poisonous by the natives. The root, too, is reckoned poisonous. It is, however, used in diseases of cattle, especially in inflammation of the lungs.—(*Wight. Roxb.*) The pulp is a powerful purgative, yet at the Cape of Good Hope the gourd is rendered so mild by pickling as to be eaten. In the West Indies it is used for killing rats.—*Agri.-Hort. Soc. Journ.* x. 3.

(571) **Triticum vulgare** (*Villars*). N. O. GRAMINACEÆ.

Common Wheat, ENG.

DESCRIPTION.—Spike tetragonal, imbricated; rachis tenacious; spikelets usually 4-flowered; glumes ventricose, ovate, truncated, mucronate, compressed under the apex, round-convex at the back; nerve prominent; flowers awned or muticous; fruit free.—*Steudel Pl. Gram.* i. 341.—*Beauv. Agr. t.* 20, fig. 4.—*Kunth En.* pl. vi. p. 360.——Cultivated in the northern parts of India.

MEDICAL USES.—Wheaten flour is demulcent and nutritive. It forms a soothing local application in erysipelatous and other external inflammations. It is also applied to burnt and excoriated surfaces, chiefly for protecting the parts from the air. Internally, flour and water are used as a chemical antidote in poisoning by the preparations of mercury, copper, zinc, tin, and by iodine. It forms a constituent in linseed and other poultices. Starch is procured from the seed. —(*Pharm. of India.*) Wheat is extensively exported from Bengal.—*V. Appendix, Table of Exports.*

(572) **Tylophora asthmatica** (*R. W.*) N. O. ASCLEPIACEÆ.

Untomool, BENG. Kaka-pulla, TEL. Codegam, Coorinja, TAM.

DESCRIPTION.—Twining; leaves opposite, ovate-roundish, acuminated, cordate at the base, glabrous above, downy beneath; peduncles short, with 2-3 sessile few-flowered umbels; flowers rather large on long pedicels, externally pale green with a faint tinge of purple, internally light purple; corolla 5-parted; follicles glabrous, divaricate; leaflets of corona fleshy, clasping the base of the gynostegium. *Fl.* All the year.—*Wight Contrib.* 51.—*Wight Icon. t.* 1277.—Asclepias asthmatica, *Roxb. Fl. Ind.* ii. 33.——Peninsula. Bengal. Mysore.

MEDICAL USES.—A very abundant and widely-diffused plant, to

be met with in nearly all situations, and in flower at all seasons. Though easily recognised, it is, from its liability to variation, difficult to define. In the recent state it is most readily distinguished from a nearly-allied species by its reddish or dull pink-coloured flowers, and the toothed leaflets of the crown, the other having greenish flowers, and obtusely-rounded, edentate, coronal leaflets. The roots partake in an eminent degree of the properties of Ipecacuanha, and are a good remedy in dysentery. Dr Roxburgh often prescribed this remedy himself, and found it answer as well as the latter. Given in a pretty large dose, it answers as an emetic; in smaller, often repeated doses, as a cathartic—and in both ways effectually. The natives also employ it as an emetic, by rubbing upon a stone 3-4 inches of the fresh root, and mixing it with a little water for a dose. It generally purges at the same time.—*Wight. Roxb.*

Among plants of this order may here be mentioned the *Asclepias Curassavica* (Linn.), a West Indian plant now naturalised in India. It is known as the *Bastard* or *Wild Ipecacuanha*, from the emetic properties of its root; but as its operation is said to be attended by powerful action on the bowels, it is little applicable in the generality of cases where a simple emetic is required. The dose of the powder of the dried root is from 20 to 40 grains. The expressed juice of the leaves is stated to act efficiently as an anthelmintic.—*Lunan*, i. 63. *Pharm. of India.*

(573) **Typha elephantina** (*Roxb.*) N. O. Typhaceæ.

Elephant-grass, Eng. Hogla, Beng.

Description.—Culms round, smooth, glossy, jointed at the insertion of the leaves, 6-10 feet; leaves linear, somewhat channelled below, exceeding the flower-bearing stem; male spadix remote from the female, both cylindric. *Fl.* Aug.—Sept.—*Roxb. Fl. Ind.* iii. 566.—*J. Grah. Cat.* 227.——Margins of tanks and beds of rivers. Concans. Peninsula. Bengal.

Economic Uses.—Elephants are fond of this grass. It is of great importance for binding the soil on the banks of the Indus with its long tortuous roots, of which great care is taken when the culms are cut down to make matting of. They are also tied in bundles and used as buoys to swim with like sedges in England. The pollen of the flowers is abundant, and if a light be applied to it a flash of fire is produced. There is another species, the *T. angustifolia* (Linn.), the leaves of which are used for making mats.—(*Roxb. J. Grah.*) Of the latter the young shoots are edible, and resemble asparagus. The flowers are used in the treatment of burns.—*Powell's Punj. Prod.*

(574) **Typhonium Orixense** (*Schott*). N. O. Araceæ.

Ghet-kuchoo, Beng.

Description.—Stemless; leaves 3-lobed; flowers sub-sessile; spathe ample, erect, longer than the spadix; filaments long and often ramous; flowers small. *Fl.* Aug.—Arum Orixense, *Roxb. Fl. Ind.* iii. 503.—*Wight Icon. t.* 801.——Peninsula. Bengal.

Medical Uses.—A native of shady mango-groves near Samulcottah, where the soil is pretty rich and fertile. The roots are exceedingly acrid, and are applied as cataplasms to discuss scirrhous tumours.—*Roxb. Wight.*

U

(575) **Ulmus integrifolia** (*Roxb.*) N. O. Ulmaceæ.

Indian Elm, Eng. Naulie, Tel.

Description.—Large tree; leaves alternate, ovate or cordate, entire, glabrous, shortly petioled, deciduous; flowers hermaphrodite and male mixed; hermaphrodite flowers, calyx 4-6 lobed, leaflets spreading, oval; stamens 7-9; pistils 2; capsule 1-celled, 1-valved, indehiscent. The first part of the flowers that appears is the reddish anthers, next the calyx increases and becomes visible, but is always very minute, and if not looked for may pass unperceived. *Fl.* Nov.—March.—*Roxb. Fl. Ind.* ii. 68.—*Cor.* i. *t.* 78.—*Wight Icon. t.* 1968.——Circar mountains. Foot of the Himalaya. Ghauts near Arcot.

Economic Uses.—The timber is of good quality, and employed for various purposes, as carts and door-frames. The forks of the branches are used by the natives to protect their straw against cattle. —*Roxb. J. Grah.*

(576) **Urena lobata** (*Linn.*) N. O. Malvaceæ.

Bun-kra, Beng.

Description.—Herbaceous; leaves roundish, with 3 or more short obtuse lobes, more or less velvety, 5-7 nerved, with 1-3 glands on the nerves; segments of involucel 5, oblong-lanceolate, equal to the expanded calyx; carpels densely pubescent, echinate; flowers middle-sized, rose-coloured. *Fl.* Aug.—Oct. —*W. & A. Prod.* i. 46.—*Roxb. Fl. Ind.* iii. 182.——Peninsula. Bengal.

Economic Uses.—This is a common shrub in the Peninsula, generally found in waste places during the rain. It abounds in strong fibres, which are considered a fair substitute for flax. The same may apply to the *U. sinuata* (Linn.), a native of Bengal.—*Royle.*

(577) **Urginea Indica** (*Kunth*). N. O. LILIACEÆ.

Indian Squill, ENG. Nurrivungayum, TAM. Addivi-tella-guddaloo, TEL. Junglie pias, HIND. Kanda, BENG.

DESCRIPTION.—Bulb perennial, truncated, white, about the size of a large apple; leaves numerous, radical, ensiform, nearly flat, smooth, 6-18 inches in length; scape erect, round, smooth, and, including the raceme, about 2-3 feet in length; raceme erect, very long; flowers remote, long-pedicelled, drooping. *Fl.* March—April.—*Roxb. Fl. Ind.* ii. 147.—Scilla Indica, *Roxb.*—*Wight Icon. t.* 2063.——Sandy shores in Malabar. Covellum, near Trevandrum.

MEDICAL USES.—The bulbous roots of this plant resemble in their appearance and qualities the root of the true squill (*Urginea maritima*), being equally nauseous and bitter. It is not so large nor so round as the latter, but it has similar fleshy scales. It is chiefly used by farriers for horses in cases of strangury and fever; it grows in abundance in waste sandy situations, in Lower India especially, near the sea. The bulb burnt is externally applied to the soles of the feet when suffering from any burning sensation.—*Ainslie.*

(578) **Uvaria narum** (*Wall.*) N. O. ANONACEÆ.

Narum-panel, MAL.

DESCRIPTION.—Climbing shrub; leaves oblong-lanceolate; flower-bearing shoots lateral, leafy; peduncles solitary, terminal; calycine lobes roundish-ovate; petals equal, roundish-ovate, concave, curved; carpels numerous, glabrous, on long stalks, red; seeds about 4, flat, smooth, shining; flowers at first brownish green, but at length becoming reddish; anthers yellow.—*W. & A. Prod.* i. 9.—U. Zeylanica, *Lam.* (not *Linn.*) —Unona Narum, *Dec.*—*Rheede,* ii. *t.* 19.——Travancore.

MEDICAL USES.—An unctuous secretion exudes from the anthers. There is a sweet-scented greenish oil obtained from the roots by distillation in Malabar, which, as well as the root itself, is used in various diseases. The roots are fragrant and aromatic, and the leaves when bruised smell like cinnamon.—*Rheede.*

V

(579) **Vateria Malabarica** (*Blume*). N. O. Dipteracеæ.

Indian Copal, Piney Varnish, or White Dammer tree, Eng. Dupada mara, Tel. Koondrikum, Velli Koondricum, Tam. Vella Koodricum, Peini-marum, Mal.

Description.—Large tree; bark whitish; young shoots and all tender parts, except the leaves, covered with fine stellate pubescence; leaves alternate, petioled, oblong, entire, slightly cordate at the base, shortly pointed or obtuse at the apex, coriaceous and smooth, petioles 1 inch in length; stipules oblong; flowers rather remote, on large terminal panicles; bracts ovate, pointed; filaments 40-50, very short; anthers not auricled at the base, terminating in a single long bristle at the apex; style a little longer than the stamens; stigmas acute; capsule oblong, obtuse, coriaceous, fleshy; seed solitary. *Fl.* Jan.—March.—*Blume Mus. Bot.* ii. 29.—V. Indica, *Roxb.* (not *Linn.*)—Chloroxylon Dupada, *Buch. Journ. Mysore,* ii. 476.——Malabar. Travancore.

Medical Uses.—A solid fatty oil, known as Piney-tallow, procured from the fruit, bruised and subjected to boiling, is of some repute as a local application in chronic rheumatism and other painful affections.

Economic Uses.—This tree must not be confounded with the *Vateria Indica* (Linn.) of Ceylon, which has larger fruit and leaves, as well as other distinguishing points. It forms beautiful avenues in Malabar and Canara, the foliage being dense and the blossom very fragrant. It was a favourite with the ancient Rajahs, and there are some magnificent old trees near Bednore. It yields the Piney gum-resin, an excellent varnish resembling copal. It is procured by cutting a notch in the tree, sloping inwards and downwards, from which the resinous juice runs, and is soon hardened by exposure to the air. It is usual, when applying it as a varnish, to apply the resin before it hardens, otherwise to melt it by a slow heat, and mix with boiling linseed-oil. It is very useful for carriages and furniture. A spirit varnish is prepared by reducing to powder about six parts of Piney and one of camphor, and then adding hot alcohol sufficient to dissolve the mixed powder. Alcohol will not dissolve Piney without the camphor, but once dissolved retains it in solution. The varnish thus prepared is good for varnishing pictures, but before being used requires to be gently heated to evaporate the camphor, which otherwise would produce a roughness on the picture in consequence of its subsequent evaporations. In addition to these uses it is made into candles on the Malabar coast, diffusing an agreeable fragrance, and giving a clear light and little smoke. For making them the fluid resin may either be run into moulds, or be rolled, while yet soft, into the required shape. The true gum-copal is not from this tree, but it generally goes under that name in India. The gum is also useful for varnishing anatomical preparations. The best specimens of the gum are employed as ornaments, under the name of Amber (*Kehroba*), to which it bears exterior resemblance. When recent it is found from pale green to a deep amber colour, with all the intermediate shades. The bark, which is bitter and astringent, is said to retard fermentation, and on that account chips are used in Ceylon when preparing jaggery from the toddy, which are thrown into the vessel to prevent fermentation taking place. The timber is used for masts and for small vessels, being proof against the *teredo navalis*.—(*Roxb. Wight.*) This is the same tree to which Dr Buchanan, in his journey through Mysore, gave the name of *Chloroxylon Dupada;* the specific name was derived by him from the Canarese name "Dupa," applied to this and probably other species of *Vateria* growing in Mysore and the western coast. From the circumstance of the *Canarium strictum* growing in the same locality arose the belief that both the White and the Black Dammer were produced from the same tree; and as the few which Dr Buchanan saw were probably *Vaterias*, he naturally concluded that this tree alone yielded both species of Dammer. The White Dammers of the Northern Circars are derived from the *Shoreas*. The Piney resin has a shining vitreous fracture, is very hard, and bears a great resemblance to amber. Its colour ranges from light green to light yellow, the green tint predominating. It is more soluble in alcohol than the Black Dammer, and burns with less smoke. It is easily distinguished from all other Indian resins by its superior hardness, its colour, and amber-like appearance. There is a variety with a cellular structure and balsamic smell, by which it may be recognised. The candles made from the resin consume the wick without snuffing. They were formerly introduced into Europe, but a very high duty having been imposed, the trade ceased.—*Jury Rep. Mad. Exhib.*, 1857.

The following is Mr Broughton's report on the Piney resin:—

This beautiful substance has long been known, and its properties and local uses have been repeatedly described. It is also not unknown in England, and I apprehend that its cost (and perhaps, also, ignorance of its peculiar properties) has prevented its becoming an article of more extended commerce. It should be remarked that the

"East Indian Dammer," which is well known among varnish-makers, though frequently confounded with this, is the product of a very different tree, and is not produced in this Presidency. The finest specimens of Piney resin are obtained by making incisions in the tree, and are in pale-green translucent pieces of considerable size. The resin that exudes naturally usually contains much impurity. In most of its properties it resembles copal, but it possesses qualities which give it some advantages over the latter. Like copal, it is but slightly soluble in alcohol; but, as Berzelius pointed out in the case of copal, it can be brought into solution by the addition of camphor to the spirit. It is easily soluble in chloroform, and thus might find a small application as a substitute for amber in photographer's varnish. It differs most advantageously from copal by being at once soluble in turpentine and drying oils, without the necessity of the preliminary destructive fusion required by that resin, a process which tends greatly to impair the colour of the varnish. The solution of the Piney resin in turpentine is turbid and milky, but by the addition of powdered charcoal, and subsequently filtering, it yields a solution transparent and colourless as water, and yields a varnish which dries with a purity and whiteness not to be surpassed. The solution in turpentine readily mixes with the drying oils. It is on these properties of the resin that its chance of becoming an article of trade will depend. In price it cannot compete with copal, whose supply to the European market is regular and abundant. Major Beddome informs me that the cost of Piney resin delivered on the sea-coast would be about 6 rupees per maund of 26 lb. The present price of the best copal in the English market is but £26, 10s. per ton.

Piney resin yields, on destructive distillation, 82 per cent of a pluresecent oil of agreeable odour, but not differing essentially from that obtained from cheaper resins.

(580) **Vernonia anthelmintica** (*Willd.*) N. O. ASTERACEÆ.

Purple Flea-bane, ENG. Caat-siragum, TAM. Catta-seragam, MAL. Adavie-zeela-kura, TEL. Kali-zeerie, DUK. Buckche, HIND. Som-raj, BENG.

DESCRIPTION.—Annual; stem erect, roundish, slightly tomentose; leaves alternate, serrate, narrowing at the base into the petioles; calyx ovate; corolla consisting of 20 or more hermaphrodite florets; flowers in panicles at the end of the branches on long peduncles thickening towards the flowers; a solitary peduncle terminates the stalk; flowers purplish. *Fl.* Nov.—Dec.—Serratula anthelmintica, *Roxb. Fl. Ind.* iii. 405.—Conyza anthelmintica, *Linn.*—*Rheede,* ii. *t.* 24.——Peninsula. Bengal.

MEDICAL USES.—The seeds are very bitter, and are considered powerfully anthelmintic and diuretic, and are also an ingredient of a compound powder prescribed in snake-bites. An infusion of them is given on the Malabar coast for coughs and in cases of flatulency. Reduced to powder and mixed with lime-juice, they are used to expel pediculi from the hair.—(*Ainslie.*) The seeds are about an eighth of an inch in length, of a dark-brown colour, covered with whitish scattered hairs, cylindrical, tapering towards the base, marked with about ten paler longitudinal ridges, and crowned with a circle of brown scales, and are nauseous and bitter to the taste. Dr Gibson regards them as a valuable tonic and stomachic, in doses of 20 to 25 grains.—(*Pharm. of India.*) It is stated by Ainslie that the *V. cinerea* (Less.) is used in decoctions by the natives to promote perspiration in fevers.

(581) **Vitex Negundo** (*Linn.*) N. O. Verbenaceæ.

Five-leaved Chaste-tree, Eng. Vellay Noochie, Tam. Ben-nochie, Mal. Wayala, Tel. Shumbalie, Duk. Nisinda, Hind. Nishinda, Beng.

Description.—Arboreous; stem twisted, 10 feet; leaves digitate, quinate, opposite, on longish petioles; leaflets lanceolate, entire, three larger petioled, two smaller sessile; panicles 2-branched; flowers blue, fragrant. *Fl.* April—June.—*Wight Icon. t.* 519.—*Roxb. Fl. Ind.* iii. 70.—*Rheede*, ii. *t.* 12.——Peninsula. Bengal. Deyra Dhoon.

Medical Uses.—This species is similar in medicinal properties to the *V. trifolia*, but somewhat weaker: the root in decoction is a pleasant bitter, and administered in cases of intermittent and typhus fevers. The leaves simply warmed are a good application in cases of rheumatism and sprains. The Mohammedans smoke the dried leaves in cases of headache and catarrh. The dried fruit is considered a vermifuge. A decoction of the aromatic leaves helps to form the warm bath for native women after delivery. The root in decoction is used as a vermifuge, and to reduce swellings in the body.—(*Ainslie. Roxb.*) Dr Fleming remarks that the leaves have a better claim to the title of discutient than any other vegetable remedy with which he is acquainted; and he adds that their efficacy in dispelling inflammatory swellings of the joints from acute rheumatism, and of the testes from suppressed gonorrhæa, are very remarkable. The mode of application resorted to by the natives is simple enough; the fresh leaves, put into an earthen pot, are heated over a fire till they are as hot as can be borne without pain; they are then applied to the parts affected, and kept there by a bandage; the application is repeated three or four times daily until the swelling subsides.—*Flem. As. Res.* vol. xi. *Pharm. of India.*

Economic Uses.—Many species of this order yield good timber. Such is the *Vitex alata* (Roxb.) and the *V. altissima* (Do.), a large tree, somewhat common in subalpine forests. Also the *V. arborea*

(Do.) The latter, when old, becomes chocolate-coloured, and is useful for many economical purposes.—*Roxb.*

(582) **Vitex trifolia** (*Linn.*) Do.

Three-leaved Chaste-tree or Indian Privet, Eng. Neer-noochie, Tam. Caranoochie, Mal. Panee ki shumbalie, Duk. Neela vayalie, Tel. Nismdha, Seduari, Hind.

Description.—Shrub, 10 feet; leaves ternate and quinate; leaflets ovate, acute, entire, hoary beneath; panicle with a straight rachis; pedicels dichotomous; flowers terminal, racemose, violet. *Fl.* April—May.—*Roxb. Fl. Ind.* iii. 69.—*Rheede,* ii. *t.* 11.——Coromandel. Concan. Deccan.

Medical Uses.—The leaves and young shoots are considered as powerfully discutient, and are used in fomentations, or simply applied warm in cases of sprains, rheumatism, and contusions, also externally in diseases of the skin and swellings. The leaves powdered and taken with water are a cure for intermittent fevers; the root, and a cataplasm of the leaves, are applied externally in rheumatism and local pains. The fruit is said by the Vytians to be nervine, cephalic, and emmenagogue, and is prescribed in powder in electuary and decoction. A clear sweet oil of a greenish colour is extracted from the root.—*Roxb. Ainslie.*

(583) **Vitis quadrangularis** (*Wall.*) N. O. Vitaceæ.

Perundei codie, Tam. Tsjangelam-parenda, Mal. Nulleroptigeh, Tel. Hasjora, Beng.

Description.—Climbing; glabrous; stem 4-angled, winged; stipules lunate, entire; leaves alternate, cordate-ovate, serrulated, short-petioled; umbels shortly peduncled; stamens 4; petals 4, distinct; fruit globose, size of a large pea, very acrid, 1-celled, 1-seeded; flowers small, white. *Fl.* Aug.—Oct.—*W. & A. Prod.* i. 125.—*Wight Icon. t.* 51.—Cissus quadrangularis, *Linn.*—*Roxb. Fl. Ind.* i. 407.—*Rheede,* vii. *t.* 41.——Peninsula. Bengal. Travancore.

Medical Uses.—The leaves and young shoots when fresh are sometimes eaten by the natives, and when dried and powdered are given in bowel affections. Forskal states that the Arabs when suffering from affections of the spine make beds of the stems.—*Ainslie.*

(584) **Vitis setosa** (*Wall.*) Do.

Barabutsali, Tel.

Description.—Climbing; clothed with scattered glandular bristly hairs, but otherwise glabrous; stem herbaceous; leaves succulent, trifoliate, without a common petiole; leaflets stalked, roundish-ovate or obovate, obtuse with numerous sharp serratures, cymes peduncled with divaricating branches; petals 4, distinct; stamens 4; style conspicuous; berries red, ovoid, hairy, 1-seeded. Flowers in the rainy season.—*W. & A. Prod.* i. 127.—*Wight Icon.* 170.—Cissus setosus, *Roxb. Fl. Ind.* i. 410. ——Rajahmundry. Mysore.

Medical Uses.—Every part of the plant is exceedingly acrid. The leaves toasted and oiled are applied to indolent tumours, to bring them to suppuration.—*Roxb.*

W

(585) **Wedelia calendulacea** (*Less.*) N. O. Asteraceæ.

Postaley-kaiantagerei, Tam. Pee-cajoni, Mal. Patsoo-poola-goonta-galijeroo, Tel. Peelabhungra, Duk. Keshoorya, Beng.

Description.—Perennial, herbaceous, creeping; leaves opposite, broad-lanceolate, obtuse, entire; peduncles axillary; flowers bright yellow. *Fl.* Aug.—Jan.—*Wight Icon. t.* 1107. —Verbesina calendulacea, *Linn.*—*Roxb. Fl. Ind.* iii. 440.—*Rheede*, x. *t.* 42.——Coromandel. Concan. Bengal.

Medical Uses.—The leaves, seeds, and flowers, which are aromatic to the taste, are considered deobstruent in decoction. The plant has a slightly camphoraceous taste.—*Roxb.*

(586) **Willughbeia edulis** (*Roxb.*) N. O. Apocynaceæ.

Luti-am, Beng.

Description.—Climbing; calyx 5-parted, small; corolla salver-shaped, with the tube thicker about the centre, 5-cleft, segments oblique; leaves opposite, elliptic-oblong, acuminated, obtuse, with parallel veins; peduncles cymose, axillary, shorter than the petioles; flowers pale pink; berry very large, globular, 1-celled, many-seeded. *Fl.* June—Aug.—*Roxb. Fl. Ind.* ii. 57.——Chittagong.

Economic Uses.—The milky viscid juice which flows from every part of this plant is converted, on exposure to the atmosphere, to an inferior kind of caoutchouc. The fruit is eatable.—*Roxb.*

(587) **Withania coagulans** (*Dunal.*) N. O. Solanaceæ.

Description.—Shrub, stellately tomentose; leaves lanceolate-oblong, unequal-sided, thickish, often somewhat twin, both sides of the same colour; flowers diœcious, aggregated in the axils; peduncles deflexed.—*Dec. Prod.* xiii. pt. 1, p. 685.—Puneeria coagulans, *Stocks.*—*Wight Icon. t.* 1616.——Seinde. Beluchistan. Mountains of Affghanistan.

Medical Uses.—The whole plant is densely covered with minute stellate hairs arranged in tufts. It is easily recognised by its dusky ash-grey hue, which in the young leafy shoots has a bluish tinge. There is not a shade of green in the whole plant. In Scinde it is known by the name of *Puneer*. The ripe fruits, when fresh, are used as an emetic. When dried they are sold in the bazaars, and are employed in dyspepsia and flatulent colic. They are prescribed in infusion, either alone or mixed with the leaves and twigs of *Rhazya stricta* (Dec.), an excellent bitter tonic, also growing in that part of the country. The dried fruit is in universal use throughout Beluchistan for coagulating milk in the process of cheese manufacture.—*Stocks in Journ. Bomb. As. Soc.*, Jan. 1849.

(588) **Withania somnifera** (*Dunal.*) Do.

Winter Cherry, ENG. Pevetti, MAL. Penerroo, TEL. Asgund, DUK. Ashwagunda, BENG. Amkoolang, TAM.

DESCRIPTION.—Perennial, 2-3 feet; stem 2-forked, flexuous; leaves ovate, entire, in pairs, pubescent; calyx 5-toothed, segments equal to the length of the tube; flowers axillary, crowded, nearly sessile; corolla campanulate, yellowish green; berry small, red, size of a pea, covered with a membranaceous, angular, inflated calyx. *Fl.* Nearly all the year.—*Wight Icon.* *t.* 853.—Physalis flexuosa, *Linn.*—*Roxb. Fl. Ind.* i. 561.—*Rheede*, iv. *t.* 55.—Coromandel. Concans. Travancore. Bengal.

MEDICAL USES.—The root is said to have deobstruent and diuretic properties. The leaves moistened with warm castor-oil are useful, externally applied in cases of carbuncle. They are very bitter, and are given in infusion in fevers. The seeds are employed in the coagulation of milk in making butter. The fruit is diuretic. The root and leaves are powerfully narcotic, and the latter is applied to inflamed tumours, and the former in obstinate ulcers and rheumatic swellings of the joints, being mixed with dried ginger and so applied. The Telinga physicians reckon the roots alexipharmic.—*Roxb. Ainslie.*

(589) **Wrightia tinctoria** (*R. Br.*) N. O. APOCYNACEÆ.

Chite-ancaloo, TEL.

DESCRIPTION.—Shrub, 10-15 feet; leaves elliptic-lanceolate or ovate-oblong, acuminated, glabrous; panicles terminal, branches and corymbs divaricate; tube of corolla twice as long as the calyx; follicles distinct, but united at the apex; flowers white, fragrant, 1½ inch in diameter when expanded. *Fl.*

March—May.—*Wight Icon.* ii. *t.* 444.—Nerium tinctorium.—*Roxb. Fl. Ind.* ii. 4.——Coromandel.

Medical Uses.—The fresh leaves when well chewed are very pungent, and are said quickly to remove the pain of toothache. They lose their property by drying.—*Wight.*

Economic Uses.—The wood is white, close-grained, and handsome in appearance, looking like ivory; much used for ornamental and useful purposes. A kind of Indigo is prepared from the leaves. This is known as *pala*-indigo, for which a prize was awarded to Mr Fischer of Salem.—*Roxb. Jury Rep.*

(590) **Wrightia tomentosa** (*Rom. et. Sch.*) Do.

Nelam-pala, Mal.

Description.—Tree; leaves oblong, acuminated, downy; corymbs terminal, small; tube of corolla longer than the calyx; corona fleshy, lacerated into obtuse segments; follicles distinct; branches downy; flowers with a white corolla and orange-coloured corona. *Fl.* May—June.—*Wight Icon.* ii. *t.* 443.—Nerium tomentosum, *Roxb.—Fl. Ind.* ii. 6.—*Rheede,* ix. *t.* 3, 4.——Circar. Concans.

Economic Uses.—A yellow juice flows from this plant, which mixed with water forms a good yellow dye. Some cloths that had been dyed with it had preserved their colour for two years as bright and as fresh as at first.—(*Roxb.*) Another species, the *W. mollissima,* grows in Cachar, the timber of which is the nearest approach to boxwood there is in that part of the country.—*Brownlow in A. H. S.,* Jan. 1864.

X

(591) **Xanthochymus pictorius** (*Roxb.*) N. O. Clusiaceæ.

Dampel, Hind. Iwara-memadee, Tel. Jwara

Description.—Tree, 40 feet; leaves linear-lanceolate, shining; calyx of 5 unequal sepals; petals 5, deciduous, alternating with the sepals; flowers lateral, fascicled, all bisexual; ovary 5-celled; fruit ovate, pointed, yellow, 1-4 seeded; flowers white. *Fl.* April—June.—*W. & A. Prod.* i. 102.—*Roxb. Fl. Ind.* ii. 638.—*Cor.* ii. *t.* 196.——Concan.

Economic Uses.—The fine yellow fruits, something like an orange, are eaten by the natives, and are very palatable, but might be much improved by cultivation. The fruit when full grown, but not ripe, yields a quantity of yellow, resinous, acrid gum like gamboge, of the consistence of rich cream. It makes a pretty good water-colour, either by itself as a yellow, or in mixture with other colour to form green. It is imperfectly soluble in spirit, and still less so in water; alkaline salt enables the water to dissolve more of the gum. —*Roxb.*

(592) **Ximenia Americana** (*Linn.*) N. O. Olacineæ.

Oora-nechra, Tel.

Description.—Shrub, 15 feet; calyx small, 4-cleft; petals 4, very hairy inside; thorns axillary or terminating the branchlets, solitary, bearing occasionally leaves or flowers, or even smaller thorns; leaves alternate, oval, emarginate; peduncles 4-6 flowered; drupe oval; flesh thick; nut crustaceous; flowers small, dull white, fragrant. *Fl.* June—Sept.—*W. & A. Prod.* i. 89.—*Roxb. Fl. Ind.* ii. 252.——Circars.

Economic Uses.—The yellow fruit, which is about the size of a pigeon's egg, is of a somewhat acid and sour taste, and is eaten by the natives. The kernels taste like fresh filberts. The rind is bitter and astringent. The wood is of a yellow colour, somewhat like sandal-wood, and its powder is used by the Brahmins on the Coromandel coast in their religious ceremonies.—*Roxb.*

(593) **Xylocarpus granatum** (*Kön.*) N. O. Meliaceæ.

Description.—Tree; leaves abruptly pinnated, leaflets 2-pair, elliptical, obtuse, entire; calyx 4-cleft; petals 4, reflexed; stamen tube 8-cleft at the apex, the segments 2-parted; style short, with a broad concave stigma; fruit spherical, 6-12 seeded, the pericarp splitting into 4 valves; seeds angled, with a spongy integument; flowers small, yellowish. *Fl.* April—May.—*W. & A. Prod.* i. 121.—*Roxb. Flor. Ind.* ii. 240.—*Rumph. Amb.* iii. *t.* 61.——Soonderbunds.

Medical Uses.—This is common in low swampy situations in all parts of the East. The bark, as well as other parts of the tree, is extremely bitter and astringent. It is much used by the Malays in cholera, colic diarrhœa, and other abdominal affections.—*Pharm. of India.*

(594) **Xyris Indica** (*Linn.*) N. O. Xyridaceæ.

Kotsjelleti-pullu, Mal. Cheena, Beng. Dali doob, Beng.

Description.—Annual, 1 foot; leaves radical, ensiform, on one edge slit into a sheath for the scape, pointed, smooth; head globular; scales roundish; scape naked, round, striated, the length of the leaves, each supporting a round, flower-bearing head; calyx 3-leaved; petals 3, unguiculate, with oval crenate borders, just rising above the scales; flowers bright yellow. *Fl.* Nov.—Dec.—*Roxb. Fl. Ind.* i. 179.—*Rheede*, ix. *t.* 71.——S. Concan. Coromandel. Malabar.

Medical Uses.—The juice of the leaves mixed with vinegar is applied externally in cases of itch. The leaves and root boiled in oil are considered useful in leprosy on the Malabar coast. In Bengal the plant is reckoned of great value as an easy and certain cure for ringworm.—*Roxb.*

Z

(595 **Zanonia Indica** (*Linn.*) N. O. CUCURBITACEÆ.

Bandolier fruit, ENG. Penar-valli, MAL.

DESCRIPTION.—Climbing; leaves alternate, large, elliptical, acute, slightly cordate at the base, 3-nerved, paler below, entire, without stipules; panicles axillary; fruit oblong, elongated, tapering from the apex to the base, slightly 3-angled; *male flowers*, calyx 3-lobed, petals 5, spreading; *female flowers*, limb of calyx 5-lobed, tube cohering with the ovary; ovary 3-celled; styles 3, spreading, 2-cleft at the apex; seeds ovate, with a large foliaceous border; tendrils axillary; flowers small, white. *Fl.* Sept.—Oct.—*W. & A. Prod.* i. 340.—*Rheede*, viii. *t.* 47, 48. ——Malabar. Alwaye, near Cochin.

MEDICAL USES.—The leaves beaten up with milk and butter are applied as a liniment in antispasmodic affections.—(*Rheede.*) This is a curious and rare plant. The fruit is fleshy, and is marked round the apex by a circular line. It is 3-celled, opening at the top by 3 valves, and is somewhat 3-angled. In each cell are 2 seeds, making six in all. The fleshy part of the placenta smells exactly like the cucumber, and the seeds are excessively bitter to the taste. The young shoots are covered with a thin, shining, light-brown cuticle, easily peeling off when handled. The bitterness of these seeds is a refutation of Decandolle's remark, that the seeds of this family never partake of the property of the pulp that surrounds them. The fruit is called the Bandolier fruit, from the form of its seed-vessels. These dried oblong capsules, open at the top, are very singular in appearance.—*Lindley. Pers. Obs.*

(596) **Zanthoxylon Rhetsa** (*Dec.*) N. O. XANTHOXYLACEÆ.

Moolleela, MAL. Rhetsa-maum, TEL.

DESCRIPTION.—Tree, 50 feet, everywhere armed with prickles; bark corky; leaves alternate, equally pinnated; leaflets 8-16 pair, lanceolate, unequal-sided, entire, glabrous; panicles terminal; petals and stamens four; capsule sessile, solitary, globose; seeds solitary, round, glossy black; flowers small, yellow; capsule 1-celled. *Fl.* Oct.—Nov.—*W. & A. Prod.* i. 148.—Fagara Rhetsa, *Roxb. Fl. Ind.* i. 417.—*Rheede,* v. *t.* 34. ——Coromandel mountains.

Economic Uses.—The unripe capsules are like small berries; they are gratefully aromatic, and taste like the skin of a fresh orange. The ripe seeds taste like pepper, and are used as a substitute. The specific name *Rhetsa* means in Teloogoo a committee, or select assembly. Under the shade of this tree the hill people assemble to examine, agitate, and determine public affairs, deliver discourses, &c. The bark is aromatic, put in food as a condiment instead of limes and pepper. It is cooked with sugar or honey; and mixed with onions, mustard-seed, and ginger, makes a good pickle. The berries are acid and succulent.—*Roxb.*

(597) **Zanthoxylon triphyllum** (*Juss.*) Do.

Description.—Small tree without prickles; leaves opposite, trifoliolate, leaflets oblong, somewhat unequal-sided at the base, acuminated; panicles axillary, longer than the petioles; capsule obovate, smooth; flowers small, white. *Fl.* April—May.—*Dalz. Bomb. Flor.* p. 45.—Fagara triphylla, *Roxb.*—Evodia triphylla, *Dec. Prod.* i. 724.—*Wight Icon. t.* 149.——Western Ghauts.

Economic Uses.—This tree yields a resin, specimens of which were sent to the Madras Exhibition, but the quantity produced did not warrant its being of importance in a commercial point of view. The capsules are smaller than those in the last species, but possess the same aromatic properties. Rumphius states that in Amboyna the women prepare a cosmetic from the bark, and apply it to improve their complexions. Of another species, the *Z. hastile* (Wall.), growing in the Himalaya, the seeds are used as an aromatic tonic, and also the bark. The small branches are used as tooth-brushes, and the larger ones to triturate the hemp-plant with. The capsules and seeds are said to intoxicate fish. The timber is used for walking-sticks and pestles. It is strongly armed with prickles. The aromatic fruit is used as a condiment.—(*Powell's Punj. Prod.*) The *Z. Budrunga* (Dec.) grows in Assam. The seeds have the fragrance of lemon-peel, and being of a warm spicy nature, are used medicinally by the natives. The fruit of the *Z. elatum* (Roxb.) growing in Rohilcund and Oude yields an aromatic essential oil.—*Pharm. of India.*

(598) **Zapania nodiflora** (*Linn.*) N. O. Verbenaceæ.

Podootalle, Tam. Bokena, Tel. Baleya eetheecannee, Mal. Bhoocokra, Hind. Chota okra, Beng.

Description.—Annual, creeping; stem roughish, with adpressed biacuminate hairs, herbaceous, filiform, ramous, procumbent, rooting at the joints; leaves cuneate-spathulate, entire at the base, above rounded, obtuse or sub-acute, equally and sharply serrated, obsoletely veined, flat; peduncles axillary, solitary, filiform, exserted; capitula ovoid and at length cylindrical; calyx 2-parted, slightly bicarinate; carinæ puberulous; flowers small, white. *Fl.* All the year.—*Wight Icon.* iv. *t.* 1463.—*Rheede,* x. *t.* 47.——Streams and banks of rivers in South India.

Medical Uses.—The leaves and young shoots, which are very bitter and astringent, are given to children in indigestion and diarrhœa. They are also occasionally recommended as a drink for women after lying-in.—*Ainslie.*

(599) **Zea Mays** (*Linn.*) N. O. Graminaceæ.

Maize or Indian Corn, Eng.

Description.—Erect, simple; culm tapering, smooth; leaves broad, flat, membranaceous; sheaths slightly compressed; ligula short, membranaceous, silky-ciliated, 2-keeled; male raceme terminal, peduncled, simple or generally furnished below with single or many spreading branches; spikelets twin, one short, one longer pedicelled; female spikes axillary, solitary, sessile; sheaths 4-5, spathiform; stigmas numerous, exserted; spikelets numerous, sessile, in many rows, rows approximated by pairs; male spikelets oblong, 2-flowered, each flower with 2 paleæ, male sessile; glumes two, externally pubescent, upper one shorter; paleæ two, nearly equal; stamens 3; filaments subulate; anthers linear, 4-sulcate, 2-celled, 2-lobed; ovary oblique, sessile, roundish-ovate, externally convex, smooth, glabrous.—*Kunth. En. Plant,* vi. 15.—*Lam. Ill. t.* 749.—Mays Zea, *Gærtn. Fruct.* i. 6, *t.* 1, *f.* 9.——Cultivated.

Economic Uses.—This is a native of the continent of America, and was not known in Europe till after the discovery of the New World. What wheat is to the natives of Europe, or rice to the inhabitants of Asia, maize is to the inhabitants of both North and South America.

The produce of this plant is very large. The stalk grows seven or eight feet in height, and bears two sorts of flowers. Those bearing the stamens are in separate panicles, at the top of the plant; whilst those bearing the pistils, which become the grain, are borne on the sides of the plant. When the grains are ripened, they are arranged in five or six rows around a common axis, and are then called cobs, which contain as many as 700 or 800 grains. There are many sorts of maize, which differ in the size of the cobs as well as in the number of the grains which they contain. Some sorts are of a pale or golden yellow, whilst others are reddish or purple. The grains are roundish and compressed, and vary in size from a grain of wheat to a kidney-bean. The maize plant is said to grow wild at the present day in the northern regions of Mexico, and in the southern districts of the Rocky Mountains.

Since the discovery of the New World, its culture has extended to every other quarter of the globe. It is extensively cultivated in Europe as high as 50 and 52 degrees north latitude. It is also produced in the West India Islands, on the coasts of Africa, and in the East Indies and China. In many of these countries its culture is rapidly extending, and it bids fair to vie with rice and wheat in feeding the human family. In the United States alone, the yearly produce of this grain is estimated at 600,000,000 bushels.

The green cobs are gathered and cooked like peas or asparagus, and afford a very agreeable article of diet. For this purpose the maize might be grown in England. This plant has also been employed in the manufacture of sugar. Like the other cereals, it contains a considerable quantity of sugar in its stem, which may be extracted in the same way as from the sugar-cane.

When the grain is ripened it is usually dried before a fire, and ground into meal, which is called "hominy." This is used like oatmeal for making porridge, or for puddings and cakes. It is a wholesome and nutritious food, and contains a larger quantity of fatty matter than other cereal grains. The grains of maize are of different colours, the prevailing hue being yellow, sometimes approaching to white, and at others deepening to red. Domestic animals, especially horses, speedily become fat when fed upon it, their flesh becoming at the same time remarkably firm.

Of all the cereals, maize is the least subject to disease. Blight, mildew, or rust are unknown to it. It is never liable to be beaten down by rain, and in climates and seasons favourable to its growth and maturity, the only enemies the cultivator has to dread are insects in the early stages, and birds in the later periods of its cultivation.

Next to rice, it forms the most important crop in the east, and is stated, and we believe correctly, to have a greater range of temperature than any other of the cereal grasses. In Bengal, which may be considered *par excellence* the country for rice, the culture of Indian corn is not carried to anything like the same extent as it is in Behar and Upper India. In the former province it forms with the Jowar, Janeera, and Shamah, the staple article of food for the bulk of the inhabitants.

The land intended for maize should be ploughed up in May, and where the soil is poor, it should receive a top-dressing of manure. A second ploughing should be given, allowing a little interval between the two, in order that the soil may derive full benefit from exposure to the sun and atmosphere. With the first showers of the rainy season sowing should commence. The seed should be sown in rows sufficiently far apart (say 4 feet) to admit of a plough being used after the plant has reached a certain height. Where it is not intended to use a plough, half that space between each row will suffice. The holes should be from 12 to 18 inches apart, with four seeds placed in each, and a thin covering of earth placed over them. When the plants are about 4 inches high, the field should be carefully hoed to remove the weeds, shortly after which it should receive its first ploughing, a second being given when the blossom appears. After the second ploughing the earth should be placed round the roots, and all shoots from the parent plant removed, as they only tend to weaken it, and yield no produce.

When the grains in the ears are formed and begin to harden, the top and leaves of the plants should be removed, and tied up (after drying two or three days) in bundles for fodder for the cattle. The grain, when hard and ripe, should be gathered, well dried, and put away in an airy place in husk, as it will keep more free from weevil in that state than if shelled, though more bulky, and occupying a larger place in the storehouse.

Such is the simple and easy mode of raising this most important crop. About six seers of seed are sufficient for sowing a piece of ground equal to an English acre. The returns vary according to soil, situation, and mode of treatment. Under very favourable conditions it will yield from four to five hundred fold. Another great advantage is, that it occupies land for not more than four months. Two crops can be raised in one year from the same land, by making the first sowings in March or April; but this is seldom done, as it necessitates irrigation for the first crop, and this adds very considerably to the expense of raising.—*Indian Field, June* 1859.

It has been said that Indian corn is free from all liability to disease. This, however, has been contradicted, for it has been asserted that a diseased state of this grain, similar in its nature to that of rye, has been met with in Columbia. The ill effects attributed, however, to ergot of maize, are by no means of so fatal a character. Its action, when administered medicinally, is said to be more powerful than that of ergot of rye. It is, however, unquestionable that the disease is of the rarest occurrence.—*Lankester.*

The leaves of the maize plant are capable of yielding a nutritive substance or bread-stuff for human food,—a fibrous material, capable of being spun and woven like flax, and ultimately a pulp, from which a most beautiful paper can be produced. The whole mass of the head-leaves yields on an average one-third of its substance for spinning, one-third for paper, and one-third for food. The whole of the fibrous substance may also be worked up into paper. The process as carried on in the Imperial Paper Manufactory at Schoegelmuehle, in Lower Austria, gives a produce of 100 lb. of paper, from 300 to 350 lb. of head-leaves, irrespective of the other materials, and one lot of such leaves costs only 6s. (3 Rs.) when delivered at the paper factory. To produce the same quantity of paper, about 160 lb. of rags would be required. According to the official returns there are 35,000,000 acres of land in Austria planted with maize, the annual product of head-leaves from which is estimated at 2,750,000 cwts. If the whole of this is worked up into paper, the yield would be enormous, exceeding 1,500,000 lb. annually. So strong and durable is maize paper, that if ground short, it is even said it can be used as an excellent substitute for glass, so great is its natural transparency and firmness.—*Powell's Punj. Prod.*

(600) **Zingiber officinale** (*Roscoe.*) N. O. ZINGIBERACEÆ.

Common Ginger, ENG. Ingie, TAM. Ischi, MAL. Ullum, TEL. Sonth, HIND. Udruck, Ada, BENG.

DESCRIPTION.—Rhizome tuberous, biennial; stems erect and oblique, invested by the smooth sheaths of the leaves, generally 3 or 4 feet high, and annual; leaves sub-sessile on their long sheaths, bifarious, linear-lanceolate, very smooth above and nearly so underneath; sheaths smooth, crowned with a bifid ligula; scapes radical, solitary, a little removed from the stems, 6-12 inches high, enveloped in a few obtuse sheaths, the uppermost of which sometimes end in tolerably long leaves; spikes oblong, the size of a man's thumb; exterior bracts imbricated, 1-flowered, obovate, smooth, membranous at the edge, faintly striated lengthwise; interior enveloping the ovary, calyx, and the greater part of the tube of the corolla; flowers small; calyx tubular, opening on one side, 3-toothed; corolla with a double limb; outer of 3, nearly equal, oblong segments, inner a 3-lobed lip, of a dark-purple colour; ovary oval, 3-celled, with many ovules in each; style filiform. *Fl.* Aug.—Oct.—*Roxb. Fl. Ind.* i. 47.—

Amomum Zingiber, *Linn.—Rheede,* xi. *t.* 12.——Cultivated over all the warmer parts of Asia.

Medical Uses.—The Ginger plant is extensively cultivated in India from the Himalaya to Cape Comorin. In the former mountains it is successfully reared at elevations of 4000 or 5000 feet, requiring a moist soil. The seeds are seldom perfected, on account of the great increase of the roots. These roots or rhizomes have a pleasant aromatic odour. When old they are scalded, scraped, and dried, and are then the white ginger of the shops; if scalded without being scraped, the black ginger. It is not exactly known to what country the ginger plant is indigenous, though Ainslie states it to be a native of China, while Joebel asserts that it is a native of Guinea.

It is still considered doubtful whether the black and white ginger are not produced by different varieties of the plant. Rumphius asserts positively that there are two distinct plants, the white and the red; and Dr Wright has stated in the London Medical Journal, that two sorts—namely, the white and black—are cultivated in Jamaica. The following account of its cultivation is given in Simmond's Commercial Products: The Malabar ginger exported from Calicut is the produce of the district of Shernaad, situated to the south of Calicut; a place chiefly inhabited by Moplas, who look upon the ginger cultivation as a most valuable and profitable trade, which in fact it is. The soil of Shernaad is so very luxuriant, and so well suited for the cultivation of ginger, that it is reckoned the best, and in fact the only place in Malabar where ginger grows and thrives to perfection. Gravelly grounds are considered unfit; the same may be said of swampy ones; and whilst the former check the growth of the ginger, the latter tend in a great measure to rot the root. Thus the only suitable kind of soil is that which, being red earth, is yet free from gravel, and the soil good and heavy. The cultivation generally commences about the middle of May, after the ground has undergone a thorough process of ploughing and harrowing.

At the commencement of the monsoon, beds of 10 or 12 feet long by 3 or 4 feet wide are formed, and in these beds small holes are dug at ¾ to 1 foot apart, which are filled with manure. The roots, hitherto carefully buried under sheds, are dug out, the good ones picked from those which are affected by the moisture, or any other concomitant of a half-year's exclusion from the atmosphere, and the process of clipping them into suitable sizes for planting performed by cutting the ginger into pieces of 1½ to 2 inches long. These are then buried in the holes, which have been previously manured, and the whole of the beds are then covered with a good thick layer of green leaves, which, whilst they serve as manure, also contribute to keep the beds from unnecessary dampness, which might otherwise be occasioned by the heavy falls of rain during the months of June and July. Rain is essentially requisite for the growth of the ginger; it is also, however, necessary that the beds be constantly kept from inundation, which, if not carefully attended to, the crop is entirely ruined; great precaution is therefore taken in forming drains between the beds, letting water out, thus preventing a superfluity. On account of the great tendency some kinds of leaves have to breed worms and insects, strict care is observed in the choosing of them, and none but the particular kinds used in manuring ginger are taken in, lest the wrong ones might fetch in worms, which, if once in the beds, no remedy can be resorted to successfully to destroy them; thus they in a very short time ruin the crop. Worms bred from the leaves laid on the soil, though highly destructive, are not so pernicious to ginger cultivation as those which proceed from the effect of the soil. The former kind, whilst they destroy the beds in which they once appear, do not spread themselves to the other beds, be they ever so close; but the latter kind must of course be found in almost all the beds, as they do not proceed from accidental causes, but from the nature of the soil. In cases like these, the whole crop is oftentimes ruined, and the cultivators are thereby subjected to heavy losses.

The rhizomes when first dug up are red internally, and when procured fresh and young are preserved in sugar, constituting the preserved ginger of the shops. Essence of ginger is made by steeping ginger in alcohol. With regard to its medical uses, ginger, from its stimulant and carminative properties, is used in toothaches, gout, rheumatism of the jaws, and relaxed uvula, with good effect, and the essence of ginger is said to promote digestion. Ginger is said to act powerfully on the mucous membrane, though its effects are not always so decided on the remoter organs as on those which it comes into immediate contact with. Beneficial results have been arrived at when it has been administered in pulmonary and catarrhal affections. Headaches have also been frequently relieved by the application of ginger-poultices to the forehead. The native doctors recommend it in a variety of ways externally in paralysis and rheumatism, and internally with other ingredients in intermittent fevers. Dry or white ginger is called *Sookhoo* in Tamil, and *Sonth* in Dukhanie; and the green ginger is *Injee* in Tamil, and *Udruck* in Dukhanie. The ginger from Malabar is reckoned superior to any other.—*Ainslie. Simmonds.*

(601) **Zizyphus glabrata** (*Heyne*). N. O. Rhamnaceæ.

Carookoova, Tam. Kakoopala, Tel.

Description.—Tree, 20 feet, unarmed; leaves alternate, ovate-oblong, obtuse, crenate-serrated, glabrous, 3-nerved; cymes axillary, scarcely longer than the petioles, few-flowered; drupe turbinate, yellow, with a soft gelatinous pulp; calyx

5-cleft; petals obovate, unguiculate; styles 2, nearly distinct; ovary 2-celled; nut hard and thick, rugose, obovate, flattened, 1-2 celled; flowers small, greenish yellow. *Fl.* April—May.—*W. & A. Prod.* i. 162.—*Wight Icon. t.* 282.—Zizyphus trinervia, *Roxb. Fl. Ind.* i. 606.——Mysore.

MEDICAL USES.—A decoction of the leaves is given to purify the blood in cases of cachexia.—*Ainslie.*

(602) **Zizyphus jujuba** (*Lam.*) Do.

Jujube-tree, ENG. Elendie, TAM. Perintoddali or Elentha, MAL. Reygoo, TEL. Beyr, DUK. Kool, BENG.

DESCRIPTION.—Small tree, 16 feet; stipulary prickles short, in pairs or solitary, often wanting, especially on the young branches; leaves elliptical or oblong, sometimes coarsely toothed at the apex, serrulated, acutish or obtuse or slightly cordate at the base, upper side glabrous, under side as well as young branches and petioles covered with dense tawny tomentum; cymes sessile or very shortly peduncled; ovary 2-celled; styles 2, united to the middle; drupe spherical, yellow when ripe; nut rugose, 2-celled; flowers greenish yellow. *Fl.* Aug.—Oct.—*W. & A. Prod.* i. 162.—*Wight Icon. t.* 99.—*Roxb. Fl. Ind.* i. 608.—Rhamnus jujuba, *Linn.*—*Rheede,* iv. *t.* 41.——Peninsula. Bengal. Travancore.

ECONOMIC USES.—The fruit is eatable. It is sweet and mealy. There is a variety of the tree which produces a long fruit, which is excellent to the taste, called in Bengal *Nari-kela-kool.* Of the former the wood is tough and tolerably strong, and is used in ordinary constructive work. The bark is used by tanners.—(*Ainslie. Stewart's Punj. Plants.*) The timber is good for saddle-trees and ornamental work, as well as for sandals. It is close and even-grained. A kind of kino is procured from the bark.—*Beddome, Flor. Sylv. t.* 149.

This is the most common species in Northern India; but in gardens there is a variety or distinct species with oblong fruit which attains a considerable size, and when grafted yields a pleasant-tasted fruit called *Ber,* which may be styled the Indian jujube. The fruit of the wild kind is dried and powdered, as was done with the lotus of the Lotophagi. This powder is called in Hindee, *Berchoonee.* This species bears a kind of lac in Northern India, called *Beree-ki-lakh,* which is used for dyeing leather, cotton, and silk. Some of the species of this order are said to possess astringent leaves, and some are remarkable for the goodness and denseness of their wood.—*Royle.*

(603) **Zizyphus xylopyra** (*Willd.*) Do.

Gotee, TEL.

DESCRIPTION.—Tree; stipulary prickles solitary, or in pairs, or wanting; leaves alternate, broadly elliptical or orbicular, slightly cordate at the base, serrulated, under side pale, softly pubescent, finely reticulated, upper side pubescent when young; cymes short; ovary 3-celled; styles 3, united below; drupe turbinate, nut globose, hard, slightly rugose, 3-celled; flowers greenish yellow. *Fl.* Aug.—Oct.—*W. & A. Prod.* i. 162.—*Roxb. Fl. Ind.* i. 611.—Z. elliptica, *Roxb.*—Z. Caracutta, *Roxb.*— Rhamnus xylopyrus, *Retz.* —— Courtallum. Cochin. Southern India generally.

ECONOMIC USES.—Cattle eat the young shoots and leaves. The kernels are edible, and taste like filberts. The wood is yellowish or orange-coloured, very hard and durable, and not heavy. The fruit is much used by shoemakers to blacken leather and to make blacking. Wight remarks that this species may always be recognised by the leaves being pale and soft beneath, and the ovary 3-celled.—*Gibson. Wight.*

APPENDIX A.

BAMBOO.

Central Provinces, *9th July* 1866.—Among the many interesting papers and circulars penned by Mr Temple during his late tour through the province, is one on the bamboo forests in the north-east of the Bhundara district. The Chief Commissioner says, in a circular to the Conservator of Forests :—

At Bhanpore, near Ilutta, on the banks of the Deo river, and on the banks of the Sonar river between Saujee and Bejaghur, and around the latter place, both localities being at the base of the eastern part of the Sautpoora range, are found the rare kind of large bamboo which particularly attracted the Chief Commissioner's attention, and to which the following remarks alone refer.

These bamboos are of great size and beauty; at the base they vary from six to ten inches in diameter, tapering up to a point of almost needle fineness at the height of eighty or ninety feet; they tower above the surrounding forests. They are invariably hollow, and the colour of their stems when in their prime is of a bright and rich emerald green. In the vernacular of the country these bamboos are called "Kuttung," which name is said to have been given them because they are covered with long sharp thorns. This may or may not be the true origin of their name, but it is quite certain that they are covered with thorns, while the common solid bamboos are not.

There is every reason to suppose—indeed it is stated by persons now living—that less than one hundred years ago the plains of Ilutta were more or less covered or studded with clumps of "Kuttungs," which have since been swept away by the advance and spread of civilisation. This fact is well preserved in the name Kuthengee, so commonly belonging to villages in this neighbourhood. The cultivation is now daily advancing, and will, unless measures are taken to prevent it, in the course of a few short years, entirely clear away the few that remain of the once innumerable "Kuttungs."

Mr Temple believes that bamboos of this kind are only to be found in three accessible places in the Central Provinces—namely, near Sironcha, at Khampare, and in the neighbourhood of Bejaghur; and in none of these places are they very plentiful. If there be any more accessible places, homes of this bamboo, we will be glad to hear of them. From Bejaghur came those noble specimens of eighty or ninety feet long which attracted so much attention at the Nagpore exhibition.

At all events, the supply from this species must be a limited one. The trees grow in clumps or clusters (*bhera*) of from thirty to fifty each. These clumps may perhaps be counted by the hundred, but not more. About the value of these "Kuttungs" there can be no question. Every year thousands are cut and sold in the bazaars, such as those of Kamptee, where there is always a good demand. The common mode of felling these bamboos is wasteful in the extreme. The first woodcutter who comes to a clump of bamboos in all probability requires just as many as he can carry away on his back; but one entire bamboo is as much as at least two men can carry, consequently the single woodcutter cuts off the upper ends of the outside bamboos to make for himself a suitable load. The next man that comes finds all the good bamboos lodged round a wall of almost useless and impenetrable stumps fifteen and twenty feet high, and is obliged to follow the example of him who came before, and content himself with merely the upper parts of the bamboos. The consequence of all this is, that not one half of the bamboos killed are brought to the market and utilised. Again, too, in most clumps the living bamboos are hampered, indeed sometimes almost weighed down, by the dead ones. The elimination of the latter would, if possible, be a great gain.

It is worthy of remark that all places where "Kuttungs" are known to abound, a river is conveniently near at hand, ready at any rate during the floods, to furnish water-carriage for the heavy produce of the forests. Near Sironcha there are the Indrawatty and the Godavery, on which timber, &c., can be floated down to the sea-coast. At Bhanpore is the Deo nuddee, which in some places is not only overhung but almost overarched by "Kuttungs," which grow along its banks. On this river, and the Sonar at Bejaghur, the "Kuttungs" could be floated down into the Bagh nuddee, and thence into the Wyngunga and Godavery to the sea, or any intermediate place they might be required.

The Chief Commissioner considers that the value of the "Kuttungs" is greatly increased by the fact that they grow so near to considerable streams. For although they are situated in very remote places, yet they can be easily reached, and, when cut, can without difficulty be transported to the markets.

Mr Temple is not aware that any arrangements have been made by the forest department for the conservation of the "Kuttungs," but is under the impression that the matter has not yet attracted much of the attention of your officers. The Chief Commissioner, therefore, requests that arrangements be made for the conservation of these bamboos. They are not situated generally on Bhalsa or Government land: where they are so situated, there will of course be no difficulty; when they are not so situated, they will of course be on the land of zemindars, who are bound to conform to instructions received regarding forestry.

In Major Beddome's Report to Government for 1869-70, he states regarding the dying out of the bamboo: "There has been a general dying out during the last two years of the large bamboos (*Bambusa arundinacea*) throughout Wynaad, Coorg, South Canara, and portions of the Anamallays, &c. In all the large tracts of this giant grass about Sultan's Battery and Manantoddy, there was nothing to be seen last cold season but dead culms,—not a single living clump; and a great portion died in 1868, the remainder in 1869. Opinions differ as to the duration at different periods, varying from twenty to eighty years; it is probably about thirty years. It may be of interest to future observers to know that the general dying out in the tracts alluded to took place during the last two years. Occasionally a single clump, or one or two culms in a clump, would be seen flowering or dying out, but these were isolated instances, and did not affect the general aspect of the jungle. Now there is not a living bamboo to be seen. The seed has already commenced to come up in many parts, but the young plant grows for a long period (one to three years) like a clump of grass, making only root-way before it begins to throw up its gigantic culms. When once these start they will sometimes grow to the length of twenty or even thirty feet in one month. There will be a great dearth of bamboos in all the forests on the western side of the presidency for the next two or three years."

A great deal has been written on the subject of the flowering and immediate dying of the bamboo. Buchanan, in his journey from Madras through the counties of Mysore, Canara, and Malabar, alluding to the trees he observed in passing through the Anamalya forest, writes thus regarding the bamboo: "Here are both the hollow and the solid kinds. When fifteen years old, they are said to bear fruit and then to die. The grain is collected by the rude tribe called Malasir, and is occasionally used by all ranks of people."

Dr Wallich alludes to the subject in a report to Government in the year 1825, in reference to the celebrated grove of bamboos which surrounds the extensive city of Rampore, in Rohilkund, to a breadth of thirty to forty feet. "I had heard," observes Dr Wallich, "a great deal about this unique object, and was therefore the more solicitous to collect all the information I could on the spot. It has been in a state of universal blossoming in 1824, so universal that there was not among its million of stems a single one to be seen which was not dead; they were all leaning on each other or fallen to the ground. I observed with peculiar pleasure that the Nawab had adopted a very effectual and judicious plan of defending the tender age of the myriads of seedling bamboos, which were seen growing on the site as thickly as you can conceive it possible, by not allowing one of the old and withered stems to be cut or in any way disturbed. I was told by some old inhabitants that the hedge was reproduced in the same manner forty years ago (I should have estimated its age at only twenty-five years), and that similar renewals have succeeded each other for ages past. I found the tree to be of the unarmed kind, and was surprised to find that the largest even were inferior in diameter as well as in the thickness of the sides."

Dr. J. D. Hooker, in the account of his excursion to Tonglo from Darjeeling, has a few remarks on the flowering of the bamboo: "At about 4000 feet the great bamboo abounds; it flowers every year, which is not the case with all others of this genus, most of which flower profusely over large tracts of country once in a great many years, and then die away, their place being supplied by seedlings, which grow with immense rapidity. This well-known fact is not due, as some suppose, to the life of the species being of such a duration, but to favourable circumstances in the season."—(*Himalayan Journals*, i. 155.)

The age to which the bamboo will attain under favourable circumstances, and whether different varieties have different ages, has never, it is believed, been accurately ascertained. Sir William Sleeman, indeed, mentions ('Rambles and Recollections of an Indian Official') that the life of the common large bamboo is about fifty years, but he does not state his authority for this assertion. Dr Wallich mentions in his report, quoted above, that he should have estimated the age of the Rampore plant at only twenty years, though the inhabitants stated it to be about forty—that is to say, a flowering similar to that he describes had not taken place for forty years. Mr Jones remarks, in his communication to the Society already cited, that the sign of bearing to which he alludes had showed itself after the lapse of twenty years, and that some very old people could not call to their recollection when it had previously borne seed. This circumstance, coupled with the fact that this bearing is not confined to the more matured plant, both old and young flowering at the same time, would almost lead one to doubt that it follows the regular course by which nature governs the other orders of vegetation; but rather that, as has been observed, it may be encouraged by particular circumstances connected with elemental changes.

In the early part of 1857, as may be remembered, many of the bamboos in Calcutta and other parts of Lower Bengal blossomed and seeded abundantly: the season had been unusually dry throughout Eastern Bengal and on to Assam, where the scarcity of grain was much felt. Mr Jones, in the paper above mentioned, observes that native superstition assigns to the appearance of the seed a certainty of impending famine—"for," say the Brahmins, "when bamboos produce sustenance, we must look to heaven for food." But he adds, "for the hundredth time, perhaps, is Brahminical prescience belied, for never was a finer crop of rice on the field than in the present season of 1836." That the scarcity of food has been partially relieved by the seeding of the bamboo we have an instance in the case cited by Mr Stewart, the collector of Canara, as also by Mr Charles Blechynden in the following words: "In the month of February of the year 1812 a failure occurred in the rice crops in the province of Orissa. Much distress was the consequence, a general famine was apprehended, and would no doubt have taken place, but for a merciful interposition of Providence in causing a general flowering of all the bamboos of the thorny kind, both old and young, throughout the district.

"The grain obtained from these bamboos was most plentiful, and gave sustenance to thousands; indeed the poorer, and therefore the greater portion, of the inhabitants, subsisted for some time solely on this food. So great was the natural anxiety that was evinced to obtain the grain, that hundreds of people were on the watch day and night, and cloths were spread under every clump to secure the seeds as they fell from the branches.

"Soon after this general flowering had taken place every bamboo died, but the country was not long denuded of this elegant tree, for such of the seeds as escaped the vigilance of the inhabitants germinated in a very short time, and a new race of bamboos sprang up to supply the place of the former generation.

"I have been informed that no other flowering has taken place since that period, now 30 years ago."—*Blechynden's Report to Beng. Govt. Sept.* 1864.

APPENDIX B.

The following is extracted from the Appendix to the Pharmacopœia of India. It was considered to be very important that all the species of known value should be introduced from South America into India; and the results of their cultivation up to 1867 have been as follows:—

I. C. CALISAYA (*Yellow bark*).—Up to last year the shrubby variety alone had been obtained; but in the autumn of 1866 a large supply of seeds of the tree variety (*C. vera* of Weddell) was received, which germinated freely. In January 1867 there were 40,000 plants of *C. calisaya* in the Neilgherry plantations. Most important results may be expected from their cultivation, which will be ascertained in the course of a few years.

II. C. SUCCIRUBRA (*Red bark*).—The trees of this species are now so large as to interlace, although 12 feet apart. They are growing at 4000 to 6000 feet above the sea. Mr M'Ivor's method of mossing the stems has increased the thickness of the bark, and, according to Mr Howard's analysis, doubled the yield of febrifuge alkaloids.

III. C. OFFICINALIS (*Brown bark*).—The plants of this species rank next in luxuriance to the red barks, and are much more hardy, growing as well upon grass as upon forest land, and flourishing even on the highest ridges of the Neilgherries, when sheltered from the full force of the monsoon.

IV. C. MICRANTHA, C. NITIDA, C. PERUVIANA, &c. (*Grey barks*).—These species grow luxuriantly with the red bark plants. A very remarkable result of their cultivation has been that, whereas in their native Peruvian forests near Huanuco they yield nothing but the comparatively useless alkaloid called Cinchonine, an analysis of specimens of their bark from the Neilgherries shows that the cinchonine has almost disappeared, and that a very large percentage of the valuable alkaloid, Quinidine, has taken its place.

V. C. LANCIFOLIA (*New Granada barks*).—There are 304 plants of this species growing on the Neilgherries, derived from a plant received from Java, and originally from seeds gathered by Dr Karsten, near Pasto. But this is not the most valuable New Granada species, and the Secretary of State for India has sanctioned the despatch of a collector to attempt once more to obtain plants or seeds of the exceedingly valuable kind that is known to grow near Popeyan and Pitayo.

EXTRACT from DR ANDERSON'S REPORT on Cinchona Cultivation at Darjeeling.—April 1865.

The progress of the cultivation and the advances made during the year will be understood by an account of the stages through which the plants pass before they are finally disposed of by planting in the permanent open-air plantations. From the stock plants of each species, which are planted in the soil in low glazed wooden frames, a crop of cuttings is obtained monthly during the cold and dry periods of the year, and twice a-month from May till October. These cuttings, prepared by a European gardener, assisted by trained natives, are planted in shallow well-drained wooden boxes in coarse sand: 100 cuttings are placed in each box. These boxes fit closely into a wooden frame with glazed lights, in every respect like a cucumber frame; while in these frames the cuttings are carefully sheltered by thin cloth nailed tightly over the glazed sashes, and also by mats which are placed over the sashes during the day. Great attention is given to the watering of the cuttings during the first month, as the slightest excess of moisture causes them to decay. Water is given sparingly, and only by means of a garden syringe provided with a very finely pierced rose. In two or three days the drooping cuttings begin to look fresh and living, and by the end of three weeks most of them have become provided with one or two delicate roots, and in three weeks more at the furthest the process of hardening the young plants commences. This is effected by removing the boxes, with the cuttings still undisturbed, to other glazed frames (principally old cutting frames, whose sashes from use and exposure do not fit tightly), into which air is admitted more and more daily, while the use of mats as protection against the sun is dispensed with. After a fortnight of this treatment, the cuttings, now two months since they were taken from their parent plants, are placed, still undisturbed, in the boxes on terraced beds, protected from the sun and rain by a low roofing of mats or tarpaulin. Twenty days' exposure to air and light in these sheds is generally sufficient to bring the plants into such a state that they can be planted in beds, where they will attain the size and condition of plants suited for permanent plantations. These beds are merely terraces formed on the slope of the hill, and in which the soil has been carefully freed from weeds. The plants are placed at a distance of about six inches from each other, and for the first twenty days after planting they are protected by mats. These are dispensed with as soon as possible, as the object all along aimed at is the inuring of the plants to all kinds of weather.

In these beds little care is bestowed on the plants. They require to be periodically cleared from weeds, and in the dry weather they receive a little water, but this is only given when it is absolutely required to save the plants from injury.

The plants remain in these beds for at least two months; but in the cold season of 1865-66 all the cuttings planted in this manner from 1st November were kept in them until April, when the permanent planting operations commenced. The ground for the plantations has been prepared by being cleared in the cold weather from all trees and vegetation, which were burned. In this land, pits 18 inches deep have been dug at 5 feet apart for *C. officinalis*, and 6 feet apart for *C. succirubra*.

The different stages described above are rendered necessary, to overcome the high state of vegetable excitability in which it is necessary to keep the stock plants. Cuttings taken from such plants, excited as they constantly are by the strongest stimulants of vegetable life—a high temperature and abundant moisture—take root rapidly, but are, when self-existing, quite unable to withstand the vicissitudes of the weather. Their delicate foliage and watery stems require to be thickened and hardened before the plants can be restored to a hardy condition. When this state is attained, the growth in the open air follows the course of vegetation which prevails in Sikhim; the plants continue at rest during the cold weather, and on the return of spring, which varies according to the height above the sea, the Cinchonas again begin to grow. In May and June, depending on the date of the setting in of the periodical rains, and aided by the considerable rise in temperature which accompanies them, the plants shoot with an astonishing vigour, growing at the rate of 1 foot a-month for nearly four months.

This process may seem a long one, but by following it, plants suitable for open-air plantations are obtained sooner than if they were raised from seeds. For example, seeds that were sown in last January cannot be planted out till the end of June; whereas cuttings made in February will be planted in the end of May.

EXTRACT from Captain SEATON'S Report on the Cinchona Plantations in the Madras Presidency.

I. *Propagation.*—The propagation of the plant is by seeds, cuttings, and buds. It is usually carried on in glass houses, by which means the failures are reduced to a minimum, compared with what would be the result if the plants were exposed to variations of temperature in the open air.

The seed is sown in pots 2½ inches deep, prepared in the following way: A piece of tile is first placed over the drain-hole, then a layer of brick-dust, and over that a mixture of sand and fine leaf-mould, but chiefly the former, the surface being kept ½ an inch below the edge of the pot, to allow of water, when poured on slowly, percolating through the soil below.

The pots are watered two or three times a-day, as may be necessary. With the temperature kept at a uniform level of 65° to 70° Fahr., germination usually takes place within two or three weeks.

When the seedlings get two or more leaves, they are put out about 1 inch apart into similar pots filled with mould and brick-dust. In this operation great care is taken not to bruise the roots. To effect this a flat small stick, with a notch at one end, is used for lifting the plants, and the earth is so opened with a round stick that they can be lowered into the holes prepared for them without risk of pressure from the hand. They are then watered carefully, and the mildew scraped off the surface of the pots daily, to prevent the plants damping off, fresh sand being sprinkled on from time to time, as that on the surface comes off in the above operation.

When an inch or two high, the seedlings are put out into hardening beds, under glass frames or thatched *pandals*, and gradually exposed to the air and sun, until sufficiently hardy to admit of removal to the nurseries, which is generally when they have four to six leaves. In the nurseries they are placed in rows 4 inches apart, and 3 inches within the rows, in soil similar to that of the main plantation for which they are destined, watered daily, if necessary, and sheltered by *tatties*, thatched with ferns, placed upon a raised framework, 5 feet high on one side and 3 feet on the other, the *tatties* being lifted more and more until the plants are well established and able to bear exposure to the sun.

The treatment of cuttings and buds is similar to that of seedlings as regards hardening and preparation for removal to the main plantations. When first taken from the parent trees they are placed in fine brick-dust over a layer of leaf-mould, and generally take root within *a month to six weeks.* If planted out in the open air, partially shaded, cuttings form roots within three or more months.

II. *Selection of sites.*—The sites are selected with reference to aspect, shelter from the prevailing winds, soil, drainage, and elevation. A northerly aspect is preferred; but at Ootacamund the various plantations have different aspects as well as degrees of exposure, which cannot be avoided, as the plantations cover a large area.

For the brown and yellow bark species, from 7000 to 8000 feet elevation is selected. For the red and grey bark, 5000 to 6000 feet elevation is deemed the best, but they will grow at a much lower elevation,—3000 feet, and as low as 2500.

Some plants, *succirubras,* two years old, are doing well in a coffee-plantation on the Carcoor Ghaut, at 2500 feet elevation, where the climate is particularly moist, the rainfall being upwards of 200 inches. As that of Ootacamund is only 40 to 50 inches, it may be assumed that a heavy rainfall compensates for elevation, and is essential to success at low elevations.

The most suitable localities on the hills for the cinchona plant appear to be the re-entering angles between the bends and spurs, where the ground was originally occupied by *sholas,* or patches of evergreen forest, and the soil consists of a dark rich vegetable loam. In such localities the red and grey bark thrive best, while the other varieties will grow on open grass-land and peaty soils. All require good superficial drainage, as well as open subsoil below.

III. *Cultivation.*—In the early part of the dry season, the trees, brushwood, &c., on the site selected, are felled and prepared for burning. After the whole has been well burnt at the close of the dry season, the ground is marked off into lines for the plants, pathways made, and catch-drains cut here and there to carry off the surface-water during heavy rains. Pits 2 feet square and 2 feet deep (7 feet apart for the red and grey barks) are then prepared, and filled with the best surface soil and burnt earth.

The ground being now ready for the reception of the plants from the nurseries, a wet showery day is selected for the work of transplanting. In this operation, to avoid touching the roots, the plants are held by the leaves; care also is taken not to embed the plant deeper than the collar or head of the roots. Immediately they are planted out, the plants have to be shaded either with a circular basket open at both ends, or with a few pieces of wood placed erect and covered with ferns. During the hot season the earth is heaped up around the billets of wood in the shape of a circular bund, but this is removed on the first fall of the rains.

In the event of the weaker plants requiring water during the hot months, this is done by watering the ground a foot or two on the slope above them, a hole being prepared for the water to penetrate readily into the soil. As they grow and require support against the wind, they have to be secured above the stem with grass ropes between two stakes. Beyond an occasional weeding, nothing more is done to the plants, which, when fairly established, can be left to themselves.

APPENDIX C.

FURTHER USES OF THE COCOA-PALM.*

It is well known that the leaves furnish material for mats, thatch, screens, *purdahs* in zenanas, &c. The finer nerves of the pinnules are employed in constructing a superior description of mat. The fibrous husk of the nut yields *kayár*, from which ropes and cables are made, and with which mattresses are stuffed. When the husk is cut across and the inner shell removed, a hard brush is formed, which is much used for polishing waxed furniture, and for many other purposes. The hard shell (endocarp), besides its use for ladles, &c., affords when burnt a good black pigment, occasionally employed in colouring the walls of houses.

The albumen and the milk are used as an ingredient in curries (and no *pillau* or curry is considered complete without them); the milk is also used in the arts. The kernel is pounded, and subjected to strong pressure, for the purpose of yielding the cocoa-oil of commerce. The manufacture of this oil constitutes a regular trade on the western coast of Hindostan. Toddy is drawn from the tree for six months of the year. The process of extracting the sap is as follows: When the spathe is a month old, the flower-bud is considered sufficiently juicy to yield a fair return to the (Sánár) toddy-drawer, who ascends the tree with surprising ease and apparent security, furnished with the apparatus of his vocation. This apparatus and the mode of ascent were described by Dr Cleghorn in his paper. A year's practice is requisite before the Sánár becomes an expert climber. The spathe when ready for tapping is 2 feet long and 2 inches thick. It is tightly bound with strips of young leaves to prevent expansion, and the point is cut off transversely to the extent of 1 inch. He gently hammers the cut end of the spathe to crush the flowers thereby exposed, that the juice may flow freely. The stump is then bound up with a broad strip of fibre. This process is repeated morning and evening for a number of days—a thin layer being shaved off on each occasion, and the spathe at the same time trained to bend downwards. The time required for this

* By Hugh Cleghorn, M.D.

initiatory process varies from five to fifteen days in different places. The time when the spathe is ready to yield toddy is correctly ascertained by the chattering of birds, the crowding of insects, the dropping of juice, and other signs unmistakable to the Sánár. The end of the spathe is then fixed into an earthen vessel, and a slip of leaf is pricked into the flower to catch the oozing liquor and convey the drops clear into the vessel. After the juice begins to flow the hammering is discontinued. A man attends to thirty or forty trees, which do not bleed so freely during the heat of the day as at night. Forty trees yield twelve Madras measures of juice, about 1½ to 2 gallons, the times of collecting being seven in the morning and five in the evening. Jaggery (coarse brown sugar) is procured by boiling down fresh toddy over a slow fire, a gallon yielding about a pound. Jaggery mixed with lime forms a strong cement, and takes a fine polish. It is to this mixture, in part at least, that the Madras Chunam owes its celebrity.

Wood.—The trunk is only used for temporary purposes; when fresh cut it possesses great elasticity, and is for this reason particularly well adapted for temporary stockades which are exposed to cannon-shot. Cocoa-palms are easily transplanted, and often with advantage. Some of the fibrous radicles are cut away, a little manure and a handful of salt being applied to the roots each time.

APPENDIX D.

ON THE CULTIVATION AND PRODUCE OF CHAY-ROOTS AND CHERINJI.

The *Hedyotis umbellata* grows spontaneously in sandy soils throughout the Carnatic, but more particularly along the Coromandel coast. The root of that which grows wild is reckoned the best, but it is also cultivated to some extent. The districts in which it is most largely produced are Rajahmundry, Masulipatam, and Guntoor. It is also obtained in Nellore, South Arcot, and Tanjore, but the information at present available is only for the three first mentioned.

For the cultivation of the plant the finest sandy soil is required, as being the most favourable to the free growth of the root, on the length of which the value of the article greatly depends.

The cultivation commences in the end of May or beginning of

June, with the first falls of the S.W. monsoon. During the space of three months the land is subjected to repeated ploughings, and is thoroughly cleaned from all weeds. Between each ploughing it is manured, and after the last ploughing it is levelled with a board, and formed in small beds of about 6 feet by 3.

The seed, which is extremely minute (so much so that it is impossible to gather it except by sweeping up the surface sand into which it has fallen at the end of the harvest), is then sown by spreading a thin layer of sand over the prepared beds. They are then kept constantly moist, and are watered gently with a sieve made of Palmyra fibres five or six times a-day, care being taken that the water is quite sweet and fresh, for which purpose it is obtained from wells newly dug in the field.

At the end of a fortnight the seeds under this treatment will have germinated freely, after which the young plants are only watered once a-day; in addition to which, liquid cow-dung, greatly diluted with water, is daily sprinkled over them.

At the end of two months the plants will have attained nearly their full height, but mixed with weeds of *Mollugo cerviana* and *Spergula trianthemum*, various kinds of *Cyperaceæ*, and other sand-loving plants. These must be carefully removed, and the beds watered again if required.

In about four months more, or at the end of six months from the time of sowing, provided the season has been good and the falls of rain regular, the plants will have reached maturity, and the roots be ready for digging. But no artificial irrigation will compensate for a failure of the natural rain, and when this happens the plants must be left for three or even four months longer, in which case the produce will be deficient both in quantity and quality. But in an ordinary season the produce of a *podu*, or plot, containing an acre and three quarters, will yield from five to ten, averaging about eight, candies of 500 lb. each.

The plants are dug up with a light wooden spade, tipped with iron, and are tied into bundles of a handful each, without cutting off the stalks. They are then left to dry; the leaves wither and fall off, and the bundles are weighed and removed. Before the digging begins, the seeds, which have now ripened, are shed, and being exceedingly minute, become inextricably mixed with the sand, the surface of which is therefore carefully scraped up, and reserved for future sowings.

The culture by means of artificial watering is called *Arntadi podu;* but there is another system called *Waka podu*, in which, when the rains are plentiful, hand-watering is dispensed with; and advantage being taken of a full (or 18-inch) fall of rain at the time of sowing, the plants are left to the chances of the season, care being only taken to keep them free from weeds.

The cost of cultivating a plot or *podu* is as follows:—

Ploughing, ...	5 Rs.
Manuring, ...	5 "
Clearing, smoothing, &c., ...	2 "
Watering, ...	6 "
(*N.B.*—If the rains are seasonable, this is proportionably diminished.)	
Weeding, ...	6 "
Digging, at so much the candy, generally about .	36 "
	60 Rs.
Add the land-tax, at 14 Rs. the acre, . . .	25 "
Total, . . .	85 Rs.

Assuming the produce to be eight candies, and the average price 16 Rs. per candy, $8 \times 16 = 128 - 85 = 43$ Rs. for the cultivator's profit, which cannot be considered large, compared with the constant care and attention required to secure a good crop.

It should be added that the assessment on such land as yields chay-root has been greatly reduced, and now does not exceed 2½ to 3 Rs.

The average price has been taken at 16 Rs., but when the demand is good it rises as high as 25 Rs.

No returns are forthcoming of the out-turn from the spontaneous Chay-root; but as the right of collecting it is farmed out, and the sum bid for it in Masulipatam only amounted to 335 Rs., the quantity cannot be large. But in Guntoor the rent sells for 7450 Rs. The same land can only be worked every third year for spontaneous produce.

Most part of the root is consumed on the spot. It is also carried by land to Velapalem, a large weaving village in Guntoor. On one occasion 22 candies were exported to Tranquebar, but the greatest part is used up in the town of Bunder, for printing chintz and dyeing cotton cloths, and most of the produce in Rajahmundry comes to the same place. Of late years the demand has greatly fallen off, both from the decay of trade at Masulipatam, and from the introduction during the last few years of a new dye.

What is known by the name of *Cherinji* is the bark of a root grown in the Dekhan. When used with a leaf called Jagi, also imported from the hill country of Ganjam, a colour is produced which is considered nearly equal to the Chay, whilst the process is far simpler and much less expensive. On the other hand, the colour is neither so fast, so bright, nor so enduring. A drop of spirit allowed to fall on Cherinji-dyed cloth takes away the colour at once, but has no effect on the Chay dye. During the last five years these articles have nearly superseded the use of Chay; but as no specimens have been sent to the Exhibition, the Jury are unable to say what they are.

The Cherinji usually sells for 20 Rs. the candy; the Jagi leaf from 30 to 45 Rs., and is all fit for use; whereas the stalks and bark of the Chay-root, included in the weight at the time of sale, have to be rejected, thus reducing the quantity very considerably. Sometimes a little Chay-root is mixed with Cherinji to improve the colour. The increasing demand for Cherinji among the native dyers has caused a serious diminution in the produce of Chay-root during the last five or six years. Thus in Masulipatam the average produce, which had been 680 candies for the five years from 1846-47 to 1850-51, fell to 425 for the next five years, from 1851-52 to 1855-56 ; and if the new dye continues to supersede it in the same proportion, it seems likely that the Chay will be driven out of the market altogether.

Not only are Cherinji and Jagi much cheaper, but the simplicity of the method of dyeing with them, compared with the complicated and tedious method involved in the use of the Chay-root process, would alone tend to bring the latter into disuse.—*Jury Rep. Mad. Exhib.*, 1855.

APPENDIX E.

The following memorandum regarding the cultivation and manufacture of Indigo, as carried on in the Benares Province, is by Claud Hamilton Brown, Esq. of Mirzapore :—

Soil.—The richest loam is supposed to give the best produce, though lighter soils frequently give finer-looking plants. Moist low soils are not suitable, but a great deal depends upon the subsoil, as the root grows vertically and to a great depth. High stony lands are to be avoided, excepting the sites of old villages, where, from the presence of lime and animal or vegetable matter, very fine crops are frequently produced, particularly in a season when the rains are heavy. Fields that have recently had heavy crops—Maize (*Holcus*), Indian corn (*Zea*), Urhur (*Phaseolus*), &c.—recently taken off them should be avoided.

Cultivation. — Immediately on the setting in of the periodical rains, say 15th to 30th June (in these parts), the lands should be well and carefully ploughed (three ploughings), the seed thrown in broadcast, at the rate of 8 lb. per *beegah*, and the land smoothed over with a *henga* (rudimentary harrow). The plant generally shows itself in three or five days. As soon as it has got two or three inches high, with six or eight leaves, all weeds must be carefully removed, and a second weeding is again requisite by the time the plant is six or seven inches high. While weeding, any place where the seed may have failed to germinate can be resown, by sprinkling the seed on the surface and dibbling it in where required. In about ninety days the plant begins to flower, and is then ready for cutting.

Manufacture.—The plant is cut at about 6 inches from the ground, and carried to the steeping-vats with as little delay as possible, strewn horizontally in the vats, and pressed down by means of beams fixed into side-posts, bamboos being placed under the beams. Water must be immediately run in, sufficient just to cover the plant. If water is not at once let in, the plant will heat, and become spoiled.

Steeping.—The time for steeping depends much on the temperature of the atmosphere, and can only be learnt by experience and careful watching of the vats; but it may be mentioned that in close sultry weather, wind east, therm. 96° in the shade, eleven or twelve hours are sufficient. In dry cool weather, wind west, fifteen or sixteen hours are sometimes requisite. If the plant is very ripe, the vat will be ready sooner than if the plant was young and unripe.

It is most important to steep exactly the proper time, the quality and quantity of your produce being dependent on this being done. As a guide, the following signs may be mentioned, as showing that the vat is ready to be let off:—

1st, As soon as the water begins to fall in the vat. 2d, When the bubbles that rise to the surface burst at once. 3d, On splashing up the surface water, it has an orange tinge mingling with the green. 4th, The smell of the water is also a great guide; when ripe it should have a sweetish pungent odour, quite different from the raw smell of the unripe green-coloured water. The first of the water, when let off into the beating-vat, has a rich orange colour; and from the depth of this you can judge whether the vat has been a proper time steeping.

Beating.—This is performed by men who enter the water (about seven to each vat) and agitate it either by the hands or by a wooden paddle, at the first gently, but gradually increasing as the fecula begin to separate, which is known by the subsidence of the froth and the change of the colour of the water from green to dark blue. The time usually necessary for beating is from one and three-quarters to three hours, but no positive rule can be given for this.

The following are common modes of testing the state of the vat:—

1st, Take a little of the water in a white plate or saucer and let it stand. If the fecula subside readily, and the water remains of Madeira colour, the beating may be stopped.

2d, Dip a coarse cloth in the vat and wring out the water, observing its colour; if green, the beating must be continued, but if Madeira or brownish colour, it is ready.

3d, When sufficiently beaten, the surface of the water will, as soon as the beating is suspended, become of a peculiar glassy appearance and the froth subside, with a sparkle and effervescence like champagne.

Three or four chatties of cold water or weak lime-water are then sprinkled over the surface to hasten the precipitation of the fecula, which does not completely take place in less than three or four hours. The water must then be drawn off from the surface through plug-holes made for the purpose in a stone slab inserted in the wall of the vat. The fecula remaining at the bottom are removed to the boiler.

Boiling.—Bring it to the boiling as soon as possible, and keep it there for five or six hours; while boiling, it must be stirred to prevent the indigo burning, and skimmed with a perforated ladle. Its being sufficiently boiled is known by its assuming a glossy appearance. When sufficiently boiled it is run off to the straining-table, where it remains twelve or fifteen hours draining; it is then taken to the press and gradually pressed. This takes twelve hours. It is then ready to be taken out, cut, stamped, and laid in the drying-house to dry. A good size of steeping-vat is 16 feet by 14 by 4¾; the beating-vat to be somewhat smaller and shallower. A beegah contains 27,224 feet. Two hundred maunds of plant do very well if they yield one maund (82 lb.) of any indigo. A vat of above size holds about 100 maunds of plants.

The plant sown, say, in June or July, is cut three months afterwards (*Now-dah*) and manufactured, and a second crop will be taken from it the following *Khoontee* (August). The second cutting gives the largest produce and best quality; the third (*Teersalee*), but it is seldom allowed to grow three years.

APPENDIX F.

EXTRACTION OF SANDAL-WOOD OIL.

The following memorandum by Dr G. Bidie on Sandalwood, and the mode of extraction of its volatile oil, is of especial interest and value, as being the result of personal observation :—

This *Santalum album* (Linn.) is a small tree, rarely exceeding 25 feet in height, and very limited in its range, being most abundant in the Mysore country, where it grows on the eastern slopes of the Western Ghauts, just beyond the limits of the Mulnaad or rain country. It is carefully protected by Government, and only the trees that have reached maturity, which they do in from 18 to 25 years, are cut down. The felling takes place in the end of the year, and the trees are then stripped of their bark and conveyed to various depots, where they are cut into billets, which are carefully dressed and sorted according to the quality of the wood. These billets form the Sandal-wood of commerce, and are sold by weight at an annual auction, native merchants congregating from all parts of India to make purchases. The pieces that are straight and have most heart-wood fetch the highest price, as the fragrance for which they are so much prized depends on the presence of essential oil, which is chiefly situated in the dark central wood of the tree. The Mysore Government has long had establishments for extracting the oil, which is sold at the annual auction along with the wood, and chiefly bought up for exportation to China and Arabia. It is procured from the wood by distillation, the roots yielding the largest quantity and finest quality of oil. The body of the still is a large globular clay pot with a circular mouth, and is about 2½ feet deep by about 6½ feet in circumference at the bilge. No capital is used, but the mouth of the still when charged is closed with a clay lid, having a small hole in its centre, through which a bent copper tube, about 5½ feet long, is passed for the escape of the vapour. The lower end of the tube is conveyed inside a copper receiver, placed in a large porous vessel containing cold water. When preparing the Sandal for distillation, the white or sap wood is rejected, and the heart-wood is cut into small chips, and distillation is slowly carried on for ten days and nights, by which time the whole of the oil is extracted. As the water from time to time gets low in the still, fresh supplies are added from the heated contents of the refrigeratory. The quantity of oil yielded by wood of good quality is at the rate of 10 oz. per maund, or 2.5 per cent. It is transparent and of a pale-yellow colour, and has a resinous taste and sweet peculiar smell, which is best appreciated by rubbing a few drops of the oil on the warm hand. Its specific gravity is about 0·980. The wood is used in various ways as a perfume by the natives, and also as a medicine, being supposed to possess cooling properties, although, from the presence and nature of the essential oil just referred to, it must be more or less of a stimulant character.—*Pharm. of India*, Append., 461.

MEMORANDUM BY C. S. KOHLOFF, ESQ., LATE CONSERVATOR OF FORESTS IN TRAVANCORE.—MAY 20, 1865.

The mode of seasoning teak timber in Travancore is by cutting five or six inches broad through the sap-wood, and about half or one inch into the sound wood round the trunk of the tree at the stem during the hot weather, from the month of November to March. In this state the tree is left to dry, which is denoted by the smaller branches dropping off in the space of two or three years, depending much on its size and the locality where it stands. If in an exposed place, and the tree is not of a large size, it will be sufficiently dry in about two years; if in a shady and damp place, it will be longer in drying. The trees when dried are felled, trimmed of the branches and sap-wood, and placed on sleepers for a year or two to render them thoroughly dry, so that they may float. If allowed to lie on the ground, the timber, by absorbing the dampness of the soil, will not turn buoyant for a length of time. This is the general practice observed in seasoning timber. Particular attention should be paid in seasoning timber: the trees ought not to be ringed when they are filled with sap, or when they are in blossom. Trees are full of sap about the full moon, and it is said to rise from the new to the full; hence the best time for ringing and felling will be during the last and first quarters of the moon. Common trees, that contain no oleaginous matter, and felled for timber during the first and last quarters, are better preserved than those felled during the other quarters of the moon. In a very few years the latter are thoroughly perforated by peculiar small bees, or are destroyed by rot. Though teak and other durable trees converted into timber are not liable to be attacked by insects, yet they are likely to crack and become somewhat brittle. Such timber is generally attributed to the nature of the wood: I should say otherwise, that it was more owing to the trees being girdled and felled when they are full of sap; and would recommend that, if particular attention is required to be paid to the seasoning of the wood, they should be girdled and felled when the trees are less impregnated with sap.

APPENDIX G.

The following is extracted from 'Remarks on Tea-Manufacture in the North-West Provinces of India,' by Mr William Bell.

In treating of tea-manufacture, leaf-plucking is the first operation requiring notice. Throughout the North-West Provinces the plucking season begins about the last week in March or the first in April, and extends to the middle or end of October (in Assam the plucking season commences earlier and lasts longer, but there both climate and soil as well as the plant cultivated are different). Each plucker is furnished with a small basket to hold the leaf, takes a single line of bushes, and is instructed to pluck young and unhealthy bushes lightly, and healthy ones moderately, not to leave any shoots fit for plucking, and not to pluck any that are not sufficiently mature, nor yet to take any that are too old and hard for making fine tea. If old hard leaves be taken along with young tender ones, in process of rolling the hard leaf breaks and chafes the tender ones, which injures the appearance of the tea. When plucking is partly done by contract (which is not unfrequently the case at the beginning of the season), it is the interest of the parties employed to bring in as many old leaves as possible, because they fill the basket more quickly and weigh heavier than young ones, but are not worth so much in the market, as the cost of plucking them and their removal injures the bushes. Hence the necessity for seeing that nothing is brought in except what is good and of uniform quality. The operation of plucking is simply the removal by the finger and thumb of the young shoots with three or four leaves. The amount of plucking depends, however, on the condition of the bush: if old and scrubby, or unhealthy, two joints of each shoot may be enough; and if vigorous, perhaps four joints of the more robust shoots. At midday the leaf is brought into the factory and weighed. The best plan is to weigh each man's gathering separately, that carelessness or laziness may at once be detected and punished. The leaf is then spread out thinly in some cool place, the object being to prevent heating, or if wet, to allow of its becoming dry before the following morning. The leaf plucked during the afternoon is weighed in the evening, and spread out in the same manner. The quantity of leaf that a man will pluck per day depends on such circumstances as the weather, the season of the year, the health of the bushes, and the quality of the leaf wanted. The amount of raw leaf required to make 1 lb. of dry tea varies according to the season. During the hot season it requires from 3 lb. 10 oz. to 3 lb. 14 oz., but after the rainy season, from 4 lb. to 4 lb. 14 oz.

I now come to the subject of tea-making proper—that is, the conversion of the leaf, plucked on the day previous, into black or green tea, as may be judged expedient. Supposing that black tea is to be made, the leaf is brought out and spread thinly on mats or carpets (anything that will prevent it from getting soiled), and turned over once or twice that it may all be fully exposed to the sun and become uniformly flaccid. This withering process is necessary, for two reasons—it improves the flavour of the tea, and prevents breakage in the process of rolling. The general test for ascertaining sufficiency of exposure, is when the points and margins of the leaves become brownish, and neither the petiole nor the blade of the leaf, when placed together and pressed by the finger and thumb, ought to crack. If the day happens to be a little dull, the whole of the leaf is withered at one opportunity; but if bright and dry, it is better to do it in portions. If too long exposed to the sun, or if it lies for any length of time after it has been properly withered, it becomes excessively difficult to roll, and the batch when finished is likely to contain a large percentage of what the brokers call flat-rolled leaves—*i.e.*, the leaf is only folded lengthwise—*not* twisted.

The next process is firing. The pans used for this purpose are of ordinary cast-metal, set in brickwork, with a high back to prevent the tea from being thrown over, and heated up to a temperature of 240° or 250°. As much leaf is put in the pan as a man can turn easily and quickly; in this operation great care is necessary to prevent burning. After a few minutes of this treatment it is brushed out, thrown on the table, and again quickly rolled while hot, and so on until the whole of the batch has been done. The same process of firing and rolling is repeated, and the leaf spread thinly over large bamboo trays, and placed in the sunshine. As the drying process proceeds, two or three of these trays may be emptied into one, and well shaken up. After the leaf has become thoroughly dry, or nearly so, it is put into sieves and placed over slow charcoal-fires for half an hour, if the day is bright—if dull, it will require a little longer; or if the day has been wet throughout, the tea is put over the fires as soon as possible after the last rolling. As the whole of the batch cannot be heated at once, that which is left is thinly spread out to prevent souring. If the tea has not been partially dried in the sun, it requires to be at least four hours over the fire before it can with safety be set aside for the night. If too quickly dried, singeing or burning is certain to be the result, which more or less injures the quality of the tea. Particular care must also be taken that nothing goes into the fire which will produce the slightest smoke; and in placing the tea over the fires, and lifting it off to turn, the danger of any particles falling through the bottom of the sieves on to the fires must be avoided. The smell of the tea shows when it has been sufficiently long over the fire. When thoroughly dry it has a pleasant, somewhat nutty smell; if not dry, the smell is bitter and disagreeable, and if stored away in that state it will become sour, and afterwards mouldy.

The next process is rolling; each man takes up as much of the withered leaf as can be easily grasped between the hands, and rolls, *not slides*, it backwards and forwards on a common deal-table, giving it an occasional *shake up* to make sure that the whole is uniformly twisted. Rolling is both slow and laborious work; 30 lb. of raw leaf, equal to about 7½ lb. of dry tea, is a hard day's work if carefully done. This operation is repeated a second and third time, but it is on the first rolling that the quality of the tea (considered as a well-finished article) entirely depends.

After rolling, the leaves are subjected to fermentation. The tea is thoroughly shaken up and thrown loosely into a heap, then covered closely with carpets or mats. The length of time it ought to lie in this state varies according to the state of the weather, the quality of the leaf, &c. If the weather be warm and dry, and the leaf of fine quality, fermentation is rapid. If the weather be dull, and the leaf a little hard, it is slower and less regular; in the one case four hours may be sufficient, in the other it may require six or eight; but whether quick or slow, it must be carefully watched and checked at the proper time. If checked too soon, the tea is somewhat coarse and astringent in flavour; if allowed to run too far, it loses the flavour partially or entirely, and has a sourish taste.

After minutely describing the process of manufacturing *Green Tea*, Mr Bell proceeds: The natives of India will not use black tea, at whatever price it may be offered; but some of the small merchants purchase damaged teas, and colour them for the local or the Central Asian markets. It is almost impossible to colour genuine black tea, so that it will pass for green; the particles require to be actually coated with colouring matter, and in the dry state that will hardly disguise its true character—a rub in the hand, or a slight infusion, shows at once what it is. But teas such as the *oolongs*, which some classify as black, are essentially green. The mode in which these are manufactured is a combination of the green and black systems; a slight dash of colour will give to these teas an appearance which will deceive any one except an expert. Teas of the *oolong* class were at one time extensively manufactured in the North-West Provinces; however, there never seems to have been a great demand for them in the London market, as persons accustomed to drink genuine black tea dislike their harsh bitter flavour, which is hardly distinguishable from that of genuine green tea. Teas of that description when coloured (made green) have been known to bring a much better price in the local markets than they would have done had they been sent to the home market as manufactured. The conversion of such teas into green can hardly be stigmatised as one of the tricks of trade, as, strictly speaking, they have more qualities in common with green than with black teas.

A correspondent of the *Hills* makes some useful remarks on tea-planting in Kumaon. He refers specially to the plantation of Konsansie, which he describes as resembling some well-cared-for estate in Scotland or Wales, rather than a forest tract in the heart of Kumaon. The soil is highly productive, and the supply of water abundant. He says that it is useless to embark in tea-planting without a capital of at least 20,000 Rs. Then the garden is not in full bearing until the seventh year; and when an abundant crop is obtained, there is the difficulty of finding a market for it. The Konsansie plantation commenced in 1857, and costing 100,000 Rs., yielded this year not quite 6000 lb. of tea, which, at 2 Rs. per lb., would be 12,000 Rs.—not nearly the expense of working the concern. Next year it expects to double its yield, and so on every year, till at the seventh year it may pay 10 or 20 per cent to the shareholders, *if they can sell the tea.* The home market is taken up by the Assam and Cachar tea. The only chance for tea in the North-West is the development of a market for it among the native population. The natives on all sides are beginning to like and buy tea. There is a market large enough amongst the native community, but they will not buy till you can manufacture at a price they can afford to give. Upon the whole, Assam and Cachar appear to have many advantages over the North-West as tea-planting districts.

TABLE showing the QUANTITIES and VALUE of the following INDIAN PRODUCTS, exported from the three Presidencies during the Years 1869-70 and 1870-71.

Botanical name of the Plant.	English name of Product.	From Bengal Presidency, 1870-71.		From Madras Presidency, 1869-70.		From Bombay Presidency, 1870-71.	
Areca catechu	Betel-nut	Cwt. 1, 68, 167	Rs. 12, 69, 554	Cwt. 441	Rs. 7, 667	Cwt. 5, 470	Rs. 65, 115
Brassica napus	Rape-seed	,, 20, 87, 790	,, 93, 94, 726	,, 220	,, 903	,, 53, 560	,, 2, 41, 024
Cannabis sativa	Hemp	,, 16, 939	,, 1, 41, 739	,, 1, 248	,, 12, 916	,, 40, 038	,, 4, 11, 740
Capsicum frutescens	Chillies	,, 5, 481	,, 43, 698	,, 6, 648	,, 1, 33, 799	,, 5, 836	,, 50, 630
Carthamus tinctorius	Safflower	,, 16, 075	,, 13, 91, 794	....	....	,, 17	,, 800
Cocos nucifera	Cocoa-nut oil	galls. 7, 818	,, 11, 772	galls. 10, 88, 857	,, 15, 19, 125	galls. 61, 735	,, 96, 561
Coffea Arabica	Coffee	lb. 9, 458	,, 2, 688	lb. 3, 73, 26, 959	,, 88, 16, 282	lb. 23, 06, 125	,, 4, 80, 277
Corchorus capsularis	Jute	cwt. 33, 43, 515	,, 2, 39, 10, 807	cwt. 34, 93	,, 15, 501	cwt. 1, 309	,, 10, 720
Coriandrum sativum	Coriander-seed	,, 16, 391	,, 65, 496	....	....	,, 379	,, 1, 839
Cuminum cyminum	Cummin-seed	,, 20, 040	,, 2, 26, 690	....	....	,, 3, 796	,, 60, 508
Curcuma longa	Turmeric	,, 59, 371	,, 2, 96, 851	,, 7, 614	,, 38, 320	,, 17, 781	,, 1, 06, 410
Elettaria cardamomum	Cardamoms	,, 67	,, 13, 428	,, 168	,, 32, 485	,, 965	,, 2, 10, 458
Gossypium herbaceum	Cotton wool	lb. 7, 86, 63, 937	,, 2, 02, 01, 688	lb. 684, 57, 798	,, 1, 91, 08, 945	lb. 48, 30, 62, 066	,, 15, 62, 16, 064
Indigofera tinctoria	Indigo	cwt. 63, 581½	,, 2, 28, 52, 025	cwt. 24, 467	,, 75, 47, 745	cwt. 1,003	,, 142, 827
Linum usitatissimum	Linseed	,, 32, 73, 576	,, 1, 63, 67, 838	,, 4, 481	,, 7, 405	,, 1, 08, 827	,, 5, 44, 135
Nicotiana Tabacum	Tobacco-leaf	,, 1, 13, 386	,, 14, 62, 485	,, 20, 552	,, 5, 97, 215	lb. 25, 90, 225	,, 4, 21, 783
Oryza sativa	Rice	,, 86, 07, 169	,, 2, 60, 98, 402	,, 14, 72, 263	,, 58, 97, 849	cwt. 4, 91, 906	,, 28, 84, 471
Papaver somniferum	Opium	chests, 48, 015	,, 5, 49, 03, 957	....	....	chests, 41, 059½	,, 5, 97, 12, 608
Piper nigrum	Pepper	cwt. 629	,, 9, 427	,, 22, 211	,, 3, 33, 217	cwt. 21, 214	,, 8, 78, 133
Ricinus communis	Castor-oil	galls 6, 55, 917	,, 7, 36, 850	galls. 48, 330	,, 49, 454	galls. 7, 217	,, 10, 358
Rubia munjista	Madder	cwt. 4, 712	,, 44, 208	....	....	cwt. 467	,, 6, 522
Saccharum officinarum	Sugar	,, 5, 28, 553	,, 67, 07, 468	cwt. 2, 08, 994	,, 15, 57, 184	,, 30, 646	,, 451, 457
Santalum album	Sandal-wood	....	....	....	....	....	,, 672
Sesamum orientale	Gingely-oil	galls. 2, 09, 188	,, 2, 50, 114	,, 7, 55, 075	,, 45, 29, 586	galls. 30, 510	,, 48, 396
Sinapis juncea	Mustard-seed	cwt. 5, 675¼	,, 25, 201	,, 1, 866	,, 8,396	cwt. 5, 703	,, 88, 524
Tectona grandis	Teak-wood	....	....	....	,, 3, 20, 340	....	,, 55, 969
Terminalia Chebula	Myrobalans	,, 10, 349	,, 34, 890	,, 56, 740	,, 1, 64, 821	,, 46, 519	,, 210, 902
Thea viridis	Tea	lb. 1, 28, 11, 618	,, 1, 07, 86, 690	lb. 6, 166	,, 9,162	lb. 841	,, 661
Triticum vulgare	Wheat	cwt. 3, 24, 978	,, 13, 06, 476	cwt. 10, 938	,, 53, 714	cwt. 60, 333	,, 3, 10, 281
Zingiber officinale	Ginger	,, 12, 579	,, 87, 780	,, 13, 492	,, 1, 66, 280	,, 8, 673	,, 105, 157

From the Annual Volumes of the Trade and Navigation of each Presidency for 1869-70 and 1870-71.

INDEX OF HINDOOSTANEE AND BENGALEE SYNONYMS.

Bagh-Dharanda, *B;* Jatropha Curcas.
Bagoon or Begoon; Solanum Melongena.
Bahura; Terminalia Bellerica.
Baingan; Solanum Melongena.
Bair; Zizyphus Jujuba.
Bakas or Bakus, *B* and *H;* Adhatoda Vasica.
Bala, *H;* Andropogon muricatum.
Bala; Sida rhombifolia.
Balam-cira; Cucumis sativus.
Baltar; Borassus flabelliformis.
Bamunhatee, *B;* Clerodendron siphonanthus.
Ban, *H;* Moringa pterygosperma.
Ban-mallica, *H;* Jasminum angustifolium.
Bans or Bansh, *B* and *H;* Bambusa arundinacea.
Bar, *H;* Ficus Bengalensis or Indica.
Baral; Artocarpus Lakoocha.
Barna; Cratæva Roxburghii.
Bartakoo, *B;* Solanum Melongena.
Basoka; Adhatoda Vasica.
Bassana, *H;* Agati grandiflora.
Bastra; Callicarpa lanata.
Bat; Ficus Indica.
Batoola; Cicer arietinum.
Bator-neboo, *B* and *H;* Citrus decumana.
Bebina, *H;* Mussænda frondosa.
Bed; Calamus Rotang.
Beedul, *B;* Bauhinia purpurea.
Beel-jhun-jhun, *H;* Crotolaria retusa.
Beel-paat.
Beemboo, *B;* Coccinia Indica.
Beertia; Panicum Italicum.
Begpoora, *B* and *H;* Citrus medica.
Behoor-bansh, *B;* Bambusa spinosa.
Behura, *H;* Terminalia Bellerica.
Bel, *B* and *H;* Ægle Marmelos.
Bel, *H;* Cratæva religiosa.
Bela; Jasminum Sambac.
Bella-wine: Semecarpus Anacardium.
Belphool, *B;* Jasminum Sambac.
Bena, *B* and *H;* Andropogon muricatum.
Beri, *H;* Zizyphus Jujuba.
Beshulyo-kurunee, *B;* Cocculus cordifolius.
Beta or Bet, *B* and *H;* Calamus Rotang.
Bhair, *H;* Zizyphus Jujuba.
Bhang; Cannabis sativa.
Bhant, *B;* Clerodendron infortunatum.
Bheela, *H;* Semecarpus Anacardium.
Bherband; Argemone Mexicana.
Bhimb; Coccinia Indica.
Bhinda-tori or Bhindea; Abelmoschus esculentus.
Bhoo-ada or Bhon-ada, *B;* Abelmoschus esculentus.
Bhoocokra, *H;* Zapania nodiflora.
Bhooe-komra, *H;* Trichosanthes cordata.
Bhooi-chumpa, *B* & *H;* Kæmpfera rotunda.
Bhooi-jamba, *B;* Premna herbacea.
Bhooin-koomra, *B* and *H;* Batatas paniculatus.
Bhooi-sunn, *B;* Crotalaria prostrata.
Bhorar: Rhizophora Mangle.
Bhorenda; Ricinus communis.
Bhuchampa, *H;* Kœmpfera rotunda.
Bhungie; Corchorus olitorius.
Bichittie, *B;* Trugia involucrata.
Bichua, *H;* Crotalaria juncea.
Bier: Zizyphus Jujuba.
Bikh; Aconitum.
Bilimbi, *B;* Averrhoa Bilimbi.
Bil-jhunjhun, *B;* Crotalaria retusa.
Bina, *B* and *H;* Avicennia tomentosa.
Bincha; Flacourtia sapida.
Birme, *H;* Trichosanthes incisa.
Birmi: Cratæva Tapia.
Bis or Bish, *B* and *H;* Aconitum ferox.
Bish-Bansh, *B;* Beesha Rheedii.
Bish-hupra; Trianthema obcordatum.
Bish-tarak; Argyreia speciosa.
Bishumba; Cucumis Colocynthis.
Biur, *H;* Zizyphus Jujuba.
Blunjeee Pat, *B;* Corchorus olitorius.
Bokenakoo, *H;* Zapania nodiflora.
Bola, *B* and *H;* Paritium tiliaceum.
Bong, *B;* Solanum Melongena.
Booien-aoonlah, *H;* Phyllanthus Niruri.
Booien-kavite; Feronia elephantum.
Boot, Boot-kaley, *B* & *H;* Cicer arietinum.
Bora, *H;* Dolichos Catjang.
Boro-joan, *B;* Ptychotis Ajowan.
Boyra; Terminalia Bellerica.
Bramee; Sarcostemma brevistigma.
Breehuti; Solanum ferox.
Brinraj bungrah, *H;* Eclipta erecta.
Buckche; Conyza anthelmintica.
Budam; Terminalia Catappa.
Budree, *B;* Zizyphus Jujuba.
Buhooari; Cordia Myxa or latifolia.
Buhura, *B* and *H;* Terminalia Bellerica.
Bukarjun, Bukayun, *H;* Melia sempervirens.
Bukkum; Cæsalpinia Sappan.
Buko, *B;* Agati grandiflora.
Bukool, *B;* Mimusops Elengi.
Bulat; Phaseolus Mungo.
Bulee, *H;* Sterculia urens.
Bulla; Terminalia Bellerica.
Bun-asarhoo; Gossypium herbaceum.
Bun-burbutee, *B* and *H;* Phaseolus rostratus.
Bun-gab, *H;* Diospyros cordifolia.
Bungrah; Acorus Calamus aromaticus.
Bun-gumuk; Cucumis pubescens.
Bun-huldi, *B* and *H;* Curcuma Zedoaria.
Bun-joma; Clerodendron inerme.
Bun-joolee; Phyllanthus multiflorus.
Bunkra, *B;* Urena lobata.
Bun-kuchoo; Colocasia antiquorum.
Bun-lubunga, *B* & *H;* Ludwigia parviflora.
Bun-marunga; Oxalis sensitiva.
Bun-mullika, *B* & *H;* Jasminum Sambac.
Bun-murich, *B;* Ammania vesicatoria.
Bun-neel; Tephrosia purpurea.
Bun-okra, *B* and *H;* Urena lobata.
Bun-pat, *B;* Corchorus olitorius.
Bunputal; Trichosanthes cucumerina.
Bunraj; Bauchinia racemosa.
Bun-shim; Lablab vulgaris.
Bun-sun; Crotalaria verrucosa.

Deb-dhanya; Sorghum vulgare.
Deeb-kanchum; Bauhinia purpurea.
Dela, *H;* Jasminum hirsutum.
Dephul Dampel, *B;* Xanthochymus pictorius.
Dephul Dampel, *B;* Artocarpus Lakoocha.
Deshi-mullika; Jasminum Sambac.
Dewudar, *H;* Sethia Indica.
Dhaee phool; Grislea tomentosa.
Dhak; Butea frondosa.
Dhan, *B* and *H;* Oryza sativa.
Dhanattar, *H;* Clitorea ternatea.
Dhanga; Coriandrum sativum.
Dhangapul, *B;* Grislea tomentosa.
Dhari; Grislea tomentosa.
Dhenroos or Dhendus, *B* and *H;* Abelmoschus esculentus.
Dhol-sumoodra, *B;* Leea macrophylla.
Dhootoora, *H;* Datura alba.
Dhub; Grislea tomentosa.
Dhunya, *B* and *H;* Coriandrum sativum.
Dier, *H;* Cocculus villosus.
Dobutee-luta, *B;* Ipomœa pes-capræ.
Doob, *H;* Cynodon Dactylon.
Doobla, *B;* Cynodon Dactylon.
Doodh-kulnee; Ipomœa Turpethum.
Doombur, *H;* Ficus glomerata.
Doorba, *B;* Cynodon Dactylon.
Dorle, *H;* Solanum Jacquini.
Duntee, *B;* Croton polyandrum.

Eesha-nungula, *B;* Gloriosa superba.
Elaich, *H;* Elettaria Cardamomum.
Elwa; Aloe perfoliata.

Falsa; Grewia Asiatica.
Falter, *H;* Borassus flabelliformis.
Faridbuti; Cocculus villosus.
Feet, *H;* Cucumis Momordica.
Felfildraz; Chavica Roxburghii.
Felfilgird; Piper nigrum.
Feringie-datura; Argemone Mexicana.
Ficki-tagar, *H;* Tabernæmontana coronaria.
Fool-sola, *B;* Æschynomena aspera.
Furrud; Erythrina Indica.

Gab, *B* and *H;* Embryopteris glutinifera.
Gach-murich, *B;* Capiscum annuum.
Gadha-buni; Trianthema decandra.
Gadha-poorna; Boerhavia procumbens.
Gandar; Andropogon muricatum.
Gandbel; Andropogon Schœnanthus.
Gangandhool, *H;* Pandanus odoratissimus.
Ganja, *B* and *H;* Cannabis sativa.
Ganjh, *H;* Andropogon muricatum.
Ganna; Saccharum officinarum.
Gawpurgee; Bixa Orellana.
Ghanur; Cynodon Dactylon.
Gheekoomar; Aloe Indica.
Ghetchoo, *H;* Aponogeton monostachyon.
Ghet-kuchoo; Typhonium Orixense.
Ghicwar, *H;* Aloe perfoliata.
Ghinalita-pat, *B;* Corchorus capsularis.
Ghoosh, *B;* Luffa pentandra or acutangula.
Ghrita-koomaree, *B* and *H;* Aloe Indica.
Ghunchi, *H;* Abrus precatorius.
Ghunta, *B;* Bignonia suaveolens.
Gilaunda, *H;* Bassia latifolia.
Gila-gach, *B;* Entada Pusœtha.
Gima Shak; Mullugo Cerviana & Spergula.
Gobhi; Cacalia sonchifolia.
Gokhoor or Gokhyoor; Tribulus lanuginosus.
Gokshura, *H;* Asteracantha longifolia.
Gol-mirch; Piper nigrum.
Gooa, *B;* Areca Catechu.
Googgul; Balsamodendron Agallocha.
Gooila; Vitis latifolia.
Gool; Cocculus cordifolius.
Goolab-jamun; Eugenia Jambosa.
Gooler, *H;* Ficus racemosa.
Gooli-turah; Poinciana pulcherrima.
Gooluncha or Goluncha; Cocculus cordifolius.
Goond; Cordia angustifolia.
Goordal-shim, *B;* Lablab vulgaris.
Goori-shyora; Ficus rubescens.
Goor-kamai; Solanum Indicum.
Goor-kha; Cocculus cordifolius.
Goorkhi-kuchoo, *H;* Colocasia antiquorum.
Gooya-babula; Acacia Farnesiana.
Gora-neboo, *B* and *H;* Citrus acida.
Govila, *B;* Vitis latifolia.
Gudgega, *H;* Guilandina Bonduc.
Guj-pippul; Scindapsus officinalis.
Gulnar; Punica Granatum.
Guma; Mullugo cerviana.
Gumbaree, *B* and *H;* Gmelina arborea.
Gundha-bela, *B;* Andropogon Schœnanthus.
Gundhabena or Gundbeyl; Andropogon Schœnanthus.
Gundhalee, *H;* Pœderia fœtida.
Gundo-bhadulee, *B;* Pœderia fœtida.
Gunna, *H;* Saccharum officinarum.
Gurcha; Cocculus cordifolius.
Gursoonder, *B;* Acacia Arabica.

Hakooch, *B;* Psoralea corylifolia.
Hakoon, *H;* Croton polyandrum.
Hakoork, *B* and *H;* Psoralea corylifolia.
Hali-moog; Phaseolus Mungo.
Har or Hara, *H;* Terminalia Chebula.
Har or Harchara, *B;* Cissus quadrangularis.
Har-cuchila; Strychnos colubrina.
Harfaroorie, *H;* Cicca disticha.
Har-kat, Harkooch kanta, *H;* Dilivaria ilicifolia.
Harpar; Polanisia icosandra.
Harsingahar; Nyctanthes Arbor tristis.
Has-jorah, *B* and *H;* Vitis quadrangularis.
Hatee-shooro, *B;* Triandrium Indicum.
Hier, *H;* Cocculus villosus.
Hijul, *B;* Barringtonia acutangula.
Hijulee budam; Anacardium occidentale.
Hijulee-mendee, *H;* Eugenia bracteata.
Hina, *H;* Lawsonia inermis.
Hingoolee, *B;* Solanum Melongena.
Hingun, *H;* Balanites Ægyptica.
Hintal, *B;* Phœnix paludosa.
Hogla; Typha elephantina or angustifolia.

Kanth-mullika ; Jasminum Sambac.
Kapas, *B ;* Gossypium herbaceum.
Karbi, *H ;* Sorghum vulgare.
Karavela, *B* and *H ;* Gynandropsis pentaphylla.
Karia-paak, *B ;* Bergera Kœnigii.
Kariari, *H ;* Gloriosa superba.
Karpassa, *B ;* Gossypium herbaceum.
Kas, *H ;* Saccharum spontaneum.
Kashiya, *B ;* Saccharum spontaneum.
Kashmulla, *H ;* Odina Wodier.
Katch-kula, *B* and *H ;* Musa paradisiaca.
Kathbel, *B ;* Jasminum hirsutum.
Katira ; Sterculia urens.
Kat-kulija, *H ;* Cæsalpinia Bonduc.
Kauchra, *B ;* Hydrolea Zeylanica.
Kawa, *H ;* Coffea Arabica.
Kayla ; Musa paradisiaca.
Kea or Kea-phool, *B ;* Pandanus odoratissimus.
Keco, *B* and *H ;* Costus speciosus.
Keera, *H ;* Cucumis sativus.
Keeramar, *B* & *H ;* Aristolochia bracteata.
Keerat, *B ;* Gentiana Cherayta.
Keeshooriya ; Wedelia calendulacea.
Keeshooriya ; Eclipta erecta.
Kela, *H ;* Musa paradisiaca.
Kelikudum, *B ;* Nauclea cordifolia.
Kendoo ; Diospyros melanoxylon.
Kental ; Artocarpus integrifolius.
Kerula, *H ;* Luffa amara.
Keshoor, *B ;* Rottlera tinctoria.
Ket, Khoet, *H ;* Feronia elephantum.
Ketgi, *B ;* Pandanus odoratissimus.
Ketukee ; Pandanus odoratissimus.
Keura-keora, *H ;* Pandanus odoratissimus.
Khagin, *H ;* Clitorea ternatea.
Khaira ; Acacia Catechu or ferruginea.
Khajoor, *B* and *H ;* Elate sylvestris.
Khajora, *H ;* Saccharum spontaneum.
Khana ; Amoora Rohituka.
Khas-khas ; Andropogon muricatum.
Khas-zahra ; Nerium oleander.
Kheeri, *B ;* Mimusops Kanki.
Kherooya ; Phaseolus Mungo.
Khikhri, *H ;* Zizyphus Jujuba.
Khira ; Cucumis utilissimus.
Khirni ; Mimusops kanki.
Khishniz ; Coriandrum sativum.
Khoodi-jam, *B* and *H ;* Antidesma paniculata.
Khoodi-okra, *B ;* Crozophora plicata.
Khoolinjan, *B ;* Alpinia Galanga.
Khor, *B ;* Andropogon muricatum.
Khuera, *B* and *H ;* Acacia Catechu.
Khugura, *B ;* Saccharum spontaneum.
Khul, *H ;* Ærua lanata.
Khurbooja, *B* and *H ;* Cucumis Melo.
Khurbuz, *B ;* Cucumis Melo.
Khuree, *B ;* Saccharum fuscum.
Khurma, *H ;* Phœnix dactylifera.
Kiew ; Diospyros melanoxylon.
Kikar, *H ;* Acacia leucophlæa.
Kingshookha, *B ;* Butea frondosa.
Kiraneli ; Phyllanthus Niruri.
Kiwach, *B* and *H ;* Mucuna prurita.
Koamoora ; Callicarpa lanata.
Kodaleya-koodaliya, *B* and *H ;* Desmodium trifolium.
Kolsi ; Solanum Indicum.
Komla-neeboo, *B ;* Citrus Aurantium.
Komol ; Nelumbium speciosum.
Koobedar ; Bauhinia variegata.
Koobell, *H ;* Andropogon Martini.
Koochila, *B* & *H ;* Strychnos Nux-vomica.
Koochila-luta, *B ;* Strychnos colubrina.
Koochunduna, *H ;* Adenanthera pavonica.
Koochuri, *B ;* Exacum tetragonum.
Kookhoora-choora ; Pavetta Indica.
Kookoora-neja ; Gloriosa superba.
Kool ; Zizyphus Jujuba.
Kooli, *H ;* Sterculia urens.
Kooli-begoon, *B ;* Solanum longum.
Koolthee, *B* and *H ;* Dolichos biflorus.
Koomaree, *B ;* Aloe littoralis.
Koomra ; Cucurbita Pepo.
Koomurka ; Smilax ovalifolia.
Koonch ; Abrus precatorius.
Koonda ; Jasminum hirsutum.
Koondoorie, *H ;* Coccinia Indica.
Kooppie ; Acalypha Indica.
Koorchi ; Wrightia antidysenterica.
Kooshoom ; Carthamus tinctorius.
Koosum ; Carthamus tinctorius.
Koosumbha, *B* and *H ;* Carthamus tinctorius.
Kootaya, *H ;* Solanum Jacquini.
Kora, Koraloo ; Panicum Italicum.
Korna-neeboo, *B* and *H ;* Citrus medicus.
Korunkoosha, *B ;* Andropogon Iwarancusa.
Kosderi ; Momordica umbellata.
Koshnanto ; Cucurbita Pepo.
Koshta ; Corchorus capsularis.
Kotoo ; Michelia Champaca.
Kovidara ; Bauhinia variegata.
Krisbanoo ; Plumbago Zeylanica.
Krishna, *H ;* Sesamum Indicum.
Krishna ; Sesamum Indicum.
Krishna-choora, *B* and *H ;* Poinciana pulcherrima.
Krishna-dhattura, *H ;* Datura alba.
Kuchoo, *B ;* Colocasia antiquorum.
Kuchoora ; Curcuma Zerumbet.
Kudoo, *B ;* Cucurbita lagenaria or Pepo.
Kudum, *B* and *H ;* Nauclea Cadamba.
Kula ; Musa sapientum.
Kulinjam, *H ;* Alpinia Galanga.
Kulkashinda, *B ;* Cassia Sophora.
Kulooa, *H ;* Saccharum officinarum.
Kumla-neboo, *B ;* Citrus aurantium.
Kumula ; Kœmpferia Galanga.
Kunchun ; Bauhinia acuminata.
Kungia, *B ;* Urena sinuata.
Kungnee, Kungoo, *H ;* Panicum Italicum.
Kungwel ; Nelumbium speciosum.
Kural ; Ocymum sanctum.
Kural ; Hemidesmus Indicus.
Kuretta, *B ;* Sida acuata.
Kurfa, *H ;* Portulaca oleracea.
Kurilla, *B* and *H ;* Momordica Charantia.
Kurish-churim, *H ;* Poinciana pulcherrima.

Murooa, *B;* Eleusine Coracana.
Musina, Musnee; Linum usitatissimum.
Musmusa, *H;* Bryonia scabra.
Mutkee-pully; Cyamopsis psoraloides.
Mutra, *H;* Sanseviera Zeylanica.
Myn; Randia dumetorum.
Mynphul; Gardenia dumetorum.

Naga, *B;* Cyperus pertenuis.
Nag-bel; Piper Betel.
Nagkeshur, *B* and *H;* Mesua ferrea.
Nagkeshura-jamba; Syzygium Zeylanicum.
Nagree; Euphorbia antiquorum.
Nagur-moothee, *H;* Cyperus pertenuis.
Nalkee, *B;* Hibiscus cannabinus.
Nalta-pat; Corchorus capsularis.
Namuti, *B;* Grangea Maderaspatana.
Nar, *H;* Amphidonax Karka.
Narang, Narangi, *H;* Citrus aurantium.
Nara shig, *B* & *H;* Euphorbia antiquorum.
Narikulee-kool, *B;* Zizyphus jujuba.
Naskel, Narii, Nargel, *B* and *H;* Cocus nucifera.
Nasurjinghi, *H;* Trianthema monogynia.
Nata, Nata-kanta, *B;* Cæsalpinia Bonduc.
Nata caranja, *H;* Cæsalpinia Bonduc.
Nayor, *B;* Icica Indica.
Nazuc, *H;* Zizyphus jujuba.
Neboo, *B;* Citrus acida.
Neel, *B* and *H;* Indigofera tinctoria.
Neel-kalmee, *B;* Pharbitis Nil.
Neel-mall, *H;* Strychnos potatorum.
Niahmooslie; Curculigo orchioides.
Nigala; Amphidonax Karka.
Nillur, *H;* Vitis quadrangularis.
Nilofar; Nymphæa pubescens.
Nim, *B* and *H;* Azadirachta Indica.
Nirbisee, *H;* Curcuma Zedoaria.
Nircha; Corchorus capsularis.
Nirgundi, *B;* Vitex Negundo.
Nirmullee, Nirmillies, *B* and *H;* Strychnos potatorum.
Nisinda, *H;* Vitex Negundo.
Nisot; Ipomœa Turpethum.
Nona, *B* and *H;* Anona reticulata.
Noncha, *H;* Portulaca oleracea.
Noonbora, *B;* Ionidium suffruticosum.
Noonya, *B* and *H;* Portulaca oleracea.
Nouka; Pontedera vaginalis.
Nubaree; Cicca disticha.
Nuckchilinie, *H;* Epicarpurus orientalis.
Nul; Amphidonax Karka.
Nuta, *B;* Amphidonax Karka.

Ocahya; Momordica Charantia.
Ochooyot, *B;* Morinda tinctoria.
Odoojatee, *H;* Justicia Ecbolium.
Ognee, *B;* Plumbago Zeylanica.
Ol, *B* & *H;* Amorphophallus campanulatus.
Oodachiretta, *H;* Exacum tetragonum.
Oodbeg, *B;* Areca Catechu.
Ook; Saccharum officinarum.
Oolut kumbul; Abroma augusta.
Orjoon; Terminalia alata or glabra.
Orol; Cajanus Indicus.
Osir; Andrapogon muricatum.

Our-chaka, *B;* Sonneratia acida.

Pakar, *H;* Ficus venosa.
Pakoor, *B;* Ficus venosa.
Palak or Palek-joohie; Rhinacanthus communis.
Pale, *H;* Maba buxifolia.
Palita-mandar; Palto-mander, *B* and *H;* Erythrina Indica.
Pan; Chavica Betel.
Pana, *B;* Pistia stratiotes.
Panch-shim; Lablab cultratus.
Panee phul; Trapa bispinosa.
Paniayala, *B* & *H;* Flacourtia cataphracta.
Panieke-shum-balie, *H;* Vitex trifolia.
Pan-kooshe, *B;* Phyllanthus multiflorus.
Papay pepya, *B* and *H;* Carica Papaya.
Paral, *H;* Bryonia chelonoides.
Paris, paris-pupil; Thespesia populnea.
Pat, *B;* Corchorus olitorius.
Pata-khuree, *B* and *H;* Saccharum fuscum.
Patchouli or Pucha-put, *B;* Pogostemon Patchouli.
Patee, *H;* Cyperus inundatus.
Patee-neeboo, *B* and *H;* Citrus acida.
Pathoor choor, *B;* Coleus Amboinicus.
Pat-kili, *B;* Hibiscus Rosa-sinensis.
Paya-tullo, *H;* Beesha Rheedii.
Peela-bhungara; Wedelia calendulacea.
Peet-shala; Pterocarpus Marsupium.
Peeyar Cheroonjie, *H;* Buchanania latifolia.
Peka Bans; Dendrocalamus Tulda.
Pendaloo; Batatas paniculatus.
Petaree, *B;* Abutilon Indicum.
Peyara; Psidium pyriferum, or pomiferum.
Phool-shoola, *B;* Æschynomene aspera.
Phulshasha, *B* and *H;* Grewia Asiatica.
Phoontee, *B;* Cucumis Momordica.
Phul-wara, *H;* Bassia butyracea.
Pilu; Careya arborea.
Pipal, *H;* Chavica Roxburghii.
Pippul, pippuloo, *B* and *H;* Chavica Roxburghii.
Pippulee, *B;* Chavica Roxburghii.
Pipul, pipal; Ficus religiosa.
Pitalee-jamai-poolishim, *B;* Lablab cultratus.
Pitoli, *B* and *H;* Trewia nudiflora.
Pitras, *H;* Curcuma longa.
Piyalee, *B;* Buchanania latifolia.
Poi, *H;* Basella alba.
Poluh, *H;* Ehretia buxifolia.
Poog; Artocarpus integrifolia, Areca Catechu.
Pooi; Basella cordifolia.
Pooin-shak, *B;* Basella cordifolia.
Poon-nag, Poon-naga; Rottlera tinctoria.
Poontureka; Nelumbium speciosum.
Post, *B* and *H;* Papaver somniferum.
Ptoon, *H;* Euphorbia Nivulia.
Pudma, *B* and *H;* Nelumbium speciosum.
Pudma-kurubee; Nerium odorum.
Pulas; Butea frondosa.
Pundaroo, *H;* Hymenodictyon excelsum.
Purush, *B* and *H;* Thespesia populnea.

Sola, *B* and *H*; Æschynomene aspera.
Soml-luta, *B*; Sarcostemma brevistigma.
Sona, *H*; Bauhinia variegata.
Sonali, *B*; Cathartocarpus fistula.
Sona-mookhee, *H*; Cassia elongata.
Sona-pat, *B*; Cassia elongata.
Son-balli, *H*; Croton plicatum.
Sonth; Zingiber officinalis.
Soodali, *B*; Cathartocarpus fistula.
Sookh-dursun; Crinum Asiaticum.
Soom; Sarcostemma brevistigma.
Soomroj; Conyza anthelmintica.
Sooparee, *B* and *H*; Areca Catechu.
Soovurnuka, *B*; Cathartocarpus fistula.
Sothali, *H*; Æschynomene aspera.
Souballi; Crozophora plicata.
Sowa, Shuta-pooshpa; Anethum Sowa or graveolens.
Sphootee, *B*; Cucumis Momordica.
Subjuya, *H*; Canna Indica.
Subzs; Ocymum Basilicum.
Sufed-baryala; Sida rhomboidea.
Suffaid or Lalkudsumbal; Canavalia gladiata.
Suffaid-mooslie; Asparagus sarmentosus.
Suffaid-muhamma; Fluggea leucopyrus.
Suffaid-toolsie; Ocymum album.
Suffet-pooin, *H*; Basella alba.
Suffet-shukurkund-aloo, *B* and *H*; Batatas edulis.
Suhoora, *H*; Epicarpurus orientalis.
Sujna; Hyperanthera Moringa.
Sukkapat; Monetia tetracantha.
Sukkur-kunda-aloo, *B*; Batatas paniculatus.
Suloopha sulpha; Anethum Sowa.
Sultan-champa, *H*; Calophyllum inophyllum.
Sundel, *H*; Santalum album.
Sung-koopie; Clerodendron inerme.
Sunn, *B* and *H*; Crotalaria juncea.
Suparee; Areca Catechu.
Suphura-koomra, *B* and *H*; Cucurbita maxima.
Suran, *H*; Amorphophallus campanulatus.
Surasaruni; Melanthesa rhamnoides.
Surba-juya, *B*; Canna Indica.
Surff-mia; Psidium pyriferum.
Surj; Shorea robusta.
Surpunka, *H*; Calophyllum inophyllum.
Surpunkha, *B*; Tephrosia purpurea.
Susha; Cucumis sativus.
Suthmoolie; Asparagus racemosus.
Sweta-koonch; Abrus precatorius.
Swet-baryala; Sida rhomboidea.
Swetu-shala; Dalbergia latifolia.

Tabaneeboo, *B* and *H*; Citrus acida.
Tala-machna; Asteracantha longifolia.
Talee, *B*; Corypha umbraculifera.
Taliera, *H*; Corypha Taliera.
Talis-putrie; Flacourtia cataphracta.
Tamarhinda, *H*; Tamarindus Indica.
Ta-moolee, *B*; Curculigo orchioides.
Tan; Zepania nodiflora.
Tapia; Cratæva Nurvala.
Tar, Talgachh, *B* and *H*; Borassus flabelliformis.
Tarbuz, *H*; Cucurbita citrullus.
Tarie; Borassus flabelliformis.
Tariyat, Tara, Talier, *B*; Corypha Taliera.
Taruni; Aloe perfoliata.
Teekor, *H*; Curcuma angustifolia.
Tekanda-jutee, *B*; Monetia tetracantha.
Tela-koocha; Coccinia Indica.
Telkaiha, *H*; Coccinia Indica.
Telnoor, *B*; Curculigo orchioides.
Tendu, *H*; Dyospyros melanoxylon.
Teora, *B*; Lathyrus sativus.
Teorie; Ipomœa Turpethum.
Thikeree; Phaseolus radiatus.
Thuhar, *H*; Euphorbia Nivulia.
Thulkuri, *B*; Hydrocotyle Asiatica.
Tidhara, *H*; Euphorbia antiquorum.
Tikhur; Curcuma angustifolia.
Tikrie; Boerhavia procumbens.
Tikta-raj, *B*; Amoora Rohituka.
Tikul, Tikoor, *H*; Garcinia pedunculata.
Tikura; Ipomœa Turpethum.
Tilea-gurjun; Dipterocarpus lævis.
Tilia-kora, *B*; Cocculus acuminatus.
Till, *B* and *H*; Sesamum orientale.
Tisi; Linum usitatissimum.
Tito-dhoon-dhool, *B*; Luffa amara.
Tittha-pat; Corchorus capsularis.
Toka-pana, *H*; Pistia stratiotes.
Tomri; Lagenaria vulgaris.
Toolsi-Toolusee, *B* and *H*; Ocymum villosum or sanctum.
Toolsoo-moodriya, *B*; Leea macrophylla.
Toombo; Cucurbita lagenaria.
Toon, *B* and *H*; Cedrela Toona.
Toong, *B*; Rottlera tinctoria.
Toor, *H*; Cajanus Indicus.
Tooti; Cucumis Momordica.
Triang-guli; Phaseolus trilobus.
Trinpali; Manisuris granularis.
Tripungkhi; Coldenia procumbens.
Tselkache; Coccinia Indica.
Tuar; Cajanus Indicus.
Tugura, *B* and *H*; Tabernæmontana coronaria.
Tula, *B*; Gossypium herbaceum.
Tulda, Bans; Dendrocalamus Tulda.
Tulidun, *H*; Solanum nigrum.
Tumal, *B*; Diospyros tomentosa.
Turanj, *H*; Citrus medica.
Turbad, *H*; Ipomœa Turpethum.
Turbooz, Turmooj, *B* and *H*; Cucurbita Citrullus.
Turooi; Luffa acutangula.
Turwur; Cassia auriculata.

Uch, *H*; Saccharum officinarum.
Udruk, *B*; Zingiber officinale.
Ukyo; Saccharum officinarum.
Ulsee, *H*; Linum usitatissimum.
Ulutchandal; Gloriosa superba.
Umbutee; Oxalis corniculata.
Umul-koochi; Cæsalpinia digyna.
Undum, *H*; Pterocarpus santalinus.
Untamool; Tylophora asthmatica.

INDEX OF TAMIL SYNONYMS.

INDEX OF TELOOGOO SYNONYMS.

Ada; Bauhinia racemosa.
Adavi-pulla; Trichosanthes cucumerina.
Adavi-zeela-kara; Vernonia anthelmintica.
Addivetella guddaloo; Scilla Indica.
Adive-cunda; Dracontium polyphyllum.
Adive-malle; Jasminum angustifolium.
Adivi-amida; Jatropha Curcas.
Adivigerenta; Sethia Indica.
Agakara; Momordica dioica.
Agunda-pacoo; Ammannia vesicatoria.
Akasa-gherooda; Bryonia epigæa.
Ali; Linum usitatissimum.
Alla-galli-gheetsa; Crotalaria verrucosa.
Allu-batsalla; Basella alba.
Amidum; Ricinus communis.
Angakara; Momordica dioica.
Annamooloo; Lablab vulgaris.
Annapa-chicureay; Lablab (a variety).
Antara-tamara; Villarsia Indica.
~~Appakozay; Bryonia rostrata.~~
Arasum; Ficus religiosa.
Aretti; Musa sapientum.
Aroe; Bauhinia parviflora.
Attika-mamadie; Boerhavia diffusa.
Avagooda; Trichosanthes palmata.
Avary; Cassia auriculata.
Avisay; Agati grandiflora.
Awatum; Spondias mangifera.

Babassa; Hydrocotyle Asiatica.
Badide-chettu; Erythrina Indica.
Ballusookura; Canthium parviflorum.
Balusoo-chettoo; Webera tetrandra.
Bandi-gooroovindza; Adenanthera pavonina.
Bapanaboori; Ehretia buxifolia.
Bapunga; Psoralea corylifolia.
Barinka; Epicarpurus orientalis.
Batsalikoora or Peddapailkura; Portulaca quadrifida.
Biddrie-nana-beeum; Euphorbia thymifolia.
Billoo; Swietenia chloroxylon.
Billoo-gaddi; Saccharum spontaneum.
Bilva; Cratæva Roxburghii.
Binda Abelmoschus esculentus.
Boarda-goomoodoo; Benincasa cerifera.
Bobra; Dolichos sinensis.
Bodatarum; Sphæranthus Indicus.
Boddama; Bryonia callosa.
Boma - papata or Commi; Stylocoryne Webera.
Bonta-jemoodoo; Euphorbia antiquorum.
Booraga; Eriodendron anfractuosum.
Boorgha; Bombax Malabaricum.
Boosee; Vitex arborea.
Botacadamie; Nauclea parviflora.
Bundaroo; Hymenodictyon excelsum.
Burong; Ficus rubescens.

Candaloo; Cajanus Indicus.
Carakaia; Terminalia Chebula.
Cassa-cassa; Papaver somniferum.
Chaga; Sanseviera Zeylanica.
Chayndpolla; Trichosanthes cucumerina.
Chendanum; Santalum album.
Cheriveloo; Hedyotis umbellata.
Chewka; Tamarindus Indica.
Chikai; Acacia concinna.
Chilta-rita; Phœnix farnifera.
Chinanghie; Lagerstrœmia parviflora.
Chini-kala-bunda; Aloe litoralis.
Chinta; Tamarindus Indica.
Chitankaloo; Wrightia tinctoria.
Chittle-bunda; Pavonia odorata.
Citra; Plumbago Zeylanica.
Condacashina; Toddalia aculeata.
Cooroo-vayroo; Andropogon muricatum.
Coraloo; Panicum Italicum.

Dadima; Punica Granatum.
Daduga; Nauclea cordifolia.
Darboojee; Cucurbita Citrullus.
Dasanie; Hibiscus Rosa sinensis.
Dellamadoo; Terminalia tomentosa.
Dewadari; Sethia Indica.
Dirishena; Acacia speciosa.
Donda; Coccinia Indica.
Doolaghondi; Tragia involucrata.
Doolagovila; Aristolochia Indica.
Doolya-gunda; Tragia cannabina.
Doombrasticum; Alpinia Galanga.
Doosratiga; Cocculus villosus.
Doskai; Cucumis utilissimus.

Eesara; Aristolochia Indica.
Ellakoora; Salsola Indica.

Gadida-guda-purra; Aristolochia bracteata.
Ganja chettoo; Cannabis sativa.
Garga; Gardenia gummifera.
Getsakaia; Guilandina Bonduc.
Ghebboonellie; Premna integrifolia.
Ghelegherinta; Crotalaria verrucosa.
Ghelijehroo; Trianthema obcordata.
Ghengheravie; Thespesia populnea.
Ghenneru; Nerium odorum.
Ghericha; Cynodon Dactylon.
Gherka; Byndon Dactylon.
Gherutti-kamma; Vernonia cinerea.

INDEX OF MALAYALAM SYNONYMS.

INDEX.

THE END.